BRIT GUIDE

ORLANDO

& Walt Disney World

© Disney

2015

Simon & Susan Veness

foulsham
LONDON • NEW YORK • TORONTO • SYDNEY

W. Foulsham & Co. Ltd
for Foulsham Publishing Ltd
The Old Barrel Store, Drayman's Lane, Marlow, Bucks SL7 2FF

Foulsham books can be found in all good bookshops or direct
from www.foulsham.com

While every effort has been made to ensure the accuracy of all the information contained
within this book, neither the author nor the publisher can be liable for any errors. In
particular, since prices, times and any holiday or hotel details change on a regular basis, it is
vital that each individual checks relevant information for themselves.

ISBN: 978-0-572-04462-6

Look out for the latest editions of Foulsham travel books:
Brit Guide to Las Vegas, Jane Anderson and the *Brit Guide* team
Brit Guide to Disneyland Resort Paris, Simon and Susan Veness
Brit Guide to New York, Amanda Statham

Dedication: To our special home-grown research team – Ben, Anthony and Mark – who help
make our work fun!

SPECIAL THANKS
Special thanks for this edition go to: Visit Orlando, Visit Kissimmee, The Walt Disney
Company, Universal Orlando, SeaWorld Parks & Entertainment and Virgin Holidays.

Our sincere thanks also go to Wendy Hobson and all the hard-working people at Foulsham
who help to bring our work to life every year.

Typeset in Great Britain by Chris Brewer Origination
Printed in Dubai

CONTENTS

Foreword

Simon says... A little more than 20 years ago, I sat down at around 2am one night to map out what I thought would be a great idea for a new Orlando guidebook, written for British visitors by a British visitor, following a memorable – but exhausting – holiday to the Theme Park Capital of the World. Now, with the 20th edition of the *Brit Guide Orlando*, I think I can safely say we know what we're doing! Things have certainly changed, a lot, in that time. We started with just 188 pages but now, with 352, this is a fair reflection of the area's continued growth, both in the breadth and depth of its hugely varied attractions. Over the past 20 years, we have charted many new arrivals, many comings and goings, and a fair few price rises (which we'll highlight at regular intervals in this 20th anniversary edition). But the bottom line is this remains a unique destination, unrivalled anywhere on the planet; its attractions are rightly world famous and, while it is not a cheap holiday, it provides (for the most part) wonderful value for money. But you need a 'good companion' to steer you through the maze of options and bewildering choices at seemingly every step, and that's where we come in. This simply isn't a make-it-up-as-you-go-along kind of place, hence the more time you spend on these pages, you more you will get from *your* holiday. Planning is an essential part of the process – more than ever with Disney's new MyMagic+ system – so be sure to take us with you!

Susan says... I count myself among the new additions to the *Brit Guide* in the last 20 years, and I've seen a fair few changes just in the last 10. One of the biggest changes happened in 2014, with the opening of the new Diagon Alley area at Universal Studios. It's not among the biggest because of what it is – although it is

absolutely mind-blowing – but because of what it represents: a whole new way of creating immersive experiences that bring guests into the story in a way that is totally, brilliantly convincing. Walk into Diagon Alley and you ARE in the world of Harry Potter. With this enchanting new land, Universal's creative team raised the bar once again (and it was pretty high after Hogsmeade!) and all of Orlando stood up and took notice. That's good news for visitors as creative competition inspires everyone in this innovation-obsessed city, and we're certain it means even more dynamic, enveloping, and – dare we say it – magical experiences in the coming years.

And if you want to make sure you get the very best out of your holiday without wasting time or money, let us help with our unique Touring Plans (p41).

So if you're ready, let's get on with the planning…!

Simon and Susan Veness
(visit us at www.venesstravelmedia.com, or email britsguide@yahoo.com, and follow Veness Travel Media on Twitter and Facebook).

1 Introduction

or Welcome to the Holiday of a Lifetime

Twenty years ago, we stated that Orlando was the nearest thing there is to an Amusement City, and nothing has changed that view since then. If anything, this area of Central Florida is now more varied, more appealing and just plain more exciting than ever, a vast mix of theme parks, smaller attractions, sport, nature, amazing dining, world class shopping, fabulous nightlife and fun, fun, fun. It is adventure rides, thrills, excitement and fantasy without equal. It appeals to families, couples and singles, young and old alike. But you must be well prepared for what's in store.

First, this is a BIG venture in every sense and it's vital you have an idea of the extensive and complex nature of this wonderland. Walt Disney World is the leading attraction and is the size of a small city, and there is a strong supporting cast, led by Universal Orlando and SeaWorld. There's something for all tastes and ages, but it exacts a high toll. You'll walk a lot, queue a lot and probably eat a lot. You WILL have a fabulous time, but you'll probably end up exhausted, too. It is a holiday – but it's also something of a military campaign!

Eight theme parks

In simple terms, there are 8 major theme parks, and several need 2 days to enjoy fully. Add a day at a water park, a trip to one of the wildlife or nature attractions and the lure of the Kennedy Space Center, and you already have 2 full weeks of pure adventure mania. Then mix in the night-time fun of Downtown Disney, Universal's CityWalk and a host of dinner shows, plus superb shopping, and you start to understand the awesome scope of the place. Even with 2 weeks, something has to give – just make sure it isn't your patience, wallet – or sanity.

So, how do you get full value from this truly magical holiday? The answer is Good Planning – read, reflect and prepare. On pages 345–46 is a handy outline guide for a typical 2-week stay. Be aware of the time demands of the parks and make sure you build in a quiet day or two by the pool or at one of the smaller attractions. With SO much on offer, it just isn't possible to 'do it all', so try to ensure you get full value from your choices. Also, don't underestimate the vast scale involved – this is a huge area and it takes time even to get from park to park. But do stop to admire the imagination and detail of what's on offer as it is all world class.

Orlando

In tourist terms, 'Orlando' has grown to encompass much of Central Florida, an area almost twice the size of Yorkshire. Yes, that big. The city itself is north of most of the parks and many people won't even see it as they charge from park to park, which is a shame as it is a bright and happening place. When Walt Disney's dream of a vast resort opened in 1971 with

Florida

0   50 miles

N

← Panama City Beach

JACKSONVILLE

Atlantic Ocean

St Augustine

Ormond Beach
Daytona Beach
New Smyrna Beach

Ocala

Mount Dora

Homosassa Springs

Sanford

Titusville

Cape Canaveral
■ Kennedy Space Center

ORLANDO

Walt Disney World

Kissimmee

Cocoa Beach

New Port Richey

Winter Haven
Legoland Florida

Melbourne

Clearwater Beach

Lakeland

TAMPA

Lake Wales
Bok Tower Gardens

St Pete Beach

FLORIDA

FLORIDA TURNPIKE

Vero Beach

Gulf of Mexico

Bradenton

Sarasota

Venice

Lake Okeechobee

Charlotte Harbor

Fort Myers

Palm Beach

Captiva

Delray Beach
Boca Raton

Sanibel

Florida

Naples

Fort Lauderdale

Marco Island

Everglades

MIAMI

Key Largo

Florida Keys

Key West

How far from Orlando to . . .

	mls	-	km
Bradenton	130	-	210
Clearwater Beach	110	-	176
Cocoa Beach	40	-	64
Daytona Beach	60	-	97
Fort Lauderdale	205	-	330
Fort Myers	190	-	306
Jacksonville	155	-	250
Key Largo	294	-	470
Key West	375	-	604
Miami	220	-	354
Naples	230	-	370
Sarasota	140	-	225
St Augustine	120	-	193
St Pete Beach	105	-	169
Tampa	75	-	120
Venice	160	-	257
Winter Haven	40	-	64

© Steve Munns 2014

the Magic Kingdom (sadly, he never saw it realised as he died in 1966), it led to a huge tourist expansion. New attractions pop up all the time and both coasts also vie for attention.

There are 7 counties in Central Florida. **Orange County**, home to the city of Orlando, with Walt Disney World in the south-west corner, part of which is also in **Osceola County**, with Kissimmee its main town; **Seminole County**, home of Orlando Sanford International Airport, north-east of Orange; **Lake County** to the north-west, with Mount Dora its principal town; **Polk** to the south-west, home to many vacation villas and Legoland Florida; and **Brevard** and **Volusia** Counties to east, home to the Kennedy Space Center and Daytona Beach.

Each year, more than 50 million people holiday in Orlando and the area boasts 115,000 hotel rooms, 26,000 vacation homes, more than 4,000 places to eat and 30 malls. Here's a taste of the main attractions.

Walt Disney World

This is where the magic really starts. This vast resort consists of 4 separate theme parks, 20 speciality hotel resorts, a camping ground, 2 water parks, a sports complex, 4 golf courses, mini-golf and a huge shopping and entertainment district (Downtown Disney). It covers 47ml²/122km² and Alton Towers and Thorpe Park would comfortably fit into its car parks! At peak periods, it holds 200,000-plus visitors. Disney does things with the most style and there are always new projects on the drawing board. It maintains a high level of customer service, where everyone who works for them is officially a Cast Member, not just staff, and they take that ethic to heart.

Magic Kingdom: The essential Disney, with the magic of its wonderful films, the adventures of the Wild West and Africa, the excitement of thrill rides like Space Mountain (an indoor roller-coaster), the eye-catching new Fantasyland and splendid parades and fireworks.

Epcot: Disney's 2-part park, with the technology-inspired Future World, plus a potted journey around the globe in World Showcase. More educational than adventurous, it has some memorable rides, including the superb Soarin', plus excellent dining.

Disney's Hollywood Studios: Ride the movies in style, meet Star Wars™, the Muppets and Indiana Jones; drop into the fearsome Tower of Terror; learn the tricks of the trade at the epic Lights, Motors, Action!™ Extreme Stunt Show; and try the Toy Story Mania ride.

Disney's Animal Kingdom: Another contrasting option, with realistic animal habitats, including a 100acre/40.5ha safari savannah, captivating shows and terrific rides, like the grand Expedition Everest.

Disney's Typhoon Lagoon Water Park: Splash down waterslides and learn to surf in the world's biggest man-made lagoon.

Disney's Blizzard Beach Water Park: The big brother of all the water parks, with a massive spread of rides in a 'snowy' environment.

Downtown Disney: Almost a mile of themed restaurants, bars, shops, a cinema multiplex, the DisneyQuest arcade of interactive games, House of Blues music venue and world-famous Cirque du Soleil® company.

Wedding Pavilion: A fairytale venue overlooking Seven Seas Lagoon for picture-perfect marriage ceremonies.

ESPN Wide World of Sports: A huge sporting venue to both play and watch top events.

The other parks

If you think Orlando is only about Disney, prepare to be amazed.

Universal Orlando: The other main resort has 2 theme parks, an entertainment district and 4 speciality hotels. At **Universal Studios** you encounter The Simpsons, the Rip Ride Rockit roller-coaster, Woody Woodpecker's KidZone, amazing TRANSFORMERS: The Ride – 3D and the new Wizarding World of Harry Potter – Diagon Alley. **Islands of Adventure** (IoA) features the original Wizarding World area, with a superb blend of thrill rides, family attractions, shows, great design and high-tech features such as the Amazing Adventures of Spider-Man.

Wet 'n Wild: On International Drive, this Universal water park offers plenty of fun rides and slides.

SeaWorld: THE place for creatures of the deep, with killer whales, dolphins and penguins, a refreshing atmosphere, the Blue Horizons and One Ocean shows, fabulous new Antarctica attraction, thrill rides like Manta and Kraken, plus an area of rides and activities just for kids.

Discovery Cove: Its exclusive neighbour offers the chance to swim with dolphins, among other things.

Aquatica: A fab water park providing even more fun and animal encounters in a colourful South Seas setting.

BRITTIP
Be realistic about the tickets you need. You simply won't get full use out of, say, a 14-day Disney ticket and the Orlando FlexTicket Plus in a 2-week holiday.

Busch Gardens: In nearby Tampa, the sister park to SeaWorld offers creatures of the land, with a good mix of rides and shows. Highlights are the Cheetah Hunt and SheiKra coasters, the new Falcon's Fury drop-tower ride, the Edge of Africa 'safari' experience and the ice-skating show, Iceplorations. A family treat, and a must for coaster fans.

The fun SeaWorld style

Other key attractions

These include: the dramatically upgraded **Kennedy Space Center**, with the new Atlantis Exhibit; the surprisingly fun and humorous **Gatorland**; **LEGOLAND Florida**, great for the 2–12 age group; **Florida Eco-Safaris**, a mix of local nature rides and high-energy zipline adventures; and **Boggy Creek Airboats** and **Wild Florida**, which provide a close-up with local nature in Kissimmee. Plus there is great **mini-golf** almost everywhere and a variety of smaller attractions along International Drive.

BRITTIP
Buy your theme park tickets in advance, NOT at the park gates. You will save time AND money, as most outlets offer an advance purchase discount.

Disney tickets

This is where things get complicated and it's important to work out what tickets you need. Most people buy one of 3 multi-day passes specifically for the UK market that allow visits to more than one park a day. They are great value for a 2 or 3-week visit and provide maximum flexibility. But they aren't cheap and, if you want to visit only 2 or 3 of the Disney parks, you have to buy a Magic Your Way ticket in Orlando. Be aware you can't walk between the parks (they can be miles apart) and trying to do more than one a day is hard work, especially in summer.

Disney's ticket system is called **Magic Your Way** and is horribly complicated (although there is a simplified choice for UK visitors; see below). Multi-day tickets offer savings against 1-day tickets but unused days expire after 14 days of first use unless you buy an upgrade.

Magic Your Way: If you just turn up at the ticket booths (or buy in advance from a US broker), you must choose:

- The number of days you want (up to 10).

- Whether you want **Park Hopping** (the ability to move between parks on the same day) for $49–60/ticket (depending on the number of days).

- If you want the **Water Park Fun & More Option** (1–10 visits to the water parks, DisneyQuest and ESPN Wide World of Sports™) for $60/ticket. Disney also offers 1 free round at 9-hole Oak Trail golf course (book in advance on 407 939 4653; club hire NOT included) and 1 free round at its mini-golf courses.

- If you want the **Non-expiration Option** (at $40–350, depending on the number of days of ticket). This can be added after the initial purchase (but before the ticket's 14-day expiration). You pay based on the original length of the ticket, so, if you buy a 7-day ticket and decide after 4 days you won't use the rest of it on that visit, you can add non-expiration for $255 and save the remaining 3 days for the future. NB: this option is only available at the park ticket booths, not online.

Per-day ticket savings increase with the more days you buy: 1 day = $94-99 plus tax; 10 days = $354 plus tax, or $35.40/day.

BRITTIP

Use the Guest Services at Downtown Disney to save time and queuing if you need to buy Disney tickets in Orlando or exchange vouchers for tickets

UK tickets: In the UK, there are 3 tickets on offer: the 7, 14 and 21-day Ultimate Ticket (see chart p11).

Other tickets

The choice is equally complicated for Universal Orlando, Wet 'n Wild, SeaWorld, Busch Gardens and Aquatica. Do check periodic special offers (see Orlando Ticket Deals, p10).

- **Orlando FlexTicket:** 14 consecutive days to both Universal parks, Wet 'n Wild, SeaWorld and Aquatica. Add Busch Gardens with the **FlexTicket Plus**.

- **1, 2, 3 or 4-day Tickets:** For Universal alone, **1 park** per day or **both parks** each day.

- **2 and 3-Park Bonus Ticket:** 14 days at Universal Studios and IoA or those 2 plus Wet 'n Wild; buy in the UK.

- **2 and 3-Park Tickets:** 14 days for SeaWorld and Busch Gardens or SeaWorld and Aquatica, or all 3.

- **Discovery Cove:** A day ticket includes a 14-Day Pass for SeaWorld and Aquatica. The **Discovery Cove Ultimate Package** adds Busch Gardens for 14 days for an extra $22.

- **Party Pass:** For Universal's CityWalk ($11.99 plus tax) or a **Party Pass with Movie** ($15 plus tax) at the 20-screen cinema.

- **14-Day Combo Pass:** Offered by many UK brokers, for Disney & Universal, or various combinations of Disney, Universal, SeaWorld, LEGOLAND and the water parks, plus a Freedom Ticket, or similar name, for all 8 parks plus the water parks. This is NOT a single ticket but a bundle of 2 or 3 tickets.

- **Go Orlando Card:** 2 or 4 days of visits within 14 days to 45 attractions and activities, including Kennedy Space Center, LEGOLAND Florida, Gatorland, WonderWorks, airboat rides, mini-golf, dinner shows and more, with a **Plus SeaWorld** option for a 1-day visit ($145–329 adults, $135–289 3–12s). It represents up to 55% in savings and comes with a handy attractions guidebook. See **www.goorlandocard.com**.

- **Eat and Play Card:** A discount card for groups of up to 4, valid for 90 days from first use. Save 10–20% off 50-plus restaurants,

Where the magic begins

from McDonald's, Denny's, Pizza Hut and TGI Friday's to upmarket choices like Big Fin Seafood, Café Tu-Tu Tango and Shula's Steakhouse, all in the main tourist areas and including alcohol in some cases; 10–30% on attractions like golf, mini-golf, Gatorland, Ripley's Believe It Or Not and more; and 10–20% off shops like Macy's and Reebok Outlet Stores, plus the Outta Control Magic Dinner Show and discounted golf. It costs a bargain $25 and covers the entire bill for up to 4 people each time, so there are significant savings possible. Available from **www.eatandplaycard.com** (or call 001 613 680 7109) or select ticket brokers and tour operators.

With annual price hikes, try to buy your tickets as soon as you can, but be aware that some discounted tickets must be used for the first time in the year of purchase (e.g. 'first use by 31 Dec 2014'). Shop around, as many outlets have sales and special offers, but use a reputable agent and use your credit card for added security. The following companies all come well recommended.

Attraction Tickets Direct: Britain's top direct-sell Florida ticket broker, with a sharp bookings team, no credit card fees, free delivery in 7 days and a promise to match any UK brochure price, plus a huge range of dinner shows, excursions, sports, theme park backstage tours and special offers, and a keen online Florida Forum and info centre to which we contribute (0800 223 0324, **www.attraction-tickets-direct.co.uk**).

Manta at SeaWorld

Ocean Florida: Independent Florida specialist also offers a well-priced ticket service, featuring all the theme parks, plus Kennedy Space Center and Miami Seaquarium (020 7939 7775, **www.ocean-florida.co.uk**).

FloridaTix: Independent ticket specialist featuring all the theme parks, plus the likes of Kennedy Space Center, Blue Man Group, dinner shows, many tours and excursions, and a low-deposit ticket offer (0844 873 0060, **www.floridatix.co.uk**).

Orlando Attractions: A UK-owned ticket service based in Orlando, it will post tickets to the UK and offers all the parks and the likes of airboat rides, fishing and other activities, plus some good combo tickets. Fully ABTA-bonded. Free shipping, price includes tax and no credit card fees (0800 294 9458, **www.orlandoattractions.com/tickets**).

Orlando Ticket Deals: A keenly priced and helpful broker that also issues real tickets (not vouchers), has a next-day delivery service and offers a significant Price Promise for all its attractions, including all the parks, dinner shows and many excursions (0800 542 1280, **www.orlando-ticket-deals.co.uk**).

There are others, including the main tour operators (p20), while you can also visit the Official Visitor Center on International Drive (**www.visitorlando.com**), but beware offers for 'free' tickets as these are purely timeshare lures. And NEVER buy resale tickets from a booth in Orlando – they are often unusable. Stick with the main brokers, who offer good products, service and local knowledge. And don't forget to plan with our sample Busy Day Guide (p346). You'll be exhausted if you try to do all the parks in one go!

✠ BRITTIP

For all your theme park tickets, be sure to check out *Brit Guide* partner Orlando Ticket Deals first, as it features an exclusive money-saving offer for our readers (see inside back cover).

Choosing a ticket

Ticket type	Park	Allowance
1-Day Ticket	Any Disney park, Universal Orlando parks, SeaWorld or Busch Gardens	Access to 1 park ONLY for 1 day; not available in advance
7, 14 and 21-Day Ultimate Ticket	All Disney parks	Unlimited access to all Disney attractions, including water parks, *DisneyQuest*, *ESPN Wide World of Sports*™ and 9-hole Oak Trail golf course (clubs not included) for 14 days after first use; NO non-expiration option; available only in advance in the UK
Annual Pass	*Magic Kingdom Park, Epcot, Disney's Hollywood Studios, Disney's Animal Kingdom;* plus discounts for shops, dining and tours	Unlimited admission and *free parking* for 365 days after purchase date. If ordered online, you get a voucher that must be activated at a park; the 365 days start on the first day you activate the pass
Premium Annual Pass	All Disney parks; plus numerous discounts for shops, dining and tours	Unlimited admission and *free parking* for 365 days after purchase date; plus discounts on sports and recreation
2, 3 or 4-Day 1-Park Ticket	Universal Studios, Islands of Adventure	Access to 1 of the Universal parks each day for 2–4 days, plus CityWalk; valid for 14 days
2, 3 or 4-Day 2-Park Ticket	Universal Studios, Islands of Adventure	Access to both Universal parks each day for 2–4 days, plus CityWalk; valid for 14 days
2-Park Bonus Ticket	Universal Studios, Islands of Adventure and CityWalk	14 consecutive days' access to both Universal parks, plus CityWalk clubs; sold in UK only
3-Park Bonus Ticket	Universal Studios, Islands of Adventure, Wet 'n Wild and CityWalk	14 consecutive days' access to all 3 parks, plus CityWalk clubs; sold in UK only
Orlando FlexTicket	Universal Studios, Islands of Adventure, SeaWorld, Wet 'n Wild, Aquatica	Access to all 5 parks, with multiple parks on same day, for 14 days from first use, plus CityWalk clubs
Orlando FlexTicket Plus	Universal Studios, Islands of Adventure, SeaWorld, Wet 'n Wild, Aquatica, Busch Gardens	Access to all 6 parks, with multiple parks on same day, for 14 days from first use, plus CityWalk clubs
2-Park Ticket	SeaWorld and Busch Gardens	14 consecutive days' access to both parks
2-Park Ticket	SeaWorld and Aquatica	14 consecutive days' access to both parks
3-Park Ticket	SeaWorld, Busch Gardens and Aquatica	14 consecutive days' access to all 3 parks

The climate

This catches out a lot of first-timers. Florida's weather varies from bright but cool with the odd drizzly spell in winter (Dec–Feb), to furiously hot and humid, punctuated by tropical downpours in summer (May–Sept). The most pleasant option is therefore spring or autumn. You will also avoid the worst of the crowds in Sept and Oct. However, as most families are governed by school holidays, Easter and July–Aug remain the most popular for British visitors, so we have plenty of advice on how to stay ahead of the high-season crush. If you do need to go in summer, opt for late Aug when the crowds drop off somewhat.

BRITTIP

The draining humidity levels – up to 100% – and daily rainstorms in summer take many visitors by surprise, so carry a lightweight rainproof jacket or buy a cheap plastic poncho locally.

The mood

Orlando is big, brash and fun, but above all it's American and that means everything is well organised, but with some cultural differences such as tipping (see below). It's clean, well maintained and eager to please: Floridians generally are an affable bunch, but they take affability to new heights in the theme parks, where staff are almost painfully keen to make sure you 'have a nice day'.

Tipping

With the exception of fast-food restaurant servers, just about everyone who serves in hotels, bars, restaurants, buses, taxis, airports and public amenities will expect a tip, not least because all service industry workers are taxed on the basis of receiving 15% in tips, whether they're given or not.

- Bars, restaurants and taxis: 15%
- Porters: $1/bag
- Chambermaids: $1/day per adult.

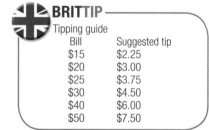

BRITTIP

Tipping guide

Bill	Suggested tip
$15	$2.25
$20	$3.00
$25	$3.75
$30	$4.50
$40	$6.00
$50	$7.50

Portofino Bay Hotel

ESTA and immigration

Anyone flying to the USA on the Visa Waiver Programme MUST register online via the Electronic System for Travel Authorization (ESTA) no later than 3 days before departure. For all flights to the USA, this has now replaced the old green Visa Waiver form (I-94W).

ESTA: ESTA is a pre-authorisation process prior to arriving at US immigration. The fee is $10 per person (plus admin and credit card fees, taking the final cost to around $15) and is valid for any visits in a 2-year span (so you do NOT pay the $10 fee again in that time).

Apply at **https://esta.cbp.dhs.gov** and fill in your basic immigration info – passport, address in the USA, flight details, email address and a few security questions. Have your holiday address details available both for the ESTA and your Advance Passenger Information for your flight online. Ask your tour operator if you don't have a specific address (e.g. for a villa allocated on arrival) as it will have a formula for this. Your application should generate an immediate response of 'Authorization Approved' or 'Pending'. If the response 'Travel Not Authorized' is generated, the applicant is unable to travel under the Visa Waiver Programme and must apply for a visa in advance. Remember to record or print your Application Number during the

process so you can amend it for future visits within 2 years.

The ESTA speeds up the immigration process and cuts out most form filling. An ESTA must be completed for each member of your group or family travelling under the Visa Waiver Programme. Those who have a US visa because they are not eligible to travel under the Visa Waiver Programme (i.e. because of a criminal record – see right) still need to fill in a white I-94 form en route (fill in the front only) but they do NOT pay the $10 entry fee. However, anyone with a US visa for work purposes and who is travelling to America for a holiday, WILL need to fill in an ESTA and pay the fee.

BRITTIP

Beware unofficial websites that offer to fill in the ESTA form for you – for a fee. Stick with the official US government website and just pay the $10/person fee (or 'Travel Promotion Act fee').

Customs: You still need to complete a white customs form en route (it'll be given to you on the plane or at check-in and it's best to complete it in advance). Fill in one customs form per family, with some of the same basic info but also the value of any goods that will stay in the USA (put $0 unless you are arriving with gifts for friends). Hand the document(s) with your passports to the immigration official who checks you through and takes a fingerprint scan and photo. The customs form will be handed back to you to present to another official when you exit the baggage hall.

BRITTIP

If you need to fill in the white I-94 immigration form for visa holders, do so carefully in block capitals. Mistakes are often sent to the back of the queue. Please be courteous to immigration officials – they do a difficult job in demanding circumstances, and jokes about terrorism are NOT appreciated.

Visa requirements

Holiday visitors to America do not need a visa providing they hold a valid machine-readable British passport (MRP). Any passport issued from 26 October 2005 must include a digital photograph (not glued or laminated). All passports issued from 26 October 2006 must include the new biometric data. Each family member must have their own passport, valid for the FULL duration of the holiday. However, British subjects, those without an MRP or those who fail to meet the photo/biometric data criteria DO need a visa ($131), and should apply at least 2 months in advance to the US Embassy.

US immigration requires ALL visitors aged 14–79 to give fingerprint and photo ID on arrival. It is a simple process, though – first the four fingers and thumb of one hand, and then the same for the other hand, then stand still for the camera. Some US gateways require a full 10-finger scan.

Some travellers may NOT be eligible under the Visa Waiver Programme and will have to apply for a special restricted visa or they may be refused entry. This applies to those who have been arrested in the past (even if it did not result in a conviction), have a criminal record

Shopping at Disney's Animal Kingdom

(the Rehabilitation of Offenders Act does not apply to US visa law), have a serious communicable illness (and the US includes AIDS sufferers in this category), or have previously been refused admission into, been deported from, or have overstayed in the US on the Visa Waiver Programme. Minor traffic offences do not count.

Contacts:

• England, Scotland and Wales: Visa Office, US Embassy, 24 Grosvenor Square, London W1A 2LQ (020 7499 9000). NB: for mailing address use postcode W1K 6AH.

• Northern Ireland: US Consulate General, Danesfort House, 223 Stranmillis Road, Belfast BT9 5GR (028 9038 6100).

• More detailed advice: 09042 450 100 (£1.23 per minute; 8am–9pm Mon–Fri, 9am–4pm Sat), **http://london. usembassy.gov**.

Travel information
Luggage is liable to random searches in the US and you are advised NOT to lock your suitcases at check-in for the flight home as TSA officials have the authority to break into them.

Using zip-lock seals that can easily be snipped open is permissible and some airlines provide them free, while you can also buy TSA-approved reusable locks at some travel shops. It is best to leave any gifts you are taking home unwrapped, just in case screening requires them to be opened; and be sure to put scissors and other sharp items in checked bags, *never* in your hand luggage.

BRITTIP
Cabin baggage restrictions often change, so check with your airline in advance for up-to-date info.

What's new?
If 2014 was the year of Harry Potter (Pt 2) at Universal Orlando, 2015 will see the advent of the Orlando Eye, Madame Tussaud's and the SeaLife Center, all at I-Drive 360. This big new complex in the heart of International Drive is due to open in March 2015, with a fabulous array of new attractions, many of them created by Merlin Entertainments (the owners of LEGOLAND Florida). With the Eye towering more than 400ft/120m high (like the London version), it promises to be an amazing new icon for

Diagon Alley at Universal Studios

Orlando as well as a great opportunity to see the area from a whole new perspective, along with additional restaurants, shops and entertainment (see full details on p237).

As far as the parks are concerned, **Universal Studios Florida** is still buzzing at the arrival of the Wizarding World of Harry Potter – Diagon Alley in summer 2014, while there were strong rumours as we went to press of a new King Kong attraction at Universal's Islands of Adventure park for 2015–16. Meanwhile, Universal's **CityWalk** district has new shopping and dining, notably with Antojito's Authentic Mexican Food, the Hot Dog Hall of Fame and Vivo Italian Kitchen, some of which was still taking shape in late 2014.

BRITTIP
If you are an Orlando aficionado and want to see just how many attractions we have reported on in the last 20 years, which are no longer open, have a look at our review on page 156 and join us in a little nostalgia!

Walt Disney World finally completed its extensive Fantasyland redevelopment in the **Magic Kingdom** in May 2014 while their two BIG projects are both ongoing, the conversion of Downtown Disney to **Disney Springs** (by 2016) and the addition of Avatarland to **Disney's Animal Kingdom** (for 2017). And talking of rumours, there is much speculation 2015 will mark the start of an expanded Star Wars area in **Disney's Hollywood Studios**.

LEGOLAND Florida is due to open the sparkling, feature-filled Legoland Hotel in late 2015 after opening their new toddler area, Duplo Valley, in May 2014.

SeaWorld will also debut an all-new sealion show in early 2015, tentatively called Clyde & Seamore: Back to School, which will add even more live-action fun.

BRITTIP
Don't forget to keep an eye out for the Brit Bonus, which features special offers and discounts with various hotels, attractions and restaurants. In addition, *Brit Guide* partners Florida Dolphin Tours now offer their exclusive 12.5% discount to our readers on a new live booking option on our website, **www.britguideorlando.net**.

Plan your visit

The next few chapters will tell you all you need to know to plan the ideal holiday. Make a rough itinerary and then fine tune it with this book. You can also take advantage of our unique Touring Plans Service (p41). Now read on and enjoy…

The Grand Carousel in Fun Town at Legoland Florida

2 Planning and Practicalities

or How to *Almost* Do It All and Live to Tell the Tale

We've been saying it from the start and it's still true today – good planning is the *only* way to tackle an Orlando holiday. This just isn't a 'make-it-up-as-you-go-along' destination (unless you enjoy being frustrated and/or exhausted!).

This huge and demanding place can pull you in a dozen directions at once, with a dazzling array of options for practically everything. Nowhere else in the world can be so complex to navigate, so it's vital to do your 'homework' in advance. Start with WHEN you want to go; WHERE you'd like to stay; WHAT sort of holiday you want; WHO to book with; and finally HOW MUCH to try to do.

When to go
To avoid the worst of the crowds, the best times to go are Oct to Dec (but not Thanksgiving week in Nov or 20 Dec to New Year); early Jan to mid-Mar (avoiding President's Day in Feb); and the week after Easter to the end of May.

Busiest times: Orlando is seldom quiet but is busiest at:

- Christmas/New Year period (about 20 Dec–4 Jan).

- Mid-Mar to week after Easter.

- From Memorial Day (the last Mon in May, the official start of the summer season) to mid-Aug, notably around 4 July.

- Labor Day weekend in early Sept, the last holiday of summer.

- Thanksgiving week (from the Wed–Sun).

The parks can close to new arrivals by mid-morning at these times – especially at Christmas.

BRITTIP
Thanksgiving is the 4th Thurs in Nov; George Washington's birthday, or President's Day, is the 3rd Mon in Feb, and both make for above-average long-weekend crowds.

Best times: The best combination of good weather and smaller crowds is in Apr (after Easter) and Oct. Rain isn't a big factor (although outdoor rides and the water parks will close if lightning threatens), but the crowds will noticeably thin out when it does rain and you can take advantage by bringing waterproofs or buying a cheap plastic poncho (all the parks sell them, but they are cheaper from

Despicable Me Minion Mayhem

© Universal Orlando

Hurricane alert?

June–Nov is officially hurricane season, but it is not anything to worry about. Even the unprecedented extremes of 2004, when 3 major storms hit Central Florida, caused no significant damage to the parks and the biggest inconvenience was losing electricity for a few days. In the unlikely event of a major storm, switch your TV to the Weather Channel or local news station WESH 2 and follow its advice.

local supermarkets). In the colder months, take a few warm layers for early morning queues. Then, when it heats up, leave them in the park lockers. When it gets hot, take advantage of the air-conditioned attractions (and drink LOTS of water). The humidity alone will knock you sideways in summer and it's vital to rehydrate at regular intervals.

Where to stay

This is equally important and, again, there's a huge choice. As a rough guide, 4 main areas make up the great Orlando tourist conglomeration.

Walt Disney World: Some of the most sophisticated, convenient and fun places to stay are Disney's own hotels.

The same imagination that created the theme parks also worked on the likes of Disney's Polynesian Resort and Animal Kingdom Lodge. They all feature free transport, resort ID (so you can charge purchases to your

room and have them delivered to the hotel), free parking and the BIG bonus of **Extra Magic Hours**. This allows Disney resort guests entry to 1 theme park each day, either 1hr before official opening or for 2hrs after closing, so you can do many of the attractions with lower crowds (though evenings can still be busy). Many also have kids' clubs and babysitting services. However, with the exception of Disney's All-Star, Pop Century and Art of Animation Resorts, its hotels are among the most expensive, especially to eat in, and are not close to other attractions you may wish to visit. They make a good 1-week base, though.

BRITTIP

Beware holiday homes (and some hotels) that insist they are 'just minutes from Disney World' – which may actually mean 30mins or more from the parks. Try to get the exact address and check it.

Lake Buena Vista: On the eastern fringes of Walt Disney World and conveniently along Interstate 4 (I-4), this features a good mix of hotels. It is handy for Disney (and slightly cheaper), with most hotels offering free transport to the parks, plus there is excellent dining and shopping.

International Drive: The ribbon development known as I-Drive lies mid-way between Disney and downtown Orlando, running parallel

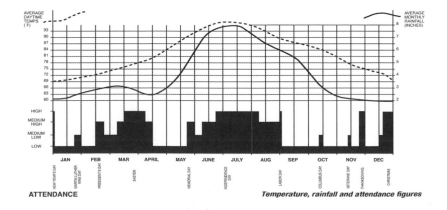

ATTENDANCE   *Temperature, rainfall and attendance figures*

Virgin's V-Room

All Virgin Holidays guests have the option of the V-Room lounge at Gatwick and Manchester, a private hideaway that includes a dedicated kids' play area, video games, big-screen TV, internet access, relaxing adults-only area, free breakfast, snacks, fruit, soft drinks, tea and coffee, and a fast-track security channel. It costs £22/adult and £12/child (2–11) in advance (£24 and £15 on day of travel), but is free with Platinum bookings.

to I-4, and is an excellent central location about 20mins' drive from Disney and close to Universal and SeaWorld. It is a well-developed tourist area in its own right, with great shops, restaurants and attractions like Wet 'n Wild, Ripley's Believe It Or Not, WonderWorks and iFLY Orlando, plus its own handy transportation service, the I-Ride Trolley. The downside is it gets congested in peak times, but it is good value and one of the few areas with extensive pavement, making it easy to explore on foot. A sub-district off I-Drive is the Universal area of Kirkman Road and Major Boulevard.

Kissimmee: Budget holiday-makers can be found in their greatest numbers along the tourist sprawl of Highway 192 (the Irlo Bronson Memorial Highway), an almost unbroken 20ml/32km strip of hotels, motels, restaurants and shops. It offers some of the best economy accommodation and is handy for Disney, though further from Universal and SeaWorld. A car is advisable here, although there is extensive pavement, landscaping, bus shelters and benches. Highway 27 is often referred to as 'Kissimmee' but is actually either in Lake County (to the north) or Polk County (to the south). This is prime holiday home territory, with numerous developments along its 25mi/40km extent.

ANNIVERSARY SPOT
20 The I-Drive area has seen the greatest growth in hotels in the past 20 years, while the eastern end of Kissimmee has struggled to keep up.

Split holidays

Florida has so much to offer, many opt to spend a week in Orlando and a week somewhere else. The Atlantic coast has great beaches an hour to the east; the Everglades are 3–4hrs to the south; and there are more wonderful beaches to the west. There's great shopping almost everywhere, stunning golf courses and opportunities to play or watch tennis, baseball and basketball, go fishing, boating or kayaking. The tour operators all offer a huge variety of packages, plus cruise-and-stay options. If you can afford it, the best option is to have 2 weeks in Orlando then a week relaxing on one of Florida's fabulous beaches. A 2-week, half-and-half split is popular, but can make for a hectic time in Orlando. Some companies offer a 10/4 Orlando/coast split, which is a better idea for 2 weeks. Fly-drives offer great flexibility, but there is a lot to tempt you and you may find it better to book a 2-centre stay that includes a car and accommodation so you can still travel but avoid too much packing and unpacking (see also Chapter 9).

Travel companies

There is serious competition for your hard-earned money – from the big boys, specialists and online agents – so choose one that best fits your needs on cost, flights, style and extras. We highlight the main ones here. Always ensure they are ABTA (for travel agents) or ATOL (for flights) bonded. During peak periods – notably the summer and Christmas holidays – it can actually be cheaper to book a package with charter flights

St Pete's Beach

Dining Plan options

Most tour operators offer the Disney Dining Plan as an optional extra with Disney hotel packages and it can be good value if you spend ALL your time in Walt Disney World, where there are few cheap dining outlets. But, because ALL members of the family must be included for the FULL length of your stay, even the Quick Service plan adds £1,232 for a family of 4 (with children 3–9) staying for 2 weeks; the main Dining Plan would be £1,680; and the Deluxe Plan a whopping £2,800. It is a LOT of food to contend with, especially when it's hot, and you often need to book the full-service restaurants well in advance. You can certainly eat cheaper elsewhere, so consider if this is a good choice before you book. However, tour operators occasionally offer the Dining Plan as a FREE perk at quieter times of the year – a BIG bonus. See more on Disney Dining Plan on p58.

rather than individual flights, hotels, etc, although it is also worth looking at flight-only prices.

The Big Boys

British Airways Holidays: A well-established and varied choice, using direct BA flights from Gatwick to Orlando International Airport and Tampa year-round, with any range of stay (0844 493 0782, **www.britishairways.com/travel/holidays-in-florida**).

Cosmos Holidays: With a long history in Florida, Cosmos focuses on the key resort areas in Orlando and the Gulf Coast. Uses Monarch Airlines from Gatwick, Manchester and Glasgow to Orlando Sanford International Airport from spring to late autumn (0483 227 1464, **www.cosmos.co.uk**).

Thomas Cook: An increasingly routine range of options from this former big mainstream operator, now offering just 7 and 14-day holidays with flights from Manchester and

Green Eggs and Ham at Islands of Adventure

Glasgow from late Mar to early Nov (0844 412 5959, **www.thomascook.com**), although their travel agent arm can still sell packages from Gatwick (just with other airlines).

Thomson: Another one of the mainstream companies, with an especially extensive range of villa choice. Flights from Birmingham, East Midlands, Edinburgh, Gatwick, Glasgow, Manchester and Newcastle to Orlando Sanford International Airport with their own Thomson Airways, many with the added bonus of the smart new Dreamliner aircraft from spring to late autumn (0871 231 4691, **www.thomson.co.uk**).

Travel City Direct: Popular budget-minded brand under Virgin umbrella and with mainly Virgin Atlantic flights (but also BA, Delta, United and Aer Lingus), with good range of beach and combo options (0844 557 6969, **www.travelcitydirect.com**).

◄■►**ANNIVERSARY** SPOT
20 Since we first started, we've said goodbye to the likes of tour operators Unijet, First Choice, Jetlife, Sunworld and Transolar.

Virgin Holidays: Britain's leading tour operator to Florida, with by far the biggest choice and multi-centre option possibilities (including cruises, beach-hopper packages and even a Miami-Cancun combo), mainly using Virgin Atlantic's award-winning service but also Delta, Air France, United and US Airways. Some exclusive extra perks, like early entry

Complete Orlando

The highly rated Attraction Tickets Direct company has a full ATOL-bonded travel operator called Complete Orlando, which is well worth trying for packages, flights, hotels, car hire and travel insurance. It offers a wide range of accommodation (usually with some great deals on Disney hotels in particular), plus handy online videos, and promises no credit card fees or hidden extras. Call 0800 294 8844, **www.completeorlando.co.uk**.

to the Wizarding World of Harry Potter at Universal Orlando and to SeaWorld, plus wedding services, vow renewals and new options on exclusive Captiva Island and Key West for 2015 (0844 557 4321, **www.virginholidays.co.uk**).

The specialists

Choose from the following smaller, specialist companies that all feature individual programmes to Florida:

- **Funway Holidays** (0844 557 3333, **www.funwayholidays.co.uk**).
- **Jetsave** (0844 415 9000, **www.jetsave.com**).
- **Kuoni** (0844 488 0561, **www.kuoni.co.uk**).
- **Ocean Florida** (020 7939 7775, **www.ocean-florida.co.uk**).
- **Premier Holidays** (0844 4937 531, **www.premierholidays.co.uk**).
- **Tour America Direct** (0845 319 4266, **www.touramericadirect.co.uk**).
- **Trailfinders** (020 7368 1200, **www.trailfinders.com**).
- **Travelbag** (0871 703 4698, **www.travelbag.co.uk**).
- **USAirtours** (020 8418 8268, **www.usairtours.co.uk**).

Online agents

The recent growth of online travel agents has been huge, and you will find some great deals in this group, for packages, flights or accommodation:

- **eBookers** (020 3320 3320, **www.ebookers.com**).
- **Dial A Flight** (0844 811 4444, **www.dialaflight.com**).
- **Expedia** (020 3564 3904, **www.expedia.co.uk**).
- **LastMinute** (0800 083 4000, **www.lastminute.com**).
- **Opodo** (0871 277 0090, **www.opodo.co.uk**).
- **Travel Supermarket** (0845 345 5708, **www.travelsupermarket.com**).

For flights only, try:

- **Cheap Flights** (**www.cheapflights.co.uk**).
- **Flight Centre** (0800 587 0058, **www.flightcentre.co.uk**).
- **NetFlights** (0844 692 6792, **www.netflights.com**).
- **Sky Scanner** (**www.skyscanner.net**).

Online search engines

The following selection search a number of travel agent sites at the same time:

- **kelkoo** (**http://travel.kelkoo.co.uk**).
- **kayak** (**www.kayak.co.uk**).
- **Travel Jungle** (**www.traveljungle.co.uk**).

Scheduled flights

The only direct non-charter flights to Orlando are with Virgin Atlantic (Gatwick, Manchester and Glasgow), British Airways (Gatwick) and Aer Lingus (Dublin). BA also flies direct to Tampa and Miami and Virgin to Miami but you can often save money on indirect flights. Choose from **American Airlines** (from Heathrow

Mulberry Street Gizmos and Gadgets at Islands of Adventure

via Boston, Dallas, New York and Washington; Manchester via New York; or Dublin via Chicago; 0844 499 7300, **www.americanairlines.co.uk**); **Delta/KLM** (Gatwick via Atlanta; Heathrow via Atlanta, Boston, Minneapolis, Detroit or New York; or Manchester via New York or Atlanta; 0871 231 0000, **www.klm.com**); **United** (Heathrow via Washington, Houston, New York or Chicago, or Manchester, Birmingham, Belfast, Dublin, Glasgow or Edinburgh via New York; 0845 607 6760 **www.united. com**); and **US Airways** (Heathrow, Manchester, Glasgow or Dublin via Charlotte, Philadelphia, Dallas, Chicago or New York; 0845 600 3300, **www.usairways.com**). **Icelandair** (from Heathrow, Glasgow and Manchester; 0844 811 1190, **www.icelandair.co.uk**) also offers a scheduled transatlantic route to Orlando Sanford Airport via Reykjavik, Iceland. In summer 2014, low-cost carrier **Norwegian** started a new route from Fort Lauderdale, near Miami, to Gatwick twice a week and once a week to Edinburgh and Manchester (all using the Dreamliner) and there were some tempting lower fares (0843 3780 888, **www.norwegian. com/uk/**). Fort Lauderdale is just 3hrs' drive from Orlando while connecting flights are also available.

The obvious drawback is the extra journey time, and the connecting flight may land you in Orlando late in the evening. However, it does break the journey and places like Detroit and Dallas often process international passengers quicker than Orlando, meaning less hassle when you arrive in Florida.

Forever Florida

What to see when

Once you arrive, the temptation is to head for the nearest theme park, then the next and so on. Except this is the best way to end up exhausted. Some days at the parks are busier than others, while you'll also need a few rest days. So here's what to do.

Using the Planner on p345 as an example (or with the Brit Guide Touring Plans service, p41), make a note of the attractions you want to see. The most sensible strategy is to plan around the 8 'must-see' parks. If you have only a week, drop Busch Gardens and focus on Disney, Universal and SeaWorld. The new-look Kennedy Space Center is also hard to overlook these days, though.

- **Magic Kingdom:** 2 days – the biggest hit with children.
- **Epcot:** 2 days – only the most fleet of foot can do it in a day, and then only with low crowds, but there are fewer rides to amuse children.
- **Animal Kingdom:** 1 day – a little short on appeal for the youngest.
- **Disney's Hollywood Studios:** 1 day – plus the evening Fantasmic! show.
- **SeaWorld:** 1–2 days.
- **Islands of Adventure:** 1–2 days.
- **Universal Studios:** 1–2 days.
- **Busch Gardens:** 1 day – extremely popular with British families, it is 75mins away in Tampa.

LEGOLAND Florida, 45mins away in Winter Haven, is also a full day's outing. Look at the detail in Chapters 5–8 before you plan.

Smaller attractions

Of the other, smaller scale attractions, **Forever Florida** is a full day out as it also involves a 1hr drive to get there, but everything else can be fitted around your Big 8 itinerary. The water parks make for a relaxing ½-day, as does the quieter **Bok Tower Gardens**. **Gatorland** (requiring at least ½ a day) is a unique look at some of Florida's oldest inhabitants and is a good combination with **Boggy Creek**

Our must-do experiences

- Soarin' and IllumiNations show (Epcot)
- Cirque du Soleil® (Downtown Disney)
- Harry Potter and the Forbidden Journey, plus the Amazing Adventures of Spider-Man and The Hulk rides (Islands of Adventure)
- Boggy Creek Airboats/Wild Florida (Kissimmee)
- Expedition Everest and Festival of The Lion King (Animal Kingdom)
- Wishes fireworks, Pirates of the Caribbean and Haunted Mansion rides (Magic Kingdom)
- Fantasmic! show and Star Tours ride (Disney's Hollywood Studios)
- Transformers: The Ride 3D and Harry Potter and the Escape from Gringotts (Universal Studios)
- Shopping!
- Antarctica: Empire of the Penguin and Blue Horizons show (SeaWorld)
- Cheetah Hunt and SheiKra coasters (Busch Gardens)
- Space Shuttle Atlantis (Kennedy Space Center)
- A Disney character meal
- A day at a water park

Airboats or **Wild Florida**. Then there are the likes of **Ripley's Believe It Or Not** museum, the **WhirlyDome** and the **WonderWorks** house of fun, both offering several hours' entertainment, the thrills of **iFLY Orlando** (an indoor 'sky-diving' wind tunnel) and the lure of old-fashioned go-karts and other fairground-type rides at **Fun Spot**, **Magical Midway** and **Old Town**. Many stay open after the theme parks close.

Disney also has **DisneyQuest**, an imaginative interactive arcade that guarantees several hours of fun (especially for older children) at Downtown Disney, while each main area is also well served with creatively designed mini-golf courses.

Evenings
The evening entertainment features a similarly wide choice. By far the best, and worth at least one evening

each, are **Downtown Disney** and Universal's **CityWalk** – the latter will keep you busy until the early hours! Dinner shows provide a lot of fun: 2hr cabarets based on themes such as medieval knights, pirates, Al Capone and murder mysteries that all include a hearty meal.

Shopping
Shopping in Orlando is world class (see Chapter 12) and your battle plan should include at least a day to visit the spectacular malls and discount centres, like the 2 excellent Orlando Premium Outlets centres, Lake Buena Vista Factory Stores, Mall at Millenia and the Florida Mall. Busy at weekends, they're handy if it rains.

What to do when
There are several guidelines for avoiding the worst of the tourist hordes, even in high season.

Avoid busy days: Most Americans arrive at weekends and head for the main theme parks first, so Sun and Mon are often bad times to visit the Magic Kingdom, while Tues is usually also busy at Epcot. New rides like Harry Potter (at Universal Studios) also create longer queues, notably at weekends. The Animal Kingdom is the hardest to navigate when crowded, while Epcot handles the crowds best. Disney's Blizzard Beach and Typhoon Lagoon water parks hit high tide at weekends, and Thurs and Fri in summer. If Walt Disney World is humming early in

SeaWorld's Journey to Atlantis

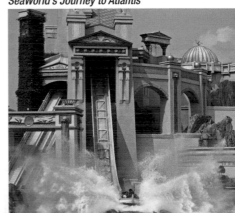

the week, that makes it a good time to visit SeaWorld, Busch Gardens or the Kennedy Space Center. Try to avoid Wet 'n Wild and Aquatica at weekends, too.

Disney's Extra Magic Hours: Allowing Disney guests early and late access (see p59) creates bigger crowds, too. So, if you are NOT staying at a Disney hotel, avoid these EMH mornings. For much of the year, they keep to the following weekly pattern: Magic Kingdom, Thurs; Epcot, Tues; Disney's Hollywood Studios, most Sat (plus some Mon); Animal Kingdom, Mon (plus some Wed). Be aware EMH days can change at short notice, and the Magic Kingdom can have multiple successive days at Easter and Christmas.

Universal Orlando: The picture is different here as only the 2 Wizarding Worlds of Harry Potter have daily early opening privileges (for guests at all of Universal's 4 hotels). This often means heavier crowds early in the week, while the parks also get busiest at weekends.

BRITTIP

If your hotel is not far away, take a mid-afternoon break from the park and return for a siesta or a swim. Your car park ticket is valid all day, and the evening is often the best time to be in the parks.

Arrive early: Getting the most out of your days at the parks is another art form, and there are several options. The opening times seldom vary

Aquatica

Medical marvels

The **Medical Concierge®** is a great choice for local medical care with doctors and paediatricians throughout the tourist areas, making house calls to hotels and villas 24/7. They also have several key clinic locations, notably close to Universal Orlando, and International Drive, Lake Buena Vista, Kissimmee and Haines City/Davenport, but you must call for an appointment. Their doctors have mobile pharmacies and even X-ray units and they specialise in providing healthcare to overseas visitors, hence their staff are familiar with dealing with Brits. They can often arrange same-day dental and other specialist appointments and take many UK travel insurance polices, meaning they deal directly with the insurance company. Their switchboard is manned around the clock with medically trained staff, ensuring you never deal with an answering machine. Call 1855 326 5252, and dial 1 to get straight through to medical care, or visit **www.themedicalconcierge.com**.

from 9am (Magic Kingdom and Animal Kingdom can be 8am at peak times), but arriving early is highly advisable. Apart from being near the head of the queues (and they are SERIOUS queues, or 'lines'), the parks occasionally open early if the crowds build up. So you can be a step ahead by arriving at least 30mins before opening time (or an hour early during peak periods). You will also be better placed to park in the huge car parks and catch the tram to the main gates.

Prioritise: Once you are in pole position, don't waste time on the shops, scenery and other frippery that will lure the unprepared first-timer. Instead, head straight for some of the main rides and get a few big-time thrills under your belt before the main hordes arrive. You will quickly work out where the most popular attractions are as the majority of early birds will flock to them. Use Chapters 5 and 6 to plan your park strategies.

Pace yourself: Disney's parks, notably the Magic Kingdom, stay open late for the main holidays, until midnight at times, and that can be a l-o-n-g

Footy frenzy

You don't need a specialist sports bar to find British football on TV these days. The Premier League is extensively covered by NBC (up to 3 games on Sat and Sun, plus the Mon night games) while the Champions League is on Fox Sports. You should check if your villa/hotel has NBC Sports for some games, though, as it is a cable channel that not everyone gets.

day for kids. It's vital to pace yourself, especially if you arrive early. There are plenty of options to take time off for a drink or a sit-down somewhere air-conditioned, and these latter are vital in summer.

Meal breaks: Benefit from the American habit of dining en masse at lunchtime (noon–1.30pm) and dinner (5.30–7pm) by planning your own meals outside those times. It pays to take an early lunch (before noon), snack in mid-afternoon and then enjoy a relative drop-off in crowds in late afternoon. But try not to have all your meals in the parks; eating here can be expensive (at least $11/person for a basic meal). A good breakfast before you arrive and a light lunch will save you $$$s!

BRITTIP
The water IS safe to drink in the US, but it might not taste great as it's heavily fluoridated. If you buy bottled water, do so at supermarkets, not at the parks, where it is exorbitantly expensive.

Comfort and clothing

You may feel jetlagged for the first day or so after your arrival, but avoiding alcohol and coffee on the plane and keeping hydrated by drinking plenty of water can reduce this.

Shoes: The most important part of your holiday wardrobe is your footwear – you'll be on your feet a LOT, even at off-peak periods. The smallest park is 'only' 100acres/40ha, but that is irrelevant to the time spent queuing. This is not the time

to break in new sandals or trainers. Comfortable, well-worn shoes or trainers are essential (many rate Croc-type shoes as ideal park footwear).

BRITTIP
Look after your feet and avoid the onset of blisters by buying some moleskin footpads from a supermarket or 'drug-store' like Walgreens and CVS.

Casual clothes: You need dress only as the climate dictates. T-shirts and shorts are appropriate in all parks and nearly all restaurants will accept casual dress. However, swimwear is not acceptable away from pool areas. If you feel the need for a change of clothes or a sweater for the evening after a long day, use the handy lockers in all the parks (unlimited use all day for a small fee).

BRITTIP
Don't be tempted to pack a lot of smart or formal clothing – you really won't need it in hot, informal Florida.

Baby services: All the parks are well equipped with pushchairs, or 'strollers', for hire (although it pays to have your own), and baby services are located at regular intervals.

Sunscreen: It is VITAL to use high-factor sun creams at all times, even during the winter when the sun may not feel strong but can still burn. Few things will ruin your holiday like severe sunburn. Orlando has a subtropical climate and you need higher factor creams than in the Mediterranean. Use sun block on sensitive areas like nose and ears, and splash on the after-sun liberally at the end of the day. You'll also need waterproof sun cream for swimming. Skincare products are widely available and usually inexpensive (at the likes of Wal-Mart, Publix and Target). Wear a hat during the day, and avoid alcohol, coffee and fizzy drinks until the evening as they are dehydrating and make you liable to heatstroke. You must increase your fluid intake SIGNIFICANTLY in the summer,

Attractions with warnings for expectant mothers

Animal Kingdom: Dinosaur!, Expedition Everest, Kali River Rapids, Kilimanjaro Safari, Primeval Whirl.

Busch Gardens: Cheetah Hunt, Congo River Rapids, Crazy Camel, Falcon's Fury, Gwazi, Kumba, Montu, Phoenix, Sand Serpent, Scorpion, SheiKra, Stanley Falls Log Flume, Tanganyika Tidal Wave, Ubanga-Banga Bumper Cars.

Epcot: Mission: SPACE, Soarin', Test Track.

Hollywood Studios: Rock 'n Roller Coaster, Star Tours, Twilight Zone Tower of Terror.

Islands of Adventure: Cat in the Hat, Dragon Challenge, Dudley Do-Right's Ripsaw Falls, Flight of the Hippogriff, Harry Potter and the Forbidden Journey, Incredible Hulk Coaster, Jurassic Park River Adventure, Popeye & Bluto's Bilge Rat Barges, Storm Force Accelatron, Dr Doom's Fearfall, The Amazing Adventures of Spider-Man.

Magic Kingdom: Big Thunder Mountain Railroad, The Barnstormer, Seven Dwarfs Mine Train, Space Mountain, Splash Mountain.

SeaWorld: Antarctica: Empire of the Penguin (Wild version of ride), Journey to Atlantis, Jazzie Jellies, Kraken, Manta, Rock Wall, Shamu Express, Swishy Fishies, Trampoline, Wild Arctic (ride portion).

Universal Studios: Disaster!, ET Adventure, Harry Potter and the Escape from Gringotts, Men in Black Alien Attack, Revenge of the Mummy, Shrek 4-D, Terminator 2: 3-D (stationary seats available), TRANSFORMERS: The Ride – 3D, Twister – Ride it Out!, Woody Woodpecker's Nuthouse Coaster.

but stick to sports drinks, such as Gatorade, and lots of water.

◀▶ BRITTIP
One of the best ways to keep cool in the sun is to buy a simple mist spray fan (about $7.99) from a supermarket.

Medical aid

Should you require medical treatment, for sunburn or other first aid, consult your tour operator's info about local hospitals and surgeries.

Falcon's Fury at Busch Gardens

In the event of a medical or other emergency, dial 911 as you would 999 in Britain. It cannot be over-stressed, however, you should take out comprehensive travel insurance (see right) for any trip to America, as there is NO National Health Service and any form of medical treatment is expensive. Keep all the receipts and put in a claim on your return home.

◀▶ BRITTIP
The summer is mosquito time and a spray-on or roll-on insect repellent is highly advisable away from the parks. Brands to look for locally are Cutter, Repel and Off!

Emergency outpatients: These can be found with **Centra Care** at Florida Hospital Medical Center in more than 20 Central Florida locations (407 200 2273; **www.centracare.org**), as well as full family and paediatric care. Open 8am–8pm (5pm at weekends), there are 4 locations open to midnight Mon–Fri, including at 12500 S Apopka-Vineland Road near the Crossroads shopping centre and Downtown Disney at Lake Buena

At-a-glance kids' height requirements

Height	Park	Rides
2ft 8in/82cm	Disney's Blizzard Beach	Chairlift
Must be with a child 3ft–4ft 8in/91–142cm	Islands of Adventure	Pteranodon Flyers
3ft–4ft 8in/91–142cm	Wet 'n Wild	The Surge, Aqua Drag Racer, Flyer, Disco H2O
3ft/91cm	Disney's Magic Kingdom	The Barnstormer
	Universal Studios	Woody Woodpecker's Nuthouse Coaster
	Islands of Adventure	The Cat in the Hat
3ft 3in/99cm	Busch Gardens	Rhino Rally (age 3 minimum)
3ft 4in/101cm	Disney's Animal Kingdom	DINOSAUR!
	Disney's Hollywood Studios	Star Tours, The Twilight Zone Tower of Terror
	Disney's Magic Kingdom	Splash Mountain, Big Thunder Mountain Railroad, Seven Dwarves Mine Train Ride (coming 2014)
	Epcot	Test Track, Soarin'
	Islands of Adventure	The Amazing Adventures of Spider-Man
	Universal Studios	The Simpsons Ride, TRANSFORMERS: The Ride – 3D, Harry Potter and the Escape from Gringotts
3ft 6in/106cm	Aquatica	Walhalla Wave, HooRoo Run, Taumata Racer
	Busch Gardens	The Wild Surge (3ft 2in/96cm with adult), Congo River Rapids, Ubanga-Banga Bumper Cars, Scorpion, Sand Serpent (age 6 minimum)
	Disney's Animal Kingdom	Kali River Rapids
	Islands of Adventure	Jurassic Park River Adventure
	SeaWorld	Journey to Atlantis, Wild Arctic (Polar Express at Christmas)
	Universal Studios	Men in Black: Alien Attack
3ft 8 in/111cm	Disney's Animal Kingdom	Expedition: Everest
	Disney's Magic Kingdom	Space Mountain
	Epcot	Mission: SPACE
	Islands of Adventure	Dudley Do-Right's Ripsaw Falls
3ft 10in/116cm	Busch Gardens	Stanley Falls
Under 4ft/122cm only	Aquatica	Kata's Kookaburra Cove
	Disney's Blizzard Beach	Tike's Peak
	Disney's Typhoon Lagoon	Ketchakiddee Creek
Under 4ft/122cm only **(with adult)**	Wet 'n Wild	Kids Park
4ft/122cm	Aquatica	Dolphin Plunge, Ihu's Breakaway Falls, Omaka Rocka
	Busch Gardens	Gwazi, Tanganyika Tidal Wave, Jungle Flyers
	Disney's Animal Kingdom	Primeval Whirl
	Disney's Blizzard Beach	Summit Plummet, Slush Gusher, Downhill Double Dipper
	Disney's Hollywood Studios	Rock 'n' Roller Coaster Starring Aerosmith
	Disney's Typhoon Lagoon	Crush 'n' Gusher, Humunga Kowabunga
	Epcot	Sum of All Thrills (non-inversion)
	Islands of Adventure	Popeye And Bluto's Bilge-Rat Barges, Flight of the Hippogriff, Harry Potter and the Forbidden Journey
	Universal Studios	Revenge of the Mummy, Disaster! A Major Motion Picture Ride…Starring YOU (unless accompanied by adult), ET Adventure
	Wet 'n Wild	Bomb Bay, Der Stuka, Black Hole, The Storm, Brain Wash
4ft 3in/130cm	Universal Studios	Hollywood Rip Ride Rockit!
	Wet 'n Wild	Wild One
4ft 4in/132cm	Disney's Magic Kingdom	Tomorrowland Speedway (for child to drive alone)
	Epcot	Sum of All Thrills (with inversion)
	Islands of Adventure	Dr Doom's Fearfall
4ft 5in/143cm	Wet 'n Wild	Knee Ski Wake-Boarding
4ft 6in/137cm	Busch Gardens	SheiKra, Kumba, Montu, Cheetah Hunt, Falcon's Fury
	Islands of Adventure	The Incredible Hulk Coaster, Dragon Challenge
	SeaWorld	Kraken, Manta

Vista (8pm Sat and Sun; 407 934 2273). Other notable tourist area locations are: 8201 West Irlo Bronson Memorial Highway (192), by Orange Lake Resort (407 465 0846); on Sand Lake Road, between John Young Parkway and Orange Blossom Trail (9am–5pm Sat and Sun; 407 851 6478); and 4320 West Vine Street, near Medieval Times (407 390 1888).

The **Dr P Phillips Hospital**, 9400 Turkey Lake Road, also has an emergency outpatients open 24hrs a day (407 351 8500).

Better still, call **The Medical Concierge®** (407 648 5252 or freephone at 1888 648 5252, or **www.themedicalconcierge.com**; see panel on p24) who make hotel and villa 'house calls' 24 hours a day.

⚑ BRITTIP

If you take regular prescription drugs, check the name with your doctor or pharmacist as many have a different name in the US (e.g. adrenaline is known as epinephrine, paracetamol is acetaminophen). Find out and carry both names in case of an emergency.

Chemists: The 2 largest chemists ('drug stores' in the US) are **Walgreens** (**www.walgreens.com**) and **CVS** (**www.cvs.com**), and the Walgreens

Diagon Alley at Universal Studios

Two-way radio rentals

Two-way radios are popular in Orlando for safety and convenience. Many families buy 'walkie-talkies' to keep in touch around the parks in preference to mobile phones. You can pick them up locally for as little as $35 in stores like Wal-Mart, Best Buy, Radio Shack, Office Depot and Staples. However, they cannot be used in the UK as they use the same frequency as our emergency services.

at 12100 S Apopka-Vineland Road (near Downtown Disney), 5935 W Irlo Bronson Memorial Highway (Highway 192 in Kissimmee), 6201, 8959 and 12650 International Drive (among others, plus the new one at the corner of I-Drive and Sand Lake Rd), are open 24 hours a day.

Travel insurance

Having said you shouldn't travel without insurance, you shouldn't pay more than you need to either. Your travel agent may imply you need to buy its policy, which might be expensive, but you are free to buy elsewhere. Your policy should cover all these options.

• Medical cover of at least £2m.

• Personal liability up to £2m (this won't cover driving abroad; you still need Supplementary Liability Insurance with your car hire firm).

• Cancellation or curtailment cover up to £5,000.

• Personal property cover up to £1,500 (but check on expensive items, as most policies limit single articles to £250).

• Cash and document cover, including your passport and tickets.

• 24hr emergency helpline.

• If you want to go horse-riding, check your policy includes dangerous sports cover.

Shop around at reputable dealers such as:

• **Allianz Assistance** (0871 200 0428, **www.allianz-assistance.co.uk**).

Measurements

US clothes sizes are smaller than ours, hence a US size 12 dress is a UK 14, or an American jacket sized 42 is a 44. Shoes are the opposite: a US 10 should fit a British size 9 foot. The measuring system is imperial, not metric.

- **American Express** (0800 587 4000, **www.americanexpress.com/uk**).
- **Aviva** (0800 051 3606, **www.aviva.co.uk**).
- **AXA** (0844 874 0360, **www.axainsurance.com/travel**).
- **Club Direct** (0845 888 8891, **www.clubdirect.com**).
- **Columbus** (0845 888 8893, **www.columbusdirect.com**).
- **Direct Travel** (0845 605 2700, **www.direct-travel.co.uk**).
- **Money Supermarket** also compares travel insurers at **www.moneysupermarket.com/travel-insurance** (0845 345 5708).

Florida with children

We are often asked what we think is the right age to take children to Orlando, and there is no set answer. Some toddlers take to it instantly, while some 6 or 7-year-olds are overwhelmed. Very often, the best attractions for young children are the hotel swimming pool or the tram ride to a park's front gates! Some love the Disney characters instantly, while others find them frightening. There is no predicting how they'll react but, at 4½, Simon's oldest boy loved just about every second of his first experience (apart from the fireworks!) and still talks about it. A 3-year-old may not remember much, but will have fun and provide you with great memories, photos and videos. Here are some top tips for travelling with youngsters.

The flight: Try to look calm (even if you don't feel it) and relaxed. Small children soon pick up on any anxieties and make them worse. Pack a bag with lots of little things for them (comics, sweets, colouring books, small surprise toys, etc.) and keep vital extras like Calpol (in sachets, if possible), a change of clothes, a small first-aid kit (plasters, antiseptic cream, baby wipes), sunglasses, a hat and sunscreen in your hand luggage.

Once you're there: Take things slowly and let your children dictate the pace to a large extent. In hot, humid summer, only the most placid children (and few under-5s, in our experience) will happily queue for an hour or more at a ride, so use Disney's FastPass+ system (p101) judiciously. The heat, in particular, can result in grizzly kids in no time, so take breaks for drinks and splash zones or head for attractions with air-conditioning. Remember to carry your small first-aid kit. Baby wipes always come in handy, and it's a good idea to take spare clothes, which you can leave in park lockers. Going back to the hotel for an afternoon snooze is a good idea – you will also dodge the worst of the heat and crowds.

◀️🇬🇧 BRITTIP

The handy Kids-eat-free card for Orlando offers a free child's meal (for 11 and under) with every adult meal or entrée purchased. It costs just $19.99/child and features more than 150 local restaurants – from the standard McDonald's and Dunkin Donuts to upmarket Cedar's and Ming Court – with potential savings of $350. It is valid for 90 days from first use. See **www.kidseatfreecard.com**.

In the sun: Carry sun cream and sun block at all times and use it often, in queues, on buses, etc. A children's after-sun lotion is also advisable. And make sure they drink a lot of water or non-fizzy drinks; tiredness and irritability are often the signs of mild dehydration.

Dining out: Look for Kids-eat-free deals in many places, as they can apply to children up to 12, and take advantage of the many buffet options (see Chapter 11, Dining Out) to fill up the family or for picky eaters.

Many restaurants do Meals To Go if you want a quiet meal in your own accommodation without the worry of the kids playing up. And try to let your children get used to the characters (especially the size of them) before you go to one of the many wonderful character meals.

Having fun: Let your children do some of the decision-making and be prepared to go with the flow if they find something unexpected – the many squirt fountains and splash zones in the parks are an example (bring swimsuits and/or a change of clothes!). The Orlando rule of 'You Can't Do It All' applies especially with kids. Be aware some youngsters find the evening fireworks too loud, but the 3 hotels around the Magic Kingdom offer a view from a distance.

Baby centres: All the parks have facilities for nursing mothers and can provide baby food and nappies on request (locations are on the park map). The centres can even provide spare children's underpants for those little accidents. All Disney hotel gift shops stock baby food and nappies. Expectant mothers are strongly advised not to ride some of the more dynamic attractions and coasters, and there will be clear warnings on park maps and at the rides.

Pushchairs: 'Strollers' are essential, even if your children are a year or so out of them. The walking wears kids out quickly and a pushchair can

Discovery Cove

save a lot of discomfort. You can take your own, hire them at the parks or, better still, buy one for as little as $20 at a local supermarket. Babysitting is available through many Disney resorts and some of the bigger hotels elsewhere.

BRITTIP

Avoid making phone calls from your hotel – they're hugely expensive. It's cheaper to buy a local phone card and use a normal payphone. British mobiles can also be costly to use in the US. To call the UK from the US, dial 011 44, then drop the first 0 from the UK area code.

Travellers with disabilities

The parks pay close attention to the needs of visitors with disabilities and Florida is extremely disabled-friendly (although Americans use the word 'handicapped' as we use 'disabled').

Access: Wheelchair availability and access is usually good (though there are a few rides that cannot cater for them) and most hotels now have disabled-accessible rooms. For hearing-impaired guests, there are assistive listening devices and reflective captioning at attractions where a commentary is part of the show. Braille guidebooks are available, plus rest areas for guide dogs, and there are special tape cassettes for blind guests. Disney, Universal and SeaWorld offer Accessibility Guides for disabled guests in all their main parks (and online). Life-jackets are always on hand at water parks. For Disney disability assistance, call 407 824 4321 (TTY 407 827 5141); for Universal, call 407 224 4233.

Guest Assistance: If you require help with queuing or have children with special needs, visit any Disney theme park Guest Relations office, with the person in question, and request a Disability Access Service card (DAS), which has replaced the old Guest Assistance Card. It doesn't provide front-of-line access, but instead

Repeat visitors

Repeat visitors are a large part of the Orlando market and are usually on the lookout for something new. Chapters 8 and 9 (Off The Beaten Track and The Twin Centre Option) are largely designed with them in mind. Here are 10 things worth doing once you have Been There and Done That:

1   Behind the scenes tours at the Disney parks.

2   Dolphin watch cruise from Dolphin Landings at St Pete Beach.

3   Wildlife eco-tour with Island Boat Lines at Cocoa Beach.

4   The scenic boat ride and Morse Museum in Winter Park.

5   Bok Tower Gardens and lunch or dinner (plus a visit to the soup cannery!) at the eclectic Chalet Suzanne in Lake Wales.

6   St John's River Cruise in Blue Spring State Park, Seminole County.

7   Boggy Creek Airboats or Wild Florida.

8   Eco-park at Florida EcoSafaris.

9   Merritt Island National Wildlife Refuge at Titusville.

10 A visit to Mount Dora, north-west of Orlando.

provides a return time based on the current queue at each attraction. As soon as the Guest finishes one attraction, they can receive a return time for another. This can be used in addition to Disney's FastPass+ service. Universal, SeaWorld and Busch Gardens provide similar assistance through their Guest Services offices.

Parking permits: To use any of the plentiful designated disabled parking areas in all public areas (including the parks), UK drivers must obtain a **Temporary Disabled Parking Permit**, which costs $15. You can either go to a local tax collection office, with your UK blue badge and passport, when you arrive (most open 8.30am–4pm Mon–Fri only), OR apply by post, fax or email at least 4 weeks in advance. You need to send a photocopy of your Blue Badge (both sides), a copy of your passport ID page, your home address and address while in Florida, arrival and departure date and a money order (in US dollars) for $15, or a non-Visa credit card (for which there is a 2.5% service fee); do NOT send cash for safety reasons. The Osceola County tax office has a special service for UK visitors with a dedicated team to deal with all requests (8am–4.30pm

Mon–Fri). By mail: Patsy Heffner Tax Collector, Attn Samantha or Holly, 1300 9th Street, Suite 101-B, St Cloud, Florida 34769, USA or by fax, 407 892 8076. By email: sjewell@osceola. org or hmccommon@osceola.org with a scanned copy of your details (as above, but NOT your credit card details) and they will email you back with a number to call to arrange payment. If you cannot reach them for any reason or don't get a response within 2 working days, try webinfo@ oscoela.org or 407 742 4000. NB: Osceola Tax Office does not accept Visa credit or debit cards.

Merrit Island

For a list of tax offices in Orange County (for the Orlando area), call 407 836 4145 (**www.octaxcol.com**, and click Office Locations); in Osceola County (for Kissimmee), call 407 742 4000 (**www.osceolataxcollector.com**). The temporary permits are valid for 90 days from issue date so it's best to apply no sooner than 5–6 weeks before travelling to ensure it will be valid for your stay. However, you may renew a permit within 12 months for no fee.

- **Suntastic Tours:** This local company can help travellers with physical and mental disabilities in many ways, including travel, arranging tours of the parks and other accessibility issues (321 284 4507, **http://suntastictours.com**).

- **Walker Mobility:** Specialises in electric scooters and wheelchair rentals, with free delivery and pick-up, even from holiday villas (407 518 6000, **www.walkermobility.com**).

- **Wheelchair Vans of America:** Has specially-equipped vans for hire for wheelchair users (1800 910 8267 or 407 977 3799, **www.wheelchairvansofamerica.com**).

◀▶ BRITTIP

'We used CARE Medical Equipment to hire a charger for our electric wheelchair as the 110v currency in the US does not work with a chair's 220v charging needs. They delivered to our villa within an hour and even stayed to make sure it worked. Some UK battery chargers will work but not all, so please check before you leave.' – Reader Lisa Smith, County Durham

Universal CityWalk

- **CARE Medical Equipment:** Another company highly recommended for sale, rent or repair of powered scooters and wheelchairs and other medical equipment (407 856 2273, **www.caremedicalequipment.com**).

The discussion forums on **www.wdwinfo.com** have a board geared to visitors with disabilities, while the excellent AllEars website has a big section on advice for a whole range of concerns, from children with ADD to vegetarian and vegan food. Visit **http://allears.net/pl/special.htm**.

Orlando for grown-ups

You don't need to have kids in tow to enjoy Orlando. There is so much clever detail and imagination, adults usually get the most out of the experience.

In fact, as many couples and singles visit the parks as do families with children. Certainly, when you look at the entertainment at Downtown Disney and CityWalk and the great range of bars and fine restaurants, it is easy to see the attraction for those 21 and over. As well as Florida being a key honeymoon destination, its friendly, sociable atmosphere is ideal for singles, while couples without children can also take advantage of late opening at the parks and clubs. Even better, the downtown area of the city of Orlando is coming back as a happening night-time venue, with a lot to recommend it for a lively evening out.

◀▶ BRITTIP

If you have a fridge in your hotel, put drink cartons in the freezer overnight and they will be cool for much of the next day in your back-pack. Better still, buy a cheap coolbag, freeze it with some water bottles in, and leave it in the car – great after a day in the parks.

Orlando for seniors

Mature travellers can also benefit from a healthy dose of the Sunshine State, as they are likely to have just as much fun, just within slightly

American-speak

Many words and phrases have a different meaning across the Atlantic. For instance, when Americans say the first floor, they mean the ground floor, the second floor is really the first, and so on. (NB: NEVER ask for a packet of fags; 'fag' is a crude, slang term for a homosexual.) Here are a few everyday words to help you:

American	English	American	English
ATM	Cash machine	Faucet	Tap
Appetizer	Starter	Fender	Car bumper
Band aid	Plaster	Freeway	Motorway
Bathroom	Private toilet	Fries	Chips
Biscuit	Savoury scone	Gas	Petrol
Broiled	Grilled	Graham cracker	Digestive biscuit
Cellphone	Mobile phone	Hood	Car bonnet
Check	Bill	Intersection	Junction
Chips	Crisps	Nickel	5 cents
Collect call	Reverse charge phone call	No standing	No parking OR stopping
		'Pound sign'	The # on a phone keypad
Cookie	Biscuit		
Cot/rollaway	Fold-up bed	Purse	Handbag
Crib	Cot	Quarter	25 cents
Diaper	Nappy	Ramp	Slip road
Dime	10 cents	Restroom	Public toilet
Divided highway	Dual carriageway	Seltzer	Soda water
Eggplant	Aubergine	Shrimp	King prawn
Eggs 'over easy'	Eggs fried on both sides but soft	Soda	Fizzy drink
		Stroller	Pushchair
Eggs 'sunny side up'	Eggs fried on just 1 side (soft)	Trunk	Car boot
		Turn-out	Lay-by
Entrée	Main course	Yield	Give way
Facecloth/washcloth	Flannel	Zucchini	Courgette

different parameters. Seniors can also take advantage of numerous discounts and special deals for their age group at the attractions, plus many restaurants and hotels. The official Visitor Center on I-Drive (p42) publishes a brochure of all the deals.

Hotels: For the older person, staying in a Disney hotel is highly recommended as it removes the stress of driving. The extra cost is offset by the convenience and relaxation factor.

Parks: There is still plenty to do here, even if the thrill rides are not a draw – just watching can be entertainment enough! Both Epcot and Disney's Animal Kingdom have much to engage the older visitor, while the

shows of Disney's Hollywood Studios make that a popular choice, too, and the Magic Kingdom, while a bit hectic, is still an essential experience.

Evenings: The Downtown Disney area can feel a bit frenetic for the senior crowd, but the Boardwalk Resort is

Red Oven Pizza Bakery at CityWalk

popular and the whole of the Epcot resort area offers much in the way of fine dining and relaxation. In fact, this is often a prime area for seniors, notably the quieter Disney's Yacht and Beach Club Resorts, and the superb Swan-Dolphin complex.

Attractions: We also highlight the following for the senior age group.

- **Animal Kingdom:** Kilimanjaro Safaris, the Maharajah Jungle Trek, Pangani Forest Trail, Finding Nemo show and Festival of the Lion King.

- **Disney's Hollywood Studios:** Jim Henson's Muppet Vision 3-D, Great Movie Ride, Indiana Jones Stunt Show, Beauty and the Beast and Fantasmic!.

- **Epcot:** Spaceship Earth, Soarin', Universe of Energy, all of World Showcase and IllumiNations (plus the superb gardens and architecture).

- **Magic Kingdom:** The Haunted Mansion, Jungle Cruise, Pirates of the Caribbean, Mickey's PhilharMagic and the monorail ride.

- **Universal Studios and Islands of Adventure:** Most of US but less of IoA.

- **Others:** Watching the children at the many parades and character greetings; dinner at the California Grill in Disney's Contemporary Resort (and other fine dining locations); shopping at Orlando Premium Outlets.

Bice

© Loews Hotels & Resorts

Top 10 romantic restaurants

1	Tchoup Chop, Universal's Royal Pacific Resort
2	California Grill, Disney's Contemporary Resort
3	Todd English's bluezoo, Walt Disney World Dolphin Resort
4	Jiko, Disney's Animal Kingdom Lodge
5	Seasons 52, Sand Lake Rd, Orlando
6	Old Hickory Steakhouse, Gaylord Palms Resort
7	Bice, Universal's Portofino Bay Hotel
8	Cala Bella, Shingle Creek Resort
9	Narcoossee's, Disney's Grand Floridian Resort
10	Park Plaza Gardens, Winter Park

- **More options:** SeaWorld remains hugely popular for seniors and even Busch Gardens, despite its many roller-coasters, has plenty to offer. The local Segway Tours (in Kissimmee, Mount Dora, St Petersburg and Clearwater Beach) are highly recommended for older visitors, while Mount Dora and Winter Park (see also Chapter 8) are also perfect senior fare.

Weather: Mar and late Oct/Nov are ideal times to visit, but the summer months are hard going for older folks. Good coats (and gloves) may still be necessary at times in winter.

BRITTIP
Don't want to take your mobile with you for fear of high charges? Hire a phone for your holiday from Adam Phones and take advantage of its special local rates for the US (0800 123000, **www.adamphones.com**).

You've got mail

You won't find post boxes in many locations and some post offices don't seem to know the fees for postage to the UK. So here's what you need to know: all the parks have post boxes and you can get stamp books from

Top things to do for FREE!

Disney's Boardwalk Resort: Free nightly entertainment includes jugglers, comedians and live music. Time your visit to coincide with the 9pm IllumiNations fireworks extravaganza at nearby Epcot.

Downtown Concert Series: 4 times a year, local radio station WMMO stages free open-air concerts in front of City Hall with the likes of Rick Springfield and Tears For Fears. Great day out, with festival atmosphere (**www.wmmo.com/s/dcs/**).

Downtown Orlando Historic Tour: From the Visitor Center on Orange Avenue, local historian Richard Forbes leads a free tour of downtown at 9.30am on the first Friday of every month from Oct–May. Must call in advance to check availability on 407 246 3789 (**http://downtownorlando.com**).

Fort Christmas Historical Park: 20ml/32km east of Orlando in the town of Christmas is this replica of an 1837 US Army fort from the Seminole Indian Wars, with tours, exhibits, video presentations and restored homes, and special events during some weekends; 8am–8pm summer, 8am–6pm winter (closed Mon and public holidays; **http://nbbd.com/godo/FortChristmas**).

Lake Eola Park: Take a walk on the mild side in downtown Orlando. The kids can play or feed the swans and summer sees live music at the Walt Disney Amphitheater; **www.cityoforlando.net/parks/lake-eola-park/**

Lake Tibet-Butler Preserve: Just 5mins from Disney but a world away from the theme park bustle (on local highway 535, Winter Garden-Vineland Road) is this local nature preserve, with quiet trails, lake overlook and interpretive centre. Open 9am–dusk (not public holidays), it is on the Great Florida Birding Trail and is a minor gem of native wildlife); **www.sfwmd.gov**.

Lakeridge Winery and Vineyards: Join one of its fun, free wine-tasting tours and you'll know why Lakeridge (in nearby Clermont) has won more than 300 awards. But designate a driver as sample sizes are generous! 10am–5pm Mon–Sat, 11am–5pm Sun (**www.lakeridgewinery.com**).

Morse Museum of American Art: This superb little museum in tranquil Winter Park, dedicated to American paintings, ceramics and representative arts from the 19th and 20th centuries, is free 4–8pm every Fri, Nov–Apr (**www.morsemuseum.org**).

Old Town, Kissimmee: The biggest vintage car parade in the US every Sat, with cars on display from 1pm and the Classic Car Cruise at 8.30pm, plus a Muscle Car Cruise 8.30pm each Fri and Country Truck Cruise each Sun with live music and line dancing 6.30–11pm (**www.old-town.com**).

Osceola County History Museum: Part of the new Welcome Center on Highway 192 in Kissimmee (by Marker 15), this offers a great insight into the region's back story and heritage (**www.osceolahistory.org**; see also p258; closed on public hols).

PLUS: Watching the participants at **iFLY Orlando** on I-Drive (p236); watching the **NASCAR** stock cars daily at the 1-mile tri-oval of the Walt Disney World Speedway (near the Magic Kingdom); the **Cornell Fine Arts Museum** at Rollins College in Winter Park (p249); and the hiking trails of **Ocala National Forest**, north of Orlando (**www.stateparks.com/Ocala.html**).

most stamp machines and City Hall at the Magic Kingdom. A standard postcard or greetings card in an envelope to the UK both require a $1.15 stamp; standard postage within the US is 49c.

The main post office for the Disney area is at 10450 Turkey Lake Road (just north of the junction of Palm Parkway and Central Florida Parkway; 8am–7pm Mon–Fri, 9am– 5pm Sat); in Kissimmee, try 2600 Michigan Avenue (8am–6.30pm Mon–Fri, 9am–4pm Sat) or 1415 W Oak Street (8.30am–5pm Mon–Fri, 9am–2pm Sat). You will also find a post office inside Mall at Millenia, off the lower level of the Grand Court.

Wedding bells

Florida is a popular choice for couples wanting to tie the knot. Its almost guaranteed sunshine and lush, natural landscape make it a huge hit as a wedding backdrop. Orlando also has terrific services, co-ordinators and venues like Cypress Grove Estate House, Winter Park wedding chapel, Casa Feliz, Leu Gardens and hotels like Wyndham Orlando Resort, Walt Disney World Swan and Dolphin and the Aloft Downtown Orlando. Even scenic golf courses such as Celebration Golf Club and Grand Cypress can stage grand occasions extremely well. More unusual ones include the Hard Rock Café, a hot-air balloon or helicopter, Danville B&B (p262) on the beach or luxury yacht, in kayaks (down at Port Charlotte), in the pit-lane of the Richard Petty Driving Experience at Walt Disney World or even at 145mph/233kph around the speedway itself! All the tour operators feature wedding options and services and offer a variety of ceremonies, or you can pick a local specialist like **Get Married In Florida** (see right). Prices vary from around £300/couple (for a basic civil ceremony) to more than £2,000.

◀️⚡️▶️ BRITTIP
Looking for essential travel accessories and useful knick-knacks, like TSA-approved locks, plug adapters and waterproof accessories? Try **www.travelbasket.co.uk**. Asda supermarkets also sell a good travel range.

Walt Disney World's Wedding Pavilion: True fairytale romance, with the backdrop of Cinderella Castle, you can opt for traditional elegance in this Victorian setting with up to 260 guests or the full Disney experience, arriving in Cinderella's coach with

Celebration Golf wedding venue

© Celebration golf.com

Mickey and Minnie as guests. Disney's wedding planners can tailor-make the occasion for you (407 828 3400) but at a price – rates START at almost $5,000 for the basic ceremony and can top $60,000!

Licence: To obtain a marriage licence, visit a local courthouse: **Osceola County Courthouse**, Courthouse Square, Suite 2000, Kissimmee (just off Bryan Street in downtown Kissimmee) 8am–4pm Mon–Fri (407 343 3500); **Orange County Courthouse**, 425 N Orange Avenue (downtown Orlando) 7.30am–4pm Mon–Fri (407 836 2067); or **Clermont Courthouse** at Minneola City Hall, 800 North Highway 27, Minneola, 8.30am–4.30pm (closed noon–1pm; 352 394 2018). All are closed on US bank holidays. Both parties must be present to apply for a licence, which costs $93.50 (in cash, travellers' cheques or by credit card) and is valid for 60 days, while a ceremony (equivalent to a British register office) can be performed at the same time by the clerk for an extra $20. Passports and birth certificates are requested and, if you have been married before, you must bring your decree absolute. After acquiring a licence, a couple can marry anywhere in Florida. It is also possible to obtain a licence BEFORE arriving in Florida (see **www. floridamarriagelicencebypost.com**). For flowers and floral design, be sure to look up **Flourish** on 407 601 4948 or **www.flourishproductions.com**.

Get Married in Florida: This local business is dedicated to organising weddings for couples from the UK and has specialised in Orlando marriages since 2002. Ideally placed to deliver great personal service, it offers the complete package for the perfect wedding (321 945 1563, **www.getmarriedinflorida.com**).

◀️⚡️▶️ BRITTIP
Phonecards, which you need to make a call from a local payphone (much cheaper than using your hotel room phone), are available from most 7-Eleven stores or from your tour rep.

Disney special occasions

Birthday badges: Free badges can be found at City Hall in the Magic Kingdom and Guest Services at Epcot, Disney's Hollywood Studios and Disney's Animal Kingdom. Cast Members like to make a fuss over children (and adults!) wearing a birthday badge.

Birthday cakes: Contact room service at your resort or Guest Services at one of the parks. All Disney restaurants can offer ready-made 15cm/6in cakes ($21 at each restaurant) or something larger ($32–120) if ordered 48 hours in advance on 407 827 2253. If someone in your group has a birthday, be sure to tell the Cast Member at check-in (or when you make your reservation), as well as hostesses and/or servers in restaurants. While not guaranteed, Disney staff often go out of their way to make the day special. If characters know it's a birthday when they sign a child's autograph book, they may add a special birthday wish.

Birthday cruise: The IllumiNations Celebration Cruise (to Epcot) provides snacks, drinks, streamers and balloons for a 90min tour, for up to 10, from Disney's Yacht and Beach Club Resort marina for $371 (407 939 7529).

Birthday parties: Disney's Polynesian Resort offers themed birthday parties with lunch options at its Neverland kids' club for ages 4 and over. A themed 2hr Premium party with cake, pizza, drinks, party activities and one Disney character is $70/person, while the Basic version (without a Disney character) is $35/person (at least a week's notice required on 407 939 7529).

Goofy Party Central: This grand 90min experience for up to 12 takes place at Goofy's Candy Company in Downtown Disney and offers a choice of Goofy's Scien-Terrific Birthday Bash or the Perfectly Princess Party, each with themed events, games, gifts and treats, plus 2 party hosts for $370 (call 407 939 2329 up to 90 days in advance).

Disney's Pirate Cruise: This 2hr adventure for kids 4–12 sails (on pontoon boats) from 4 of the resorts (Grand Floridian, Yacht/Beach Club, Port Orleans and Caribbean Beach at 9.30am) to find pirate 'booty' at different ports of call, with a final stop for lunch; $35 per child (407 939 7529, up to 180 days in advance).

Money matters

You'll need to carry ID for both cheques and some credit card purchases (take your UK driving licence card).

◄⧫► BRITTIP

American banknotes are all the same size and primarily green, with just the occasional splash of colour in the newer notes. The only real difference is the picture of the president and the denomination in each corner.

Cash: It is worth separating larger notes from smaller ones in your wallet to avoid flashing all your money in view. Losing £300 of travellers' cheques shouldn't ruin your holiday – but losing $600 in cash might. All the theme parks have ATMs (cash machines).

Credit cards: Having a credit card is almost essential (especially for car hire) as they are accepted everywhere and provide extra buying security. Visa, Mastercard and American Express are all widely accepted.

FairFX card: Perhaps the best option is this convenient card, which you preload to a chosen amount (**www.fairfx.com**). The exchange rate is fixed at loading and you can save 5–10% on High Street currency rates.

Travellers' cheques: Dollar travellers' cheques can be used as cash almost everywhere (though a few places, like Golden Corral restaurants, no longer accept them) and can be replaced if lost or stolen, so it is not necessary (or advisable) to carry lots of cash. Sterling travellers' cheques can be cashed only in major banks.

Safety and security

While crime is not a serious issue in Florida, this is still big-city America, so don't leave your common sense at home. Tourism is such a vital part of the economy, the authorities have a highly safety-conscious attitude. However, it would be foolish to ignore the usual safety guidelines for travelling abroad.

BRITTIP

For your journey to the US, use a business rather than your home address on your luggage. It is less conspicuous and safer should any item be lost or stolen.

Commonsense tips: A bumbag (Americans say 'fanny pack'!) is better than a handbag or shoulder bag. Try not to look too much like a tourist – the map over the steering wheel is a giveaway, but other no-nos are wearing loads of jewellery and carrying lots of camera equipment. The biggest giveaway is leaving a camera or camcorder on view in the car (which the heat may ruin).

The VERY strong police advice in the unlikely event of being confronted by an assailant is: DO NOT resist or

CityWalk

Simon and Susan

Apart from the *Brit Guides* to Orlando and Disneyland Paris, we contribute to a wide range of media on many travel subjects. Find out more about our work at **www.venesstravelmedia.com** or see us on Facebook and Twitter at Veness Travel Media.

'have a go', because this can often make a bad situation worse. However, it is comforting to know Orlando does not have any no-go areas in the main tourist parts. The nearest is the portion of the Orange Blossom Trail south of downtown Orlando (a selection of strip clubs and 'adult bars' that can be downright seedy) and the Parramore area south-west of downtown.

TOPS: International Drive has its own dedicated police unit (the Tourist Oriented Policing Squad, a division of the Orlando City Police), with officers patrolling this long tourist corridor, arranging crime prevention seminars with local hotels and ensuring I-Drive takes good care of its visitors. You'll often see these police out on mountain bikes, and they are a polite, helpful bunch.

Christmas cheer

We're often asked our favourite time of year here and it has to be the festive season, from late Nov–1 Jan. Every park adds a fab Christmas overlay and there is more to enjoy everywhere, even at the smaller attractions and places like *Downtown Disney* and town of Celebration. It can get seriously crowded 20 Dec–4 Jan, but visit in early Dec and you get all the festivities with fewer crowds. Here's what to enjoy.

Walt Disney World: Every park has its own extensive decorations and magnificent Christmas tree, with a daily lighting ceremony at the **Magic Kingdom**, plus Mickey's Once Upon A Christmastime Parade, the Castle Dream Lights (a stunning effect on Cinderella Castle) and the chance to meet Santa, as well as the extra-ticket event of Mickey's Very Merry Christmas Party (p118). At **Epcot**, the standout feature is the Candlelight Processional, a choral retelling of the Christmas story with a guest narrator, as well as Holidays Around The World, with traditional storytellers at each World Showcase pavilion. Mrs and Mrs Claus visit at the American Adventure pavilion, where vocal group Voices of Liberty become carollers for the season. The daily IllumiNations show also has a special Yule finale. At **Disney's Hollywood Studios**, the dazzling Osborne Family Spectacle of Dancing Lights is a marvel – with 5 million twinkling, themed fairy lights that draw huge crowds – and at **Disney's Animal Kingdom** Santa Goofy's Holiday Village should return despite no longer having Camp Minnie-Mickey as its location, while the giant Christmas Tree outside the park is one of the best. **Downtown Disney** features Festival Of The Seasons, with Santa's chalet, school choirs and more lavish decorations. Each resort also boasts plenty of Christmas cheer, with the best being **Disney's Grand Floridian**, offering a life-size Gingerbread House.

Universal Orlando: Miles more garland, lights and tinsel are on offer here, plus 2 daily features. At **Universal Studios**, Macy's Holiday Parade is the highlight, a fabulous cavalcade of floats, giant balloons, Father Christmas (and his Rockette-style dancers!) and a tree-lighting ceremony at dusk each day, as well as strolling carollers, hot cocoa kiosks and a Christmas Village of traditional fare and gifts. **Islands of Adventure** offers Christmas Dr Seuss style, with Grinchmas all around Seuss Landing, including the epic, family-friendly stage show of *The Grinch Who Stole Christmas*.

SeaWorld: Arguably the biggest Christmas celebration can be found here, with magnificent shows, special effects and extravagant theming throughout. It starts with a Polar Express makeover for the Wild Arctic ride and continues with the Sea of Trees, an eye-catching sequence of well-lit 'trees' spread over the main lagoon. A Christmas Marketplace highlights one end of the park, while 2 unmissable seasonal shows are Winter Wonderland On Ice and O Wondrous Night, a nativity tale with a difference. Both the Shamu and Sea-Lion shows have their own festive additions, and nightly 'snowfalls,' dancers, musicians and the Christmas Celebration fireworks round out a glittering seasonal occasion.

Busch Gardens: The highlight here is **Christmas Town**, another separate-ticket event, featuring an eye-catching variety of themed areas, shows and decorations (each Fri, Sat and Sun 6–11pm from late Nov; $29.99 for adults, $9.99 for 3–9s). Highlights include the Carol of the Bells, an Ice Show, the Three Kings Journey and a lavish array of seasonal dining and shopping, plus Santa's 'North Pole' home! Yes, it costs extra but it is an event well worth considering.

Gaylord Palms Resort: equally astounding is their annual ICE! exhibition, a mind-boggling presentation of 2 MILLION pounds of ice in marvellous tableaux, hand-carved by 40 Chinese artisans in the special 'Florida Freezer,' including 4 huge ice slides. There are festive presentations, shows, musicians, tree, kids' activities, character meet-and-greets from Dreamworks and the chance to meet Santa, making for an amazing Christmas offering. It MUST be booked in advance, though, at **www.marriott.com/hotels/travel/mcogp-gaylord-palms/**

Celebration: this pretty Disney-inspired town offers nightly 'snow-falls' 6–9pm on Market Street in Dec and also features ice-skating for kids, horse-drawn carriage rides, carollers and other festive touches.

And more: downtown Orlando is well worth a visit for its many festive touches, notably around **Lake Eola**, which has Christmas trees, ice-skating and the nightly Holiday Lights show. The child-sized fun of **LEGOLAND Florida** boasts a superb array of decorations and the daily Tree Lighting, while all the **dinner shows** add in suitably festive theming and extra Christmas elements. One final amazing event is staged at the huge First Baptist Church on John Young Parkway just off I-4, where **The Singing Christmas Trees** is a stunning choral show presentation of music, stage and lighting each Fri, Sat and Sun for the first 2 weeks in Dec. Find out more at **www.firstorlando.com/Worship/Singing_Trees.aspx**.

Hotel security: While in your hotel, always use door peepholes and security chains when someone knocks at the door. DON'T open the door to strangers without asking for identification, and check with the hotel desk if you are still not sure. It is stating the obvious, but keep doors and windows locked and always use deadlocks and security chains. Always take cash, credit cards, valuables and car keys when you go out (or put them in the room safe), and don't leave the door open, even if you just pop down the corridor to the ice machine. Most hotels now have electronic card-locks for extra security and can offer deposit boxes in addition to the standard in-room mini-safes. Don't be afraid to ask reception staff for safety advice for surrounding areas or if you are travelling somewhere you are not sure about. Safety is a major issue for the Central Florida Hotel & Lodging Association (**www.cfhla.org**) and hotel staff are well briefed to be helpful.

◀█▶ BRITTIP
If your room has already been cleaned before you go out for the day, hang the 'Do Not Disturb' sign on the door. Always keep your valuables out of sight, whether in the hotel or the car.

Christmas at Animal Kingdom

Car safety: Make the basic safety checks of your hire car straight away and familiarise yourself with the car's controls BEFORE driving away. Try to memorise your route in advance, even if it's only a case of knowing the road numbers. Most hire firms now give good directions to all the hotels, so check them before you set off (or, better still, hire a GPS system). Make sure the fuel tank is well filled and never let it get near empty so you risk running out of 'gas' in an unfamiliar area. If you do stray off your pre-determined route, stick to well-lit areas and ask for directions only from official businesses like hotels and petrol stations, or the police. Try to park close to your destination where there are plenty of lights and DO NOT get out if there are suspicious characters around. Always keep windows closed (and air-con on), and don't hesitate to lock the doors from the inside if you feel threatened (larger cars have doors that lock automatically as you drive off). Don't forget to lock the car when you leave it – and note that not all rental cars have central locking.

◀█▶ BRITTIP
Remember, if you are calling Orlando (area code 407) from the UK, you must put the international dialling code for the USA, 001, first.

More info: For more info on safety, contact the Orange County Police (407 254 7000 or www.ocso.com) or the International Drive police team office (407 351 9368).

Emergencies

Emergency services: For police, fire department or ambulance, dial 911 (9-911 from your hotel room). Make sure your children know this number.

General: For smaller-scale crises (e.g. mislaid tickets, lost passports or rescheduled flights), your holiday company should have an emergency contact number in the hotel reception.

Let us take the stress out of your holiday ...

...with our unique Touring Plans

The *Brit Guide* Touring Plans will ensure you get the most out of your time in central Florida. This is a service no one else can offer, as we provide you with daily touring plans for the parks, attractions and shopping in central Florida.

Your full Touring Plan (which usually runs to 40 pages for a 2-week holiday) will: walk you through your day so you make the most of your time and your tickets; highlight any rides that may be closed for refurbishment; include shopping guides if you plan to take advantage of all the savings to be had at the malls and outlets; provide key advice right from the source of the fun, as well as a host of Brit Tip Extras and Brit Picks (our special favourites) we can't fit into the book, plus a special Busy Day Guide for your visit. Just go to **www.britguideorlando.net** and click Touring Plans.

Fill out the online form with your travel dates, choose the type of Plan you need (be sure to see our FAQ to help you decide which Plan is right for you), and indicate which parks/shopping/etc you want to fit into your visit. Submit the form, with your payment, and you'll receive, by email, your unique Touring Plan, which will consist of:

1   An official *Brit Guide* welcome from Susan and Simon Veness.

2   A daily plan for each of the parks, water parks and shopping centres you will visit.

3   Touring strategies in each day's plan to help you avoid the longest queues and take advantage of the latest developments.

4   Alternative suggestions in case of bad weather.

5   A note of any rides/shows that are closed during your visit (please see our FAQ for further info).

6   A special selection of Brit Tip Extras and local advice.

7   Our Brit Picks – a guide to a range of personal favourites, from restaurants to shops.

8   The ultimate insider knowledge, as Susan and Simon are based in the heart of the Orlando magic and are fully up to date on all developments.

9   Our special bonus: an EXCLUSIVE Platinum VIP Passport for Orlando Premium Outlets (not available to the public), with extra savings at select stores at this great shopping venue.

10 Best of all, you will receive a Busy Day Guide especially for your holiday dates so that you can assemble the best possible day-by-day plan.

All in all, it adds up to the most comprehensive package of specialised holiday info anywhere, and it represents the secret to the most fun, in the most hassle-free way, in the most exciting place on earth. What more could you ask for? Just check out our website and we'll do the rest.

Please note: There is a minimum order period, so check online and apply in good time before your holiday (*at least* 10 days). Book owners receive a discount on the price of the Touring Plans, so have it with you when you register as you'll need a password from the book.

The password is random and expires on 31 Dec of the edition's year, NO EXCEPTIONS. We are not a travel agency or ticket service and you MUST know your park and shopping requirements in advance.

We urge you to read our FAQ before ordering, as it will assist you in choosing the right plan for your holiday, answer the most common questions we receive, and ensure you order with confidence.

Independent travellers: If you run into passport or other problems that need help from the British Consulate, its main office is now at 1001 Brickell Bay Drive, Miami, Florida 33131 on 305 300 6400, but there is still a small office in downtown Orlando offering consular services, such as lost documents and aid for those hospitalised or arrested and detained, on 407 254 3300 (**http://ukinusa.fco.gov. uk**).

You'll find masses of info on all things Orlando on the discussion forums at **www.attraction-tickets-direct.co.uk** and, as we are both Moderators on the site, you can come and 'talk' to us and pass on your own ideas and experiences. It's a fun, friendly community and we're always happy to see new faces.

Know before you go

Here are the best sources for additional info before you go.

- **Experience Kissimmee:** More useful online info and an e-guide to download (**www.experiencekissimmee. com**).

- **Fan websites:** The biggest and best of these is **www.thedibb.co.uk** ('Disney with a British accent'), the fully comprehensive **www.allears. net** (notably for its Disney dining section) and **www.wdwinfo.com**.

- **Orlando Attractions mag** (which we also write for) offers a superb

website full of features and videos at **www.attractionsmagazine.com**, plus a weekly magazine-style programme called *The Show*.

- **Official sites:** Not bad for opening hours, rides, parades, and bookings, though Disney's is ridiculously hard work: **www.disneyworld.co.uk**, **www.universalorlando.com**, and **www.seaworldparks.co.uk**.

- **Orlando Sentinel:** The online local paper (**www.orlandosentinel.com**) is packed with info (especially for shopping, dining and nightlife), while the free **Orlando Weekly** is also worth checking (**www.orlandoweekly.com**).

- **Orlando Visitor Center:** It's worth checking Orlando's ONLY official Visitor Center, 8.30am– 6.30pm daily at 8723 International Drive (407 363 5872 or email info@ visitorlando.com) for discounted attraction tickets, and free brochures, accommodation advice, info pamphlets and maps.

- **Visit Florida:** Offers a free info pack, as well as many online e-brochures (01737 644 882, **www.visitflorida.com/en-uk.html**).

- **Visit Orlando:** has a 24hr info line, plus a website where you order its free Holiday Planning kit (0800 018 6760, **www.visitorlando.com/uk/**).

Now, on to the next step of the holiday, your transport…

The wacky Seuss Landing at Universal's Islands of Adventure

3 Getting Around

or The Secret of Driving on the Wrong Side of the Road!

Arriving and driving in Orlando are among the biggest concerns for visitors, especially first-timers, but there's no need to worry. Although most people begin their holiday by leaving the airport in a newly acquired, automatic, left-hand-drive hire car on roads that can appear bewildering, driving here is a lot easier and more enjoyable than in the UK. Anyone familiar with the M25 should find Florida FAR less stressful.

Before you get to your hire car, though, you need to be aware of the arrival process at the 2 airports.

BRITTIP
Don't forget you must have filled in your ESTA form and immigration details online before you travel (see p12). For country of residence put UNITED KINGDOM; for Passport Issuing Country, put UK – BRITISH CITIZEN. You must give a valid US address for your accommodation.

Orlando International

This is one of the most modern and enjoyable airports in the world, but it can be confusing for newcomers. All flights arrive at one of 4 satellite terminals and you then take a shuttle tram (like a mini monorail) to the main terminal. Allow around an hour from landing to ground transportation.

International arrivals: If you arrive with British Airways, Virgin Atlantic or Thomas Cook, you disembark at the satellite for Gates 60–99. First, you go through Immigration. Join one of the 2 main queues that feed into the individual immigration kiosks, and wait for the official to call you to the next open kiosk. Once through Immigration, collect your baggage from the carousel and go through the Customs check. The airport now has a series of self-service electronic processing kiosks, allowing you to input your flight info and passport details, fingerprints and photo before reaching the Immigration officer, which can save considerable time for whole flights at a time. Just follow the instructions and take your receipt, with your passports and customs form, to the officer after completing the kiosk process. NB: Children under 14 cannot be processed by the electronic kiosks and will need to be checked by the Immigration officer.

BRITTIP
Visit **www.orlandoairports.net** for a photo preview of the arrival process at Orlando International Airport (click Airport Guide, then Arrivals Guide) and other info.

Then you have a choice. **Option 1:** Deposit your checked luggage on a second conveyor belt to take it to the main terminal while you go upstairs to the shuttle with your hand luggage only. Once in the main terminal you are on Level 3 and you follow signs down to Baggage Claim B on Level 2, unless you took a **Virgin** flight, in which case you cross over to the A-side and go down to Level 1.

Option 2: If you can manage your luggage without a trolley, take it on the escalator up to the shuttle and go straight to pick up your transport on Level 1 (or, if a specific driver is meeting you, Level 2).

Domestic arrivals: For anyone arriving on a US domestic flight (from another US gateway), you disembark at the satellite terminal and proceed straight to the main terminal on the shuttle to collect your baggage on Level 2 (either A or B side, depending on arrival gate). Once at the main baggage claim, porters can help you to Level 1 (for a $1/bag tip) for car hire, shuttles and buses. Trolleys need $3 in change (or a credit card) to operate.

◀■▶ ANNIVERSARY SPOT

20 The biggest change in Orlando International Airport in the past 20 years is with the new automated arrivals process and the number of car hire companies now on site (most used to need a shuttle bus to their depot). Orlando Sanford Airport wasn't even operating when we started!

Transfers: Kerbside pick-up is just outside the doors on Level 2. If a driver is meeting you, he or she will wait on Level 2, either at the bottom of the escalators or by your baggage reclaim. Several tour operators have help desks here, too, while Virgin has a reception desk on Level 1. The public bus system, Lynx (p46), operates ONLY from the A side of Level 1 (6am–10.30pm; 9.30pm on Sundays and public holidays), in spaces 38–41. Links 11, 41 and 51 depart every ½hr (less often on Sundays and bank holidays) for Orlando city centre (about 45mins), while Link 42 serves International Drive (about a 1hr journey) and Link 111 goes to Walt Disney World (Hotel Plaza Boulevard and the Transportation &

Ticket Center) via the Florida Mall and I-Drive (Canadian Court). Fares are $2 one-way.

Car hire: All the main hire companies are on site (with 18 off-airport). The main 11 to choose from include *Brit Guide* partner Alamo (with new automated self-service kiosks), Dollar, National, Thrifty, Hertz and Avis, and all offer a full service. After completing your paperwork, simply walk out of Level 1, across the road to the multi-storey car park to collect your car.

If you arrive late, consider staying overnight at the Hyatt Regency hotel at the airport rather than driving tired. You will be far more ready to drive next day (and the car hire queues will be shorter). Several tour operators also offer an arrival-day transfer, with car hire pick-up arranged the next day.

◀■▶ BRITTIP

If you are hiring a car from one of the on-airport companies, save time by sending the driver to complete the paperwork BEFORE collecting your luggage on Level 2.

Leaving the airport: When you drive out of the airport, DON'T follow signs to 'Orlando'. The main tourist areas are south and west of the city, so follow the signs for your accommodation.

The Martin Andersen Beachline Expressway (528) and Greeneway (417) are both toll roads, so make sure you have some US currency before leaving the airport. Toll booths hate to change notes above $20, while some auto-tolls take ONLY coins.

- For International Drive (or I-Drive), take the North Exit and the Beachline Expressway (Route 528) west until it crosses I-Drive just north of SeaWorld (you will need $2.25 in toll fees). Most hotels on I-Drive are to the north, so keep right at the exit.

- For Kissimmee, Disney and villas in Clermont/Davenport: Take the

Welcome Sunrail!

Summer 2014 saw the long-awaited debut of Central Florida's first commuter rail system, Sunrail, and, while it is not extensive enough to be fully relevant to visiting tourists, it offers a few possibilities.

Sunrail currently operates over a 32-mile, 12-station stretch from east Sand Lake Rd (at the junction with S Orange Ave) to DeBary in the north. A northern extension is due in 2015/16 to DeLand and south to Poinciana (south of Kissimmee). From Sand Lake Rd station, it runs straight to downtown Orlando (3 stations, including Church St Station) and up to Winter Park, providing a handy way to visit these areas without driving. However, it ONLY operates Mon–Fri, every 30mins in peak periods and every 2hrs otherwise, 5.30am–10pm.

Fares are extremely modest ($3.75/adult for a round-trip from Sand Lake Rd to Winter Park while a weekly SunCard is $34 for unlimited 7-day use) and tickets can be purchased via the machines at each station using cash or credit card. Once you have your ticket, you 'tap on' by tapping it against one of the 6 validator machines on the platform before you board the train, then 'tap off' when you reach your destination. There are also Lynx bus connections at every Sunrail station, including Link 111 from SeaWorld and Link 42 from I-Drive to the Sand Lake Rd station, plus the free Lymo bus service in downtown Orlando. Look up more at **www.sunrail.com**.

South Exit for 3ml/5km and pick up the Central Florida Greeneway (Highway 417) west.

- For most Disney resorts: Take exit 6 and follow the signs ($3 in tolls).
- For Animal Kingdom resorts: Use exit 3 and take Osceola Parkway west ($3.75).
- For eastern Kissimmee: Come off Highway 417 at exit 11, the Orange Blossom Trail (Highway 17/92), and go south ($2.25 in tolls).
- For west Kissimmee and Clermont/Davenport (Highway 27): Take exit 2, turn right on Celebration Avenue and left (west) on Highway 192 all the way to Highway 27 (you will need $3.75 in toll fees).

BRITTIP
For traffic news and reports, tune to 96.5FM (WDBO). Dial 511 on a tri-band mobile phone for traffic info on I-4.

Orlando Sanford International Airport

Arriving at Sanford (in Seminole County) couldn't be easier. The list of airlines visiting this easy-to-use airport currently includes Thomson Airways, Monarch and Icelandair.

It generally takes only 30–40mins from arrival to leaving the baggage hall, but there may be delays in peak season when several planes arrive at once, as its handling capacity is limited. It's a short walk from the plane to the immigration hall (where there are 2 queues that feed through to the kiosks); you then collect your baggage, pass through Customs and walk straight out to car hire, shuttle or taxi pick-up.

BRITTIP
Don't want to drive? Consider a multi-centre stay within Orlando itself, staying first at, say, I-Drive or Universal Orlando and then a Disney resort, to get the best of the free or cheap transport options.

2nd Street Sanford

Car hire: As you exit the Customs Hall, the welcome desks for Thomas Cook and Thomson are across the road in front of you, next to the Car Rental centre, which houses all the car hire companies plus the Cosmos welcome desk. The one exception is for *Brit Guide* partner Alamo, which has its own centre via a covered walkway and boardwalk behind this building, and its British-dedicated operation is very smooth. Look up more on **www.orlandosanfordairport.com**.

Leaving the airport: It may be 35ml/56km to the north and involve more driving (and taxis and shuttles are much more expensive – a town car service would be around $140 one-way to Walt Disney World and a taxi $100, while Orlando Carriers charge $49/person on their shuttle; www.orlandocarriers.com), but you usually save time by your quicker exit. There is just one main road out, on to Lake Mary Boulevard, and you then take Seminole Expressway (Highway 417, which becomes Central Florida Greeneway in Orange County) south. The slip road to this toll motorway is just under the flyover on your LEFT, and you need $8 to reach Disney or Kissimmee or $6.50 for I-Drive (via the Beachline Expressway). You can avoid the tolls by staying on Lake Mary Blvd for 6ml/10km until you get to I-4, but you're likely to hit heavy traffic through the city centre. The Expressway/Greeneway is an excellent, easy-driving introduction to Orlando, even if it does cost a few dollars.

Disney's monorail terminus

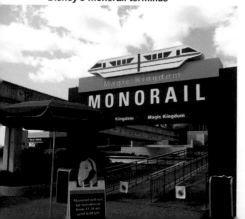

ORLANDO WITHOUT A CAR

Although being mobile is advisable, it is certainly possible to survive without a car. However, few attractions are within walking distance of hotels, and taxis can be expensive. You also need to plan with greater precision to allow for extra travelling time (and with children, taking buses can be tiring). For non-drivers, your best base is either Walt Disney World itself (free transport throughout, but harder to get to the rest of Orlando) or International Drive for its location, 'walkability' and the great I-Ride Trolley. Many hotels have free shuttles to some of the parks or a cheap, regular mini-bus service. There are 4 main options: public transport; shuttle services; town cars and limousines; and taxis.

Public transport

Lynx bus system: Reliable and cheap but slightly plodding, it covers much of metro Orlando. Its online system map shows all its routes (or 'links') and main attractions (407 841 5969, **www.golynx.com**).

- **Link 18:** From Kissimmee to downtown Orlando (from Osceola Square Mall, east on Highway 192 and north on Boggy Creek Road, Buenaventura Boulevard and Orange Avenue).

Park Maps

For a detailed look at the layout of the parks, each of the park maps contains a QR code that you can scan with your smartphone or tablet to take you to a high-res online map. You'll need a QR reader, which you can get free from Apple at **https://itunes.apple.com/gb/app/ qr-reader-for-iphone/id368494609?mt=8** or for Android at **https://play.google.com/ store/apps/details?id=me.scan.android. client&hl=en**.

- **Link 38:** I-Drive to downtown Orlando (from the Convention Center via Wet 'n Wild, Kirkman Road and I-4).

- **Link 42:** From Orlando International Airport to I-Drive.

- **Link 50:** From Disney's TTC to downtown Orlando via SeaWorld and I-4.

- **Link 55:** Kissimmee's Highway 192 from Osceola Square Mall west to Four Corners via the Summer Bay Resort.

- **Link 56:** From Kissimmee to Disney (from Osceola Square Mall, along Highway 192 via Old Town and Celebration to Disney's Transportation & Ticket Center (TTC) by the Magic Kingdom).

- **Link 300:** From Downtown Disney via I-4 to downtown Orlando.

- **Link 304:** To Disney from the top of I-Drive (Oak Ridge Road to Downtown Disney, via Sand Lake Drive).

◀▮▶ BRITTIP

Lynx buses use the Downtown Disney West Side Transfer Center as their Disney hub, with Links 301, 302 and 303 spreading out from there to the theme parks and resorts.

Lynx fares are $2 a ride (transfers are free) or $16 for a weekly pass (children 6 and under go free with a full-fare passenger). The service is every 30mins in the main areas, every 15mins 6–9am and 3.30–6.30pm, but you must have the right change. Lynx stops are marked by pink paw-print signs and all buses are wheelchair accessible. There can be long queues for buses at Disney at closing time, so you could take Disney transport to Downtown Disney (via one of the resorts or the TTC), then get a taxi back to your hotel (about $30–35 to I-Drive).

I-Ride Trolley: Great-value service for the I-Drive area, it operates 2 routes along a 14ml/23km stretch of this tourist corridor.

- **The Main/Red Line:** With 77 stops, this runs from the Orlando Premium Outlets at the top of I-Drive to SeaWorld and Aquatica via Westwood Boulevard and Sea Harbor Drive, and on to Orlando Premium Outlets (Vineland Ave).

- **The Green Line:** With 33 stops, this goes from the Universal resort area (Windhover Drive and Major Boulevard) south to Orlando Premium Outlets via Universal Boulevard, the Convention Center and SeaWorld.

Running every day, 8am–10.30pm at roughly 20-min intervals (30mins on the Green Line), it costs $2/trip ($1 kids 3–9, 25c for seniors) – please have the right change – or you can buy Unlimited Ride Passes for 1, 3, 5, 7 or 14 days at $5, $7, $9, $12, $18. If you need to transfer between routes, ask for a transfer coupon when you board (not needed with Unlimited Ride Passes). All trolleys have hydraulic lifts for wheelchairs. Passes are sold at more than 100 locations in the I-Drive area, including the Official Visitor Center and most hotel desks, plus online, but NOT on the trolleys themselves (407 248 9590 or US freephone 1866 243 7483, **www. iridetrolley.com**). I-Ride has a high-tech vehicle location system that allows riders to check arrival times, maps and other info live on their mobile devices. It can be accessed on their mobile website **www.iDrive2Go.mobi** or if you text the code at each trolley stop.

Busch Shuttle Express: This regular daily service operates from SeaWorld to Busch Gardens in Tampa, with 7 departure points, 8.15–9.40am daily. It costs $10/person but is FREE if you have Busch tickets in advance (included in the FlexTicket Plus or 3-Park Ticket with SeaWorld and Aquatica). For more info, call 1800 221 1339 in Orlando toll-free.

 BRITTIP

The cheapest way to get from I-Drive to Disney is the $2 Lynx bus Link 50 from SeaWorld – 6600 Sea Harbor Drive – to the Transportation & Ticket Center next to the Magic Kingdom. All Disney transport then operates from there. Use the I-Ride Trolley to get to SeaWorld.

Shuttle services

Alternatives to public transport are the well-organised firms offering set-fee shuttles to the attractions that pick up at hotels. There are more than a dozen, with everything from stretch Hummer limos to buses.

Florida Fun Shuttle: An excellent range of attraction shuttle options (round-trip transportation only), with tours to the likes of St Augustine, Daytona and Cocoa Beach, plus winery excursions, a new Craft Beer tour, kayaking trips, sports events and other one-off trips. They can even do one-way visits to the beaches, with pick-ups a few days later, and Port Canaveral transfers (321 231 0005, **www.floridafunshuttle.com**).

Mears: The most comprehensive service, with a 1,000-vehicle fleet from limousines to town cars and coaches. Typical round-trip shuttle fares would be: airport to Walt Disney World, $36 adults, $27 under-12s, under-4s free ($22 and $17 one way); airport to I-Drive, $32 and $24 ($20 and $15 one way); airport to Highway 192 in Kissimmee $38 and $29 ($22 and $17 one way); Walt Disney World to Universal Orlando, $20 round trip; I-Drive to Walt Disney World, $20; I-Drive or Walt Disney World to Kennedy Space Center, $36. You can book a shuttle on arrival at the Mears'

desks in the luggage halls, but it can be a longish trip if it has a full van stopping at several hotels before yours (407 423 5566, **www.mearstransportation.com**).

Maingate Transportation: Another option from the Highway 192 area ($15 round-trip to Universal or Wet 'n Wild, $12 to SeaWorld and $11 to Disney parks; 407 870 5553, **www.maingatetaxi.com**).

Omega Transportation: with a full range of shuttle and airport transfer services from most hotels (1800 997 9489, **www.shuttlesinorlando.com**).

Shopping mall shuttles: Lake Buena Vista Factory Stores collects guests free each day from 60 hotels in the Orlando and Kissimmee areas (407 363 1093, or **www.lbvfs.com**); Orlando Premium Outlets Vineland Ave has a free shuttle from 15 Lake Buena Vista area hotels or for $11 round-trip from Kissimmee hotels (call at least 2hrs in advance on 407 858 3008).

Excursions: There are also excursion services offered by the likes of Brit Guide partners Florida Dolphin Tours (407 352 5151, **www.floridadolphintours. com**) and Gray Line Tours (p264).

Town cars and limos

When it comes to limousine, town car and other transport services, there is again a huge choice (more than 150 at the last count). The following all earn a *Brit Guide* recommendation:

BRITTIP

A 'town car' means a deluxe saloon, such as a Cadillac or Lincoln.

Quick Transportation: A good bet for airport transfers and tailor-made transport packages, its town cars comfortably cope with a family of 4, while luxury vans cater for larger parties and all offer a ½hr grocery stop for an extra $20. Luxury van rates (for up to 7) one-way from Orlando International Airport range from $75 to the I-Drive area up to $120 for the farthest parts of Walt Disney World. Up to 11 can use a van for a small additional fee per person. Larger parties may need a luggage trailer for $25 extra each way. Town car rates are $120 from the airport to anywhere in Greater Orlando and $230 for a round trip, while stretch limos are $195 and $380. It serves all the parks and attractions and offers online quotes for all services, while it can also supply vehicles for the disabled (407 354 2456 or 1888 784 2522, **www.quicktransportation.com**).

Sky Limousine: This company has one of the largest selections of vehicles in town, from Lincolns and executive vans to the amazing Hummer limo. One-way airport transfers from $80 (plus a 20% driver gratuity), and vehicles can also be hired by the hour from $60/hour. Other options cover much of central Florida, offering cruise transfers, a night on the town, all-day services, beach trips, concerts and tailor-made excursions (407 352 4644, **www.skyorlando.com**).

FL Tours: This well-established and popular company specialises in both airport–Disney routes and Port Canaveral transfers. One-way trips start from $70 and round trips from $129 ($125 and $235 from Orlando Sanford International Airport), plus gratuity; it also offers a free ½hr grocery stop, free kids' booster and car seats, 24hr online reservation access, and no extra charge for late pick-ups (407 857 9606, **www.fltours.com**).

Taxis
For groups of 4 or 5, taxis can be more cost-effective than the shuttles. Orlando International Airport to I-Drive would be around $40 (plus tip); $50–60 for the Kissimmee area; $65 to Magic Kingdom resorts and $60 for the Epcot resort area; $15–20 from I-Drive to Universal Orlando; and $25–35 from I-Drive to Downtown Disney. You'll find plenty of taxis in ranks at the parks, hotels and shopping centres, but they don't cruise around looking for fares, so it's often best to book in advance. You also need to ensure you choose a reliable, fully insured company. Check

the name and phone number of the cab company is clearly displayed on the side, the driver's ID and insurance are visible and the rates are shown on the window or inside the car. Some drivers look for fares in the airport baggage hall, which is strictly illegal; all legitimate taxis should be in the rank on Level 1.

Mears: A group of 3 firms – Checker Cabs, Yellow Cabs and City Cabs (407 422 2222) – all of which are reliable. Mears is the main taxi company for Orlando Sanford International Airport, and you can pre-book cabs for around $105 to I-Drive, $120 to Lake Buena Vista and $125 to Disney hotels. Most taxis are metered but it is also acceptable to ask in advance what the fare will be.

Other reputable firms: Ace Metro Cab (407 855 1111), Star Taxis (407 857 9999) and Diamond Cab (407 523 3333). Several hotels have town cars at their ranks and these won't have meters, so you can either ask for the fare or call one of the companies listed above.

THE CAR
Ultimately, having a car is the key to being in charge of your holiday and, on a weekly basis, car hire tends to be quite reasonable: weekly rates can be as low as $120 for the smallest car. The scale of the car hire operation is huge, with as many as 1,000 visitors arriving at a time.

BRITTIP
Your first call for car hire should be to *Brit Guide* partner Alamo. See inside the front cover for our special offer.

The cars will be mainly American – Chevrolet, Dodge, Buick, Chrysler, Ford, Mercury and Lincoln, plus some other makes like Kia, Hyundai and Nissan.

BRITTIP
Check you have both parts of your driving licence BEFORE you leave home. You will simply NOT be given a hire car without all of it.

- **Economy or Subcompact:** The smallest cars are usually a Vauxhall Corsa-sized hatchback.

- **Compact:** Next up is a small family saloon like a Nissan Versa.

- **Midsize or Intermediate:** A more spacious 4-door, 5-seater like a Toyota Corolla.

- **Fullsize:** This would be a larger-style executive car like a Ford Fusion.

- **Premium, Luxury, Convertible, SUV and Minivan:** All more upmarket options, while the Minivan is a Ford Galaxy or Renault Espace type.

Most holiday companies offer 'free car hire', but that doesn't mean it won't cost you anything. Only the rental cost is free and you must still pay the insurances and taxes (which makes the all-inclusive packages more attractive).

BRITTIP
Be firm with the car hire company check-in clerk. Some can push you into having extras, like car upgrades, you simply won't need.

Also beware low starting rates – there are essential insurances, taxes and surcharges that can take the weekly rate above $300. However, all the big rental companies now offer all-inclusive rates, which can work out cheaper if booked in advance in the UK, and you also benefit from easier processing in Orlando, making the whole business quicker.

Serengeti Railway at Busch Gardens

Enter Mapman

By far the best and most up-to-date area map is a British production, created by Disney fan and cartographer Steve 'Mapman' Munns. It is superbly detailed for the I-4 corridor, Highway 192 and *Walt Disney World*, with special sections on I-Drive and villa locations. All the main attractions, hotels and even many restaurants are clearly indicated and there is accompanying text and photos, while the website adds updates and insider tips. We think it's the perfect companion to the *Brit Guide* and you won't go wrong with it at only £7.40 (plus £1.10 p&p). Go to **www.orlandomaps.co.uk** (online orders only). It's also available as an iPhone/iPod/iPad App from the iTunes store for £2.99. Called iOrlando Tourist Map, it is offline so there are no roaming charges, but it does include a searchable database to find places quickly. Even better, Steve is our resident 'mapman' for the *Brit Guide*.

Car rental companies: Alamo is our *Brit Guide* partner and offers excellent rates and service (see inside front cover). You also benefit with Alamo from being able to choose your own car from the different ranges, where most other companies assign you a specific car. For alternatives, try Dollar (020 3468 7685), Avis (0844 581 0147), Budget (0844 544 3439) or Thrifty (01494 751 500), or try the comparison website **www.carrentals. co.uk**.

BRITTIP
The boot (trunk) size of American cars tends to be slightly smaller than the British equivalent. Plus you won't get 7 adults AND all their luggage in a 7-seat people carrier ('van')!

Insurance: Having a credit card is essential, and there are 2 main kinds of insurance, the most important being the Loss or Collision Damage Waiver (LDW or CDW). This costs $25–27/day and covers you for any damage to your hire car. You can do without it, but the hire company will insist on a deposit around $1,500 on

The satnav solution

The best way to navigate is by a GPS or satnav system. All car hire companies offer this as an extra (at around $90/week) or you can bring your own. If your system has only the base-level (i.e. UK) maps loaded, download the maps for south-east USA for around £35. If you are thinking of buying a GPS system, the likes of Wal-Mart offer new systems, fully loaded for the US, for less than $200.

your credit card (and you are liable for ANY damage). You will also be offered Supplemental Liability Insurance (SLI) or Extended Protection at $13–15 a day, which is not essential but does cover you for most damage you might cause. Another option is Underinsured Motorists Protection (in case someone with minimal cover runs into you) at around $8 a day.

BRITTIP

Unless you have accepted the SunPass pre-pay auto-toll option from the car rental firm, you cannot drive through the toll booths marked 'Sunpass' or 'E-Pass' only. You must stop at the booths marked 'Change Given' (in green) or 'Exact Change Only' (in blue).

Those on a budget can cut costs by taking insurance through specialists like **Insurance4CarHire** (0844 892 1770, **www.insurance4carhire.com**), whose US and Canada cover offers up to 60 days' continuous rental, including CDW/LDW and SLI, for £100. You may still need to leave a credit card imprint with the hire firm, but it should accept these policies (check in advance).

Other costs: Drivers must be at least 21, and those under 25 have to pay an extra $25 a day. Other costs include local and state taxes, plus Airport Access and 'Facility' fees, which can add more than $40 a week. Many companies also offer a Roadside Plus (around $5/day), which covers flat tyres, running out of fuel or locking your keys in the car, but this is again totally optional.

Fuel: Then there is 'gas', though this is still cheaper than in the UK. You can either pre-pay for a full tank (so you bring it back empty; the charge is usually slightly under the local rate/gallon for this); fill it up yourself so you have a full tank on return; or pay a fuel surcharge at the end for the company to refill the tank (the most expensive option).

Pre-pay tolls: You can also opt for the SunPass auto-pay system for toll roads, so you just drive through without stopping; all your tolls are auto-recorded for payment when you return the car (plus a $2–3/day convenience fee). Dollar and several other hire companies call it Pass24 and charge a flat-rate fee of $5–8/day (max $41.99/week).

Getting used to your car

Most people soon find driving in America is a pleasure, mainly because nearly all hire cars are automatics and nearly new. And, because speed limits are lower (and rigidly enforced), you won't often be rushed into taking a wrong turn.

- All cars have air-conditioning, which is essential for most of the year. Turn on the fan as well as the A/C button or it won't work! A small pool of liquid will form under the car from condensation.

- Power steering is universal.

- Larger cars have cruise control, so you can set the desired speed and take your foot off the accelerator. There will be 2 buttons on the steering wheel, one to switch on cruise control, the other to set the speed. To cancel, either press the first button or touch the brake.

- Some cars have an extra pedal to the left of the brake, and you need to push this to engage the handbrake. To release it, you pull the tab just above it, if there is one, or give a second push on the pedal.

- Keep your foot on the brake when you are stationary as automatics tend to creep forward. Always put the gear lever in 'P' (Park) when switching off.

- The car probably won't start unless the gear lever is in 'P'. To put the car in 'D' for Drive, depress the brake pedal. D1 and D2 are extra gears for steep hills (none in Florida!).

- Not all cars have central locking, so make sure you lock ALL the doors before leaving it. With an automatic, you won't be able to take the keys out of the ignition unless you put the gear lever in 'Park'.

Fuel: All local gas stations are self-service and you usually pay before filling up. However, the pumps should allow you to pay by credit card without having to visit the cashier (some stations ask for a local zip code with a credit card swipe, which means you DO need to go inside). To activate the petrol pump, you may need first to lift the lever underneath the pump nozzle. RaceTrac and Hess petrol stations are often the cheapest. The 3 Hess stations in Walt Disney World are, surprisingly, among the cheapest in the area, while the Wal-Mart on Vineland Road is also a cheaper option. Petrol stations just outside Disney and the airport are the MOST expensive.

Finding your way

Your car hire company should provide you with a basic map of Orlando, plus directions to your hotel – insist they do, as all the hire companies make a big point of this in their literature.

◀▌▶ BRITTIP

Be organised – get your directions in advance off the internet at sites like **www.mapquest.com** or use Google Earth to source maps, directions and even check out the lie of the land in advance. Download it free from its website at **http://earth.google.com**.

Signposting: You can't fail to find the main attractions, but retracing your steps can be tricky as the exit road may be different from the way in. It is vital to familiarise yourself with the main roads in advance and learn to navigate by road numbers (as it's mainly those that are given on the signposts), exit numbers off the main roads, and directions around the attractions so you know where you're heading (i.e. if you want I-4 east or west or 192 as you exit Walt Disney World).

Lanes and exits: Exits off motorways can be on EITHER side of the carriageway, not just on the right, but you can overtake in ANY lane on multi-lane highways. Therefore, you can sit in the middle lane until you see your exit. You don't get much advance notice of turn-offs, though.

Road names: Around town, road names are displayed at every junction suspended ABOVE the road underneath the traffic lights. This road name is NOT the road you are on, but the one you are CROSSING. Once again there is little advance notice of each junction and the road names can be hard to read as you approach, especially at night, so keep your speed down if you think you are close to your turn-off to allow time to get into the correct lane. If you do miss a turning, most roads are on a grid system, so it's easy to work back.

Occasionally you will meet a crossroads where no right of way is obvious. This is a 4-Way Stop, and the priority goes in order of arrival. So, when it's your turn, just indicate and pull out slowly (America doesn't have many roundabouts, so this may be the closest you get to one).

Local maps: The maps supplied by the car rental companies are pretty basic, as are the free maps in the tourist areas. AA members have their own map options (p54), but we highly recommend getting the Orlando Map by Steve Munns (p50).

Rules and regulations

As well as the obvious difference of driving on the 'wrong' side of the road, there are several differences in procedure.

Tolls: For toll roads, have some change handy in amounts from 25c to $2. They all give change (in the GREEN lanes), but you will get through quicker if you have the correct money (in the BLUE lanes). On minor exits of Osceola Parkway and the Greeneway, there are auto-toll machines only, so keep some loose change to hand.

BRITTIP
On nearly all toll roads, for the manned toll booths you have to pull in to a slip road on the right to pay. It is SunPass/E-Pass only on the main carriageway. This can catch you out when you have just left the airport.

Traffic lights: The most frequent British errors occur at traffic lights (which are hung above the road). At a red light, you can still turn RIGHT providing there is no traffic coming from the left. Stop, check there are no pedestrians crossing and make your turn – unless there is a sign indicating 'No turn on red'. Turning left at the lights, you have the right of way with a green ARROW but must give way to traffic from the other direction on a SOLID green. The recent addition of a YELLOW flashing arrow means it is OK to turn left providing the way is clear.

Left turns: The majority of accidents involving overseas visitors take place on left turns, so take extra care. There is also no amber light from red to green, but there IS from green to red. A flashing amber light at a junction means proceed but watch for traffic joining the carriageway, while a flashing red light indicates it is okay to turn if the carriageway is clear.

BRITTIP
The Osceola Parkway toll road (522) that runs parallel to Highway 192 is a better route in to Walt Disney World from eastern Kissimmee and costs only $1.75. Use Sherberth Road for Disney access from west 192 or the new Western Beltway (Highway 429).

Speed limits: Speed limits are always well marked with black numbering on white signs and the police are pretty hot on speeding, with steep on-the-spot fines. There are varying

limits of 55–70mph/88–113kph on the Interstates, where there is also a 40mph/64kph minimum speed limit. It can also be just 15–25mph/24–40kph in built-up areas.

Seat belts: These are compulsory for all passengers, while child seats must be used for under-4s and can be hired from the car companies at $10–15 a day (so bring your own or buy one locally for $70–80). From 4–5, they can use regular car seatbelts if they are at least 49in/124cm tall; otherwise use a booster seat.

Parking: It is illegal to park within 10ft/3m of a fire hydrant or a lowered kerb, and never park in front of a yellow-painted kerb – they are stopping points for emergency vehicles and you will be towed away. Never park ON a kerb, either. Park bonnet first – reverse parking is frowned upon because number plates are only on the rear of cars and police then can't see them. If you park parallel to the kerb, you must point in the direction of traffic.

Other traffic laws: Flashing orange lights over the road indicate a school zone and school buses must NOT be overtaken in either direction when they are unloading and have their hazard lights on. U-turns are forbidden in built-up areas and where there is a solid line down the middle of the road. You must pull to the side of the road to allow emergency vehicles to pass, in either direction, when they have lights and/or sirens going. Also, on multi-lane highways in Florida, the Move Over law means you must pull into an adjacent lane

Disney's car park tram

if you see a police car on the hard shoulder, or slow down if you can't move over. And you must put on your lights in the rain.

Finally, DON'T drink and drive. Florida has strict laws, with penalties of up to 6 months in prison for first-time offenders. The blood-alcohol limit is lower than in Britain, so it is safer not to drink at all if you are driving. It is also illegal to carry open containers of alcohol in the car.

Bonus for AA members: Your membership is recognised by the equivalent AAA in the US and you benefit from various special offers. Take your AA card and produce it where you see the AAA 'Show & Save' signs in to enjoy the same discounts as the locals. Visit **www.aaasouth.com** and click AAA Discounts for the full range, which includes shopping and dining, like 10% off at Hard Rock Cafe and Dennys restaurants (use the zip code 32819 when prompted). You can also get maps and books from their office in Lake Mary in Seminole County (near Sanford).

There are no fixed speed cameras in Florida (although many traffic lights DO have cameras to catch red-light offences), but the police often go out with hand-held radar guns.

Accidents

In the unlikely event of an accident, no matter how minor, you must contact the police before the cars can be moved (except on the busy I-4). Car hire firms will insist on a full police report for the insurance. If you break down, there should be

Hard Rock Café

an emergency number for the hire company in its literature or, if you are on a main highway, raise the bonnet and wait for one of the frequent police patrol cars to stop (or dial *FHP on your mobile). Always carry both parts of your driving licence and your car hire forms in case you are stopped by the police.

Key routes

All main motorways are prefixed I, the even numbers going east–west and odd numbers north–south. Federal Highways are the next grade down, with black numerals on white shields, while state roads are prefixed SR (black numbers on white circular or rectangular signs).

All American motorways have their junctions numbered in mileage terms, which makes it easy to calculate journey distances. I-4 starts at exit 1 in Tampa and goes to exit 132 at Daytona, 132ml/211km away. In Orlando, the main junctions run from exit 55, at Highway 27, to exit 83 (downtown Orlando) and exit 101 for the Seminole Expressway (417) and Orlando Sanford International Airport.

Interstate 4: I-4 is the main route through Orlando, a 4, 6 or 8-lane motorway linking the coasts. Interstates are always indicated on blue shield-shaped signs. For most of its length, I-4 travels east–west but, around Orlando, it swings north–south, though directions are still given east (for north) or west (for south). All the attractions of Walt Disney World, plus SeaWorld and Universal Orlando are well signposted from I-4. LEGOLAND Florida in Winter Haven, Lake Wales and Bok Tower Gardens are a 45min drive from Orlando west on I-4 and then south on Highway 27, while Busch Gardens is 75–90mins down I-4 to Tampa. Be aware I-4 can be packed with traffic for long sections in the morning and evening rush hours. You can check for major roadworks on **www.cflroads.com**.

International Drive: I-Drive is the second key local roadway, linking a 14½ml/24km ribbon of hotels, shops, restaurants and attractions like Wet 'n Wild, Pointe Orlando and Orlando Premium Outlets (I-Drive South, from Highway 192 in Kissimmee north to Route 535 is NOT the main stretch and the 2 sections are linked via Route 535 and World Center Drive). From I-4, take exits 71, 72, 74A or 75A going east, or 75B, 74A or 72 going west. To the north, I-Drive runs into Oak Ridge Road and the South Orange Blossom Trail, which leads to downtown Orlando (junctions 82C–84 off I-4). I-Drive is also bisected by Sand Lake Road and runs into World Center Drive (536) to the south, also convenient for Disney.

◀▮▶ **BRITTIP**

Stand by for some MAJOR roadworks on I-4 from Sand Lake Rd to north of downtown starting in 2015. It is a road widening project that will also add toll lanes for the first time. Completion date? 2021!

I-Drive is a major tourist centre and makes an excellent base, especially around the Sand Lake Road junction, as it is fully pedestrian-friendly. It's a 20min drive to Disney and 10mins from Universal. However, at peak times, heavy traffic means it's best to avoid the stretch from the Convention Center north. Use Universal Boulevard instead.

Kissimmee: The other main tourist area, south of Orlando and south-east of Disney, its features are grouped along a 20ml/32km stretch of the Irlo Bronson Memorial Highway (192), which intersects I-4 at junction 64B, and is close to Walt Disney World (though a good 25mins from SeaWorld and Universal). Downtown Kissimmee is off Main Street, Broadway and Emmett Street, and is ideal for walking.

Highway 192: A handy visual along here is the Marker Series from Formosa Gardens (number 4) to just past Medieval Times (number 15). These highly visible signs are good locators for hotels, restaurants and attractions, and much of this stretch is also walkable (though few places are close together). Try

to avoid the area of the 192 east of Marker 15, though; it is rather run-down and unappealing. For downtown Kissimmee (which we DO recommend) use the Osceola Parkway and S Orange Blossom Trail (441). The unique Disney-inspired town of Celebration is also here (just south of Walt Disney World).

Highway 27: This is at the west end of Highway 192, running north to Clermont and south to Davenport (and Haines City). A major area of holiday villa developments, these are generally quite convenient for Disney. Many home owners claim they are only '5mins from Disney' but it is at least 10mins from Highway 27 to the edge of Disney property; often more. The area is also starting to add shops and restaurants, notably in the Cagan Crossings junction (just north of where 192 meets 27), where there is also a large Wal-Mart, and Berry Town Center (to the south).

Western Beltway: Highway 429 provides a western Orlando bypass, avoiding the often-crowded I-4 to link with the Florida Turnpike and Apopka to the north. It also offers a western gateway to Walt Disney World at Exit 8 (Western Way), which is handy for the Davenport/Clermont areas. This junction is also destined for development in the next 10 years as an area called Flamingo Crossings at the junction of the 429 and Western Way (**www.flamingocrossings.com**).

Now, let's go on to the next vital step – your holiday accommodation…

SheiKra at Busch Gardens

4 Accommodation

or Making Sense of American Hotels, Motels and Condos

Metro Orlando has the second highest concentration of hotels in the world (after Las Vegas) and more are being built all the time. There are currently 118,000 rooms, and counting, not to mention 26,000 villas for rent. Therefore, what follows is only a general guide to the various types, plus our recommendations and favourites.

The main choice is between a traditional hotel option and one of the many self-catering types of accommodation, which can be villas/ vacation homes, town homes or condos.

Disney's All-Star Movies Resort

BRITTIP
Don't make calls from your hotel – most add a 45–70% surcharge (Disney resorts even add a connection fee), while you can be charged for an unanswered call if it rings 5 or more times. Buy a phonecard instead (p30 and 34).

HOTELS

Many American hotels, particularly in the tourist areas, tend towards the motel type, where everything is not necessarily located in one main building. Your room may be in one of several blocks sited round the pool, restaurant or other amenities. Room size rarely alters, even from 2

to 4-star hotels; their amenities and services form the basis of their star ratings. A standard room usually has 2 double beds and will accommodate a family of 4 (couples without children should ask for a king room, with an extra-size bed), while most rooms are now completely non-smoking. Motel-type accommodation can also lack a restaurant as they operate on a room-only basis.

Most hotels are big, clean, efficient and great value. You'll find plenty of soft-drink and ice machines (though it's cheaper to buy drinks from a supermarket), with ice buckets in all rooms. All accommodation will be air-conditioned and, when it is hot, you have to live with the drone of the A/C unit at night. If you need a more spacious room, look for one of the many suite hotels, which provide sitting rooms and mini-kitchens, as well as 1, 2 or even 3 bedrooms.

Deals and bookings: If you've just arrived and need a hotel, visit the official Visitor Center on I-Drive just north of Pointe Orlando (on the corner of Austrian Court; 8.30am–6.30pm daily; closed 25 Dec; 407 363 5872), where they have brochures on all current deals. There are also many online hotel specialist agents like **www.priceline.com**, **Expedia** (020 3564 3904, **www.expedia.co.uk**), **Hotels.com** (**www.hotels.com**), **Orbitz** (1800 649 9920 in the US only, **www.orbitz.com**) and **Hotwire** (**www.hotwire.com**).

◄► **BRITTIP**
Buy soft drinks at the supermarket, and (if your hotel room doesn't have a fridge) a polystyrene cooler for about $5 that you can fill from your hotel ice machine to keep drinks cold.

Prices: Hotel prices are always per room (not per person) and they will be cheaper out of the main holiday periods, with special deals at times. Always ask for rates if you book directly and check if special rates apply during your visit (don't be afraid to ask for their 'best rate' at off-peak times, which can be lower than published or 'rack' rates). There

may be an additional charge ($5–15 per person) for more than 2 adults sharing a room, plus there is state tax and, sometimes, a sneaky resort fee that can add $10–15/day.

There is no widely accepted star rating, so (with the exception of Disney's resorts), we group hotels into 4 ranges: where the (rough) price groups/night will be:

- Budget   =   up to $50
- Value   = $51–99
- Moderate = $100–160
- Deluxe   = $161 plus

The main factor is the extra facilities. Thus, a Deluxe rating will include the highest level of facilities and service, while a Budget will be a basic motel-type. A key pricing factor is location (the closer to Disney and other parks, the higher the price), so you can save if you don't mind a longer journey.

Suite things
Suites hotels provide a combination of hotel and apartment, with extra value for large families or groups. Typically, a suites room gives you a living room and kitchenette, including microwave, coffee-maker, fridge, cutlery and crockery, while many offer a complimentary continental breakfast (or better). All have pools and grocery stores or snack bars and several have restaurants. They vary only in the number of bedrooms and can usually sleep 6–10.

Disney hotels
Our review of Orlando's hotels starts with Walt Disney World. Sited conveniently for all its attractions – and linked by an excellent free transport system of monorail, buses and boats – Disney's hotels, suites and campsites are all magnificently appointed and maintained. It also groups them into 5 types: Value, Moderate and Deluxe Resorts, then the Deluxe Villas (Disney's timeshare properties) and the Campground of Fort Wilderness (with a strong element of self-catering for the latter

Disney Dining Plan

This is another perk of staying onsite with Disney. Hotel guests can pre-pay most meals at a set fee per day. However, it is an EXPENSIVE option if you are staying for a week or more. There are 3 different Plans to choose from (prices shown as of summer 2014):

Quick Service Dining Plan: Provides 2 counter-service meals and 1 snack a day, plus 1 refillable resort mug/person. Counter-service meals are defined as 1 entrée or combo meal, plus 1 dessert and 1 (non-alcoholic) drink for lunch or dinner, and 1 juice, 1 entrée or combo meal and 1 drink for breakfast. Snacks can be any item such as an ice-cream, popcorn, pastry, a piece of fruit, a bag of crisps, a bottled drink, a medium soda or tea/coffee. Cost: $41.99/day for adults, $16.03 for 3–9s (children must order off the Children's Menu).

Disney Dining Plan: Provides 1 table service meal, 1 counter-service and 1 snack per person per day. Table-service meals are 1 entrée, 1 dessert and 1 (non-alcoholic) drink, or 1 juice, 1 entrée and 1 drink OR a full buffet for breakfast. Cost: $60.64 and $19.23/day (slightly more in peak season).

Deluxe Dining Plan: Provides 3 meals (either table or counter-service) and 2 snacks per person per day, plus 1 refillable resort mug per person. Cost: $109.53 and $29.86/day (slightly more in peak season).

All meals do NOT have to be used per day and can be spread over the duration of your stay, so you can miss a table-service meal one day, then use 2 table-service credits another day for a signature restaurant or dinner show. Gratuities are NOT included. When you check in at a Disney hotel, your MagicBand is loaded with all your Dining Plan meals and that monitors your daily usage. The Dining Plans CAN be used for Character Meals, when 1 table-service meal is required per person (2 at ultra-popular Cinderella's Royal Table in Magic Kingdom), and for the 13 Signature Restaurants in Walt Disney World (notably Jiko at Animal Kingdom Lodge, California Grill at the Contemporary Resort and Citricos at the Grand Floridian Resort), which all require 2 table-service meals. They can even be used at Disney's Dinner Shows (p295), subject to availability, at 2 table-service meals per person.

However, ALL members of the group must book the Plan for the full duration of the stay and inclusive of park tickets. It is also advisable to pre-book (on 407 939 3463) full-service meals well in advance as the sit-down restaurants usually book up early. Not all restaurants are on the Plan but you still have 100 options. If you have used it before, be aware there were substantial price increases in 2014, making the Dining Plans even more expensive, in our view. More info at **www.disneyworld.co.uk**, where you can book all table service restaurants online.

2). They range from the swanky Grand Floridian Resort & Spa to the more basic but still fun style of the Pop Century Resort. And Disney's imagination and attention to detail here are as good as at the parks. There are more than 22,000 rooms, while Fort Wilderness has 1,195 campsites and cabins. All Disney hotels are non-smoking, with designated smoking areas outside.

Grand accommodation comes at a price, though. A regular room at the Grand Floridian can be over $800 a night in high season (suites can top $2,000) and even the Moderate Port Orleans Riverside can be $300 a night. Dining at resort hotels is not cheap either, and you'll find few fast-food outlets on site. However, staying with the Mouse is one of the great thrills, for the style, service and extras. The 20 resorts offer a superb array of facilities that children especially love. The benefits are:

- **MagicBand:** Every guest receives this new wristband, which is the room key, theme park entry, FastPass+ entry and PhotoPass collector, as well as a 'charge card' for almost all on-site purchases. Disney hotel guests can also book FastPass+ 60 days in advance instead of 30.

- **Package delivery:** Park purchases can be sent back to your hotel.

- **Free parking:** At all the parks.

- **Free Wi-fi:** At the parks.

- **Refillable mugs:** All Disney resorts sell collectable drinking mugs, which are well worth buying (from $8.99 for a 1-day stay to $17.99 for 4 or more days) as you then get free refills at their self-service cafés.

- **Dining priority:** Many Disney restaurants hold tables for resort guests, while you can also book 180 days in advance plus the length of your stay (i.e. 194 days if you're going for 2 weeks). Call 407 939 3463 (non-Disney hotel guests can book only 180 days in advance).

- **Children's services:** All resorts have in-room or group babysitting (subject to availability) and 8 of the 9 Deluxe resorts have supervised activity centres and dinner clubs (around $15/child per hour), usually open until midnight.

- **Mickey on call:** An alarm call from the Mouse himself.

- **Extra Magic Hours:** The BIG bonus is getting into one of the parks each day either an hour early or for 2 hours after regular park closing to enjoy rides with reduced crowds.

- **Disney's Magical Express Service:** The free airport transfer service for guests at Disney hotels. Book at least 10 days before arrival through **www.disneyworld.co.uk** or a travel agent.

◄■► ANNIVERSARY SPOT

20 Disney had just 13 resorts when we published our first edition. Since then, they have added The Boardwalk, Coronado Springs, Saratoga Springs, Pop Century, Art of Animation, Bay Lake Tower, Animal Kingdom Lodge (both parts of it), and the Vacation Club villas at the Yacht and Beach Club, Wilderness Lodge and the Grand Floridian.

Value resorts

Disney's All-Star Resorts: Here you can stay in one of the 5 Sports-themed blocks centred on a massive food court, 2 swimming pools, a games arcade and shops; the Music-themed version; or the

Movies complex – possibly the most imaginative, with its Fantasia pool and kids' play areas, the most popular blocks being Toy Story and 101 Dalmatians.

Standard rooms are bright and compact (read 'tight' for families with older children), but well designed for those who want the Disney convenience but not the price. The All Star Music Resort (Jazz and Calypso buildings) also has 192 impressive 2 room Family Suites (combining 2 standard rooms) that sleep up to 6. Each suite has 2 bathrooms, a well-stocked kitchenette, a lounge and private master bedroom, making the space much more flexible.

All 3 centres, with 5,794 rooms, have pool bars, shops, laundry facilities, video games rooms and a pizza delivery service. Close to the entrance is a large McDonald's if the resort's food courts don't appeal. All resort transport is provided by an efficient bus service.

◄■► BRITTIP

To make a reservation at any Walt Disney World hotel call 407 934 7639 or see **www.disneyworld.co.uk**.

Disney's Pop Century Resort: In a similar vein, themed round the decades of the 2nd half of the 20th century, here are 5 blocks with giant icons – such as yo-yos, Rubik's cubes and juke-boxes – and a riot of period sayings and visual gags. Opened in 2003, it features a pool like a 10-pin bowling lane (others shaped like a

The Rosen Center

computer and a flower), a huge table football set-up and open-air Twister mats. Blocks are grouped around a main building housing the check-in area (with a large-screen TV showing Disney films), an imaginative food court, a lounge (with quick-breakfast bar), a Disney store and a games arcade. The 177acre/72ha complex also features a central lake and lots of bright landscaping. It also has a well-organised bus service to the parks. The drawbacks? Long queues to check in and a rather hectic feel, even late in the evening. You need to request a hairdryer from reception and rooms are, again, rather small.

Disney's Art of Animation Resort:
New in 2012, this Budget-priced suites-style resort builds on the popularity of the Family Suites at the All Star Music Resort. Originally intended to be part of the Pop Century Resort, it is a 4-part, 1,984-room complex (1,120 suites, 864 standard rooms) based around classic animated films *The Lion King*, *The Little Mermaid*, *Finding Nemo* and *Cars*, and with an elaborate main pool and children's play areas themed with *Finding Nemo* characters, 2 'quiet' pools, the animation-themed Landscape of Flavors food court with 4 sections (themed to the 4 movies and one of Disney's best), enormous games arcade and the Ink and Paint gift shop. The 4 different courtyards are heavily themed for each of the films, with larger-than-life icons,

Disney's Art of Animation Resort

interactive sculptures, fountains, extensive photo ops, and other play features, and theming in all the rooms (look for fun 'character reveals'), with the suites offering a master bedroom, 2 bathrooms and 3 separate sleeping areas in the living space, including the 'Inovabed' – a piece of furniture that converts from a table or work-desk into a bed, plus a small kitchenette with mini fridge, microwave, and coffee maker. The main pool area is vivid and colourful with plenty of kid-appeal as it even features an underwater sound system! Like Pop Century, all park transport is by bus.

Moderate resorts
Disney's Caribbean Beach Resort:
This 2,112-room complex is spread over 5 Caribbean 'islands' (with an inter-island bus service). The resort's basic rooms are relatively plain, but comfortably sleep 4, while the new Pirate Rooms (which need to be requested at booking) take the swashbuckling theme to a fantastic level, with ship-shaped beds and other decorations. The Market Street food court, main restaurant Shutters and outdoor activities (with a lakeside recreation area with themed waterfalls, slides, games arcade, bike and boat rentals) are a big hit with kids. The 6 Market Street outlets at the Old Port Royale resort hub can get busy in the morning, and the Trinidad South and Barbados 'islands' are a fair walk from the centre. Trinidad South rooms feature the pirate theming (for a supplement) and there are other imaginative touches, like Parrot Cay Island with its tropical birds and play area. Transport to all the parks is solely by bus.

Disney's Coronado Springs Resort:
Possibly the best value of this trio, it has slightly more facilities for its 1,921 rooms spread over 125acres/50ha: 4 pools (including the massive Lost City of Cibola activity pool with waterslide), 2 games arcades, restaurant, food court and café/convenience store, lounge bar, gift shop, beauty salon and health club, business centre and 2 launderettes. The chic and upscale Rix Lounge

Kidsuites = happy families

Orlando has pioneered a great family accommodation style, worth seeking out if you have kids who enjoy bunk beds. Basically, a kidsuite is a separate area within the hotel room that gives the kids their own 'bedroom' (with bunks), usually also with their own TV and games console.

– a bar/nightclub serving unique cocktails and appetisers – gives the resort another claim to fame. Constructed on a scenic Mexican/Spanish theme in 3 'villages' (Casitas, Ranchos and Cabanas), Coronado is an often-overlooked treasure. Check out the Maya Grill and its New Latino cuisine; sample the offerings of the Pepper Market food court; or grab a drink and soak up the splendid lake views from the outdoor terrace. Coronado Springs is only 5mins from Disney's Animal Kingdom and is well served by the bus network.

◀◼▶ BRITTIP

Disney resort restaurants can (and, we think, should) be visited even if you aren't staying there. Advance book at any of the parks, call 407 939 3463 or visit **www.disneyworld.co.uk**.

Disney's Port Orleans Resort: This is a 2-part complex. The 2,048-room Riverside has a steamboat reception area, a great Riverside Mill food court, Boatwright's full-service restaurant,

the River Roost lounge (with live entertainment on certain nights) and an old-fashioned General Store (gift shop). It also features the new Royal Guest Rooms, themed for Princes and Princesses right down to headboards that perform fibre-optic fireworks! Also at this resort, the 1,008-room French Quarter has the Sassagoula Floatworks and Food Factory court, 2 bars, a games room and shopping arcade.

The Riverside includes the magnificent Ol' Man Island, a 3½acre/1.5ha playground with swimming pool, kids' area and a fishing hole, while the French Quarter has Doubloon Lagoon, with Mardi Gras dragon slide, alligator fountains and a play area. The eye-catching landscaping and design vary from rustic Bayou backwoods to turn-of-the-century New Orleans. Transport for both is by bus to the parks and bus or boat to Downtown Disney.

Deluxe resorts

More than anything, Disney specialises in high-quality hotels with all manner of grand design features, amenities and restaurants. All 9 offer a Concierge level, which adds an exclusive, personalised service, and a private lounge with meals and snacks.

Disney's Animal Kingdom Lodge: This stunning 'private game lodge' is set on a 33acre/13ha animal-filled savannah, which many rooms overlook. The pervasive African theme and the effect of opening your curtains to a vista of giraffes and

Disney's Animal Kingdom Lodge

zebras is immense. The lavishness and detail are superb, right down to the guides who can tell guests about the animals and their habitats, the African folklore stories around the outdoor fire pit and the chance for children to become junior safari researchers while Mum and Dad do some wine-tasting (the hotel boasts a huge collection of South African wines).

All this creativity comes before you consider the amenities: 2 restaurants, café, bar, elaborately themed 'watering-hole' main pool (with waterslide) and kids' pool, massage and fitness centre, large gift shop, children's play area and an awesome 4-storey atrium.

The main restaurant, Jiko, is spectacular, but there is also the superb buffet-style Boma, a 'marketplace' restaurant featuring African-tinged dishes from a wood-burning grill and rotisserie for breakfast and dinner.

◀▦▶ BRITTIP

Jiko at Disney's Animal Kingdom Lodge offers an imaginative New World cuisine menu, attentive service and authentic ambience, and is a wonderfully romantic choice.

Rooms range from standard doubles to 1 and 2-bedroom suites, some of which have bunk beds. Part of the main building, Jambo House, has been converted into studios and 1 and 2-bed villas (the latter with full kitchens) for Disney Vacation Club guests, sleeping 4–12, but these are also available to regular guests when not in use by DVC. The newer **Kidani Village** wing adds still more (p68). Simba's Cubhouse is for 3–12s (4.30pm– midnight), and all transport is by bus (with the Animal Kingdom barely 5mins away).

Disney's Boardwalk Inn and Villas: One of the Crescent Lake resorts next to Epcot is this 45acre/18ha extravagant Inn and entertainment 'district'. It features a 512-room hotel, 383 villas, 4 themed restaurants, a TV sports club and 2 nightclubs, plus an array of shops, sports facilities and a huge, free-form pool with a waterslide, all on a semi-circular boardwalk around the lake. The effect is stunning, and the in-room attention to detail excellent, notably in the 'summer cottage' Villas (also part of the Disney Vacation Club).

For dining, the Big River Grille is a great bar/restaurant with its own micro-brewery while the Flying Fish is an upmarket seafood option with a hugely creative menu (if a bit pricey). Italian restaurant Trattoria al Forno was due to open in December 2014, replacing Kouzzina, with wood-oven pizza and risottos. You can also try the

The beautiful Boma restaurant at Disney's Animal Kingdom Lodge

Boardwalk Bakery for a snack. It's a delightful place to visit for a meal, the nightlife (especially Jellyrolls piano bar and ESPN Club) or just to wander along the boardwalk. Transport is by boat to Epcot and Disney's Hollywood Studios and bus to the other parks.

Disney's Contemporary Resort: On the monorail next to the Magic Kingdom, this 15-storey resort boasts 655 rooms, a cavernous foyer, 5 shops, 4 restaurants, 2 lounges, a real sandy beach, a marina, 2 pools (1 with waterslide), 2 tennis courts, a video games centre and health club – and fabulous views, especially from the superb, hotel-top California Grill (one of the most romantic settings in Orlando; try to get a reservation to coincide with the park's fireworks), completely refurbished in 2013. Don't miss Chef Mickey's for a breakfast or dinner buffet with your favourite characters, while the monorail runs right *through* the hotel – great for kids. Rooms are some of Disney's largest, with elegant décor, dark-wood furniture and comfy duvets. Chic restaurant/lounge The Wave features a modern bar and dining area with a highly varied menu and is well worth trying for dinner or just a cocktail, while the Contempo Café adds a light meal option 6am–midnight. Within walking distance of the Magic Kingdom, transport to other parks is by bus.

Disney's Grand Floridian Resort & Spa: This true 5-star hotel is built like an elaborate Victorian mansion, with 867 rooms, an impressive domed foyer and staff in period costume. Again on the monorail, one stop from the Magic Kingdom, the rooms and facilities are truly luxurious – hence the mega prices, though it's worth a look even if you're not staying. Its 6 restaurants include the top-of-the-range Victoria and Albert's (where the set 6-course dinner with wine costs $200, or you could sample the Chef's Table at $315 – with wine – per person), the chic seafood-based Narcoossee's (one of our favourites), with its excellent view over Seven Seas Lagoon, and Mediterranean-styled Citricos. There are also 4 bars

and impressive sports and relaxation facilities, notably the fabulous Senses Spa. There's a wonderful second pool area, complete with zero-depth entry and waterslide, while the main pool has been heavily remodelled. The Mouseketeer Club caters for 4–12s (4.30pm–midnight) and the 1900 Park Fare restaurant is hugely popular for character breakfasts and dinners, plus various children's activities (p102). The Garden View Lounge serves a variety of traditional Afternoon Teas 2–5pm daily, $15–38/person. Transport to the Magic Kingdom is by boat and monorail; by bus to the other parks.

BRITTIP

Watch out for the free nightly Electrical Water Pageant on Bay Lake and Seven Seas Lagoon, on view from all the Magic Kingdom resorts.

Disney's Polynesian Village Resort: This is a South Seas tropical fantasy – with modern sophistication and comfort. Beautiful beaches, lush vegetation and architecture are home to 853 rooms built in wooden long-house style, all with balconies and superb views. Also on the monorail opposite the Magic Kingdom, it boasts a lovely 3-storey atrium, with 75 varieties of tropical plants, koi ponds and a waterfall. The large rooms have been extensively refurbished to revive the Pacific isles theme, with custom-made furniture, tapestries and warm colours. The eating is excellent: 'Ohana is a stylish dinner venue with lively character breakfasts, while the Kona Café is

Disney's Grand Floridian Resort at Christmas

less formal but still with an extensive menu and Captain Cook's Snack Company has more basic counter-service fare. Then there are canoe rentals, a beautiful 'Volcano' pool area with waterslide, games room, shops and children's playground. The Neverland Club caters for 3–12s (4pm–midnight). Catch the monorail or boat to the Magic Kingdom and buses to the other parks. The Poly is also home to the Spirit of Aloha dinner show (p295), which is open to non-resort guests and makes a great evening among the torch-lit gardens. The Resort's beach is a great area from which to view the nightly Magic Kingdom fireworks. A major renovation to add Disney Vacation Club villas and lakefront bungalows (some on stilts over the water) is due for completion in late 2015, including Trader Sam's Grog Grotto bar and lounge, serving signature cocktails and snacks.

Disney's Wilderness Lodge: One of the most picturesque and romantic resorts, this is a re-creation of a National Park lodge, from the stream running through the massive wooden balcony-lined atrium into the gardens, past the swimming pool (with hot and cold spas) to a geyser that erupts each hour. Offering backwoods charm with luxury, the resort is connected to the Magic Kingdom by boat and bus (and buses

to the other parks). Rooms are all spacious and well furnished, while the Courtyard View rooms are the best of the regular rooms (though at a slight premium). Deluxe rooms sleep up to 6 and the suites (at up to $1,600/night) are sumptuous. It also has 2 restaurants: the brilliant Artist's Point (lunch and dinner) and the Whispering Canyon Café (lively breakfast and huge all-you-can-eat family meals) – plus a snack bar and pool bar. The Cubs' Den is for 4–12s (4.30pm–midnight). The Villas at Wilderness Lodge is a Disney Vacation Club development of 136 studios and 1 and 2-bed villas. Facilities include living areas, kitchens, private balconies and whirlpool baths. There is a quiet pool area, a spa and health club.

Disney's Yacht and Beach Club Resorts: Disney added more refined quality with this duo, featuring 630 and 580 nautical-themed rooms respectively. Set around Crescent Lake next to the Epcot park, they help to form a massive resort area that is a delight to walk around at any time but especially at night. For dinner, the Yachtsman Steakhouse offers friendly, elegant dining at the Yacht Club, while the sister hotel features Cape May Café for lovely character breakfasts and a nightly New England-style clambake buffet. Beaches & Cream can also be found here, a classic 1950s-style diner for burgers, shakes and sundaes. Both resorts are set along a white-sand beach like a tropical island paradise and share water fun at Stormalong Bay, a superb 2½acre/1ha recreation area with waterslides and a sandy lagoon. You can go boating or catch a water-shuttle to Epcot or Disney's Hollywood Studios; other park transport is by bus. The Sand Castle Club here caters for youngsters aged 3–12 (4.30pm–midnight).

Disney's Yacht & Beach Club

BRITTIP

Look out for the nightly Disney film shows on the big outdoor movie screen by the beach at the Yacht and Beach Club Resorts.

Walt Disney World and Lake Buena Vista Accommodation

© Steve Munns 2014

N

Big Sand Lake

I-4 PALM PARKWAY

Hilton Garden Inn
Residence Inn
Embassy Suites
Hampton Inn & Suites
Quality Suites Lake Buena Vista
Floridays
Barton Inn
Comfort Inn
Extended Stay America
Hawthorn Suites
Courtyard Orlando
Crossroads Center
Hilton Grand Vacation Suites
Radisson Lake Buena Vista
Marriott Village
Courtyard by Marriott, Fairfield Inn, SpringHill Suites
Holiday Inn LBV Resort
Blue Heron Beach Resort
Bryan's Spanish Cove
Grand Beach Resort
Caribe Royale
Buena Vista Suites
Nickelodeon Family Suites

APOPKA - VINELAND ROAD

Cypress Pointe Resort
Staybridge Suites
Fairfield Inn & Suites
Sheraton LBV Resort
Crowne Plaza
Hyatt Regency Grand Cypress
Doubletree Guest Suites
Best Western LBV
Wyndham LBV Resort
Holiday Inn
Hilton Orlando Resort
B Resort Lake Buena Vista
Buena Vista Palace
Saratoga Springs Resort & Spa, & Treehouse Villas
Old Key West Resort
Vistana Resort
Orlando World Center Marriott Resort
Marriott Vacation Club

LBV

DOWNTOWN DISNEY

BUENA VISTA DRIVE

Typhoon Lagoon

Four Seasons Hotel and Disney's Golden Oak Villas

Port Orleans Riverside Resort
Port Orleans French Quarter Resort

EPCOT CENTER DRIVE

Car Park

Epcot

Waldorf-Astoria, Hilton Orlando and Wyndham Grand Resort at Bonnet Creek

Caribbean Beach Resort

Pop Century Resort

Disney's Art of Animation Resort

Beach Club
Boardwalk
Yacht Club
Dolphin
Swan

Disney's Hollywood Studios

Walt Disney World

Fort Wilderness Resort & Campground

Wilderness Lodge

Contemporary Resort & Bay Lake Tower

Bay Lake

Seven Seas Lagoon

Magic Kingdom

Grand Floridian Resort & Spa

Polynesian Resort

Transportation & Ticket Center

Car Park

monorail

WORLD DRIVE

BAY LAKE

WESTERN WAY

Blizzard Beach

Coronado Springs Resort

BUENA VISTA DRIVE

Animal Kingdom

Animal Kingdom Lodge Resort & Kidani Village

OSCEOLA PARKWAY

All-Star Resorts

INTERNATIONAL DRIVE SOUTH

WORLD CENTER DRIVE

APOPKA - VINELAND ROAD

Toll road

Walt Disney World Swan and Dolphin Resort: These unmistakable twin hotels, while not actually owned by Disney, still conform to the same high standards. They have some of the most extensive facilities, a great location, fab restaurants and a night-time view second to none, while they are usually slightly cheaper than most Deluxe resorts. They're within walking distance of Epcot and Disney's Hollywood Studios, Disney's Boardwalk Resort and the Fantasia Gardens Miniature Golf Courses, but also have a boat service to both parks (and bus to the others). The unique architecture is extensive, with the Swan topped by a 45ft/14m statue, as well as 756 large rooms (including 55 suites), while the Dolphin (1,509 rooms, 112 suites) is crowned by 2 even bigger statues. Both have been extensively refurbished to include the Westin Heavenly Bed® and high-speed wi-fi. The Dolphin also boasts the Balinese-inspired Mandara Spa, with a relaxing tea garden and Meru Temple. This resort has 17 restaurants and lounges, 4 tennis courts, 5 pools (one an amazing grotto pool with hidden alcoves and waterslide), a kids' pool and white-sand beach, 2 health clubs, bike and paddle boat rentals, a great range of shops, a video arcade and the Camp Dolphin centre for 4–12s (5.30pm–12am, $10/hour per child). Even for non-guests, Shula's Steak House and celebrity chef Todd English's Bluezoo

(both Dolphin) are worth seeking out, along with Il Mulino Trattoria, New York's top Italian restaurant (in the Swan). Fresh, the Dolphin's Mediterranean-style market, serves breakfast and lunch, featuring all made-to-order menu items and both à la carte and tableside dining. The decor and atmosphere at the Swan's Garden Grove Café is inspired by the gardens of Central Park, and it serves à la carte or buffet breakfasts, with Disney characters each evening and breakfasts at the weekend. The intimate Kimonos, in the Swan, offers sushi and a karaoke bar. Picabu in the Dolphin is open 24 hours with all-American favourites. With its ideal location and amenities, this is possibly the perfect resort (407 934 4000, www.swandolphin.com).

Four Seasons Resort: (see Golden Oak, p68).

> ### BRITTIP
> Most Disney hotel rooms will accommodate only 4, with the exception of Port Orleans Riverside (which can take an extra child on a trundle bed). For larger groups, consider Old Key West, Saratoga Springs, the Boardwalk Villas, the villas at Animal Kingdom Lodge, Wilderness Lodge Villas, Fort Wilderness cabins or 2-room suites at the All Star Music Resort and Art of Animation Resort.

Campground and cabins

Disney's Fort Wilderness Resort & Campground: This is possibly the best value of all the Disney properties. Situated on Bay Lake across from the Magic Kingdom, it offers impressive camping facilities and chalet-style cabins housing up to 6 in a 750acre/304ha spread of countryside. Two 'trading posts' supply fresh groceries and there are 2 bars and cafés plus a range of on-site activities, including 2 swimming pools, the thrice-nightly Hoop-Dee-Doo Musical Revue, Mickey's Backyard Barbecue (a seasonal character buffet dinner), campfire programme, open-air films, sports, games and a prime position to view the nightly

Disney's Fort Wilderness Resort

Electrical Water Pageant. You can rent bikes or boats or take horse rides around the country trails, while the Tri-Circle D ranch has a small petting zoo. There is even a Segway Tour (the great 2-wheeled personal transports), the Wilderness Back Trail Adventure, providing a unique 2-hr trundle around the many trails ($96/person, over-15s only; 8.30 and 11.30am Tue–Sat; call 407 939 8687 to book). The Trails End restaurant (sit-down and takeaway) offers a great value buffet breakfast, à la carte lunch and buffet dinner, while Crockett's Tavern serves pizza and appetisers (dinner only). Buses and boats link the resort with other areas (and the short boat ride to the Magic Kingdom is a great start to the day). If you need a break from the Magic Kingdom, hop on the boat here and try the family-friendly Trail's End for lunch or the dinner buffet ($27 for adults, $15 3–9s).

Disney Vacation Club resorts

Disney's Old Key West Resort: Disney's first Vacation Club resort, this is primarily a 5-star holiday ownership scheme (one of 8 such timeshares), but the 1, 2 or 3-bed studios in a Key West setting can also be rented nightly when not in use by members. Facilities include 4 pools, tennis courts, a games room, shops and a fitness centre, plus the lovely Olivia's restaurant. Transport to all parks is by bus.

◀▶ BRITTIP

Looking for a handy diversion from Downtown Disney? Take the boat to Old Key West and try a meal at Olivia's for a lovely, laid-back holiday vibe.

Disney's Saratoga Springs Resort & Spa: The most extensive DVC resort, this 65acre/26ha apartment complex is opposite Downtown Disney, has some wonderful views over the lake and is next to scenic Lake Buena Vista Golf Course. It boasts 828 units, from standard 2-bed hotel-style studio rooms to massive 2-storey, 3-bed

apartments sleeping 12. The theme is the 1880s' New York resort of the same name, with a peaceful, gracious look and a great array of facilities, from the free-form, zero-depth entry main pool (with waterslide and squirt-fountains), a smaller quiet pool, the health-conscious dining room (the Artist's Palette, offering breakfast, lunch and dinner, plus food shop), a large video arcade, tennis courts and a wonderful full-service spa and gym. All but the hotel-style studios have a kitchen (with dishwasher and microwave), washer-dryer, whirlpool bath and DVD player, with TVs in each living room and bedroom. The resort includes room service, babysitting and childminding services plus a water taxi to the shops and entertainment at Downtown Disney. Rates for the 3-bed villas top $1,900 a night, but the 1-bed units are more modestly priced and, although it is a Vacation Club property, rooms are usually available to the public.

Also here are 60 3-bed **Treehouse Villas**, beautiful chalets raised 10ft/3m off the ground and set among a heavily wooded area next to Sassagoula River. Sleeping up to 9, they feature some sumptuous furnishings, including granite counter-tops and flatscreen TVs, as well as 2 full bathrooms and outdoor barbecue grills. They also have their own leisure pool and whirlpool spa. Transport to all parks is by bus.

Bay Lake Tower at Disney's Contemporary Resort: This resort is linked to the Contemporary Resort by a 5th-floor bridge and features its own pool, waterslide and whirlpool spa, plus kids' water-play area,

Disney's Vacation Club

shuffleboard and bocce courts. The 14-storey, 295-room Tower offers modern decor throughout, including the studio rooms and spacious 1, 2 and 3-bed villas. The studios (sleeping up to 4) all have small fridges, microwaves and coffee-makers, while the villas (sleeping up to 12) have full kitchens and laundry facilities. The Tower superbly complements its neighbour resort and affords wonderful views over the Magic Kingdom and nightly fireworks from its exclusive rooftop lounge and viewing deck (DVC members only). There is also a gourmet coffee bar and easy access to the restaurants of the Contemporary Resort. Transport by monorail or bus (or on foot to Magic Kingdom).

Disney's Animal Kingdom Lodge – Kidani Village: An addition to the Animal Kingdom Lodge, this is divided into hotel-room studios (sleeping up to 4) and 1, 2 and 3-bed villas (sleeping 5, 9 or 12), all offering full kitchens and laundry facilities. The low-rise architecture and decor continue the resort's eye-catching African theme and the 3-bed villas are magnificently spacious. There is a separate wildlife preserve in 4 animal savannah areas, a fabulous pool and kids' play area, and another restaurant, Sanaa, which continues the Lodge's reputation for fine dining. The stunning Samawati Springs – a huge zero-depth entry pool – is also open to guests at the Lodge, while children will make a beeline for Uwanja Camp, a 3-part interactive water playground (for ages 4 and under, 5–7s, and 8 and over). Other amenities include a video arcade,

Disney's Contemporary Resort

basketball court, fitness centre, gift shop and animal programmes, from flamingo-feeding to campfire story-telling. Transport to all the parks is by bus.

Grand Floridian Villas: New in late 2013 were these sumptuous additions to the DVC inventory, providing 147 stylish 1 and 2-bed villas sleeping 5–9, plus 'grand villas' that sleep 12 and include a media room with home theatre system. The elegant building, with subtle Mary Poppins theming, has its own reception, children's water-play area and private beach.

Golden Oak: Now being built in an ultra-exclusive corner of Walt Disney World is this small-scale community of holiday homes for private sale. Like most villa developments, it has its own luxurious Clubhouse, but homes are NOT rented out and feature VIP perks such as concierge service, private transport to the parks and special events. The price is equally exclusive – they START at $1.4m!

Four Seasons Resort: Within the gates of Golden Oak but a separate entity (and also open to non-guests for its spectacular dining opportunities), the first Central Florida hotel of this fabulous 5-star brand opened in August 2014 and features 444 capacious rooms and even larger suites, all with marbled bathrooms. Built in Spanish Revival style and with luxury throughout, it has an amazing array of amenities, including 5 restaurants, 3 pools, a lazy river and water-play area, tennis courts, extensive spa, state-of-the-art gym and its own golf course. The huge kids club (for 5–12s, open 9am–5pm) is free to guests and offers a superb spread of games and activities and there is a good choice of inter-connecting family rooms, as well as adults-only rooms with luxurious king beds and great views to both sides. Rooms with views of the parks – and the Magic Kingdom fireworks – come at a premium while the rooftop Spanish steakhouse restaurant Capa is one of Orlando's most spectacular. Authentic Italian restaurant Ravello, with its show kitchen, is another show-stopper and the golf clubhouse diner Plancha features Cuban-American cuisine in a lakeside setting. It offers a full Disney Planning Centre, grab-and-go café, teen hangout and the kind of deluxe 'extras' – including a shoe-shine service, twice-daily housekeeping, refrigerated private bar and unobtrusive service – that go with the brand. However, regular room rates start at $545/night and reach $12,000/night (!) for the 9-bedroom Royal Suite (1800 267 3046, **www.fourseasons.com/orlando/**).

BRITTIP
Book dinner at Capa at the Four Seasons to coincide with the nightly Wishes show at the Magic Kingdom and you will have a superb high-level view of the fireworks.

Disney Hotel Plaza

If Disney's hotel prices are out of your range, consider the 7 'guest' hotels that are on site but come with a less hefty price-tag, on Hotel Plaza Boulevard on the doorstep of Downtown Disney. There's a free bus service to the parks, guaranteed admission (even on the busiest days), and you can make reservations for shows and restaurants before the general public. The convenience of being able to walk to Downtown Disney and the Crossroads shopping plaza is also handy.

BRITTIP
Look out for a 'Free Breakfast' and special Advance Purchase offers at the Holiday Inn Walt Disney World. Book 7 nights or more and qualify for free breakfast for 2 adults (there's also Kids-eat-free options). Look them up on **www.hiorlando.com/specials.htm**.

Take your pick from the well-priced **Best Western Lake Buena Vista** (407 828 2424; Value); the new-look **B Resort** (407 828 2828; Moderate; see also p76); the outstanding **Buena Vista Palace Hotel & Spa** (407 827 2727; Moderate); the versatile **DoubleTree Suites by Hilton** with its array of 2-room suites (407 934 1000; Moderate); the **Hilton Orlando Resort** (the only hotel here to benefit from Disney's Extra Magic Hours programme; 407 827 4000; Moderate); the South Beach vibe and excellent dining of the **Holiday Inn** (407 828 8888; Moderate); and the recently renovated **Wyndham Lake Buena Resort** (407 828 4444; Moderate). For more info on these 7, go to **www.downtowndisneyhotels.com**.

20 ANNIVERSARY SPOT
The Accommodation chapter was a mere 16 pages in our first edition but is now more than 40, indicating another of Orlando's major growth areas.

Beyond Disney

Once you move away from Walt Disney World, your hotel choice becomes more diverse. The Budget and Value types are most common, and the area you stay in also has an effect on price: the further you go from Disney on Kissimmee's Highway 192, the cheaper (and more basic) the hotel/motel, while parts of I-Drive are more expensive than others (north of Sand Lake Road is usually cheaper). Facilities vary little and what you see is usually what you get. All the chain hotels can be found here, with rates as low as $35/room off-peak (but remember the local sales tax). Some also have rooms with a kitchenette (an 'efficiency'). Be prepared to shop

Doubletree by Hilton at Universal Orlando

Hotel Plaza Highlight

Looking for something different, hotel-wise? Formerly the Royal Plaza Resort, the **B Resort at Walt Disney World** is its new-look replacement after a total refurbishment in 2014, offering 394 rooms in 5 categories, with suites accommodating up to 5 and family rooms with kids' bunks. It features fresh, contemporary decor and excellent personal amenities in the upscale-but-relaxed style of the new B brand. There is a high-quality signature restaurant called American Q (serving barbecue specialities at dinner), a Grab 'n Go deli-café, landscaped pool (with interactive water elements) and pool bar, 4 tennis courts, stylish Aveda Spa, fitness centre, coin-op laundry and kid-zone area with films and games. Standard rooms have a sitting area while the magnificent 2-room suites boast a huge lounge and all feature clean, crisp design, the trademark Blissful beds, 47in/120cm flatscreen TVs, mini-fridge and superb bathrooms. Other signature elements include free technology amenities like high-speed Internet access throughout the resort, courtesy iPads, game consoles and Monscierge®, a digital touchscreen concierge and destination guide. The attention to detail and that 'something different' style is highly noticeable here but be aware there is a $20 resort fee and self-parking is $16/day (407 828 2828, **www.bresortlbv.com**).

around, especially on Highway 192, where many hotels advertise their rates, and feel free to ask to see a room before you book. Here are the main options.

◀🇬🇧▶ **BRITTIP**

Coffee-makers are standard in most hotel rooms, but tea-making facilities are rare. Bring your own teabags or look for PG Tips and Yorkshire Tea in the International aisles at Publix and Wal-Mart.

Budget hotels

Chain hotels can be found at their most numerous in this category and you'll find few frills. All have pools, but not many have restaurants, bars or lounges (though some provide a free continental breakfast and many offer fridges and microwaves).

B Resort at Walt Disney World

- **America's Best Value Inn:** Basic motel type with some newer properties that are worth seeking out, with free wi-fi and continental breakfast (1888 315 2378, **www.americasbestvalueinn.com**).

- **Days Inn:** Chain that varies widely from tired older hotels to smart newer ones, and with free continental breakfast (1800 225 3297, **www.daysinn.com**).

- **Econo Lodge:** Also with free wi-fi and continental breakfast (1877 424 6423, **www.econolodge.com**).

- **Howard Johnson:** Mainly older properties, many with a Kids-eat-free option and free breakfast, but rooms are often more spacious (1800 221 5801, **www.hojo.com**).

- **Knights Inn:** Several smarter choices in the Orlando area (1800 477 0629, **www.knightsinn.com**).

- **Motel 6:** 'Bargain basement' choice (1800 466 8356, **www.motel6.com**).

- **Red Roof Inn:** Several renovated properties in Orlando, plus free wi-fi (1800 733 7663, **www.redroof.com**).

- **Rodeway Inn:** Chain that has slipped from Value to more Budget territory, but still offers a free breakfast (1877 424 6423, **www.rodewayinn.com**).

- **Super 8 Motel:** Chain varies a lot, but has several newer motels

Our Budget recommendations

Hotels we rate as above average for this category include:

Champions World Resort: Converted Howard Johnson on west Highway 192, a sound budget choice with 3 pools, free theme park transport and wi-fi (1800 638 7829, **www.championsworldresort.com**).

Destiny Palms Hotel Maingate East: Well situated for Disney, this pleasant motel also offers free wi-fi and a continental breakfast (407 396 1600, **www.destinypalmshotel.com**).

EconoLodge Inn International Drive at Universal: Basic, clean and reliable, with free wi-fi, coffee and pastries, and a nice picnic area (407 313 1090, **www.econolodge.com**).

Golden Link Resort Motel: On Highway 192, this quaint little retro motel with free breakfast and wi-fi consistently gets rave reviews (407 396 0555, **www.goldenlinkresortmotel.com**).

Super 8 Kissimmee/Maingate: Well above average for this low-cost chain, with good customer feedback (407 396 8883, **www.super8maingate.com**).

Travelodge Suites East Gate Orange: Higher quality from a basic chain motel, with wi-fi, microwave and fridge in all rooms, a good pool and kiddie pool (407 396 7666, **www.travelodge.com**).

(notably on American Way, just off I-Drive) and all offer free breakfast; look for its 'Pride' hotels, which are above average (1800 454 3213, **www.super8.com**).

- **Travelodge:** With an excellent property on American Way, plus free breakfast and wi-fi (1800 525 4055, **www.travelodge.com**).

There are dozens of smaller, independent outfits that offer special rates periodically, especially a battery of cheap and cheerful motels along Highway 192 in Kissimmee (but try to stay west of Marker 14).

◀╬▶ BRITTIP

Hotels designated Maingate East or Maingate West should be close to Disney's main entrance on Highway 192, though it is wise to check.

Value hotels

At first glance there may not seem much difference here between these Value options and the Budget category, especially as some are still motels, and the big chains dominate. They should have smarter facilities, but not all have their own restaurant.

- **Baymont Inn & Suites:** Highly worthwhile group, boasting several new properties in the area, all with free breakfast and wi-fi (407 354 3996, **www.baymontinns.com**).

- **Choice Hotels:** Group comprising Comfort Inn, which is a bland chain, but offers a free breakfast; Comfort Suites, which has some smart, newer properties; Quality Inn, with a reputation for good value, some with an exercise room and free continental breakfast; and the smarter Clarion Inn (and Suites), often including restaurants, though the age of the properties varies (1877 424 6423, **www.choicehotels.com**).

- **Extended Stay America:** No-frills, clean and consistent chain with more space than many in this group, a free grab-and-go breakfast and wi-fi, plus fully equipped kitchens (1800 804 3724, **www.extendedstayamerica.com**).

Econolodge Kissimmee

Our Value recommendations

Notable properties in this range:

Avanti Resort: This former EconoLodge in the heart of I-Drive has been heavily refurbished to provide an individual touch, with a fabulous new resort pool area (including kids' water fun section), interactive games room, state-of-the-art fitness centre, coffee shop and poolside bar & grill. Rooms have been given a sleek new look and vary from standard queen doubles to a king Jacuzzi room, while double queen and king rooms can be connected to sleep a family of 6, all with free wi-fi and flatscreen TVs. There are free daily shuttles to Universal, SeaWorld and Epcot, as well as Wet 'n Wild and Aquatica (407 313 0100, **www.avantiresort.com**).

Drury Inn & Suites: New in 2013, this smart choice includes a lot for your money (like free wi-fi, parking, hot breakfast, phone calls, snacks and drinks at their daily 5.30pm Kickback sessions and popcorn and soft drinks in the lobby 3–10pm). Well situated for I-Drive, Universal and Sand Lake Road, room choice includes 2-room suites and there is an indoor/outdoor pool and fitness centre (407 354 1101, **www.druryhotels.com**).

Extended Stay America Orlando-Universal Studios: A high-quality choice in this chain, in a great location for Universal and I-Drive, with all rooms recently renovated (407 370 4428, **www.extendedstayhotels.com**).

Galleria Palms Hotel: In Kissimmee at Maingate West, just off Highway 192, has a smart, contemporary look, ultra-comfy rooms, a great location close to Disney, free shuttle to the parks, free breakfast and wi-fi, and a relaxing pool area (there is no restaurant but plenty nearby; 407 396 6300, **www.galleriakissimmeehotel.com**).

Holiday Inn Maingate East: In Kissimmee (between Markers 8 and 9), offering well-maintained rooms (including kidsuites) in 2 high-rise towers, plus an oversized pool, kids' pool, waterslides, gym, children's theatre, food court and lobby lounge, plus a Kids-eat-free programme (407 396 4222, **www.holidayinnmge.com**).

Ramada Plaza Resort & Suites: Top value-for-money choice in a good I-Drive location with a free continental breakfast, wi-fi and Disney transport, plus over-sized rooms all with fridge, microwave and coffee-maker (407 345 5340, **www.michotel.com**)

Palms Hotel & Villas: Just off Highway 192 in Kissimmee (close to I-4), resort with spacious 1 and 2-room suites with full kitchens, 2 large pools and kiddie pool, sports court, free shuttle to Disney parks and free breakfast (407 396 2229, **www.thepalmshotelandvillas.com**).

Wyndham Orlando Resort: Heavily remodelled in the heart of I-Drive and with great facilities, this boasts 2 pools, a delightful poolside bar and restaurant, ice-cream shop, new fitness centre and sauna, all set in landscaped grounds but without the high price tag you might expect. There is also a free shuttle to Universal and SeaWorld but be aware there is ongoing construction next door through early 2015. The $16/day resort fee includes parking and wi-fi (407 351 2420; **www.wyndham.com**).

- **Fairfield Inn:** Budget version of the Marriott chain, usually with newer hotels, many with gyms and most with free breakfast (1800 1927 1927 in the UK, 407 581 5600 in the US, **www.marriott.com**).

- **Hampton Inn and Suites:** Usually above average in this category, with free wi-fi, hot breakfast and tea/coffee in the lobby 24hrs (1800 426 7866, **www.hamptoninn.com**).

- **Ramada:** Good value at this level, many have free wi-fi and breakfast or a restaurant (1800 854 9517, **www.ramada.com**).

There are more options at the upper end of the category.

- **Best Western:** Good, family-style facilities with more amenities (0800 393 130 in UK, 1800 780 7234 in US, **www.bestwestern.com**).

- **Holiday Inn and Holiday Inn Express:** Recently rebranded to be more upmarket, there are still bargains in Value/Moderate territory as they offer Kids-eat-free (with parents) at all properties and many include sophisticated pools and extra facilities such as games rooms (0800 405060 from the UK, 1888 465 4329 in the US, **www.holidayinn.com**).

- **La Quinta Inn and Suites:** Some notably smart hotels in Orlando (1800 753 3757, **www.lq.com**).

- **Radisson:** Possibly the best overall value here, this group has some excellently priced hotels, all with above-average amenities and services, free wi-fi and well situated for the parks (0800 374 411 in UK, 1800 976 9033 in the US **www.radisson.com**).

- **Wingate Inn:** Modern chain, with gyms, free breakfast and wi-fi (1800 337 0077, **www.wingatehotels.com**).

BRITBONUS

Enjoy a special *Brit Guide* rate of $69/night, plus resort fee and tax, at the Palms Hotel & Villas on Parkway Boulevard in Kissimmee (just off Highway 192). This includes: full suite (sleeping 1–5) with kitchen and living space, free hot breakfast daily, free wi-fi, use of recreational facilities and parking. Use code BRIT2015 when calling (407 396 2229) or email palmshotelandvillas@gmail.com. Offer valid until 31 Dec 2015.

Moderate Hotels

This is a category with fewer of each brand, so we highlight a few worthy individuals as well as the chains. All properties provide a good pool (often with extras like a waterslide, kids' pool and/or playground), at least one restaurant, bar and café, and extra in-room comfort.

Main chains:

- **Country Inn & Suites:** A smart choice, with spacious rooms and a pleasant country-house lobby, with an extensive free breakfast (0800 973 217, **www.countryinns.com**).

- **Hyatt Place:** A chic, contemporary choice with stylish, comfortable rooms, free continental breakfast (or hot breakfast upgrade), 24-hour café and evening bar service, plus free wi-fi (1888 492 8847, **www.hyatt.com/hyatt/place**).

- **Residence Inns:** Identikit but consistent, with free breakfast and exercise rooms, plus microwave, fridge and tea/coffee-making facilities (00800 1927 1927, **www.marriott.com/residence-inn/travel.mi**).

- **Springhill Suites:** Also part of the Marriott group, they offer reliable, comfortable value (00800 1927 1927, **www.marriott.com/springhill-suites/travel.mi**).

BRITTIP

Not all hotels provide hairdryers, though they can often be ordered from the front desk. For your own, you will need a US plug adaptor (with 2 flat pins). The voltage is 110–120AC (ours is 220) so UK appliances will be sluggish.

More upmarket

- **Crowne Plaza Hotels:** Some eye-catching properties featuring great pool areas, smart restaurants, fitness centres and ultra-comfy rooms (www.ihg.com/crowneplaza/). The Crowne Plaza Orlando-Universal is a fine example, with 398 rooms and suites in 2 stylish blocks and a spectacular

Country Inn & Suites

Coming up Rosen

One notable local operator in Orlando is the **Rosen Hotels & Resorts** group, with a good variety of 7 well-run, value-conscious properties. Four are budget-minded, the Brit-popular **Rosen Inn** at Pointe Orlando (formerly the Quality Inn Plaza), **Rosen Inn International** (ex Quality Inn International) and Rosen Inn (ex Rodeway Inn) on I-Drive, and the **Clarion Inn Lake Buena Vista** (formerly a Comfort Inn). All have been impressively refurbished and offer standard amenities but thoughtful touches, like family-style buffet restaurants, kids facilities, plenty of pool choice and free wi-fi. The other hotels are the flagship **Deluxe Rosen Shingle Creek Hotel** (p81), and the Moderate pair of **Rosen Centre Hotel** and **Rosen Plaza Hotel**, a distinctive 800-room property with excellent facilities – including 2 restaurants, a pizza shop, deli, fitness centre and nightclub – and spacious, well decorated accommodation (1866 337 6736, **www.rosenhotels.com**).

atrium. Two restaurants, a cocktail lounge and fitness centre, plus a huge heated pool add up to quality and value in an ideal location on Universal Boulevard's junction with Sand Lake Road (407 355 0550, **www.cporlando.com**).

BRITTIP

It is usual to tip hotel chambermaids by leaving $1/adult each day before your room is made up.

- **Doubletree by Hilton:** A contemporary, upscale choice with fewer frills but spacious, ultra-comfy rooms featuring their Sweet Dreams sleep experience and signature welcome cookies, plus a rare B&B option (1800 222 8733, **http://doubletree3.hilton.com/en/index.html**). A good example is the **Doubletree by Hilton Orlando at SeaWorld**, a recently remodelled hotel just off I-Drive set in 28acres/11ha. It offers 3 pools, 2 kids' pools, a playground, mini-golf and extra-large suites. Limited

Cabana Bay Beach Resort

dining, but tropical grounds give it a luxury feel (407 352 1100, **www.doubletreeorlandoidrive.com**).

- **Hilton Garden Inn:** The Hilton chain has really struck the right note with this modern, comfortable and family-friendly brand, with a number of attractive, modern hotels (1877 7829 444, **http://hiltongardeninn3.hilton.com/en/index.html**).

- **Marriott:** Another well-represented group, with some of the smartest hotels in this category, often providing extra facilities and more landscaped grounds, a choice of restaurants and some of the largest standard rooms. Features include its signature Revive beds for a guaranteed good night's sleep (00800 1927 1927, **www.marriott.com**).

- **Sheraton hotels:** These boast a smart, revamped look. Several are themed and feature extra facilities and good dining (1800 325 35353, **www.starwoodhotels.com/sheraton**). The **Sheraton Lake Buena Vista Resort** remains a popular choice with Brits, with spacious, well-furnished rooms, a spectacular pool complex and fitness centre, and impressive restaurant and lounge. (1800 325 3535, **www.sheratonlakebuenavistaresort.com**).

Notable individuals:

There are only a few non-chain properties in the Moderate category.

- **Cabana Bay Beach Resort:** New in March 2014, Universal's first

The Sky's the limit

For a good cross-section, from Value hotels to villas and community resorts, try **Sky Hotels & Resorts**, a specialist management company. Its one-stop shop includes the reliable **Enclave Suites** just off I-Drive, **Hawthorn Suites Lake Buena Vista**, the excellent **Lake Buena Vista Resort Village & Spa** (p90) and the highly rated **Coral Cay Resort** in Kissimmee, a well-designed gated development of 3 and 4-bed town-homes (terraced villas), plus the spectacular views of the 3-star **Hawaiian Inn** at Daytona Beach. An interesting prospect is their own branded **StaySky Suites** just off I-Drive on Canada Avenue. A converted Hawthorn Suites property, it features 1 and 2-bed suites, all with full kitchens and sleeping 4–8. There is free breakfast, shuttle transport to the parks and wi-fi, as well as a fitness centre, heated pool and hot tub, games room and free parking (1866 455 4062, **www.staysky.com**).

fully Moderate hotel is split into 2 impressive parts either side of a central reception area with classic 1950s styling. There are 1,800 standard rooms and family suites with kitchenettes that sleep up to 6, set either side of an efficient 600-seat Food Court, with a variety of food stations, including burgers and milk shakes, salads, pizza and pasta, a bakery, sandwiches and a Grab & Go section. There are also 4 huge video screens showing period TV shows and vintage holiday home movies! Other options include a retro Starbucks coffee shop, lobby bar and 2 elaborate pool bars offering signature frozen drinks and smoothies. The Lazy River Courtyard also offers the Hideaway Bar & Grille for lunch and dinner. Guests can even have pizza delivered to rooms that feature all mod cons, with flatscreen TVs, mini fridge, free wi-fi and a clever bathroom arrangement that features two wash-basins as well as a bathtub/shower. Amenities include a 10-lane bowling alley, which has its own bar/restaurant, and 2 feature-packed resort pool areas, with zero-depth entry, sandy beaches, waterslide and Universal's first lazy river, while the period theming is extensive and all-pervading. Other notable extras include a large video games room and themed fitness centre with lockers and showers (very handy if your room isn't ready yet and you want to change for the parks). However, this is the one Universal resort that does not benefit from the free Universal Express pass perk, although there is still early entry to the parks. It also requires its own shuttle bus to CityWalk (or a 15min walk). The bright, retro styling, while a touch monolithic with the sheer size of the resort, goes well with the neighbouring parks and there may even be enough to keep kids amused here all day, too (1888 430 4999, **www.loewshotels.com/Cabana-Bay**).

BRITTIP

Need a Moderate hotel that is truly family friendly? Consider the CoCo Key Hotel and Water Resort, one of the most thoughtful and feature-packed hotels we've seen in ages.

- **CoCo Key Hotel & Water Resort Orlando:** This ultra-family-friendly option offers excellent amenities, notably the extensive water park. It has been transformed from

CoCo Key

Our Moderate recommendations

Crowne Plaza Lake Buena Vista: Extensively renovated in 2013/14, this essentially new hotel in the Crossroads area (formerly the Orlando Vista) is perfectly situated just outside Disney and offers beautiful, spacious rooms and excellent amenities, including outdoor pool with pirate ship play area, fitness centre and free shuttle to all the parks. In best boutique hotel style, Sapore d'Italia Restaurant features menus with a continental flair and fun options for kids (407 239 4646, **www.ihg.com/crowneplaza/**).

Embassy Suites International Drive South: A consistent 'old faithful' in the heart of I-Drive, with spacious rooms (either standard 2-room suites sleeping 4 or double-doubles for 6) providing 2 TVs, coffee-maker, fridge and microwave. There's a great outdoor pool deck, kids' splash pool and indoor pool, plus a sauna and gym and good dining options, with a free breakfast. It is rare in this area in offering a free shuttle service to Disney, Universal and SeaWorld (407 352 1400, **www.embassysuitesorlando.com**).

Four Points By Sheraton Orlando Studio City: A 21-storey I-Drive icon near Universal Orlando, this features a heated tropical pool and paddling pool, games room, mini-golf, fitness room and free shuttle to Disney and Universal. All 301 well-appointed rooms have coffee-makers, Nintendo games and free wi-fi, plus superb views (ask for a Universal view if possible). The Tropical Palms restaurant is a minor gem, with a fun ambience for breakfast, lunch or dinner, and an imaginative dinner menu, while you can also grab a drink at the Oasis Lounge or Tropical Breezes patio pool bar (407 351 2100, **www. fourpointsorlandostudiocity.com**).

Radisson Hotel Lake Buena Vista: A dramatically remodelled property, convenient for Disney and the Crossroads area, with sleek rooms and furnishings, the stylish Liquid Bar & Grill, a small gym and free wi-fi. Extra-spacious rooms feature a fridge, microwave, coffee-maker, large, flatscreen TV and the signature comfy Sleep Number bed (407 597 3400, **www.radisson.com**).

Rosen Center Hotel: This spectacular 24-storey property, one of the area's largest, caters heavily to the Convention Center next door but also offers excellent facilities. It has a huge swimming grotto, tennis courts, an exercise centre, high-quality restaurants (the excellent steak-and-seafood Everglades and casual 24-hour deli, Café Gauguin), the chic Banshoo Sushi bar and new 98Forty Tapas & Tequila bar. The style is luxurious, yet prices aren't (1800 204 7234, **www.rosencenter.com**).

We also rate the renovated **Holiday Inn** at Walt Disney World (p69) very highly.

an old Ramada in every respect, from the chic new lobby area to the 391 rooms (all with flatscreen TVs, smart bedding and furniture, coffee-maker and free wi-fi). There is a quiet adults' pool, with fountain and Jacuzzi, buffet breakfast room (Tradewinds), food court (Callaloo Grill, featuring Pizza Hut), indoor sports bar and outdoor Tiki Bar overlooking the Key West-themed water park, with a canopy roof to protect from the sun (but also an uncovered play area and terrace). There is a fitness centre, extensive games arcade, gift shop and convenience store, private rooms for birthday parties and a kids' club. The water park is a marvel, with 4 areas: Parrot's Perch, an interactive jungle-gym; Minnow Lagoon, for pre-school kids, with a zero-depth entry pool and water cannons with mini-slides and other small-scale fun (with life-jackets, and life-guards on duty); Coral Reef Cove, the teen activity pool, with the Cyclone body-slide; and the outdoor Water-Park, with nine different slides, including the Over The Falls and Surfer Splash body-slides and Boomerango double-rider tube slide. There is a 'resort fee' for use of the water park, but at $22/room/day, it isn't unreasonable. Day guests are also allowed when the resort is not full, at $23–25/person (kids under 3ft are free) (407 351 2626, **www.cocokeywaterresort.com**).

- **Monumental Hotel:** A converted Crowne Plaza hotel and still ultra-stylish, with a Key West theme, 94

The SeaWorld bonus

For anyone planning on a lot of SeaWorld and Aquatica visits, consider a **SeaWorld Official Partner Hotel** for a range of benefits and money-saving offers. All 7 feature *free* Quick Queue at SeaWorld, a free behind-the-scenes Rescue Tour, free shuttle service to SeaWorld and Aquatica, early park entry on select days, 10% off dining and 10% off merchandise purchases of $50 or more. These benefits are available at each of the Renaissance Orlando, Doubletree by Hilton, Hilton Garden Inn, Hilton Grand Vacations, SpringHill Suites, Fairfield Inn & Suites and Residence Inn, all at SeaWorld. Be sure to pick up a Benefits Card when you check in at any of these hotels. Alternatively, there are another 10 hotels near by that offer the early entry and 10% discounts, as well as $5 off the QuickQueue pass. See details at **http://seaworldparks.com/en/seaworld-orlando/vacations/hotels/benefits/**.

spacious, well-equipped rooms, beautiful pool area and Pineapple Grill Restaurant for daily breakfast and dinner Fri and Sat (1877 239 1222, **www.monumentalhotelorlando. com**).

Deluxe hotels

When it comes to the best hotels, it is largely a question of individuals. The growing selection of genuinely deluxe properties in this area are all highly distinctive, with excellent facilities, outstanding service and, usually, at least one 5-star restaurant. They can be divided into 5 main areas: Universal Orlando, International Drive, Lake Buena Vista, Kissimmee and Further Afield.

Universal Orlando

Universal teamed up with the Loews group to create its hotels, and the 3 upscale offerings come with the Universal Express front-of-queue bonus to the main attractions with your key card. Universal resort guests also enjoy other benefits, like a resort ID card (for buying food, merchandise, etc. throughout the resort), priority seating at most restaurants (show your room key card), package delivery to your room, special golf privileges at 4 nearby courses, and early entry to the Wizarding World of Harry Potter in both parks. The deluxe 3 all feature boat transport to the parks, plus kids' activity centres with a meal option (for 4–14s; 5–11.30pm Sun–Thurs, to midnight Fri and Sat; $15/hour per child, plus $15 for meal). Anyone booking a Universal hotel package via their reservation system (**www. universalorlandovacations.com**) can also add a daily Dining Plan to the park experience (p20). For all Universal hotels, call 1888 430 4999 or visit **www.universalorlando.com**.

Hard Rock Hotel: Possibly the coolest hotel in Orlando, this icon of rock chic is themed as a former rock star's home, with 650 rooms and suites in California mission style. High ceilings,

Hard Rock Hotel

© Universal Orlando

Suite choice

These are our top-rated suites hotels.

Embassy Suites: With smart interior courtyards, good restaurants and relaxing pool areas (1800 362 2779, **http://embassysuites3.hilton.com/en/index.html**).

Homewood Suites: Provide extra room for larger families in 1 and 2-bed suites with full kitchens, free breakfast and an upmarket feel with mid-range pricing (1800 225 54663, **http://homewoodsuites3. hilton.com/en/index.html**).

Hawthorn Suites by Wyndham and Staybridge Suites: Both feature spacious 1 and 2-bed suites that sleep up to 6 and fully fitted kitchens, plus a hearty free breakfast, wi-fi and free local phone calls (1800 337 0202, **www.hawthorn.co**m or 1877 424 2449, **www.ihg.com/staybridge/**). Sister properties the **Buena Vista Suites**, a well-appointed and more individual choice, and **Caribe Royale Resort** (1800 823 8300, **www.cariberoyale.com**) are on World Center Drive just off the lower end of I-Drive. The former is the more basic type, with spacious 2-room suites, a free full breakfast, heated pool, whirlpool, tennis courts, gift shop, mini-market and the Vista Bistro. The Caribe Royale is more luxurious, with a choice of 1-bed suites and 2-bed villas, a tropical pool with waterslide, tennis courts and 2 fitness rooms. Award-winning Venetian Room restaurant is a treat for lovers of fine continental cuisine, and there are 4 other cafés and lounges.

Nickelodeon Family Suites: Not so much a hotel as a theme park resort is this striking, kid-friendly choice on I-Drive South. With loads of character interaction, daily activities, shows and celebrations, this has huge kids appeal, especially as the facilities – including 2 huge water-play areas, video arcade, mini-golf and various shops – are all child-friendly. Rooms come in 1-bed kitchen suites and 2 and 3-bed kidsuites, with living room and bathroom, microwave and fridge (and full kitchen with some). Nicktoons Café offers buffet dining (plus à la carte in the evening), while the character breakfast with Spongebob and pals or the Teenage Mutant Ninja Turtles costs $14/ages 4–13 and $24/adults. Plus there is a food court, pool bar and grill, and adult-friendly Nick@Nite Lounge (407 387 5437; **www.nickhotel.com**).

Sonesta ES Suites: Newly converted from Staybridge Suites on I-Drive (right opposite the I-Drive 360 complex), this refreshing, spacious and Brit-friendly choice features 146 1 and 2-bed suites sleeping 4–8 in 3 configurations, including full kitchens and a master bedroom with its own bathroom. The versatile Trio 2-bed suite features a master bedroom, two double beds in the second bedroom and a sleeper sofa in the lounge. A hot and cold breakfast buffet is included and the new pool area and hot tub provide a great retreat at the end of the day. The inviting bar area extends to an outdoor patio that guarantees a good social gathering and there is also a fitness centre, snack shop, coin-op laundry and daily housekeeping. There is free wi-fi and a daily shuttle to the parks (407 352 2400, **www.sonesta. com/orlando**).

wooden beams, marble floors and eclectic artwork give an eye-catching style, with a rock-star theme to most public areas, music memorabilia, black-suited foyer staff and fairly constant music. The 14acre/6ha site includes 3 bars (including the ultra-cool Velvet Bar), 2 restaurants (the full-service The Kitchen and the 5-star, dinner-only Palm Restaurant), plus a takeaway café, fitness centre, gift shop and games room. The lido area features a huge, free-form pool and 240ft/73m waterslide, 2 Jacuzzis, a beach volleyball court, shuffleboard and life-size chess and draughts. The pool even has an underwater sound system! The 650 rooms (including 12 kidsuites and 10 king suites) are big, beautifully furnished in the hotel's chic style and superbly comfortable.

◀🇬🇧▶ BRITTIP

Hard Rock Hotel guests – and music fans – should make a note of the monthly Velvet Sessions at the hotel, live gigs by well-known bands ('rock 'n' roll cocktail parties' as they call them), on the last Thurs of each month. There's music, free drinks and finger foods. Book tickets at **www.velvetsessions.com**.

Portofino Bay Hotel: The stunning jewel in Universal's crown is a splendid re-creation of the famous Italian port. The elaborate porticos, trompe l'oeil painting, harbourside piazza and faithful ornamentation of the waterfront make it one of Florida's most memorable settings. The 750 rooms were all completely refurbished in 2012–13 and are impeccably appointed, with lashings of Italian style. Standard rooms are sumptuous, with huge beds, spacious bathrooms, mini-bar and coffee facilities, ironing board and hairdryer, while the 94 Club Rooms feature concierge service with private lounge, extra room amenities and free entry to the Mandara Spa fitness centre. There are 18 superbly-themed Despicable Me kidsuites with separate bedrooms each (complete with missile beds!) with their own TV. The resort facilities are equally breathtaking – a Roman aqueduct-style pool with waterslide (and poolside films on Sat evenings), an enclosed kids' play area and wading pool, a separate quiet pool, Jacuzzis, the beautiful Mandara Spa, business centre, an array of gift shops and a video games room. The Portofino also has an amazing 8 restaurants and lounges, including the 5-star (and very romantic) Bice Ristorante (p324), the boisterous Trattoria del Porto (with themed character dinners on Fri 6.30–9.30pm), Mama Della's, an authentic Italian family dining experience (watch out for Mama herself!), an aromatic deli, a pizzeria, gelateria and swanky Bar American. It is only a short way from the parks, but is light-years away in terms of its tranquil ambience.

Royal Pacific Resort: This 53acre/21ha, 1,000-room resort has an exotic 1930s South Seas style, and you feel as if you have stepped into another world as you cross the bamboo bridge into the elegant lobby, faced by the splendid Orchid Garden courtyard. Extensive use of rich, dark woods, cool stone floors and masses of greenery give the place an opulent, colonial feel. Standard rooms feature hand-carved Balinese furniture among many refined touches, and there is also a Club level, with separate lounge and extended facilities, and 51 superlative suites – including 8 Jurassic Park-themed kidsuites (dinosaurs not included!). The Islands Dining Room offers breakfast, lunch and dinner in a setting of oriental simplicity (children have their own buffet area with TV screen, plus character dining on select nights), while fine dining is taken to a new dimension by a magnificent restaurant run by celebrity chef Emeril Lagasse called Tchoup Chop (possibly the best in Orlando; p326). There's a pool snack bar and luau garden area, with the Wantilan Luau Saturday nights, featuring an eye-catching Polynesian feast and dinner show ($63–70 adults, $35–40 under-13s; 407 503 3463 to book). The huge freeform pool is ideal for kids, with zero-depth entry at one

Royal Pacific Resort

end and a boat-shaped interactive play area of squirting fountains. Add a health club (with Jacuzzi, sauna and gym), kids' club (with computer games, TVs and organised activities), video arcade and 2 shops and you have excellent value, even at this end of the scale.

International Drive

There are 4 eye-catching hotels here that take advantage of I-Drive's great location.

Hilton Orlando: This impressive 1,400-room hotel on I-Drive next to the big Convention Center and set in 26acres/10.5ha boasts superb leisure facilities. It features upscale steakhouse, Spencer's, along with David's Club bar and grill, casual dining at The Bistro, a 24hr Marketplace and an inviting pool bar and grill. A full-service spa, a large state-of-the-art fitness centre, 2 pools, lazy river (in a wonderful 'tropical island' setting), tennis, volleyball and basketball courts, and a neat 9-hole putting golf course complete the impressive amenities. The Resort pool boasts a waterslide and kids' fountain, while the Quiet pool has several Jacuzzis and both have cabanas, with fridges and TVs, for hire. Rooms feature Hilton 'Serenity' bedding, 37in HD TVs and high-quality toiletries, while an executive level includes a private lounge and extra services (407 313 4300, **www.thehiltonorlando.com**).

BRITTIP
Spencer's at the Hilton Orlando offers some of the best dry-aged steaks in Florida, and a unique monthly cooking class with Chef Eric Szymczak, including wine from its exclusive cellar.

Hyatt Regency Orlando: Formerly the Peabody and, sadly, no longer with its trademark ducks, this remains an upmarket choice right in the heart of I-Drive, appealing largely to convention business but also well-stocked for holiday fun. The original 891-room tower has an Olympic-size pool, tennis courts and 2 superb restaurants in the gourmet Italian of Fiorenza and the amazing 24-hour B-Line Diner. Larger-than-average rooms and huge suites add to the quality, but conference business can make this side of the hotel a bit hectic.

BRITTIP
The impressive 2,178m²/22,000ft² The Spa at the Hyatt Regency features a blissful array of treatments and make-up services, plus a full-service nail and hair salon, and all-day spa packages with lunch, all open to non-hotel guests on a daily basis.

The relatively new 34-storey tower adds real cutting-edge sophistication and holiday appeal, with another 1,641 luxurious rooms; a lushly landscaped 3acre/1.2ha recreation area with 3 pools (and you'll feel a million miles from busy I-Drive), with tropical pool bar and cabanas; a Napa Valley wine-themed restaurant; a chic cocktail bar, Rocks (perfect in the evening, with live music); a grab-and-go Café; lobby coffee bar; and a superbly stylish spa and fitness centre. All the new rooms (and 193 massive suites) come with LED motion-censored night lights, 42in LCD TVs, iPod docking stations, a Hyatt Grand Bed, fridges, cordless phones and even mini LCD TVs in bathroom mirrors! (407 284 1234, **www.orlando.regency.hyatt.com**).

Renaissance Orlando Resort: This superb resort (788 rooms on Sea Harbor Drive, next to SeaWorld) completed a $35m renovation in 2012 that added a wonderful 2-part children's water-park, complete with 2 120ft/36.6m slides, water-jets rain-tree and more. It gives the outdoor amenities a real boost (parents may struggle to get their young 'uns out of here!) and creates more of an adults-only vibe to the main pool area and gardens. It has a massive 10-storey atrium lobby and some equally large rooms and suites, that renovated pool area with bar and grill, a lavish Neu Lotus Spa and fitness centre and a video arcade. All rooms feature extra bathroom

Condo hotels

A condo-hotel is a cross between a villa and a hotel. People buy 'rooms' in these big properties (which look like resort hotels), which they then own – unlike timeshare, where you just 'own' a time period for a resort. All rooms are identically furnished, unlike villas, and feature 1, 2 or 3 bedrooms, living/dining room and kitchen or kitchenette. A management company then rents them out on behalf of the owners. For guests, they are booked as you would for any hotel. Some are owned by hotel groups such as Starwood while others are just managed by hotel specialists to ensure they maintain the right standards. They are usually built in tower blocks around communal facilities like the Clubhouse check-in and swimming pool (often with elaborate water features), and can include restaurants, fitness centres and even spas.

amenities, flatscreen TVs and Marriott's Revive bedding. The dining line-up consists of Mist Sushi & Spirits (cocktails and full-service dining, plus an amazing 'aquarium' video wall), Boardwalk Sports Bar, the upscale but casual Tradewinds for breakfast, lunch and dinner, Palms Pool Bar & Grill, a smart Starbucks café and ice-cream parlour. The hotel offers great packages in conjunction with SeaWorld, which is a 2min walk across the car park, and its rates are often the best in Deluxe territory (1800 327 6677, **www.renaissanceseaworldorlando.com**).

Rosen Shingle Creek Hotel: This 230acre/93ha resort ranks among the grandest for its location, quality and style. In the middle of the award-winning Shingle Creek Golf Club on lower Universal Boulevard, it boasts 1,500 rooms and suites, all with sumptuous decor and comfort, as well as a full-service spa and fitness centre. Rooms vary from standard doubles to presidential suites, but all with fabulous flatscreen TVs, wi-fi, fridges and first-class toiletries. Amenities include 5 restaurants, 4 bars, a lounge, coffee house, deli and ice-creamery, plus 3 outdoor pools, tennis, basketball and volleyball courts and nature trails. There is also a shopping gallery and babysitting service. The resort is built in a 1900s Spanish revival style and offers flawless service (especially at concierge level). Don't miss A Land Remembered, one of the best steakhouses in the state, in the Golf Clubhouse, and Cala Bella, a fine-dining Italian restaurant, with heavenly desserts from its renowned pastry chef (407 996 9939, **www.shinglecreekresort.com**).

Westin Imagine Orlando: Also on Universal Boulevard, this chic condo-hotel property features 315 king rooms and 1 and 2-bed suites, with either kitchenettes or full kitchens, and the trademark Westin Heavenly bed and bath, plus distinctive decor and extras like flatscreen TVs and marble-topped desks. Signature Italian restaurant Fiorella's Cucina

Rosen Shingle Creek

© Rosen Shingle Creek

Toscana features delicious casual lunches and upmarket dinners surrounded by unique decorative glass designs, with the option of al fresco dining. The bar area is equally distinguished plus there is a huge South Beach-style pool with Tiki Bar and a modern fitness centre to complete a very fresh and modern offering (407 233 2200, **www.westinimagineorlando.com**).

◀🇬🇧▶ BRITTIP

Looking for a quiet resort that is still close to the main attractions? The Westin Imagine is superbly situated close to I-Drive but away from the hustle and bustle. Don't miss lunch at Fiorella's Cucina Toscana for some stylish cuisine at modest prices.

Lake Buena Vista

Moving to the next major resort area, there is a growing range of Deluxe choice here, too.

Hilton at Bonnet Creek Resort: This rare and extensive development is in a unique position inside Walt Disney World but privately owned (the only piece of land Walt was unable to buy from the original landowners in 1966). It is part of a 482acre/194ha resort complex with the Waldorf-Astoria (below) and shares some of the same facilities. The Hilton features 1,000 rooms, 4 restaurants, a lagoon pool complex with lazy river and waterslide, 18-hole golf course, tennis courts and the adjoining full-service European spa and fitness centre. The chic modern Italian-themed La Luce restaurant provides

Hyatt Regency Grand Cypress

fine dining, while the Harvest Bistro offers the main alternative (with kids 12 and under eating free with a full-paying adult), along with the Muse grab-and-go deli (with coffee bar), Zeta bar/lounge and Beech Pool Bar and Grill. One of its prime draws, though, is that it is just minutes from the Disney parks, and benefits from the full Hilton package of stylish accommodation and excellent kids' activity programmes, as well as some blissfully comfy rooms (407 597 3600, **www.hiltonbonnetcreek.com**).

◀🇬🇧▶ BRITTIP

The Hilton Bonnet Creek Resort's splendid La Luce restaurant is usually featured in Orlando's Magical Dining Month each September, when a selection of the best restaurants offer three-course prix fixe dinners for a bargain $30/head. See more at **www.visitorlando.com/magicaldining** (and p304).

Hyatt Regency Grand Cypress: The area's first genuine Deluxe hotel in 1984, this is still one of the best. A mature 1,500acre/608ha resort with a unique mix of facilities, it has a rare 9-hole pitch-and-putt golf course, 27 holes of regular golf (designed by Jack Nicklaus), a golf academy, boating lake and superb pool complex. The resort completed a grand $60m refurbishment in 2013 that included a kids' water park, with a rock-climbing wall, 17ft/5m slide, water pavilion and snack bar. Other extensive enhancements were made to every guest room, the fitness centre and the restaurants. The elegant lobby boasts Zen-inspired décor with some highly relaxing touches, while all 750 rooms have been given a bright, contemporary finish, with large, flatscreen TVs, large shower units and elaborate lighting. The dining choice is among the best of any Orlando resort, and the location remains ideal, almost on the doorstep of Disney yet blissfully reclusive (on Winter Garden-Vineland Road, around the corner from the Crossroads area). The huge freeform swimming pool boasts Jacuzzis, waterfalls and slide, while the white sand beach and magnificent

International Drive Accommodation

Steve Munns 2014

restaurants make for a sumptuous stay, especially Hemingway's, its Key West-styled dinner spot, and Cascade American Bistro, the all-day option with its 2-storey atrium and beautiful lake views. There is also the On The Rocks pool bar and deli-style Palm Café; an inviting lobby lounge and sushi bar; and an eye-catching art gallery. Watersports – such as boating, kayaking or fishing on scenic Lake Windsong with its white-sand beach – and other activities like tennis and bike rentals are covered by the one-off resort fee. And, once among its richly landscaped grounds, you could easily be light years from the theme-park bustle (407 239 1234, http://grandcypress.hyatt.com).

Orlando World Center Marriott: We love this impressive landmark on Disney's outskirts, set in landscaped 200acres/810ha and surrounded by a beautiful golf course. With 2,000 rooms and suites (most boasting fabulous views up to 28 storeys high), 6 restaurants and a series of pools, including a huge freeform tropical pool and three amazing water slides, it is a monumental prospect, set among landscaped foliage and with fabulous facilities, including a Bill Madonna Golf Academy, tennis courts, volleyball, basketball, spa and state-of-the-art gym. Highlights are the Mikado Japanese Steakhouse, Hawk's Landing Steakhouse, Siro Urban Italian Kitchen and High Velocity Sports Bar, while there are excellent children's amenities and programmes. It gets busy with convention business, but the picturesque pool complex offers true relaxation bliss and there were

Orlando World Center

extensive renovations in 2013/14 (407 239 4200, **www.marriottworldcenter.com**).

Waldorf-Astoria: The second part of the huge Bonnet Creek development, this 497-room hotel was the first US Waldorf outside New York and added a new level of luxury to the Orlando scene when it opened in 2009. Stately and serene, the famous-name hotel features 313 standard rooms with Italian marble bathrooms and HD flat-screen TVs, plus 185 truly grand suites with butler service. The zero-entry pool boasts cabanas and waiter service, while the dining choice is superb, from the poolside grille and classic Bull & Bear Steakhouse to the small-plate cuisine of Peacock Alley, gourmet style of signature Oscar's brasserie and private club atmosphere of Sir Harry's Lounge. The Spa by Guerlain is also unashamedly 5-star. Other amenities include basketball and tennis, jogging trails, bike rentals, a state-of-the-art fitness centre (with personal trainers), yoga and aerobics classes and boutique shops on a par with the Waldorf's luxury cachet. Even children aren't forgotten, with the WA Kids Club providing active, creative fun for 5–12s (10am–5pm, $15/hour per child) and the After Dark programme with dinner and games 6–10pm at $75/child (407 597 5500, **www.waldorfastoriaorlando.com**).

Kissimmee

The more budget-oriented area of Osceola County also now has its share of upmarket properties.

Bohemian Hotel: In the Disney-inspired town of Celebration just off Highway 192, this unique hotel offers refreshing small-town America style that is a long way from the usual tourist hurly-burly. With just 115 rooms in its 1920s' wood-frame design, it has a classy ambience and a wealth of high-quality touches, notably in the ultra-comfy rooms: Standard or Lake View (with either a king or 2 queen-size beds), Studio or a 2-room suite, all beautifully furnished. Lovely artwork, courteous staff and a good array of facilities

Kissimmee Accommodation

– pool, Jacuzzi and fitness centre, plus the highly-regarded Bohemian Bar & Grill (excellent for breakfast, it becomes a signature steakhouse at night) – mark out this hotel as a real gem. In addition, it is within a short stroll of the town's shops, restaurants and lakeside walks and makes a great romantic choice (407 566 6000, **www.celebrationhotel.com**).

Gaylord Palms Resort: One of the most dramatic hotels, with 1,406 rooms, is on the junction of I-Drive South and Osceola Parkway (ideal for Disney). A cross between a convention centre and a vast turn-of-the-century Florida mansion, it features 4½acres/2ha of indoor gardens, fountains and 'landscaped' waters under a glass dome, with live entertainment nightly. Three themed indoor areas bear witness to great creativity and the resort offers every creature comfort, with an array of restaurants and bars (including the spectacular 2-level Wreckers sports bar, with more than 50 HDTVs and a 20ft/6m high video screen), full-service spa and children's centre. The Cypress Springs Family Fun Water Park adds a huge zero-entry pool featuring 4 water slides, a massive multi-level water play structure, lagoon, toddler splash area, and 'dive in' family-friendly movies. Grown-ups will appreciate the relaxed ambience of the eye-catching South Beach Pool (with the option of private cabanas). Standard rooms are some of the smartest and most spacious, while the suites are enormous. The central Emerald Bay offers even more choice with a concierge level. One area is landscaped like the Everglades (with alligator feeding!); another copies St

Gaylord Palms

Augustine's old-world charm, with a replica Spanish fort; and the third is eclectic Key West, with a mock-up marina and sailboat. To walk into the resort's marbled lobby and cavernous interior at night is like entering a future world. Then there is the signature fine dining, with the choice of Old Hickory Steakhouse, Sunset Sam's (fine seafood), the Mediterranean buffet-style Villa de Flora (with an excellent Sun brunch and Shrek-Fest character breakfast featuring Shrek and friends from the DreamWorks animated movie Shrek; Sat–Sun 8am–10.30am, $29.95 ages 13 and up, $19.95 ages 4–12) and SORA Sushi Bar. The Relâche Spa is one of the area's largest, with 25 treatment rooms, fitness centre and beauty salon. Find unique shopping along the indoor 'retail street', plus the Cocoa Bean coffee shop and Honeybells Frozen Yoghurt. The hotel stages regular special events and is a great wedding venue (407 586 0000, **www.gaylordpalms.com**).

BRITTIP
The Gaylord Palms features the stunning Christmas celebration ICE!, a wonderland of ice sculptures, snow scenery and ice slides, plus other festive touches. Early Nov–3 Jan, tickets $30 adults, $28 over-55s and $16 4–12s.

Meliã Orlando Hotel (formerly Mona Lisa Suites Hotel): One of the finest condo-hotels, on Highway 192 at the entrance to Celebration, this is a luxury 5-storey, 240-unit property set around a spectacular 'vanishing edge' swimming pool and boasting upmarket dining at the Gastrobar, with its small-plate dining and signature sangrias, and Fuego Restaurant with its Latin flavours. The 1 and 2-bed suites feature beautifully furnished living areas, full kitchens and ultra-comfy bedrooms, with designer toiletries. Balconies overlook the infinity pool or lush landscaping. There is a free shuttle to all the parks and privileged use of the Celebration Spa and Golf Club (407 964 7000; **www.meliaorlando.com**).

◄◄► **ANNIVERSARY SPOT**
20 Names change in the Orlando hotel
◄◄► business, often from year to year. Of
the 7 Downtown Disney hotels, only 2 have
the same name as in our 1st edition – the
Hilton and Buena Vista Palace, and the latter
was also known as the Wyndham Palace
from 1998–2006.

Further afield

Grande Lakes Orlando: You'll find
extensive luxury at this 500acre/200ha
combination of a 584-room, 5-star
Ritz-Carlton Hotel, a 1,000-room JW
Marriott Hotel, grand spa, 18-hole
Greg Norman-designed golf course,
tennis centre and an upscale range
of shops and restaurants, like the
outstanding Norman's, featuring the
'new world' cuisine of celebrity chef
Norman Van Aken. Located on the
edge of a forestry preserve, it feels
secluded and remote – quite a feat in
this area. It is slightly off the beaten
track – at the junction of John Young
and Central Florida Parkway – yet is
only 10ml/16km from Disney and
Orlando International Airport.

JW Marriott: This flagship hotel of the
Marriott group has Spanish-Moorish
design, a formal restaurant featuring
fresh, organic produce, an American
brasserie, Starbucks lounge, Sushi Bar
and a pool bar and grill. It has a great
lazy river mini-water park, plus a kids'
pool and splash fountain. Rooms are
plush and ultra-comfortable; 70%
have balconies and there are 64 grand
suites.

Ritz-Carlton: This offers a wonderful
blend of scale and detail, with lush
gardens, abundant lakes and streams,
Venetian-inspired architecture and a
wealth of genuine antiques. It has a
large, sloped-entry pool, kids' pool,
3 floodlit tennis courts, a signature
shop and 5 dining choices, plus a
separate children's check-in and
the excellent Ritz Kids Club (5–12s;
also for JW Marriott guests), while
all restaurants offer child menus. As
well as the highly rated Norman's,
the restaurants include The Vineyard
Grill steakhouse (try its excellent
Sun champagne brunch at $65/

adults and $29/children), Fairways
Pub and Bleu pool bar and grill. The
rooms are beautifully furnished,
with high-quality products in the
marbled bathrooms, plasma-screen
TVs, radio/CD, mini-bar, slippers
and robes, and all have balconies.
There are 66 spacious suites and 92
Club rooms on the top 2 floors, with
concierge and butler service, food
and drink presentations in the Club
Lounge and Bulgari amenities. Two
kidsuites feature a separate bedroom
and bathroom, with toys, games,
TV and video games for 100% child
appeal. The golf course is immaculate
and offers a Caddie Concierge
programme for the ultimate in
service. The beautiful citrus-tinged
spa boasts a huge fitness centre and
aerobics studio, lap pool (all free to
guests at both hotels), lovely spa-
cuisine restaurant and a huge array of
massages and therapies. The pricing
is suitably upmarket, but it is a rare
treat (407 206 2300/2400,
www.grandelakes.com).

**Omni Orlando Resort at Champions
Gate:** A real golfing paradise,
this offers 720 rooms and suites
overlooking a superb golf set-up with
2 Greg Norman-designed courses.
An imposing hotel with impressive
facilities, including the HQ of the
renowned David Leadbetter golf
academy, main swimming pool
and activity pool (including a lazy
river, fountains and waterslide), 4
restaurants (notably the superb Asian
cuisine of Zen and the chic David's
Club bar-restaurant), coffee bar,
deli, 3 lounge bars, state-of-the-art
health club and full-service spa. Just
15mins south of Disney off I-4, this is
well situated yet off the beaten track
for those (especially golfers) looking
for something different. Set in 1,500
landscaped acres/607ha and with
a magnificent vista as you walk in,
it suits both business travellers and
leisure-seekers. It also has 59 superb
2 and 3-bed villas, affording a more
private stay, with full kitchens and
opulent furnishings (407 390 6664,
www.omnihotels.com).

Park Plaza Hotel: Tucked away well
off the beaten tourist track in the

heart of Winter Park is this lovely family-run boutique-style hotel, boasting a traditional touch, 28 individually decorated rooms and a superb restaurant. Built in 1921, it continues to be a haven of old-fashioned charm – albeit with mod cons – and offers rare single rooms as well as 4 beautiful honeymoon suites. All rooms are non-smoking but smoking is permitted on balconies. The (separately managed) Park Plaza Gardens restaurant is a well-established local gem for lunch and dinner and there is great additional dining choice within a short stroll, while a basic breakfast (tea, coffee, orange juice and fresh muffins served either in-room or in the lobby), wi-fi and valet parking are all included. Probably not ideal for a full Orlando stay but definitely a wonderful get-away-from-it-all option for a few days. Children under 5 are not accepted, hence it makes for a more grown-up ambience (407 647 1072, **www.parkplazahotel.com**).

◄🇬🇧► **BRITTIP**
Head for the Ritz-Carlton's lobby lounge for afternoon tea or drinks in style with a magnificent view, especially at sunset.

Doubletree by Hilton at Orlando Airport

Airport convenience

If you need to stay near the airport, either if you have a late arrival or if you'd prefer the convenience of collecting your hire car in the morning rather than straight after a long flight, consider this duo.

Hyatt Regency: It doesn't get more convenient than a hotel inside the airport, and this is a great choice as well for its 2 excellent restaurants, recently renovated pool deck, fitness room, lounge and business centre. Rooms are ultra-spacious, particularly the corner rooms, and many feature internal balconies overlooking the airport atrium. We especially enjoy dining or just drinks at McCoy's (breakfast, lunch and dinner) restaurant, with its newly revamped menu and sushi bar, while Hemisphere, on the 8th floor, boasts award-winning steaks and seafood (breakfast and dinner only) as well as great views. There is no noticeable aircraft noise and none of the bustle you expect at an airport hotel and staying here is a real boon if you're looking for a stress-free arrival (407 825 1234, **http://orlandoairport.hyatt.com**).

Doubletree by Hilton at Orlando Airport: This impressive hotel is just 5mins north of the airport and especially well equipped after a big renovation completed in early 2014. A great pool area provides a lot of relaxation potential while all the ultra-spacious rooms are fully refurbished, with the latest flatscreen TVs, wi-fi, coffee-makers and either a king bed or two doubles. The junior suites add a living area, larger TV, kitchenette and dining table. The all-new lobby features welcome cookies (a Doubletree speciality) and a combination lounge-bar and restaurant that is especially inviting at night. There is also a modern fitness centre and business centre with computers. Bistro 436 features the trademark Wake-up Doubletree breakfast buffet, plus lunch and dinner. Extremely disabled-friendly, it used to be the Crowne Plaza but benefits more from the Hilton brand name (407 856 0100, **www.OrlandoAirport.DoubleTree.com**).

Self-catering definitions

To avoid confusion, here's the correct terminology for self-catering accommodation (but check with the operator for the exact type if it's not clear):

Villa: Detached vacation home, usually with its own screened-in pool, in self-contained residential communities.

Townhome: 2-storey terraced-style house, rarely with its own pool; found in many Resorts.

Condo: 1, 2 or 3-bed apartment-style unit, usually in a low-rise block but sometimes 10 or more storeys.

Studio: 1-room accommodation unit that includes kitchen facilities.

Resort: Collection of condos (or townhomes) built around central features like pools, recreation facilities and (sometimes) a restaurant/bar or 2.

SELF-CATERING

Once you venture beyond pure hotel territory, your choice varies through a range of 'Resorts' to timeshares, villa communities, studios and condos, all of which are essentially self-catering (although some still offer restaurants and other hotel-type amenities). They all tend to be further away from the parks, but they represent a flexible option, especially for larger groups.

Bahama Bay Resort: A wonderful location on Lake Davenport in Davenport (west on Highway 192, then south on Highway 27 to Florence Villa Grove Rd, or via Westside Rd), this is spread over 70acres/28ha, with 498 condos in 38 2 and 3-storey buildings. The community is woven with tropical landscaping that includes water features, a recreation centre and clubhouse, Tradewinds restaurant and Mambo's Poolside Bar & Grille, internet café, fitness centre, fabulous Eleuthera Spa & Salon, tennis, basketball, volleyball, billiard tables, 4 heated pools and kiddie pools. You can fish in the lake, which has a sandy beach, plus there are nature trails. Shuttle transport to the parks can be arranged for a small

charge. The 4 types of condo offer 2-bed, 2-bath (sleeping 6, with a sofa-bed in the lounge) and 3-bed, 2-bath (sleeping 8, again with sofa-bed), with fitted kitchen, laundry room/washer-dryer, living room and dining area. The Grand Bahama 3-bed condo has 1,739ft2/162m2 of space and is one of the most elegant (1877 299 4481 or **www.wyndhamvacationrentals.com**).

Barefoot'n Resort: This boutique timeshare of 40 1-bed condos is nicely tucked away next to Old Town in Kissimmee and was dramatically enhanced in 2009 with another 42 1 and 2-bed units. There's a main pool, kids' pool, whirlpool, children's play area, volleyball and barbecue stations. (407 589 2127, **www.barefootn.com**).

Blue Heron Beach Resort: A superb complex of 2 high-rise towers (16 and 21 storeys) on Apopka-Vineland Rd (Highway 535) in Lake Buena Vista, this features 283 beautifully furnished 1 and 2-bed condos, all with 2 bathrooms, a balcony and fully equipped kitchen, including washer-dryer. There are bunk beds for kids in the spacious 1 and 2-bed units, which can comfortably sleep 6–8. All master bedrooms also include a whirlpool tub in the en-suite bathrooms. All have balconies overlooking scenic Lake Bryan while the 2 bed Deluxe suites have a second balcony with a Disney firework view.

BRITTIP

If you prefer a tranquil Lake View room at the Blue Heron Beach Resort, you can still get a view of Disney's fireworks at night from the outdoor corridor/terrace on each floor.

There is a superb lido deck, with a large freeform pool, kids' pool, hot tub and Tiki Bar, plus a boardwalk fronting the lake and watersports (jet-skis and water-skiing, for an extra charge), with the 36-hole Hawaiian Rumble mini-golf course outside (for a fee). There is a video games room and 2 fitness centres, but no restaurant (but plenty nearby, including a CiCi's Pizza, Starbucks,

Dunkin' Donuts and Subway in front). As a self-catering resort, daily housekeeping is available only for a charge, but there is a free daily shuttle to Disney and SeaWorld and for $12/person to Universal (407 387 2200, **www.blueheronbeachresort.com**).

BRITBONUS

Get 7 nights for the price of 5 or 14 for the price of 10 at the Blue Heron Beach Resort. Book online or call 407 387 2200, extension 4, and use booking code 'BRIT75'. Valid until 31 Dec 2015; not valid with any other discount or coupon. Based on availability and certain blackout dates.

Floridays Resort Orlando: One of the smartest of the area's condo-hotels, this is well situated in a quieter part of I-Drive but close to Orlando Premium Outlets and with a free shuttle service to the parks. The full site consists of 6 condo blocks (each with 72 rooms), 2 pools (including the elaborate main zero-depth entry pool and great water-play area), a pool bar and grill, fitness centre, stylish Welcome Center, kids' activity centre and games room, a small grocery store, plus concierge services, business centre and meeting facilities. The 2 and 3-bed grand suites are beautifully furnished, sleep 6–10, and have either a balcony or patio. Living rooms include large plasma TVs, high-speed internet, games console and stereos, while each bedroom also has a TV. There's also a delivery service (8am–10pm) from the Café & Marketplace, which serves Starbucks coffee. All rooms are wheelchair-accessible and some are adapted for the disabled with roll-in showers (1866 994 6321, **www.floridaysresortorlando.com**).

Renaissance Orlando Resort

Fountains Resort: This high-quality timeshare is on the quieter stretch of I-Drive (south of SeaWorld). It has superb 2-bed, 2-bath condos, with full kitchens, plus a huge pool area with waterslides and poolside bar, all in a beautiful tropical environment, complete with the large Clubhouse boasting a games room, kids' activity centre, bar, coffee lounge and spa services (1800 456 0009, **www.bluegreenrentals.com**).

Hapimag Orlando Resort: An unusual combination of vacation home and resort, this is the Swiss timeshare operator's only US property (but with NO timeshare solicitation), inside the mature Lake Berkley villa community in Kissimmee (almost behind Medieval Times). It encompasses a self-contained circle of 2 and 3-bed town-homes, grouped around a busy clubhouse with pool, volleyball court, small fitness centre and gift shop.

BRITBONUS

Stay 6 nights in a row at Hapimag Orlando Resort and the 7th is free. Special rates for 1, 2 and 3-bed units of $92, $103 & $124/night low season and $115, $125 & $146/night high season; and $135, $146 & $167 at Christmas (plus tax). All offers valid to end 2015; subject to availability; some blackout dates apply. Just quote code 'Brit Guide 2015' when booking on 407 390 9083 or email www.orlando@hapimag.com..

There are also a handful of fully furnished 4-bed villas elsewhere in the community, which also has its own clubhouse and smart pool area with kids' pool, plus another gym, games room and internet room. There is then a scenic walkway around the lake, with 2 white-sand beaches (407 390 9083, **www.orlando-hapimag.com**).

Lake Buena Vista Resort Village & Spa: This stylish condo-hotel features 5 tower blocks of 2, 3 and 4-bed condos, next to Lake Buena Vista Factory Stores on Highway 535. The impressive facilities include a superb freeform swimming pool, with pirate play-ship, a second quiet pool, a state-of-the-art fitness centre, video games room and Kids' Club. There is a convenience store and gift shop, a Pizza Hut Express, specialist bar-restaurant Frankie Farrell's Irish Pub & Grille and Lani's Luau, the pool-side bar and grill, as well as a shuttle to the main theme parks (as part of the resort fee). The rooms (all with full kitchens, Jacuzzi tubs, digital TVs and internet) are comfortable and stylish, with the 4-bed condos very spacious. Housekeeping services are available either daily or weekly for a charge, while the resort fee covers a grocery delivery and dry-cleaning service, although all rooms come with their own washer and dryer. The blissful Reflections Spa & Salon offers some wonderfully relaxing treatments (407 597 0214, **www.lbvorlandoresort.com** or **www.staysky.com**).

BRITTIP

Visiting Lake Buena Vista Factory Stores? Relieve aching limbs by popping next door to the Resort Village for the Reflections Spa for a soothing pedicure, massage or other spa treatment (407 597 1695).

Liki Tiki Village: On the western fringe of Highway 192, this timeshare set-up often has good-value condos to rent on a weekly basis. It features spacious 1, 2 and 3-bed condos, all with well-equipped kitchens (including coffee and ice-makers), while the 64acre/26ha complex boasts 2 pools, a mini water park, tennis courts, paddle boats, mini-golf, pool-bar and grill, free wi-fi and kids activity programmes Mon–Fri (407 239 5000, **www.likitiki.com**).

Mystic Dunes Resort & Golf Club: This holiday ownership property is tucked away in a quiet corner of Kissimmee and offers hotel-type rentals, often at terrific rates. It features just about every facility, including 4 resort pools, water-slide and water-play area, plus an impressive array of 1, 2 and 3-bed condos that sleep up to 12, a championship-quality golf course and mini-golf (1877 747 4747, **www.mystic-dunes-resort.com**).

Orange Lake Resort: This vast resort on west Highway 192 offers a mixture of well-furnished 1, 2 and 3-bed condos (NB: Orange Lake refers to them as 'villas' but they are definitely apartment-type) and studios that sleep 4–12, plus golf, watersports and cinema. Then there are kids' activities, exercise classes, tennis, racquetball, mini-golf and a Marketplace of general store, pizzeria and golf shop. The amazing River Island water park has a lazy river, 2 zero-depth entry pools, mini-golf, whirlpool tubs, waterfalls and a clubhouse, arcade and fitness centre, while the Water's Edge beach Club adds a restaurant, pool bar, cabañas, stage and gift shop, plus an Olympic-size pool with beach-style entry. There is also a Publix supermarket, and this resort gets consistently good feedback, if occasionally a bit strong on the timeshare sales (407 239 0000, **http://experienceorangelake.com/**).

Palisades Resort: A real find out at the rural western end of Highway 192 in Kissimmee, this smart condo-hotel features spacious 1, 2 and 3-bed condos that sleep 4–8, with fully equipped kitchens, including washer-dryers, and private balconies. Each unit offers generous living and dining areas, 2 bathrooms (master bed with oversized bath) and flatscreen TVs.

Palisades Resort

The tropical lido deck has a large outdoor pool in lush surroundings, plus there is a sauna, fitness centre, small shop for sundries and free wi-fi. It is close enough to benefit from the shops and restaurants along Highway 192 (and be just 10mins from Disney), but still be tranquil. There is no bar or restaurant, but a Publix supermarket is only 5mins away and its rates in 2014 ($116/night for a 3-bed condo in low season) were amazing (321 250 3030, **www.palisadesvacations.com**).

Regal Oaks at Old Town: This mix of stylish town-homes, from 3-bed, 2-bath units to grand 4-bed, 3-bath villas, follows the successful blueprint of accommodations set around an elaborate clubhouse, with fabulous water features (zero-entry pool, waterslide, whirlpool and lazy river), Tiki Bar and other facilities. Right next to all the fun and shopping of Old Town in Kissimmee, it offers terrific value (407 997 1000, **www.regaloaks.com**).

Regal Palms Resort & Spa: Next door to the serene Highlands Reserve villa community on Highway 27 is this mix of 3 and 4-bed townhomes and 4 and 5-bed villas set around a beautiful Clubhouse that includes a mini water park (with lazy river and waterslides), pools, Jacuzzis and extensive sun terraces, as well as free wi-fi. The sister resort to Regal Oaks, it also features a pub that shows live UK sports, a business centre, gym and gift shop/grocery store, plus an indulgent Spa & Health Club (407 965 3887, **www.regalpalmsorlando.com**).

Regal Palms Resort & Spa

Reunion Resort & Club: One of the most extensive resorts, this will be of interest to golfers who appreciate the chance to stay where they play. On Highway 532 in Kissimmee (just off exit 58 of I-4 south of Disney), this 'community' boasts a vast line-up of condos, town-homes and luxury villas set around 3 superb golf courses (designed by Arnold Palmer, Tom Watson and Jack Nicklaus). The choice is deluxe, featuring 1, 2 and 3-bed condos (many with stunning golf course views); a range of private homes, from modest 3-beds to mansion-style 8-beds; a stylish golf clubhouse with excellent bar and restaurant; a full-service spa, with a superb array of treatments; the scenic Seven Eagles pool, complete with The Cove bar and grill, Jacuzzis, fitness room and kids' play centre; floodlit tennis courts; an amazing water park consisting of lazy river, slides, pools, waterfalls and interactive kids' area; and miles of biking and hiking trails. High-rise condo, the Reunion Grande, features 82 luxurious 1 and 2-bed suites, magnificent Italian cuisine restaurant Forte, a state-of-the-art fitness facility and ultra-chic rooftop pool and bar, Eleven, offering American fare, cocktails and panoramic views. It all comes with concierge service and even private in-room dining that marks this out as one of Florida's most upmarket resorts. Only those staying here or members can play on the courses, but the scale of the resort is superb (407 662 1000, **www.reunionresort.com**). Reunion is also home to the state-of-the-art ANNIKA Academy, created under the direction of top golfer Annika Sorenstam.

◀▨▶ **BRITTIP**

At both Sheraton Vistana properties, for a nominal fee, you can arrange to have your condo pre-stocked with food and laundry products.

Sheraton Vistana Resort: This sprawling family-friendly timeshare set-up in Lake Buena Vista, close to Walt Disney World, is a mature

Rental Accommodation

Walt Disney World

MAGIC KINGDOM

EPCOT

ANIMAL KINGDOM

HOLLYWOOD STUDIOS

SEAWORLD

Kissimmee

Celebration

Champions Gate

Remington

Windsor Park

Buena Ventura Lakes

Nagic Landings

Kissimmee Pines

Whispering Oaks

Country Creek
Creekside

Bass Lakes
Lake Berkley
Indian Point

Eagle Point
Liberty Village
Fiesta Key
Cumbria Lakes

Villas at Somerset
Chatham Park
The Hamlets
Montego Bay
Sweetwater Club
Sierra Lago
Bella Vida
Seasons
Terra Verde

St James Park
Trafalgar Villas

Doral Woods

Royal Bay
Windward Cay
Laguna Bay
Crystal Cove

Cane Island
Hamilton's Reserve

Barefoot'n & Regal Oaks

Poinciana

Countryside Manor

Crescent Lakes

Blackstone Landing

Poinciana Boulevard

Ronald Reagan Parkway / Loughman Road

Old Lake Wilson Road

*Terrace Ridge & Lake View also at Town Center

Terraces at Reunion

Lake Wilson

Sandy Ridge

Thousand Oaks

Paradise Woods

Oak Point
Grand Reserve
Robbins Rest
Wildflower Ridge

Avana
Providence
Watersong

Davenport, Haines City

Reunion

Bridgewater Crossing
Bentley Oaks

Windwood Bay
Loma Linda
Briargrove
Sunridge Woods

Ashley Manor
The Proper Pie Co.
Arrowhead Lakes
Royal Palms
Aylesbury
Regency Place

Haines City

Ridgewood Lakes

Marbella

Vizcay

Indian Ridge
Mystic Dunes
Tempus Palms
Rolling Hills
Oakwater
Windsor Hills
Formosa Gardens
Arcadia Estates
Oak Island

Marketplace Supermarket

Orange Lake
Vista del Lago
Grand Palms
Lindfields
Encantada
Emerald Island
Indian Creek
Windsor Palms
Lake Davenport Estates
Bahama Bay

Summer Bay, Lighthouse Key, Liki Tiki Resort
Palisades
Legacy Dunes

Glenbrook Resort
Sunrise Lakes
Woodridge, Clear Creek, Silver Creek
Riverside Bank

Cagan Crossings
High Grove

Berry Town Center

Westchester Villas
Greater Groves
Eagle Ridge
Mission Park
Weston Hills
Orange Tree
Clermont
Siena Ridge
Sawgrass Bay

Westridge (Durango Gold)
Windmill V'llage
Eass Lake
Tuscan Hills
Legacy Park
Wellington

Polo Park
Polo Park East
Esprit
Davenport Lakes

Highlands Reserve

The Ridge

Hampton Lakes
Palm Key
Solana

The Gardens
Santa Cruz
Loma Del Sol

Florida Pines
Calabay Parc
The Preserve
Four Corners
West Stonebridge
Tuscan Ridge
Pines West
Bella Toscana
Dunston Hills

West Haven
Loma Vista

Posner Park

Tivoli Manor
Westbury
Sunset Ridge
Silver Palms

Champions Gate

Indian Wells

TOLLS

417 TOLLS

435

192

429

Tampa

3 miles

0

N

© Steve Munns 2014

Wal-Mart
Publix
Winn Dixie
Walgreens
Target

development of roomy 1 and 2-bed/2-bath condos (sleeping 4–8; again, they are called 'villas' but are definitely apartment-type) with fully equipped kitchens and magnificent resort facilities. Furnishings and facilities are all modern, with multiple TVs, DVD player and a screened-in private patio or balcony, plus large washer-dryers, which all serves to underline the great self-catering value of this type of accommodation. There are 7 giant pools, 13 floodlit tennis courts, smart Marketplace deli (with Starbucks coffee), Food Court, casual café/restaurant and 3 pool bars, plus massage treatments. There is complimentary scheduled transport to select Disney parks and lots of family-orientated activities, including poolside parties, crafts and more (407 239 3100, **www.sheraton. com/vistanaresort**).

BRITBONUS

Stay in a 1 or 2-bed villa at the Sheraton Vistana Resort or Sheraton Vistana Villages and receive $50 in resort credit. When making your reservation mention special code '50RC', and then show your Brit Guide upon check in. Valid on stays over 3 nights, no cash value/no refund on any unused portion.

Sheraton Vistana Villages: The sister property, located on I-Drive south of SeaWorld, this upmarket family resort offers spacious 1 and 2-bed/2-bath condos with fully equipped kitchen or kitchenette, dining area, washer-dryer and more, all in 5 and 6-storey blocks and all set around scenic landscaping or pool areas. The beautiful lobby opens on to a stunning main pool boasting waterfalls, Jacuzzis and children's play areas, while there is also the smart Flagler Station Bar & Grill for breakfast, lunch and dinner and a mini-market/deli for quick snacks and light shopping. Less than 6ml/10km from Disney, guests enjoy extensive amenities like complimentary scheduled transport to select Disney parks, daily scheduled activities, 3 pool areas (some with slides and water-

play areas), a state-of-the-art fitness centres, games rooms, basketball and tennis courts and a grocery store, plus there is a big Publix supermarket and the Premium Outlets shops nearby (407 238 5000, www.sheraton.com/ vistanavillages). All rooms at both Sheraton Vistana resorts have also been heavily renovated recently, ensuring they stay fresh and inviting.

BRITTIP

As the Sheraton Vistana resorts are both timeshare properties, you may well be asked if you'd like to take their property tour, but there is no pressure to sign up or hard-sell if you do.

Summer Bay Resort: Out on west Highway 192 is a mix of hotel (The Crown Club Inn), and 1 and 2-bed condos sleeping 4–8. The 700 rooms spread over 400acres/162ha are all smart, while the facilities include outdoor heated pools and kiddie pools, pool bars, an elaborate children's water-play area, mini-golf, clubhouse with volleyball, tennis, basketball, shuffleboard and fitness room, video arcade, gift shop and snack bar. New in 2014 was the family Adventure Park activity centre, featuring zip-lines, bungee jumping, wipe-out style Inflatable Zone, rock-climbing wall, bumper boats and picnic area. The lake provides jet-skis, paddleboats, waterskiing and more, plus daily kids' activities and organised sports. Even those in The Crown Club Inn (which has its own pool and breakfast area) benefit from the clubhouse facilities, while next door is a Denny's diner and Publix supermarket, plus another 12 restaurants within a few miles (352 242 1100, **www.summerbayresort.com**).

Tuscana: This Mediterranean-inspired condo-resort bordering the Champions Gate golf courses offers 288 elegant, oversized 2 and 3-bed condos, each with 2 full baths, balcony, fully equipped kitchen, washer and dryer. The excellent clubhouse boasts the Tuscana Tavern bar and grill, tiki snack bar, elegant pool, kiddie pool, cabanas, fitness centre and spa treatments (407 787 4800, **www.tuscanaresort.com**).

Villas at Grand Cypress: Arguably Orlando's top golf resort, this is also a wonderfully upmarket option in a beautiful setting behind Walt Disney World, making it among the most convenient villa options in all of Orlando. It offers 146 single-room club suites and 1, 2, 3 and 4-bed condo-style villas, all recently renovated and furnished in luxury style, with fully equipped kitchens and patios or balconies. There is a blissful Villa Pool, with poolside saunas and bar, bike rentals and 2 restaurants (The Club sports bar and fine-dining Nine18 overlooking the North-South golf course), the Golf Academy for personalised lessons, plus 24hr room service. Villa guests also get full use of all the amenities of the nearby Hyatt Regency Grand Cypress (p82), a 5min ride on the free on-demand shuttle service. Literally just minutes from Disney, the villas' relaxed ambiance and lush surroundings make you feel as if you're a million miles away (407 239 4700, **www.grandcypress.com**).

Vista Cay Resort: This recent timeshare development offers some of the most extensive facilities in the I-Drive/Universal Boulevard area (behind the Convention Center North). Convenient for all the attractions but away from the main bustle, it has beautiful accommodations (2 and 3-bed executive suites and 3-bed town-homes), plus a large clubhouse with a pool set in lush, tropical landscaping; whirlpool spa, kids' pool and basketball court; games room, business centre and fitness centre. Apartments range from 1,500ft²/140m² to 2,300ft²/214m² and offer fully equipped kitchens, large HD TVs with DVD players and Sony PlayStations, dining rooms, master bedrooms (with separate Roman tubs and showers), private balconies and free wi-fi (407 996 4647, **www.vistacayholidays.com**).

Windsor Palms Resort: Just off west Highway 192 in Kissimmee,

this popular gated community has a mix of 2-bed condos, 2 and 3-bed town-homes, and 3–6-bed private pool villas. Amenities include a large clubhouse and fitness centre, tennis courts, an Olympic-sized pool, a kiddie pool and spa, basketball, billiard room, volleyball court, video arcade, playground and a 58-seat cinema showing recent films. The (slightly newer) sister resort Windsor Hills on Old Lake Wilson Road offers the same accommodation choice and impressive amenities, like its huge lagoon-style pool with waterslide and state-of-the-art fitness centre and is even closer to the Disney parks (407 409 8035, **www.globalresorthomes.com**).

HOLIDAY HOMES

This is in many ways the biggest area of accommodation in Orlando, especially for UK visitors, as there has been a huge development of holiday homes, or villas, in the last 20 years. They provide a valuable way for large families and groups to stay together – the largest can sleep 16 – and cut costs by self-catering. The homes – individual or groups in residential communities – are sometimes gated, and most have a private pool, while some have access to communal facilities like pools and recreation areas. They are always equipped with microwaves, multiple TVs and washer-dryers. Some are classed as 'executive', and this usually means more facilities (games rooms, barbecues, Jacuzzis, etc.) rather than an increase in size. A hire car is usually essential, but the savings can

Villas at Grand Cypress

be significant. Prices can be as low as $450/week off-peak, but expect to pay at least $1,600/week for a 5 or 6-bed villa in high season. A word of warning: once you've experienced pool-at-home life, you may never go back to a hotel!

If you book independently, there are several key questions to ask. Do you need to go to an office some way away to pick up the keys or is there a combination lockbox at the house? Is there a local contact if anything goes wrong (most owners do not live in Florida) and is the property maintained by a local company? Does it offer a secure bonding for your booking, and is it a member of a reputable organisation, such as the Better Business Bureau of Central Florida? In winter, is the pool heated, and what is the charge for heating? Finally, is it as close to Disney as it says (some can be in Polk County, 30mins away, but still insist they are 'just minutes from Disney')?

There are more than 25,000 villas on offer, spread across Kissimmee and out in Polk and Lake Counties to the west and south-west of Disney, most in well-established developments (Highlands Reserve is a good example). Be aware that homes within a particular community can still vary in quality depending on the care and attention of owners and/or property managers, hence just being in, say, stylish Cumbrian Lakes, is not a guarantee of executive quality. You can rent direct from the owners or a property management company that will look after multiple villas. For direct villa rentals, check sites like **www.vrbo.com**, **www.lastminutevillas. net** and **www.thedibb.co.uk**, plus Owner

The Proper Pie Company

Pool heat

To heat or not to heat is a common question for those renting a villa in Florida. Typically, pools will NOT need heating from mid-May to mid-Oct, when the sun is usually enough to heat them to at least 80°F/26.6°C. But, at other times of the year, and especially Nov–Apr, you will almost certainly need pool heating. Systems can be electric or (propane) gas, with the latter usually more expensive. Expect to pay anywhere $25–30/day for electric heating and $30–40/day for gas. It can also take up to 48hrs to heat a pool to 85°F/28°C during the colder months and, if the air temperature drops below 55°F/13°C, the heating may not function fully to more than 15°F above air temperature. Pool heat will also be in addition to the villa rental cost.

Direct, who offer villas worldwide and have a well-vetted Orlando selection of more than 500 properties and are often good for last-minute deals at **http://www.ownerdirect.com/ accommodation/disney-world-central- florida**.

Ironically, there are increasing numbers of terrace-style townhomes (so developers can fit in more); for a 'detached' house, ask for a 'single family home'. The bottom line is you must do your homework, shop around as you would for any big purchase, and check with organisations like the Central Florida Vacation Rental Managers Association. This is the only acknowledged umbrella organisation for the holiday home business and helps to provide a level of credibility.

BRITTIP

For home-cooking comforts, the British-owned The Proper Pie Company on Ridge Center Drive (on Highway 27 in Davenport, just south of the junction with I-4) offers a fab array of home-made pies and pasties, plus British groceries, from Walkers crisps to Sharwood's chutney. See more at **www. properpiecompany.com** or call 863 438 2705. They also offer fresh fish 'n' chips every Friday!

PROPER PIE CO.

The following companies all pass the *Brit Guide* credibility test.

Advantage Vacation Homes: In the villa rental business for more than 20 years and one of the largest companies, few of its 2–6 bed homes (the majority on west Highway 192 and Highway 27 in Clermont and Davenport) are more than 10yrs old, while many are 4–5yrs at most. It also manages a range of condos (in the Bahama Bay and Venetian Bay resorts) and town-homes. It offers 24hr management, with courteous and efficient staff at its office just off west Highway 192 (plus an attraction ticket service), open 9am–10pm daily. Its holiday homes are rated Silver, Gold or Platinum, with the difference measured in the extras rather than size (larger-screen or plasma TVs, tiled floors rather than carpeting, a Jacuzzi or games room, etc), though some of the more exclusive villas might be situated on a golf community or have tennis courts (0871 711 9531 in the UK, 407 396 2262 in the US, **www.advantage vacationhomes.com**).

BRITBONUS

Stay in a fully furnished home with Advantage Vacation Homes, with 6-bed pool homes and rates starting at $119/night. Visit **www. advantagevacationhomes.com** or call 407 396 2262 and mention the *Brit Guide*. Offer valid until 20 December 2015; not valid with any other offers (based on availability and certain blackout dates; restrictions apply).

Alexander Holiday Homes: Family-owned Alexander manages more than 200 properties in Kissimmee, from standard 2, 3 and 4-bed condos to luxury 7-bed executive homes sleeping 14, all with pools and immaculately furnished, within 15–20mins of Disney, including some of the closest to the parks. This company was the first of its kind in Orlando (in 1981) and still offers a personable, efficient service. It was only the third management company to earn the distinguished AAA (American Automobile Association) 3 Diamond rating, as well as being fully accredited with the official Walt Disney World Vacation Rental Home Connection (where homes are inspected quarterly) and definitely gets our approval. It shows prices in UK and US currency and even offers an airport meet-and-greet service to ensure you get to your home, as well as arrival grocery packages, barbecue rentals, scooter and wheelchair hire. Its informative website provides photo tours of all its homes, useful blogs and other features (0871 711 5371 in the UK, 1800 621 7888 in the US, **www.floridasunshine.com**).

BRITTIP

Thinking of buying an Orlando holiday home? Check first with *Brit Guide* partner British Homes Group (**www.britishhomesgroup.com**) who are a one-stop shop for all home-buying queries (see also inside back cover).

Florida Leisure Vacation Homes: Another company we know well and can recommend, it is British-owned and pays great attention to detail, with an upscale, almost boutique approach, which sets them apart from the larger, more mass-market operators. With 100 homes (3–7 beds) in the Kissimmee area, most just a few years old and many in the highly regarded Cumbrian Lakes community, it prides itself on a personal touch (even down to providing personal chef, massage and concierge services) and offers some of the biggest and newest properties, as well as a full online booking system. Many are in the Executive range, with the fullest array of amenities in addition to their private, screened pools, and often in gated communities. All properties have lockboxes, so you don't need to visit the management office to check in. You can see all its homes online (in extended photo and video) plus lots of local info, while its new testimonial sections provide first-hand feedback. The sister website **www.floridaleisure.com** includes a regular blog, free newsletter and other useful features. Also accredited to the Walt Disney World Vacation Rental Home Connection, its office is handily placed on east Highway 192 in Kissimmee, just past Osceola Square Mall (407 870 1600; **www.floridaleisurevacationhomes.com**).

Loyalty Homes: For a luxury touch, all these homes (2–6 bedrooms) are no more than 4ml/6.5km from Disney and all offer the true 'executive' style, with the likes of digital door locks (so no key collection required), cable TV and many with games rooms. The website offers video tours, too (call 0121 468 0016 in the UK or 407 397 7475 in the US, **www.loyaltyusa.com**).

Park Square Homes: This is actually operated by the home builder, hence it features the complete resort communities of Encantada and Bella Vida, both just off Highway 192 in Kissimmee, with a series of well-built and beautifully furnished 3 and 4-bed town-homes, plus larger villas at Bella Vida, all with private pools. The 2 tropically styled resorts benefit from a central clubhouse, with a large pool, cyber café, exercise room and arcade, while Encantada also has a lakefront gazebo and Romy's Bistro wine bar (1866 930 0444/1800 520 8070, **www.bvrmanagement.com** and **www.encantadaorlandoresort.com**).

Premier Vacation Homes: A good range of spacious properties with 2–7 bedrooms, sleeping up to 14, in secure residential communities within a 15–20min drive of Disney. All are privately owned and have been furnished as holiday homes, with screened pools, 2 TVs, fully equipped kitchens (including dishwasher, washer-dryer, microwave and coffee-maker), at least one king or queen bed and free local phone calls. Maid service can be added for a fee. The Luxury homes (2–4 beds) are standard accommodation, while Executive homes (3–6 beds) are bigger, with an extra TV, VCR and barbecue, and there's also a town-home and condo choice (407 396 2401, **www.premiervacationhomesorlando.com**).

BRITTIP
You'll find Marmite, Ribena, McVities and a handful of other British groceries at Publix and Winn-Dixie supermarkets, and most Wal-Marts (International aisle).

Villa Direct: Another major Orlando specialist, and one of the biggest, with an extensive range of properties in the area, from 2-bed condos to luxury 7-bed villas, and a good user-friendly website, plus an excellent range of guest services, including arrival groceries, a personalised concierge service, car hire and even mobility equipment rental. Also on the Walt Disney World Vacation Rental Home Connection, its welcome centre is easily found on west Highway 192 in Kissimmee while the head office is close by in Celebration, just off I-4 (407 409 8038, **www.villadirect.com**).

OK, that's enough accommodation advice. Now it's on to the parks…

Doubletree at Orlando Airport

5

The Theme Parks: Disney's Fab Four

or Spending the Day with Mickey and the Gang

By now you should be prepared to deal with the main business of any visit to Orlando: Walt Disney World. This is the heart of all the excitement and fun in store (along with the other big theme parks of Universal Orlando, SeaWorld and Busch Gardens).

In our opinion, 2 weeks are barely enough to see all of Disney on its own, let alone the other theme parks and smaller scale attractions, so you start to realise the awesome scope of an Orlando holiday!

BRITTIP
Before you leave home, photocopy the back of your park passes and your passport. If your tickets are lost during your holiday you will need the information on the back of each ticket to have them replaced. A copy of your passport will suffice as photo ID in the parks, or if your passport becomes lost.

Buying your tickets in advance is highly advisable (it saves time and is often better value), but work out your requirements first – you won't get full use out of, say, a 14-day Ultimate ticket AND an Orlando Flex Ticket Plus in just a fortnight. Try to use your credit card for all purchases – there is built-in additional security (for our list of recommended ticket outlets; p10).

Discount options: You will find a welter of discount coupons for many of the smaller attractions in tourist publications distributed in Orlando (or from your hotel Guest Services desk – it's often worth asking), while the tour operators' welcome meetings usually have special offers and tickets for the latest excursions.

BRITTIP
Offers of 'free' Disney tickets usually mean timeshare firms, which also claim to have 'official' visitor centres. I-Drive has the only genuine Official Visitor Center.

Check out the **Official Visitor Center** for discounts at 8723 International Drive in the Gala Center on the corner of Austrian Row (407 363 5872, **www.visitorlando.com/uk**). The Universal Attractions booths at several shopping malls also have great deals (3 days for the price of 2, 2-for-1 drinks etc.) from time to time. It IS possible to bag free tickets by attending timeshare presentations but they can easily take a ½ day of your precious holiday and do you really want the hard-sell hassle?

Welcome to The Magic Kingdom

If you DO want to check out timeshare options, look first at **Disney Vacation Club** for the guarantee of memorable holidays. A tour (for which you will be picked up) will take around 3 hours, but you will be given a small parting gift (dining coupon, etc). Call 407 566 3300, 1800 500 3990 or visit **http://disneyvacationclub.disney. go.com.**

> 🇬🇧 **BRITTIP**
> Smoking is not permitted in the restaurants or in the parks, apart from in a handful of designated areas. Check park maps for their exact locations.

Ratings

We judge all the rides and shows on a unique rating system that splits them into thrill rides and scenic rides. Thrill rides earn **T** ratings out of 5 (hence a **TTTTT** is as exciting as they get) and scenic rides get **A** ratings out of 5 (an **AA** attraction is likely to be twee and missable). It is a matter of opinion to some extent but you can be sure a **T** or **A** ride is not worth your time, a **TT** or **AA** is worth seeing only if there is no queue, a **TTT** or **AAA** should be seen if you have time, but you won't miss much if you don't, a **TTTT** or **AAAA** ride is a big-time attraction that should be high on your 'must do' list, and a **TTTTT** or **AAAAA** attraction should not be missed! The latter will have the longest queues, so you should plan your visit around them. Some rides have height restrictions and are not advisable for people with back, neck or heart problems or for expectant mothers. Where this is the case we

Crystal Palace for character dining

say, for example, 'R: 3ft 6in/106cm'. Height restrictions (strictly enforced) are based on the average 5-year-old being 3ft 6in/106cm tall, those aged 6 being 3ft 9in/114cm and 9s being 4ft 4in/132cm. You can also refer to our Height Restriction Guide, p27.

My Magic+

In 2013, Disney introduced this high-tech system of guest interaction, designed to personalise and enhance many aspects of park visits. Free for Disney resort guests, but available for offsite guests to buy, the MagicBand wristband acts as an all-purpose ticket, optional payment card, FastPass+ and PhotoPass card, and allows various special features, like pre-booking FastPass+, providing personal greetings on some rides and in ride queues and having the characters greet you by name (great for kids!). It works in conjunction with My Disney Experience (see below), where you fill in your trip details (as much or as little as you prefer) and use the mobile app for all the latest info, such as queue wait times and dining reservations. MagicBands also come in different colours and styles and are designed to be collectible. Intended to be 'transformational' in the way we enjoy the parks, it can be difficult to navigate, somewhat glitchy, and the need to pre-book 60 days in advance for onsite guests or 30 days in advance for offsite guests makes people feel they need to plan every day in advance (thus, actually taking some of the fun out of the whole experience), so check out the website carefully before you sign up. All Disney parks have free Wi-Fi, too. You do not have to sign up for My Magic+, but you will not be able to access all of the perks available if you choose not to participate in the programme.

Disney has an App for that

Get all the latest park updates on your mobile phone or tablet, including park hours, wait times, menus, reservations, attraction info and

Character dining

Having a meal with Mickey and Co is one of the great Disney experiences – even without children! It is also often the best way to meet your favourite characters without a wait. Reservations can be made up to 180 days in advance by phoning 407 WDW DINE (939 3463), calling at any Guest Services desk in a hotel, or by touching *88 on any Disney pay phone or 55 from a Disney resort room phone.

Some meals are difficult to get. Breakfast at Cinderella's Royal Table at the Magic Kingdom usually sells out within minutes of the 180-day window being open. Chef Mickey's and the Princess Storybook meals also go quickly. If you cannot book in advance, try calling the day you'd like to dine or, as a last resort, show up to see if there have been any cancellations. You must check in at the podium 10mins prior to your time and you will be given the next available table. Some characters don't enter the restaurant so, if they are in the lobby, you'll want to meet them before you are seated. Dining is all-you-can-eat, served buffet, pre-plated or family-style. Inside the restaurant, characters circulate among the tables giving attention to each group (particularly when children are holding the camera!). Character interaction is top-notch, especially if you dine off-hours when the restaurant is quieter. Be sure to bring your autograph book, a fat pen or marker (easier for the characters to hold) and an extra digital card. Some characters are huge, and children may be put off by them. If you aren't sure how they'll react, see how they are with the characters in the park before booking. Price range: breakfast $22–58 adults, $13–35 children; lunch $32–60 and $18–38; dinner $41–73 and $21–43 (NB: beware the peak season price rises – Disney has resorted to raising its rates in high season and even at weekends, and some of those children's prices for lunch and dinner are outrageously high, in our opinion.).

FastPass+ reminders, plus games and more. Available free for iPhone and Android, from **https://disneyworld. disney.go.com/plan/mobile-apps/**.

My Disney Experience

My Disney Experience is the online platform that allows guests to make dining reservations, schedule FastPass+ times, add Photopass, and link their Disney resort reservations and theme park admission. You must have a My Disney Experience account and valid theme park admission to schedule FastPass+ selections in advance. Using the online system, guests are also able to connect Friends and Family in-park experiences. To create an account, visit **https://disneyworld.disney.go.com/ plan/my-disney-experience**

Disney's FastPass+

One essential aid to queuing is Disney's FastPass+ system, or FP+, (free with admission). Most of the attractions have this, allowing you to roam while you wait for your scheduled ride time. How it works: Onsite guests can schedule 3 FP+ times in 1 park per day, up to 60

days in advance (30 days for offsite guests) using the online My Disney Experience system or Disney's free mobile app. Guests may also schedule FP+ times at in-park kiosks. Simply purchase your park passes, create a My Disney Experience account, and follow instructions for scheduling FP+, booking dining reservations, and adding 'reminders'. You can then link your experiences to others in your party, make changes as needed, and customise your account with additional options. However, each guest can choose their own FP+ selections if they would like to experience attractions separately.

BRITTIP

Disney's new FastPass+ system makes it essential to schedule your ride times well in advance. It is likely FP+ times for the major attractions will be gone if you leave it until the day, especially in peak seasons.

Additional FP+ times can be scheduled in the park, once you have used your 3 FP+ allotments. Park Hopping is allowed, but you must use your initial 3 FP+ in one park only, so

Character Dining: the meals

MAGIC KINGDOM: Crystal Palace for breakfast, lunch or dinner with Winnie the Pooh and Co – especially good for smaller children; and **Cinderella's Royal Table** for the (expensive) Once Upon A Breakfast, with Cinderella and her Princess Friends; Fairytale Lunch (Cinderella and Friends); and Dreams Come True Dinner (Fairy Godmother only). Breakfast (off-peak) is $53 adults, $35 children; lunch $57 and $36; dinner $67 and $41. Credit card payment in full is required to book and you WILL be charged if you cancel less than 24hrs in advance (photo package and gratuity included, additional photos for a fee).

EPCOT: Garden Grill for lunch or dinner with Farmer Mickey, Pluto, Chip and Dale; Princess Storybook Dining at **Restaurant Akershus** (Norway) for breakfast, lunch and dinner; an alternative to Cinderella's, with some of Belle, Jasmine, Snow White, Mulan, Aurora (Sleeping Beauty) and Mary Poppins. Breakfast $42 adults, $25 children; lunch $43 and $26; dinner $48 and $26. Credit card needed to book; full charge applied for cancelling less than 24hrs in advance.

DISNEY'S HOLLYWOOD STUDIOS: Hollywood & Vine for breakfast or lunch with the Disney Junior Pals, including JoJo and Goliath from JoJo's Circus and Leo from *Little Einsteins*.

DISNEY'S ANIMAL KINGDOM: Donald's Dining Safari Breakfast and Lunch at **Tusker House** with Donald, Goofy, Pluto and sometimes Daisy and Mickey.

DISNEY RESORTS:

Beach Club Resort: At Cape May Café, breakfast with Goofy, Minnie and Donald.

Contemporary Resort: At Chef Mickey's, breakfast or dinner with Mickey, Minnie, Goofy, Pluto, Chip and Dale – peak times book up quickly.

Fort Wilderness: At Mickey's Backyard Barbecue, $60 (adults) and $36 (3–9s), games, storytelling, live entertainment, music and dancing with Mickey, Minnie and Co; chicken, hot dogs, burgers, ribs, beer, wine, iced tea and lemonade (Thurs and Sat only, 6.30pm, Mar–Dec).

Four Seasons Hotel: At Ravello, Thurs and Sat breakfast with Goofy and pals.

Grand Floridian: At 1900 Park Fare, breakfast with Alice, Mary Poppins and Mad Hatter; dinner with Cinderella, Anastasia, Drizella, Lady Tremaine and, sometimes, Prince Charming – book early. Wonderland Tea Party 2–3pm Mon–Fri, 4–12s only, $52.19, meal, activities and storytelling with Alice and friends ($10 no-show). Perfectly Princess Tea Party with Princess Aurora, 10.30am–12pm (not Tues and Sat), 3–11 with an adult, $290 for 1 adult with 1 child age 3–11. Meal (tea, cake, finger sandwiches), singalong, story time, Disney Girl doll, bracelet, tiara, scrapbook page, and Best Friend certificate.

Polynesian Resort: At 'Ohana, breakfast with Lilo, Stitch, Pluto and Mickey.

Walt Disney World Swan: At Garden Grove Café, Mon–Fri, Timon and Rafiki; Sat and Sun breakfast with Goofy and Pluto.

we advise making it the park in which you begin your day. If you cancel your existing FP+ times (via Guest Services or Disney's mobile app), you cannot schedule new FP+ times until the last time scheduled for your cancelled FP+ has expired.

Take note, Epcot and Disney's Hollywood Studios both use a tiered system for FastPass+. Tier 1 indicates attractions from which you must choose only 1; Tier 2 allows you to schedule 2 attractions. Watch for FP+ (choose 2) and FP+1 (choose 1) indications in our attraction descriptions. Guests who opt out of My Disney Experience can still use their regular ticket for park admission.

Onsite guests will each receive a MagicBand (waterproof wrist band with RFID chip) in place of an admission ticket, which can also be used to open their room door, charge purchases (if desired), allow FP+ access, and more. MagicBands will not be shipped overseas, but will be presented upon check-in. However, FP+ can still be booked in advance with a confirmation code. Offsite guests can purchase MagicBands to replace their admission tickets, if desired.

With young ones

All Disney's parks offer pushchair ('stroller') hire, and you can save money by purchasing a multi-day rental at your first park. Children of ALL ages seem to get a big thrill from collecting autographs from the various Disney characters, and most shops sell handy autograph books. Parents wanting healthier dining options for kids in Disney parks and resorts should look for the **Mickey Check**, a standard for more nutritious meals. Every counter service and full-service restaurant should be able to provide at least 1 Mickey Check choice, which adheres to prescribed nutrition guidelines. Look for the Mickey Check icon on menus and learn more at **www.disneymickeycheck. com**. Equally, the **Power Pack** lunch at some counter service options, notably in Disney's Hollywood Studios, serves up healthier snacks in neatly boxed packs, containing things like juice, yoghurt, string cheese, Goldfish crackers, carrots and apple sauce.

PhotoPass

This unique and worthwhile scheme is available in all Disney's parks and (occasionally) in Downtown Disney. Disney photographers take photos of guests and, instead of receiving a paper claim ticket, they receive a Disney PhotoPass that links all their photos on one online account for easy viewing. There is no charge for obtaining a PhotoPass or for viewing (though there is if you want to download and print them), while each photo can be enhanced with Disney characters and special borders. There are also 'magical' photos where photographers ask guests to pose in a fun way and Tinker Bell (or Figment, or Simba or Mickey) balloons will magically appear. Guests have 30 days after the photos were taken to decide if they want to buy them (visit **www.disneyphotopass. com**), or you can visit a PhotoPass shop (one at each of the parks, plus

Downtown Disney Marketplace and most of the Deluxe resorts). Collect up to 300(!) and have them burned onto an Archive Disc for $169.95. There are many other products you can have your photos transferred on to, including mugs, mouse pads and calendars. Or try Memory Maker, which includes PhotoPass photos, on-ride photos and character dining photos for $199.95 ($149 online advance purchase).

Cast Members

Disney employees are called Cast Members or CMs (never 'staff' as they all play a 'role' in the entertainment) and they're renowned for their helpful, cheerful style, always willing to assist, offer advice or just chat. So, if you've had exceptional service or a CM has gone out of their way to help, let Disney know as it values such feedback (plus CMs get credit for it). Call in at Guest Relations or City Hall.

Child Swap

Where families have small children, but Mum and Dad still want to try a ride with height restrictions, you DON'T have to queue twice. When you reach the entrance to the queue, tell the operator you want to do a Child Swap. This means Mum can ride while Dad looks after junior in a quiet area and, on her return, Dad can have his go. At some attractions you may be given a Child Swap ticket while you wait.

Park security

All visitors with bags are required to go through a security bag-check before reaching the turnstiles. This is a fairly cursory (but compulsory) inspection but there is a separate lane for those without bags. When you put your ticket (or MagicBand) across the new electronic terminal, you are also required to give a finger scan (which stops others from using your ticket).

Goofy's Barnstormer

Magic Kingdom Park

The starting point for any visit has to be the Magic Kingdom, the park that best embodies the genuine enchantment Disney bestows on its visitors. It's the original development that sparked the Orlando tourist boom in 1971. In comparative terms, the Magic Kingdom is similar to the Disneyland Park at Disneyland Paris and Disneyland California. Outside those, it has no equal as a captivating day out for all the family. However, although a few rides are the same as those in Paris or LA, there are key differences, notably on Pirates of the Caribbean, Big Thunder Mountain Railroad and Haunted Mansion. And Space Mountain is a completely different ride from the one in Paris. And, even if a couple of attractions are closed for refurbishment, you won't be short of things to do! We will now attempt to steer you through a typical day at the park, with a guide to the rides, shows and places to eat; how to park, how to avoid the worst of the crowds – and how much you should expect to pay. The Magic Kingdom takes up just 107acres/43ha of Disney's near 31,000acres/12,555ha but attracts almost as many as the rest put together. It has 6 separate 'lands', like slices of a cake, centred on Florida's most famous landmark, Cinderella Castle. More than 40 attractions are packed into the park, plus shops and restaurants. It's easy to get overwhelmed, especially as it gets so busy (even the fast-food restaurants have long queues in high season), so plan around what most takes your fancy, but do look out for the new interactive queues at some rides, including Big Thunder Mountain Railroad, Haunted Mansion, Space Mountain, Little Mermaid, Winnie the Pooh and Seven Dwarfs Mine Train.

Magic Kingdom Park at a glance

Location	Off World Drive, Walt Disney World
Size	107 acres/43ha in 6 'lands'
Hours	9am–7pm off peak; 9am–10pm President's Day (see Brit Tip, p17), spring school holidays; 8am–11pm or midnight high season (Easter, summer holidays, Thanksgiving and Christmas)
Admission	Under-3s free; 3–9 $93 (1–day base ticket), $284 (5–day Magic Your Way), £264 (14–day Ultimate); adult (10+) $99, $304, £279. Prices do not include tax.
Parking	$17
Lockers	To the right of the main entrance $12 small, $14 large ($5 deposit each)
Pushchairs	$15 and $31 (underneath Main Street Train Station); length-of-stay, $91/week, $130 10 days single, $189/$270 double
Wheelchairs	$12 or $70 ($20 deposit refunded) underneath Main Street Train Station
Top attractions	Splash Mountain, Space Mountain, Mickey's PhilharMagic, Big Thunder Mountain Railroad, Pirates of the Caribbean, most rides in Fantasyland
Don't miss	Festival of Fantasy Parade, Main Street Electrical Parade or SpectroMagic (certain nights) and Wishes fireworks (most nights)
Hidden costs	**Meals** — Burger, chips and coke $12.18; 3-course dinner (Be Our Guest) $27.67–$50.67; Kids' counter service meal $5.49–5.99
	T-shirts — $21.95–36.95 Kids $12.95–27.95
	Souvenirs — $1.45–3,750
	Sundries — Chalk colour portraits $17.95, or Silhouettes $8, with oval frame $15.95

Location

The Magic Kingdom is situated at the innermost end of Walt Disney World, with its entrance Toll Plaza three-quarters of the way along World Drive, the main entrance off Highway 192. World Drive runs north–south, while the Interstate 4 (I-4) entrance, Epcot Drive, runs east–west. Unless you are staying at a Disney resort or an Annual Pass holder, you must pay the $17 parking fee at the Toll Plaza to bring you into the massive car park.

🇬🇧 **BRITTIP**

For the smoothest entry by road from Highway 192, take Seralago Boulevard (opposite the Seralago Hotel & Suites next to Old Town), turn left on to a non-toll stretch of Osceola Parkway and follow the signs to your chosen park. On West 192, turn off on Sherberth Road, go north to the first traffic lights and turn right, then pick up the Disney signs.

The majority arrive from 9.30–11.30am, so the car parks are busiest then, which is another good reason to get here EARLY. If you can't make it by 9am during peak periods, you might want to wait until after 1pm, or even later when the park is open as late as midnight. Remember to note exactly where you park: there are 2 sides to the 'parking lot', Heroes and Villains, with subsections for Woody, Simba, Rapunzel, Aladdin, Peter Pan and Mulan, then Ursula, Jafar, Zurg, Hook, Scar and Cruella. Be sure to note which side you're on and then if you're in Ursula row 94, Hook 77, etc, as many hire cars look the same!

A motorised tram takes you from the car park to the Transportation and Ticket Center at the heart of the operation. Unless you already have your ticket (which will save valuable time), you visit the ticket booths here. Then, either the monorail or ferryboat will bring you to the Magic Kingdom itself. The monorail (straight ahead) is quicker if there isn't a queue, otherwise bear left and take a slower ferryboat. If you're staying at a Disney hotel, the resort buses deliver you almost to the front door (or the monorail or boat will if you are staying at one of the Magic Kingdom resorts). Finally, the Magic Kingdom is the only 'dry' park – that is, there's NO alcohol on sale (except at the Be Our Guest restaurant at dinner).

🇬🇧 **BRITTIP**

An easy way to remember where you parked is to take a picture of the Section and Row number on your digital camera or phone. Then simply delete it when you get back to your car.

'it's a small world'

Main Street USA

Right, we've finally reached the park itself… but not quite. Hopefully, you've arrived early and are among the leading hordes aiming to swarm through the entrance. The published opening time may say 9am, but the gates can open up to 45mins earlier.

Main Street is the first of the 6 'lands' and, at opening time, there is an informal Welcome Parade, with costumed singers and dancers, and the Character Train arrives at Main Street Station to bring a variety of characters for a meet-and-greet in Town Square (get those autograph books ready!). A family is then chosen at random to sprinkle some 'pixie dust' to open the park officially for the day. On your right is Town Square Theater, the special place to meet **Magician Mickey** and **Tinker Bell**.

BRITTIP
Meet Mickey without the long wait by scheduling your time in advance using the FastPass+ system.

On your left is **City Hall**, where you can pick up a park map and daily schedule (if you haven't already got one en route) and book restaurants (highly advisable at peak periods). You can also find out where and when the characters will appear. Ahead is **Town Square**, where you can take a 1-way ride on a horse-drawn bus or fire engine, or visit the **Car Barn** mini museum. The Street itself houses the park's best shopping (check out

Town Square Theater

the massive Emporium), and the **Walt Disney World Railroad** AAA, a Western-themed steam train that circles the park and is one of the better attractions when queues are long elsewhere (though Town Square station is often the busiest).

Sorcerers of the Magic Kingdom: This interactive game takes place throughout the park (except Tomorrowland) but has its HQ at The Firehouse in Town Square (with a second station at Ye Olde Christmas Shoppe in Liberty Square), where guests sign up for a role in saving the Magic Kingdom from various Disney villains. With the help of role-playing cards, players visit special 'portals' (cleverly disguised video screens) to discover their task and use their cards to help Merlin defeat the villains. It is designed for all ages and has the ability to get quite complex for serious role-playing gamers, using multiple cards to cast 'spells' that ward off evil-doers and save the day in each land. Like an interactive scavenger hunt, it is aimed at children but adults get a kick out of it, too. AAA½

Dining: The Italian-style **Tony's Town Square Restaurant** serves lunch and dinner; **The Plaza Restaurant** offers salads and sandwiches (lunch and dinner); and **The Crystal Palace** (breakfast $24.99 adult, $13.99 ages 3–9; lunch $27.99 & $14.99; dinner $37.99 & $17.99) is buffet-style food with Winnie the Pooh and Co. Quick bites can be bought from **Casey's Corner** (hot dogs, chips and soft drinks), **Main Street Bakery** (a new Starbucks coffee shop, also serving wonderful pastries), **Main Street Confectionery** (chocolate and sweets) and the **Plaza Ice Cream Parlor**. Disney characters also appear periodically throughout the Square.

Info: Check the Guest Information Board at the top of Main Street (on the left) as it gives waiting times for all the attractions. The **Baby Center** (for nursing mothers) is also at the top of Main Street, to the left next to Crystal Palace, along with the **First Aid** station.

ADVENTURELAND

1 Swiss Family Treehouse
2 Jungle Cruise
3 Magic Carpets of Aladdin
4 The Enchanted Tiki Room
5 Pirates of the Caribbean

FRONTIERLAND

6 Splash Mountain
7 Big Thunder Mountain Railroad
8 County Bear Jamboree
9 Raft to Tom Sawyer Island

LIBERTY SQUARE

10 Liberty Tree Tavern
11 Liberty Square Riverboat
12 The Haunted Mansion
13 The Hall of Presidents

FANTASYLAND

14 'It's a Small World'
15 Prince Charming Regal Carrousel
16 Mad Tea Party
17 The Many Adventures of Winnie The Pooh
18 Princess Fairytale Hall
19 Dumbo The Flying Elephant
20 Mickey's PhilharMagic
21 The Barnstormer starring The Great Goofini
22 Casey Jr Splash 'n' Soak Station

23 Peter Pan's Flight
24 Castle Forecourt Stage
25 Cinderella's Royal Table
26 Brave – Meet Merida
27 Enchanted Tales with Belle
28 Be Our Guest Restaurant
29 Under The Sea – Journey of the Little Mermaid
30 Ariel's Grotto
31 Seven Dwarfs Mine Train

TOMORROWLAND

32 Space Mountain
33 Tomorrowland Indy Speedway
34 Walt Disney's Carousel of Progress
35 Astro Orbiter
36 Tomorrowland Transit Authority
37 Stitch's Great Escape!
38 Buzz Lightyear's Space Ranger Spin
39 Monsters Inc. Laugh Floor
40 Club 626 Dance Party

TRANSPORT

41 Walt Disney World Railroad Stations
42 Boat Dock
43 Monorail Station
44 Bus Station

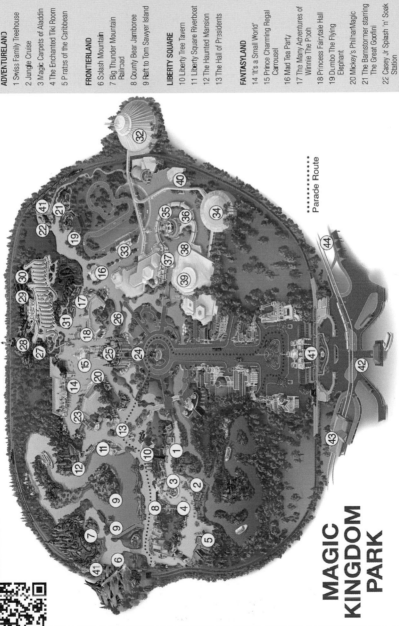

Parade Route

MAGIC KINGDOM PARK

BRITTIP

Can't find Mickey and Co? This is often one of the main laments of those who arrive unprepared. At City Hall they can tell you where to find the characters. In fact, City Hall is your best friend for many queries, from baby facilities to meal bookings (but there are NO baby facilities at City Hall itself). Character meet-and-greets are also shown on all park maps with a 'Mickey glove' icon.

Beating the queues: Unless you are late, skip Main Street and head for the end of the street to the real entrance to the park. This is where you await the official opening hour, and you should adopt 1 of 3 tactics, each aimed at doing some of the most popular rides before the queues build up (wait times of 2 hours for Splash Mountain are not unknown). 1: If you fancy the 5-star, log-flume ride Splash Mountain, keep left in front of the Crystal Palace with the majority, who will head for the same place. 2: If you have young children who can't wait to try the Fantasyland rides, stay in the middle and pass around the Castle. 3: If the thrills of indoor roller-coaster Space Mountain appeal, move to the right by The Plaza Restaurant and go straight into Tomorrowland. Now you'll be in pole position for the initial rush (and it will be a rush; take care with children).

BRITTIP

The Move It! Shake It! Celebrate It! Street Party begins in Town Square, but the real action takes place around the Castle Hub. Stake out a spot in advance if you want an up-front view.

Other entertainment: Watch out for the **Move It! Shake It! Celebrate It! Street Party** up to 3 times daily, from Town Square, along Main Street, ending up in the Hub area as Disney characters, stilt walkers and dancers lead guests in a high-energy street party. The **Main Street Trolley Show** happens 3 or 4 times a day, with the horse-drawn trolley arriving on Main Street for a 6min song-and-dance

interlude. The fun barbershop quartet the **Dapper Dans** and brass band **Main Street Philharmonic** (who also play in Storybook Circus) add lively musical interludes throughout the day, as does **Casey's Corner Pianist**, and don't miss the **Glass Blowing Demonstrations** at Crystal Arts Shop. There is also a daily **Flag Retreat** at 5pm each day, with a military veteran helping the Security Colour Guard to bring down the national flag.

Adventureland

If you head left (going clockwise round the park), you enter Adventureland. If you're going to Splash Mountain first, pass the Swiss Family Treehouse on your left and bear right through an archway (with toilets) into Frontierland, where you turn left and Splash Mountain is ahead. Stopping in Adventureland, these are the attractions.

Swiss Family Treehouse: This imitation banyan tree is a clever replica of the treehouse from Disney's 1960 film Swiss Family Robinson. It's a walk-through attraction where the queues (rarely long) move steadily if not quickly, providing a neat glimpse of the ultimate tree house. **AA**

BRITTIP

The special deal on autograph book and fat pen combo can be cheaper than buying them separately.

Jungle Cruise: It's not so much the scenic, geographically suspect boat ride (where the Nile suddenly becomes the Amazon) that is so amusing here as the patter of your boat's captain, who spins a non-stop yarn about your adventure. Great detail but long queues, so visit either early morning (opens 10am) or late afternoon (evening queues are shortest, but you'll miss some of the detail in the dark). **AAAA FP+**

Pirates of the Caribbean: One of Disney's most impressive attractions that involves Walt's pioneering work in audio-animatronics, life-size figures that move, talk and, in this instance, lay siege to a Caribbean island! Your 8min underground boat ride visits a typical pirate adventure and the world of Captain Jack Sparrow and nemesis Captain Barbossa as they search for buried treasure. It's terrific family fun (though perhaps a bit spooky for young children, with one small drop in the dark). Queues are longest from late morning to mid-afternoon. AAAAA (TTTT under-10s) FP+

The Enchanted Tiki Room: A classic bird-laden, South Seas audio-animatronic show (rethemed to its original 1971 version in 2011) starring various parrots, macaws and other tropical feathered friends – plus the angry Tiki Gods! Queues are rare and it is air-conditioned. AA

Magic Carpets of Aladdin: Here, in an Agrabah-themed area, this ride spins you up, down and around as you try to dodge the spitting camel! Your 'flying carpet' tilts as well as levitates, simple stuff geared for younger children (virtually identical to the Magic Carpets of Agrabah in the Walt Disney Studios in Disneyland Paris). TT (TTTT under-5s), FP+.

A Pirate's Adventure: Treasure of the Seven Seas: A variation on the Sorcerers of the Magic Kingdom interactive card game (p106), this new quest opened in 2013, with the chance to help Captain Jack Sparrow fight off his various foes and locate different treasures around Adventureland, using a pirate map

and magic talisman. Visit the special kiosk through the archway past the Pirates ride to get started. AAA½

Other entertainment: Outside the Pirates of the Caribbean ride (and a must for young swashbucklers), **Captain Jack Sparrow's Pirate Tutorial** runs several times daily. Captain Jack and sidekick Mack invite youngsters to join them in sword fights and treasure hunting, ending with the Pirate Oath to become honorary buccaneers. **Disney characters** also turn up at the Adventureland entrance (Peter Pan) and next to the Magic Carpets ride (characters from Aladdin).

Shopping and dining: The best shopping is in the **Pirates Bazaar**. Here, the **Pirates League** (9am–4pm) offers a macho version of the Bibbidi Bobbidi Boutique that lets young swashbucklers transform into fully-fledged pirates. Choose from 4 packages ($29.95– 49.95), *Jake and the Neverland Pirates; First Mate; Empress;* and *Mermaid,* with a variety of accessories, including earrings, eye patches, swords, removable teeth (!), coin necklaces and temporary tattoos (photos sold separately). For food, you have **Aloha Isle** (yoghurt and ice-cream), **Sunshine Tree Terrace** (fruit, snacks, yoghurt, tea and coffee), and the more substantial beef or vegetarian tacos, empanadas and taco salads of **Tortuga Tavern** (open seasonally).

Magic Carpets of Aladdin

Frontierland

This Western-themed area is one of the busiest and is best avoided from late morning to late afternoon.

Splash Mountain: Based on the 1946 classic Disney cartoon Song of the South, this is a watery journey into the world of Brer Rabbit, Brer Fox and Brer Bear. The first part is all jolly cartoon scenery and fun with the main characters and a couple of minor swoops in your 8-passenger log boat. The conclusion, a 5-storey plummet at 45° into a mist-shrouded pool, seems like you are falling off the edge of the world! A huge adrenalin rush, but busy almost all day (try it first thing or during one of the parades to avoid the longest queues). Some riders also get VERY wet! R: 3ft 4in/101cm. TTTT FP+

Big Thunder Mountain Railroad: When Disney does a roller-coaster it will be one of the classiest, and here it is – a runaway mine train that swoops, tilts and plunges through a mock abandoned mine filled with clever scenery. You have to ride it at least twice to appreciate all the detail, but again queues are heavy, so go first

Big Thunder Mountain Railroad

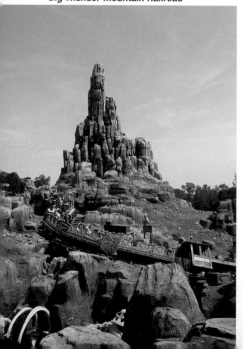

thing (after Splash Mountain) or late in the day. R: 3ft 4in/101cm. TTTT FP+

Country Bear Jamboree: Now here's a novelty: a 16min musical revue presented by audio-animatronic bears! It's great family fun with plenty of novel touches (watch for the talking moose head). Crowds are rare, so it's a good one when it's busy elsewhere. AAA

Frontierland Shootin' Arcade: The park's single attraction that costs extra ($1 for 35 shots), as you take aim at a series of animated targets. T

Tom Sawyer Island: Take a raft over to an overgrown playground of mysterious caves, grottos and mazes, rope bridges and Fort Sam Clemens, where you can fire air guns at passing boats (opens 9am). A good choice in early afternoon when the queues are long elsewhere. Aunt Polly's Dockside Inn allows time off your feet, but the only drinks here are from a vending machine. TT

Other entertainment: The comic trio of **The Notorious Banjo Brothers and Bob**, and the **Frontierland Hoedown**, with the Country Bears provide musical interludes. Disney characters can be found by the Liberty Square bridge (*Princess & The Frog*) and next to Splash Mountain (*Toy Story*).

Shopping and dining: Frontierland shops sell cowboy hats, guns and badges, as well as Native American and Mexican crafts. Look out for the nicely themed **Briar Patch** and **Prairie Outpost** for interesting gifts. For food, try **Pecos Bill Tall Tale Inn & Café** (salads, sandwiches and burgers), **Golden Oak Outpost** (chicken nuggets, chicken sandwich, desserts, flatbread, fries and drinks) or **Turkey Leg Cart** (massive, smoke-grilled turkey legs).

Liberty Square

The clockwise tour brings you next to a homage to post-independence America. A lot of the historical content will go over the heads of British visitors, but it still has some great attractions.

Liberty Square Riverboat: Cruise America's 'rivers' on an authentic paddle steamer, be menaced by river pirates and thrill to the stories of How the West Was Won (10am–8pm). This is also good at busier times of the day, especially early afternoon. AAA

The Haunted Mansion: A clever delve into the world of Master Gracey's ghostly bride that is neither too scary for most kids nor too twee for adults. Not so much a thrill ride as a scenic adventure. Watch out for the fun touch at the end when the 'hitch-hiking ghosts' might drop in! Longish queues for much of the day, however, so try to visit late on. AAAA (TTTT under-6s), FP+

The Hall of Presidents: This is the attraction likely to mean least to us, a 2-part show that is a film about the Constitution and an audio-animatronic parade of all 44 US presidents (opens 9am). Technically impressive, but it may bore young 'uns (though it is air-conditioned). AAA

Shopping and dining: Shopping includes **Ye Olde Christmas Shoppe** and **The Yankee Trader**; eating options are the full-service **Liberty Tree Tavern** (hearty soups, salads, and traditional dishes like roast turkey, carved beef and smoked ham), **Columbia Harbor House** (counter-service fried chicken or fish and some good soups, salads and sandwiches, notably for vegetarians) and **Sleepy Hollow** (a picnic area serving snacks, fruit and drinks).

Fantasyland

Leaving Liberty Square, you come into the park's spiritual heart, the area with which young children are most enchanted. The attractions, in 3 separate areas, are designed with kids in mind, but the shops are quite sophisticated and the **Tangled** 'village' (basically just a courtyard with restrooms) is wonderfully scenic.

'It's a Small World': This could almost be Disney's theme ride, a family boat trip around the world, each represented by 100s of dancing, singing audio-animatronic dolls in delightful set-piece pageants. If it sounds twee, it actually creates a surprisingly striking effect, accompanied by an annoyingly catchy theme song that young children adore. Crowds peak in early afternoon. AAAA FP+

BRITTIP

Get more value for your money at the parks by ordering sodas 'without ice' to get a full cup.

Peter Pan's Flight: This may seem a rather tame ride but is another Walt classic and a big hit with kids. Its novel effect of flying with Peter Pan is good fun and there's a lot of clever detail as your ship sails to Neverland. AAA (AAAAA under-6s) FP+

Mickey's PhilharMagic: This fun-tastic 10-min 3-D film show has a host of special effects as Donald tries to conduct the Enchanted Orchestra – to comic effect. It features a 150ft/46m wide screen to immerse guests in the 3-D world of *Beauty and the Beast*, *The Little Mermaid*, *The Lion King*, *Peter Pan* and *Aladdin*, with hapless Donald surviving a string of adventures before Mickey brings him back to earth. The lavish theatre, artistic animation, special effects (you can 'smell' the food!) and all-round family entertainment make for a hugely enjoyable attraction. There is no scare factor (though the sudden plunge into darkness at one point and noise of the 'orchestra' can spook young children), while you'll

Liberty Square Riverboat

be enchanted when Tinker Bell seems to fly out of the screen in front of you. AAAAA FP+

Prince Charming Regal Carrousel: The Fantasyland centrepiece shouldn't need any more explanation other than it is a vintage carousel that kids love. Long queues for much of the day, though. T (TTT under-5s)

The Many Adventures of Winnie the Pooh: Building on the timeless popularity of Pooh, Piglet and Co, this family ride offers a musical jaunt through Hundred Acre Wood with some clever effects (get ready to 'bounce' with Tigger!) and an original soundtrack. Wait times are made easier by hands-on elements throughout the queue. AAA (AAAAA under-5s) FP+

Mad Tea Party: The kids will insist you take them in these spinning, oversized tea cups that have their own 'steering wheel' to add to the whirling effect. Actually, they're just a heavily disguised fairground ride. Again, go early or expect crowds. Characters from Alice in Wonderland also visit periodically. TT (TTTT under-5s) FP+

Princess Fairytale Hall: This elaborate 'royal' residence features a dramatic castle gallery area where visitors gather before they are summoned for an audience with some of the Disney princesses (choose from *either* Cinderella and 1 of Rapunzel, Aurora, Snow White, Jasmine or Tiana) or mega-popular

Seven Dwarfs Mine Train

Frozen duo Anna and Elsa. AAA (AAAAA under 13 girls!) FP+

BRITTIP
Anna and Elsa draw HUGE queues, while their FP+ option also books up 30–60 days in advance.

Enchanted Tales with Belle: A glorified (but extremely clever) character meet-and-greet, here you visit Maurice's Workshop, nestled in the shadow of Beast's Castle, and guests are transported via a magic mirror to the Castle Library for a memorable interactive story-time with Belle and Lumiere. AAAA FP+

Under the Sea – Journey of the Little Mermaid: Be a part of her world as you journey under the sea with Ariel in this lovely, gentle ride aboard stylised clamshells, past colourful scenes from the much-loved animated movie. Ariel, Prince Eric, Flounder, Scuttle, Sebastian, King Triton and evil sea witch Ursula all make appearances, while favourite songs from the hit movie add to this charming adventure (with some surprising special effects!) that is sure to have a happy ending. AAAA. FP+

Ariel's Grotto: Next door is the elaborate setting for a character meeting with the Little Mermaid herself. FP+

The Seven Dwarfs Mine Train: It's 'off to work we go' with the Seven Dwarfs in this charming dark ride through a gem-laden mine. Your trip begins as a family-friendly outdoor coaster, enters the mine for a gentle (and slightly dark) journey past the Dwarfs as they dig, dig, dig, then plunges back outside as a coaster again for the grand finale. The mine cars have the swaying motion of a real mine train (though you actually feel very little sway, as the banked turns overpower it), all the charm of the fairytale from which it originates, and the sense of being 'in the film' is completely convincing. Watch for the surprise visitor at the end! TTT (TTTTT under 10s) FP+

Storybook Circus

The former Toontown area of Fantasyland is now themed for the classic film Dumbo and features more family-friendly fun.

Dumbo the Flying Elephant: Young children cannot pass this one by and, thankfully, with all-new dual Dumbos (doubling the capacity of the old ride) and a clever interactive, air-conditioned queue, parents should be less put off by the prospect of a long wait. It's a 2min ride on the back of a swooping, circling, flying elephant, and its charm is undeniable. **TT** (**TTTT** under-5s) **FP+**

The Barnstormer: Get ready for a junior-sized coaster in the company of classic stunt pilot The Great Goofini as this surprisingly whizzy (but very short) ride takes some sharp twists and turns in best circus style. **R:** 2ft 11in/89cm. **TTT** (**TTTTT** 4–8s) **FP+**

Casey Jr Splash 'n' Soak Station: The Circus Train has pulled into a siding – and sprung a leak! In fact, it is just a cleverly disguised water-play area, with all manner of squirting fountains, pop-jets and dumping buckets guaranteed to get the kids good and wet – so don't forget swimsuits OR a change of clothes. **AAAA** (under 10s)

Pete's Silly Sideshow: More themed fun under the Big Top as Minnie, Goofy, Donald and Daisy (in circus-style character) line up for a clever meet-and-greet. **AAA**

Other entertainment: The superb **Dream Along With Mickey** show is staged up to 6 times a day on the Castle Forecourt Stage, a 20min fantasy featuring Donald, Mickey, Minnie, Goofy and various Princesses and their Princes. Peter Pan and Wendy join the battle against Maleficent and Captain Hook to help Donald remember the power of believing in your dreams (**AAA**). In Storybook Circus, look out for featured clown **Wowzer**, while the **Giggle Gang** are a whole posse of wacky clown fun. The **Royal Majesty Makers** are another group of strolling performers, in the Castle Courtyard, with a variety of regal routines (including the revived Sword in the Stone ceremony) and **The Fairy Godmother** meets with children periodically at Cinderella's Fountain. Other **character experiences** include Meet Merida from the 2012 film *Brave* in the Fairytale Garden, Pooh and friends next to the Winnie the Pooh ride, Gaston outside Gaston's Tavern and Alice in Wonderland characters next to the Mad Tea Party.

Shopping and dining: Shop at **Castle Couture**, the excellent **Sir Mickey's, Fantasy Faire**, **Pooh's Thotful Shop**, **Big Top Souvenirs** and **Bonjour! Village Gifts**. There is also an outlet of the **Bibbidi Bobbidi Boutique** here (the other is in Downtown Disney), where 'little princesses' who are over 3 can choose from 4 makeover styles ($58–207) the Coach, Crown, Courtyard and Castle packages with 3 different hairstyles, Disney Diva, Pop Princess and Fairytale Princess, from 8am–8pm (reservations highly recommended on 407 939 7895).

Eating opportunities are at **Pinocchio Village Haus** (flatbreads, salads, chicken nuggets, pizza and pasta), **Storybook Treats** (ice-cream), the **Cheshire Cafe** (iced drinks and juices), **Big Top Treats** (sweets and pastries) and **Friar's Nook** (hot dogs, chicken baskets, crisps and frozen drinks). **Cinderella's Royal Table** is a fine setting for the popular character breakfast, lunch and dinner with various Disney princesses (Cinderella greets guests in the foyer only). The majestic hall, waitresses in costume and well-presented food – salads, seafood, roast beef, prime rib and

Pinocchio Village Haus

chicken – provide a memorable experience. It's pricey, though – $178 for a family of 4 for breakfast, $197 for lunch and a massive $233 for dinner, including photo and gratuity. Be aware you pay in FULL by credit card when you book, there is a $10 per person fee if you cancel more than 24 hours in advance, and, if you cancel less than 24 hours in advance, there is NO refund. More fun (and better value) is the spectacular **Be Our Guest** restaurant inside the Beast's Castle, a unique 550-seat counter service lunch option by day and a full service restaurant by night, with the addition of beer and wine (the only Magic Kingdom venue that serves alcohol). Divided into 3 themed sections – the Ballroom (complete with snow on the outdoor terrace!), Rose Gallery and the dark and moody West Wing – it is one of Disney's most ornate dining options. At lunch, choose from soups, salads, quiche, sandwiches and braised pork, while dinner offers a richer range of French-influenced dishes like Ratatouille and thyme-scented Pork Rack Chop. Dinner books up FAST, though, so try to get a reservation at the 180-day mark (407 939 3463 or online at www.disneyworld.com; credit card deposit required, $10 charged per person if you don't turn up), lunch is first come, first served. **Gaston's Tavern** is a counter-service offering featuring an eclectic menu of snacks, drinks, pastries and their signature Roasted Pork Shank, again with some great Beauty and the Beast theming.

Prince Charming's Carrousel

BRITTIP

Two people can easily make a meal of the massive Pork Shank at Gaston's Tavern while the unique Le Fou's Brew (frozen apple juice with marshmallow) is a must-try drink!

Tomorrowland

This area's cartoon-like space-age styling, novel shops and varied rides provide guaranteed all-round appeal.

Space Mountain: One of the 3 most popular attractions, its reputation is deserved. Launching from Starport 75, this is a high-thrills, tight-turning roller-coaster, completely in the dark save for occasional flashes as you whiz through the galaxy. Don't do this on a full stomach! The only way to beat the crowds is to go either first thing, late in the day or during one of the parades (or, of course, get a FastPass+). Ride photos are available for $18.95–49.95. Children are also likely to gravitate towards the Tomorrowland Arcade as you exit. **R:** 3ft 8in/111cm. TTTTT FP+

Tomorrowland Speedway: Despite the long queues, this is a rather tame ride on supposed race tracks that just putt-putts along on rails with little real steering required (children must be 4ft 4in/132cm to drive alone). T (TTTT under-6s) FP+

Astro Orbiter: A jazzed-up version of Dumbo in Fantasyland, this ride is a bit faster and higher and features rockets. Long, slow-moving queues are a reason to give this a miss unless you have young children. TT (TTTT under-10s).

Walt Disney's Carousel of Progress: This will surprise, entertain and amuse. It is a journey through 20th-century technology with audio-animatronics in a revolving theatre that reveals different periods in history. Its 22min duration is rarely threatened by crowds (open only at peak periods). AAA

Tomorrowland Transit Authority: A neat 'future transport system', this offers an elevated view of the area, including a glimpse inside Space Mountain, in electro-magnetic cars. Short queues. AAA (TTT under-8s)

Stitch's Great Escape: This 15min experience receives mixed reviews – some like it for the audio-animatronic prequel to Disney's Lilo & Stitch, with visitors being recruited into the madcap Galactic Federation prison service (where things go hilariously wrong as Stitch arrives and causes havoc), while others find it puzzling and rather lame. Young children can also be scared by the complete darkness at times. There are 2 pre-show areas before recruits are ushered into the sit-down chamber (with shoulder restraints) where Stitch is let loose to bounce, dribble and even belch over the unwary audience. R: 3ft 2in/101cm. AA

Buzz Lightyear's Space Ranger Spin: Ride into action against evil Emperor Zurg and the robot army – and shoot them with laser cannons! A sure-fire family winner, especially as you get to keep score. TTT (TTTTT under-8s) FP+

Monsters Inc Laugh Floor: This innovative show is based on the hit Pixar film *Monsters Inc*. With 'live' animation, special effects and high-tech voice links, guests can meet and match wits with the likes of Mike, Sulley and Roz and be entertained by their patter and amusing antics.

Billy Boil opens the show, introducing various comedians (including 2-headed jokester Sam-n-Ella), with the aim of capturing the audience's laughter. Guest interaction is integral to the show. Watch the screen – you may be featured! AAA FP+

Other entertainment: Incredibles fans should enjoy the **INCREDIBLES Super Dance Party** (high season) with the chance to bop along with a live DJ and various Incredibles characters, led by Mr & Mrs Incredible, while Disney characters are often on hand by the Carousel of Progress, notably Buzz Lightyear.

Shopping and dining: Shopping highlights are provided by **Mickey's Star Traders** and **Merchant of Venus**. For food, try **Cosmic Ray's Starlight Café** (good burgers, chicken, sandwiches, soups, salads and flavoured iced coffees), **Auntie Gravity's Galactic Goodies** (ice-cream, smoothies and juices), the **Lunching Pad** (speciality hot-dogs, pretzels and frozen drinks) or **Tomorrowland Terrace** (burgers, pasta, sandwiches and salads; open seasonally).

Having come full circle you're now back at Main Street USA and it's best to return here in the afternoon to avoid the crowds and enjoy the impressive shops.

Monsters Inc Laugh Floor

Disney parades

If there is one thing Disney knows how to do well, it's a parade. Coupled with its range of special seasonal events, there is always much more to look forward to than just the rides.

Festival of Fantasy Parade: A completely new procession of imaginative floats, costumes, dancers and music that is simply unmissable. The 7 featured floats include The Little Mermaid, Disney Princesses (including *Frozen*'s Anna and Elsa), Maleficent (with a magnificent fire-breathing steam-punk style dragon!), Tangled and Peter Pan and friends, plus a special balloon-like vehicle for Mickey and Minnie. The energetic dancers, stilt-walkers and rather menacing outfits of the 'Raven' men all combine for added dramatic effect. AAAAA FP+ for special viewing area.

To watch a parade, sit on the left side of Main Street USA (facing the Castle) to stay in the shade if it's hot, or stake out a spot in the Hub or Frontierland. People start staking out the best spots an HOUR in advance.

Main Street Electrical Parade: A mind-boggling light and sound festival full of glitter and razzamatazz, with the Disney characters at the centre of a multitude of fibre-optic effect floats. It is classic Disney, using the latest technology to enhance the heart-tugging impact of this sparkling cavalcade. Tinker Bell leads the procession, with each successive float a visual and audio treat, and the music a real highlight. A brilliant end

Festival of Fantasy Parade

to any Magic Kingdom day. When the park is open late (during peak periods and weekends), there are 2 showings per night, and the second is less crowded. AAAAA

Main Street USA closes 30mins after the rest of the park, so you can avoid the inevitable mad rush for the car parks by lingering here to shop or enjoy an ice-cream.

Celebrate The Magic!: This stunning nightly state-of-the-art projection show uses the Cinderella Castle as its backdrop, incorporating a series of animated special effects and video that make the castle seem to come alive, transforming again and again with a sequence of Disney characters and films in vivid, dynamic colour. Look for the castle's turrets to become 'rockets,' or a vine-covered fantasy or a fiery inferno as the imagery weaves visual trick after trick in a kaleidoscopic pattern that will leave your eyeballs breathless! AAAA

Wishes: Most nights also finish with this spectacular fireworks show over the Castle. With a clever soundtrack narrated by Jiminy Cricket and featuring memorable moments from various Disney classics, it is magnificently choreographed and culminates in a sequence of dazzling pyrotechnic explosions (many designed especially for this show). Starting with an appearance by Tinker Bell (from the Castle's top turret), it continues for 12mins of typical Disney emotional appeal; the perfect pixie-dust farewell to a memorable day. AAAAA FP+

> **BRITTIP**
> After the fireworks crowd exits, you are allowed to take the Resort Only monorail back to the Transportation & Ticket Center, rather than queue for the main Express monorail.

Wishes Cruises: If you prefer not to fight the crowds for a fab view of Wishes, book one of 3 speciality cruises to view the fireworks from Seven Seas Lagoon. The **Basic Cruise** holds up to 8 guests onboard

MAGIC KINGDOM PARK with children

Here is a rough guide to the attractions that appeal to different age groups (height restrictions have been taken into account):

Under-5s

Buzz Lightyear's Space Ranger Spin, Prince Charming Regal Carousel, Country Bear Jamboree, Dream Along With Mickey, Dumbo the Flying Elephant, Enchanted Tales With Belle, The Enchanted Tiki Room, 'It's a Small World', Jungle Cruise, Liberty Square Riverboat, Main Street Vehicles, Many Adventures of Winnie the Pooh, Mickey's PhilharMagic, Monsters Inc Laugh Floor, Move It! Shake It! Celebrate It! Street Party, Peter Pan's Flight, Tomorrowland Speedway (with a parent), Tomorrowland Transit Authority, Walt Disney World Railroad, Main Street Electrical Parade, Journey of the Little Mermaid, Festival of Fantasy Parade.

5–8s

Astro Orbiter, The Barnstormer, Big Thunder Mountain Railroad, Buzz Lightyear's Space Ranger Spin, Country Bear Jamboree, Dream Along With Mickey, Enchanted Tales With Belle, The Enchanted Tiki Room, Haunted Mansion, Jungle Cruise, Liberty Square Riverboat, Mad Tea Party, Magic Carpets of Aladdin, Many Adventures of Winnie the Pooh, Mickey's PhilharMagic, Monsters Inc Laugh Floor, Move It! Shake It! Celebrate It! Street Party, Pirates of the Caribbean, Seven Dwarfs Mine Train Ride, Space Mountain (with parental discretion), Splash Mountain, Stitch's Great Escape!, Swiss Family Treehouse, Tom Sawyer Island, Tomorrowland Speedway (with a parent), Tomorrowland Transit Authority, Walt Disney World Railroad, Walt Disney's Carousel of Progress, Main Street Electrical Parade, Journey of the Little Mermaid, Festival of Fantasy Parade.

9–12s

Astro Orbiter, Big Thunder Mountain Railroad, Buzz Lightyear's Space Ranger Spin, Country Bear Jamboree, The Haunted Mansion, Mad Tea Party, Mickey's PhilharMagic, Monsters Inc. Laugh Floor, Move It! Shake It! Celebrate It! Street Party, Pirates of the Caribbean, Seven Dwarfs Mine Train Ride, Space Mountain, Splash Mountain, Stitch's Great Escape!, Tomorrowland Indy Speedway (without a parent), Main Street Electrical Parade, Journey of the Little Mermaid, Festival of Fantasy Parade, Wishes fireworks.

Over-12s

Astro Orbiter, Big Thunder Mountain Railroad, Buzz Lightyear's Space Ranger Spin, Haunted Mansion, Mad Tea Party, Mickey's PhilharMagic, Move It! Shake It! Celebrate It! Street Party, Pirates of the Caribbean, Festival of Fantasy parade, Seven Dwarfs Mine Train, Space Mountain, Splash Mountain, Stitch's Great Escape!, Main Street Electrical Parade, Wishes fireworks.

a 21ft/6m pontoon boat and costs $292 (includes water, soft drinks and snacks); the **Premium Cruise** holds up to 10 on a 25ft/7.6m pontoon boat (for $346), including water, soft drinks, snacks and an audio feed to the Wishes music; or splash out for the **Celebration Cruise**, which adds special occasion decorations to the Basic Cruise for a total of $325 and the Premium Cruise for $375. All can be booked 90 days in advance.

Pirate and Pals Fireworks Voyage: This kid-friendly Wishes cruise includes meeting Mr Smee and Captain Hook before cruising the Seven Seas Lagoon to view the Electrical Water Pageant and Wishes. Snacks and drinks are provided while you enjoy a retelling of the Peter Pan story, then meet Pan himself at the end of your voyage ($57/adult, $33/3–9; can be booked 180 days in advance).

BRITTIP

For a final bit of typical Disney entertainment, head outside the Magic Kingdom at 10.25pm and catch the Electrical Water Pageant passing by on Seven Seas Lagoon in front of the park.

Leaving the park: When it comes to leaving, the monorail is quicker than the ferry but it can still take up to an hour to get back to your car. Also, if the crowds get too heavy during the day, you can escape by leaving in the early afternoon (your car park ticket is valid all day) and returning to your hotel for a few hours' rest or a dip in the pool. Alternatively, catch a boat to one of the Disney resorts. Fort Wilderness is especially fun for kids and boasts the good value Trails End restaurant for lunch or dinner.

Halloween and Christmas

Two additional annual events in the Magic Kingdom provide a separate, party-style ticketed event 7pm–midnight, with most of the rides open and extra themed fun and games.

Mickey's Not So Scary Halloween Party: Sept–Oct sees many visitors dress up for the typical American trick-or-treat fun, with plenty of treats for youngsters along the way. With special music, storytelling, parades and the HalloWishes fireworks (plus some wonderful lighting effects), tickets go on sale about 5 months in advance and sell out quickly.

Mickey's Very Merry Christmas Party: The Christmas party (Nov–Dec) sees 'snow' on Main Street and an array of magnificent festive decorations and theming. There is

Halloween at the Magic Kingdom

free hot chocolate and cookies, as well as a special parade and more fireworks. The atmosphere is truly enchanting, though the evening can be prone to unfriendly weather.

BRITTIP
Although the special evening parties don't start officially until 7pm, you can use the ticket to gain entry to the park from 4pm, which gives you 8 full hours to enjoy all the attractions.

Park tours: Finally, one of the park's little-known secrets is the **Keys to the Kingdom**, a 4–5hr guided tour of many backstage areas, including the service tunnel under the park, and entertainment production buildings. It's an extra $79 (including lunch; not available for under-16s) but is a superb journey into the park's creation. **Disney's Family Magic Tour** is a 2hr guided adventure that takes you on a search for clues throughout the park at $34/person, or you can experience the 3hr **The Magic Behind Our Steam Trains Tour** ($54/person; no under-10s) as you join the crew that prepares the park's trains each day. **Walt Disney: Marceline to Magic Kingdom** is a 3hr tour focusing on how the inspiration of Walt's early years in Marceline, Missouri, culminated in the creation of the Magic Kingdom ($30/person; no under-12s).

Epcot

Epcot originally stood for 'Experimental Prototype Community of Tomorrow', but it might be more accurate to say Every Person Comes Out Tired. For this is a BIG park, with a lot to see and do, and much legwork required to cover its 300acre/122ha extent. Actually, it is not so much a vision of the future as a look at the world and technology of today, with a strong educational and environmental message. At almost 3 times the size of the Magic Kingdom Park, it is more likely to require a 2-day visit (though under-5s might find it less entertaining) and your feet in particular will notice the difference!

Location

Epcot opened in October 1982 and its giant car park can hold 9,000 vehicles, so a tram takes you from your car to the main entrance (though if you are staying at a Disney hotel you can catch the monorail, boat or bus service to the gates; International Gateway is a separate entrance for guests at the Epcot resort hotels). Don't forget to note where you have parked (e.g. Create, row 49). If you have your ticket or MagicBand, you pass through the gate area and wait in the immediate entrance plaza for Rope Drop, which is signalled by Mickey and Co arriving to greet guests.

Beating the queues: Epcot is divided into 2 distinct parts arranged in a figure of 8 and there are 2 tactics to help you avoid the worst of the crowds. The first or lower half of the '8' consists of Future World, with 6 pavilions arranged around Spaceship Earth (which dominates the skyline) and the 2 Innoventions centres.

Epcot at a glance

Location	Off Epcot Drive, Walt Disney World		
Size	300 acres/122ha in Future World and World Showcase		
Hours	9am–9pm Future World (except Universe of Energy, Imagination, Innoventions, 9am–7pm), 11am–9pm (World Showcase)		
Admission	Under-3s free; 3–9 $88 (1–day base ticket), $284 (5–day Magic Your Way), £264 (14–day Ultimate); adult (10+) $94, $304, £279. Prices do not include tax.		
Parking	$17		
Lockers	Through the main entrance to the right hand side and at International Gateway $12 small, $14 large ($5 deposit each)		
Pushchairs	$15 and $31 to the left after the main entrance and at International Gateway; length of stay $91/week, $130 10 days, $189/$270 double		
Wheelchairs	$12 or $70 ($20 deposit refunded) with pushchairs		
Top attractions	Mission: SPACE, Test Track, Spaceship Earth, Soarin'™, Universe of Energy, American Adventure		
Don't miss	IllumiNations: Reflections of Earth, Disney Character Spot, Turtle Talk With Crush, live entertainment (including Off Kilter in Canada, JAMMitors in Innoventions Plaza and Voices of Liberty in America), and dinner at any of the World Showcase pavilions		
Hidden costs	**Meals**	Burger, chips and coke $11.72 3-course dinner $37.25–47.25 (La Hacienda, Mexico) Kids' meal $5.99	
	T-shirts	$21.95–36.95 Kids' T-shirts $16.95–29.95	
	Souvenirs	$1.45–6,800	
	Sundries	Epcot 'Passport' $9.95	

Future World

1 Universe of Energy
2 Mission: SPACE
3 Test Track
4 Odyssey Center
5 Imagination!
(including
Captain Eo)
6 The Land (including
Soarin'™)
7 The Seas with
Nemo and Friends
8 Spaceship Earth
9 Innoventions West
10 Innoventions East

World Showcase

11 Mexico
12 Norway
13 China
14 The Outpost
15 Germany
16 Italy
17 The American
Adventure
18 Japan
19 Morocco
20 France
21 International
Gateway (to Epcot
resort hotels)
22 United Kingdom
23 Canada
24 Friendship Boats
to Italy and
Morocco
25 America Gardens
Theater
26 Showcase Plaza
27 Monorail Station
K Kidcot Fun Stops

EPCOT

The second part, or top of the '8', is World Showcase, a potted journey around the world via 11 international pavilions that feature a taste of each country's culture, history, entertainment, shopping and cuisine. Once through the entrance plaza, aim to get the 3 big-time rides – Test Track, Mission: Space and Soarin'™ – under your belt first, then move into World Showcase for its 11am opening. Continue around World Showcase until 4 or 5pm, then return to Future World to catch up on the other attractions there, as the majority will have moved on (apart from at the 3 main rides). As a general tactic, head first for the magnificent Soarin'™, then go across to the other side of Future World for Test Track, if you haven't got a FastPass in advance (and you can book only 1 of them with the two-tiered FP+ system). While you wait for your ride time, you can queue for Mission: SPACE and perhaps even take in Universe of Energy. Alternatively, if the rides don't appeal quite so much as a visit to such diverse cultures as Japan and Morocco, spend your first couple of hours in the Innoventions centres (busy from mid-morning), then head into World Showcase at 11am and you'll be ahead of the crowds for several hours. The other thing you should do early on is book lunch or dinner at one of the fine restaurants around World Showcase (Mexico, Italy, France and Morocco are all highly recommended). The best reservations go fast, but check in at Guest Relations (on the left after Spaceship Earth) for advice and bookings.

Planning your visit
If you plan a 2-day visit, it makes sense to spend the first day in World Showcase, arriving by 11am and going straight there while the majority stay in Future World, booking your evening meal for around 5.30pm, then lingering around the lagoon for the evening entertainment. For your second visit, try arriving in mid-afternoon and then doing Future World in a more leisurely fashion.

Queues at most of the pavilions are almost non-existent for rides like Universe of Energy, Spaceship Earth and Journey into Imagination, though Test Track, Soarin'™ and Mission: Space stay busy all day. You CAN do Epcot in a day – if you arrive early, put in some speedy legwork and give some detail a miss. But, of all the parks, it is a shame to hurry this one. Browse in the shops (almost 70 in all), when the rides are busiest.

Kidcot Fun Stops: At 11 activity centres around Epcot (each country in World Showcase), children can play games and collect a special Epcot Passport to get stamped as they visit each Stop.

Future World
Here's what you'll find in the first part of your Epcot adventure.

Universe of Energy: There is just one attraction here but it is a stunner. Ellen's Energy Adventure is a 35min show-and-ride with comedienne Ellen DeGeneres and Bill Nye the Science Guy exploring the creation of fuels from the age of dinosaurs to their modern-day usages. The film elements make it seem you are in a conventional theatre, but then your seats rearrange themselves into 96-person solar-powered cars and you are off on a journey through the prehistoric era, with some realistic dinosaurs! Queues are steady but not overwhelming from mid-morning.
AAAAA

Epcot's China pavilion across the lagoon

Mission: SPACE: This is more high-tech Disney imagination, a journey into the future at the International Space Training Center. The space-age building prepares you for a major adventure as you enter through Planetary Plaza, with its giant replica planets (check out the model showing the moon landings). At the entrance you have a choice of 2 queues – Standby (the main queue), and FastPass+ Return, and the clever organisation keeps queues moving. As you enter the training facility, there are some superb models and graphics (like the giant revolving Gravity Wheel) to look at while you queue to reach Team Dispatch. Here, the 4 ready rooms form you into teams of 4 for the ride, and you will be either Navigator, Engineer, Pilot or Commander, each with different functions to perform. You also have the choice of either the full, dynamic version of the ride (the 'orange' version) or a toned-down alternative that avoids the 'spinning' effect (the 'green' version). Once briefed (by actor Gary Sinise), you enter the Preparation Room to learn your mission – a flight to Mars. And then it's into the ride vehicle – capsules that close down tightly with outer doors, shoulder restraints and screens that move forward to just 18in/46cm from your face (this is NOT a good ride for those with claustrophobia or prone to motion sickness). The sense of realism, with the control consoles, individual speakers and countdown is magnificent.

ANNIVERSARY SPOT

20 Universe of Energy and The Land pavilions are the only ones still mainly intact from 20 years ago. All Epcot's other Future World pavilions have been closed, re-built or heavily re-themed.

For those on the full version, the blast-off feels VERY real as you experience some of the genuine forces of a rocket launch (thanks to its huge centrifuge, which is part-ride and part-simulator). Each member of the team has to perform their duties on cue and you experience a simulated sling-shot around the moon and on to Mars, where the landing is an adventure in itself. It's a truly original, aggressive ride, but you should heed the advice to keep your head still and look straight into the screen or you WILL feel sick (unless you are on the tamer version, where the capsules just tilt and turn). We think the full-on experience is too intense for young children, and there is no backing out once you blast off (parents could try it first), while it is definitely not for expectant mothers. **R: 3ft 8in/112cm. TTTTT FP**

Spaceship Earth

As you exit the ride, there is an elaborate post-show and activities. **Space Base** is an excellent play area for children who can't ride (and those who just like to climb, slide and crawl); **Space Race** is a great game for 2 teams of 60 players to propel a rocket back to Earth via a series of on-screen challenges; **Expedition Mars** is a computer game to rescue stranded astronauts; and, in **Postcards from Space**, you can email a 'space video' to friends and family. There is then the inevitable (and well-stocked) gift shop. All in all, it's a terrific experience.

Test Track: This equally big-scale production – a 5½min whirl along Disney's longest, fastest track – was extensively rethemed in 2012 to offer a journey into the world of Chevrolet car design and technology. It starts with an interactive queue that invites riders to design their own car according to Capability, Efficiency, Responsiveness and Power, which they then carry on to their prototype vehicle. Once aboard, it is off through an elaborate digital computer world of performance tests, with the car put through its paces on hair-pin bends, rough-road surfaces, extremes of heat and cold and a final high-speed section outside the building at up to 67mph/108kph! Each guest's car design is computer tested alongside the vehicle and scored according to how it fares. The final post-ride area is set up to show more about the testing process and its 4 key design elements. The vivid lighting, which makes you feel as if you're inside a computer (like the film Tron), sharp twists and turns and other special effects add up to a unique whirl through this high-tech world (complete with Chevy gift shop), but it does draw BIG queues and the FP+ option can run out well in advance during busy seasons. If you're on your own or don't mind your family being split up, the Single Rider option is handy here. **R:** 3ft 4in/101cm. **TTTT** (TTT teens) **FP+1**

The Odyssey Center: Baby-care, first-aid, telephones and restrooms.

Imagination!: The 2-part attraction here starts with Journey into Imagination with Figment, an uneven but quirky ride into experiments with imagination in the company of Eric Idle (as Dr Nigel Channing of the Imagination Institute) and the cartoon dragon Figment. The sight laboratory sees Figment having fun with a vision chart, the sound lab is a symphony of imaginative melodies and Figment's house is a truly topsy-turvy world (watch out for the skunk in the smell lab!). It's gentle fun and rarely draws a crowd. **AAA FP+** You exit into **Image Works – The 'What If' Labs**, an interactive playground of sight and sound, which usually amuses kids more than adults (though you might be tempted to buy various cartoon images and select your-own CDs).

Captain EO: Come out and turn right for an encore presentation of this fun 3-D musical film show starring Michael Jackson, which originally debuted in Epcot in 1986 but was replaced by Honey I Shrunk The Audience in 1994. Now digitally remastered and sound enhanced, it is a 17min romp through space as Captain EO and his band of ragtag renegades set out to save the universe by bringing a special gift to the evil Supreme Leader. Jackson's signature dancing and the show's We Are Here To Change The World message keep the tone upbeat, but some of the darker thematic elements may frighten young children. It's a visually thrilling trip down memory lane for Disney fans, as good conquers evil – naturally! **AAAA FP+** Outside, kids are always fascinated by the Jellyfish and

Test Track

© Floridaleisureblog.com

PRESENTED BY **CHEVROLET**

Serpentine Fountains that send water squirting from pond to pond. Have your cameras ready!

The Land: This pavilion combines 3 elements for an entertaining but educational experience on food and nutrition – plus the spectacular thrill-ride of Soarin'. **Living with the Land** is an informative 14min boat ride well worth the sometimes long queue. A journey through food production may sound dull, but it is informative and enjoyable, with plenty to make children sit up and take notice of its 3 ecological communities, especially the greenhouse finale. AAAA FP+ After the ride, you can also take the **Behind the Seeds** 1hr guided tour through the greenhouse complex and learn more about Disney's horticultural projects ($20 adults, $16 3–9s). FP+

The Circle of Life: This 15min animated tale features characters from The Lion King explaining ecological concerns that are easily digestible for kids. Queues are rare. AA

Soarin'

Soarin'™: One of Disney's most imaginative attractions, this 'flight simulator' offers an exhilarating ride for all ages, a breathtaking swoop over Californian icons, complete with 'aromavision' (smell those orange groves!). An elaborate queuing area leads to the departure lounge, with passengers embarking on rows of seats that are hoisted into the air over a giant screen. The feeling is like taking a hang-glider ride as the special film, sounds and scents become all-encompassing. Feet dangling, you soar over the Golden Gate Bridge, sweep through a redwood forest and glide above Napa Valley. The finale includes a close encounter with a Disney theme park in Los Angeles! The ride's realism, magnificent music and superb technology ensure a 5-star experience – but also long queues. FastPass+ may be difficult to secure on the day, so be sure to book well in advance or visit early. **R:** 3ft 4in/101cm. AAAAA FP+1

Dining: The **Sunshine Seasons** Food Court offers the chance to eat some of Disney's home-grown produce, while the **Garden Grill** restaurant is a slowly revolving platform that offers more traditional food, including roast meats, pasta, seafood and a vegetarian selection, all in the company of Mickey, Goofy, Pluto and Chip 'n' Dale.

BRITTIP

Anyone looking for organic or gluten-free treats and snacks should look for the selection on offer at the entrance to the Sunshine Seasons food court.

The Seas with Nemo & Friends: This pavilion does for the oceans what The Land does for terra firma, in the company of the characters from the Pixar film *Finding Nemo*. You start with the signature ride, The Seas With Nemo and Friends, which takes riders on an underwater journey in 'clam-mobiles' to meet Nemo and Co (who are brilliantly interwoven into the huge aquarium, apparently swimming with the real fish!). Nemo has gone missing (again), hence the ride becomes a quest to reunite him with teacher Mr Ray and the rest of the class in a rousing musical finale. **AAAA FP+** You then exit into **Sea Base**, a 2-level development offering 6 modules presenting stories of undersea exploration and marine life, including a research centre that provides a close encounter with the endangered manatee. Plenty of interactive elements and educational touch-screens are on offer, plus additional tanks displaying Caribbean reef fish, jellyfish and cuttlefish, while there is an excellent demonstration of a diving chamber. Crowds are steady, but queues rarely get too long – with one exception. **Turtle Talk With Crush** is a brilliantly interactive meet-and-greet with the surfer dude turtle and his friend Dory from the film Finding Nemo. Crush is the star of the show as he swims up and engages children in the audience with some fun live banter. **AAAA FP+** Next door, **Bruce's Sub House** is a kids' play area including great photo opportunities with more of the Nemo characters (**TTT** under-6s). **Nemo and Friends** is more hands-on fun for kids, while **Mr Ray's Lagoon** showcases some real stingrays.

Dining: The pavilion includes the highly recommended **Coral Reef Restaurant** that serves great seafood, as well as providing a grandstand view of the massive aquarium. Dinner will be $26.48–45.98 (starter and main), depending on your choices, which isn't cheap, but the food is first class (kids' menu $8.99–10.99).

Spaceship Earth: Spiralling up 18 storeys, this attraction is a convincing time-travel story into various technologies narrated by Dame Judi Dench. From cave paintings to the internet (with a superb depiction of Michelangelo's Sistine Chapel), the gentle ride unfolds in imaginative historical stages, culminating in an interactive finale that invites riders to 'predict' the future. Sponsor Siemens (the electronics giant) has added a post-show interactive demonstration area (including predictive surgery and a driving challenge), which makes for an entertaining diversion after

the 15min ride. Queues are heavy all morning, but almost non-existent late in the day. **AAAA FP+**

Innoventions: These 2 centres of hands-on exhibits are fun and educational, with interactive exercises into things like recycling, fire prevention and energy use, as well as future technologies and some of the latest video games. **Innoventions East:** Don't miss **The Sum of All Thrills** experience, where budding mathematicians and engineers can design and create their own ride using physics principles and touchscreen technology. Then, hop aboard the motion simulator for a hair-raising ride! **R:** 4ft/122cm for non-inversion ride, 4ft 6in/138cm with inversions. **TTT**. Other novelties include **Test the Limits Lab**, **Vision House** (a 15min walk through new home technologies) and **Storm Struck** (experience a violent storm from a special viewing theatre). New in 2013 was **Habit Heroes**, a clever series of interactive games that focus on healthy eating habits and encourage guests to have a more active lifestyle (although most kids just want to play the games!), with computers outside to record your own 'secret code'. **AA Innoventions West:** Kids tend to gravitate to the selection of free Disney video games but parents will probably enjoy **THINK – by IBM**, a short film and interactive

China pavilion

stations demonstrating how progress is shaped. Worth waiting for is the 20min **Where's The Fire?**, an interactive game exploring home fire hazards, with a race against the clock to extinguish pretend fires. For those concerned about their finances, the humorous **Great Piggy Bank Adventure** teaches the importance of setting financial goals and saving.

BRITTIP

Innoventions East and West are good places in which to spend time if you need to cool down, or if it's raining. They are usually quiet in the afternoon, too.

Other entertainment: Live fun is also provided periodically around Future World by the unique **JAMMitors** percussion group, while the **Epcot Character Spot** (across from Innoventions West, 9am–9pm at peak times, 10am–6pm off-peak, FP+1) offers a fabulous themed meet-and-greet with many Disney characters. Daisy Duck and Goofy can often be found just inside the main entrance. The majestic **Plaza Fountain** choreographs to musical performances every 15min.

Dining and shopping: Food outlets include the counter-service **Electric Umbrella Restaurant** for lunch and dinner (sandwiches, burgers and salads) and the **Fountainview Café** for signature Starbucks coffees, cold drinks, pastries and sandwiches. Look out also for **Club Cool** presented by Coca-Cola®, where you can enjoy international Coke products and souvenirs, along with various free tastes from around the world (beware

Restaurant Akershus

the Beverly!). For shopping, **Mouse Gear** in Innoventions East features a massive variety of Epcot and Disney merchandise (and don't miss the wacky ceiling architecture!), while the **Art of Disney** features superb signature art and animator drawings.

World Showcase

If you found Future World amazing, prepare to be astounded by the equally imaginative pavilions around the World Showcase Lagoon. Each features a glimpse of a different country in dramatic settings. Several have rides or films to showcase their main features, while the restaurants offer some outstanding fare and many character greeting spots can be found in each country (check the daily Times Guide for locations and timings).

Agent P's World Showcase Adventure: 11am–8.15pm. look out for the sign-up station for this interactive and highly family-friendly challenge game, based on the *Phineas & Ferb* TV series, on the bridge over to World Showcase (and with other stations at International Gateway, Norway and Italy). With the aid of the Field Operative Notification Equipment (or FONE), guest 'agents' follow the clues around each World Showcase pavilion to help the boys' pet platypus Perry (Agent P) in his bid to foil his nemesis Dr Doofenschmirtz. Complete all the tasks on your FONE and you foil the evil Dr and free Perry from his predicament.

BRITTIP

Disney's cuddly character, Duffy the Bear, meets and greets guests in his own location just after you enter World Showcase, turning left toward Mexico.

Mexico: Starting at the bottom left of the circular tour of the lagoon and moving clockwise, your first encounter is inside the spectacular pyramid of Mexico. Here you have the amusing boat ride Gran Fiesta Tour Starring The Three Caballeros, a 9min journey through the people and history of the country with Donald

Duck, Panchito and José Carioca as your guides. Queues build up in mid-afternoon but are usually light otherwise. **AAA**

Other entertainment: As in all of the World Showcase pavilions, there is live entertainment, with periodic 25min music shows from **Mariachi Cobre**, while **Donald Duck** puts in character appearances.

Dining and shopping: Much of the pavilion comprises market-style gift shops, while the **San Angel Inn** is a romantic Mexican restaurant and **La Cava del Tequila** has tempting cocktails, light bites and signature tequilas. Outside, choose from the revamped counter service **Cantina de San Angel** (open-air lunch from 11am, serving tacos, nachos and tortillas) and full-service **La Hacienda de San Angel** (dinner from 4pm) serving a rich variety of authentic Mexican fare with a superb lagoon view and grandstand seat for the nightly IllumiNations show. This gets our thumbs-up as a stand-out choice.

Norway: Next up is the best ride in World Showcase, the Viking-themed **Maelstrom**. This 4-min longboat trip through Norway's history and scenery features a short waterfall drop and a North Sea storm. It attracts longish queues from early afternoon, so the best tactic is to go soon after World Showcase's 11am opening or use FP+. **TTT FP+1** There is an engaging Viking-themed exhibit in the reconstructed **Stave Church** while the pavilion is designed as a reproduction of Oslo's Akershus Fortress.

◀◀▶ **BRITTIP**

If you can't get a booking for Cinderella's Royal Table in the Magic Kingdom, the Akershus Royal Banquet (8.30am–8.30pm; $42–48 for adults, and $25–26 kids 3–9) is the next best thing and should keep most young 'princesses' happy! Call 407 939 3463 up to 180 days in advance or book online at **www.disneyworld.com**.

Dining and shopping: The **Akershus Royal Banquet Hall** offers the

Princess Storybook dining for breakfast, lunch and dinner, complete with a host of Disney Princesses, while the **Kringla Bakeri Og Kafé** serves sandwiches, pastries and drinks. **Puffin's Roost** is a large gift shop for all things Norwegian.

China: The spectacular landscapes of China are well served by the main attraction of this pavilion, the stunning **Reflections of China**, a 360° film in the circular Temple of Heaven. Here you are surrounded by the sights and sounds of one of the world's most enigmatic countries in an eye-catching production. Queues build up to 30mins during the main part of the day (but it is fully air-conditioned). **AAAA**

Other entertainment: Don't miss the periodic shows from the spectacular **Jeweled Dragon Acrobats** on the plaza in front of the temple, while Disney characters from *Mulan* also appear throughout the day.

Dining and shopping: Two restaurants, the **Nine Dragons** and the counter-service **Lotus Blossom Café** offer tastes of the Orient, while **Yong Feng Shangdian Dept Store** is a warehouse of Chinese gifts and artefacts.

The **Outpost** between China and Germany features hut-style shops and snacks, with crafts from Africa and the Caribbean.

Hotel du Canada

Germany: This provides more in the way of shopping and eating than entertainment, though you still find a magnificent re-creation of a Bavarian **Biergarten**, with lively **Oktoberfest** shows featuring the resident **Musikanten** brass band at regular intervals. It also offers hearty portions of German sausage, sauerkraut and rotisserie chicken. The **Sommerfest** is fast food German-style (bratwurst and strudel), while there are more shops (8 in all) than anywhere else in Epcot, including chocolates, wines, crystal, porcelain, toys and cuckoo clocks.

◀▮▶ BRITTIP

With seating for 400, Biergarten often takes walk-ups even when Disney's reservations system indicates the restaurant is full.

Other entertainment: An elaborate outdoor model railway is popular with children, and look out for character appearances from Snow White.

Italy: Similarly, Italy has pretty, authentic architecture, including a superb reproduction of Venice's St Mark's Square, 3 gift shops stocking wine, chocolates, Armani collectables, fine crystal, porcelain and Venetian masks, and 2 full-service restaurants. **Tutto Italia** is the fine dining option, designed like the Medici Palace, complete with a gluten-free menu and a splendid cellar-style wine bar, **Tutto Gusto**, that offers small plates and light bites (reservations not required for the wine bar), while the superb **Via Napoli** is a delightfully

China pavilion

authentic pizzeria, featuring wood-burning ovens and genuine Neapolitan style, with 300 seats, including an outdoor terrace.

Other entertainment: Watch out for the fun entertainment of **Sergio**, a madcap juggler who loves to involve his audience.

The American Adventure: At the top of the lagoon and dominating World Showcase is this huge edifice, not so much a pavilion as a celebration of the country's history and Constitution. A colonial Fife & Drum Corps and wonderful singing group add authentic sounds to the 18th-century setting, overlooked by a reproduction of Philadelphia's Liberty Hall. Inside, you have the **American Adventure** show, a magnificent ½hr film and audio-animatronic production that details the country's founding, its struggles and triumphs, presidents, statesmen and heroes. It's a glossy, patriotic display, featuring some outstanding technology and, while some of it will be unfamiliar to foreign visitors, it's difficult not to be impressed. A good choice at most times of the day – and it's all in the cool! AAAA If you have time to spare, check out the special exhibitions in the **American Heritage Gallery**.

Other entertainment: Superb *à capella* group **Voices of Liberty** appear in the pavilion's rotunda several times a day, while the **Spirit of America Fife & Drum Corps** put on a show out front. The **America Gardens Theater**, next to the lagoon, presents concerts from international artists during the Flower & Garden Festival, Sounds Like Summer series and Food & Wine Festival.

Dining and shopping: Antiques and handcarts provide touches of nostalgia, along with the **Heritage Manor Gifts** store, while **Liberty Inn** offers fast-food lunch and dinner.

Japan: Next up on the clockwise tour, you are introduced to typical Japanese style and architecture, including a five-storey 8th century Pagoda, some magnificent art exhibits, notably in the **Bijutsu-kan**

Gallery, featuring art and insights into Japanese history and culture, a tranquil Bonsai garden (complete with carp pond) and landmark Torii gate.

Other entertainment: Live shows are key here, with periodic presentations from the superb **Matsuriza** taiko drummers.

Dining and shopping: Great food is a real highlight, and the restaurant line-up consists of the wonderful fine dining of **Teppan Edo** (with its traditional chefs at each table) and **Tokyo Dining**, a venue featuring typical cuisine and ingredients, showcasing sushi and innovative presentation. **Katsura Grill** is its fast-food equivalent, with great soups, teriyaki and sushi dishes while the **Garden House** serves sake, beer, plum wine, tea and soft drinks. The huge **Mitsukoshi** store adds fascinating shopping, from traditional calligraphy, tea kettles and wind chimes to Hello Kitty souvenirs.

Morocco: As you would expect, this is another shopping experience, with bazaars, alleyways and stalls selling a well-priced array of carpets, leather goods, clothing, brass ornaments, pottery and antiques. All the building materials were faithfully imported for the pavilion, which was hand-built to give Morocco a greater degree of authenticity, even by World Showcase's high standards. **The Gallery of Arts and History** offers more historical and cultural insights, while the **Fez House** depicts a typical Moroccan home.

Other entertainment: Characters from Disney's *Aladdin* appear from time to time, while live musical show **MoRockin'** presents a variety of Arabic rhythms in fun style, including an eye-catching belly-dancer!

Dining: Restaurant Marrakesh provides a full dining experience, complete with traditional musicians and their own belly dancer. It's rather pricey but the lively atmosphere is entertaining. Better value can be had at **Tangierine Café**, with its healthy array of roast lamb, hummus, tabbouleh, couscous, lentil salad and Moroccan breads ($8.99–14.99; kids' meals $7.99). New in 2014 was **Spice Road Table**, a clever indoor/outdoor café and bar offering superb small-plate meals and snacks with a Mediterranean style, including two samplers at $16 each, plus signature cocktails and other drinks, all with a great Lagoon view (select tables are ideal for the nightly IllumiNations show).

BRITTIP

The Tangierine Café in Morocco is a peaceful haven in which to enjoy a quiet, healthy lunch, especially if you are vegetarian, plus there is a tempting coffee and pastry counter.

France: Predictably overlooked by a replica Eiffel Tower, this is a clean and cheerful pre-World War I Paris, with comedy street theatre adding to the rather dreamy atmosphere and pleasant gardens, plus stylish shopping and great dining options. Don't miss **Impressions de France**, a big-film production that serves up all the grandest sights of the country to the music of Offenbach, Debussy, Saint-Saëns and Satie. Crowds get quite heavy from mid-day. AAAA

Other entertainment: Look out for the visual comedy and amazing balancing act of **Serveur Amusant** (not when it's too windy), while Princess Aurora (Sleeping Beauty) makes regular appearances, along with *Beauty and the Beast* characters and Marie from *The Aristocats*.

Mexico pavilion

Dining and shopping: This is THE pavilion for a gastronomic experience provided by 3 restaurants, of which **Les Chefs de France** and **Monsieur Paul** are major discoveries. The former is a classic, full-service establishment featuring top-quality French cuisine for lunch and dinner, while the latter, upstairs, is named (and themed) for famous chef Paul Bocuse, with his well-trained team in charge of both. Monsieur Paul is a touch more formal and upscale, with a 4-course prix fixe menu ($89/person), and, while an expensive meal (dinner only; appetisers from $14–29 and main courses $38–42), it is a truly fabulous choice. Also here is the **Les Halles Boulangerie Patisserie**, a genuine French patisserie featuring authentic freshly-made baguettes, croissants, salads, quiches and wonderful pastries, and **L'Artisan des Glaces**, an artisan ice-cream and sorbet shop, with everything made fresh in-house every day (and with liqueur treats for grown-ups!). Shopping is suitably chic, with an authentic **Wine Shop** and elegant **Guerlain** and **Givenchy** perfumeries (ask about the free perfume tour during the Flower and Garden Festival).

BRITTIP

The special dining events in the France pavilion are often the highlight of the annual Food & Wine Festival and are worth signing up for.

United Kingdom: The least inspiring of all the pavilions, and certainly with little to entertain those who have ever visited a pub or shopped for Royal Doulton or Burberry goods, it is partly offset by some good live entertainment and pleasant gardens, but that is about it.

Other entertainment: Live music is provided by **British Revolution**, offering the sounds of the 60s, 70s and 80s up to 5 times a day, while the **Pub Musician** performs several times daily and the lively **World Showcase Players** add madcap street theatre. Mary Poppins, Winnie the Pooh, Tigger and Alice in Wonderland can also be found here.

Dining and shopping: The **Rose and Crown Pub** is antiseptically authentic but you can get better elsewhere at these prices (grilled sirloin steak $26.99, bangers and mash $14.99 or fish and chips $14.99, and a pint of Bass for a whopping $8.50). There's also a takeaway **Yorkshire County** fish and chippie. The best shops are the **Tea Caddy**, the **Queen's Table**, **Crown and Crest** (perfumes and heraldry), **Sportsman Shoppe** (sweaters, kilts, football shirts) and **Toy Soldier** (traditional games and toys), but prices are WAY above what you'd pay at home.

Canada: Completing the World Showcase circle, the main features here are Victoria Gardens, based on the world-famous Butchart

Mission: Space

EPCOT with children

Here is our rough guide to the attractions that appeal to different age groups:

Under-5s
Circle of Life, Gran Fiesta Tour Starring The Three Caballeros, Journey into Imagination with Figment, Kidcot stops, Living with the Land, The Seas with Nemo and Friends, Soarin'™ (if tall enough), Spaceship Earth, Turtle Talk with Crush, Universe of Energy.

5–8s
All the above, plus The American Adventure, Captain EO (with parental discretion), Image Works, Innoventions, JAMMitors, Maelstrom, Test Track, Agent P's World Showcase Adventure.

9–12s
All the above, plus Impressions de France, Matsuriza Drummers, Mission: SPACE, O Canada!, Sergio, Le Serveur Amusant, Reflections of China.

Over-12s
Living with the Land, The Seas with Nemo and Friends, Soarin'™, Spaceship Earth, Universe of Energy, The American Adventure, Captain EO, Innoventions, JAMMitors, Maelstrom, Test Track, Impressions de France, Matsuriza Drummers, Mission: SPACE, O Canada!, Reflections of China, Bijutsu-kan Gallery, Off Kilter (Canada).

Gardens on Vancouver Island, some spectacular Rocky Mountain scenery, a replica French gothic mansion, the Hôtel de Canada, and another stunning 360° film, **O Canada!** As with China and France, this showcases the country's sights and scenery in a terrific, 17min advert for the Canadian Tourist Board led by comedian Martin Short. It's at its busiest in late afternoon. AAA

Other entertainment: Resident band **Off Kilter** are one of the most entertaining acts we've seen anywhere and they perform 30min sets up to 5 times a day. Want to hear rock 'n' roll bagpipes? This is the group for you!

BRITTIP

Best way to tour World Showcase? Start in Canada and continue anticlockwise or jump on the Friendship Boats and go straight to Italy or Morocco.

Dining and shopping: Le Cellier Steakhouse is an excellent dining room, offering great steaks, prime rib, seafood, chicken and several vegetarian dishes for lunch and dinner. **The Trading Post** and **Northwest Mercantile** provide a range of Canadian clothing and

souvenirs, notably wonderful glass ornaments, Deauville perfume – and Off Kilter CDs!

IllumiNations: Reflections of Earth

The day's big finale and an absolute show-stopper, this firework and special-effects extravaganza is awesome even by Disney standards. British composer Gavin Greenaway provided the original music for a 15min performance of vivid brilliance. Some 2,800 firework shells are launched as a celestial backdrop to a series of fire-and-

Epcot monorail

water effects on the World Showcase Lagoon. The central icon is a 28ft/9m video globe of Earth that opens in a spectacular climax of choreographed pyrotechnics. However, people start staking out the best lagoon-side spots up to 2 HOURS in advance. FP+1 for special viewing area. The ultimate way to view IllumiNations is by private boat on one of 2 speciality cruises from Disney's Boardwalk or Yacht and Beach Club Resorts, and the Grand Floridian (for non-residents, too). The price range is $325–1148 per boat (holding 4–10 guests) and can be used for special celebrations. The Basic Cruise costs $325 and the boat holds up to 10. It includes water, soft drinks and snacks (call 407 824 2682 up to 90 days in advance to book).

Epcot After Hours Wind Down: Stay in the park after closing time, choosing from 4 lounges (Mexico, UK, Morocco, Italy) where 1 drink flight and small snacks add to the relaxed ambiance ($35pp, reservations and park admission required).

Behind-the-scenes tours

Epcot also has a big range of tours. Book all tours on 407 939 8687.

Dolphins in Depth: This is a 3hr dip into the research areas of The Seas pavilion, including a chance to meet the dolphins ($199, with refreshments, photo and T-shirt; 13–17s must be accompanied by an adult; swimming costume required).

Undiscovered Future World: A 4½hr journey into the creation of Epcot, Walt's vision for the resort and

Epcot's amazing IllumiNations show

backstage areas like IllumiNations ($64).

Behind the Seeds: This 1hr tour, every 45mins from 9.45am–4.30pm at The Land pavilion, looks at Disney's innovative gardening practices ($20 adults, $16 3–9s).

Dive Quest: A 3hr experience, with a 40min dive into The Seas aquarium, plus a backstage look at the facility at 4.30 and 5.30pm daily, Must have scuba certification; park admission not required ($175/person, 10 and over, includes T-shirt and certificate).

Seas Aqua Tour: A similar tour without the scuba diving, daily at 12.30pm ($140/person, 8 and over; under-18s must be accompanied by an adult).

Backstage Magic: The most comprehensive tour goes behind the scenes of Epcot, Magic Kingdom and Disney's Hollywood Studios on a 7hr foray into little-seen aspects, such as the backstage areas of the Studios and the tunnels below Magic Kingdom ($249, 16 and over).

Annual festivals

There are 2 main annual Epcot events to watch out for.

International Flower and Garden Festival: This literally puts the whole park in full bloom with an amazing series of set-pieces, topiaries, seminars and mini-exhibitions from early Mar to mid-May. All exhibits and some lectures are free, and they add a beautiful aspect to an already scenic park, along with new food kiosks around World Showcase that offer regional tastes and drinks.

Food and Wine Festival: From late Sept to around 12 Nov, this showcases national and regional cuisines, wines and beers, with the chance to attend grand Winemakers' Dinners and Tasting Events, or just sample the offerings of more than 20 food booths dotted around World Showcase. Both festivals also offer free concerts several times a day at the America Gardens Theater (weekends only for Flower & Garden).

Disney's Hollywood Studios

Welcome to a journey into the world of film and TV, an epic voyage of adventure, creation – and fun. Here you will learn plenty of tricks of the trade; movie-making secrets and behind-the-scenes glimpses that have been cleverly turned into rides, shows and other attractions with guaranteed entertainment appeal. Rather bigger than the Magic Kingdom at 154acres/62ha but smaller than Epcot, Disney's Hollywood Studios is a different experience yet again with its rather chaotic combination of attractions, street entertainment, film sets and smart gift shops. Like the Magic Kingdom, the food may not win awards, but some of the restaurants (notably the Sci-Fi Dine-in Theater and 50s Prime Time Café) have imaginative settings. The park also has more to occupy smaller children than Epcot, but you can still easily see most of it in a day unless the crowds are heavy.

Location

The entrance arrangements will be fairly familiar if you have already visited the other parks. Disney's Hollywood Studios is located on Buena Vista Drive (which runs between World Drive and Epcot Drive) and parking is $17. Remember to make a note of where you park before you catch the tram to the main gates, where you must wait for the official opening time. If the queues build up quickly, the gates will open early, so be ready for a running start.

Once through the gates, you are into Hollywood Boulevard, a street of gift shops, and you have to decide which of the main attractions to head for first, as these are the ones where the

Disney's Hollywood Studios at a glance

Location	Off Buena Vista Drive or World Drive, Walt Disney World		
Size	154 acres/62ha		
Hours	9am–7pm off peak; 9am–10pm high season (Easter, summer holidays, Thanksgiving and Christmas)		
Admission	Under-3s free; 3–9 $88 (1–day base ticket), $284 (5–day Magic Your Way), £264 (14–day Ultimate); adult (10+) $94, $304, £279. Prices do not include tax.		
Parking	$17		
Lockers	From the Crossroads kiosk through the main entrance; $12 small, $14 large ($5 deposit each)		
Pushchairs	$15 and $31 Oscar's Super Service Station; length of stay $91/week, $130 10 days, $189/$270 double		
Wheelchairs	$12 or $70 ($20 deposit refunded), from Oscar's		
Top attractions	Toy Story Mania, Twilight Zone™ Tower of Terror, Rock 'n' Roller Coaster Starring Aerosmith, Star Tours, The Great Movie Ride, Voyage of the Little Mermaid, Jim Henson's Muppet*Vision 3-D, Lights, Motors, Action!™ Extreme Stunt Show		
Don't miss	Indiana Jones™ Epic Stunt Spectacular, American Idol Experience, Fantasmic!		
Hidden costs	**Meals**	Burger, chips and coke $11.72 3-course lunch $37.73 (Mama Melrose's) Beer $5.50–8.50 Kids' meal $5.99	
	T-shirts	$21.95–36.95 Kids' T-shirts 19.95–27.95	
	Souvenirs	$1.45–5,000	
	Sundries	Special effects make-up $12.45	

1 The Great Movie Ride
2 American Idol Live!
3 Indiana JonesTM Epic Stunt Spectacular
4 Star Tours
5 Jim Henson's Muppet*Vision 3-D
6 Honey, I Shrunk the Kids Movie Set Adventure
7 Catastrophe Canyon on Disney's Hollywood Studios Backlot Tour
8 Studio Backlot Tour
9 The Legend of Captain Jack Sparrow
10 Toy Story Mania
11 Walt Disney: One Man's Dream
12 Voyage of the Little Mermaid
13 The Magic of Disney Animation
14 Disney Junior – Live on Stage!

15 Rock 'n' Roller Coaster Starring Aerosmith
16 The Twilight Zone™ Tower of Terror
17 Beauty and the Beast – Live on Stage
18 Fantasmic!
19 Guest Information Board
20 Toy Story Pizza Planet
21 Lights, Motors, Action!™ Extreme Stunt Show
22 Premier Theater
23 '50s Prime Time Café
24 Hollywood and Vine
25 Hollywood Brown Derby
26 Mama Melrose's
27 Sunset Ranch Market
28 Sci-Fi Dine-in Theater Restaurant

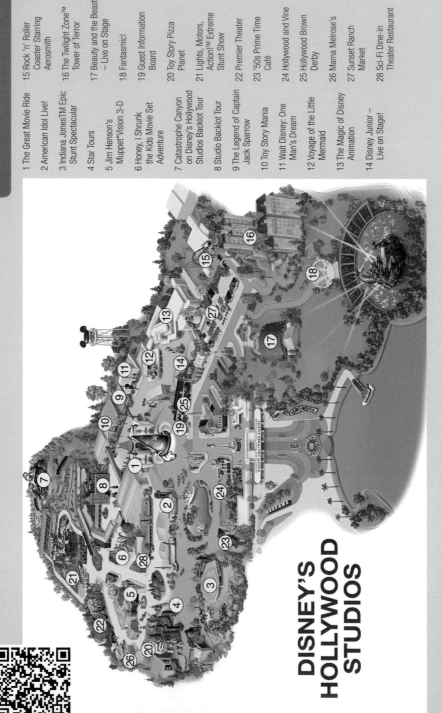

DISNEY'S HOLLYWOOD STUDIOS

queues will be heaviest most of the day. Try to ignore the lure of the shops as it is better to browse in the early afternoon when the attractions are at their busiest.

BRITTIP

It is crucial to schedule your Hollywood Studios FastPass+ times 60 days in advance if you are staying onsite, or 30 days in advance if you are staying offsite. Main attraction Toy Story Mania books up well in advance.

Incidentally, if you thought Disney had elevated queuing to an art form in its other parks, wait until you see how clever they are here. Just when you think you have reached the ride itself, there is another twist to the queue you hadn't seen or an extra element to the ride that holds you up. The latter are 'holding pens', which are an ingenious way of making it seem you are being entertained instead of queuing. Look out for them in particular at the Great Movie Ride, Twilight Zone™ Tower of Terror and Jim Henson's Muppet*Vision 3-D.

The main attractions

The park is laid out in a rather more confusing fashion than its counterparts, with their neatly packaged 'lands', so have your map handy to keep your bearings.

Beating the queues: The opening-gate crowds will all surge in one of 3 directions, which will give you a pretty good idea of where you want to go. By far the biggest attraction here is **Toy Story Mania**, and it's important to head here first if you don't have a FastPass+ time scheduled. The other crowd-pullers are **Twilight Zone™ Tower of Terror**, a magnificent haunted hotel ride that ends in a 13-storey drop in a lift, where queues hit 2hrs at peak periods, and **Rock 'n' Roller Coaster Starring Aerosmith**. Head straight up Hollywood Boulevard, turn right into Sunset Boulevard and you'll see it them at the end of the street. They are both FP+ rides (p101).

Star Tours, the remodelled Star Wars™ simulator ride is another of the park's serious queue-builders (and, happily, also a FP+ attraction). If you are not up for the really big thrills, grab a FP+ for **Toy Story Mania** if there are any available, then head for Star Tours (across the main square past the Indiana Jones™ show). After Star Tours and Toy Story Mania, another gentler experience (and also worth doing early on) is the hysterical **Muppet*Vision 3-D** show, which is another big draw later in the day. It has the benefit of being air-conditioned, too, for when you need a rest. The park's big stunt show, **Lights, Motors, Action!™ Extreme Stunt Show**, plays 2–3 times a day and is a good one to catch early on or later in the day.

One other thing to watch for in late afternoon if you love to meet the characters is an unscheduled meet-and-greet held in one of 3 locations from around 4.45–6.20pm and featuring up to 8 well-known and lesser seen characters (from Jafar and Captain Hook to the Queen of Hearts and Stitch). Ask about it inside the Magic of Disney Animation (at the end of the attraction, where the other characters are on show; you can also enter via the back of the Animation Gallery shop), or on the Streets of America or around Echo Lake.

The Magic of Disney Animation

Hollywood Boulevard

Moving around the park in a (roughly) clockwise direction, you start in the Hollywood Boulevard area. As with the Magic Kingdom, your entry here is along a street of shops and services that are best visited in early afternoon when it's busier elsewhere. Immediately to the left through the turnstiles are the Guest Relations and First Aid offices, plus the Baby Care centre. An up-to-the-minute check on queue times at the attractions is kept on a Guest Information Board on Hollywood Boulevard, just past its junction with Sunset Boulevard, where you can also book restaurants. To the right is Oscar's Station for pushchair and wheelchair hire, while locker hire is obtained at the Crossroads kiosk in front of you.

The Great Movie Ride: This faces you (behind the Hat icon) as you walk in along Hollywood Boulevard and is a good place to start if the crowds are not too serious. An all-star audio-animatronics cast re-creates a number of box office smashes, including Jimmy Cagney's *Public Enemy*, Julie Andrews in *Mary Poppins*, Gene Kelly in *Singin' in the Rain* and many more masterful set-pieces as you undertake your conducted tour. Young children may find the menace of *The Alien* too strong, but otherwise the ride has universal appeal and features some clever live twists (there are 2 variations on this ride, a cowboy and a gangster version – ask a Cast Member if there's one you especially want to do). AAAA FP+

Other entertainment: A series of **Citizens of Hollywood** acts enliven Hollywood Boulevard throughout the day, staging impromptu movie shoots, casting calls or even detective investigations. Have fun with them – you just might end up the star of the show! Also by the Hat, look out for **Disney characters** during the morning.

Shopping and dining: Hollywood Boulevard has the best of the park's shopping (9 of the 21 stores), including **Sid Caheunga's One-of-a-Kind** (rare movie and TV items, including celebrity autographs), **Keystone Clothiers** (some of the best apparel), **Mickey's of Hollywood** (all your souvenirs and gift items) and **The Darkroom** (for camera items). **The Brown Derby** is the park's signature restaurant, offering fine dining in best vintage Hollywood style (reservations usually necessary).

On the Streets of America

Star Tours

Echo Lake

Turn left out of Hollywood Boulevard
and you find another area that pays
homage to the movie world of the
1930s and 40s.

American Idol Experience: An
exciting audience participation
show based on the TV reality series.
Guest performers undergo the full
Idol experience, from audition to
preparation (with a vocal coach and
hair and make-up artists) to the
performance, with those who score
highest returning for an end-of-day
Grand Finale show. The show features
3 contestants with varying degrees
of talent (from 'exceptional' to 'good
sport') and, while the judges' critiques
are a bit canned, the experience is
suitably realistic. *NB: This attraction
will close in Jan 2015.* AAA FP+

**Indiana Jones™ Epic Stunt
Spectacular:** Consult your park
Times Guide for the various times
this stunt cavalcade hits the stage. A
special movie set creates 3 different
backdrops for Indiana Jones'™ stunt
people to put on a dazzling array of
scenes and special effects from the
films. Audience participation is an
element and there are some amusing
sub-plots. Queues for the 30min show
begin up to ½hr beforehand, but the
auditorium holds more than 2,000 so
everyone usually gets in. TTTT FP+

Star Tours: The popular Star Wars™
simulator ride has had a complete
revamp, returning in 3-D as The
Adventure Continues. Climb into
your StarSpeeder 1000 for a stunning
high-speed journey through the
worlds created by George Lucas in
his award-winning films, including
Coruscant, Naboo, Kashyyyk (the
Wookiee planet) and Tatooine,
where riders blast into the Boonta
Eve Classic Podrace with convincing
and dramatic results. New robot
characters AC-38 ('Ace') and Aly San
San prepare you for your flight, but
predictably it all goes wrong, and
droids R2-D2 and C-3PO must save
your Speeder from disaster as they
evade the Imperial Forces and a very
determined bounty hunter. Master
Yoda, Boba Fett, Darth Vader and a
new branch of stormtroopers, called
'Skytroopers', join the pursuit, and
you never know how it will all work
out. With the option to change the
story at 4 points, making for 54 ride
options, the repeat factor here is
huge! The realism of the Star Wars™
world, from the queue to the post-
ride gift shop, is brilliant and lots of
fun. **R:** 3ft 4in/101cm, no under-3s.
TTTT AAAAA FP+

50s Prime Time Café

Other entertainment: Kids should make a beeline for the **Jedi Training Academy**, on the stage outside the Star Tours ride up to 8 times a day. Here, young Jedi hopefuls get to try their light sabre technique under the eyes of a Jedi master, before taking on Darth Vader himself. Great fun just to watch, too (**TTTT** for under-12s).

There are ongoing rumours of a major Star Wars expansion, but no confirmation as yet. Watch this space!

Shopping and dining: Shop for Star Wars™ goods at **Tatooine Traders** (at the exit to Star Tours) and Indiana Jones souvenirs at the **Indy Truck and Adventure Outpost**. There are also 3 good dining choices: the **'50s Prime Time Café** is a fun experience as you sit in mock stage sets from 1950s American TV sitcoms and eat meals 'just like Mom used to make' (the waiters all claim to be your aunt, uncle or cousin and warn you to take your elbows off the table – good fun!); the **Backlot Express** features superb burgers, hot dogs and sandwiches, while a varied buffet dinner is served up at **Hollywood & Vine** in addition to the Play 'n Dine character breakfast and lunch with the Disney Junior Pals, available from 8am–2.25pm ($24–32 adults, $14–17 3–9s).

Streets of America

Three of the park's bigger attractions can all be found here, along with an often-overlooked gem of a restaurant.

Muppet*Vision 3-D: The 3-D is crossed out here and 4-D substituted in its place, so be warned strange things are about to happen! A wonderful 10min holding-pen pre-show takes you into the Muppet Theater for a 20min experience with all of the Muppets, 3-D special effects and more – when Fozzie Bear points his squirty flower at you, prepare to get wet! It's a gem, and the kids love it. Queues build up through the main parts of the day, but Disney's queuing expertise makes them seem shorter. **AAAAA FP+**

Honey, I Shrunk the Kids Movie Set Adventure: This adventure playground gives youngsters the chance to tackle massive blades of grass that turn out to be slides, crawl through caves, investigate giant mushrooms and more. There can be long queues here, so arrive early if the kids demand it. **TTTT** under-10s.

Premier Theater: This fully enclosed theatre is used for the Star Wars™ Weekend meet and greets and other set-piece special events.

Backlot Express

Lights, Motors, Action!™ Extreme Stunt Show: A direct import from the Walt Disney Studios in Paris, this is one of the most remarkable shows you will see anywhere, full of genuine high-risk stunts featuring cars, motorbikes, jet-skis and stuntmen of all kinds, that will leave you shaking your head in amazement. The magnificently crafted set is based on a Mediterranean village and seating starts 30min prior to a show. There is some amusing pre-show chat before the serious stuff starts, when you are treated to a 33min extravaganza of daredevil stunts, with a Car Ballet sequence, a Motorbike Chase and a Grand Finale that features some surprise pyrotechnics to complete an awesome presentation (keep your eyes on the windows below the video screen at the end). Each scene – featuring a secret-agent and various baddies – is explained by a movie director and the results of each shoot are played back on screen to show how the effects were created.

BRITTIP
If you have young children, be aware there is some (loud) mock gunfire in the Lights, Motors, Action!™ Extreme Stunt Show, which can upset sensitive ears, while the motorbike scene includes a rider catching fire, which can be frightening for them, too.

All the cars were specially built by Vauxhall and there are some extra tricks between the main scenes. It was all designed by Frenchman Rémy Julienne, the doyen of film car stunt sequences from James Bond films *Goldeneye* and *Licence to Kill* and other action epics like *The Rock, Gone in 60 Seconds* and *Enemy of the State*. The exit can be quite a scrum, though, as 5,000 people have to leave together, and it can take 15mins to clear the auditorium, hence if you can sit towards the front, you will be out quicker. Because it involves so much live co-ordination, it makes for a thrilling experience and you may want to see it more than once – another reason to see it early on. **TTTTT FP+**

Studio Backlot Tour: Before you board the special trams for a look at the off-limits part of the studios in this 35min walk-and-ride tour, you are treated to some special effects (involving an amusing water tank with a mock Pearl Harbor attack). The tram takes you round the production backlot and then to Catastrophe Canyon for a demonstration of special effects that try both to drown you and blow you up! **AAA TTTT** You exit into the American Film Institute showcase of costumes and props from recent films.

BRITTIP
Don't queue for the Backlot Tour when Lights, Motors, Action! has just ended – it will be far too crowded.

Other entertainment: Live music is provided periodically on the main street by the spectacular comedy rock band **Mulch, Sweat and Shears** (**AAA**; sometimes in front of the Sorcerer's Hat at the top of Hollywood Boulevard), while this is also a great place to meet **Disney characters** – look for *Cars* friends Lightning McQueen and Tow Mater at Luigi's Garage, and a *Monsters University* set-piece starring Sulley and Mike from the 2013 movie prequel in the building to the right of Lights, Motors, Action! Extreme Stunt Show. Disney TV stars Phineas & Ferb can be found near Luigi's Garage.

Phineas and Ferb

Toy Story Midway Mania

Shopping and dining: Shop for Christmas items at **It's A Wonderful Shop**, **Stage 1 Company Store** for Muppet and Sesame Street souvenirs and **Writer's Stop** for books and speciality coffees. **Mama Melrose's Ristorante Italiano** is a wonderful table-service Italian option (one of our favourites), while there are also the counter-service offerings of **Toy Story Pizza Planet** (average pizza, salads and drinks) and **Studio Catering Co.** (sandwiches, chicken wraps, salads and its own bar – with beer $7.50–8.50, wine $6.95–7.50 and cocktails $8.50–10.75).

Pixar Place

Commissary Lane

This is just a small link between the Streets of America and the central plaza by the Sorcerer's Hat, and contains only 2 eating opportunities. The **Sci-Fi Dine-In Theater Restaurant** is a big hit with kids as you dine in a mock drive-in cinema, with cars as tables, car-hop waitresses and a big film screen showing old black-and-white science-fiction movie clips. The menu features gourmet burgers, ribs, chicken, pasta and sandwiches, as well as signature milkshakes and sodas ($31.47 for 3-course lunch, $8.99 kids' meal). The counter-service option **ABC Commissary** serves up a multi-ethnic choice that includes a chicken curry, Cuban sandwich and Asian salad.

Pixar Place

This area is styled after the real-life Pixar film studios in California, and houses one of the most popular rides.

Toy Story Midway Mania: A real family fun fiesta, a 3-D ride into a fantasy fairground of games with the *Toy Story* characters. To start with you are 'shrunk' to toy-size and board carnival vehicles (each equipped with individual spring-action shooters) to go through Andy's Bedroom, where the toys have set up a Midway Games Play Set with 5 challenges, plus a practice round. Thanks to a pair of

3D glasses, riders can 'see' everything their shooter fires at the sequence of targets (while, with the magic of Disney's special effects, they might also 'feel' objects whirring past as they burst out of the screens; and, if you hit a water balloon, watch out!). Throw virtual eggs at barnyard targets, launch darts at prehistoric balloon targets, break plates with baseballs, land rings on Buzz Lightyear's alien friends and finish up in Woody's Rootin' Tootin' Shootin' Gallery (with a bonus roundup) before totting up your scores and comparing with fellow riders. All the time, the Toy Story characters cheer you on (and pass on hints to boost your score, so it works for all abilities) and provide some amusing commentary. At times it is a touch raucous and chaotic, but kids are sure to love the shooting game element and the whole family can enjoy the amusing ride through the toys' world. Even the queuing area is fun, with a huge animatronic Mr Potato Head acting as a fairground barker to entertain while you wait (AAA TTTT FP+1). It draws some HUGE queues, so use the FastPass+ option here (it is crucial you book these as far in advance as possible).

Other entertainment: Look out for the *Toy Story* characters meet-and-greet here.

Shopping and dining: For souvenirs and gifts from your favourite Pixar films visit the **Camera Dept**, while **Hey Howdy Hey Take Away** offers counter-service ice-cream, snacks and drinks.

Animation Courtyard

Get ready for a series of wonderful family-friendly shows in this area of the park.

Voyage of the Little Mermaid: A 17min live performance that is primarily for children who have seen the Disney cartoon. It brings together a mix of actors, animation and puppetry to re-create the film's highlights. Parents will still enjoy the special effects, but queues tend to be long, so go early or late. There is also the likelihood you will get a little wet. AAA (AAAAA under-9s; FP+)

BRITTIP
Try to sit at least halfway back in the Mermaid Theatre, especially if you are with young children, as the stage front is a bit high.

The Legend of Captain Jack Sparrow: A walk-through experience into the world of the famous *Pirates of the Caribbean* film character. Telling the full story of Cap'n Jack himself (not just a 'behind-the-scenes' look, either), it adds to the pirate's story and surrounds guests with the whole world of the Johnny Depp character. AAA FP+

Voyage of the Little Mermaid

Walt Disney: One Man's Dream: This interactive show-and-tell exhibit chronicles Walt himself and his lifetime of accomplishments. From archive school records to a model of the Nautilus from *20,000 Leagues Under the Sea*, the story of the man behind the Mouse comes to vivid life. The homage ends with a preview of Disney's future developments, plus a 10min film encapsulating all Walt achieved and dreamed about. AAAA

The Magic of Disney Animation: An amusing and entertaining 30min show-and-tour through the making of cartoons. It starts with a theatrical performance by Mushu, the Eddie Murphy-voiced dragon from the film *Mulan*. From there, you exit into a hands-on area of interactive fun (especially for children); **Ink & Paint** is a colouring challenge; at **Sound Stage** you can try a voiceover; and **You're a Character** will tell you which Disney character you most resemble. From there, you have the choice of joining the **Animation Academy** for a tutored class in cartoon art or stopping for a meet and greet with Disney characters, including Mickey Mouse and *The Incredibles*. You exit via the **Animation Gallery**, which has some fabulous gifts. Queues are rarely serious, so it's a good afternoon choice. AAAA

Disney Junior – Live on Stage!: Mickey, Goofy, Donald and Daisy are throwing a surprise birthday party for Minnie, but need the help of friends like Jake and the Neverland Pirates, Doc McStuffins and Sofia the First to make this the best celebration ever. It's colourful and entertaining and pre-schoolers just love it. AA (AAAAA under-5s) FP+

Other entertainment: Youngsters can meet all their favourite **Disney Junior characters** in Animation Courtyard, several times daily and take part in the lively **Disney Junior Dance Party**, while Minnie Mouse has her own meet-and-greet in the Drawing Room in the post-show area of the Magic of Disney Animation.

Sunset Boulevard
The final part of the park contains the 2 high-thrill rides, and the big night-time finale, but it's also the busiest area from midday on, so try to visit here first or use FastPass+.

Rock 'n' Roller Coaster Starring Aerosmith: Disney's first big-thrill inverted coaster is a sure-fire draw for the adrenalin ride addicts, with a magnificent indoor setting and nerve-jangling ride. It features a clever holographic-style film show starring rock group Aerosmith in

Disney Junior – Live on Stage

DISNEY'S HOLLYWOOD STUDIOS with children

Here is our guide to the attractions that appeal to the different age groups in this park:

Under-5s

Beauty and the Beast – Live on Stage, Fantasmic!, Honey I Shrunk the Kids Movie Set Adventure, The Magic of Disney Animation, Disney Junior–Live On Stage!, Voyage of the Little Mermaid.

5–8s

Beauty and the Beast – Live On Stage, Fantasmic!, Honey I Shrunk the Kids Movie Set Adventure, Indiana Jones™ Epic Stunt Spectacular, The Legend of Captain Jack Sparrow, Lights, Motors, Action!™ Extreme Stunt Show, The Magic of Disney Animation, Muppet* Vision 3-D, Jedi Training Academy, Studio Backlot Tour, Toy Story Mania, Voyage of the Little Mermaid.

9–12s

American Idol Experience, Beauty and the Beast – Live on Stage, Fantasmic!, The Great Movie Ride, Indiana Jones™ Epic Stunt Spectacular, The Legend of Captain Jack Sparrow, Lights, Motors, Action!™ Extreme Stunt Show, The Magic of Disney Animation, Muppet*Vision 3-D, Rock 'n' Roller Coaster Starring Aerosmith, Jedi Training Academy, Star Tours, Studio Backlot Tour, Twilight Zone™ Tower of Terror, Toy Story Mania. *Remember: American Idol closes Jan 2015.*

Over-12s

American Idol Experience, Fantasmic!, The Great Movie Ride, Indiana Jones™ Epic Stunt Spectacular, Lights, Motors, Action!™ Extreme Stunt Show, The Magic of Disney Animation, Muppet*Vision 3-D, Rock 'n' Roller Coaster Starring Aerosmith, Star Tours, Studio Backlot Tour, Toy Story Mania, Twilight Zone™ Tower of Terror, Walt Disney: One Man's Dream, The Legend of Captain Jack Sparrow.

their recording studio. That leads to the real fun, set to specially recorded tracks from the band itself and with outrageous speaker systems, as riders climb aboard Cadillac cars for a memorable whiz through a mock Los Angeles (watch out for a close encounter with the Hollywood sign!). The high-speed launch and inversions ensure a dynamic coaster experience. Go first thing or expect serious queues, and don't forget to check out your ride photo ($18.95–49.95). **R:** 4ft/124cm. TTTTT FP+1

BRITTIP

If only 1 or 2 in your group want to ride Rock 'n' Roller Coaster, or you want to save significant time waiting, opt for the Single Rider queue. You will be split up, but the wait will be much shorter.

The Twilight Zone™ Tower of Terror: This 199ft/60m landmark invites you to experience another dimension in the strange Hollywood Tower Hotel that time forgot. The exterior is intriguing, the interior is fascinating,

the ride is scintillating and the queues are huge! Just when you think you are through to the ride, there's another queue, so spend your time inspecting the superb detail. There's a lot more to this than just the big 13-storey drop, however, as the 'Twilight Zone' theme adds a real element of invention. Your elevator car twists and turns unexpectedly before it is time to 'drop in', and the random drop sequence provides hair-raising thrills before you exit! **R:** 3ft 4in/101cm. TTTTT FP+

Honey, I Shrunk the Kids

Beauty and the Beast – Live on Stage: An enchanting live musical song and dance performance of the highlights of this Disney classic will entertain the whole family for 30min in the Theater of the Stars. Check the daily schedule for show times, which are up to 5 times a day, usually starting at 11.45am. **AAA FP+1**

Fantasmic!: This special-effects spectacular is simply not to be missed. Staged nightly (twice nightly in peak periods) in a 6,900-seat amphitheatre, it features the dreams of Mickey, portrayed as the Sorcerer's Apprentice, through films such as *Pocahontas, The Lion King* and *Snow White*, but hijacked by the Disney villains, leading to an epic battle, with Our Hero emerging triumphant. Dancing waters, shooting comets, animated fountains, swirling stars and balls of fire combine in a breathtaking presentation, especially the giant, fire-breathing dragon! The 25min show begins seating up to 2hrs in advance and it's best to head there at least 30min before (watch out for the splash zones!). **AAAAA FP+1**

Other entertainment: Sunset Boulevard is also home to more of the park's **Citizens of Hollywood** characters.

BRITTIP
You can get a plain burger without all the trimmings at Backlot Express and Rosie's. Just ask when you reach the cashier. It's not on the menu, but it is available.

Star Wars Weekends

Rock 'n' Roller Coaster Starring Aerosmith

Shopping and dining: The best shopping here is provided by **Legends of Hollywood**, **Planet Hollywood Super Store** and the **Sunset Boulevard** shops (for limited edition watches, clothing and other collectibles). **Rosie's All-American Café** (chicken, burgers and salads) and **Catalina Eddie's** (pizza) are the best of Sunset Boulevard's 5 market-style eateries.

Skywalker and Co

Star Wars™ film fans will want to make a beeline for the Studios during weekends in late May and early June when the park becomes a playground for characters, film stars, photo-opportunities, competitions and other memorabilia based on anything to do with Luke Skywalker and Co, plus a nightly fireworks display. Much of the event is scheduled in and around the Premier Theater in the Streets of America area. There is no additional fee to rub shoulders with (and get autographs from) various Star Wars™ personalities, and the Studios take on an extra dimension each weekend (though the park is also at its most crowded). Some Star Wars Weekend character meets and events are FP+1. New in 2014 were the **Star Wars Dine-In Galactic Breakfast** at the Sci-Fi Dine-In Theater ($48 adults, $30 3–9) and **Jedi Mickey Star Wars Dine** at Hollywood and Vine for dinner ($56 adults, $34 3–9) featuring Jedi Mickey and Darth Vader Goofy. **A Feel the Force Premium Package** includes special parade and fireworks viewing, snack and beverage, dessert party, plus Photopass card.

Disney's Animal Kingdom Theme Park

Disney's newest and smartest theme park opened in 1998 representing a completely different experience. With an emphasis on conservation and nature, it largely eschews the non-stop thrills and attractions of the other parks and instead offers a change of pace, a more relaxing motif, as well as Disney's usual seamless entertainment style, but still with some excellent rides, including one of its very best. The attractions are relatively few, with just 6 out-and-out rides, but there are then 2 elaborate wildlife trails, 4 shows (including 2 that are almost worth the entry fee alone), an extravagant adventure playground, conservation station and a petting zoo.

It is also outrageously scenic, notably with the 145ft/44m Tree of Life, the Kilimanjaro Safaris and the Asian village of Serka Zong (home to the gigantic Expedition: Everest™ ride), but it won't overwhelm you with Disney's usual grand fantasy. Rather, it is a chance to explore and experience; to learn and understand; and to soak up the gentler more natural ambience. It is not a zoo in the conventional sense, but it is home to 200-plus species of birds and animals (in some wonderfully naturalistic settings). The educational tone is fairly strong, but children in particular may pick up easily on the essential conservation undertones of things like Kilimanjaro Safaris and Maharajah Jungle Trek. However, the park does get crowded, the walkways can be congested and there are fewer places to cool down. It is definitely a good idea to be here on time and use FastPass+ to minimise queuing.

Disney's Animal Kingdom Theme Park at a glance

Location	Directly off Osceola Parkway, also via World Drive and Buena Vista Drive
Size	500 acres/203ha divided into 6 'lands'
Hours	9am–5 or 6pm off peak; 8am–8pm in high season
Admission	Under-3s free; 3–9 $88 (1–day base ticket), $284 (5–day Magic Your Way), £264 (14 day Ultimate); adult (10+) $94, $304, £279. Prices do not include tax.
Parking	$17
Lockers	Either side of Entrance Plaza; $12 small, $14 large ($5 deposit each)
Pushchairs	$15 and $31 at Garden Gate Gifts, through entrance on right; length of stay $91/week, $130 10 days, $189/$270 double
Wheelchairs	$12 or $70 ($20 deposit refunded) with pushchairs
Top attractions	DINOSAUR!, Kilimanjaro Safaris, It's Tough To Be A Bug!, Kali River Rapids, Festival Of The Lion King, Finding Nemo – The Musical, Expedition: Everest™
Don't miss	Pangani Forest Exploration Trail, Maharajah Jungle Trek, Rafiki's Planet Watch, dining at Rainforest Café
Hidden costs	**Meals** — Burger, chips and coke $11.72 / 3-course meal at Yak & Yeti $35-50 (kid's entrée and dessert $8.49) / Beer $6.50–8.00 / Kids' meal $5.99
	T-shirts — $21.95–39.95 Kids' T-shirts $12.99–29.99
	Souvenirs — $1.49–2,000
	Sundries — Face Painting: $12–18

The Oasis

1 The Oasis Tropical Garden

Discovery Island

2 The Tree of Life
3 It's Tough To Be A Bug
4 Discovery Island Trails
5 Flame Tree Barbecue
6 Pizzafari
7 Adventurers' Outpost

11 Chester And Hester's Dino-Rama!
12 TriceraTOP Spin
13 Primeval Whirl
14 Restaurantosaurus

Africa

15 Harambe
16 Kilimanjaro Safaris
17 Rafiki's Planet Watch
18 Pangani Forest Trail
19 Tusker House Restaurant
20 Festival Of The Lion King

Camp Minnie-Mickey
(Closing 2013–14)

Dinoland USA

8 DINOSAUR!
9 The Boneyard
10 Finding Nemo – The Musical

Asia

21 Flights Of Wonder
22 Kali River Rapids
23 Maharajah Jungle Trek
24 Expedition: Everest™
25 Yak 'n Yeti Restaurant
26 Rainforest Café

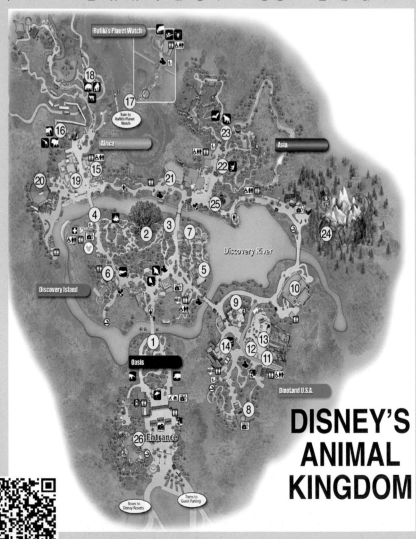

DISNEY'S ANIMAL KINGDOM

Location

If you are staying in the Kissimmee area, Disney's Animal Kingdom is the easiest of the parks to find. Just get on the (toll) Osceola Parkway and follow it all the way to the toll booths. Alternatively, coming down I-4, take exit 65 on to Osceola Parkway. From West Highway 192, come in on Sherberth Road and turn right at the first traffic lights. If you arrive early (which is advisable), you can walk to the Entrance Plaza. Otherwise, the usual tram system takes you in, so make a note of the row you park in (e.g. Unicorn, 67). The entrance plaza is overlooked by the Rainforest Café, with its 65ft/20m waterfall, which is open for breakfast, lunch and dinner (but is busy 12.30–3.30pm and an hour before closing). With Orlando so hot in summer, you need to be here as early as possible to see the animals before they hide in the shade.

BRITTIP

An early start is especially advised for Kilimanjaro Safaris in summer. You will see far more animals in the first few cooler hours of the day than during the hotter afternoon when they seek the shade.

Beating the queues: For the early birds, here is your best plan of campaign. Once through the gates, animal lovers should head first for **Kilimanjaro Safaris**, through the Oasis, Discovery Island and Africa. After the Safari, go straight to **Pangani Forest Exploration Trail** and you will have experienced 2 of the park's best animal encounters before it gets too hot. Alternatively, thrill-seekers should walk straight through Discovery Island for Asia, where the **Expedition: Everest**™ ride is the big draw. Then head to Kilimanjaro Safaris or the nearby **Kali River Rapids** raft ride, followed by the scenic **Maharajah Jungle Trek**. The best combination for the first arrivals is to get a FastPass+ for Expedition: Everest™ (if you don't already have one), then ride Kilimanjaro Safaris and, once you have done that (and depending on your FP+ time), either

do your Everest ride or go straight to Kali River Rapids. Check your show schedule for **Festival of the Lion King** and try to catch one of the first 2 performances, as the later ones draw sizeable queues. The wait time board at the entrance to Discovery Island is helpful. Those are your main tactics – here is the full rundown.

The Oasis

Tropical Garden: A gentle, walk-through introduction to the park, this is a rocky, tree-covered area featuring animal habitats, streams, waterfalls and lush plant life. Here you meet miniature deer, a giant anteater, exotic boars, macaws, waterfowl, a Patagonian cavy and wallabies in an environment that leads you across a stone bridge to the main park area. Visit in early afternoon when many of the rides are busy. AAA

Shopping and dining: Stop at **Garden Gate Gifts** (on the right) for pushchair, wheelchair and locker hire, while **Guest Relations** is on the left. The fun **Rainforest Café** also has an entrance inside the park here. If you haven't seen the one at Downtown Disney, you should call in to view the amazing jungle interior with its audio-animatronic animals, waterfalls, thunderstorms and aquariums. A 3-course meal costs $29–$52, but the setting alone is worth it and the food is above average. Try breakfast or an early dinner to avoid the crowds.

The Asia panorama

Discovery Island

This colourful village is the park hub, themed as a tropical artists' colony, with animal-inspired artwork, nature trails, 4 main shops and 2 eateries. You will also find the **First Aid** station here (look for the 'ladybird' lights) and the Baby Center.

The Tree of Life: This arboreal edifice is the park centrepiece, an awesome creation that seems to have a different perspective from wherever you view it. The trunk and roots are covered in 325 carvings representing the Circle of Life, from the dolphin to the lion. Trails lead round the tree, interspersed with habitats for flamingos, otters, ring-tailed lemurs, macaws, axis deer, cranes, storks, ducks, porcupines, kangaroos and tortoises. The tree canopy spreads 160ft/49m, the trunk is 50ft/15m wide and the diameter of the roots is 170ft/52m. It has 103,000 leaves (all attached by hand) on more than 8,000 branches! **AAAA**

It's Tough To Be A Bug!: Winding down among the Tree's roots brings you 'underground' to a 430-seat theatre and another example of Disney's artistry in 3-D films and special effects. This hysterical 10min show, in the company of Flick from the Pixar film *A Bug's Life*, is a homage to 80% of the animal world, featuring grasshoppers, beetles, spiders, stink bugs and termites (beware the 'acid' spray!) as well as several tricks we couldn't possibly reveal. Sit towards the back in the middle (allow a good number of people in first as the rows are filled up from the far side) to get the best of the 3-D effects. Queues build up from midday, but they do move quite steadily. Don't miss the 'forthcoming attractions' posters in the foyer for some excruciating bug puns on famous films. **AAAAA FP+**

BRITTIP

The dark, special effects and mock creepy-crawlies in It's Tough To Be A Bug! can be extremely scary for young 'uns. Use caution.

Other entertainment: The Island is home to the lively **Viva Gaia Street Band** and various **Disney characters**, notably Daisy Duck at Character Landing (opposite Flame Tree Barbecue), Pocahontas on Discovery Island Trail, and two of the characters from *UP!* near Disney Outfitters. **Adventurers Outpost** is the new setting to meet Mickey and Minnie. **FP+** Children can also sign up for the novel **Wilderness Explorers**

The Tree of Life

Harambe Village

programme here (also based on *UP!*), with the chance to visit 30 locations around the park for interactive lessons and animal experiences, earning sticker badges along the way that act as a gentle educational story. **Winged Encounters – The Kingdom Takes Flight** free-flight macaw show takes place over Discovery Island several times daily.

Shopping and dining: You will find a huge range of merchandise, souvenirs and gifts here, notably in **Disney Outfitters** (artwork and collectables) and **Island Mercantile**. Counter-service restaurants **Pizzafari** (pizza, salads and sandwiches) and **Flame Tree Barbecue** (barbecued ribs, beef and pork, chicken sandwiches and salads) are both good choices. If it's not too hot, the **Flame Tree** is a picturesque option, set among pretty gardens and fountains on the Discovery River; the air-conditioned Pizzafari is better in summer months.

Camp Minnie-Mickey: This area is now closed as part of the ongoing development for the Avatar project due to open in 2017.

Africa
The largest land in the park, it recreates the forests, grasslands and rocky homelands of East Africa's most fascinating residents in a

richly landscaped setting that is part rundown port town and part savannah. The central area, Harambe Village, is a superb Imagineer's eye-view of a Kenyan port town, complete with white coral walls and thatched roofs, and is the starting point of your adventure. The Arab-influenced Swahili culture is also depicted in the native tribal costumes and architecture.

BRITTIP

The best (i.e. the most jolting) ride with the Kilimanjaro Safaris is at the back of the truck. There is less to see from midday to late afternoon in summer when many animals take a siesta.

Discovery Island

Festival of the Lion King

Festival of the Lion King: This not-to-be-missed high-powered 25min production (up to 10 times a day in peak periods, 7 at quieter times) brings the hit animated film to life in spectacular fashion, with giant moving stages, huge animated figures, singers, dancers, acrobats and stilt-walkers, plus some fun audience participation. All the well-known songs are given an airing in a fiesta of colour and sound, and it underlines the quality Disney brings to its live shows. However, queuing often begins an hour in advance for the new 1,000-seat (air-conditioned) theatre, so use FastPass+ or try to take in one of the early shows. AAAAA FP+ Sign language shows are performed

Kilimanjaro Safaris

at 4pm each Tue and Sat; arrive at least 25 mins early and ask to sit in the Warthog section, but check with a Cast Member on arrival.

Kilimanjaro Safaris: The queuing area alone earns high marks for authenticity, preparing you for the sights and sounds of the 110acre/45ha savannah beyond. You board a 32-passenger truck, with your driver relaying information about the flora and fauna on view and a bush ranger-pilot overhead relaying facts and figures on the wildlife, including the dangers threatening them in the real world. Scores of animals are spread out in various habitats, with no fences in sight (the ditches and barriers are all well concealed) as you splash through fords and cross rickety bridges, and you should get good close-ups of lions, rhinos, elephants, giraffes, antelope, hippos and ostriches. Once again, the authentic nature of all you see (okay, some of the tyre 'ruts' and termite mounds are concrete and the baobab trees are fake) is breathtaking, with the spread of the vegetation and landscaping. The animals roam over a wide area, though, and can disappear from view. Not recommended for expectant mothers or anyone with back or neck problems. AAAAA FP+

Pangani Forest Exploration Trail: As you leave the Safari, you turn on to a serious nature trail that showcases gorillas, hippos, okapi, zebras, meerkats and rare tropical birds. You wander the trail at your own pace and visit 'research' stations to learn more about the animals, including the underwater view of the hippos (check out the size of a hippo skull and those teeth!) and the savannah overlook, where giraffes and antelope graze and the meerkats frolic. The walk-through aviary gives you the chance to meet the carmine bee-eater, pygmy goose, African green pigeon, ibis and brimstone canary, among others, but the real centre-piece is the silverback gorilla habitat (in fact, 2 of them). The family group is often just inches away from the plate-glass window, while the bachelor group further along can prove more elusive. Again, the natural aspect of the trail is fabulous and it provides a host of photo opportunities. Do this early or save it for late in the day when most of the crowds will have moved on. AAAAA

Rafiki's Planet Watch: This subsection of Africa involves a (rather dull) rustic train ride, with a peek into some of the backstage areas, as a preamble to the park's interactive and educational exhibits (especially for children). The 3-part journey starts with **Habitat Habit!**, where you can see cotton-top tamarins and learn how conservation begins in your own back garden. **Conservation Station** offers a series of exhibits, shows and information stations about the environment and threats to its ecology. Look out for **Sounds of the Rain Forest** (in special listening booths) and the **Live Animal Cams** that show many of the park's inhabitants in their back-stage areas. Then observe the park's **Veterinary Treatment Center** (including a hatchery and neo-natal care) and **Training Exhibits**. You can easily spend an hour absorbing the information here, inspired by Disney's Worldwide Conservation Fund. Finally, the **Affection Section** petting zoo consists of a collection of goats, sheep and a miniature donkey. ΛΛΛ

Other entertainment: There's plenty more to enjoy here, with the splendid African sounds of **The Burudika Band** and the pageantry and rhythms of **Tam Tam Drummers of Harambe**. With luck you'll also spot the wonderful **DiVine**, a 'moving' part of the foliage (also in The Oasis at times). Rafiki's Planet Watch is also home to roving musician **Gi-Tar**

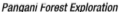
Pangani Forest Exploration

© Andrew Dean

Dan and his fun songs, which he can personalise at the drop of a hat!

Shopping and dining: Harambe is home to the **Mombasa Marketplace/ Ziwani Traders**, where you can suit up safari-style, while Rafiki's Planet Watch has **Out of the Wild** for more gifts and souvenirs. **Tusker House Restaurant** (featuring Donald's Dining Safari for Breakfast at $30 adults, $16 children, and Lunch at $32 and $17) is one of the best diners in the park, with a mouth-watering array of salads, a hot carvery, rotisserie chicken, stews and vegetarian dishes ($33 and $16 for dinner, without characters). There are also 4 snack and drink bars, most notably the **Kusafiri Coffee Shop** (muffins, pastries, coffee), while **Tamu Tamu Refreshments** offers some tasty sandwiches, salads and drinks, plus bagels, French toast sticks and coffee for breakfast and the **Dawa Bar** is a great place to sit with a beer or cocktail and soak up the scenery.

Asia

The next 'land' is elaborately themed as the gateway to the imaginary south-east Asian region of Anandapur, with temples, ruined forts, landscape and wildlife. The element of reality is startling and the architecture is full of faithful representations of genuine locations. The elaborate ruined temple showcases for the gibbons and siamangs are worth looking out for – and you may well hear them wherever you are in the park!

Maharajah Jungle Trek

Flights of Wonder: Another wildlife show, this portrays the talents and traits of the park's avian inhabitants. A trainer showcases the behaviours of various birds, including macaws and hawks, before being interrupted by a bumbling tour guide, who needs to be reminded of key conservation issues. This is the cue for some frolics with our feathered friends, including vultures, eagles, toucans and a singing parrot. The Caravan Stage is not air-conditioned, though, and can be hot in summer. AAA

Kali River Rapids: Part thrill-ride, part scenic journey, this bouncy raft ride will get you pretty wet (not great for early morning in winter). It starts out in tropical forest territory before launching into a scene of logging devastation, warning of the dangers of clear-cut burning. Your raft then plunges down a waterfall (and one unlucky soul – usually the one with their back to the drop – gets seriously damp) before you finish more sedately. Queues can be long through the main part of the day, so use FastPass+ here. R: 3ft 6in/106cm (a few rafts have adult-and-child seats allowing smaller children to ride). TTT AAAA FP+

Maharajah Jungle Trek: Asia's version of the wildlife trail is another picturesque walk past decaying temple ruins and animal encounters. The first few exhibits – the Malayan tapir, Komodo dragon and a bat enclosure (including the flying fox bat, the world's largest) – lead to the main viewing area, the 5acre/2ha Tiger Range, whose pool and fountains are a popular playground early in the day for these magnificent big cats. An antelope enclosure and walk-through aviary complete this breathtaking trek (which rarely draws heavy crowds). AAAAA

> ✚ **BRITTIP** ────
> Although Expedition: Everest™ is a FastPass+ ride, its popularity means FP+s often run out, so schedule in advance, if possible. Don't leave it too late.

Expedition: Everest™: A major attraction, this clever roller-coaster takes you deep into the Himalayas for an encounter with the mythical Yeti. The queuing area alone will convince you of its authentic location (try to do the main queue at least once rather than FastPass to appreciate all the fine detail) as it delivers you to an old abandoned tea plantation railway station. Here you undertake the ride to the foothills of Mount Everest, but you must first brave the perils of the Forbidden Mountain – lair of the Yeti. Will the beast be in evidence? You bet! The ride becomes a typically fast-paced whiz (but no inversions), forwards AND backwards, as you attempt to escape the creature's domain. The final encounter with a massive audio-animatronic Yeti is jaw-dropping and underlines the splendidly creative nature of this ride. It has proved to be a fabulous attraction but draws equally impressive crowds all day, so make it one of the first things you do. You can also take advantage of a Single Rider queue here (at the FP entrance) if you don't mind your group being split up. You can get ride photos here, too ($18.95–49.95). **R:** 3ft 8in/115cm. **TTTTT** FP+

Other entertainment: Have fun with **DJ Anaan** and his Bangra Dance Party next to the Local Foods Café, along with the **Chakranadi** duo, sitar and tabla musicians, while *Jungle Book* characters can be found at Upcountry Landing.

Shopping and dining: The retail options are limited in Asia (just 2 minor kiosks), but it is home to the fab **Yak and Yeti** combination diner. Outside is the counter-service **Local Foods Café** (honey chicken, beef lo mein, egg rolls, chicken salad and sweet and sour chicken), while inside the 2-storey structure is the full restaurant. Yak and Yeti offers some imaginative cuisine, from a Dim Sum basket to Maple Tamarind Chicken and a Malaysian Seafood Curry, as well as more standard Asian-fusion dishes, like Crispy Mahi Mahi and Spring Rolls. A good range of drinks and cocktails complement this superior eatery. Extra incentive to visit: a full range of bar drinks to go, while you can just sit at the bar for a drink or a full meal. The **Anandapur Ice Cream Truck** is also popular and the **Royal Anandapur Tea Company** features a great range of speciality teas, coffees and soft drinks.

DinoLand USA

The final area of the park is somewhat at odds with the natural theme of the rest, a full-scale palaeontology exercise, with the accent on a 'university fossil dig'. Energetically tongue-in-cheek (the students who work the area have the motto 'Been there, dug that', while you enter under a mock brachiosaurus skeleton, the 'Oldengate Bridge' – groan!), it still features some glimpses into genuine research and artefacts.

DINOSAUR!: Renamed after Disney's big animated film (it was initially called Countdown to Extinction), this is a herky-jerky ride experience, rather dark and intense (and often too scary for young children). It is also a wonderfully realistic journey back to the end of the Cretaceous period, when a giant meteor put paid to dinosaur life. You enter the high-tech Dino Institute for a multimedia history show that leads to a briefing room for your 'mission' 65 million years in the past. However, one of the Institute's scientists hijacks your trip to capture a dinosaur, and you career back to a prehistoric jungle in a 12-passenger Time Rover. The threat of a carnotaurus (quite frightening for children; try to sit them on the inside of the car) and the impending doom of the meteor add

Expedition Everest

up to a breathtaking whirl through a menacing environment. You will need to ride at least twice to appreciate all the detail, but queues build up quickly, so go either first thing or late in the day. **R:** 3ft 4in/101cm. **TTTT AAAA FP+**

The Boneyard: A hugely imaginative adventure playground, it offers kids the chance to slip, slide and climb through the 'fossilised' remains of triceratops and brontosaurs, explore caves, dig for bones and splash through a mini waterfall. The amusing signage will be wasted on most kids, but it's ideal for parents to let their young 'uns loose for up to an hour (though not just after the neighbouring Finding Nemo show has finished). **TTTT** (kids only).

Finding Nemo – The Musical: This lovely show is a first for Disney entertainment, taking a regular animated feature and turning it into a full musical. The show combines colourful puppets, dancers, acrobats and animated backdrops with innovative lighting, sound and special effects.

◀◀▶ **BRITTIP**

Finding Nemo – The Musical is a popular addition, but although it draws long queues, the theatre seats 1,500, so most people usually get in.

The basic idea remains faithful to the story of Nemo, his dad Marlin and friends Dory and Crush and features larger-than-life puppetry, plus rod,

The Festival of The Lion King Show

bunraku and shadow puppets, all designed by Michael Curry, who created the award-winning Broadway version of Disney's The Lion King show. It's a spectacular combination of music and grand staging, and the 30min show performs up to 5 times a day. **AAAA FP+**

Chester & Hester's Dino-Rama!: This mini-land of rides, fairground games and stalls adds a rather garish element to the park. Its main icon is a towering concretosaurus (!), and it is designed to have a quirky, tongue-in-cheek style reminiscent of 1950s' American roadside attractions. The rides are: **TriceraTOP Spin:** another version of the Dumbo/Aladdin rides in the Magic Kingdom, where a flying, twirling, spinning top bounces you up and down with a surprise at the top. **AA** (**TTTT** under-5s); and **Primeval Whirl:** coaster fans will get a laugh out of this wacky offering that sends its riders through a maze of curves, hills and (quite sharp) drops that make it seem faster than it actually is. It's basically a lampoon of the DINOSAUR! ride, a mock journey 'way back in time', with plenty of cartoon frippery. Extra fun is provided by the fact that the cars spin, which gives an unpredictable element to each 3min ride. The queuing area is a riot of visual gags, but the ride is not recommended for anyone with back or neck problems. **R:** 4ft/122cm. **TTTT FP+**

Other entertainment: Dino-Rama also features the **Fossil Fun Games**, 6 fairground-type stalls (costing $4 each) designed to tempt you to try to win a cuddly dinosaur. **Disney characters** Goofy and Pluto meet guests across from TriceraTop Spin, with Donald Duck nearby.

Shopping and dining: Chester and Hester's Dinosaur Treasures (the 'Fossiliferous Gift Store' – groan!) offers a wide range of dino-related souvenirs. You can get a counter-service meal at the (you've guessed it!) **Restaurantosaurus** (burgers, hot dogs, sandwiches, chicken nuggets and salad) or ice-cream and pastries at **Dino Bite Snacks**.

DISNEY'S ANIMAL KINGDOM THEME PARK with children

Here is our guide to the attractions that appeal to the different age groups in this park:

Under-5s
Affection Section, The Boneyard, Character Greeting Trails, Discovery Island Trails, Festival of the Lion King, Finding Nemo – The Musical, Kilimanjaro Safaris, Maharajah Jungle Trek, Pangani Forest Exploration Trail, TriceraTOP Spin.

5–8s
All the above, plus Conservation Station, DINOSAUR! (with parental discretion), Flights Of Wonder, Habitat Habit!, It's Tough To Be A Bug (with parental discretion), Kali River Rapids, Primeval Whirl.

9–12s
All the above, plus Expedition: Everest™.

Over-12s
DINOSAUR!, Expedition: Everest™, Festival of the Lion King, Flights Of Wonder, It's Tough To Be A Bug!, Kali River Rapids, Kilimanjaro Safaris, Maharajah Jungle Trek, Pangani Forest Exploration Trail, Primeval Whirl.

Other Entertainment

While Mickey's Jammin' Jungle Parade has been discontinued, a new evening show is due to debut in 2015, called **Rivers of Light**. Set on the lake between Discovery Island and Expedition Everest, it will feature live music, fountains, floating lanterns, boats and an immense water-screen effect with elaborate animal imagery, all presented before an amphitheatre viewing area. AAAAA (expected).

Harambe Nights: Remain in the park after closing time and enjoy a (rather pricey) special show, with a guest narrator, based on The Lion King, along with a street party featuring live music, food, beer, wine and soda (7pm–10.30pm select nights; reservations required on 407 939 1319 or online; $119 adults, $70 9 and under, $135/$94 premium seating).

Tours: Finally, for a behind-the-scenes look at the park, **Backstage Safari** is a wonderful 3hr journey into the handling and care of all the animals (Mon, Wed, Thurs, Fri; $72, no under-16s), while **Wild By Design** offers a 3hr tour of the park's art, architecture and history and how it was all created (Mon, Wed, Thurs, Fri; $60, no under-14s). For something really different, try the **Wild Africa Trek**, a 3hr ride-and-trek into the African savannah. From a precarious rope bridge crossing high above Harambe Reserve to a VIP safari in special open-air vehicles and a visit to Harambe's private camp, this exclusive experience, in groups of no more than 12, is open to ages 8 (minimum 4ft/122cm tall) and up, 6 times daily. Closed toe shoes required, dresses/skirts not advised; weight limit 310lb/141kg. Seasonal pricing $189–249. Book tours on 407 939 8687.

That's the full Disney theme park story, but there is still PLENTY more in store…!

Triceratop Spin

A 20th Anniversary recollection

While we have marked many new developments during our 20 years, we've said goodbye to many attractions, too, with a lot of fond memories for our regular readers over the years. Attractions have started up and fallen away, while some long-running shows – such as Arabian Nights – have recently failed to last the distance. Here's a look back at many things we have reported on in the past two decades that are no longer a part of the Orlando scene:

Walt Disney World

Discovery Island closed in 1999 and River Country water park in 2001 while the Disney Institute ran from 1996-2003 and Pleasure Island effectively shut down in 2008. In the parks: Diamond Horseshoe Saloon Revue, Frontierland Stunt Show, Mike Fink Keelboats, 20,000 Leagues Under The Sea (replaced, eventually, by Fantasyland expansion), Snow White's Adventure (replaced by Princess Fairytale Hall), Legend of the Lion King (replaced by Mickey's Philharmagic), Dreamflight (replaced by Buzz Lightyear's Space Ranger Spin), Transportarium (replaced by Metropolis Science Center, and now Monsters Inc Laugh Floor), Mickey's Starland (which became Mickey's Toontown and was then replaced by Storybook Circus), Skyway and Galaxy Palace Theatre (all Magic Kingdom); Wonders of Life pavilion, Journey Into Imagination (now Imagination!), Honey I Shrunk The Audience, Food Rocks, Caribbean Coral Reef Ride at Seabase Alpha (replaced by Nemo and Friends), World of Motion (now Test Track), Horizons (now Mission: Space); El Rio Del Tiempo (now the Gran Fiesta Tour) and Miyuki the Candy Lady (all at Epcot); Superstar Television (now American Idol Live), The Monster Sound Show (later Sounds Dangerous starring Drew Carey), Inside the Magic (now part of the Backstage Studio Tour) and Power Rangers (all at Disney's Hollywood Studios); Disney's Animal Kingdom arrived in 1998 but has since lost Camp Mickey-Minnie (to the Avatarland development) and the Discovery Island boat ride, while Tarzan Rocks became the Finding Nemo Show.

Universal Orlando

Hitchcock's 3-D theatre (now Shrek 4-D), Nickelodeon Studios (now the Blue Man Group theatre), Funtastic World of Hanna-Barbera (which became the Jimmy Neutron Ride and now Despicable Me), The Murder She Wrote Mystery Theatre (also Xena and Hercules; finally redeveloped as Transformers Ride), Ghostbusters (now Twister), Kongfrontation (now Revenge of the Mummy), Wild, Wild, Wild West Stunt Show (now Fear Factor Live), Earthquake – The Big One (now Disaster! A Major Motion Picture, Starring You), Jaws (now the Diagon Alley expansion), Back To The Future (now The Simpsons Ride), the Boneyard, Production Tram Tour and the Adventures of Rocky and Bullwinkle show (all at Universal Studios); Islands of Adventure opened in 1999 and has since closed the Triceratops Encounter and Pandemonium Cartoon Circus, while part of the Lost Continent became the Wizarding World of Harry Potter in 2010.

SeaWorld

Mission: Bermuda Triangle (replaced by Wild Arctic), SeaWorld Theater (Water Fantasy, now the Pets Ahoy show), Clydesdale Hamlet (now Sea Garden), Hospitality House (now the Terrace Garden Buffet), Tropical Reef and Hawaiian Rhythms show. The Waterfront was added in 2003, Journey to Atlantis in 1998, Kraken in 2000, Manta in 2009, Turtle Trek (replacing the Manatees, The Last Generation) in 2012 and Antarctica: Empire of the Penguin in 2013 (replacing the Penguin Encounter). All the shows here have changed at least once, too.

Busch Gardens

Monorail ride, Python (replaced for SheiKra), Sandstorm (now Falcon's Fury), Dolphin Theater (replaced by 3-D theatre and now Pantopia animal show), Claw Island (now Jungala), Akbar's Adventures and, of course, the Anheuser-Busch brewery. All the shows have changed more than once. Edge of Africa was added in 1997, Sesame Street Safari of Fun in 2010 and Cheetah Hunt in 2011.

International Drive

The Mercado, Skull Kingdom, Mystery Fun House, Guinness World Records Experience, Hard Rock Vault, Movie Rider, Belz Factory Outlets (now Orlando Premium Outlets) and King Henry's Feast dinner show.

Kissimmee

Jungleland Zoo, Splendid China, Haunted Castle, Water Mania, and the American Gladiators, Fortune Feast, Buffalo Bill's and Arabian Nights dinner shows.

Other changes

The wonderful Church Street Station in downtown Orlando shut in 2001, while Cypress Gardens is now LEGOLAND Florida, Silver Springs in Ocala closed in 2013 and the Fantasy of Flight attraction (which opened in 1995) shut in 2014.

6 Five More of the Best

It's time to leave the wonderful world of Disney and explore the rest of Central Florida's great attractions. And there's still a terrific amount in store, including some of the most thrilling rides and dazzling creativity. Yes, Universal Orlando and the SeaWorld parks are that good.

Universal has developed astronomically in recent years, with new hotels, entertainment, restaurants and, above all, headline attractions. In 2014, it opened the massive Cabana Bay Beach Resort, completed a major expansion of the CityWalk district and debuted the most eye-catching themed area in 15 years with the **Wizarding World of Harry Potter – Diagon Alley**. And, we believe, there is more in store. Much more. In fact, while it can't match Disney for size, it seems increasingly set on one-upping The Mouse for ambition and innovation

With 4 hotels, all connected by boat, bus or path to the CityWalk hub, from where the 2 parks radiate, Universal is an increasingly dynamic proposition, and more centralised than Disney. It also owns the Wet 'n Wild water park (with more plans for expansion there) and its tie-up with the SeaWorld parks via the **Orlando FlexTicket** offers amazing value. For UK visitors,

Harry Potter and the Escape from Gringotts

Universal Dining Plan

New in 2013 was the option to add a daily meal allowance to your hotel booking, or a daily Quick Service meal plan if you are just visiting the parks. The full **Dining Plan** can only be booked via Universal's own reservation system – **www.universalorlandovacations. com** – and offers 1 Table Service meal (entrée, dessert and soft drink), 1 Counter Service meal (entrée and soft drink), 1 Snack (popcorn, ice-cream, etc) from food carts or counter service restaurants, and 1 additional soft drink per day for $52/adult and $19/child. It can be used at most dining venues in the parks and 10 in CityWalk. The Quick Service option costs $20/adult and $13/child per day and offers 1 counter service meal (entrée and soft drink), 1 snack and 1 soft drink per day. The **Quick Service** option can be purchased on the day or in advance online. There is also the **Coca-Cola Freestyle cup** at $12/person (plus $10 for additional days) with unlimited free refills all day at the special Coca-Cola Freestyle outlets (5 in each park), offering more than 100 different drinks. NB: the old Universal all-day Meal Deal has been discontinued.

the 2- and 3-park Bonus Tickets are also extremely well priced. It does not offer a free FastPass+ system like Disney but you can buy the **Universal Express** pass that covers a one-time front-of-queue access to nearly all the rides (but not the 3 headline Harry Potter attractions). It is not cheap – from $30–100 depending upon time of year and $36–120 for both parks, but can save a lot of queuing at peak periods. A limited number go on sale after park opening and are snapped up, but they can also be bought online for a specific day at **www.universalorlando.com** or in the parks themselves for another day. The Park-to-Park Ticket + Unlimited Express provides park admission AND unlimited Express access for 1, 2, 3 or 4 days, from $190–340/adult, $185–328/child (online only).

Universal hotel guests (except those at Cabana Bay Beach Resort) benefit from Express ride priority all day by showing their room key and all 4 enjoy the major perk of early access to The Wizarding Worlds of Harry Potter each day. In addition, some rides have Single Rider queues, which save time if you want to go by yourself or don't mind splitting up your group. Once again, height/health restrictions (R) are noted in ride descriptions. Universal is also home to some of the best (and most grisly!) Halloween celebrations on earth, with their Halloween Horror Nights programme (p167).

Hollywood Rip Ride Rocket

Universal Studios Florida®

Universal opened its first Florida park in June 1990 (its original Los Angeles movie site opened to the public in 1917!) and quickly became a serious rival to Disney. For the visitor, it means a consistently high standard and good value (though the choice can be bewildering), but there are few similarities to the LA Studios. Universal is also a different proposition to Disney, with a more in-your-face style that appeals especially to teens. Younger children are still well catered for, though. Universal parks can also need more than a full day in high season. Strategies are the same, though: arrive EARLY (up to 30mins before opening), do the big rides first, avoid main meal times and take time out for an afternoon break (try shopping, dining or visiting the cinemas at CityWalk) if it gets too crowded.

Location

Universal Studios Florida® is divided into 7 main areas, set around a lagoon, but there are no great distinguishing features. The main resort entrance is just off Interstate 4 (I-4 eastbound take exit 75A; westbound take exit 74B) or via Universal Boulevard from I-Drive by Wet 'n Wild. Parking is in its massive multi-storey car park and there is quite a walk (with moving walkways) to the front gates.

◄█►ANNIVERSARY SPOT
20 For a price comparison, in our 1st edition, a 1-day adult ticket was $37, parking was $5, a typical burger-fries-and-coke meal was just $6.20 and lockers cost only 50 cents!

Universal Studios Florida® at a glance

Location	Off exits 75A and 74B from I-4; Universal Boulevard and Kirkman Road
Size	110 acres/45ha in 7 themed areas
Hours	9am–6 or 7pm off peak; 9am–10pm high season (Washington's birthday, Easter, summer holidays, Thanksgiving, Christmas)
Admission	Under-3s free; 3–9 $90 (1-day ticket), $166 (2-day Park-to-Park ticket), $300 (FlexTicket), $340 (FlexTicket Plus); adult (10+) $96, $177, $320, $360. Prices do not include tax.
Parking	$17 (preferred parking $22; valet parking $30)
Lockers	Immediately to left in Front Lot $8
Pushchairs	$15 and $25, kiddie cars $17.99 and $27.99 next to locker hire
Wheelchairs	$12 and $50 (with photo ID as deposit), with pushchairs
Top attractions	Harry Potter and The Escape From Gringotts, Hogwarts Express, Revenge of the Mummy, Men in Black, Despicable Me: Minion Mayhem, TRANSFORMERS: The Ride – 3D, The Simpsons, Hollywood Rip, Ride Rockit!
Don't miss	Universal's Cinematic Spectacular, Universal's Superstar Parade, Curious George Playground (for kids), The Blues Brothers, Tales of Beedle the Bard
Hidden costs	**Meals** Burger, chips and coke $10.69–11.78 3-course dinner $25–39 (Lombard's) $5.99 ($6.99–8.99 in Finnegan's)
	T-shirts 21.95–34.95
	Souvenirs 95c–$1,500
	Sundries Temporary tattoos $7–10

Production Central
1 Main Entrance
2 Shrek-4D
3 Despicable Me
4 Hollywood Rip, Ride, Rockit!
5 Meet Shrek & Donkey
6 Monsters Café
7 Transformers: The Ride – 3D

New York
8 Twister
9 Revenge Of The Mummy
10 The Blues Brothers
11 Finnegan's Bar and Grill
12 Louie's Italian Restaurant

San Francisco
13 Disaster! A Motion Picture Ride… Staring YOU!
14 Beetlejuice's Graveyard Revue
15 Lombard's Seafood Grill

The Wizarding World of Harry Potter – Diagon Alley
16 Hogwarts Express

17 The Leaky Cauldron
18 Diagon Alley
19 Harry Potter and the Escape from Gringotts
20 Carkitt Market

World Expo
21 Men in Black – Alien Attack
22 Fear Factor Live!
23 The Simpsons Ride
24 Kang amd Kodos' Twirl 'n Hurl
25 Duff Brewery & Shop

KidZone
26 Animal Actors on Location!
27 Fievel's Playland
28 A Day in The Park with Barney
29 ET Adventure
30 Woody Woodpecker's Nuthouse Coaster
31 Curious George Goes To Town

Hollywood
32 Universal's Horror Make-Up Show
33 Terminator 2: 3-D Battle Across Time
34 Lucy A Tribute
35 The Brown Derby

Photo connect

Universal's photo sharing system allows guests to collect all their ride photos in one source and is cheaper than buying them individually. Just ask for a Photo Connect card when you buy your first ride photo and all subsequent ones will end up on the same account for that day. You can then download your pics, add fancy borders and other features, share or have them put on posters, keychains, mugs and more at the Photo Connect kiosk when you leave. Or look for the Star Card, which allows you to compile ALL your Universal photos (include ride ones) on the 1 card account for either 1 day ($49.95), 1 week ($59.95), an Annual Pass ($59.95) or a 14-day Digital Package ($99.99). You can pre-order it with a discount at **https://photoconnect. amazingpictures.com/** and share it on social media with their Amazing Pictures app.

⚡🇬🇧 BRITTIP

A good way to enjoy the Universal Express perk is to book a night's stay at one of their 3 deluxe hotels. Check in early (they will store bags for you) and you get your hotel room key, with Express feature, for use that day AND the next day.

Beating the queues: With the opening of The Wizarding World of Harry Potter – Diagon Alley, this has become THE place to visit first, with heavy queues building up quickly and lasting all day. It is at the back of the park, so try to avoid all the other attractions if this is your top target. Turn right on Rodeo Drive, continue through Sunset Boulevard and the Springfield area of The Simpsons, and go left across the bridge straight to the Wizarding World. If you are not a Potter fan (although you should still give Diagon Alley a look at some stage) and want some of the big-time thrills, stop first at Hollywood Rip Ride Rockit (on your left in Production Central) and then take in TRANSFORMERS: The Ride – 3D and the nearby Revenge of The Mummy in New York. For interactive fun, take in

Despicable Me first, then head back to the Springfield area and do The Simpsons and Men In Black. Many of the other attractions are now easy to do with the crowds flocking to Diagon Alley.

Here's a full guide to the Studios (for CityWalk, see Chapter 10). Watch out for the helpful mobile electronic Wait Times boards around both parks, too.

Production Central

Coming straight through the gates brings you into the administrative centre, with a couple of large gift stores plus **Studio Sweets**. Call at **Guest Services** for guides for disabled visitors, TDD and assisted listening devices, and to make restaurant bookings, which can also be made at a kiosk to the right after the turnstiles, next to the Beverly Hills Boulangerie. First aid is available here (and on Canal Street between New York and San Francisco), while there are facilities for nursing mothers at **Family Services** by the bank through the gates on the right. In addition, Universal Studios hosts **IMPACT Wrestling** (periodically), with free tickets available on a first-come, first-served basis (call 407 224 8000 for more details, or visit the Studio Audience Center – the Lost & Found office in the Guest Services courtyard through the gates to the right). Coming to the top of the Plaza of the Stars brings you to the business end of the park.

Shrek 4-D: This adds a new dimension to 3-D films as the original cast (Mike Myers, Eddie Murphy, Cameron Diaz and John Lithgow) reprise their Oscar-winning roles. The amusing 7min pre-show leads into the 500-seat main theatre, where you don your Ogre Vision 3-D glasses and prepare to enter a new world. The film is funny enough as Shrek and Donkey save the Princess, but the special effects (watch out for the spiders!) and moving seats add a startling extra element that is hugely entertaining. State-of-the-art digital projection and audio systems, lighting effects and smoke (plus a hilarious finale featuring an out-of-control Tinker Bell) ensure a real laugh-fest. Queues stay long for much of the day. AAAAA+

ANNIVERSARY SPOT

20 In 1995 there was only 1 Universal park, and no CityWalk. And, of all the Universal Studios attractions, only 4 remain as they were then – Lucy: A Tribute, the ET Adventure, Fievel's Playland and A Day In The Park With Barney.

Despicable Me – Minion Mayhem:
This outrageously funny 3-D simulator ride is based on the 2010 animated film starring Steve Carell. You enter the home of super-villain Gru and visit his lab where you are 'shrunk' to undergo Minion training. In the company of Gru's daughters, Margo, Edith and Agnes, the zany scheme goes awry and his 'recruits' suffer some hair-raising adventures that need Gru's intervention to save the day. It ends happily, of course, with a fun Minion dance party (and gift shop). With dynamic, motion-based seats, things can get bumpy, so those with heart, neck, or back problems should ask for the stationary seats. TTT + AAAA (TTTTT under-10s)

Hollywood Rip Ride Rockit!: This iconic ride is a high-tech colossus, with an onboard system that allows you to select your own ride music – then take home the DVD. Orlando's highest and fastest roller-coaster at a daunting 167ft/51m and almost 70mph/113kph, you can't miss this vivid red steel beast as it loops right through the width of the park! It starts with a video intro while you

Transformers: The Ride – 3D

queue that reveals 5 music choices (Rap/Hip Hop, Country, Classic Rock/Metal, Pop/Disco and Club Electronica), each with 6 tracks. You're then strapped into an open-sided car that goes straight up a 17-storey vertical lift-hill, then into a steep dive followed by the signature Double Take, the world's first non-inverted loop (you don't actually go upside-down but it feels like it!). You will soar over the heads of people in the queue, dive below ground level and fly around a 150° banked turn, all in the course of the 1min 40sec ride. The innovative open cars make the whole experience feel even faster and more dynamic, while the mix of pounding music (from your headrest and speakers along the track) and concert-style lighting (flashy during the day, stunning at night) ensures this is a ride that really rocks. You can buy the ride video, complete with your musical selection captured by multiple cameras (for $34; ride photos $20–25). It looks more frightening than it actually is, but it is truly exhilarating. Leave this for later in the day when queues tend to drop off. R: 4ft 3in/130cm. TTTTT+

BRITTIP

If you don't empty your pockets before riding Rip Ride Rockit, you'll find them empty by the end of the ride! Put ALL loose items in the free lockers.

TRANSFORMERS: The Ride – 3D:
The latest generation of Universal's dramatic 3-D technology allied with a dynamic ride vehicle, this puts guests at the heart of an explosive battle between the Autobots, led by Optimus Prime and the evil Decepticons of Megatron. It feels like walking into a movie as the long, elaborate queuing area prepares riders for joining the planet-defending forces of NEST, and then a larger-than-life whirl through a Decepticon attack in a bid to defend the AllSpark – and the earth's existence! The combination of ultra-HD film, real scenery and dramatic special effects is breathtaking (if loud). Even those who have never

seen one of the films will not feel left out as the whole scenario is explained while you queue. Crowds build up quickly, hence you need to ride early on or late in the day. **R:** 3ft 4in/101cm. **TTTT**

Other entertainment: Optimus Prime, Bumblebee and Megatron have a brilliant set-piece **Transformers photo spot** next to the ride, or meet Shrek, Fiona and Donkey at **Meet Shrek/Donkey**, well worth catching for the amusing patter. You'll find **Minion photo ops** in the Super Silly Stuff shop.

Shopping and dining: Great shops here, including **Supply Vault** for all things Transformer, On Location (film, clothes, sundries and 2-way radio rentals), **Super Silly Stuff** (*Despicable Me* merchandise), the massive **Universal Studios Store** (with everything) and **It's A Wrap** (discounted items). The main eating outlet is the wonderful **Monsters Café** (peak season only) offering salads, lasagne, meatloaf, burgers, hotdogs and pizza. The counter-service area is themed like Frankenstein's lab, with the dining areas showing black-and-white horror film clips.

New York

Now head to New York with its impressive architecture and detail – just too clean to be totally authentic!

Twister: Based on the hit film, this brings audiences 'up close and personal' with the awesome forces of a tornado. The 5-storey terror shatters everything in its path, with a splintering climax (watch for the flying cow!), but the noise can be a bit much for under-10s. The pre-show area is a work of art but do it early or late in the day. **TTT**

Revenge Of The Mummy: This superb offering is a high-thrill, high-fun journey into the Ancient Egypt of *The Mummy* film series, fusing coaster technology with space-age robotics and special effects. It starts out as a slow, dark ride through curse-ridden Hamunaptra, but soon takes an ingenious launch into something

more dynamic, using the novel idea of the film studio becoming a full archaeological discovery, with a host of special effects and audio-animatronics as you brave the Mummy's realm. The high-speed whiz in the dark (backwards to start with) doesn't involve inversions but is still a thrill with its tight turns and dips, while there are several clever twists (the front row may get slightly damp!). It is a hugely immersive experience and rates 5-star with the elaborate queuing area, but may be too scary for under-8s. Preview your ride photos ($20–25) as you enter the gift shop. **R:** 4ft/122cm. **TTTT½**

> **BRITTIP**
> For the best ride experience on Revenge Of The Mummy, try to get a back row seat. You are not allowed to carry anything on the ride – loose items must be left in the (free) lockers provided.

The Blues Brothers: Fans of the film will not want to miss this live show as Jake and Elwood Blues (or pretty good doubles anyway) put on a stormin' performance on New York's Delancey Street several times a day. They cruise up in their Bluesmobile and go through a series of the film's hits before heading off into the sunset, stopping only for autographs. **AAAA**

Other entertainment: The energetic can try the **42nd Street Wall Climb** (rock wall) on 5th Avenue ($5). New York also boasts the inevitable amusement arcade. Or just grab a drink at Finnegan's bar and listen to the live music from their fun singer-guitarist.

Revenge of the Mummy

© Universal Orlando

Shopping and dining: Check out **Sahara Traders** for Mummy souvenirs, as well as jewellery and toys, **Rosie's Irish Shop** for all things Irish and **Aftermath** for Twister souvenirs. For dining, you have 2 main restaurants: **Finnegan's Bar and Grill** offers shepherd's pie, fish and chips, corned beef and cabbage, along with steak, burgers, fries and a good range of beers, plus Irish-tinged entertainment and Happy Hour 4–7pm ($3.50 Miller Light; $4.50 imported beers), while **Louie's Italian Restaurant** has counter-service pizza and pasta, ice-cream and tiramisu. There's also a **Ben and Jerry's** store for ice-cream and smoothies, and a Starbucks for coffee and pastries.

San Francisco

Crossing Canal Street brings you right across America to 2 smaller-scale attractions.

Disaster! A Major Motion Picture Ride… Starring YOU: This funny 3-part adventure rarely gets too busy and goes behind the scenes into film special effects in the mythical Disaster Studios. Christopher Walken, playing Studios boss Frank Kincaid in high style, sets the scene for the Sound Stage (a sequence of amusing set-pieces using audience volunteers) and then the Disaster Set – an underground train ride into a San Francisco earthquake, with YOU as the 'extras'. Tremble as walls and ceilings collapse, trains collide, fire erupts and a tidal wave of water pours in. Finally, check out how you did on the screen at the end, which reveals some hilarious results! It's probably a touch scary for small children, while those with bad backs or necks or expectant mothers should not ride the final scene. R: 4ft/122cm (unless accompanied by an adult, with parental discretion). AAAA TTT

Beetlejuice's Graveyard Revue: Disney's Hollywood Studios has *Beauty and the Beast* and *The Little Mermaid*; Universal goes for *Dracula, Frankenstein, The Wolfman* and *Frankenstein's Bride* in this 20min live song-and-dance show compèred by Beetlejuice himself. The raucous concert shuns the prettiness of Disney's attractions yet still comes up with a fun family show (re-worked in 2014), as the graveyard characters perform specially adapted 1980s rock and pop anthems with a mock-horror theme in a great setting. AAA

Other entertainment: Although the Jaws ride is gone, you can still get a photo with the 'Great White' next to the Chez Alcatraz dockside bar, or try the **Amazing Pictures** kiosk and have your face added to a famous view or magazine ($29–59).

Shopping and dining: Visit **San Francisco Candy Factory** for fab pick-n-mix or try the park's best dining choice, **Lombard's Seafood Grille** (high season only; reservations accepted) for great seafood, steak, pasta and sandwiches, all accompanied by a wonderful view over the Central Lagoon. **San Francisco Pastry Co** offers desserts and coffee and **Richter's Burger Co** has some tempting burgers.

The Wizarding World of Harry Potter – Diagon Alley

Put simply, this is the most amazing theme park experience in the world today. The second part of Universal's hugely impressive Potter-verse not only repeats the immersive, film-like setting of Hogsmeade in Islands of Adventure (with a unique link between the two), it goes even deeper into JK Rowling's creation and leaves you in awe of the design and innovation. And that's before you get to the 2 rides, the live entertainment and the food offerings!

Diagon Alley: Hidden behind a realistic setting of The Embankment lies the secret wizarding street and a full array of complex theming, with the entrance next to a façade of Leicester Square tube station. The external design is modern London, right down to the ¼-scale King's Cross Station and a working version of Piccadilly's Eros Statue, where you will also find the iconic Knight Bus. Other elements include Grimmauld Place and the Wyndham Theatre but then visitors walk through the jumbled red-brick barrier next to the tube station and emerge in the jaw-dropping recreation of Diagon Alley, where the towering shop-fronts and mysterious businesses envelop visitors with the full visual effect of the films. Also here is the brooding Knockturn Alley, where the dark arts rule and every nook and cranny is suitably sinister as it is always night-time. Another area, Carkitt Market was created by JK Rowling purely for Universal. It is all new yet it LOOKS like it has been here for 150 years. Its mix of shops and dining are all jumbled together in a seamless way, making this as much of an attraction as the rides themselves. **AAAAA+**

Harry Potter and The Escape From Gringotts: Prepare to be mesmerised as you enter the vaults – and dangers – of the wizarding world's bank. A fire-breathing dragon sits high atop the building and, if that doesn't take your breath away, the stunning entry hall will as realistic goblins – the bank staff – lift the animatronic art to new heights, including an ultra-realistic head clerk who talks to visitors while you wait. The queue twists and turns through the filing office and backrooms before reaching Bill Weasley's office, where you learn you have arrived during the famous episode when Harry, Ron and Hermione break into the vaults. Then you take the elevator deep underground and climb a long flight of steel stairs into a vast cavern that only *feels* like it's miles below the bank. Here you board the ride to share in the perils of Harry and Co as they search for a crucial Horcrux. Half coaster and half 3-D simulator ride, it changes pace from scene to scene as riders brave the various guardians of the vaults, including the dangerous Bellatrix Lestrange, a fire-breathing dragon, an enchanted waterfall, assorted goblin guards and, finally, a close encounter with Lord Voldemort himself (which may be a touch intense for young children).

Riders do escape, of course, and the sense of realism will have you coming back for more – just be aware this draws the longest queues in the park from first thing, so head here straight away or expect a l-o-n-g wait. **R.** 3ft6in/106cm. **TTTTT+**

Hogwarts Express: This neat, realistic ride operates between the 2 parks, as guests journey to Hogsmeade from King's Cross Station. Again, the sense of realism is superb and, after what seems like the longest queue in theme park history, you arrive at Platform 9¾ to board an amazing replica of the famous Hogwarts train, complete with separate compartments and pulled by a Hull-class locomotive. While it runs on a special track backstage, the enclosed carriage 'windows' show highlights of the long journey north to Scotland, including a close encounter with Hagrid on his flying motorcycle, the flying Ford Anglia – and some dangerous Dementors. Oh, and look out for Harry, Hermione and Ron on the train! As this ride goes from park to park, you will need a multi-park ticket to ride, hence there is a real ticket office to check you through, or sell you a ticket to complete the journey. The queue area here is vast but waits rarely top 30mins. **AAAAA+**

Other entertainment: Look out for two completely original shows in Carkitt Market, where **Celestina Warbeck & The Banshees** take the stage several times a day to deliver a rollicking four-song performance. The 'Singing Sorceress' is not dissimilar to Shirley Bassey in a 1940s big-band jazz style, and the songs are all originals, including the classics 'You Stole My Cauldron But You Can't Have My Heart' and 'Beat Back Those Bludgers,

Wiseacre's Wizarding Equipment

© Universal Orlando

Boys and Chuck That Quaffle Here'! **AAAA**. Also on the Market stage is the elaborate story-telling of **Tales Of Beedle The Bard**, a combination of live actor and puppetry show, with the intricate puppets created by award-winning designer Michael Curry. It's especially engaging for children, and Potter fans. **AAA**. Other live entertainment is provided by the essential wizard's shop of **Ollivander's**, where "the wand chooses the wizard' and all manner of strange goings-on highlight this fun actor-staged show. **AAA**. Look out also for the **Knight Bus Conductor**, who will engage visitors as they enter the Wizarding World, and don't miss the bus's Talking Shrunken Head, as his wisecracks might just be aimed at YOU!

Dining and shopping: The essential reality of the Wizarding World is continued into the main dining outlet of **The Leaky Cauldron**, a superb recreation of Diagon Alley's hallmark pub. The food may seem standard pub fare, but the Cottage Pie is excellent, as is the Beef, Lamb and Guinness Stew, while their Ploughman's Platter is positively indulgent with its array of 3 cheeses, pickle, salad, scotch egg and fresh bread (priced variously from $12–15). There is also Toad in the Hole (which Simon may just have helped with!), Fish 'n Chips, two types of sandwich (sausage and chicken) and a Fisherman's Pie. Kids can choose from a mini-pie, mac and cheese and their own fish 'n chips ($7.99). There are then 3 tempting desserts, of which the Sticky Toffee Pudding is to die for. All this can be washed down with signature drinks such as Fishy Green Ale (a variation on bubble tea and non-alcoholic), Otter's Fizzy Orange Juice, Tongue-Tying Lemon Squash and Gilly Water, as well as 2 outstanding beers – the IPA-like Dragon Scale Ale and porter-style Wizards Brew. You order at the counter and are then given a 'magical' candle and shown to a table, where the food will find you thanks to a clever GPS device in the candle! There is a separate menu for breakfast. Still hungry? Head for **Florean Fortescue's**

Ice Cream Parlour where Universal's culinary wizards have come up with a superb array of flavours that are all worth trying, including Earl Grey & Lavender, Apple Crumble, Chocolate Chilli and Clotted Cream. You can also grab a drink – alcoholic and otherwise – at the **Hopping Pot** and **Fountain of Fair Fortune**.

Shopping is another key experience, with 8 immersive stores to please the eye and tease the wallet. **Weasley's Wizard Wheezes** is a multi-storey joke shop with all manner of gags, then there is **Wiseacre's Wizarding Equipment** (for all your essential school gear), **Quality Quidditch Supplies**, **Madam Malkin's Robes** (school uniforms and accessories), **Borgin & Burkes** (the Dark Arts store in Knockturn Alley), **Magical Menagerie** (a soft toy emporium – listen for the animals scurrying about in the upper levels!) and **Scribbulus**, for other Hogwarts mementoes. The shops also feature interactive windows that work with the **special wands** on sale at Ollivander's and Wands By Gregorovitch at $45 each. Look for the markers in the pavement, say the magic command and wave your wand for a host of surprises. You can even change dollars into wizarding notes at the **Money Exchange**, complete with a Goblin host. Be ready to spend a fair bit of time here, as well as money!

World Expo

Continuing around the park brings you to an extensive area that is home to Fear, Aliens and The Simpsons.

Men in Black – Alien Attack: This combination thrill/dark ride takes up where the hit films, starring Will Smith, left off. Visitors are introduced to the MIB Institute in an inventive mock-futuristic setting and enrolled as trainees for a battle around the streets of New York with a horde of escaped aliens. Your 6-person car is equipped with laser zappers for an interactive shoot-out that is like a real-life arcade game, as the aliens can also shoot back to send your car spinning. The finale features a close

Halloween Horror Nights

Universal's massively popular Halloween celebration occurs through late Sept and all of Oct each year and is a wonderfully bloodthirsty – and thoroughly entertaining! – series of evening events. The Horror Nights have become a real trademark and add a suitably grisly touch to park proceedings. The park is transformed with imaginative set pieces from various horror movies, plus live shows and character interaction. The general mix is 7 indoor Scare Houses, each with its own macabre theme (such as *The Walking Dead* and *American Werewolf in London* in 2013), plus open-air Scare Zones, with atmospheric dry ice and characters (zombies, chainsaw guys and various beasts!) lurking in dark corners, and 2 or 3 live presentations, including the signature *Bill & Ted's Excellent Halloween Adventure* (an annual comedy special that heavily satirises pop culture icons). All horror genres are well represented, and the Scare Houses feature some superb 'scare actors' and special effects. The rides are all open (and often with fairly short queues), adding more novelty to the park experience, but this over-the-top (and occasionally downright gruesome) extravaganza is definitely not for kids, especially as the atmosphere can get a bit raucous late in the evening as alcohol is widely available. It goes down a treat with adults with the right sense of humour, though, and begins every evening at 6.30pm–midnight, 1 or 2am. It is a separate event costing between $68 (off-peak Sun–Thurs) and $95 (Fri and Sat) per person, and it is advisable to book in advance at **www.universalorlando.com**. There is even a Frequent Fear Pass for multiple visits on selected evenings (not Fri and Sat, when crowds are heaviest and queues for the Scare Houses can reach 2 hours) and a HHN Universal Express pass for $45–110 (depending on dates), plus a $200 VIP Pass that includes Universal Express access to all the Scare Houses and rides, and a separate buffet and lounge. No costumes are allowed on any evening, though.

encounter with a giant bug that is all mouth. Only your collective shooting skills can save the day, and there are numerous ride variations according to your accuracy. Fast, frantic and a bit confusing, you'll want to come back until you can top 250,000 (for Defender status). **R:** 3ft 6in/106cm. **TTTT**

BRITTIP

For a big score in Men In Black, when you meet the Big Bug – push the big red button!

Fear Factor Live: (high season only) This live-action version of the reality TV show asks audience volunteers to take part in some hair-raising (and stomach-churning!) challenges, with a head-to-head competition to find the biggest daredevil. Auditions take place 70mins before each show, and the audience then gets to see the chosen few battle it out, with clips from the TV show interspersed with live action. Some of the stunts are distinctly off-colour (anyone for a maggot milkshake?) and may not be good for young children (or anyone of a weak disposition!). **TTT**

The Simpsons Ride: The headline attraction in the Springfield sub-area of World Expo, this brings the TV characters to vibrant life in a colourful and amusing production, even if you're not a fan of The Simpsons. It is themed as Krustyland amusement park, brainchild of irascible Krusty the Clown, a bizarre funfair that is the setting for a hectic, breathtaking ride in the company of the Simpson clan. A wicked sound system and state-of-the-art motion simulator technology ensure a frantic race through outlandish attractions (watch out for the Tooth Chipper!). The feel of the 'ride' is amazing and the huge domed

The Leaky Cauldron

screen ensures an outrageously comical sensory experience. However, this can also be a big draw, hence you should visit early or expect a serious wait. **R:** 3ft 4in/101cm. **TTTTT**

Kang and Kodos' Twirl 'n' Hurl: A standard fairground whirligig with some clever touches as the alien duo take 'foolish humans' into 'orbit' and provide a challenge as you twirl. **TT** (**TTTTT** under 6s).

Other entertainment: In Springfield, chance your hand at a series of fairground-type games that require $3–5 to play, like the groan-inducing Sledge-Homer. Look out for Simpsons character meet-and-greets at regular intervals, and **photo ops** with Springfield icons like the Lard Lad Donuts statue, Founders statue and The Seven Little Duffs.

Shopping and dining: Visit **MIB Gear** (at the exit to the ride) for Men In Black-themed clothing and souvenirs (plus photo opportunities with the MIB themselves), while Expo Eats offers drinks and snacks. To complete the immersive Springfield effect, visit the **Kwik-E-Mart** for Simpsons souvenirs (plus more gags), then try the clever counter-service offerings of the food-court. Here you can dine in true Homer fashion (albeit with better quality) at **Krusty Burger, Luigi's Pizza, Frying Dutchmen, Cletus' Chicken Shack** and **Moe's Tavern** (complete with the non-alcoholic Flaming Moe cocktail). For a specially-made brew, you can visit the **Duff Brewery & Shop** with a fab view of the Lagoon. **Bumblebee Man's Taco Truck** completes the heavily remade picture here.

Kang and Kodos' Twirl 'n' Hurl

© Universal Orlando

BRITTIP

Along the lagoon in the Springfield/ KidZone area is East Green, a quiet spot where you can stop to take a break for a while.

KidZone

This is a great place to let the kids loose on their own, but it does also feature several great family attractions.

Animal Actors On Location!: An amusing mix of video, animal performance and audience interaction, several children are invited to help present some unlikely feats and stunts featuring a range of wildlife, from parakeets and pigs to cats, dogs and an orang-utan. Many have been rescued from animal shelters and gone on to feature in films before finding a home at Universal. The theatre also provides an escape from the queues. **AAAA**

Fievel's Playland: Strictly for kids, this playground, based on the enlarged world of the cartoon mouse, offers the chance to bounce under a 1,000-gallon hat, crawl through a giant boot, climb a giant spider's web and shoot the rapids (a 200ft/61m waterslide) in Fievel's sardine can. **TTTT** (young 'uns only!)

A Day in the Park with Barney: Again strictly for the younger set (2–5), the purple dinosaur from kids' TV is brought to super-dee-duper life in a large arena that features a pre-show before the 15min main event, plus an interactive post-show area. **AA** (**AAAAA** under-5s)

ET Adventure: This is as glorious as scenic rides come, with a picturesque queuing area from the film and then a spectacular leap on the trademark flying bicycles to save ET's home planet. Steven Spielberg has added some special effects and characters, and you have an individual ET greeting at the end. The masses often overlook this corner of the park, hence it's a good afternoon choice. **R:** 4ft/122cm to ride alone, but smaller children can ride with parents. **AAAAA**

UNIVERSAL STUDIOS with children

Our guide to the attractions that generally appeal to the different age groups:

Under-5s
Animal Actors On Location!, Curious George Goes To Town, A Day In The Park With Barney, ET Adventure, Fievel's Playland, Kang & Kodos' Twirl 'n' Hurl, Universal's Superstar Parade.

5–8s
All the above (minus Barney), plus Disaster! and TRANSFORMERS: The Ride – 3-D (with parental discretion), Despicable Me, Hogwarts Express, Men In Black, Shrek 4 D, The Simpsons and Woody Woodpecker's Nuthouse Coaster, Universal's Cinematic Spectacular.

9–12s
All the above, plus Hollywood Rip Ride Rockit, Beetlejuice's Graveyard Revue, Fear Factor Live!, Harry Potter and The Escape From Gringotts, Revenge Of The Mummy, Terminator 2: 3-D Battle Across Time, and TRANSFORMERS: The Ride – 3-D, Twister.

Over-12s
Hollywood Rip Ride Rockit, Beetlejuice's Graveyard Revue, The Blues Brothers, Disaster!, ET Adventure, Fear Factor Live, Despicable Me, Men In Black – Alien Attack, Revenge Of The Mummy, Shrek 4-D, The Simpsons, Terminator 2: 3-D, and TRANSFORMERS: The Ride – 3-D, Twister, Universal's Cinematic Spectacular, Universal's Horror Make-Up Show.

Woody Woodpecker's Nuthouse Coaster: Anchoring the excellent under-10s adventure land is this child-sized but still quite racy roller-coaster. The ride reaches only 28ft/8m high and 22mph, but it seems the real deal to young 'uns. However, the height restriction is still 3ft/91cm. TTTT (juniors only)

BRITTIP
If you want to let your youngsters loose in the Curious George playground, it is advisable to bring swimsuits or a change of clothing.

Curious George Goes To Town: Kids of all ages love this adventure playground with plenty of ways to get wet. It combines toddler play, water-based play stations and a huge interactive ball pool, and is a real bonus for harassed parents. The town theme includes buildings to climb, pumps and hoses to spray water, a ball factory in which to shoot, dump and blast thousands of foam balls and – the tour de force – 2 huge buckets of water that flood the street below at regular intervals. TTTTT (under-12s) Curious George roams the KidZone from time to time, while other characters make regular appearances.

Other entertainment: young 'uns should head for **Barney's Backyard**, a neat indoor play area for those under 36in/91cm tall, including a photo opportunity with Barney himself (in addition to the one at the end of each show). It also has the parental benefit of being in the air-conditioned cool!

Shopping and dining: Shop at the fun **Spongebob Storepants** for everything to do with Spongebob and friends in an immersive environment, complete with character photo opportunity, plus the **Barney Store** and **ET's Toy Closet and Photo Spot**. For a quick bite, **Kidzone Pizza Company** offers pizza and chicken fingers.

Hollywood
Finally, your circular tour of Universal returns you to the main entrance via Hollywood (where else?).

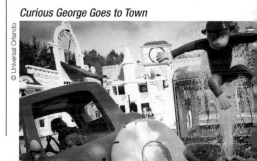

Curious George Goes to Town

© Universal Orlando

Universal's Horror Make-Up Show: Not recommended for under-12s, this demonstrates some of the ways in which films have terrorised us, from classic black-and-white examples to modern horror movies. Using film clips and 2 special effects 'experts', the audience is treated to a slapstick approach to horror make-up. It's a 20min show, queues are rarely long and the special effects are largely amusing. AAA

Terminator 2: 3-D Battle Across Time: Another first-of-its-kind attraction, this is part film, part show, part experience but all action, and usually leaves its audience in awe. The 'Wow!' factor works overtime as you go through a 10min pre-show representing a trip to the Cyberdyne Systems company from the Terminator films and then into a 700-seat theatre for a 'presentation' on its latest robot creations. The show is interrupted, though, by John and Sarah Connor and mayhem ensues, with the audience subjected to an array of (loud) special effects, including real actors interacting with the screen and the audience, indoor pyrotechnics and a climactic 3-D film finale that takes the Terminator story a step further. TTTTT

Lucy: A Tribute: This attraction will mean little to all but devoted fans of the late Lucille Ball and her 1960s TV comedy *The Lucy Show*. Classic shows, home movies, costumes and scripts are paraded, but youngsters will find it tedious. AA

Terminator 2 – 3D

© Universal Orlando

Other entertainment: The Hollywood Character Zone provides numerous character appearances throughout the day along Hollywood Boulevard, from Scooby Doo and Shaggy to Dudley Do-Right, The Flintstones and Lucille Ball. Characters from the **Superstar Parade** appear periodically next to Mel's Drive-In.

BRITTIP
Budding magicians should make a bee-line for the small Theater Magic shop next to Mel's Drive-In, with merchandise and some terrific small-scale magic shows several times daily.

Shopping and dining: Look for Terminator gifts and clothing in **Cyber Image**, all manner of headgear in **The Brown Derby**, Hollywood legends' jewellery in **Studio Styles** and movie memorabilia, notably for Betty Boop and Lucille Ball, in **Silver Screen Collectibles**. There are 4 contrasting eateries: **Mel's Drive-In**, a re-creation from the film *American Graffiti*, serving burgers and hot dogs (though Richter's has better burgers); **Café La Bamba** for the daily Parade Character Breakfast (p171); **Schwab's Pharmacy**, with traditional ice-cream, milkshakes and sundaes; and **Beverly Hills Boulangerie** for a range of sandwiches, cheesecake, pastries, juices and coffee.

Parade time!

The daily outing of Universal's Superstar Parade takes place each day at 2 or 5pm in a vibrant and lively style, with dozens of performers and interactive characters. The 4 main sets of 'superstars' are led by Gru and his Minions from *Despicable Me* and followed by Spongebob Squarepants and his Bikini Bottom pals, including skaters and stilt walkers – and with the world's biggest pineapple! EB and the bunnies from 2011 film *Hop* take over, including some snazzy live drumming, while Nickelodeon stars Dora and Diego from *Dora The Explorer* and *Go, Diego, Go!* complete the line-up, with aerialists and other high-energy performers. The huge floats – especially for the Minions – are feature-packed, and the parade has 2 dance stops to allow characters to meet guests. It is just 15mins but there are up to 4 other meet-and-greet performances during the day when specific floats come into the park for their own Street Parties, while the characters also come out individually along Hollywood Boulevard. AAAA

BRITTIP
The 2 best viewing spots for the Parade are halfway along the main New York street (opposite the Palace Arcade) or on Hollywood Boulevard, outside the Cyber Image shop.

The Parade also has a **Character Breakfast** 8–10.30am daily, with the chance to meet the Minions, pose with Spongebob, get autographs from Dora and Diego and enjoy a full breakfast at **Café La Bamba** ($25 adults, $11 3–9s). Those booking the breakfast also receive VIP viewing for the Parade and early access to selected rides.

Universal's Cinematic Spectacular: the nightly finale is this 20min film, firework, fountain and special effect-laden performance on the Main Lagoon. With 3 'stages' and numerous water effects, it celebrates 100 years of Universal movies with clips choreographed to some spectacular fountains and pyrotechnics. See how many movies you can spot, as well-known moments from the likes of *E.T.*, *Apollo 13*, *Jurassic Park*, *The Mummy* and *The Fast & The Furious* are projected on to the fountains, all with narration by Morgan Freeman. The show culminates in a firework frenzy, underscored by dramatic music (on 300 outdoor speakers) and superb digital projection for a truly original presentation. There is a seasonal version for Christmas, too. TTTT

For VIP viewing of the Spectacular, book the Cinematic Dining Experience with dinner at Lombard's Seafood Grille and reserved seats in the new VIP area on the Springfield

waterfront ($45 for adults, $13 3–9s). Book on 407 224 7554 or at **www.universalorlando.com**.

BRITTIP
You need to be facing one of the 3 stages (they are double-sided, so can be seen from both sides of the Lagoon) of the Universal Cinematic Spectacular for a good view, notably along the waterfront of the World Expo area or in the East Green park.

Special programmes

Universal Studios features some brilliant extra seasonal entertainment for **Mardi Gras**, with a hectic, bead-throwing parade, plus music, street entertainment and authentic New Orleans food each Sat at 6pm mid-Feb–mid-Apr (and free with park admission). The day culminates in a live concert with well-known acts (including Kool & The Gang, Nelly and Robin Thicke in 2014), but it does draw HUGE crowds. Universal also throws a party for **Fourth of July**, when the park presents a major firework spectacular, while the Summer Concert Series runs on Sat in June and early July, with stars such as ZZ Top and Big Time Rush. And don't miss the Studios at Christmas (p39).

Character dining at The Kitchen at the Hard Rock Hotel

© Universal Orlando

Islands of Adventure

With the arrival of Diagon Alley at Universal Studios, you'd think there might be slightly less focus on the original Harry Potter development here but not a bit of it. In fact, with the Hogwarts Express ride now connecting the two areas, it's possible this will be busier than ever in 2015, especially if the new King Kong attraction is ready before the end of the year.

The Islands of Adventure opened in 1999 under the supervision of creative consultant Steven Spielberg, and it provided one of the most complete and thrilling theme parks you could imagine, containing an upbeat collection of high-adrenalin rides, shows and entertainment, plus some fine dining. Then JK Rowling's boy wizard arrived and added a whole new 'world' of excitement.

The park has a full range of attractions, from out-and-out thrills to pure family entertainment. OK, so they aren't really islands (the areas form a chain around the central lagoon), but that's the only illusion. And you get a lot for your money here, unless you have extremely timid children or under-5s. Seuss Landing will usually keep preschoolers amused for several hours, while Camp Jurassic is a clever adventure playground for 5–12s, but the rest of the park, with its 8 5-star thrill rides and other attractions, is primarily geared to kids of 10 and over, their parents and especially teenagers. There are 6 elements that look alarming, but don't be put off – they all deliver immense fun as well as terrific spectator value! If any one ride sums up IoA, it is Harry Potter and the Forbidden Journey, which took theme

Islands of Adventure at a glance

Location	Off exits 75A and 74B from I-4; Universal Boulevard and Kirkman Road
Size	110 acres/45ha in 6 'islands'
Hours	9am–6, 7 or 8pm off peak; 8 or 9am–9 or 10pm high season (Washington's birthday, Easter, summer holidays, Thanksgiving, Christmas)
Admission	Under-3s free; 3–9 $90 (1-day ticket), $166 (2-day Park-to-Park ticket), $300 (FlexTicket), $340 (FlexTicket Plus); adult (10+) $96, $177, $320, $360. Prices do not include tax.
Parking	$17 (preferred parking $22; valet parking $30)
Lockers	Immediately to left through main gates; $8
Pushchairs	$15 and $25, kiddie cars $17.99 and $27.99 next to locker hire
Wheelchairs	$12 and $50 (with photo ID as deposit)
Top attractions	Harry Potter and the Forbidden Journey, Hogwarts Express, Amazing Adventures Of Spider-Man, Dragon Challenge, Incredible Hulk Coaster, Jurassic Park River Adventure
Don't miss	Eighth Voyage Of Sindbad, Jurassic Park Discovery Centre, If I Ran The Zoo playground (for toddlers), Three Broomsticks restaurant and Ollivander's Wand Shop
Hidden costs	**Meals** Burger, chips and coke $10.69 3-course lunch $20–35 (Confisco Grill) Kids' meal $5.99–6.99 (drink not included)
	T-shirts $21.95–34.95
	Souvenirs 95c—$6,500
	Sundries Caricature drawings $15–41 (black and white and airbrush colour); Butterbeer $4.50 regular, $5.50 frozen

park ride technology to a whole new level.

Private nursing facilities, an open area for feeding and resting (with high chairs) and nappy-changing stations, can be found at the Family Service Facility at Guest Services (to the right inside the main gates), while ALL restrooms throughout the park are equipped with nappy-changing facilities. First aid is provided in Sindbad's Village in the Lost Continent, just across from Oasis Coolers, and in Port of Entry.

Port of Entry

You arrive for IoA as you do for Universal Studios, in the big multi-storey car parks off I-4 and Universal Boulevard and pass right through the CityWalk area, where you come to the main entrance plaza (head for the huge Pharos Lighthouse). As with Universal Studios, you can purchase the Universal Express pass for Islands of Adventure ($30–100, depending on time of year) at various locations throughout the park and at Guest Services. Once through the gates, the lockers, pushchair and wheelchair hire are on your left as the Port of Entry opens up before you. This elaborate 'village' consists of shops and eateries, so push straight on until you hit the main lagoon.

Shopping and dining: Later in the day, return to check out the extensive retail experience at places like **IoA Trading Company** and **Ocean Trader Market** for a full range of Islands of Adventure merchandise. You can enjoy a coffee and pastry at the inevitable **Starbucks** or the **Croissant Moon Bakery** (also with croissants and sandwiches), or sample the huge cinnamon rolls and pastries of **Cinnabon**. Alternatively, try lunch or dinner at **Confisco Grille** with tastes from around the world including Italian, Mexican and Asian as well as American, and a good range of dishes from sandwiches and burgers to salads, Fajitas, ribs, pizza and pasta. Or just grab a beverage and a snack at the **Backwater Bar** (Happy Hour 4pm–closing time). Above all, be sure to take in the wonderful architecture throughout Port of Entry, which borrows from Middle East, Far East and African themes and uses bric-a-brac from all over the world.

Beating the queues: At the end of the street, you will need to decide which way to head first as there are 9 attractions where the queues build up quickly and remain that

Backwater Bar

Port of Entry
1 Ocean Trader Market
2 Confisco Grille

Marvel Super-Hero Island
3 Incredible Hulk Coaster
4 Dr Doom's Fearfall
5 Café 4
6 Captain America Diner
7 The Amazing Adventures of Spider-Man
8 Storm Force Accelatron

Toon Lagoon
9 Popeye And Bluto's Bilge-Rat Barges
10 Dudley Do-Right's Ripsaw Falls
11 Me Ship, The Olive
12 Comic Strip Café
13 Toon Lagoon Amphitheater

Jurassic Park
14 Jurassic Park River Adventure
15 Pteranodon Flyers
16 Camp Jurassic
17 Discovery Center
18 Thunder Falls Terrace

The Wizarding World of Harry Potter
19 Harry Potter and the Forbidden Journey
20 Filch's Emporium
21 Flight of the Hippogriff
22 Olivander's
23 Dervish and Banges
24 Three Broomsticks
25 Zonko's
26 Dragon Challenge
27 Hogwart's Express

The Lost Continent
28 Mythos Restaurant
29 Mystic Fountain
30 The Eighth Voiage of Sindbad
31 Poseidon's Fury

Seuss Landing
32 Circus McGurkus Café Stoo-pendous
33 High In The Sky Seuss Trolley Train Ride
34 Caro-Seuss-el
35 If I Ran The Zoo
36 The Cat In The Hat
37 One Fish, Two Fish, Red Fish, Blue Fish

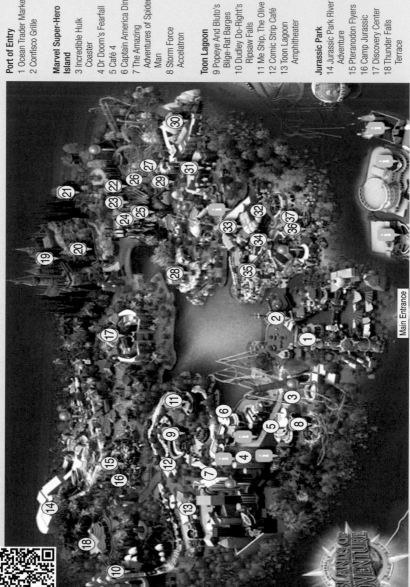

Main Entrance

way. If you are among the majority lured by Harry Potter, turn right (through Seuss Landing and The Lost Continent; bear in mind you may be directed into Jurassic Park to queue just to get into Wizarding World, especially in peak season, which underlines the need to arrive early). If you're after the big thrill rides, turn left into Marvel Super-Hero Island and head straight to Spider-Man, then do Dr Doom's Fearfall and the Incredible Hulk Coaster.

BRITTIP

There are 2 entrances to the Wizarding World of Harry Potter: from Jurassic Park and The Lost Continent. The latter is much more dramatic and offers the full Hogsmeade Village panorama.

Dinosaur fans should go left around the lagoon to Jurassic Park for the River Adventure before the majority arrive. Once you are nice and wet, go back to Toon Lagoon for Ripsaw Falls and the Bilge-Rat Barges. Or, if you have younger children, turn right into the multicoloured world of Seuss Landing and enjoy The Cat In The Hat and High In The Sky Seuss Trolley Train Ride prior to the main crowd build-up.

Turning right, in an anti-clockwise direction, here's what you find.

Seuss Landing

There is not a straight line to be seen in this vivid 3-D working of the books of Dr Seuss. The characters may not mean much to those unfamiliar with the children's stories, but everyone can relate to the fun here (though queues build up quickly). Take your time and try not to miss the clever detail, from squirt ponds to beach scenes, while the lagoon-front area provides a quieter corner to escape the crowds.

Caro-Seuss-el: This intricate carousel ride on some of the Seuss characters – cowfish, elephant-birds and dog-a-lopes, for example – has rider-activated features that are a big hit with children. **AA** (**AAAA** under-5s).

One Fish, Two Fish, Red Fish, Blue Fish: A fairground ride with a twist as you pilot these Seussian fish up and down according to the rhyme that plays while you ride. Get it wrong and you get squirted! More fun for the younger set. **TTT** (**TTTTT** under-5s)

The Cat in the Hat: Prepare for a ride with a difference as you board these crazy 6-passenger 'couches' to meet the world's most adventurous cat and friends Thing One and Thing Two. You literally go for a spin through this storybook world, and it may be a bit much for very young children. The slow-moving queues are a bit of a drag, so try to get here early or leave it until later in the day. **AAAA**/**TTT**

If I Ran the Zoo: Interactive playgrounds don't get much better for the pre-school brigade than with these Seuss character scenarios, some of which can be pretty wet! Hugely imaginative and great fun to watch. **TTTTT** (under-5s)

The High in the Sky Seuss Trolley Train Ride: This fun family adventure high above Seuss Landing has terrific

One Fish, Two Fish

appeal to youngsters as you board a trolley to journey into the world of the Sneetches, visiting the Inking and Stamping Room, the Star Wash Room and a tour inside the Circus McGurkus Café Stoo-pendous. It is slow-paced and scenic, but it does draw slow-moving queues, so head here early with under-9s. AAAA

Other entertainment: Look out for character appearances by The Cat In The Hat, Thing One and Thing Two and The Grinch outside the Circus McGurkus, and the character-filled celebration of the Oh! The Stories You'll Hear street show.

Shopping and dining: If the land has captivated you, you can buy the books at Dr Seuss' **All The Books You Can Read Store**, or a full variety of character merchandise at the **Mulberry Street Store**. **Snookers and Snookers Sweet Candy Cookers** is a super sweet shop, while snacks and drinks can be had at **Hop On Pop Ice Cream Shop**, **Moose Juice Goose Juice** and **Green Eggs and Ham Café** (sandwiches and burgers). The **Circus McGurkus Café Stoo-pendous** is a mind-boggling eatery for fried chicken, lasagne, spaghetti, burgers and pizza – with clowns and pipe organs.

The Lost Continent
This land underwent a rather drastic reduction to accommodate Harry Potter, but it still offers some eye-catching locations.

The Eighth Voyage of Sindbad: This stunt and special effects show is fun for both elaborate staging and

Circus McGurkus Café Stoo-pendous

Mythos Restaurant

performance. Mythical adventurer Sindbad and side-kick Kabob tackle evil witch Miseria in a bid to rescue Princess Amoura, and the action springs up in surprising places. There are several loud bangs that could scare young children but otherwise it's good family fun. The cast appear for photos and autographs post-show. TT AAAA

Poseidon's Fury: A walk-through show that puts its audience at the heart of the action as a journey in the company of a hapless young archaeologist takes a turn for the worse in the lost temple of Poseidon. You pass through an amazing water vortex before your expedition awakens an ancient demon. There is an element of suspense, but the special effects showdown between Poseidon and the demon is amazing. Queuing is tedious, but it is inside. TTT

Other entertainment: Try a bit of mystic manipulation with the **Psychic Readers**, while the Shop of Wonders houses **Theatre Magic**, with continuous live shows from 11am. But beware The Mystic Fountain; it can strike up a conversation – and then soak you!

Shopping and dining: Find some original souvenirs at **The Coin Mint** (watch coins forged and struck) and **Coat Of Arms** (explore the history of your family name and coat of arms),

Treasures of Poseidon (jewellery, clothing), and **The Pearl Factory** (pick an oyster). Food options include **The Fire-Eater's Grill** (chicken fingers, hotdogs, salads, fries and drinks) and **Frozen Desert** (sundaes and sodas). The ornate **Mythos Restaurant** provides the best dining in IoA; the food (seafood, salads, grills, pizza and pasta) is first class, but the setting (inside a dormant volcano with fountains and clever lighting) is a real attraction (3-course meal $21–37, kids' meals $5.99–10.99).

Wizarding World of Harry Potter – Hogsmeade

This 'Island' has significantly boosted the park's attendance since it opened in 2010 and draws BIG crowds. The magnificent edifice of Hogwarts Castle looms large over the 20acre spread of the famous Wizarding World but the whole area is completely immersive as it uses the design genius behind the films. Entering from The Lost Continent area provides the grand view, through Hogsmeade and with Hogwarts seemingly towering above (the use of architectural perspective is masterful), and you are drawn into an all-encompassing realm where chimneys smoke, icicles glitter, owls roost, visitors are warned to 'Observe the spell limits' and Butterbeer is real!

Hogsmeade Village: Walk through the grand archway into the Wizarding World and a powerful sense of realism envelops you. This is a shimmering, snow-covered version of the magical settlement Harry, Ron and Hermione inhabit. It is the shopping and dining heart of the Wizarding World, but is an attraction in itself. Here you will find a wonderful photo opportunity with the Hogwarts Express, while nearly all the shop windows feature 'wizardly' animatronic touches. The Owl Clock comes to life every 15mins; the wooden-raftered Owlery is a work of art; and you may just encounter Moaning Myrtle in the loos! Numerous other clever effects and design touches all help to transform this corner of Florida into J K Rowling's authentic creation (see also Shopping and dining). AAAAA+

Dragon Challenge: This towering coaster delves into the Goblet of Fire story involving the big contest between the wizarding schools of Hogwarts, Durmstrang and Beauxbatons, represented by the

Hogsmeade Arch

billowing banners at the entrance. The long, elaborate queuing area (we LOVE the Corridor of Candles!) sets the scene for your 'flight' on either a Chinese Fireball or Hungarian Horntail dragon, with perils aplenty. You choose which dragon to ride (the tracks differ slightly) and this is a suspended coaster, so your legs dangle free – the initial drop is therefore like going into free-fall! Coaster aficionados reckon the best ride is in the back of the Hungarian (blue) dragon, but both offer an awesome experience. The coaster features a 100ft/30m drop, 5 rapid-fire inversions among the intertwined tracks and hits a top speed of 60mph/96kph. **R:** 4ft 6in/137cm; all loose items must be left in the lockers by the entrance. **TTTTT+**

◀◀▶ **BRITTIP**
The lockers for Dragon Challenge are in the Hogsmeade train station, but are free only for the duration of your ride. Make a note of your locker number!

The Flight of The Hippogriff:
This junior-sized coaster is aimed primarily at youngsters and features a journey into Hagrid's realm, where his love of outlandish creatures gives rise to this swooping ride. Hagrid offers instructions and warnings as you wind through the queue, and you may even hear Fang barking from inside his hut. There are no big drops, but it delivers a surprisingly fast-paced whirl. Be sure to bow to the Hippogriff at the start of the ride. **R:** 3ft 4in/92cm. **TTT (TTTT** for 6–12s)

Harry Potter and the Forbidden Journey:
This is the Big One: a trip inside the legendary halls of Hogwarts, and a breathtaking plunge on a state-of-the-art ride, Quidditch and all. The basic premise is that 'muggles' (non-wizarding types, i.e. you!) have been invited to tour the school for the first time and see much of the castle's interior. The queuing area is part discovery, part storytelling and part entertainment as it winds through, out, around and back in again for some 1,500ft/400m before you even get to the ride! Be ready for a LONG time on your feet as you traverse the corridors, traipse through the greenhouse, tiptoe along the Portrait Hall (where the paintings of the 4 founders of Hogwarts come to life in magical fashion) and tread the stone floors of the Gryffindor common room. Along the way, you'll

Harry Potter and the Forbidden Journey

© Universal Orlando

be greeted by Professor Dumbledore in his study (complete with more talking portraits), be accosted by the Fat Lady (another painting-come-to-life) and enter the Defence Against the Dark Arts classroom, where Harry, Ron and Hermione urge visitors to abandon their 'boring' tour and come to the Quidditch match (with the aid of a magic spell).

BRITTIP
Once again, this is an unpredictable, dynamic ride, with sudden twists, turns and tilts. You are strongly advised to leave all loose items in the free-to-use lockers just inside the castle.

Finally, you reach the Room of Requirement (past the Sorting Hat), where your mode of transport to the match is revealed – magical flying benches. With some pre-ride warnings, you are then strapped in to your 'bench' and are up, up and away. Only things don't go as planned and, before you can say 'Expecto Patronum' you're on a crazy dash through some of the young wizard's most dangerous adventures. Your unique ride vehicle – which moves on a giant robotic arm – sweeps you through dramatic settings that combine clever film technology with full-scale, all-encompassing scenery, creating a totally convincing effect as you move up, down, backwards, forwards and even sideways.

BRITTIP
Look for the Single Rider queue at Harry Potter and the Forbidden Journey – it can save a LOT of time.

There is a close encounter with a fire-breathing dragon, an army of giant spiders, a Death Eater and a narrow escape from the clutches of the Whomping Willow before the big finale in a spooky underground cavern where it's up to Harry, naturally, to try to save the day. The 4min whirl will seem a LOT longer as the ride's breathtaking sequence of special effects make this an eye-popping extravaganza of sound,

movement and high-tech dynamics. It is an astounding theme park experience, but it WILL scare small children (and those with arachnophobia!), and it draws HUGE queues – in excess of 2hrs at peak times – so you are strongly advised to do this early in the day. **R:** 4ft/122cm. **TTTTT+** NB: Universal's Express Pass does NOT cover this ride. You exit through Filch's Emporium of Confiscated Goods, where you'll find plush Hedwig owls, Crookshank cats, Scabbers rats and 3-headed dogs (watch out, he growls!), plus a range of tempting Azkaban and House-related clothing and gifts. You also pick up your ride photos here ($24.95–49.95).

BRITTIP
Look out for the Marauders Map in Filch's Emporium, plus other clever Hogwarts signature gadgets and gizmos among the merchandise.

Hogwart's Express: This is the new element in Hogsmeade, the 'northern' end of the famous train ride from King's Cross Station. With its own station (and queue area), it provides the full effect of arriving at or departing from this mythical

The Flight of the Hippogriff

Scottish village. The station is almost completely enclosed to allow the designers to build up the illusion, and then you pass through a small section of the Forbidden Forest to reach Hogsmeade itself and enjoy your first full view of the village with Hogwarts towering behind it. The ride from Hogsmeade to King's Cross is also different, screen-wise, from the one that brings you here, with more scenes of London and some of Harry's other exploits from the films. Don't forget, you need a 2-park ticket to ride the Express, or you can pay the extra fee at the ticket office. AAAAA+

Other entertainment: The **TriWizard Spirit Rally** celebrates the upcoming tournament, with the Beauxbatons Academy ribbon dancers and staff-fighting wizards from Durmstrang Institute. Hogwarts is represented by the Frog Choir (4 students and 2 enormous frogs!), an ensemble whose vocal talents result in an entertaining show.

BRITTIP

Butterbeer is non-alcoholic and comes in 2 sweet varieties, 'regular' and frozen (slushie style). Try both, as they taste quite different! It's also usually easier to get served in the Hog's Head rather than at the busy street carts.

Shopping and dining: As with all things here, the level of detail given to shopping and dining locations is so intricate they are attractions in their own right. Many items can be found only here in Hogsmeade, but whether

Honeydukes

Hogwart's Express

you pull your wallet out or not, be sure to have a wander through each to soak up the atmosphere.

When shopping, be sure to visit the famous sweetshop **Honeydukes**, the place to buy Cauldron Cakes, Bertie Bott's Every Flavour Beans, Chocolate Frogs and more. Find 136 varieties of sweets, many from the Harry Potter films or well-known British favourites (including jelly babies, humbugs and sherbet lemons). **Dervish and Banges** supplies 'students' with Quidditch gear and school related clothing, Luna Lovegood's 3-D Quibbler, and even the Nimbus 2001 broomsticks. **Owl Post:** Buy your wand here after visiting Ollivander's, and don't miss sending a letter by owl! Your mail will receive 1 of 4 different Hogsmeade postmarks, a detail friends and family back home can enjoy. Also here are stationery and owl-related gifts. Every wizard needs a wand, and **Ollivander's** has 13 varieties to choose from. Here, 'the wand also chooses the wizard,' with surprising special effects similar to those Harry experienced when choosing his wand. Because the environment is interactive and the shop is small, a limited number are allowed inside for each 'show' and wait times are long all day. AAAAA

There is only one sit-down dining location here, but it's a corker. A 'Cathedral to Butterbeer', the **Three**

© Universal Orlando

Broomsticks menu features British favourites such as shepherd's pie, fish and chips and Cornish pasties, along with the Great Feast, a family-style meal of salad, ribs, chicken, roast potatoes and corn on the cob ($49.99 party of 4; $12.99 per extra person). Entrées $7.99–15.99, with desserts $3.49–3.99, including strawberry and peanut-butter ice cream, found only in the Wizarding World. They also serve a different menu for breakfast. Next door is the **Hog's Head Pub**, complete with animatronic boar's head, where you'll find Hog's Head Brew ($7.46).

BRITTIP

Of all the buildings, the Three Broomsticks is a must-see experience of dramatic interior design and special effects. Look up in the rafters for arriving owls, magical maids and the roaming House Elf!

All in all, it's an immense collection of dramatic and charming elements (witness the animated Prisoner of Azkaban poster in Hogsmeade) that add up to a vivid portrayal of J K Rowling's work. You don't need to be a fan to enjoy the Wizarding World and,

like the Diagon Alley area in Universal Studios, the only snag is the huge crowd it draws for much of the day, as most of the shops are quite small and quickly feel congested. Arriving early is highly advisable (hence the early entry perk with Universal hotels is so valuable here), but you should also try to see it after dark, when the lighting effects make it even more dramatic.

Jurassic Park

Now travel back to the Cretaceous age and the make-believe dinosaur film world where extravagant scenery will have you looking over your shoulder for stray dinos.

Jurassic Park River Adventure: From scenic splendour, the mood changes to hidden menace as your journey into this magnificent waterborne realm brings you up close and personal with some seriously realistic dinosaurs. Inevitably, your passage is diverted from the safe to the hazardous, and the danger increases as the 16-person raft climbs into the heights of the main building – with raptors loose everywhere. You are aware of something large lurking in the shadows – will you fall prey to the T-Rex, or will your boat take

Pteranodon Flyers

© Universal Orlando

Jurassic Park Discovery Center

the 85ft/26m plunge to safety (plus a good soaking)? Queues usually move briskly but will top an hour in mid-afternoon. **R:** 3ft 6in/106cm. The ride photo comes in various packages ($19.95–25). **TTTT**

BRITTIP

Automobile Association members receive a 10% discount on all ride photos at Universal Orlando.

Pteranodon Flyers: The slow-moving queues are a major turn-off, especially for a fairly average ride, which glides gently over much of Jurassic Park (though it reaches a height of almost 30ft/9m). **R:** It is designed mainly for kids, and anyone

Pteranodon Flyers

© Universal Orlando

OVER the height range of 3ft–4ft 8in/91–142cm (usually 11+) must be accompanied by a child of the right height. **TT** (**TTTT** under-9s). The Universal Express pass is not valid here, either.

Camp Jurassic: More excellent kids' fare with the mountainous jungle giving way to an 'active' volcano for youngsters to explore, climb and slide down. Squirt guns and spitter dinosaurs add to the fun (for kids, but parents can explore!). **TTTT**

Discovery Center: This indoor centre offers various interactive games, like creating a dinosaur via DNA sequencing, mixing your own DNA with a dino on a touch-screen, seeing through the eyes of various large reptiles and handling 'dino eggs', plus other hands-on exhibits. It's ideal in summer as it's fully air-conditioned (10am–4pm; 5pm peak season). **AAA**

Other entertainment: The more adventurous can try the Rock Climbing Wall (just outside River Adventure) for an extra $5.

Shopping and dining: Visit **Dinostore** and **Jurassic Outfitters** for the best shopping, while you can try **Burger Digs** (huge burger platters), **Pizza Predattoria**, **Thunder Falls Terrace** (counter service rotisserie chicken, ribs, burgers, turkey legs and salads, plus a great view of River Adventure) or the **Watering Hole** (hot dogs, snacks and drinks).

King Kong/Skull Island: Behind the Thunder Falls Terrace at the Toon Lagoon end of Jurassic Park, look for all the construction going on under cover of large green fences. This will be the King Kong 360 3-D attraction that had not been officially announced as we went to press but which is widely rumoured to be the park's next attraction. It's hard to imagine it being completed before the end of 2015 at the earliest but, if it is, prepare for a ride into Skull Island, lair of the mighty gorilla, where your tram vehicle gets caught in the middle of a battle between three marauding Vastatosaurus Rex and Kong himself. With 3-D film effects, motion and a vast sound system, this will be an epic journey into the prehistoric world created by Peter Jackson for his King Kong remake in 2005.

Toon Lagoon

The thrills continue here with a watery theme and more comic-book elements from (US) newspaper cartoon characters. Children will also love the fountains, squirt pools and overflowing fire hydrants!

Popeye And Bluto's Bilge-Rat Barges: Every park seems to have a variation on the white-water raft ride, but this is one of the wettest! Fast, bouncy and unpredictable, it has water coming at you from every direction, a couple of sizeable drops and a whirl through the Octo-plus Grotto that adds to the fun. If you don't want to get wet, don't ride, because there is no escaping the deluge here. This is also one of the top 5 for long queues (at least when it's hot), but it's worth the wait. **R:** 4ft/ 122cm. Look for the Water Blasters (for 25c) on the bridge to give riders a wet start. **TTTTT**

BRITTIP

A change of clothes is often advisable after the Barges, unless it's mega hot. Bring a waterproof bag for your valuables or leave them in a locker.

Dudley Do-Right's Ripsaw Falls: A flume ride that sends its passengers on a wild (and steep!) journey in the company of guileless Mountie Dudley Do-Right, bidding to save girlfriend Nell from the evil Snidely Whiplash. The action builds to an explosive finale at the top of a 75ft/27m abyss that drops you through the roof of a

Dudley Do-Right's Ripsaw Falls

ramshackle dynamite shack to the lagoon below. Wet? You bet! **R:** 3ft 8in/111cm. **TTTTT** More Water Blasters on the bridge overlooking the final drop get riders even wetter.

Me Ship, The Olive: This purpose-built kids' playland is designed as a 3-storey boat full of interactive fun and games, including water cannons, bells and slides (ideal for squirting riders on the Bilge-Rat Barges below), in best Popeye style. **TTTT** (for youngsters)

Other entertainment: Comic Strip Lane is the place to meet the Classic Comic Book Characters like Beetle Bailey, Hagar the Horrible, Betty Boop, Popeye, and Dudley Do-Right. You can also try various fairground stall games for $5–10.

Shopping and dining: There is the usual array of character shops, like **Gasoline Alley**, **Boop Oop A Doop** and **Toon Extra**, while you can grab a humongous sandwich at **Blondie's** (home of the Dagwood), a trademark burger at **Wimpy's,** sample the food court of **Comic Strip Café** (burgers, fish, chicken, Chinese dishes, pizza and pasta), something cool at **Cathy's Ice Cream** or a cold beverage at **Ale To The Chief.**

Marvel Super-Hero Island

Finally, you arrive at total immersion in the elaborate comic-book pages of the super-heroes, with some of the best rides in the park.

The Incredible Hulk Coaster: Roller-coasters don't come much more dramatic than this giant green edifice that soars over the lagoon, blasting 0–40mph/64kph in 2secs, and reaching a top speed of 65mph/105kph. It looks awesome, sounds stunning and rides like a demon as you enter the gamma-ray world of Dr David Banner, aka the Incredible Hulk, and zoom into a weightless inversion 100ft/30m up.

> **BRITTIP**
> At the Hulk Coaster, keep left where the queue splits up and you will be in line for the front car for an even more extreme Hulk experience.

Just watching is mind-boggling, and the effects are brain-scrambling! You will need to deposit ANY loose articles in the lockers at the front of the building as the ride is guaranteed to shake anything out of your pockets. Crowds build up rapidly but queues

The Incredible Hulk Coaster

ISLANDS OF ADVENTURE with children

Our guide to the attractions that generally appeal to the different age groups:

Under-5s

Caro-Seuss-el, The Cat In The Hat, High In The Sky Seuss Trolley Train Ride, If I Ran The Zoo, Jurassic Park Discovery Center, Me Ship, The Olive, One Fish, Two Fish, Red Fish, Blue Fish.

5–8s

All the above, plus Amazing Adventures Of Spider-Man, Camp Jurassic, Eighth Voyage of Sindbad, Flight of the Hippogriff, Jurassic Park River Adventure (with parental discretion), Pteranodon Flyers, Storm Force Accelatron, Harry Potter and the Forbidden Journey (if tall enough), Hogwarts Express.

9–12s

Amazing Adventures Of Spider-Man, Camp Jurassic, The Cat In The Hat, Dr Doom's Fearfall, Dudley Do-Right's Ripsaw Falls, Dragon Challenge, Eighth Voyage Of Sindbad, Flight of the Hippogriff, Harry Potter and the Forbidden Journey, Hogwarts Express, Incredible Hulk Coaster, Jurassic Park Discovery Center, Jurassic Park River Adventure, Popeye And Bluto's Bilge-Rat Barges, Pteranodon Flyers, Storm Force Accelatron.

Over-12s

Amazing Adventures Of Spider-Man, Dr Doom's Fearfall, Dudley Do-Right's Ripsaw Falls, Dragon Challenge, Eighth Voyage Of Sindbad, Harry Potter and the Forbidden Journey, Hogwarts Express, Incredible Hulk Coaster, Jurassic Park Discovery Center, Jurassic Park River Adventure, Popeye And Bluto's Bilge-Rat Barges, Storm Force Accelatron.

move reasonably quickly. **R:** 4ft 6in/137cm. You can also buy the DVD of your ride for $25, with extra park footage, or photo packages from $20–25. **TTTTT**

Dr Doom's Fearfall: This is where, oh hapless visitor, you wander into the lair of the evil Dr Doom – arch-enemy of the Fantastic Four – and his sinister cohorts. His latest creation is the Fearfall, a device for sucking every iota of fear out of his victims, and YOU are about to test it as 16 riders at a time are strapped into chairs at the bottom of a 200ft/60m tower. The dry ice rolls, and whoosh! Up you go at breakneck speed, only to plummet back seemingly even faster, with an amazing split second when you feel suspended in mid-air. Summon up the courage to do this and we promise an astonishing (if brief!) experience. There are substantial queues from mid-day. **R:** 4ft 4in/132cm. **TTTTT+**

The Amazing Adventures Of Spider-Man: Get ready for another signature ride, with a visit to the *Daily Bugle*, home of ace reporter Peter Parker (aka Spider-Man) that turns into a

Dr Doom's Fearfall

mission in a 'Scoop' vehicle – and an audio-visual extravaganza. This roving 3-D motion simulator takes you into a battle with various super-villains that includes a convincing 'drop' off a skyscraper as the contest hots up. There are special effects aplenty and the whole ride is loaded with the 'wow' factor. Go early on or wait until late in the day – queues often top an hour by mid-morning. **R:** 3ft 4in/101cm. **TTTTT+** PS: If this seems similar to the TRANSFORMERS ride at Universal Studios, it's because they use the same type of ride vehicle.

> **BRITTIP**
> You can beat some of the queues on the Spider-Man ride at busy times by opting for the Single Rider queue.

Storm Force Accelatron: This ride, primarily for kids, puts you in the middle of a battle between X-Men heroine Storm and arch-nemesis Magneto. It's basically an updated spinning-cup ride but with some neat twists (like a 3-way rotation where the cars look set to collide). **TTT (TTTTT under-12s)**

Storm Force Accelatron

> **BRITTIP**
> For some of the park's best shopping bargains, visit Port Provisions right by the exit gates (to the left as you come through) where all the merchandise is 30–50% off.

Other entertainment: The **Marvel Super-Heroes** appear here periodically for photos and autographs, while Spider-Man has his own meet 'n' greet booth at The Marvel Alterniverse Store. A high-energy video arcade can be found at the exit to Dr Doom's Fearfall.

Shopping and dining: Each ride has its own character merchandise, while the **Comic Book Shop** and **Marvel Alterniverse Shop** sell other souvenirs. For a bite to eat, try the Italian buffeteria **Café 4** (pizza, pasta, sandwiches and salads) or a burger, chicken fingers or salad at the **Captain America Diner**.

And that, folks, is the full low-down on arguably the world's most thrilling and complete theme park. Not to be missed!

SeaWorld

SeaWorld is firmly established with British visitors as one of the most popular parks for its more peaceful and naturalistic aspect, the change of pace it offers and the general lack of substantial queues. It is large enough to handle big crowds well (though it still gets busy in peak season) and is a big hit with families in particular, but it has some fabulous rides and imaginative attractions too, including the Antarctica: Empire of the Penguin, the park's biggest expansion to date and a world-class exhibit.

Part of the SeaWorld Parks & Entertainment group, along with sister parks Busch Gardens in Tampa, with its animal encounters and roller-coasters (p204); Discovery Cove, an exotic tropical 'island' with dolphin, coral reef and snorkelling adventures (p200); and water-park Aquatica (p247), this makes for excellent multi-day tickets, notably Discovery Cove's

Ultimate Ticket, which includes all 4 parks. SeaWorld's recent additions and brilliant Christmas overlay (p39) mean this remains a wonderfully fresh and invigorating place to visit.

Happily, this is still a park where you can proceed at a relatively leisurely pace, see what you want without too much jostling and yet feel you have been well entertained (even if the restaurants get crowded at mealtimes). SeaWorld is a good starting point if this is your first Orlando visit as it gives you the hang of negotiating the vast areas, navigating by the various maps and learning to plan around the show times. There are special offers for booking online at **www.seaworld.com**, where you can print your tickets to save waiting in the queue, plus a website for UK visitors – **www.seaworldparks.co.uk**.

SeaWorld at a glance

Location	7007 SeaWorld Drive, off Central Florida Parkway (Junctions 71 and 72 off I-4)
Size	More than 200 acres/81ha, incorporating 26 attractions
Hours	9am–6pm off peak; 9am–7 or 8pm some weekends; 9am–10pm high season (Easter, summer holidays, Thanksgiving, Christmas)
Admission	Under-3s free; 3–9 $87 (1-day ticket), $124 (2-park ticket, with Aquatica), $134 (2-park ticket with Busch Gardens), $300 (Orlando FlexTicket), $340 (Orlando FlexTicket Plus); adult (10+) $92, $129, $139, $320, $360.
Parking	$17, $22 preferred parking
Lockers	Inside Entrance Plaza (next to Sweet Sailin' Candy), $8 and $10 (rent from Pushchair and Wheelchair location)
Pushchairs	$15 and $25, to right of Guest Services inside park
Wheelchairs	$12 and $45; with pushchairs
Top attractions	TurtleTrek, Antarctica: Empire Of The Penguin, One Ocean, Shark Encounter, Journey To Atlantis, Kraken, Manta, Wild Arctic, Blue Horizons
Don't miss	Reflections (high season), Manatee Rescue, behind-the-scenes tours, A'Lure Call of the Ocean show, dining at Sharks Underwater Grill

Hidden costs	**Meals**	Burger, chips and coke $11.68 3-course lunch $37–60 (Sharks Underwater Grill) Kids' meal $6.69; $13 at Sharks Underwater Grill
	T-shirts	$19.95–35
	Souvenirs	$0.99–1,500
	Sundries	Ride photos $19.99–35

1 Entrance plaza
2 Key West at SeaWorld
3 Stingray Lagoon
4 Flamingo Habitat
5 Dolphin Cove
6 Blue Horizons
7 Dolphin underwater viewing
8 Turtle Trek
9 Journey To Atlantis
10 Kraken
11 The Manta
12 Antarctica: Empire of the Penguin
13 Pacific Point Preserve
14 Sea Lion and Otter Stadium
15 The Waterfront
16 Seaport Theater
17 Seafire Inn
18 Sky Tower
19 Dolphin Nursery
20 Voyager's Smokehouse
21 Shark Encounter
22 Nautilus Theatre – A'lure
23 Sharks Underwater Grill
24 Terrace Garden Buffet
25 Animal Connections at Sea Garden
26 Shamu Stadium
27 Shamu's Happy Harbor
28 Wild Arctic
29 Mango Joe's Café
30 Bayside Stadium

Hotel bonus

Before you even head here, you should consider the eco-friendly park's great variety of behind-the-scenes tours, which provide great insight into its superb conservation and research programmes, as well as its entertainment resources. Book in advance (advisable): online, call 1888 800 5447 or visit the Guided Tours counter first thing when you arrive.

VIP Tour: 6hr tour with individual tour guide and reserved seats for the 3 main shows, All-Day Dining Deal, QuickQueue and animal feeding ($79/adult, $59 3–9s;).

Private VIP Tour: Similar to the above but just for your family or group, including preferred parking, animal interactions and lunch at Sharks Underwater Grill ($299/person).

Dolphins Up-Close Tour: Fascinating 1hr glimpse backstage at the training and care of the stars of the Blue Horizons show, as well as a look into the dolphin-care facilities, finishing with a Q&A session with a trainer and the chance to touch one of the residents ($59 adults, $39 3–9s).

Sea Lions Up-Close Tour: A 1hr walking tour focusing on the care and training of the stars of the Clyde & Seamore show, including a photo with them and a chance to feed the Pacific Point Preserve sea lions ($39 and $19).

Penguins Up-Close Tour: This 45min family walk goes behind the scenes at Antarctica: Empire of the Penguins to learn the proper care for these cute birds and gives visitors the chance to interact with and touch a penguin ($59 and $19).

Wild Arctic Up-Close Experience: An interactive 60min tour into the care and animal interactions with the walrus, seals and beluga whales at this in-depth exhibit ($59/person, ages 8 and up only).

Family Fun at Christmas Tour: A 4hr guided tour of the top children's attractions, feeding dolphins and stingrays, with reserved seats at the One Ocean show, a light meal and front-of-line access to the Polar Express Experience, finishing with an exclusive meet 'n' greet with Santa Claus ($79 and $59).

Marine Mammal Keeper Experience: An interactive programme, this takes 2 visitors daily to discover the care needed to rehabilitate injured manatees, plus bottle-feed some of them, meet the seals and walruses and prepare meals for the beluga whales (starts at 6.30am; lasts around 8hrs; $399/person including lunch, T-shirt, special book, souvenir photo and 7-day SeaWorld pass; must be 13 or older).

Beluga Interaction Program: A unique chance to meet some of the park's biggest but most benign denizens in their own environment. Swimming isn't necessary but guests must be comfortable in the water as touching, feeding and using hand signals are part of this informative tour ($119/person; no expectant mothers; must be 10 or older). NB: All prices can vary seasonally.

Manatee Rescue

Location

SeaWorld is located off Central Florida Parkway, between I-4 (exit 71 going east or 72 heading west) and I-Drive. It is still best to arrive before the opening time so you're in a good position to book a backstage tour, dash to one of the attractions that draws a crowd, like Manta and Antarctica, or buy QuickQueue, the park's limited number of paid-for passes that provide front-of-the-line access to each of the main rides (priced seasonally at $19–29). There is also a **Signature Show Seating** option at $19–29/person.

The park covers more than 200acres/81ha, with 6 shows, 5 major rides, 10 large-scale continuous viewing attractions and 7 smaller ones, plus a smart range of shops and restaurants. Try to eat before midday or after 2.30pm for a crowd-free lunch, and before 5.30pm if you want a leisurely dinner (better still, book Sharks Underwater Grill).

SeaWorld is not organised into neat 'lands' like the others and it often requires much to-ing and fro-ing to catch the various shows, which can be wearing. Keep a close grip on your map and schedule and take regular breaks. Going in a clockwise direction, here's what you find.

◄20► ANNIVERSARY SPOT
Since we first started writing about SeaWorld only TWO of their attractions, rides and shows have stayed the same – Pacific Point Preserve and Wild Arctic.

Ray Lagoon

Entrance plaza

Coming through the turnstiles brings you to the park's main business area, including the Information & Reservations kiosk, Lost & Found, and lockers, pushchair and wheelchair hire. You will also find some good shopping and snack options here. Look for **Shamu Emporium** for the full range of SeaWorld souvenirs, while **Adventure Photos** provides all your park pictures taken by the SeaWorld photographers. You can grab a quick breakfast (tasty pastries and coffee) at **Cypress Bakery** or something colder from the **Polar Parlor Ice Cream**. This is also the place for a photo opportunity with Shamu and friends.

Also worth considering is the **All Day Dining Deal**, a wristband giving unlimited visits to 6 restaurants (Spice Mill, Voyager's – excluding their baby-back ribs – Mango Joe's, Seaport Pizza, Seafire Inn and Terrace Garden Buffet), claiming an entrée, side dish or dessert and standard non-alcoholic drink each time ($32.99 and $17.99). It's good value if you eat at least twice in the park and can be booked at the Information & Reservations desk.

Key West at SeaWorld

A whole collection of exhibits is grouped together here under the clever Key West theme, starting with **Stingray Lagoon**, where you can feed (for $5) and touch fully grown rays, including a nursery for newborn rays. The centrepiece, though, is the 2.1acre/0.8ha Dolphin Cove, a spectacular, naturalistic development that offers the chance to feed this community of frisky Atlantic bottlenose dolphins (for $7 at specific times of the day; or you can just watch). There is also an excellent underwater viewing area, and park photographers are ready to snap you at play with the dolphins (a 6x8in/15x20cm photo is $19.99; add a frame for $5, or get 3 for $35).

The whole Key West area is designed in the eclectic, tropical flavour of America's most southerly city, but it also underlines the environmental message through interactive graphics and video displays, and children will find it a fun, educational experience. AAAA

◀◼▶ **BRITTIP**
If you drop your fish on the ground when feeding the dolphins, seals or sea lions you are asked to throw it away, for the animals' health and safety.

Shopping and dining: There are 5 gift shops and kiosks here, the best being **Coconut Bay Trader** (apparel and soft toys) and **Sandcastle Toys 'n Treats**. You can grab a turkey leg, cheese nachos or chicken tenders at **Captain Pete's Island Eats**.

◀◼▶ **BRITTIP**
For a great soft drink deal, buy any souvenir cup at one of the restaurants for $7.99–9.99 and get refills with it for just 99c for the rest of the season.

Dolphin Theater

The first large-scale encounter is the setting for a magnificent show, plus the TurtleTrek experience.

Blue Horizons: This wonderful production serves up a big helping of dramatic animal behaviour in best Broadway style. It features dolphins, exotic birds (including an Andean condor), and a lot more besides as the general (and rather abstract) theme of a girl's dream about maritime wildlife is brought to life. The elaborate set design has a 40ft/12m sea-meets-sky backdrop that also conceals the setting for a host of additional performers, from high divers to bungee jumpers and trapeze-like aerialists. There is subtle interaction between trainers and animals as the show moves from one scene to the next, both above and below the water, but there is plenty to admire as the stage is filled with graceful and daring action. A stirring score by the Seattle Symphony Orchestra underpins the complex staging and Broadway-style costumes and it makes for a magnificent 25mins that often draws a huge ovation. AAAAA

TurtleTrek: Right behind the Dolphin Theater is this thrilling experience that is part exhibit and part show. You enter down a ramp that introduces you to the undersea world of the sea turtle and marine conservation, passing by two huge man-made lagoons, the first for the endangered manatee and then some of SeaWorld's rescued turtles. A marine life host introduces the next part of the Trek and the doors open to reveal a domed cinema where you don 3-D

Blue Horizons

glasses. Suddenly, you are in the world of the sea turtle, sharing the life-cycle journey from the dangers of leaving the egg to life in the open ocean and then the final return to the same beach where it was born. It all takes place in a immersive 3-D environment (you have to remember not to hold your breath!) with amazingly graphic encounters with a marauding crab, sharks and dolphins. You exit back up another ramp to 2 open-air pools (the top view of the lagoons you see below) where you can learn more about sea turtle life and see them and the manatees being fed. There is also a TurtleTrek video game for kids, and another open-air exhibit showcasing some Florida alligators. **AAAAA** NB: The menace of the crab in the early scene may be a bit scary for very young children.

Shopping and dining: Stock up on all your sea turtle and manatee souvenirs at **Trek Treasures**, while there are also 2 drinks carts.

Ride central

Continue past Dolphin Theatre and you come to the park's serious thrill quotient.

Journey to Atlantis: Unique in Orlando, this terrific water-coaster gave SeaWorld its first 5-star thrill attraction in 1998. The combination of extra elements makes it a one-off, with some illusory special effects giving way to a high-speed water ride that becomes a runaway roller-coaster. The discovery of Atlantis in your 8-passenger 'fishing boat' starts gently through the lost city. But evil spirit Allura takes over and riders plunge into a dash through Atlantis, dodging gushing fountains and water cannons, with hundreds of dazzling holographic and laser-generated illusions before the 60ft/18m drop, which is merely the entry to the roller-coaster finale back in the candle-filled catacombs. Be ready to get soaked, which is great in summer but not so clever first thing on a winter morning. **R:** 3ft 6in/106cm. **TTTTT**

Kraken: This is one of Florida's most breathtaking roller-coasters. Based on the mythical sea monster, Kraken is an innovative pedestal ride (you are effectively sitting in a chair without a floor) that plunges an initial 144ft/44m, hits 65mph/105kph, dives underground 3 times, adds 7 inversions (including a vertical loop, a diving loop, a zero-gravity roll and a cobra roll) and a flat spin before riders escape the beast's lair. The ride from the front row, especially down an opening drop at an angle best described as ludicrous, is positively blood-curdling, and sitting in the rear is thrilling, too. **R:** 4ft 6in/137cm. **TTTTT+**

Kraken

Antarctica

Getting back to the animal side of the park brings you to the newest development (opened May 2013), and one of the most eye-catching sections of any park. It is both an extensive, themed area in its own right – and an amazing ride. It is the biggest expansion in SeaWorld history and their most immersive environment to date, an epic journey into the snow and ice-covered realm of the South Pole and its inhabitants.

Antarctica: Empire of the Penguin: Once you walk between the towering ice-and-snow-capped 'mountains,' the (indoor) ride awaits. It begins with a dramatic presentation about penguin life and then takes visitors on a unique expedition into the heart of the continent, following the story and guidance of Puck, a young Gentoo penguin. Guests board special vehicles in groups of 8 and choose their own level of ride experience, either 'Mild' or 'Wild', and then set off on this first-of-its-kind ride, featuring real motion, simulation and film elements that offer a realistic taste of the polar region, above and below the penguins' icy world, moving seemingly at random and with no obvious track. The dangers – including a typical Antarctic storm – and beauty of life in this extreme realm are graphically depicted as you track Puck's own life journey through the world's most extreme landscape before you then step out through a real penguin colony (cleverly but minimally screened off) to experience more of their 'empire.' And guess what? It is cold; like, *really* cold (the

Manta

Manta: This ride turns high tech coaster into a unique mixture of ride and animal encounter. The elaborate queuing area winds through cool, rocky caverns, passing waterfalls and floor-to-ceiling windows showcasing some 300 rays and thousands of fish, which lead through to the 'undersea world' of the manta ray. Themed like a giant ray, riders are swung into a face-down position before being launched into an exhilarating series of 4 inversions along 3,359ft/1,024m of track, reaching nearly 60mph/96kph and 140ft/43m high as well as skimming the surface of the lagoon. The 'flying' nature of the coaster and smooth ride vehicles make this a true original. It has great spectator appeal and there is a separate walk-though aquarium with its own entry. Lockers located near the queue entry are available for use during your ride (50c and $1). **R:** 54in/137cm. **TTTTT**. For the most powerful effects of the Manta G-forces, opt for the back rows.

Shopping and dining: Don't miss the **Golden Seahorse** and **Jewel of the Sea** as you exit Journey to Atlantis, a combination gift shop and aquarium full of tropical fish (remember to look upwards), while there are coaster-orientated souvenirs in **Kraken Gifts** and **Manta Gifts**. **High Seas Market** offers convenient grab-and-go snacks and drinks.

Antarctica

temperature drops during the ride, reaching to below freezing by the end) and you may want to visit the gift shop for a scarf or some gloves before you set off! The 'Wild' version of the ride is more fast-paced, with various bumps, slides, spins and rolls, but 'Mild' is still designed for all the family, with no height restriction. AAAAA+ This is also easily the park's most popular attraction, hence if it appeals to you, go here *first*.

BRITTIP

Take a look at the main 'mountain' in Antarctica. Does the shape look familiar? Yes, that's right – the whole edifice has been shaped like a towering mother penguin on the left, with her baby to the right.

Other entertainment: Once you have ridden the ride (or if you don't want to), there is a spectacular 2-storey **underground viewing area** where you can see the 4 different species of penguin – Rockhopper, King, Adelie and Gentoo – at play. Then, back out in 'Antarctica,' you can marvel at this realistic environment, which includes a special 'Penguin Wall' for photo opportunities, and flatscreen TVs that offer more info about the region's main inhabitants. It even has its own original musical score

Sea Garden animal encounter

that evokes images of the windswept frozen continent. The many exterior 'icebergs' and 'icicles' all started as liquid acrylic and SeaWorld has had to come up with special paints and coatings for their snowy environment to withstand the Florida sun, ending up with the most realistic tableaux it is possible to create outside the Polar regions.

Shopping and dining: Lone gift shop **Glacial Collections** has a huge selection of all things penguin-orientated and cuddly, while **Expedition Café** provides Italian, Asian and American food choices from their show kitchen which you can then enjoy in one of two clever 'Quonset Huts' that provide a South Pole setting.

BRITTIP

Be sure to come back to Antarctica at night to see how the brilliant blue lighting makes the whole setting even more impressive.

Sea Lions & more

Sea Lion and Otter Stadium: The venue for another live show, this will be all-new in 2015 (provisionally titled Clyde and Seamore: Back To School) and features the resident sea lions and their pals the otter and walrus, along with the inevitable human fall-guys. The 25 min performance will showcase a variety of slapstick fun and watery stunts. AAAA (expected).

Pacific Point Preserve: This rocky habitat shows the park's seals and sea lions at their most natural. A hidden wave machine adds the perfect touch while park attendants provide lively talks. You can also buy smelt ($5 per tray or 5 trays for $20) to throw to these ever-hungry mammals. AAA

Shopping and dining: Stitches is the best of the shops here, while **Seaport Pizza** offers cheese and pepperoni pizza and there are drinks carts and an ice-cream counter.

The Waterfront

Backtracking slightly (or turning right after the Entrance Plaza area) brings you to this beautiful 5acre/2ha seafront 'village' of restaurants and shops, which is a great place to spend some time when other parts are busy, especially for lunch or dinner.

Pets Ahoy!: Just inside the Waterfront is the air-conditioned haven of the Seaport Theater, which hosts this cute 25min giggle featuring an unlikely menagerie of dogs, cats, birds, rats, pot-bellied pigs and others, most from local animal rescue shelters. AAA The Theater is also home to the seasonal show **Elmo Rocks!** when the Sesame Street characters get together for their own rock 'n roll concert. AAA

The Tower: The centrepiece of the Waterfront, this 400ft/122m landmark offers slowly rotating rides for a bird's-eye view of the park and surrounding areas. It used to cost extra but is now open to all-comers. NB: It will close if windy. AAA

Other entertainment: The **Dolphin Nursery** provides close-up views with some of the park's younger dolphins, and look out for the zany antics of **The Longshoremen** periodically, as the hapless trio try their hand at various maintenance tasks.

Shopping and dining: This has some of the best in SeaWorld, starting with 4 interlinked boutique-style shops that offer a stylish range of souvenirs and other gift items (notably **Allura's Treasure Trove** and **Artisans Hall**). The unique **Oyster's Secret** shop features resident pearl divers who can be viewed underwater as they collect the pearl-bearing oysters on request, to be incorporated into jewellery pieces by the shop's artisans. The 3 excellent eateries are: **Seafire Inn** (sandwiches, wraps, pasta, fish and chips and chicken stir-fry); **Voyagers** (smoked chicken, barbecue ribs, salads, turkey sandwich and a children's menu with chicken nuggets, hot dog, macaroni and cheese or junior portion of ribs); and **The Spice Mill** (flame-grilled burgers, salads, sandwiches and flatbreads, plus a low-fat vegetarian chilli). There are also 3 snack bars: **Café de Mar** for pastries, coffees, smoothies and soft drinks; **Smugglers Feast** for smoked turkey legs; and Freezas for frozen yoghurt and other drinks. The **SandBar** is a water's edge hideaway, serving beer, wine and snacks – THE place to watch the sun go down.

BRITTIP

Grab an evening meal at The Spice Mill, then head out on to its open-air terrace for one of the best seats in the house to experience the Reflections summer nightly finale.

The Waterfront

Sharks and Co

Continuing the clockwise tour brings you towards the back of the park (which usually doesn't open until 11am). Here you find more animal encounters – and a wonderful show.

Shark Encounter: Top of the bill, the world's largest collection of dangerous sea creatures can be found here, brought dramatically to life by the walk-through tubes that surround you with more than 50 prowling sharks (including sand tigers, black tips, nurse sharks and sandbars), sawfish, tropical fish and gigantic groupers. It's an eerie experience, but brilliantly presented and highly informative. Queues build up here at peak times. AAAA TTTT

A'Lure, the Call of the Ocean: This imaginative 30min show in the Nautilus Theater features acrobatic feats, engaging live music, yo-yo artists, aerialists, clever lighting and special effects. The show tells the story of a fisherman who is pulled into the ocean to an undersea world ruled by a tyrant queen. He becomes the unwilling pawn in her battle against a beautiful Siren for control of the ocean kingdom. AAAA

The theatre is also home to weekend events throughout the year, notably **Jack Hanna's Animal Adventure**.

◄❚❱► **BRITTIP**

Looking for a quiet spot for a break? Seek out the terrace along the lagoon (with tables and chairs) directly behind Fins gift shop and across from Sharks Underwater Grill.

Shamu Stadium

Other entertainment: The flamingo pedal-boats on the lagoon rent for $5 per 20min (for 2 people). You can also feed the sharks and stingrays outside Shark Encounter ($5 per tray). Also nearby is the revamped **Sea Garden**, a lovely spot for some time off your feet. As well as several clever sea-creature sculptures made completely out of reclaimed rubbish washed up on America's beaches by **http://WashedAshore.org**, the Animal Connections meet-and-greets here allow for encounters several times daily with various rescued and rehabilitated animals, including two small ponies, a possum, various hawks, a Kookaburra, a great horned owl, a Crested Caracara, a groundhog and others. Bring your camera, as photos are encouraged.

Shopping and dining: The 3 shops here (**Shark Attack Photo**, **Fins** and **Gulf Breeze Trader**) are relatively small-scale but, at the entrance to Shark Encounter is the top dining choice, **Sharks Underwater Grill**. Not only do you have an amazing backdrop for your meal in a subterranean environment (check out the mini-aquarium bar), but the upmarket menu features appetising 'Floribbean' cuisine, blending local and spicy Caribbean fare. The emphasis is on seafood – wonderful creations with shrimp, salmon, scallops and a fresh Catch of the Day – plus pasta, steaks and chicken, as well as fab desserts, cocktails (including non-alcoholic) and menus for under-10s. Open from 11am to park closing, it's busy at lunch but quieter in late afternoon, so we advise booking (at the restaurant itself) as soon as you arrive. The **Lakeside Panini Bistro** (high season only) offers fresh-grilled panini sandwiches, salads and drinks while the Terrace Garden Buffet features an all-you-can eat pizza, pasta and salad buffet ($14.99 adults, $9.99 3–9s), while the **Terrace Bar** has a selection of beers. Sadly, it no longer offers free tastes of Anheuser-Busch products.

SEAWORLD with children

The following gives a general idea of the appeal of the attractions to the different age groups:

Under-5s
Antarctica: Empire of the Penguin, One Ocean, Blue Horizons, Clyde And Seamore Take Pirate Island, Elmo Show, A'Lure, the Call of the Ocean, Pacific Point Preserve, Pets Ahoy!, Shamu's Happy Harbor, Waterfront entertainment, Wild Arctic (without the ride).

5–8s
All the above, plus Turtle Trek, Reflections, Shark Encounter, Wild Arctic (with the ride).

9–12s
All the above, plus Journey to Atlantis, Manta and Kraken.

Over-12s
Antarctica: Empire of the Penguin, One Ocean, Blue Horizons, Clyde And Seamore Take Pirate Island, Journey To Atlantis, Manta, Kraken, Reflections, A'Lure, Shark Encounter, Wild Arctic, Turtle Trek.

Shamu central

The other main area of the park features the iconic Shamu Stadium and a fabulous kids play area, plus another engaging ride/animal attraction.

◀⚡▶ BRITTIP

The first 14 rows at Shamu Stadium get VERY wet (watch out for your cameras) – when a killer whale leaps into the air in front of you, it displaces a LOT of water on landing. In fact, the Splash Zones should be renamed Soak Zones!

Shamu Stadium: 'What can one person do?' That is the message One Ocean brings to SeaWorld in a spectacular show filled with brilliant splashes of colour – especially of the black and white variety! In the past, the whales' relationship with their trainers was the main focus, and while that bond remains strong, the heart of One Ocean lies with the relationship between the whales themselves. Behaviours common to whales in the wild combine with learned behaviours in a celebration of joyful play, reminding us we are all connected and, when we pull together, we can do amazing things. And if the biggest thrills in past Shamu shows came from seeing these magnificent animals jump, spin, and cover the Soak Zone in a wall of water, you're in for a real treat! Even better, the charming Side By Side scene features the connection between mother and baby, so have those cameras ready. Shamu Stadium is extremely popular, so try to take in an early show. And, if you think it looks good during the day, return in the evening (in high season) for an even more dramatic, music-orientated presentation under the lights, **Shamu's Celebration: Light Up The Night**. AAAAA+

◀⚡▶ BRITTIP

Be sure to arrive early for One Ocean, especially if you have a smart-phone. You may get a sneak peek behind the scenes during the pre-show!

All guests can then enjoy the backstage **Underwater Viewing area**.

Shamu's Happy Harbor: 4acres/1.6ha of brilliantly designed adventure playground and rides await youngsters of all ages here. Activities include a 4-storey net climb, 2 tented ball rooms to wade through, a giant trampoline tent, a mock pirate ship and a water play area, **Water Works** (great on a hot day). The signature junior-sized coaster **Shamu Express** offers mild thrills over more than 800ft/245m of track (and a framed ride photo for $19.99). The **Jazzy Jellies** is a jellyfish-themed samba tower ride that lifts and spins, while **Swishy Fishes** features oversized seats that spin round a giant waterspout. **Flying Fiddler** (a 20ft/6.1m tower ride on a jumping giant crab), **Ocean Commotion** (a rocking tug ride), junior-sized **Seven Seas Railway** and **Sea Carousel** (a traditional carousel featuring 65 sea creatures) complete the line-up. The area gets busy from midday, but the kids seem to love it at any time. Next door is the arcade and **Games Area**, a series of fairground-type stalls ranging from $1–10 as you head toward the Nautilus Theater. **TTTT**. At the back of the Harbor is a well equipped, comfortable **Baby Care Center** and the park's **First Aid** station.

Wild Arctic: This interactive ride-and-view is an exciting simulator jet helicopter journey into the white wilderness, where passengers see seals, beluga whales and walruses. This one is not to be missed (but avoid just after One Ocean when the hordes descend). **R:** 3ft 6in/106cm. **TTTT AAAAA.** Those who don't want to do the (quite dynamic) ride can just walk to the Base Station.

BRITTIP

Any purchases can be sent to Package Pick-up in Shamu's Emporium to collect on your way out, if you give at least an hour's notice.

Shopping and dining: The **Arctic Shop** is the best of the 3 stores here. For dining, **Mango Joe's Café** offers grilled fajitas, speciality salads and sandwiches, while **Coconut Cove** offers drinks and snacks in **Shamu's Happy Harbor** and the **Soft Serve** shop has some fab ice-cream treats. Weary parents will enjoy the convenience of **Harbor Market** grab-and-go snacks and drinks. Killer whale fans may also want to splash out (!) on the **Dine With Shamu** experience, backstage at Shamu Stadium, where a buffet lunch or dinner featuring seasonal, organic and sustainable menu items is served while some of the trainers meet with guests and show off more of the whale behaviours in spectacular, close-up fashion (times changes seasonally, with prices from $29–34 for adults and $19–24 for children; book in

Live entertainment outside Mango Joe's

Shamu's Celebration: Light Up The Night

advance on 1888 800 5447, online at **www.seaworldparks.com** or at the Information Kiosk when you arrive).

Bayside Stadium

The final part of SeaWorld is this large outdoor arena facing the central Lagoon. It's home to an array of seasonal entertainment, including the nightly finale of the Reflections fireworks show in summer and other holiday periods, the Bands, Brew & BBQ concerts and the ice-skating show at Christmas.

◄◼► **BRITTIP**
Learn more about SeaWorld's conservation and environmental efforts at **www.seaworld.org**.

Summer extras

During the official summer season (mid-June–mid-Aug), SeaWorld has extended hours to 10pm and offers an array of extra live entertainment as part of its **Summer Nights** programme. The 'rock 'n' roll' party atmosphere is generated by live DJs and other entertainers and features extra shows, notably **Shamu's Celebration: Light up The Night**, which adds a more high-energy version of the main show, including new, original music and production elements, as well as new killer whale behaviours and dramatic lighting. Then, over at Sea Lion & Otter Stadium, there is a second evening show, Sea Lions Tonite, which serves up a fun parody of other SeaWorld

shows. Summer Nights Central, on the Bayside Stadium pathway, features live DJs (and bands at weekends) to add a family-friendly dance party from 6pm.

It all leads up to the big Reflections finale on the Waterfront lagoon. This is a neat mix of pyrotechnics and special effects, with towering fountains (up to 100ft/30m high), mist sprays, unique fireworks and an epic soundtrack. View from the Waterfront, or arrive early for seating at the Bayside Stadium. AAAA

For SeaWorld's amazing Christmas Celebration (late Nov–31 Dec each year), see our Christmas section, p39.

And there's more

Other seasonal events (all FREE with park admission) include **Bands, Brew & BBQ**, weekends in Feb and Mar that provide a festival atmosphere with live music, barbecue kiosks and craft beer stalls, as well as a special guest concert (beer and barbecue extra, including a 'Sampler' package for $21/person); **Just For Kids**, each Sat mid-Mar to mid-Apr, with live shows, games, new characters and the Rockin' Rockhopper Party at Antarctica: Empires of the Penguin; the Apr–May weekends of **Viva La Musica Latin** festival (with more live bands and food offerings); and the ultra child-friendly **Halloween Spooktacular**, when there are fun activities for kids of all ages, including trick-or-treating, Penelope's Party Zone, sweet treat decorating and strolling entertainers.

Discovery Cove

Fancy a day in your own tropical paradise, with the chance to swim with dolphins, encounter sharks, snorkel in a coral reef and dive through a waterfall into a tropical aviary? Well, Discovery Cove is all that and more. The only drawback is the price. This mini theme park comes at a premium because it is restricted to just 1,300 guests a day, creating an exclusive experience that is reflected in the admission fee.

The weather can get distinctly cool in the winter, but the water is always heated (apart from the dolphin lagoon, which remains at 72ºF/22ºC) and full wetsuits are available to keep out the chill. The attention to detail is superb, guest ratings are extremely high and it is hugely popular with British visitors. However, if any element falls below expectations, it's worth bringing it to the attention of a manager as they are always keen to rectify any oversights.

The costs

In 2014, the Dolphin Swim package was $229–379/person, or you could choose the Day Resort package, without dolphin swim, for $169–269, all depending on day and season (under 3s free; 3–5s cannot do the dolphin swim but must pay the Day Resort price). So, just what do you get for your money? Well, as you would expect, it's a supremely personal park. You check in at the beautiful entrance lobby as you would for a hotel rather than a theme park, and you have a guide to take you in and get you set. All your basic requirements – towel, mask, snorkel, wet-jacket, lockers, beach umbrellas, food and drink – are included, and the level of service is excellent. A pass for SeaWorld AND Aquatica is also included (valid for 14 consecutive days before or after your Discovery Cove visit), or you can upgrade to the **Ultimate Package**, which provides 14 days at SeaWorld,

Discovery Cove

Aquatica AND Busch Gardens for just $22 extra (superb value). A full breakfast, snacks, beverages (including beer and cocktails) and an excellent lunch at the Laguna Grill are all included. But gift shop and photo prices reflect the entry fee – expensive. It is also an extra $125–275 (seasonally) to hire one of their swanky cabañas for the day (which include tables, chairs, loungers, towels and a fridge stocked with soft drinks) depending on position and view (must be booked in advance).

Therefore, for all its style and dolphin appeal, Discovery Cove will take a BIG bite out of your holiday budget. A family of 4, with children old enough to do the Dolphin Swim, would pay $1,516 in peak season. Even with a free SeaWorld and Aquatica pass, it's a big outlay. The charge for ages 3–5 is also pretty steep, in our opinion. Your sundries can add up, too. A 6x8in/15x20cm photo is $20; then there are photo packages at $60 and $139, while the DVD of your experience (which includes 30mins of park highlights) costs $50 and the Ultimate Package (7 6x8 photos, 1 4x6 photo, 2 key chains, digital photo CD, Interaction video, photo album, 16x24 poster) is $219. Poster-size photos (16x24 and 24x36) are $25 and $35, while a marble photo-tile is $39. However, despite the fees, the feedback we get is almost unfailingly positive and most people are captivated by the experience. One handy free perk, though, is the **Horticulture Tour**, twice a day, which takes guests through the care and maintenance of the park's tropical plant and tree life (sign up at Guest Relations).

BRITTIP
Try to pick up your Discovery Cove photos before 4pm or you might find everyone else trying to do the same!

Trainer for a Day: This programme is an exciting opportunity to go behind the scenes into the park's training, feeding and welfare. You get to work with the experts as they interact with dolphins, birds, sharks, stingrays and tropical fish, including a behavioural training class, the chance to experience a double-foot push (ride on the front of 2 dolphins), a souvenir shirt, dolphin book and waterproof camera. Participants must be at least 6 and in good health, and it costs $428–578 (seasonally). For all Discovery Cove bookings, call 407 370 1280 (freephone 00800 3344 1818 in the UK) or visit **www.discoverycove.com**.

Location
Situated on Central Florida Parkway, almost opposite the SeaWorld entrance (open year-round 9am–5.30pm; parking free), the whole 30acre/12ha park is magnificently landscaped, with thatched buildings, palm trees, lush vegetation, white-sand beaches, gurgling streams – even hammocks to chill out in. The overall effect is of being transported to a relaxing tropical paradise away from the hurly-burly. The 5-star resort feel is enhanced by a high staff-to-guest ratio, there are no queues (though the restaurant may get busy at lunchtime), and the highlight Dolphin Encounter is world class. Visitors with disabilities are well catered for, with special wheelchairs that can move in sand and shallow water, and an area of the Dolphin Lagoon that allows those who can't enter the water still to touch a dolphin.

The main attractions
Freshwater Oasis: This combination of animal environment, walking trails and pools offers the chance to get a close-up of the park's otters and marmosets in realistic, natural habitats. Children especially love watching the otters, and the way the animals are incorporated into the lush tropical scenery is a real gem of clever design. AAAA

Wind-away River: This 800yd/732m circuit of gently flowing bath-warm water is a variation on the lazy river feature of many of the water parks, though with a far more naturalistic aspect and none of the inner tubes. It is primarily designed for snorkellers and features rocky lagoons, caves, a beach section, a tropical forest segment and sunken ruins. The lack of fish makes it a bit bland after the Grand Reef, but it is as much about relaxing as having fun. It is up to 8ft/2.4m deep at points, so non-swimmers are advised to use a flotation vest. It finishes in the freeform Serenity Bay pool, which provides more idyllic relaxation. AAA

Explorer's Aviary: This 3-part adventure is both an area in its own right and a 120ft/37m section of the Tropical River. You can walk in off the beach or swim in through the waterfall from Wind-away River, fun for snorkellers. Some 250 tropical birds fill the main enclosure and, if you stand still, they are likely to use you as a perch. There is a small-bird sanctuary – full of finches, honeycreepers and hummingbirds – and a large-bird enclosure, featuring toucans and the red-legged seriema. Guides will introduce you to specific birds (which you can hand-feed) and tell you about their habitats and conservation issues. AAAA

Dolphin Swim: The big headline attraction is the encounter with the park's Atlantic bottlenose dolphin community. A 20min orientation programme in one of the beach cabañas, with a film and instruction from 2 trainers, sets you up for this thrilling experience. Groups of 6–8 go into the lagoon with the trainers and, starting off standing in the waist-deep (slightly chilly) water as one of the dolphins comes over, you gradually become more adventurous until you are swimming with them. Timid swimmers are well catered for and there are flotation vests for those who need them. The lagoon is up to 12ft/3.6m deep so there is a real feeling of being in the dolphins' environment. You learn how trainers use hand signals and positive reinforcement to communicate, and get the chance to stroke, feed and even kiss your dolphin. The encounter concludes dramatically as you are towed ashore by one of these awesome animals (which weigh up to 600lb/272kg), though activities vary according to their attention span. You spend around 30mins in the water

Discovery Cove

and it is totally unforgettable. Under-6s are not allowed in the lagoon. TTTTT+

The Grand Reef: This area features a massive 2.5acre/1ha artificial reef with 125 species of sea creatures, including fish, rays, eels, sharks, urchins, and lionfish (the dangerous ones are behind glass!). White sand beaches, meandering pathways and scenic bridges lead to shallow wading areas, waist-deep paddling pools and deep-water snorkelling, while underwater canyons and inviting grottos combine with brightly coloured artificial coral reefs for a convincing and utterly exhilarating experience. It's like paradise, only better!

For an extra element of relaxation, stake out a hammock on the central island or consider hiring one of 8 private waterside cabañas (with table, chairs, loungers and towels). There is a drinks kiosk here but no food outlets. AAAAA

BRITTIP

The Sea Venture area is not accessible to snorkellers during tours, but you can swim there when a tour is not running.

Sea Venture: One of the most innovative features of the Grand Reef is this underwater walking tour. Equipped with special dive helmets, guests make a 20min trek along the bottom of the reef, passing sharks and lionfish and interacting with schools of fish and gentle rays. This is a totally immersive experience and a sensation like no other (how often can you explore underwater while standing up straight?). There are handrails throughout the journey, which takes groups of 4–9 at a time. Total tour time is 1hr, including preparation and underwater trek (for an extra $59 per person). Ages 10 and up only. TTTT

Discovery Cove 'extras'

This isn't a cheap day out, but the extra quality is everywhere. The Laguna Grill lunch is excellent and you can visit as often as you want, while a Calypso band adds to the tropical paradise feel. **Conservation Cabaña** allows guests to meet a neat selection of the park's small mammals (like an anteater and tree sloth); parking is free and you also receive an 8x6in/15x20cm welcome photo. While official opening time is 9am, they will check you in as early as 8am for the free breakfast.

Special occasions

Discovery Cove has a range of options that involve dolphin interaction and private beach cabañas.

The **Celebration Package** ($129) includes 6x8in/15x20cm photo, photo frame or plush toy, bag, T-shirt, souvenir buoy delivered by a dolphin and 25% off Ultimate photo package, while a Premium Package ($229) adds a private cabaña.

The **Elite Package** ($359) includes a buoy with personalised message delivered by a dolphin; signature tote bag; choice of deluxe photo frame or plush toy; a private cabaña; Ultimate Photo Package.

Park admission and dolphin swim package are required with all special occasion packages. You are advised to book at least 3 months in advance as they do sell out in peak periods and, in winter, the park is closed on some midweek days. There is also a 10% advance discount periodically for online bookings. See **www.discoverycove.com**.

Discovery Cove

Busch Gardens

While the Orlando parks may get more publicity, the 335acre/136ha Busch Gardens in Tampa offers just as much in terms of attractions and – especially – Brit appeal. In fact, the sister park to SeaWorld, which started as a mini-menagerie for the wildlife collection of the brewery-owning Busch family in 1959, is often one of the most popular of all Florida attractions with UK visitors for its nature appeal – and superb roller-coasters. It is a major, multi-faceted family park, the biggest outside Orlando and just an hour from International Drive. It is rated among the top 4 zoos in America, with more than 2,700 animals representing over 320 species of mammals, birds, reptiles, amphibians and spiders. But that's just the start. It boasts a safari-like section of Africa spread over 65acres/26ha of grassy veldt, with special tours to hand-feed some of the animals. Interspersed among the animals are more than 20 bona fide theme park rides, including the mind-numbing coasters Kumba, SheiKra, Montu and Cheetah Hunt, plus the dramatic new drop-tower ride, Falcon's Fury, with guaranteed fun for coaster addicts, plus plenty of scaled-down rides for children. Then there are animal shows, musicians and big-stage show productions.

The overall theme is Africa, hence the park is divided into areas like Nairobi and Morocco, and dining and shopping are just as good as the other parks. It doesn't quite have the pizzazz of Epcot or Universal, and the staff are a bit more laid back, but it has guaranteed 5-star family appeal, especially with its rides just for kids. It's a bit like the big brother of Chessington World of Adventures in Surrey, though on a grander scale

BUSCH GARDENS at a glance

Location	Busch Blvd, Tampa; 75–90mins' drive from Orlando
Size	335 acres/136ha in 11 themed areas
Hours	9 or 10am–6 or 7pm off peak; 9am–8pm Easter, Thanksgiving, Christmas; 9 or 9.30am–10.30pm summer
Admission	Under-3s free; 3–9 $87 (1-day ticket), $134 (2-park ticket with SeaWorld), $154 (3-park ticket with Aquatica and SeaWorld), $340 (Orlando FlexTicket Plus); adult (10+) $92, $139, $159, $360.
Parking	$17, $22 preferred parking, $28 valet
Lockers	$7, in Morocco, Congo, Egypt and Stanleyville
Pushchairs	$15 and $20
Wheelchairs	$15, $45 and $55, with pushchairs
Top attractions	Congo River Rapids, Kumba, Montu, Cheetah Hunt, Rhino Rally, SheiKra, Tanganyika Tidal Wave, Iceploration show, Falcon's Fury
Don't miss	Jungala, Edge of Africa, Madagascar Live! Operation: Vacation, Animal Care Center, Myombe Reserve, Meet The Keepers talks
Hidden costs	Meals	Burger, chips and Pepsi $10.20 3-course meal $22-35, family-style diner $16.99 & $9.99 (Crown Colony House) Kids' meal $6.50
	T-shirts	$19.95–32.95
	Souvenirs	99c–$2,100
	Sundries	Face Painting $7–13

Morocco
1 Marrakesh Theater
2 Moroccan Palace Theater
3 Myombe Reserve
4 Gwazi

Cheetah Hunt
5 Cheetah Run
6 Cheetah Hunt and Skyride Station

Bird Gardens
7 Gwazi Pavilion
8 Lory Landing
9 Walkabout Way

Sesame Street Safari of Fun
10 Air Grover
11 Sunny Day Theater
12 Big Bird's 123-Smile With Me

Stanleyville
13 SheiKra
14 Stanley Falls Flume
15 Tar'ganika Tidal Wave
16 Stanleyville Theater
17 Skyride Station
18 Zambia Smokehouse

Jungala
19 Jungle Flyers, The Wild Surge and Treetop Trails
20 Tiger Habitat
21 Orang Outpost

Congo
22 Kumba
23 Congo River Rapids
24 Ubanga-Banga Bumper Cars

Pantopia
25 Falcon's Fury
26 Sand Serpent
27 The Phoenix
28 Grand Caravan Carousel
29 Pantopia Theater

Nairobi
30 Rhino Rally
31 Serengeti Plain
32 Jambo Junction
33 Edge of Africa
34 Elephant Habitat
35 Animal Care Center

Egypt
36 Montu

BUSCH GARDENS

(and in a better climate). Busch Gardens is the only park to offer 1-day Tickets with a rain guarantee, which means if you get rained out on your visit, you can return FREE within 7 days. Look for self-serve machines to the right of the park entrance to save time at ticket booths.

BRITTIP

Like SeaWorld, Busch Gardens offers QuickQueue, the limited number front-of-the-line pass for all the park's main rides. Price varies (seasonally), $19.99–39.99 for One-Time use, $34.99–59.99 for Unlimited use.

All Day Dining Deal: For just $32.99 ($16.99 3–9s) you can enjoy all-you-care-to-eat-and-drink privileges at 5 restaurants throughout the park. With your special wristband, choose 1 entrée, 1 side or dessert and a soft drink each time you pass through the dining queue (child's price valid for kids' meal only; baby back ribs excluded).

Meet The Keeper: Look out also for sessions around the park where the animal handlers explain various features of animal husbandry, notably with the gorillas, elephants and hippos. You will find them at the Alligator Habitat, Myombe Reserve, Edge of Africa, Jungala, Elephant and Rhinoceros Habitats and Jambo Junction (where they feature various small-animal encounters).

Animal Care Center

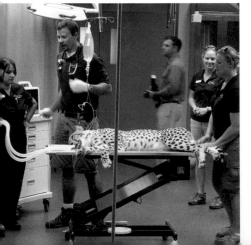

Location

Busch Gardens can be hard to locate on the sketchy local maps as the sign-posting is not as sharp as it could be, but from Orlando the directions are simple. Head west on I-4 for almost an hour (it is 55ml/88km from I-4's junction with Highway 192) until you hit intersecting motorway I-75. Take I-75 north for 3½ml/5.5km to the exit for Fowler Avenue (Highway 582). Go west on Fowler for another 3½ml/5.5km, then, just past the University of South Florida on your right, turn LEFT into McKinley Drive. A mile/1.6km down McKinley Drive, the car park is on your left, where it costs $17 to park (those with disabled badges should continue on then turn right).

Those without a car can use the Busch Gardens Shuttle Express bus, which makes several $10 round trips a day from Orlando (FREE if you have a multi-day ticket). You board at SeaWorld, Orlando Premium Outlets, Universal Studios, Ramada Maingate West, Best Western Lakeside or Old Town in Kissimmee and pick-up times range from 8.30 to 9.40am, returning at 6 or 7pm. Book at Guest Services at SeaWorld or call 1800 221 1339.

ANNIVERSARY SPOT

20 Back in our first edition, a child's 1-day ticket to Busch Gardens was $28.20 while an adult's was $34.60. It was only $3 to park!

Beating the queues: Don't think you've left the high-season Orlando crowds behind. It's still advisable to be here at opening time, if only to be first in line to ride the dazzling roller-coasters, which all draw big queues (especially SheiKra and Cheetah Hunt). The Congo River Rapids, Stanley Falls Log Flume ride and Tanganyika Tidal Wave (all opportunities to get wet) are also prime draws in peak season. But queues take longer to build here, so for the first few hours you can enjoy a relatively crowd-free experience.

Adventure Tour Centre: On your left through the main gates, go here first (better still, book in advance on 1888 800 5447 or online at www.buschgardens.com) if you'd like to do the wonderful Serengeti Safari or other Adventure Tours (p215). Busch Gardens is divided into 11 main sections, with the major rides all a bit of a hike from the main entrance. Check your park map for times and locations of various small-animal encounters throughout the park – then watch for passing flamingos as they take the first of their twice-daily promenades in the main courtyard!

Coaster fans flock in serious numbers to SheiKra, the world's second highest and fastest dive coaster, and queues can top an hour by mid-afternoon in peak season. So, if you are tempted by this first, bear left through Morocco past the Zagora Café, through the Bird Gardens and up into Stanleyville. Then continue through Stanleyville to Congo for Kumba, and retrace your steps to do Congo River Rapids and the other 2 water rides. If you would like to start with the superb new Cheetah Hunt coaster, veer right into Morocco and go past the Moroccan Palace Theater, where the loading area for the ride faces Crown Colony. After riding the Cheetah, you should take the SkyRide to Stanleyville and take on the other big rides there. Here is the full layout of the park in a clockwise direction.

Morocco

Coming through the main gates brings you into the home of all the guest services and a lot of good shops. Epcot's Moroccan pavilion sets the scene better, but the architecture is still impressive and this version won't tax your wallet as much as Disney's! Turning the corner brings you to the first animal encounter, the alligator pen. Morocco is also home to 2 of the park's biggest shows.

Marrakesh Theater: In summer 2014, this venue presented **Soundsational!**, a fun and fast-paced *a capella* singing 'competition' between two contrasting vocal groups up to 4 times a day (not Tue or Wed), with a chance to meet the performers after the show. AAA

Moroccan Palace Theater: The setting for the lavish production Iceploration, a fabulous 25min stage show featuring ice skating, elaborate puppetry, trampoline artists and 20 live animals (including a Siberian lynx), plus in-theatre special effects. It tells the story of a technology-overdosed teen who gets to travel the world with his grandfather and learn the real-life mysteries of the African Serengeti, the Great Barrier Reef, the Arctic and the Amazon rainforest. With vivid costuming, scintillating music and eye-catching performers – plus some wonderfully cute huskies! – it offers yet another dimension to the park's live entertainment 3–4 times a day. AAAAA Stay around to meet some of the performers; you can also buy a CD of the original music.

Myombe Reserve: One of the largest and most realistic habitats for the threatened highland gorillas and chimpanzees of Central Africa, this 3acre/1.2ha walk-through has a convincing tropical setting with high temperatures, lush forest landscaping and water mist sprays. Take your time, especially as there are good, seated vantage points, and catch these magnificent creatures on their daily routine. It is also highly informative, with attendants on hand to answer any questions. AAAAA

Gwazi: The future of Busch's classic wooden roller-coaster looks to be limited as half of the ride (the Tiger track) was shut down permanently in 2013, leaving the Lion half to shake,

Sesame Street Safari of Fun

rattle and roll its riders around the 7,000ft/2,134m of track. Insiders insist the whole ride will eventually be closed to make way for a major new high-speed coaster in 2016.
R: 4ft/122cm. **TTTTT**

Gwazi Gliders: This gentle circling 'hang-gliding' ride is purely for the pre-school crowd. **T** (**TTT** under-6s)

Other entertainment: Basketball fans can try the Hoops Challenge (for $5) next to Gwazi.

Shopping and dining: Choose from 4 main shops, with **The Emporium** and **Marrakesh Market** the pick of the bunch. For a quick meal, try **Zagora Café**, especially at breakfast. Alternatively, the enticing **Sultan's Sweets** serves coffee and pastries.

Cheetah Hunt

This sub-area next to Morocco features the park's wonderful cheetah habitat – and signature ride.

Cheetah Hunt: Like a cheetah in hot pursuit of its prey, this beast of a coaster re-creates the thrill of a high-speed chase. Launching from the loading station out across the savannah, the hunt is on. A second launch spirals you 10 storeys up the ride's signature figure-of-8 tower (with an astonishing view of the landscape) before taking an exhilarating 130ft/40m plunge into a subterranean gorge. Then you're off again, low and fast along the Serengeti. A final launch zips back across the grasslands (leaping over the heads of onlookers below and above the SkyRide!) and, just before you're completely out of breath, the hunt comes to an end. It lasts just 2mins but the effect is sensational. The smooth nature of the coaster, extensive theming and superb eye-appeal mark this out as possibly Florida's finest but it draws BIG queues, so try to do it early on.
R: 4ft/120cm; **TTTTT**

Cheetah Run: Here you have the chance to see these magnificent cats up close in a 250ft sprint (chasing their favourite toy alongside Cheetah Hunt!), or just lounging around the splendid new habitat designed

especially for them. Sprints occur up to 4 times daily (check park map for times). Then, take time to learn more about cheetahs and the park's conservation efforts through nearby touch-screen technology.

Shopping and dining: Grab a souvenir at **Cheetah Gifts** or quick bite or drink from **Cheetah Snacks**.

Bird Gardens

The most peaceful area and the original starting point of the park in 1959, it is possible to unwind here from the usual theme-park hurly-burly. The exhibits and shows are all family-orientated, too, with live shows, an elaborate kids' playground and more animal exhibits.

> **BRITTIP**
> The Bird Gardens area is a good place to visit in mid-afternoon when most of the rides are busy.

Lory Landing: Walk through this tropical aviary featuring lorikeets, hornbills, parrots and more, with the chance to become a human perch and feed the friendly lorikeets. A cup of nectar costs $5, but makes for a great photo opportunity. **AAA**

Walkabout Way: This charming Australia-themed attraction offers the chance to feed the free-roaming kangaroos and wallabies ($5, ages 5 and up only) and meet other Down Under denizens like the emu. It is a surprisingly captivating area, perfect for a relaxed stroll. **AAA** Other encounters include the lush, walk-through **Aviary**, **Flamingo Island** and the **Backyard Wildlife Habitat**.

Other entertainment: Gwazi Park is home to the seasonal live musical entertainment during summer and other special events, like **Viva La Musica** (Sun Apr/May) and the excellent **Bands, Brews and BBQ** (Sun Feb/Mar), with free concerts from the likes of Barenaked Ladies and The Doobie Brothers.

Shopping and dining: A real novelty here is the eye-catching **Xcursions**

eco-friendly gift shop. Its live frog and gecko displays and conservation info on interactive touch-screens make it worth visiting whether you buy or not (but all proceeds contribute to the Busch Gardens Conservation Fund). **Garden Gate** is another imaginative shop. A pizza-and-pasta buffet with salad, dessert and non-alcoholic drinks (beer and wine extra) is on offer at the pleasant **Garden Gate Café** (excellent value at $14.99 per adult, $9.99 under 9s).

Sesame Street Safari of Fun

This impressive children's interactive play area is the cheerful 'home away from home' for much-loved Sesame Street characters, dressed in best African Safari finery. You will be hard pressed to get pre-schoolers away when they catch sight of this land's 7 rides (including a junior-sized coaster, a gentle flume ride and character-themed fairground style rides), entertaining stage show and the wonderfully extensive water play and climb-and-slide areas. The huge treehouse climb, ball pools and adventure play structures alone will keep most kids busy for hours! But there's more:

Air Grover: A whizzy little dip-and-turn coaster packing plenty of junior-sized thrills, piloted by everyone's favourite blue guy, Grover. R: 2ft 9in/97cm accompanied; 3ft 5in/104cm unaccompanied.

Sunny Day Theater: Elmo, Abby, Zoe, Grover and Cookie Monster star in A is for Africa, a delightfully zany stage show that brings tales of adventure to life, with a gently uplifting message. Children (and adults!) can't help but sing and clap along, and it is a great photo opportunity as the characters arrive and then come out for a meet-and-greet afterwards.

BRITTIP
Arrive early and find a seat in the first 5 rows for an unobstructed view at the Sunny Day Theater. Seat children on the ends for the best character interaction.

Big Bird's 1-2-3 Smile with Me: Big Bird and friends have their own meet-and-greet area, near Air Grover. The big bonus here is 1-on-1 time with the character in a quiet, air conditioned room (photo packages $20–30).

Bert and Ernie's Watering Hole: Thoughtfully designed with even the smallest guests in mind, this gentle

Cheetah Hunt

water-play area is filled with bubblers, water jets, dump buckets, geysers and splash tubs. Swimwear and sun block are available at Cookie Monster's Trading Post if you forgot yours. Convenient seating surrounds the area. TTTTT (young 'uns only!)

Shopping and dining: Look for **Abby Cadabby's Treasure Hut** and **Cookie Monster's Trading Post** for Sesame Street gifts and souvenirs. For a quick bite here, try **Snack-n-Getti Tribal Treats.** The big opportunity, though, is **Dine with Elmo & Friends,** where visitors can enjoy lunch with Elmo and his chums in an outdoor covered dining area. A kid-friendly buffet along with a character song-and-dance show make this a delight for the younger set, with loads of time to meet their favourite characters ($22 for adults, $15 3–9s, including a 6x8in/15x20cm photo per family; not on weekdays in low season).

◀▦▶ BRITTIP
Dine with Elmo has a great Birthday option, with reserved seats, a cake and special birthday wishes from Elmo and the gang for an additional $45. Call 1888 800 5447 or visit **www.SesameStreetSafariofFun.com**.

Stanleyville
This brings you back into true ride territory, with the park's biggest coaster, as well as several water rides and a fabulous new show. You'll also find one of the 3 Train Stations here (next to SheiKra), for a gentle 35min journey round the park.

SheiKra

SheiKra: The park's outstanding big-thrill attraction is the giant steel structure of this monstrous coaster. At 200ft/62m tall and hitting 70mph/112kph, this is the ride to put Alton Towers' fearsome Oblivion in the shade. Higher, longer and faster, it features an initial drop at an angle as near vertical as makes no difference (with a delicious moment of stop-go balance as you teeter on the edge!), a second drop of 138ft/42m into an underground tunnel, an Immelman loop (an exhilarating rolling manoeuvre) and a water splashdown over 0.6ml/1km of smooth-as-silk track. As if all that isn't enough, a 2007 modification removed the coaster's floor, so there is nothing between you and the track but air! The whole ride lasts less than 3min and is almost as much fun to watch as to ride. It also draws big queues, so get here early or expect a long wait (or use the paid-for QuickQueue system). You can buy the video of your ride for $25, a 6x8in/15x20cm photo for $16.50 or packages from $20–35. **R:** 4ft 6in/137cm. **TTTTT+**

Stanley Falls: Almost identical to Log Flume rides at Chessington, LEGOLAND, Thorpe Park and Alton Towers, this guarantees a good soaking at the final 40ft/12m drop. **R:** 3ft 10in/116cm. **TTT**

Tanganyika Tidal Wave: A distinctly more scenic ride, this takes you on a journey along 'uncharted' African waters before tipping you down a 2-stage drop that lands with tidal-wave force. **R:** 4ft/122cm. **TTTT**

◀▦▶ BRITTIP
Don't stand on the bridge by Tanganyika Tidal Wave or by the SheiKra splashdown – unless you want to get seriously wet!

Stanleyville Theater: This newly enclosed venue (and, therefore, air-conditioned!) debuted with the 20min **Madagascar Live! Operation: Vacation** show in 2013, featuring live song-and-dance performances from the stars of the *Madagascar* film series. It follows the antics of Alex the

Lion, Gloria the Hippo, King Julien, Mort and the Penguins during their holiday adventures, backed by music from a live band rocking through both classic and original songs. Superb staging, vivid lighting and the show's singers and dancers (plus the lovable penguins and outrageous King Julien) combine to provide an infectious, sing-along style that should appeal to children and anyone who enjoys the Madagascar humour. The characters are also available for meet-and-greets after the show. AAAA

Skyride: The other end of the park's cable-car ride (from Morocco), it offers spectacular views over the Serengeti Plain (with a thrilling moment as Cheetah Hunt races above!). However, it closes when it's windy and queues can build up here in late afternoon. AA

Other entertainment: Try Bahati Hoops and other fairground games (next to SheiKra) for a small fee.

Shopping and dining: The **Kariba Marketplace** has the best of the shopping, while, for a hearty meal (and a great view of SheiKra), try **Zambia Smokehouse**, where its wood-smoked ribs platter is a delight among a heavily barbecue-orientated menu (also with salads, sandwiches and kids' meals).

Jungala

One of the park's biggest expansions, this 4acre/1.6ha land opened in 2008 adding a couple of small-scale rides, some superb animal habitats and a hugely elaborate children's play area, designed with older children in mind (where Sesame Street Safari of Fun is primarily for under-6s). It also gets busy in the afternoon, so visit either early on or late in the day.

Jungle Flyers: This kids' ride (6–13s) is a junior-sized zipline journey over part of the Jungala area, a 1-seat there-and-back trip from the upper level of Treetop Trails. Great fun for kids, but a rather short ride, and queues build up quickly and move slowly most of the day. **R:** Maximum height 4ft 8in/145cm. **TTT**

The Wild Surge: Get ready to 'surge' 4 storeys into the air on this tower ride from inside a giant waterfall providing a (brief!) glimpse over Jungala before bouncing back down again. Be aware that queues here are also long and slow-moving as the ride takes just 14 at a time. **R:** 3ft 6in/106cm to ride solo (3ft 2in/96cm with a parent). **TTT** (**TTTTT** under-12s)

Treetop Trails: Climbing nets, elaborate bridges, crawl tubes and a multi-level maze are the basis of this fab 3-storey children's playground, with smaller-scale adventures at ground level, including squirt fountains and other watery fun (swimsuits or a change of clothes are advisable). It cleverly mixes in 2 different animal habitats, for the fun-loving gibbons, flying fox-bats and the rare tomistoma (an Asian crocodile). **TTTT** (young 'uns only)

 BRITTIP
The toddler play area in Treetop Trails is very thoughtfully in the shade.

Tiger Habitat: One of the park's most creative animal environments is this multi-level tiger exhibit (including its rare white tigers). It is divided into Tiger Lodge, an air-conditioned overlook including conservation info and issues, and Tiger Trail, a walkthrough section with various close-up opportunities, including a unique pop-up turret (which has a separate queue) in the main enclosure and a rope-pull for guests to 'test their strength' (periodically) against the big cats. Huge windows

Treetop Trails

provide maximum viewing of the animals at play, especially in their plunge pool. AAAA

Orang Outpost: Another brilliant animal habitat, this showcases the park orang-utans, who love to look in on guests, viewing them as much as vice versa. A series of close-up windows, including a glass floor over a hammock play area and a kids' tunnel, provide superb observation of the specially designed forest environment. AAAA

Other entertainment: Look out for **Kareebu Jungala**, colourful stilt-walkers around the village area periodically (see map for times).

Shopping and dining: Shop for gifts at **Tiger Treasures** (organic cotton T-shirts and conservation-related items) and **Cubs Closet** (kids' clothing), and then stop to eat at **Bengal Bistro** (fish, burgers, veggie wraps, salads and sandwiches) or the more snack-orientated **Orang Café** (chicken strips, hot dogs, fries, and funnel cakes).

Congo

As you continue into the Congo, this is primarily about just 3 rides, plus a stop on the Serengeti Railway.

Kumba: Another of the park's signature coasters, this unmistakable giant turquoise structure looms over the area. It's one of the largest and fastest in south-east USA and, at 60mph/97kph, features 3 high-thrill elements: a diving loop plunging a full 110ft/33m; a camel-back, with a 360° spiral; and a vertical loop. For good measure, it dives underground!

Pantopia

It looks terrifying close up but is absolutely exhilarating, even for non-coaster fans. R: 4ft 6in/137cm. TTTTT

Congo River Rapids: These look pretty tame after Kumba, but don't be fooled. The giant rubber rafts will bounce you down some of the most convincing rapids outside of the Rockies, and you will end up with a fair soaking. R: 3ft 6in/106cm. TTTT

Ubanga-Banga Bumper Cars: Fairly typical fairground dodgems, you won't miss anything if you pass them by. R: 3ft 6in/106cm. TT

Shopping and dining: There is just the **Congo River Outfitters** gift shop here, plus 3 refreshment kiosks.

Pantopia

This redeveloped land opened in summer 2014 with a dramatic new look, name (it was formerly Timbuktu) and the park's most eye-catching ride. There is also a full back-story, as Pantopia was created by a mystical Key-Master who arrived by hot air balloon to create a place where travellers could meet. The doors of Pantopia tell a tale of the original owners and travellers who passed this way and the land includes clever kinetic sculptures and re-purposed vehicles, like an Asian tuk-tuk and various bikes and wagons. Another highlight is **The Sitting Place**, a modern-day watering hole where visitors can sit, relax and enjoy the views, as well as the signature food and drink offerings.

Falcon's Fury: The land's signature ride, this awe-inspiring tower lifts 32 riders at a time (slowly) up to its 300ft/91m height, tilts them *forward* so they are face down – then drops in best free-fall style. Yes, it's the world's highest drop-tower ride and it's for adrenalin addicts only as it really has that sky-dive feeling for several seconds before the brakes kick in and bring you more gently back to earth. It is aptly named for the vertical dive of a falcon (which can hunt its prey at up to 160mph) and provides an amazing view from the top – if you can keep your eyes open. We think it's as much a spectator opportunity as something you'll actually want to ride but it does provide an iconic look to the park. It's a relatively brief experience and queues move slowly, so you may want to try this early on – or chicken out completely! **R:** 3ft 6in/106cm. **TTTTT**

Sand Serpent: This family-orientated 'Crazy Mouse' style coaster is surprisingly energetic, rising as it does some 46ft/14m and adding tight turns and swift drops. Top speed is only 22mph/35kph, but it seems faster and thrills younger kids. **TTT** (**TTTTT** under-10s)

The Phoenix: A positively evil invention that involves sitting in a gigantic, boat-shaped swing that eventually performs a 360° rotation in dramatic, slow-motion style. Don't eat just before this one! **R:** 4ft/122cm. **TTTT**

Scorpion: A 50mph/80kph roller-coaster, this features a 62ft/19m drop and a 360° loop that is guaranteed to dial D for dizzy for a while. It lasts just 120secs, but seems longer. Queues build here from late morning. **R:** 3ft 6in/106cm. **TTTT**

Grand Caravan Carousel: Join this 'Bedouin caravan' in its layers of tapestries and tenting for a genuine kiddie carousel ride. **TT** (**TTTT** under 5s)

Pantopia Theater: This all-new indoor entertainment arena (replacing the former 3-D cinema) features a terrific animal show. Opening Night Critters. It follows the exploits of 2 wannabe stage presenters and their host of critter side-kicks, including dogs, cats, birds, pigs, a skunk and even a kangaroo, and is sure to raise a lot of laughs with all the family, while you can also meet some of the stars of the show afterwards. **AAAA.**

Other entertainment: The **Games Area** offers fairground-style games that require a few extra dollars, while the **Pantopia Grill Theater** – a Moroccan-influenced nightclub that is Pantopia's gathering place for artists from around the world – offers

a show while you dine (or just sit and watch). In summer 2014 it was Burn The Floor: Untapped, a lively dance competition featuring flamenco, tango, tap dancers and more, with a chance to meet the cast after the show.

Shopping and dining: This has been heavily redesigned for the Pantopia theme, with the **Painted Camel Bazaar** offering a wide range of creative merchandise, some of it made from recycled materials from around the world, as well as Falcon's Fury and other souvenir items. Headline restaurant the **Pantopia Grill** serves great sandwiches, salads, pasta, baby back ribs and kids meals while, outside, the **Dragon Fire** features ribs, sausages and kebabs. **Twisted Tails Pretzels** is a delightful new offering of fresh-rolled pretzels (don't miss the signature Bacon Pretzel Fury, along with the beer mustard sauce!), artisan sandwiches, pizza and pretzel dogs, as well as craft beers. **Lynx Frozen Treats** adds snowcones, smoothies and other icy delights and **Kettle Corn** is a haven for popcorn-lovers as well as serving turkey legs, potato twisters, chicken strips and drinks.

Nairobi

It's back to the animals as we enter this area, with 5 different habitats, plus an animal adventure ride.

Rhino Rally: This off-road jeep safari has been heavily modified in recent years (losing part of its run to make room for Cheetah Hunt), but is still an engaging whirl through 'the wilds of Africa' to encounter elephants, rhinos, crocodiles, antelope and more. Your driver adds to the fun with some amusing spiel, but it does draw slow-moving queues through the middle part of the day. **R:** 3ft 3in/99cm. **AAAA**

Serengeti Plain: A 49acre/20ha spread of African savannah, this is home to buffalo, antelope, zebras, giraffes, wildebeest, ostriches, hippos, rhinos and many exotic birds, and can be viewed for much of the journey on the Serengeti Express, a full-size, open-car steam train that chugs slowly from its main station in Nairobi to the Congo, Stanleyville and back. **AAA**

BRITTIP
Take the Serengeti Railway from Nairobi (or Congo or Stanleyville) in mid-afternoon to give your feet a rest when it's busy elsewhere.

Jambo Junction: The park's nursery is an interesting animal encounter, with some friendly flamingos, small critters (lemurs, sloths, possums and babies needing extra care) on view through the large windows. This is the place to meet the park's Animal Ambassadors for education and conservation issues. **AA**

Animal Care Center: This is a peek into the way Busch Gardens cares for its residents, even down to performing live surgical procedures. The state-of-the-art facility is in 3 parts, for the Treatment Room, Nutrition Center and Pathology Lab, with live audio links to the vets and technicians working behind the big glass windows and keepers on hand to answer questions, whether it's a snake getting an ultrasound check-up or the daily preparation of mealworms for the possums! **AAAA**

Edge of Africa: This is a 15acre/6ha 'safari experience', which can also be accessed through Egypt, guarantees a close-up almost like the real thing. The walk-through puts you in an authentic setting of native wilds and villages from which you can view giraffes, lions, baboons, meerkats, crocodiles, hyenas and vultures, and even an underwater hippo habitat. Wandering naturalists offer informal talks, and the attention to detail is superb.

BRITTIP
Edge of Africa offers some fantastic photo opportunities but, in the hot months, come here early in the day as many animals seek refuge from the heat later.

Other entertainment: Look out for the **Elephant Habitat** and periodic sessions with animal staff (notably the afternoon Elephant Wash), while you can see more park inhabitants at the **Reptile House, Curiosity Caverns** (nocturnal animals) and **Tortoise Habitat**. The meeting area for the Serengeti Safari is also here, next to Kenya Kanteen.

Shopping and dining: Caravan Crossing (safari apparel and hats) has the best shopping here while **Kenya Kanteen** offers drinks and snacks.

Egypt

The final area of Busch Gardens is somewhat tucked away, so it's best visited either first thing or late in the day (sooner rather than later if you want to ride Montu). It sits in the park's bottom right corner and much of it is re-created pharaoh country, dominated by suspended coaster Montu, named after an ancient Egyptian warrior god. You can also take the SkyRide cable car to Stanleyville (with a great look at Rhino Rally en route).

Montu: You cannot miss the area's main attraction, another breathtaking inverted coaster, covering nearly 4,000ft/1,219m of track at up to 60mph/97kph and peaking with a G-force of 3.85! Like Kumba, it looks terrifying but really is a 5-star thrill as it leaves your legs dangling and twists and dives (underground at 2 points) for almost 3min of brain-scrambling fun. **R:** 4ft 6in/137cm. **TTTTT**

Other entertainment: Youngsters can make their own excavations in the Shifting Sands, a neat sand play area or try some more fairground-style games.

Shopping and dining: The high-quality **Golden Scarab** offers hand-blown glass and cartouche paintings while you can grab other souvenirs at **Montu Gifts**. For dining, Victorian-style **Crown Colony Restaurant** overlooks Serengeti Plain and offers counter-service salads, sandwiches and pizzas in the Café downstairs (with a pub bar, too) or full-service dining upstairs, including family-style fried chicken and fish, gourmet sandwiches, burgers and salads, with magnificent views of the animals. For a memorable meal (11.30am until an hour before park closing), head here for lunch (it doesn't take bookings) or, even better, come back at early evening and see the animals visit the waterhole.

BRITTIP

We find Crown Colony Restaurant a blissful lunch stop in the hotter months when its cool interior and elegant ambience offer a welcome change of pace after all the rides.

Special tours

Busch Gardens features a wide range of behind-the-scenes tours and adventure expeditions that add an extra dimension to the park. For all tours, book at the Adventure Tour Center in Morocco or, better still, book in advance on 1888 800 5447 or at **www.seaworldparks.com**.

Serengeti Safari: A 30min excursion (5 times a day, up to 20 at a time) aboard flat-bed trucks, takes you to meet some of the Serengeti Plain's residents and feed the beautiful giraffes while learning about the park's environmental efforts. It tends to fill up quickly and costs $19–39/person seasonally (children must be at least 5; 5–15s must be accompanied by an adult). The **Serengeti Night Safari** (park admission not required) is a 2hr after-dark excursion into the Serengeti, with appetisers and hot and cold drinks (Nov–May, $69/person, 21 and over only).

Guided Adventure Tour: This takes just 15 at a time on a 5hr VIP trek, with your own guide, reserved seating at the Moroccan Palace Theater, front-of-line access for major rides, counter-service lunch and close encounters with many of the animals, including the Serengeti Safari ($99 adults, $89 children)

Elite Adventure Tour: A personal 7hr park tour with front-of-line access to all rides, the Serengeti Safari, reserved seating at shows, free bottled water throughout and lunch at Crown Colony ($199/person, 5 and over).

Keeper for a Day: An exclusive 6½hr behind-the-scenes tour where you join the keepers as they feed, train and care for giraffes and antelope, then move on to assist the avian team on the Serengeti ($250/person, including park admission and lunch; 13 and over only, must book at least 2wks in advance).

Elephant Insider: A 45min group walking tour behind the scenes with the elephant handlers and their charges ($29/person, ages 10 and up).

Roller Coaster Experience: Unique 8am tour into how the park builds and maintains its amazing rides, with front-row rides for all (10 and over only; must be 4ft 6ins/137cm tall to ride; $69/person).

Jungala Insider: A fascinating 45min group visit behind the scenes in Jungala to meet the keepers, see how they care for the magnificent tigers (you might even help to weigh one!) and orang-utans, and learn some zoo husbandry secrets ($29/person, ages 5+).

Animal Care Center Behind The Scenes: A 75min tour with the park's vet and zoological staff, with hands-on opportunities, as they showcase medical check-ups and other treatments ($29/person, ages 8+).

Montu

© Jeremy Thompson

Heart of Africa Tour: A 90min behind-the-scenes walking tour to get close to hippos, cheetahs and lions with their keepers ($39/person, ages 10+).

Special programmes

Busch Gardens is open until 10pm for the **Summer Nights** programme (June–Aug), featuring outdoor food and drink, live entertainment (notably at the Pantopia Grill and Gwazi Pavilion), music and DJs, plus clever lighting effects on coasters like SheiKra. A superb nightly high-energy finale, **Kinetix**, brings together live musicians, singers, dancers and acrobats for a 30min contemporary rock show enhanced by innovative lighting and with an all-new fireworks spectacular at the end.

And don't miss **Howl-O-Scream**, the park's special Halloween presentation each Sept–Oct. A separately ticketed event ($55–85/person; see online for early-booking discounts) offering grisly goings-on and themed houses, it also offers the chance to ride all the big coasters at night (7.30pm–midnight or 1am). It features some imaginative shows with all the shock-horror effects, plus a dance party, but it is definitely not advised for young children. It is similar to Universal's Halloween Horror Nights programme (p167), with 8 elaborately themed haunted houses – like Blood Asylum and Zombie Mortuary – plus

a series of scare zones that change annually. The Busch Gardens version is more spread out and less frenetic than Universal's, but you may well want to try both. See more at **www.howloscream.com**.

For the Christmas period, see p39.

For a really full family day out, you can combine Busch Gardens with sister water park **Adventure Island** (on McKinley Drive), which is blissful when it hots up. The 25acres/10ha of watery fun, in a Key West theme, offer a full range of slides and rides, such as the **Wahoo Run** raft ride, a 210ft/64m plunge on the body slide **Gulf Scream**, the exciting 4-lane mat slide **Riptide** and spiralling tube ride **Calypso Coaster**. Adventure Island is open mid-Mar to late Oct (weekends only Sept and Oct) 10am–5pm (9pm in summer). Tickets are $47 (adults) and $43 (3–9s), while a Busch Gardens–Adventure Island combo is $135 and $120 (but only $92pp online).

◀▶ BRITTIP

The Anheuser-Busch factory at Busch Gardens is long gone BUT you can still get a (free) brewery tour (and samples!) at the nearby Yuengling Brewery on neighbouring 30th Street (p280).

Well, that's the low-down on all the main theme parks, but there is still MUCH more to discover…

Busch Gardens at Christmas

If you think you can 'do' Orlando just by sticking to the main theme parks, think again! There is still a LOT more to discover, starting with Kennedy Space Center, which we rate as an essential place to visit these days. It will easily demand a day of your attention.

Then there's LEGOLAND Florida – ideal for the 3–12 brigade – and Gatorland, which provides another great-value experience with its alligators and shows. There are unique venues like WonderWorks, Orlando Science Center and Ripley's Believe It Or Not and, for more individual tastes, the amazing 'skydive' experience of iFLY Orlando and WhirlyDome fun centre, plus some magnificent water parks. The choice is yours, but it's an immense selection. Let's start with One Giant Leap for Mankind.

Kennedy Space Center

Welcome to the past, present and future of NASA's space programme, and one of the most fascinating places in Florida. The KSC has undergone huge redevelopment in recent years, culminating in 2013 with the opening of their Space Shuttle Atlantis exhibit to showcase the last orbiter in the Shuttle programme that gives the whole Visitor Complex

Kennedy Space Center

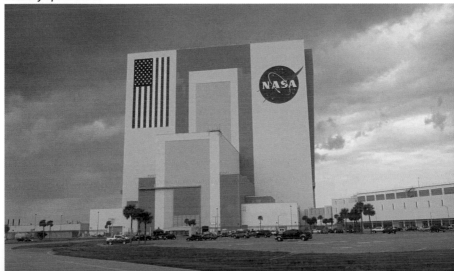

Orlando's Other Attractions

✈ Sanford International Airport

Sanford Airport via Interstate 4 has no tolls, but can be far busier, especially during rush-hour

Sanford Airport via 417 has a few tolls, but is much quieter

Mount Dora

Daytona

ALTAMONTE SPRINGS

Sanford-Central Florida Zoo

94

4

436

Toll road (from 50c to $5)

Lake Apopka

Winter Park

Black Hammock Fish Camp

Leu Gardens

429

190

441

88

87

417

OCOEE

WINTER GARDEN

50

50

WEST COLONIAL DRIVE

84

Amway Center

Downtown Orlando
Lake Eola

408

EAST - WEST EXPRESSWAY

83

Citrus Bowl Stadium

82

WINDERMERE

FLORIDA TURNPIKE

KIRKMAN RD

80

79

429

78

441

Universal Studios

77

Islands of Adventure

75

SEMORAN BOULEVARD

74B

Pirates Dinner Adventure

Cocoa Beach

SAND LAKE RD

74A

Port Canaveral →

Sleuth's Mystery
Dinner Shows

528

BEACHLINE

Mickey's Backyard Barbecue,
Hoop-Dee-Doo Musical Revue

INTERNATIONAL DRIVE

Orlando
Watersports
Complex

✈ Orlando
International
Airport

Magic Kingdom

535 **435**

TURKEY LAKE RD

71

SeaWorld

Richard Petty
Driving Experience

4

Lake Buena Vista

423

Epcot

68

Buena Vista Watersports

JOHN YOUNG PARKWAY

ORANGE BLOSSOM TRAIL

BOGGY CREEK ROAD

CENTRAL FLORIDA GREENEWAY

Disney's Hollywood
Studios

Fantasia Gdns Mini-golf

67

WESTERN BELTWAY

429

535

Winter-Summerland Mini-golf

417

Animal Kingdom

65

MainGate
West

64

OSCEOLA PARKWAY

Toll road

BOGGY CREEK ROAD

BOGGY CREEK ROAD

63

KISSIMMEE

Capone's Dinner Show

East Lake Fish Camp
(Boggy Creek Airboats)

Celebration

Osceola County Historical Museum

62

Medieval Times

192

IRLO BRONSON

East Lake
Tohopekaliga

Osceola County Pioneer Museum

Silver Spurs Arena

Warbird Adventures & Museum

Kissimmee Airport

60

Champions
Gate

Green Meadows Petting Farm

Kissimmee Scenic
Lake Tours

FLORIDA TURNPIKE

MEMORIAL HIGHWAY

58

17

Forever Florida,
Reptile World
Serpentarium

OLD LAKE WILSON RD

WORLD DRIVE

EPCOT CENTER DRIVE

← Dinosaur World

55

**Tampa, Clearwater,
Gulf Coast**

ST CLOUD

© Steve Munns 2014

Horse World Riding Stables,
Boggy Creek Airboat Rides

0   5 miles

Lake
Tohopekaliga

Miami

N

a fresh, new look. This underlines its place among the first rank of local attractions and provides even more reason to justify an all-day visit. Apart from the Space Shuttle, there are a series of exhibits and shows (including 2 splendid IMAX films), a children's play area, an art gallery, the captivating daily Astronaut Encounter, the sombre Astronaut Memorial, and the essential Space Center bus tours, which all add up to great value. There is also the brilliant Astronaut Training Experience, an extra programme into real-life astronaut missions and simulations at the neighbouring US Astronaut Hall of Fame. However, there is now a $10 parking fee, when it used to be free.

You start at the vivid new Entrance Plaza, bringing visitors in via the Rocket Garden, an eye-catching selection of the actual hardware that put NASA on the space map. They include Atlas and Titan rockets that formed the cornerstone of the Gemini and Apollo programmes.

 BRITTIP

Don't miss the clever water show at the Space Center's entry plaza. It runs every 15 minutes.

Once inside the Visitor Complex, the attractions are as follows. You should certainly start with the new Space Shuttle Atlantis, as this has proved THE big draw since it opened in June 2013. Late arrivals should do the Bus Tour first, though, then visit the Shuttle complex.

Atlantis: This dramatic $100m, 65,000ft²/6,000m² exhibit is the core experience of the new-look KSC, offering the 30-year history of the Shuttle programme through a mix of interactive media. Both hands-on and immersive, it features 1 of the 3 surviving orbiters (*Discovery* is on show at The Smithsonian in Washington and *Endeavour* at the California Science Center in Los Angeles). The 6-storey building is clad in orange and gold, to symbolise

KENNEDY SPACE CENTER at a glance

Location	Off State Road 405 in Titusville		
Size	Visitor Complex 70 acres/28.3ha		
Hours	9am–5 or 6pm) year-round (except Christmas Day)		
Admission	Under-3s free; 3–11 $40; adult (12+) $50; Atlantis annual pass $89/$71; Explorer annual pass $139/$109. Prices do not include tax but include admission to US Astronaut Hall of Fame.		
Parking	$10		
Lockers	$5, just inside turnstiles to left.		
Pushchairs	Available on a complimentary basis (with photo ID as deposit) inside the Information Center		
Wheelchairs	Available on a complimentary basis (with photo ID as deposit) inside the Information Center		
Top attractions	Space Shuttle Atlantis; Shuttle Launch Experience; IMAX films; Astronaut Encounter; KSC Bus Tours		
Don't miss	Apollo-Saturn V Center on Bus Tours; Astronaut Memorial; Rocket Garden; Angry Birds Space Encounter		
Hidden costs	Meals	Burger, chips and coke $11.98 Kids' meal $5.99	
	T-shirts	$15.99–35.99	
	Souvenirs	79c–$4,800	
	Sundries	Bus tour photos – $15 and $25	

the fiery glow of atmosphere re-entry, and is dominated outside by full-size replicas of the external fuel tank and solid rocket boosters, with their 184ft/56m height illustrating the power needed to put the Space Transport System (STS) in orbit. Visitors wind up a gently-sloped ramp to a film pre-show into how and why the Shuttle programme was devised, and then doors open into the main theatre, offering a vivid sense-surround presentation into the life and missions of *Atlantis* (stand about two-thirds of the way back to get the full effect of the wrap-around screens). The specially written musical score reaches an emotional crescendo that is accompanied by a real 'Wow' moment as…no, we won't reveal it, you'll just have to see it for yourself! It is a breathtaking show that leads into the main exhibit hall, with the orbiter displayed in ultra-dynamic form, with its payload bay doors open and robotic arm extended alongside an elevated viewing platform. The hall is then subdivided into areas for the International Space Station, Hubble Space Telescope and Astronaut Training Simulation Gallery (complete with the chance to land a Shuttle and dock with the Space Station). In all, there are more than 60 interactive touch-screen experiences and simulators, many with high-tech elements, and the climb-through Space Station, with its clear plastic tube suspended 2 storeys up, is quite a challenge. There are also parts of the launch platform and other support elements on show, while kids can try the Shuttle 'landing slide' and a jump-around hydrogen 'energy' game. You

Kennedy Space Center

can easily spend 2hrs in here and we strongly advise heading here first as queues build up quickly on the entry ramp. AAAAA+ The gift shop offers a great variety of souvenirs.

Shuttle Launch Experience: After seeing *Atlantis*, visitors should also walk up the long gantry for this well-made presentation into a real-life launch – with you on board! A clever pre-show, with dry ice, moody lighting and sound and vibration effects pave the way to the 'ready room' to prepare for your own blast-off. The 4 capsules look like crew cabins in the cargo hold of the Shuttle, and you go through the launch procedure as the vehicle moves into a near vertical position for take-off. On the command 'Go for engine start', you are at the heart of a 5min simulation providing the features of a realistic launch, with vibration generators, sound effects, cabin movements and screen visuals. You get a taste of the G-forces involved, the Rocket Booster and External Tank separations, and a moment of 'weightlessness' as you enter Earth's orbit. Finally, the cargo doors open to reveal an awe-inspiring view. There is then a 'space walk' back to Earth via a spiral walkway surrounded by the stars and more satellite views of the planet. Don't miss the plaques to mark every Shuttle flight – and the memorials to the *Challenger* and *Columbia* tragedies. **R:** 3ft 8in/112cm. **TTT** AAAAA

◀▶ **BRITTIP**

All of the Shuttle Launch Experience is fully wheelchair-accessible, and there is a seat outside for potential riders to test their comfort level. For anyone wary of the full ride (although there is no need to be), there is a bypass room where you can experience the attraction without the motion.

Bus tours: The KSC's signature coaches depart every 15mins from 10am and are fully narrated to provide a full overview of the Space Center. They make 2 stops in addition to driving around much of the working areas, including past the shuttle launch pad. The first is the LC39 Observation Gantry (Fri and Sat only), just 1ml/1.6km from shuttle launch pad 39A, a combination 4-storey observation deck and science centre. The exhibits consist of a 10min film into how launches were prepared, plus models and videos of a countdown with touch-screen info on the shuttle programme. Next is the Apollo/Saturn V Center, one of the KSC's great exhibits, where you can easily spend 90mins. It highlights the Apollo missions and first Moon landing with 2 impressive theatrical presentations on the risks and triumphs, a full-size 363ft/111m Saturn V rocket and a hands-on gallery of space exploration. Allow 2–3hrs to do the tour justice but be aware the last bus leaves the Visitor Center at 2.20 or 2.50pm, depending on season. AAAAA

IMAX films: Back at the Visitor Complex are the IMAX cinemas, twin 55ft/17m screens that give the impression of sitting on top of the action. Space Station 3-D, narrated by Tom Cruise, is a slice of science fact, living with the crew of the International Space Station and affording a heart-stopping look at the construction process. Hubble 3-D (narrated by Leonardo DiCaprio) is a fabulous 43min journey through the universe as seen by the Hubble Space Telescope. Float beside astronauts as they adjust and repair Hubble, marvel at the sensation of moving through galaxies and experience the profound dynamics of the cosmos. This presentation dazzles with the spirit of human achievement and you may feel the urge to stand up and cheer at the end! AAAA Also in the IMAX building, you'll find **Eye on the Universe: The Hubble Telescope Exhibit**, featuring still images taken by Hubble.

Astronaut Encounter: This engaging feature is a daily talk and Q&A session, with personal observations and stories from various veterans of the space programmes, including Shuttle astronauts. It is an insightful

and engrossing programme, up to 3 times a day at the Astronaut Encounter Theater. AAAA

Angry Birds Space Encounter: This fun-packed game centre is dedicated to the angry avians and their eternal battle with those pesky piggies. Mainly for kids (but grown-ups get to play, too!), it features 5 different sections, with a real Angry Bird slingshot, computer stations (create your own Angry Bird), a maze and laser maze, plus a chance to play the computer game itself. AAAA

Robot Scouts: This walk-through display-and-show is done in the company of Starquester 2000, your 'robot host', who explains the history of NASA's unmanned space probes in a surprising and amusing style. AAA

Early Space Exploration: A clever walk-through trip into the space programme's past, including the Hall of Discovery, the Mercury Mission Control Room – the original consoles from America's first manned space flights – and the Hall of History. AAA

Exploration Space: An interactive exhibit and showcase featuring the Explorers Wanted show, an engaging NASA presentation geared toward children. Check out the computer photo stations for a neat souvenir to take home. AAA

Other exhibits: Nature and Technology (which showcases the unique balance the Center maintains with the local environment), the **Center for Space Education** (an interactive learning centre), the **Space Walk of Honor** and **NASA Art Gallery** (exhibits and artwork).

Entrance Plaza, Kennedy Space Center

Youngsters have their own playground, the covered **Children's Play Dome**, which has a range of climbing/crawling/sliding elements. Finally, head back to the **Rocket Garden**, which has a kids' splash fountain and an Apollo capsule gantry, to give the feel of astronauts boarding the Saturn V rocket. Free tours are given up to 4 times a day (times vary). Don't forget to stop at the **Astronaut Memorial**, a moving tribute to the men and women who have died in the course of the space programme. AAA

Shopping and dining: The Visitor Complex has an excellent **Space Shop** (the world's largest store for space memorabilia and gifts – enter at your peril!), the smaller **Voyagers** just outside the main exit and **The Right Stuff Shop** at the Apollo/Saturn V Center. Stop for lunch at **Orbit Food Court**, a cafeteria-style diner serving fresh salads, burgers, pasta, pizza and sandwiches. The excellent **Rocket Garden Café** offers a tasty selection of sandwiches, salads, pizza and nachos. Quick bites can be found at the **Pastry & Espresso Retrieval Kiosk** (or PERK truck) and Shuttle Plaza Snacks, plus various carts for snacks and drinks. You'll also find the **Moon Rock Café** at the Apollo/Saturn V Center on the bus tour.

A Space Center exhibit

The Center then has 5 optional extra tours and 3 other features.

KSC Up-Close: Explore Tour: Travel nearly a ¼mile/800m within the perimeter security fence of Launch Pad 39-A and get a close view of the amazing complex, including the flame trench and emergency escape system. The highlight of the tour is the photo opportunity during a stop at the pad. Other sites on the tour include drive-by views of Launch Pad 39-B, the Vehicle Assembly Building, mobile launch platforms and a stop at the Apollo/Saturn V Center ($25 adults, $19 for 3–11s).

KSC Up-Close: The Launch Control Center Tour: Go inside Firing Room 4, from which all 21 shuttle launches since 2006 were controlled. See the engineers' working computerised launch control systems, main launch countdown clock and large video monitors on the walls, then enter the 'bubble room' with its wall of interior windows through which the management team viewed all of the proceedings ($25 and $19).

Cape Canaveral: Then and Now: If you want to learn more about NASA history, here is a 2hr-plus guided tour (daily at noon) into the early days of space exploration around the older part of the facility. Highlights include the Air Force Space & Missile Museum, Mercury launch sites and Memorial, original astronaut training facility and several active launch pads, all of which are otherwise off-limits. For this tour, international guests (including children) must present a valid passport to participate. You must check in at the Information Counter at least 30min prior to your tour ($25 and $19). Reserve online or call 1866 737 5235.

Astronaut Training Experience (ATX): Away from the main attractions, you have the choice of a thrilling ½day programme into Shuttle training, using a sequence of simulated hands-on preparations, with the input of various NASA veterans. The training provides activities from the multi-axis trainer and 1/6 gravity chair, to operating a Shuttle mock-up and taking the helm in Mission Control. You must be at least 14 (under-18s must be accompanied by a parent). Hardwearing clothes and athletic shoes are advised, and 'recruits' should be free of neck and back injuries. It costs $145 (including ATX gear) but guarantees a memorable day for 'space cadets'.

ATX Plus: This adds admission to the Space Center and the option for a special-interest tour and lunch with an astronaut ($175). **Family ATX** is a chance for children as young as 7, with a parent, to participate in a ½day course. The session includes building and launching rockets, riding realistic simulators, meeting a veteran NASA Astronaut and working on a shuttle mission to the International Space Station in 'Mission Control.' It's $145/person and you can book in advance on 321 449 4830 or online (see below).

◀▮▶ BRITTIP

Although there are no more Shuttle launches, the KSC still has an active rocket launch programme. Check out **www. nasa.gov** and **www.spacecoastlaunches. com** for all the details.

Getting there: Take the Beachline Expressway out of Orlando (Route 528, and a toll road, see map p218) for about 45mins, bear left on SR 407 (don't follow signs to Cape Canaveral or Cocoa Beach at this point) and turn right at the T-junction onto SR 405. The Visitor Center is located 9ml/14km along on the right. Tours and IMAX presentations start at 10am (**www.KennedySpaceCenter.com** – be sure to check the website for periodic online ticket discounts).

Lunch with an astronaut

For another fully engrossing feature at the Kennedy Space Center, a small group gets to dine with the star of the daily Astronaut Encounter. The featured person gives their own special briefing, adding extra insight into their space missions, plus answers individual questions, gives autographs and poses for photos.

It is $30 adults and $16 children at noon daily, and tickets may be bought online or by calling 1866 737 5235. It's a highly worthwhile opportunity and one we strongly recommend. The buffet-style lunch is pretty good, too!

US Astronaut Hall of Fame

While the Space Center tells you primarily about the machinery of putting men and women in space, the Astronaut Hall of Fame (on SR 405, just before the main entrance to KSC) gives the low-down on the people involved, with engaging memorabilia, exhibits and explanations. A chronological approach divides it into 5 sections, from **Entry Experience**, visions of space flight; **Race to the Moon**, the stories of the Mercury, Gemini and Apollo missions; Space Shuttle: The **Astronaut Experience**, a unique collection of testimonials, personal experiences and authentic artefacts; **Astronaut Adventure** room, with space-walk 'chairs', a G-force simulator, moon exploration, interactive computers and Mars Mission experience; and on to **Science on a Sphere**, a fascinating 3-D exhibit exploring the Earth, moon and the planets in our solar system as viewed from space. Admission: Included with Kennedy Space Center or $27 adults, $23 3–11s on its own. Open noon–5pm. If you enjoyed the KSC, try to spend a couple of hours here (it is busiest towards the end of the day). AAA

US Astronaut Hall of Fame

LEGOLAND Florida

Children aged 2–12, their parents and probably their grandparents will all want to make a beeline for this wonderfully bright and expansive park, which opened in 2011. In a beautiful lakeside setting on the site of the former Cypress Gardens attraction – and including the old tropical gardens – it offers 150acres/60ha of guaranteed fun with its extensive main park and new Water Park. In fact, while the typical LEGOLAND age range is 2–12, the Floridian version probably appeals to kids as old as 14 with its bigger rides and water flumes. There is plenty to do, with no fewer than 30 rides, 3 main shows, an extensive adventure play area, the amazing Miniland, farm-themed Conservatory and, of course, great LEGO shopping, hence they offer a 2-day ticket, which is great value. Even the dining options are fresh, healthy and appealing, and there are plenty of quiet corners and gardens in which to chill out and enjoy your holiday!

It does require a lot of legwork to see it all, though, as it is spread round the southern shore of Lake Eloise in rather sprawling fashion and, when it's hot, there aren't so many places in the air-conditioned cool. But there is definitely something for all but older teens here and we really enjoy the clever landscaping and fun use of LEGO characters and features.

Location and tactics

LEGOLAND Florida is in the town of Winter Haven, about 45min south-east of the Disney/Kissimmee area. To get there, take I-4 west to Exit 55, then Highway 27 south for 18 miles to State Road 540, and the park is 4 miles along on the left. If you are staying in the Highway 27 area, it is even simpler as you just head south to 540. Shuttle service is available from the new I-Drive 360 complex on International Drive at 9am next to the multi-storey car park, for $5/person round trip, reservations required on 1877 350 5346 or the Legoland website.

LEGOLAND FLORIDA at a glance

Location	Off State Road 540 in Winter Haven		
Size	150acres		
Hours	10am–6, 7 or 8pm in high season (Easter, summer, Thanksgiving and Christmas), 10am–5pm off peak; closed Tues and Wed off peak; Water Park 10am–5, 6 or 7pm in summer, 10am–5pm May, Sept, Fri–Sun only; noon–5pm Oct, Sat and Sun only.		
Admission	Under-3s free ($3 for water park); 3–12s and Seniors (60+) $77 (1-day ticket); $92 (1-day plus water park or 2-day ticket); $107 (2-day plus water park); adults (13-plus) $84, $99, $114.		
Parking	$14		
Lockers	$5, $7 and $12		
Pushchairs	$10 and $15		
Wheelchairs	$12 and $37 ($47 with canopy)		
Top attractions	The Dragon, Coastersaurus, Technic Coaster, Driving School, Boating School, Wave Racers, Island in the Sky, The Quest for CHI, Royal Joust, Safari Trek		
Don't miss	Miniland, Fun Town 4-D Theater, Pirates Cove Water Ski Show, Cypress Gardens		
Hidden costs	Meals	Burger, chips and coke $9.89 Kids' meal $5.99	
	Kids' T-shirts	$14.99–26.99	
	Souvenirs	$0.50–200	
	Sundries	Face painting $10–15; Photopass $39.99	

You arrive into the large car park where the parking fee is $14 and then walk to the entrance. Its 150acres/60ha spreads people out well but still draws queues at peak periods, hence your best bet is to head for LEGO Kingdoms, Land of Adventure, World of Chima and new DUPLO Valley, returning to Fun Town and Miniland later in the day. For day 2, start with your favourite rides then cool down in the Water Park (which closes an hour before the main park). Once through the gates, here's what you'll find, moving in an anti-clockwise direction (advisable). NB: All ratings are indicated for younger children rather than adults!

The Beginning: This offers the ticket centre, Guest Relations and functional elements like the lockers, pushchair and wheelchair hire. There are no shows but the one ride, Island in the Sky, is a breathtaking 150ft/46m lift into the air on a gently revolving platform that affords a magnificent view over the park, lake and surrounding areas Under 4ft/122cm must be accompanied by adult. AAAA

Shopping and dining: Immediately to the left of the entrance is **The Big Shop** (one of the largest LEGO merchandise stores in the world). Dining is found at **The Market Restaurant** (soups, salads, sandwiches; gluten free, fresh chicken and Asian stir-fry selections) with a quick-bite counter and coffee bar.

Fun Town: Here is where the squeals of delight really begin! In true LEGOLAND style, you have entered a charming village complete with a working factory, 4-D cinema and carousel. Take a Factory Tour and watch working machinery as it goes through the process of making LEGO bricks, from moulding to packaging, then let the kids ride **The Grand Carousel** (TT; under 4ft/122cm must be accompanied by adult). Just beyond is **Fun Town Theater**, featuring 3 12min 4-D movies daily including the LEGO Chima 4-D Movie Xperience – all of which provide some clever special effects as well as great film fun for kids (TTT). **Fresh From**

Florida Greenhouse is another LEGO set-piece exhibit showcasing the value of local farm produce in a fun and engaging way for youngsters. AA

BRITTIP

Fun Town Theater is a blissful air-conditioned haven in summer and ideal for visiting during the hottest parts of the day.

Shopping and dining: All of your favourite themed merchandise can be found at **LEGO Studios**, including Star Wars, SpongeBob, Indiana Jones, and Batman, the **Minifigure Market** and **Pick A Brick**, while the **Garden Shop** adds novel gift ideas from the land. **Granny's Apple Fries** serves up the park's signature dessert (apples, cinnamon and a creamy sauce), and **Sunny's Ice Cream Shop** offers great cold treats. **Fun Town Pizza & Pasta Buffet** is a value-conscious choice if you have a hungry tribe to feed.

DUPLO® Valley: Next up as you turn right out of Fun Town is the perfect place for toddlers to let their imaginations run wild as they explore a village sized just for them. Completely re-themed in 2014, this area features a junior-sized train that winds through the 'countryside', passing farms, campgrounds, and fishing holes. Toddlers will love helping the 'farmer' find missing animals and plough the fields, and then cool down in the water play area. TTTT under 6s

Duplo Valley

World of Chima: This is where the large-scale fun starts for the 6-plus brigade, with the newest area of the park themed for the LEGO Legends of Chima toy range, as brought to life by the Cartoon Network. Here, visitors enter the fabulous Lion Temple on **The Quest for CHI**, a challenging water ride where they battle Cragger the Crocodile King with water cannons as he bids to steal the CHI energy orbs. The journey travels through the full mystical animal world, including imaginative habitats for **Gorilla Forest** and **Raven's Roost**. TTTT Also here is the **Speedorz™ Arena**, where players can build LEGO Speedorz and compete to win the precious supply of CHI in group challenges. For watery fun, check out **Cragger's Swamp**, a children's play area featuring an array of interactive water spouts and fountains. Kids can then meet Laval the Lion Prince and Cragger at a special **character meet-and-greet** station.

Shopping: Having ridden the ride, of course, you can then buy the LEGO at the **World of Chima** store.

LEGO Kingdoms: The next large-scale land features 3 major rides and a cool play area. Climb aboard **The Dragon** for a backstage view of life in an enchanted castle, then take off on a thrilling flight as this scenic dark ride becomes a dynamic outdoor coaster! **R:** 4ft/122cm or 3ft 4in/102cm with adult. Child Swap and ride photo available. TTTT Then, saddle up on LEGO-themed horses for **The Royal Joust**, where youngsters gallop though an enchanted forest, jousting with LEGO knights along the way. **R:**

World of Chima

3ft/91cm; max 12 yrs and 170lb/76kg. TT Also here is **Merlin's Challenge**, a fairly standard but quite whizzy fairground circular ride (4ft/122cm or 3ft 4in/102cm with adult). TTT Kids will also want to spend time in **The Forestmen's Hideout**, a multi-level climb, scramble and crawl treehouse adventure with ropes and slides. AAAA There are also the **Jester's Games** for a few extra dollars.

Shopping and dining: The Kings Market and **Princess Palace** are 2 suitably themed gift opportunities while **Castle Burger** serves up tasty burgers and chicken sandwiches.

Land of Adventure: Next up is another BIG land, with 2 more major rides and 3 other great kiddie attractions. The excitement continues at **Lost Kingdom Adventure** as you hunt for treasure while fighting off baddies with laser blasters. Youngsters will want to ride several times to better their score. **R:** 4ft 6in/137cm or 2ft 10in/86cm with adult. TTT Child Swap, ride photos available. Next up is another top thrill in the form of **Coastersaurus**, a classic wooden coaster that zips through a prehistoric jungle and past animated dinosaurs (made from LEGO, of course!). **R:** 3ft/91cm or 4ft/122cm with adult. TTTTT Then you can just let young 'uns loose at **Pharaoh's Revenge** multi-level climbing structure, with the added fun of being able to shoot soft foam balls at each other. Beetle Bounce shoots riders 15ft/4.5m high on this kid-friendly tower ride (**R:** 3ft/91cm; TTTT) while **Safari Trek** is the classic children's car ride, albeit through a clever LEGO-themed African savannah full of lurking animals. **R:** 2ft 10in/86cm, or 4ft/122cm with adult, max age 12; TTT The **Adventure Games** are more fairground side-stalls for an extra few dollars.

Dining: The Adventure Trailer is a good choice for hot dogs, nachos and cheese, and beverages and **Waffle Spears** offers tasty desserts.

LEGO City: The first thing you see in this next area is the large-scale stage fun of **The Big Test Show**, where the madcap members of the City Volunteer Fire Department prove they are not quite a crack fire-fighting force (but also deliver some key fire safety advice) several times a day. AAAA

🇬🇧 **BRITTIP**

Those sitting in the first few rows on The Big Test Show may just get a bit wet as the 'firemen' often miss their target!

The scaled-down elements of a real working town continue with **Rescue Academy**, where families race each other to 'put out the fire'. But these fire trucks only move when you pump the levers! **R:** 4ft/122cm or 2ft 10in/86cm with adult; guests in wheelchairs must transfer. **TTT** LEGOLAND's ultra-popular **Driving School** (ages 6–13) and **Junior Driving School** (3–5s) and **Boating School** (4ft/122cm or 2ft 10in/86cm with adult) are all here too, giving kids the chance to navigate electric cars and small boats to earn official LEGOLAND driving licences. **TT–TTTT** For something more dynamic, try **Flight School**'s suspended steel coaster, one of the biggest thrills in the park and a major hit with coaster fans. **R:** 3ft 8in/111cm or 4ft 4in/130cm with adult. **TTTTT**

Shopping and dining: Pick up some more souvenirs at **City Shopping** and grab a tempting chicken lunch or dinner at the indoor **Fried Chicken Co** or a light bite and drink at **City Stage Snack Bar**.

🇬🇧 **BRITTIP**

See LEGOLAND's website for periodic discounts. They sometimes offer $15 off ALL tickets if booked in advance for a specific day.

LEGO Technic: This area is packed with fun and thrills for older children as it offers 3 super rides. The LEGO **Technic Coaster** is the stand-out offering, a tall, fast-turning steel coaster where riders race, brake and bank in life-size LEGO Technic cars. **R:** 4ft/122cm or 3ft 6in/99cm with adult; **TTTTT** Ride the waves and

dodge soaking blasts of water on the airboat-style **Aquazone Wave Racers**, a ride so cool you'll want to queue up straight away for another go! **R:** 4ft 4in/132cm or 3ft 4in/102cm with adult; **TTTT**). Kids can also try the more sedate **Technicyle (TT)** and have a go at the **Extreme Games** (for a few extra dollars).

Shopping and dining: With a great view overlooking Lake Eloise, the **Extreme Zone** offers surf-style clothing and gifts while the neighbouring **Lakeside Sandwich Co** is a fab choice for fresh sandwiches, wraps, salads and drinks. **Robot Pit Stop** features hot dogs, nachos, novelty ice creams, and drinks.

🇬🇧 **BRITTIP**

Have kids who are nervous about coasters (even the junior kind)? LEGOLAND has a unique programme to help parents with 'Roller Coaster Readiness' tips, available online at http://florida.legoland.com/PageFiles/1107/LLFBrochureWeb.pdf and at the front gate.

Imagination Zone: Next up is the creative heart of the park, where kids put their imaginations to work at 4 hands-on stations. **Hero Factory** offers the chance to create and build your own galaxy-defending LEGO Heroes (and meet leader Preston Stormer periodically); build and race a LEGO car at **Build & Test**; or assemble a robot at **LEGO Mindstorms**. **Kid Power Towers** then burn off excess energy as kids (and adults!) use ropes and pulleys to ascend colourful towers – and

The Daytona section of Miniland

let go for a 'free fall' back down. **R:** 4ft/122cm or 3ft 4in/100cm with adult; **TTT** Child swap available, guests in wheelchairs must transfer. The **Warner Bros Game Zone** provides more fun here.

Dining: Grab a tasty toasted sandwich, salad and drink at **i-Zone Panini**.

Cypress Gardens: Just behind and to the right of the Imagination Zone are the beautiful gardens this park was originally known for, now lovingly restored and a peaceful haven for strolling, complete with beautiful gazebo and tropical displays (and yes, that banyan tree is real, unlike the Disney version!). **AAAA**

Pirates Cove: Come back out of the Gardens and you'll find the place where swashbuckling meets water in an exciting battle on the 'high seas' in **The Battle for Brickbeard's Bounty**. LEGO characters and a life-sized pirate ship add to the fun of this water stunt show, with water-skiers, ski-jumping and other stunts that young children will not want to miss. **AAA**

Dining: Grab a burger, chicken sandwich or snack before or after the show at **Capt Brickbeard's Burgers**.

Miniland USA: Completing the big LEGOLAND tour brings you to the park's other crown jewel, an iconic area featuring 8 themed US locations in miniature – and the big bonus of a Star Wars-themed area. **Florida** shows off some of the state's gems, with separate areas devoted to a magnificent replica of the **Kennedy Space Center** (complete with Shuttle countdown!) and the huge Daytona International Speedway, where youngsters can race LEGO dragsters. **Las Vegas** boasts the glittering resorts and other icons of Nevada's most famous city while **Washington DC** re-creates the White House, US Capitol, Smithsonian museum and the Washington and Jefferson monuments. Look closely and you'll see an animated parade and the cherry trees that bloom each spring. No mini-land would be complete without **New York City**, and this representation includes Rockefeller Plaza (complete with squirt fountains!), Times Square, Lady Liberty, the Empire State building, Bronx Zoo and Grand Central Station. Finally, there is a section devoted to the ever-popular subject of **Pirates**, and another miniland that highlights the state of California, plus the **Star Wars** zone, complete with scenes from all 6 films, as well as 1 from animated series the Clone Wars. Miniland's detail is amazing, with a riot of visual gags and fun touches (try to spot the surprised gent in the loos at Grand Central Station!), and you can easily spend an hour or more browsing here.

BRITTIP

There is no shade in the Miniland area, so be SURE to apply lots of high-factor suncream before spending time here.

Pirates' Cove

Haven dining

Water Park: This fabulous extra (for $15/person) is an opportunity to have fun in best LEGO style. Not as large as the likes of Blizzard Beach and Aquatica, but designed completely with young children in mind and easier to negotiate, it offers the full array of lockers, changing rooms, towel rental and gift shop (with swimming costumes for sale if you make a late decision to try it), plus its own restaurant, complete with shaded Tiki bar for tired parents! There are 5 main areas and it will require at least half a day of your time. As ever, have plenty of high-factor, waterproof suncream.

DUPLO Splash Safari: This is Toddler Central, featuring small-scale slides and interactive DUPLO creatures, all in just 6in/15cm of water (and within view of the Tiki bar!). AAAA

Joker Soaker: Older children will be captivated by this huge water-feature adventure playground and its array of slides, fountains, climbs, squirt guns and more, including a 300-gallon bucket that fills and tips periodically! **R:** 3ft/91cm on 3 lower slides, 3ft 6in/99cm on upper 4; under 3ft 6in/99cm must be accompanied by an adult. AAAAA

Build A Raft River: an imaginative variation on the lazy-river idea, with riders able to build their own floating raft with special LEGO bricks and then complete the 1,000ft/330m-long 3ft/91cm deep circuit. AAA

LEGO Wave Pool: enjoy some gentle surf fun in this wide, walk-in pool that allows young children to splash happily while their older siblings can brave the 3ft 4in/100cm-plus depths. AAA

Twin Chasers: older children will love the chance to ride these double flumes – one open, one enclosed – on individual rafts that sloosh down the 375ft/114m tubes, with a grand splash-down at the end. **R:** 4ft/122cm; TTTT

Splash Out: the ultimate thrill-ride for kids, a selection of 3 intertwined body-slides with a drop of 60ft/18m that afford a great view of the surrounding area – before you 'drop in'! **R:** 4ft/122cm; TTTTT

Take note: LEGOLAND closes on Tue & Wed at quiet times of the year and the Water Park is only open in the hotter months (and closes weekdays in the spring and autumn). Check in advance on 1877 350 5346 or **http://florida.legoland.com**.

The new **LEGOLAND Hotel** is scheduled to open in late 2015, offering the chance to stay in the heart of all this creativity and enjoy their 152 brightly coloured rooms and suites, all with plenty of LEGO style. There will be various interactive play areas, an imaginative pool and toddler water-play area, and a restaurant. It will also make the park a more inviting multi-day opportunity.

Oriental Pool at Legoland

Gatorland

For a taste of Florida wildlife, this is as authentic as it gets and is popular with children of all ages. The 'Alligator Capital of the World' was founded in 1949 and is still family owned, so it possesses a natural, homespun charm few of its big-name rivals can match. And, when the wildlife consists of several thousand menacing alligators and crocodiles in various natural habitats and 3 fascinating shows – plus a fabulous Zip Line attraction that is now disabled accessible – you know you're in for a different experience (although there is a LOT more to Gatorland than just gators – including their new Bobcat Bayou). Overall, Gatorland is something you're unlikely to get anywhere else, and the sense of being in the 'real' Florida is terrific.

> **BRITTIP**
> If you have an evening flight home from Orlando International, visit Gatorland for half a day on your final day as it is just 20mins' drive from the airport.

Tours and attractions: Start by taking the 15min **Gatorland Express** railway around the park to get an idea of its 110acre/45ha expanse. This has an added fee but is good for multiple rides, is fully narrated (usually in amusing style) and is especially fun for kids. You also get a good look at the native animal habitat, which features whitetail deer, wild turkey and quail. Wander the natural beauty of the 2,000ft/610m **Swamp Walk**, as well as the **Alligator Breeding Marsh Walkway**, where a

Gatorland

3-storey observation tower gives a neat overview of these reptiles. Ask yourself: are they hanging around in the hope someone might 'drop in' for lunch?

> **BRITTIP**
> If you are at Gatorland first thing in the morning, take the Swamp Walk straight away. There will be far more wildlife activity then and the peaceful ambience is quite invigorating.

Breeding pens, baby alligator nurseries and rearing ponds are also situated throughout the park to provide an idea of the growth cycle of the gator and enhance the overall feeling that it is the visitor behind bars here, not the animals. **Jungle Crocs** features some of the deadliest animals of Egypt, Australia and Cuba, with authentic lairs and brilliant presentation (look out for Sultan and his 'harem' of lady crocs from the Nile). Many of the small-scale attractions have been designed with kids in mind and there is plenty to keep everyone amused. **Allie's Barnyard** is a petting zoo, while you can feed some friendly lorikeets at the **Very Merry Aviary**, and view the pink inhabitants of **Flamingo Island**.

Don't miss the remarkable **White Gator Swamp**, showcasing 4 rare and completely white alligators, which are totally leucistic (without pigment), with startling blue eyes, not pink like albinos. Other animals to see include owls, turtles, flamingos, tortoises, snakes, spiders, emus and deer. The park is also home to hundreds of wading birds, providing a fascinating close-up of the nests during Mar–Aug.

> **BRITTIP**
> Lucy and Neiko, brother and sister panthers who live at Gatorland, are at their most lively first thing in the morning when they have been let out of their night quarters — just like any domestic cat!

New in 2014 was the elaborate habitat, **Bobcat Bayou**, home to the park's newest residents, 2 gorgeous young bobcats, while the park also showcases two rare Florida panthers in the **Panther Springs** exhibit.

Shows: The 800-seat Wrestling Stadium sets the scene for some real cracker-style feats (a 'cracker' is a Florida cowboy) as Gatorland's resident 'wranglers' catch a medium-sized gator and proceed to point out the animal's features, with the aid of some daredevil stunts that will have you questioning their sanity. The **Gator Jumparoo** is another eye-opening spectacle as some of the park's biggest creatures use their tails to 'jump' out of the water and be hand-fed tasty morsels, like whole chickens! **Up-Close Encounters** is another amusing showcase of creatures, from the expected snakes to less obvious cockroaches and scorpions. Great photo opportunities for brave children!

Gator Gully: This superb little water park features numerous ways for kids to cool down, get wet and generally have fun. The ½acre/0.2ha park features 5 elements, including a giant jalopy with water jets for spokes and a fountain radiator, an old shack that 'explodes' with water, and giant gators with squirt guns. The neighbouring dry play area and chairs and tables allow parents to sit and watch their offspring expend some energy, perhaps with a drink from one of the kiosks.

But wait… that's not all!

Screamin' Gator Zip Line: Gatorland has fixed its eyes firmly on the brave of heart, introducing a first-of-its-kind zipline experience, with 4 zips soaring high above the park's most notorious residents. At 1,200ft long and up to 56ft high, the lines afford spectacular views of jumping Cuban Crocodiles and the scenic Alligator Breeding Marsh. Start at Tower One, where the 'bunny hill' builds up your courage (and your excitement). Tower Two soars over 2 croc pools (look down – the view is outrageous!); Tower Three is the tallest launch point at 75ft/23m, and its 600ft/182m run zips straight over the breeding marsh at up to 35mph/56kph. (Are you feeling the adrenaline rush? Yes, you are!) Take the walking bridge over to Tower Four where you're met by a double zipline for a final (and utterly thrilling) race to the finish.

BRITTIP

Book the Screamin' Gator in advance to avoid disappointment. Capacity is limited to groups of 12 4–7 times a day and demand is high. Reserve by phone or online.

The experience includes orientation, full equipment check, the zipline and a trek across a swinging bridge. There is a separate fee, but at $69.99/person, it includes all-day admission to the park. A photographer will also chart your journey for purchase back on terra firma! **R:** Min weight 75lb/34kg, max 250lb/113kg. Must be able to climb stairs. Wear closed toe shoes and trousers or long shorts. New in 2014, Gatorland installed a brilliant wheelchair accessible, one-segment zip line for guests with lower-body disabilities (must transfer to specially designed harness), providing a thrilling 350ft glide over the gator marsh.

Shopping and dining: In addition to 3 gift stores around the park and the amusing **Gator & Snake** photo opportunity, you should visit the **Gift Shop** complex at the entrance, which incorporates the trademark Gator Mouth entryway. You can grab a bite or drink at 3 snack bars, try **Gator Jake's Fudge Kitchen** or dine on smoked gator ribs and fried gator nuggets (as well as burgers and hotdogs) at **Pearl's Smokehouse**, with excellent kids' meals at $6.49.

Gatorland's Gator Jumparoo show

Special events: Some unique options if you really want to get to know your gators are: **Trainer for a Day**, with the chance to work behind the scenes at the park 8am–10am, finding out what it takes to handle such dangerous animals, behavioural training and novice gator wrangling ($125 12s and over, max 5 people; includes park admission); **Gator Night Shine**, which takes guests into the Breeding Marsh after dark for a 1hr tour with one of the park's senior gator experts, with torches and gator food to lure the 'locals'. You can then marvel at how gator eyes shine like red beacons in the torchlight and learn more about the habits of these amazing animals – a real family treat, which kids seem to love (dusk, around 8.15pm summer, 6.30pm autumn and winter; $20 all ages; bug spray provided; reservations required); and **Adventure Hour**, a chance to go truly 'behind-the-scenes' in the Breeding Marsh to feed and pose for photos with the gators here ($10/person). **Rookie Wrestling** is every kid's chance to show his or her bravery and have the picture to prove it ($10 to kneel over a gator's back; extra for the photo).

Getting there: Gatorland is on the South Orange Blossom Trail, 2ml/3km south of the Central Florida Greeneway and 3ml/5km north of Highway 192 (see map p14). Admission: $26.99 adults, $18.99 3–12s, 10am–5pm, parking free.

Ripley's Believe It or Not

Annual passes are only $45.99 and $31.99 if you plan more than 1 visit (407 855 5496, **www.gatorland.com**). Check website for current coupons.

20 ANNIVERSARY SPOT — Our 1st edition highlighted a brand new aviation museum attraction in central Florida but, sadly, Fantasy of Flight closed in 2014 in its 20th year.

INTERNATIONAL DRIVE

The 14½ml/23km tourist corridor of I-Drive (see maps p14 and 218) continues to be an ever-changing source of hotels, restaurants, shopping and fun. There are more than 42,000 hotel rooms, 150+ restaurants and almost 500 shops, as well as 15 attractions, including 6 mini-golf courses. The **I-Ride Trolley** links it all in transport terms and the website **www.internationaldriveorlando. com** highlights all the options. Its Official Visitors Guide has an I-Ride map and valuable money-off coupons, which you can download to get you started, plus a hotel booking facility. The I-Ride Trolley section provides 'NextTrolley' info as well as maps and listings of what is near each trolley stop. Access to the mobile site, with live options for dining, shopping or attractions, is obtained by QR scanning, SMS texting or by simply going to **iDrive2Go.mobi** on a smart phone.

Here's a look at the area's attractions (see also Chapter 10, Orlando By Night, and Chapter 12, Shopping, to get the full picture).

BRITTIP

Ripley's, Titanic, iFly Orlando, WonderWorks and WhirlyDome are all handy retreats to keep in mind for a rainy day or if you need time out of the sun.

Ripley's Believe It Or Not

You can't miss this particular attraction and its extraordinary tilted appearance as it's designed to seem as if it's falling into a Florida 'sinkhole'. However, once inside you soon get back on the level and, for an hour or so, you can wander through this quirky museum dedicated to the weird and wonderful. Robert L Ripley was an eccentric explorer and collector (a real-life Indiana Jones) who for 40 years travelled the world to assemble a collection of the greatest oddities known to man. The Orlando branch of this chain features 8,900ft²/830m² of displays in 16 galleries, including authentic artefacts, interactive exhibits, illusions, video presentations and music. The elaborate re-creation of an Egyptian tomb showcases a mummy and 3 rare mummified animals, while the Primitive Gallery contains artefacts (some quite gruesome) from tribal societies around the world. There are then Human and Animal Oddities, Big and Little galleries, Illusions and Dinosaurs, plus extra interactive elements. The collection of miniatures includes the world's smallest violin and a single grain of rice hand-painted with a tropical sunset. Larger-scale exhibits include a balloon-powered chair that flew over the Rocky Mountains, a 2/3-scale 1907 Rolls-Royce built in matchsticks and a 26ft/8m tall 'painting' of Van Gogh made out of postcards! You can also attempt various puzzles and brain teasers, and try the shooting gallery with its odd array of targets. **Admission:** $19.99 adult, $12.99 4–12s; 9am–12am (last entry 11pm; 407 345 0501, **www.ripleys.com/orlando**). AAA Included with Go Orlando Card.

BRITTIP

Receive a $3 discount/adult, $2/child (age 4–12) on the regular admission price at Ripley's Believe It Or Not by visiting their website.

Titanic – The Experience

Go back in time at this fascinating attraction just north of Sand Lake Road. Weave through the redesigned Experience featuring full-scale re-creations of the *Titanic*'s famous rooms, including her grand staircase, first class parlour suite, Veranda Café and the Marconi Room, third class cabin and bridge. Actors in period costume portray such notables as Captain Smith and Molly Brown, sharing stories of passengers and crew during a 1hr guided journey of the famous ship. The 17-gallery attraction features an interactive Underwater Room, including a 15ft/4.5m 'iceberg' and a detailed replica of the vessel as she appears on the bottom of the Atlantic today. More than 400 artefacts and treasures, including memorabilia from James Cameron's blockbuster movie *Titanic* are also on display here, notably some ultra-rare pieces, including the 2nd-largest piece recovered from the wreck site. Both engaging and moving, it consistently gets good reviews from locals and tourists alike.

Admission: $21.95 adults, $12.95 3–11s ($2 off online; under-3 free); tours 10am–6pm (8pm or 9pm peak seasons; **www.titanictheexperience.com**). AAAA Also with Go Orlando Card.

Titanic

For something special, try the **Titanic Dinner Event** (each Sat), a 3hr theatre/dining occasion with the cast of the Experience. Starring Molly Brown, Captain Smith and Thomas Andrews and other high-society luminaries, it offers each table a front row seat for the whole Titanic story, setting the scene and delivering a dinner party with a difference, all in period style. Enjoy a sumptuous 3-course meal, featuring fillet of beef and chicken, with tea, coffee and soft drinks (extra for unlimited beer and wine) in a splendid atmosphere. The 1st Class Gala Dinner recreates Titanic's first-night sailing, every Fri. $69.95 for adults, $42.95 for 6–11s. (not recommended for under-6s); book in advance on 407 248 1166.

Fun Spot America

Just off I-Drive on Del Verde Way (look for the 250ft/76m SkyCoaster past the junction with Kirkman Road), the first phase of a huge expansion in 2013 added a whole raft of family fun with coasters, go-karting, kiddie rides and arcade action. The go-kart thrills come from 4 challenging tracks, including the enlarged Quad Helix, the triple level corkscrew track of Conquest, the fiendish Thrasher and multi-level Commander. Then there are bumper cars and boats, 4 daring fairground-type rides (including the whizzy Scrambler and Paratrooper), one of the largest and most up-to-date video arcades in Florida, a Big Wheel, 8 Kid Spot rides – including a classic 2-storey carousel – and a Cadet track for the little ones. Fun Spot also boasts the world's second-

Fun Spot America

largest SkyCoaster (a massive, free-fall swing) and three coasters – the impressive long steel-wooden hybrid of White Lightning, which races along at up to 48mph/76kph with a max drop of 75ft/23m; the tight-turning suspended ride of Freedom Flyer; and the child-friendly Sea Dragon. Another newcomer was the high-spinning Enterprise, and an all-new Food Court, serving hotdogs, burgers, salads, pizza, nachos, popcorn and ice-cream. A water-splash area for children was added in 2014. Parking and admission are free, with a series of ride Passes geared around children's height (above and below 4ft 4in/1.32m), with younger children getting free run of all the rides (and as a passenger on the 2-seater go-karts with an adult).

Admission: Free; Go-Karts $9, other rides $3/ticket; Go-Kart Armband (all day on all 4 tracks, plus all rides and unlimited Free Play arcade) $40; Rides Armband (all day on all rides plus unlimited Free Play arcade) $30; Kid Spot Armband (all day on Kid Spot rides plus unlimited Free Play arcade) $15; 4-Ride Track Sampler $27. Height requirements: over 4ft 4in/1.32m for Quad Helix, Conquest, Commander; 4ft 6in/1.37m for Thrasher. Open daily 10am–midnight; (407 363 3867, **www.funspotattractions.com**). **TTTT** Also with Go Orlando card.

Magical Midway

Magical Midway back on I-Drive (just north of Sand Lake Road) offers more go-karts, games and thrill rides, including the Sling Shot (400ft straight up!), the unique StarFlyer, a 230ft/70m tower with chair swings that lift and rotate for a dizzying view at 54mph and Space Blast, another vertical-launch monster! The 2 elevated kart tracks, the double uphill corkscrew of The Avalanche and sharply-banked Alpine are its signature rides (you must be at least 12 and 4ft 8in/147cm tall to drive, at least 16 to drive a passenger, and at least 5 and 3ft/91cm to be a passenger). Fast Track, a flat concrete track with a 25° bank turn (riders must be 12 and 4ft 8in/147cm to drive; single cars only) complete the line-up. There are also bumper cars, boats, a merry-go-round, trampolines, a large arcade, a pizza parlour and ice-cream counter.

Admission: Free, then 3hr Armband (unlimited go-karts and midway rides for 3hrs, not Sling Shot) $25; All-Day Unlimited Armband (not Sling Shot) $32. Or $25 Sling Shot, $7 Starflyer (ride DVD $15), $7 go-karts, $3 all other rides. Must be 4ft/121cm for Bumper Cars, 3ft 6in/106cm for Bumper Boats and Kiddie Track; 2–12pm Mon–Fri, noon–midnight Sat–Sun (407 370 5353, **www.magicalmidway.com**). **TTTT** See website for $2.50 off Go-Karts.

BRITTIP

WonderWorks, Fun Spot, Magical Midway and WhirlyDome are all open until at least midnight in high season, long after most theme parks are shut, so you can have a day at the park, then let the kids loose here to tire them out completely!

WonderWorks

This interactive entertainment centre is I-Drive's most unmistakable landmark, a 3-storey chamber of family fun with a host of novel elements. Unmistakable? The 82ft/25m building is upside-down! That's right, the entire edifice is constructed from the roof up! The basic premise is that WonderWorks is a secret research facility into unexplained phenomena that was uprooted by a tornado experiment and dumped in topsy-turvy fashion in the heart of this busy tourist district (yeah, right!). You have to give full marks for imagination and, with various enhancements since it opened in 1998, there's a lot here, especially for 6–12s.

You enter through an 'inversion tunnel' that orientates you the same way round as the building (look out of the window to check!) and then progress to various chambers of entertaining and mildly educational hands-on experiences that demand several hours to explore fully. Without ever using the words 'science' or 'museum', WonderWorks steers you through various 'labs' of interactive activities, including natural disasters (earthquakes, hurricanes, famous disasters) and Google Earth virtual globe and map; physical challenges (Bubble Lab, Mind Ball bio-feedback challenge, Bed of Nails and the chance to make an impression of your entire body in 40,000 plastic nails at Wonderwall!); illusions (with a computer ageing process and 'elastic surgery', ethnicity changer and a 'couple's morph' that combines 2 faces to see what the resulting children would look like!); and Space Discovery, where you have Jet

WonderWorks

Fighters (virtual reality F18 fighter jet), Shuttle Landers (your chance to pilot the Discovery Space Shuttle), a Mercury capsule mock-up, an astronaut spacesuit and Wonder Coaster (a pair of enclosed 'pods' that let you design and ride your own coaster). There is also a 3-storey indoor rope climbing structure with 20 obstacles, and the XD Theater 4-D Extreme Motion Experience simulator ride, plus the WonderWorks Gift Shop and Café. A Lazer Tag game on the top floor adds even more appeal for kids. If you have already seen DisneyQuest, WonderWorks may seem tame, while it isn't as educational as the Orlando Science Center, but it has different features from either, including the fun of **The Outta Control Magic Comedy Dinner Show** (p298), with a good-value combo ticket.

Admission: $24.99 adults, $19.99 seniors (55+) and 4–12s (includes 1 4-D Motion Ride and Ropes Course); $9.99 just for 4-D Motion Ride and Ropes Course; $6.99 for Lazer Tag; $24.99 and $19.99 for The Outta Control Dinner Show; $43.99 and $33.99 for WonderWorks/dinner show; $27.99 and $22.99 for WonderWorks/Lazer Tag; $44.99 and $34.99 for all 3; Extreme Play Pass – 1 4-D Ride, Ropes Course and 1 Lazer Tag game – $19.99; 9am–midnight (407 351 8800, **www.wonderworksonline. com/orlando**). **TTT** Also with Go Orlando Card.

WhirlyDome

iFLY Orlando

At the junction with I-Drive and Kirkman Road is this unmistakable blue and yellow funnel that houses one of the most fun 'rides' in town. It is billed as a 'free-fall skydiving adventure' but is much more than that – a fun, addictive, difficult but exhilarating 'flying' experience, with the bonus of a great spectator sport! It's basically a huge vertical wind tunnel, which provides the feeling of a freefall. The standard 1hr programme provides a full briefing with an instructor, then you're given helmet, pads, goggles, earplugs and flight suit, and your group of 8–12 returns to the flight deck, where you get two 1min supervised 'flights' (which seem a lot longer!) Just watching makes it seem all too easy but, as soon as you hit the tunnel, you discover how fiendishly tough it is to just 'hang' in this 125mph/200kph column of air. However, before long it becomes a fun and absorbing experience and it's almost guaranteed to make you want to try again. There is no fee for non-participating members of your group to watch from the observation deck, and you can also just turn up to see for yourself at any time (you might even see sky-dive groups practising).

Admission: Standard flight, which includes a certificate, is $59.95; add a DVD and photo CD for $19.99. Discount coupons (for return visitors) and gift certificates can be found on its website. Try a Spread Your Wings Package (double your flight time) for $99.95, Spread Your Wings for Two at $129.95, or a Family Package for up to 5 at $269.95, (all including DVD). For real addicts, a new Take Flight package offers 10 1min flights or 5 double-flights for $222.90 (including DVD). Open 10am–10pm daily, reservations recommended (407 903 1150, **http://orlando.iflyworld.com**). **TTTT**.

WhirlyDome

This indoor fun centre boasts a unique game, full-service restaurant, arcade and other novel elements. Their stock in trade is the hilarious

WhirlyBall game, a cross between bumper cars, basketball and lacrosse (!) as 2 teams of 5 battle for possession of a whiffle ball and try to hit a target at either end. There are 2 courts of 4,000ft²/370m² and the centre provides a ref. It is open to all-comers or groups and games are timed in periods of 10min. Guests must be at least 12 and 4ft 6in/137cm to play but it is easy to pick up and the Whirlybugs, like fancy bumper-cars, are easy to drive. It is free just to turn up and watch (and is great spectator fun). Playing time is $8/player for 10min, or you can hire the court at $250/hr. In addition, the Dome also offers America's only genuine **F1 race simulator**, the SYM 06 from Italy ($8/3min), a huge **Laser Tag** venue ($8/15min) and a novel **Laser Frenzy** room, where players try to navigate a maze of laser beams, haze and mirrors ($3). More arcade games, 2 self-serve bowling lanes (bowling shoes not required; $5/person) and billiards and pool in the upstairs Bar fill out the entertainment, while the **Bloodhound Brew Pub & Eatery** is a surprisingly smart restaurant, with great local microbrews and a tempting menu (Happy Hour 4–7pm and 10pm–close daily). The Dome is open 4pm–12am Tues–Thurs, 4pm–2am Fri, 11am–2am Sat, 11am–12am Sun, just south of Wet 'n Wild. See more, including Monthly Specials, at **www.whirlydome.com** (407 212 3030).

I-Drive 360

Due to open in spring 2015 is this grand multi-level entertainment, restaurant and shopping complex (on the old site of the Mercado Center), boasting the 400ft/122m **Orlando Eye** observation wheel (like the London Eye), a **Madame Tussauds**, **SeaLife Aquarium**, elaborate landscaping, water features and more. There will be a 4-D film pre-show for the Eye, which will command views as far away as the Kennedy Space Center on a clear day, while both the international waxworks museum and the interactive SeaLife centre – like the 14 in the UK – will feature unique Floridian touches. Dining options – opening through 2014 – include the unique **Sugar Factory** restaurant and design store (**www.sugarfactory.com**), the **Tin Roof** live music bar (**www.tinroofbars.com**), **Cowgirls** Country & Western bar, **Bar Jour** wine bar, **The Yard House** brew-pub and restaurant (**www.yardhouse.com**), the lively style of **Dick's Last Resort** (**www.dickslastresort.com**), a **Pretzelmaker/ Great American Cookie** combo store and outlets of the **Outback Steakhouse**, **Carabbas Italian Grill**, **Buffalo Wild Wings** sports bar and **Ben & Jerry's** ice cream. I-Drive 360 is anchored by a free multi-storey car park and, while pricing and other details were unknown as we went to press, you can look up more at **www.i-drive360.com**.

Sea Life 360 Degree Ocean Tunnel

Also part of the complex is **Kings Bowl**, which is either a bowling centre with great dining or an eye-catching restaurant and bar where you can also bowl. With a plush 1950s vibe but modern styling – notably with 22 high-tech bowling lanes – it offers a grown-up atmosphere that is also family-friendly. Its elegant multi-bar and dining room set-up features 60 big-screen HDTVs, billiard tables, shuffleboard, bocce ball, serve-yourself beer booths and great cocktails. The food – from standard diner fare like burgers, pizza and fish and chips, to succulent steaks and scallops, is well above average and worth coming in for on its own, while the beer list is impressive and the desserts and sundaes are nothing short of decadent. Bowling is offered from 11–2am daily, at $5/person before 6pm and $6 after 6pm ($7 after 6pm on Fri and Sat). Shoe hire is $3 and it is 21 and over only after 8pm (407 363 0200; **http://kingsbowlamerica. com/orlando/**). Parts of Kings Bowl can also be booked for private parties.

◄█► **BRITTIP**

Call ahead for a Priority Lane Reservation when you dine at Kings Bowl and your group will be bumped up to the next available lane once you have finished eating.

Helicopter rides

These are another local staple, and you can try any one of 9 tours with **Air Florida Helicopters** at 8990 International Drive (just north of the big Convention Center). A minimum of 2 people are required, and then

Air Florida Helicopters

it's just a question of whether you want the local 8ml/12.87km tour, a trip over Universal and SeaWorld, the chance to see Disney from the air, a view of Downtown Orlando or a mega 30ml/48km grand journey that adds flying over the homes of the rich and famous in Windermere. Prices vary from just $20 for the short flight to $355 for the longest, plus a $4/person fuel surcharge ($20–325 for children; see website for discounts). No need to book; just turn up and go. They fly 9.30am–7pm daily (407 354 1400, **www.airfloridahelicopter.com**).

Mini-golf

For those in need of more holiday fun, don't miss the 6 mini-golf outlets along International Drive (see p268).

Kissimmee

Old Town: In the heart of tourist Highway 192 in Kissimmee is this shopping and entertainment attraction. The shopping part is covered in Chapter 12, but there are also 14 rides, from the standard and rather tame **Happy Days** bumper cars, go-karts and large **Ferris Wheel** to the **Windstorm** roller-coaster and **Super Shot** (a free-fall-style ride of over 140ft/43m), plus the exciting 4-storey **AMPVenture** course, a challenging and energetic mix of ropes, 35ft/10m climbing wall and zipline. There is a **Fun Town** area of junior rides, plus a Laser Tag game, and tickets are sold separately for most rides ($1 each), but if you plan to do several, go for the Valuepak at 20 for $22, 30 for $30, 45 for $40 or 60 for $50 (save $5 online). Ride prices vary from 2 tickets (Ferris Wheel and Fun Town kiddie rides) to 4 (Tilt-aWhirl and Super Shot), 5 (Windstorm) and 3–8 (AMPVenture). There are separate fees for bumper cars ($5), Laser Tag ($5) and go-karts ($7). For a different kind of fun, try the 2-storey **Legends: A Haunting at Old Town**, a clever, atmospheric and totally convincing walk-through haunted house with state-of-the-art horror scenes, live 'scare actors' and special effects that come straight out of Universal's Halloween Horror Nights play-book

($15/person; not recommended for under 14s). The rides are open 2–11pm Mon–Fri, noon–midnight Sat and noon–11pm Sun (407 396 4888, **www.old-town.com**). TTTT

20 ANNIVERSARY SPOT

In 1995, Old Town featured a ferris wheel, go-kart track, carousel and haunted house. Now it features 16 rides, 6 attractions, and 4 popular car and truck cruises, including the Saturday Classic Car cruise, which draws visitors from around the world.

Fun Spot USA: Next door to Old Town (but not connected) is another area of rides and fun owned by Fun Spot Attractions. There are a good selection of 9 thrill rides, a Kid Spot of 8 junior-sized rides, 2 high-adrenalin signature rides (which are real one-offs) and 4 go-kart tracks. **RockStar Coaster**, formerly in Cypress Gardens, adds another terrific ride to the line-up. But the big daddy of them all is the amazing **SkyCoaster**, a 300ft/90m tower that sends up to 3 riders at a time on a free-fall plunge (for the first 120ft/37m) that turns into a giant swing – at 85mph/136kph! The more down-to-earth rides consist of 2 flat go-kart tracks, Slick and Road Course, and 2 multi-level tracks, the labyrinthine Chaos and Vortex, with its challenging banked bowl section. The other 9 rides are almost as much fun – like the more fairground style of Flying Bobs, Fun Slide, Surf's Up and the Paratrooper, the giant swing of the Hot Seat and the tower-ride Screamer. More swinging fun is provided by the **Screamer** and **YoYo**, while standard **Bumper Cars** complete the line-up. There is a well-stocked **Snack Bar** (with free soft drinks) in the outdoor rides section, drinks and snacks at **SkyCoaster** and an indoor food court. Children will also gravitate to the arcade, with 60 games (perfect for a wet day or the heat of summer).

Admission: Free, then per-ride prices are Multi-level Tracks $9, Flat Tracks $6, Extreme Thrill Ride $6, Most Thrill and Family Rides $3; an Adult Armband is $40 (go-karts and other rides all day), Youth Armband (less than 54in/1.37m tall) $30, and a Track Sampler $27 (4 goes on go-karts or rides), plus there is a Chauffeur Armband (for a parent to drive or accompany a young 'un on various suitable rides) at $10. The SkyCoaster is $40 for one rider ($35 for a second ride), $70 for 2, $90 for 3. Open 10am–midnight (407 397 2509, **www.funspotattractions.com**). There is also a special 2-park Armband for Fun Spot America and Fun Spot USA at $60.

BRITTIP

Visiting the Orlando Information Center? Take exit 82B off I-4 and there are 4 multi-storey car parks nearby, including the Library park (take 4th right on Central Boulevard). Or just go straight across South Street (the first main road you come to), and park on the left, underneath I-4 after Church Street, where it is just $1/hr (pay-and-display).

DOWNTOWN ORLANDO

The last few years have seen a major revamp of Orlando's city centre ('downtown'), with new offices, apartments, shops and restaurants. This has also enhanced some notable tourist attractions and is well served by the Information Center on Orange Avenue (10am–5pm, Mon–Fri; 407 246 3789, **www.downtownorlando.com** – click 'Visit Downtown'). Start here to get a full overview, with a 3-D city model and ultra-helpful staff (plus free wi-fi). They can provide free maps of the area, a Historic Walking Tour guide and info on riding the free Lymmo bus service around downtown. There is also a free guided tour at 9.30am on

Downtown Orlando

the first Fri of each month with local historian Richard Forbes (not June–Sept). More development is taking place in the old Church Street district, **www.churchstreetdistrict.com**.

Orange County History Center

This smart part of the downtown scene offers an imaginative journey into central Florida history, from the wildlife and Native Americans to today's tourist issues and space programme. The accent is on the interactive, with hands-on exhibits and audiovisual presentations, and it is very much a journey through time, starting with the Natural Environment and First Peoples exhibits and moving on to the 1800s, with an authentic pioneer 'cracker' home, tales of Florida's ranching days, a Seminole settlement, and tourism pre-Disney to modern times. Aviation explores World War II bombers to the outer reaches of space. Orlando Remembered is a journey from the 19th century to the edge of the 21st while an exhibit on African American history and a series of travelling exhibits round things off.

Getting there: On E Central Boulevard (exit 82B off I-4, go across South St and take 3rd right; see also map p218), park at the Public Library multi-storey car park on Central

Orange County History Center

Blvd. Admission: $9 adults, $7 seniors (60+), $6 5–12s; 10am–5pm Mon–Sat, noon–5pm Sun (407 836 8500, **www.thehistorycenter.org**).

Getting around: Everywhere is walkable here, but the free **Lymmo** bus service connects the central area along Magnolia Avenue, from South Street and City Hall up to the Centroplex area. Or you could try the **Orland Bike Share** service, a bike-sharing scheme that allows bike rentals from specific hubs around the city centre, for as little as $5/hr (**http://orlandobikeshare.com/**).

Theatre and more

Orlando loves its theatre, and those wishing to take in a performance should look for the lavish new **Dr Phillips Center for the Performing Arts** (407 839 0119; **www.drphillipscenter.org**); the amazing **Amway Center**, home to the Orlando Magic basketball team, Orlando Predators Arena League outfit and Orlando Solar Bears minor-league ice-hockey team, plus major concerts (407 440 7000; **www.amwaycenter. com**); the improv of **SAK Comedy Lab** at Eola Capital Loft on S Orange Avenue (407 648 0001, **www.sak.com**); and **City Arts Factory** featuring local and national artists and a city-wide Gallery Hop on the third Thurs each month from 6–9pm (407 648 7060, **www.orlandoslice.com**). Don't miss the eclectic **Mad Cow Theatre** on Church Street, which presents major plays and theatrical events, including an annual Cabaret Festival (Apr–May; 407 297 8788, **www.madcowtheatre.com**).

Dining: The restaurant/bar choice is also pretty good here, too. Take your pick from **Frank & Steins** (with 300 craft beers, 40 on tap), **Wall Street Plaza** (a lively collection of bars and lounges that are the heart of downtown nightlife), the upscale supper-club style of **Kres Chophouse**, and **Church Street Station**, the remains of the old entertainment district, which still includes a cluster of fine restaurants and bars, notably the stylish Spanish cuisine of **Ceviche**, the fun **Harry Buffalo** and

Hamburger Mary's Bar & Grille. See more in Orlando By Night.

◀🇬🇧▶ BRITTIP

In party mode? Head for Wall Street Plaza, between Orange Ave and N Court Ave, on any Thurs, Fri or Sat night and bar-hop with the locals all night long! (http://wallstplaza.net/). Or try Nickel (5c) Beer Night at Big Belly every Wed, 5–9pm (www.churchstreetbars.com/big-belly).

Lake Eola: Once you have sampled the heart of downtown, head out here, with more restaurants and shops, plus a beautiful lakeside walk, children's play area, Swan paddle-boats, new artwork and a peaceful ambience. There are regular open-air concerts and storytelling at the **Disney Amphitheater** and the **Sunday Farmers Market** (around Lake Eola, 10am–4pm) is another focal point, with vendors including local artists as well as wonderful fresh produce.

Dining: Stop for a great meal, with a view, at **310 Lakeside** (407 373 0310, **www.310lakeside.net**) or **Spice Modern Steakhouse** (407 481 9533, **www. spicesteakhouse.com**). Continue on to the Thornton Park area and enjoy the most happening part of Orlando, with **Thornton Park Central** (at the junction of Summerlin Avenue and Central Boulevard, just south-east of

Lake Eola) offering a mix of unique boutiques and trendy restaurants. **Cityfish** is a casual seafood café/bar (407 849 9779, **www.cityfishorlando. com**), **Anthony's Pizzeria** is a great upmarket pizza restaurant (407 648 0009, **www.anthonyspizza.com**), **Dexter's** is a smart café/wine bar with a fab Sunday brunch (407 648 2777, **http://thorntonpark.dexwine.com**) and **Wildside BBQ** is another lively locals' hangout (407 872 8665, **www.wildsidebbq.com**).

◀🇬🇧▶ BRITTIP

Don't miss the annual Spring and Fall Fiestas around Lake Eola, with hundreds of vendors, live entertainment and special fun for kids, the first weekend in April and Nov (**www.fiestainthepark.com**).

Loch Haven Park

Continue north and you travel the 'Cultural Corridor' to Loch Haven Park and the area's fine collection of theatres, museums and the Orlando Science Center. Also here is the extensive **Orlando Museum of Art** (407 896 4231, **www.omart.org**), the diverse **Mennello Museum of American Art**, with a permanent collection by painter Earl Cunningham (407 246 4278, **www.mennellomuseum.com**), the **Orlando Philharmonic Orchestra**

Loch Haven Park

(407 770 0071, **www.orlandophil.org**) and **Orlando Shakespeare Theater** (407 447 1700, **www.orlandoshakes.org**). Parents should also note the superb **Orlando Rep**, a fabulous company specialising in family theatre, with youth academies and summer camps for kids. Their 2014/15 season includes *The Borrowers, A Christmas Story* and *Shrek The Musical* TYA (407 896 7365, **www.orlandorep.com**). Highly recommended.

Orlando Science Center: The Orlando Science Center is more than a mere museum and far more fun than the average science centre. Here you are given a series of hands-on experiences and habitats that entertain as well as inform, and school-age children in particular will benefit greatly from it. It has 9 main permanent exhibits, a night sky observatory, an inviting café, Science Store and a giant screen cinema.

NatureWorks: This is an immersion-style exhibit creating 6 typical Florida habitats, complete with native plants and animals (with field stations such as how sea turtles make their nests and a live beehive); **KidsTown** has plenty of junior-sized fun and games for under-6s; **DinoDigs** was a gift from the Walt Disney Company of its former Dinosaur Jubilee exhibit in Disney's Animal Kingdom, re-created in the OSC with 8 full skeleton replicas and some genuine fossils; **Science Park** is a hands-on adventure into the worlds of physical science and technology, including a hurricane simulator and Dr Dare's Laboratory; and **Our Planet, Our Universe** encourages interactive learning

Orlando Science Center

about planets, the sky, black holes, and cosmic collisions. Don't miss the hands-on Mars Rover experience and the chance to Ask An Astronomer (via video kiosk). Preschoolers will appreciate **All Aboard**, with child-sized trains, planes and automobiles, and **Adventures with Clifford**, an immersive experience on Birdwell island. Each Jan also sees the fun Otronicon, a 4-day event celebrating the best in video game technology. If you like the game Rock Band, you'll LOVE **Otronicon!** In addition, the centre has several programmes in **Dr Phillips CineDome**, a 310-seat cinema that surrounds its audience with large-format films and digital planetarium shows. The **Digital Adventure Theater** adds educational films and **Science Live!** real-life experiments and interactive programmes in partnership with National Geographic.

BRITTIP

Visit the Crosby Observatory (selected times only; be sure to call in advance) on top of the Science Center to gaze through the region's largest publicly accessible refractor telescope.

Getting there: On Princeton Street in downtown Orlando, just off exit 85 of I-4 (go east on Princeton; the Center is on the left but the multi-storey car park is on the RIGHT, see map p218). Admission: $19 adults, $17 seniors (55+) and students with ID, $13 3–11s; parking $5, includes 1 mainscreen film (Fri, Sat and Sun). 10am–5pm daily (closed Wed, Easter Sunday, Thanksgiving, Christmas Eve and Christmas Day; **www.osc.org**) AAA

THE WATER PARKS

Florida specialises in elaborate water parks, and Orlando boasts the very best. Predictably, Disney has the 2 most sophisticated ones, but SeaWorld's Aquatica adds real competition, while Universal-owned Wet 'n Wild is also adept at providing hours of watery fun. They adopt a variety of styles that owe much to the flair of the theme park creators, and

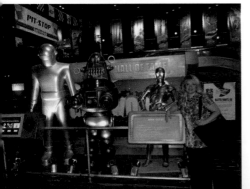

are imaginative for both the rides and imagery around them. All require at least ½ a day of splashing, sliding and riding to get full value from their rather high prices. Lockers are provided for valuables and you can hire towels.

◀↑▷ BRITTIP
Want a day of watery fun but don't want to purchase an extra pass for a water park? Consider CocoKey Water Resort on International Drive. You can purchase a day pass for $22.95–24.95; it's great for the pre-school to 10-year-old crowd, and it's partly covered, to protect kids from the harsh Florida sun (**www. cocokeywaterresort.com**).

Disney's Typhoon Lagoon Water Park

When Typhoon Lagoon opened in 1989, it was the biggest and finest of Florida's water parks. And, although it has since been superseded, in high season it is still the busiest, so be prepared for more queues. You should definitely arrive half an hour early if possible as entry often begins before the official opening hour. The park's 56acres/23ha are spread out around the 2½acre/1ha lagoon fringed with palm trees and white-sand beaches. It is extravagantly landscaped and the walk up Mount Mayday provides a terrific overview as well as adding scenic touches like rope bridges and tropical flowers. Sun loungers, chairs, picnic tables and even hammocks are provided to add to the comfort and convenience of restful areas like Getaway Glen. However, you need to arrive early to bag a decent spot. Or, for $58 extra(!) you can reserve 2 beach loungers, 2 towels, an umbrella and a small table by stopping in at High 'n Dry Rentals (or calling in advance). Really want to splash out? Opt for a Beachcomber Shack (cabaña), which includes a locker, drinks mug, cooler with ice, bottled water, towels, loungers and table, and waiter service. Full day rental for up to 6 guests will set you back $345 (admission not included). Reserve

in advance on 407 939 7529 (we're fans of arriving early and getting your loungers for free!).

◀↑▷ BRITTIP
While water parks provide a great way of cooling down, it is easy to pick up a 5-star case of sunburn. So don't forget the high-factor waterproof suncream, and reapply often.

Beating the crowds: To avoid the worst of the summer crowds (when the park's 7,200 capacity is often reached), Mon morning is best (steer clear of weekends at all costs) and, on other days, arrive either before opening or in mid-afternoon, when many decide to dodge the daily rainstorm. Early evening is also pleasant when the park lights up.

◀↑▷ BRITTIP
Want to learn to surf? Typhoon Lagoon offers Surfing School 2hrs before park opening every day. Call 407 939 7529 in advance to book at $165/person.

Slides and rides: The park is overlooked by **Mount Mayday**, on top of which is perched the luckless *Miss Tilly*, a shrimp boat that legend has it landed here during the typhoon that gave the park its name. Watch out for the water fountains that shoot from *Miss Tilly's* funnel at regular intervals, accompanied by the ship's hooter, signalling another round of fun big waves in the **Surf Pool**. Circling the lagoon is **Castaway Creek**, a 3ft/1m deep, lazy flowing river offering the chance to float idly along on rubber tyres.

The slides and rides are all clustered around Mt Mayday and vary from the breathtaking body slides of **Humunga Kowabunga** that drop you 214ft/65m at up to 30mph/48kph down some pretty steep inclines (make sure swimming costumes are securely fastened!) to **Ketchakiddee Creek**, which offers a selection of slides and pools for youngsters under 4ft/122cm. In between, you have the 3 **Storm Slides**, body slides that twist and turn through caves, tunnels and waterfalls, **Mayday Falls**, a wild 460ft/140m single-rider inner-tube flume down a series of banked drops, **Keelhaul Falls**, a more sedate tube ride that takes slightly longer, and **Gangplank Falls**, a family ride inside rafts that take up to 4 people down 300ft/90m of mock rapids.

The fun **Crush 'n' Gusher** is a fabulous trio of 'water-coaster' tube rides, plus a large heated pool with zero-depth entry (great for toddlers). It also has an extensive sandy beach, ideal for sunbathing. The 3 different slides feature tubes for 2 or 3 riders at a time that whoosh you down and UP several inclines before dropping you into the pool with a significant splash. This is busy from midday. The imaginative (but chilly) **Shark Reef** is an upturned wreck and coral reef in which you can snorkel among 4,000 tropical fish and a number of (harmless) nurse sharks. Those not brave enough to get in can still get a close-up through the underwater portholes of the sunken ship. The Reef is closed during the winter. Substantial queues build up from late morning, so do this early.

BRITTIP
'Buy a disposable waterproof camera to tie around your wrist when you visit the water parks. We bought one cheap at Wal-Mart and have some lovely photos from Typhoon Lagoon,' says reader Judith Bingham.

Typhoon Lagoon

Keeping out of the sun can also be a problem as there's not much shade. A quick plunge into Castaway Creek usually prevents overheating but do remember your sunscreen. There are height restrictions (4ft/122cm) on Humunga Kowabunga and Crush 'n' Gusher and they're not suitable for anyone with a bad back or neck, or expectant mothers.

Shopping and dining: If you have forgotten a sunhat or bucket and spade for the kids, or even your swimsuit, they are all available at **Singapore Sal's**. You CAN'T bring your own snorkels, inner tubes or rafts, but snorkels are provided at Shark Reef, **Lowtide Lou's** and **Let's Go Slurpin'** both offer snacks and drinks, while **Typhoon Tilly's** and **Leaning Palms** serve a decent mix of sandwiches, burgers, salads and ice-cream. Avoid main mealtimes if you want to eat in relative comfort. You can bring your own picnic (unlike the main parks), although no alcohol or glass.

BRITTIP
As the busiest of the water parks, Typhoon Lagoon can hit capacity quite early in the day in summer. Call 407 824 4321 in advance to check on the crowds.

Getting there: On Buena Vista Drive, ½ml/800m from Downtown Disney (see map, p218). Admission: $56 adults, $48 3–9s (under-3s free); included with Ultimate tickets; parking free; 9am (10am off season)–dusk daily. **TTTT AAAAA**

Disney's Blizzard Beach Water Park

Ever imagined a skiing resort in the middle of Florida? Well, here it is. This park opened in 1995 and is still the largest, with all 66acres/27ha arranged as if it were in the Rocky Mountains rather than the subtropics! That means snow-effect scenery, Christmas trees and waterslides cunningly converted to look like skiing pistes and toboggan runs. The same 'premium' offer at Typhoon Lagoon applies here for 2 beach loungers, 2 towels, an umbrella and a small table for $58. Or, if the price doesn't scare you off completely, you can hire a **Polar Patio** (cabaña), which includes a locker, drinks mug, cooler with ice, bottled water, towels, loungers and table, and waiter service. Full day rental for up to 6 guests is $345 (admission not included). Reserve in advance on 407 939 7529 (once again, we're fans of arriving early and getting your loungers for free).

> ### ◄⚑► BRITTIP
> Adjacent to Blizzard Beach are the amazing Winter Summerland Miniature Golf Courses (where Santa's elves hang out!), with 2 elaborate courses that are a great diversion for children (p267).

Slides and rides: Main features are **Mount Gushmore**, a 90ft/27m mountain down which all the main slides run. A ski chair-lift operates to the top, providing a magnificent view of the park and surrounding areas. Don't miss the outstanding rides, including the world's tallest free-fall speed slide, the terrifying 120ft/37m **Summit Plummet**, which rockets you down a 'ski jump' at up to 60mph/97kph. For those not quite up to the big drop, the brilliantly named **Slush Gusher** is a slightly less terrifying body slide. Then there is **Teamboat Springs**, a wild family inner-tube adventure and arguably the best of all the water rides; **Runoff Rapids**, a choice of 3 tube plunges; **Snow Stormers**, a daring head-first 'toboggan' run; and **Toboggan Racers**, the chance to speed down the 'slopes' against 7 other head-first riders. All 4 provide good-sized thrills without overdoing the scare factor. The side-by-side **Downhill Double Dipper** tubes send you down 230ft/70m tubes in a timed race, with a real jolt half-way down! **Tike's Peak** is a kiddie-sized version of the park's slides and a mock snow-beach, and **Ski-Patrol Training Camp** is a series of challenges and slides for pre-teens. **Melt-Away Bay** is a 1acre/0.4ha pool fed by 'melting snow' (actually

blissfully warm), and **Cross Country Creek** is a lazy-flowing 1½ml/800m river round the whole park that also floats guests through a chilly 'ice cave' (look out for the ice-water waterfalls!).

Shopping and dining: There is a 'village' area with a **Beach Haus** shop and **Lottawatta Lodge** fast-food restaurant (pizzas, burgers, salads and sandwiches), offering a grandstand view of Mount Gushmore. Snacks are also available at **Avalunch** (ouch!), the **Warming Hut**, **Polar Pub** and **Frostbite Freddie's Frozen Refreshments**.

Getting there: Just north of Disney's All-Star Resorts off Buena Vista Drive (see map p14). Admission: $56 adults, $48 3–9s (under-3s free); included with Premium and Ultimate tickets; parking free; 9am (10am off-season) to dusk daily. TTTTT ΛΛΛΛΛ

Wet 'n Wild

If Disney scores highest for scenic content, Wet 'n Wild, the world's first water park in 1977, goes full tilt for thrills and spills of the highest quality, with several major experiences and a fabulous kids' water-play area. This park will certainly test your swimsuit material to the limit!

Wet 'n Wild is one of the best-attended water parks in the country, and its location in the heart of I-Drive makes it a major draw. Consequently, you will encounter some crowds here, though the 15 slides and rides, Lazy River attraction, elaborate Blastaway Beach kids' park, Surf Lagoon, restaurant and picnic areas absorb a lot of punters before queues

Wet 'n Wild

develop. Waits of more than a ½hr at peak times are rare, but it is packed at weekends and throughout June and July as well. However, the park offers an Express Pass for limited queuing for an extra $20/person (1-time use per ride) or $50 (unlimited use).

◄■► ANNIVERSARY SPOT
20 In 1995, Orlando's water park offerings consisted of Disney's River Country, Typhoon Lagoon, and Blizzard Beach, plus Wet 'n Wild and the long-gone Kissimmee park Water Mania.

Slides and rides: You are almost spoilt for choice of main rides, from popular group inner-tube rides of **The Surge** and **Bubba Tub** to the more demanding **The Flyer**, **The Blast** and single-rider **Mach 5** (head-first on a mat-slide). For body slides, try the high-energy plunge of **The Storm** and the sheer terror of **Der Stuka** and **Bomb Bay**. The latter duo are definitely not for the faint-hearted. Basically, they are 276ft/23m near-vertical body slides. Der Stuka is the straightforward slide, while Bomb Bay adds the extra terror of being allowed to free-fall on to the top of the slide. Strangely, only a minority of visitors pluck up the courage to try it! There are 4ft/122cm height restrictions on Bomb Bay and Der Stuka. New in summer 2014 was **Aqua Drag Racer**, a terrific 4-lane, head-first toboggan-mat plunge down 350ft/107m of twisting track, ending in a big splash-down. Another standout is **Black Hole: The Next Generation**, a pulsating 2-person ride down an enclosed flume, with a dynamic lighting package and other special effects.

Our favourites? We like the thrilling toboggan-like Flyer, which takes 4 passengers in 8ft/2m in-line tubes down more than 450ft/137m of banked curves and straights, and The Blast, with its 1 or 2-passenger tubes that surprise you with sudden twists and turns, explosive pipe bursts and drenching waterspouts, leading to a final waterfall plunge. And don't miss The Storm, a pair of identical circular

slides billed as 'body coasters' – the enclosed tubes (complete with storm sound and light effects) send the rider plunging into a circular bowl, around which they spin at high speed before landing in the splash-pool below. Possibly the funniest, though, is **Disco H2O**, a superbly themed family raft ride that plunges down an enclosed tube into a swirling 'disco bowl' (featuring lights and mirror ball!) before spitting you out through a waterfall. It is all accompanied by 1970s music and commentary to add to the fun (big queues from midday to late afternoon). Equally, **Brain Wash** is a 65ft/20m funnel ride that sends riders on 2, 3 or 4-person tubes down an enclosed flume into a huge funnel that washes the tube wildly backwards and forwards before setting it up for the final splashdown.

Families should definitely head for the **Blastaway Beach** area, a full 1acre/0.4ha play structure themed like a giant sandcastle. This amazing adventure playground features a huge array of junior-sized slides and flumes, with all manner of soakers, jets, waterfalls and cannons to keep kids amused for hours. There are 2 pool areas, with 17 slides ranging from just a few ft/m to more than 2 storeys in height. More importantly, it has its own seating area, set amid some lush tropical beach landscaping to allow parents to relax while they supervise or just watch. There is only one exit/entry, hence it is an ideal self-contained area for younger children. It is the largest structure of its kind in Florida – at 60ft/28m high and covering a full 1acre/0.4ha – but is also extremely popular with youngsters, hence you should head here first if you have children under 12.

The neighbouring lake is also part of the fun (May–Sept, noon–dusk only), adding the options for cable-operated **Knee Ski**, **Wake-Skating** and **Paddle Boarding** (all for a small extra fee). Take a breather in the slow-flowing **Lazy River** as you float past palms and waterfalls, or head for one of several picnic areas (though they can be crowded). The energetic can play beach volleyball. Lockers, showers and tube and towel rentals are all available; if you bring your own equipment, you must have it checked by the lifeguards.

Shopping and dining: Sportswear, swimwear, sunglasses, hats and more can all be found at the **Beach Shop**. For food, **Bubba's Fried Chicken 'N Ribs** serves chicken, ribs, fries and drinks, the **Surf Grill** features burgers, hotdogs, salads, chicken and sandwiches, and **Manny's Pizza** has pizza and subs. **Riverside BBQ** (summer only) offers an 'Unlimited visit' BBQ option ($19 adults, $11 3–9s) while the **Wild Tiki Lounge** is a covered Polynesian-style restaurant and bar, **Carnival Treats** features various sweet treats, including candy floss and funnel cakes and 6 additional snack bars offer ice-cream, beer and more. You can also bring your own picnic, but not alcohol or glass containers.

◀▶ BRITTIP

For all the water parks, it's a good idea to bring a pair of water shoes or sandals that can be worn in water. All the local supermarkets sell them cheaply.

Getting there: Wet 'n Wild is ½ mile/800m north of I-Drive's junction with Sand Lake Road at the intersection with Universal Boulevard (see map p14), just off exit 75A and 74B of I-4. Admission: $56 adults, $51 3–9s (half-price after 2, 3, 4 or 5pm seasonally; buy online in advance and save $10/person), under-3s free (included with Orlando FlexTicket and Universal 3-Park Ticket). Towels $5 ($3 deposit) and lockers $6–11 ($3 deposit); cabañas for up to 6, from $119–275; parking $13; open 9.30–9pm in summer, 10am–5, 6 or 7pm at other times (**www.wetnwildorlando. com**). TTTTT AAA

Aquatica by SeaWorld

This eye-catching water park has a wonderful range of children's attractions and facilities, innovative rides and an all-you-can-eat-meal option, spread over 59acres/24ha of South Seas-inspired landscaping.

Slides and rides: Aquatica's signature attraction is the **Dolphin Plunge** (4ft/122cm), a twin body slide that sends riders down 300ft/91.5m of tubes and through a lagoon of playful, black-and-white Commerson's dolphins (it's a touch gimmicky as you catch only the briefest glimpse of them on the way down, but it is an exhilarating slide). You can then view the Dolphins at the end of the ride through the huge lagoon window, where the inhabitants often hang out to look at their human visitors! The other standout attraction is the new **Ihu's Breakaway Falls**, with 3 enclosed tubes featuring break-away floors (complete with heartbeat effect while you're waiting for the drop!) and 1 outrageous non-breakaway tube that is every bit as scary. Each offers a completely different ride. **Whanau Way** is a quadruple raft ride with 2 distinct variations that twist and turn before landing with a resounding splash, while **Tassie's Twisters** are double bowl rides that send riders down 1 and 2-person tubes into giant bowls before splashing back into the **Loggerhead Lane** lazy river (which also incorporates a cool coral reef viewing section). **Taumata Racer** (3ft 6in/107cm) is a fast-paced mat slide set up like an 8-lane racing toboggan run, partly enclosed and then with a double drop into daylight (queues can look long here but they usually move quickly). Family raft ride **Walhalla Wave** features a winding, enclosed section before a big splash finale; while **HooRoo Run** is a shorter, and straighter ride – with 2 distinct drops on the way (4ft/122cm must wear a life vest)! **Omaka Rocka** features 2 high-speed single-rider tube flumes, each with 3 sets of funnels that send you coursing up one side and down the other with a sensational 'feel it in your tummy' weightlessness before final splash-down. **Big Surf Shores** wave pool offers big dynamic waves, while sister wave-pool **Cutback Cove** features gentler rolling surf. A huge sandy **Beach** offers a large array of sun loungers and umbrellas, and private cabañas ($60 for Standard, $80 Pool or River View or $120

Premium in low season; or the Ultimate Cabaña, including upgraded furniture, dining table and a second cabana with couch, coffee table and additional seating for up to 8, at $300–600 seasonally). Call 1888 800 5447 to book or go online.

BRITTIP

Head for the Beach area when you first arrive to stake out a place to base yourselves and try to grab one of the bigger fixed umbrellas that offer the most shade.

As well as the gentle **Loggerhead Lane** (under 4ft/122cm must wear life vest), you should try the dynamic **Roa's Rapids** (under 51in/129cm must wear a life vest), which provides a helter-skelter whirl along this river feature, with a series of fountains, jets and other watery boosts to keep you bobbing along with no effort at all. Free life vests are on offer here and it is worth trying one for the feeling of floating along in high style!

Kids' features: The big success of the park, though, is its extensive features for children, from the youngest to young teens. **Kata's Kookaburra Cove** is an exclusive area for those under 4ft/1.2m tall, with a whole range of scaled-down slides, rides, pools and fountains to provide a gentler experience for the young 'uns. By contrast, **Walkabout Waters** is a vast and frenzied 60ft/18m-high water play structure with every kind of climb, slide and water eruptions and outpourings, including 2 giant buckets that fill and dump in spectacular fashion over those below. Small animal encounters are also designed to appeal to children,

Aquatica at SeaWorld

so watch out for these around the park (featuring macaws, leggy spoonbills, anteaters, tortoises and a kookaburra).

Shopping and dining: The imaginative **Kiwi Traders** is the biggest of the 4 shops, but both **Adaptations** and **Beachies** are worth a look. For dining, try **Waterstone Grill** (chicken tenders, burgers, salads, sandwiches, wraps), **Mango Market** (chicken tenders, sandwiches, salads, fries and desserts) or **Banana Beach Cookout** buffet (pizza, pasta, chicken, pork, hotdogs, salads, desserts, non-alcoholic drinks; all-day pass $18 adults, $13 ages 3–9; add refillable souvenir bottle for $5). Aquatica also offers a pre-purchased Family Picnic (choose main course, side, dessert, and beverage at Mango Market) for $9 adult, $6 child, or $30 'family size,' feeding up to 6 people.

BRITTIP

Youngsters can learn to swim at Aquatica, with a week-long course of 45min lessons by water safety instructors at $49/student. Book online or call 1888 800 5447.

Aquatica features elements that no other park has, like Roa's Rapids and Kookaburra Cove. And, if you buy the 2-park ticket with SeaWorld, it's great value in summer, as you can spend much of the day in Aquatica and then hop over to SeaWorld for the evening.

Getting there: Just across the road from SeaWorld on International Drive, exit 71 or 72 off I-4. Admission: $56 adults, $51 3–9s; 2-Park Ticket (with SeaWorld) $129 and $124; (save $10 by booking online; included with Orlando FlexTicket); parking $12, locker rental $20 and $35 (plus refundable $5), towels $4; 9am–6, 7 or 8pm (late May–Aug) or 10am–5pm (winter, spring and autumn; 407 351 3600, **www.aquaticabyseaworld.com**) TTTT AAAAA

That sums up the large-scale attractions on offer, but let's explore some alternatives to the mass-market experience…

8 Off the Beaten Track

or When You're All Theme-Parked Out

Orlando's main attractions are undoubtedly a lot of fun, but they can also be extremely tiring and you may well need a break from all the hectic theme park activity. Or you may be visiting again and looking for a different experience. If either is the case, this chapter is for you.

Hopefully, you will already have noted the relatively tranquil offerings of Gatorland in the previous chapter, but to enhance your view of the area further, the following are all guaranteed to take you off the beaten tourist track. This chapter could easily be subtitled 'A Taste of the Real Florida', as it introduces the towns of Winter Park, Celebration and Mount Dora, plus the natural delights of the area, including the state parks, day-trips, eco-tours and sports.

ORLANDO/Orange County

Foremost among the 'secret' hideaways is the elegant northern suburb of **Winter Park**, little more than 20mins from the hurly-burly of I-Drive yet a world away from the relentless tourism. It offers museums and art galleries, boutique shopping, numerous restaurants, walking tours, a delightful 50min boat ride around the lakes and, above all, a chance to slow down. Take exit 87 from I-4, Fairbanks Avenue; turn right on Fairbanks and go east for 2ml/3km and turn left at the junction with Park Avenue.

Morse Museum of American Art: A must for admirers of American art pottery, American and European glass, furniture and other decorative arts of the late 19th and early 20th centuries, as it includes one of the world's foremost collections of works by Louis Comfort Tiffany. The dazzling chapel restoration from the 1893 Chicago World Expo is on display in its original form for the first time since the late 19th century and is worth the entrance fee alone. It also has special Christmas exhibitions and periodic family programmes (9.30am–4pm Tues–Sat, 1–4pm Sun, also 4pm–8pm Fri only Nov–April; adults $5, Seniors $4, students $1, under-12s free; free 4–8pm each Fri Nov–April; **www.morsemuseum.org**).

BRITBONUS
Bring your *Brit Guide* to the Cornell Fine Arts museum and receive a 10% discount on all purchases in the museum store.

Park Avenue: The heart of Winter Park is a classy street of restaurants, fine shops and a shaded park. At one end is Rollins College, a small but respected arts education centre housing the beautiful **Cornell Fine Arts Museum**, with the oldest collection of paintings, sculpture and decorative arts in Florida (10am–4pm Tues–Fri, 12am–5pm Sat and Sun, closed Mon and holidays; admission is free; **www.rollins.edu/cfam**).

You should also take the **Park Avenue Walking Tour**, with free maps provided by the Welcome Center (on W Lyman Ave; 8.30am–5pm Mon–Fri, 9am–2pm Sat; 407 644 8281). The shops of Park Avenue are a cut above most and, while you may find the prices equally distinctive, just browsing is an enjoyable experience with the charm of the area highlighted by the friendliness hereabouts. For shops both unique and fun, look for **Simmons Jewellers**, **Ten Thousand Villages** (international arts and crafts), **Bebe's** (children's clothes), the eclectic **The Doggie Door/Unleashed** (pet accessories), **Siegel's** (men's clothing) and **Kathmandu** (imported goods from all over the world), plus **Peterbrooke Chocolatier**. Regular craft fairs and art festivals add splashes of colour to an inviting scenario. Street parking allows 3 hours free, but there is a multi-storey car park on the corner of Comstock and Park Avenue, which is a better ½-day option. Keep an eye out for the **Taste of Winter Park** in Apr and Autumn Art Festival in Oct (**www.cityofwinterpark.org**).

Scenic Boat Tour: Started in 1938, this is located on East Morse Boulevard and offers a charming, 12ml/19km narrated tour around the lakes and canals, giving a fascinating glimpse of some stunning homes, boat houses and lakeside gardens (property prices start at around $1m and several top $10m!). Tours run every hour 10am–4pm daily (closed Christmas) at $12 for adults and $6 for 2–11s, cash only; and this is one of the most relaxing hours you can spend in Orlando (407 644 4056; **www.scenicboattours.com**).

In south-west Orange County (just north of Disney), **Lake Tibet-Butler Preserve** is a small nature reserve on SR535 (Winter Garden-Vineland Rd) that features 4ml/6.5km of trails and elevated boardwalks where the cypress swamps, freshwater marshes, scrub and pine flatwoods are home to gopher tortoises, turtles, armadillos and especially birds (it is on the Great Florida Birding Trail). Stop by the Visitor Center to pick up a map and see its wildlife exhibits and enjoy an

A dining delight

Winter Park boasts some of the best upmarket dining in Orlando. **Park Plaza Gardens** specialises in a modern mix of American and Continental cuisines, plus a wonderful Sunday brunch. **310 Park South** offers the epitome of elegant, European café culture. We are also big fans of the pavement bistro of **Briarpatch** (breakfast and lunch), the Italian style of **Pannullo's**, and the fabulous **Luma on Park**, a 'gastropub' featuring fresh, daily specials from simple burgers to gourmet offerings and a superb wine list (**www.lumaonpark.com**). The **Ravenous Pig** on Orange Avenue has a similar wide-ranging pub choice, from its fine micro-brewery to wonderful steaks and seafood and earns top marks from leading local restaurant critic Scott Joseph (**www.theravenouspig.com**).

hour or 2 of peace and quiet (10am–5 or 6pm Wed–Sun).

MOUNT DORA/ Lake County

Immediately to the west and north of Orlando is this large, rural county that is home to more unspoiled Florida charms and several small-scale attractions, including a notable state park and well-known winery.

Mount Dora: This smallish town on beautiful Lake Dora is one of Florida's hidden gems; a day here is a breath of fresh air with its unique mix of pleasant shops, restaurants, bars, inns and tours. Mount Dora is also renowned as a festival city, with 19 annual galas. Visit www.mountdora.com to see if there is one during your visit (4 July and Christmas are especially notable, while the Sail Boat Regatta each April is one of Florida's finest).

Start with the **Mount Dora Trolley** from the Lakeside Inn, a 1hr narrated trundle around the streets (11am, noon, 1 and 2pm Mon–Sat, $15 adults, $13 2–13s; 352 385 1023), a fascinating tour of one of the 'Top 100 Great Towns of America', and a former key stop on the now-defunct Florida railroad. Then stroll round the compact centre, which is full of quaint shops, cafés and bars. Antique hunters are spoiled for choice but should visit **Village Antique Mall**, with more than 80 vendors, and **Pak Ratz**, plus **Uncle Al's Time Capsule**, for film and celebrity memorabilia, while other unique stores include a **Walk in the Woods** (for clothing and Crocs shoes), **Gold In Art** (jewellery) and **Thee Clockmaker Shoppe**. The town even boasts the **Rocking Rabbit Brewery**, with live music on Fri and Sat 8pm–11pm (**www.mountdorabrewing.com**). Other stops of interest include **Mount Dora Historic Museum** (the former town jail!), which displays more (free) local history, and the Museum of Speed, a homage to high-powered American sports cars of yesteryear (plus other memorabilia such as vintage juke boxes and Coca-Cola machines; 10am–5pm Mon–Fri; $10/person or $12 with tour, no under-14s, no credit/debit cards; 352 385 0049, **www.classicdreamcars.com**).

Possibly the best way to see Mount Dora is with the fully narrated **Guided Tours of Segway of Central Florida**. They use unique, state-of-the-art, 2-wheel Segways to take small groups downtown, on to the iconic Mount Dora lighthouse and around scenic Palm Island Park. They pass some of the city's many fine B&Bs (including the award-winning **Magnolia Inn** on East 3rd Avenue) and the genteel 125-year-old **Lakeside Inn**, on the National Register of Historic Places, where you can stop for a drink in **Tremain's Lounge** or dine in the **Beauclaire Dining Room** (great Sunday brunch – **www.lakeside-inn.com**). The Segway is easy to master (after a brief hands-on lesson) and ideal for the quiet streets. If you enjoy the 1hr tour, there is a second guided tour of nearby Dogwood Mountain. Both cost $55/person and tours run Tues–Sun 10am, noon, and 2pm (reservations advised; 352 460 2039, **www.segwayofcentralflorida.com**; save $6 if booking online). Riders must be 18 (16 with parent) and no more

than 260lb/118kg. This is one of our favourite activities.

Premier Boat Tours: You can see more via the *Captain Doolittle* from the Lakeside Inn for a fascinating eco-tour of the lakes and Dora Canal. As well as gators, you may see raccoons, turtles, otters, birds of prey and other nesting birds along this beautiful waterway. There are narrated 2hr tours daily at 11am and 2pm ($27 adults, $15 children) and 1hr Sunset Tours 45min before sunset daily ($17 and $12, bring your favourite beverages; reservations advised on 352 434 8040, **www.doracanaltour.com**). Pontoon rentals are also available.

CraigCat Tours: Offer 2hr narrated guided tours along Lake Dora and the Dora Canal aboard CraigCat motorised 2-person watercraft. Bottled water and lifejackets provided. No experience necessary, drivers must be 21 and up with valid driving licence, passengers must be 12 and up. Non-marking soft-soled shoes or sandals required ($99/person; 407 227 3388; **www.craigcattours.com**; check website for periodic discounts).

Getting there: On US Highway 441 north-east of Orlando, take the (toll) Florida Turnpike to exit 267A for the (toll) Western Beltway (429), and the Beltway north to its junction with 441, from where Mount Dora is 10ml/16km further north. For more info, contact the excellent Mount Dora Chamber of Commerce on 352 383 2165 or **www.mountdora.com**. The visitor centre is at 341 Alexander Street.

$ BRITBONUS

Take a kayak tour with Central Florida Nature Adventures and, when you book for 3, the fourth person paddles free! Just remember to quote the *Brit Guide* offer when you book and show your copy when you turn up.

Central Florida Nature Adventures: Head north from Mount Dora to Eustis, from where this company offer guided tours of the Dora Canal and the Lil' Amazon in Lake County, Rock Springs Run and the Wekiva River in Seminole County, Blackwater Lake in Marion County and the Silver River in Ocala; plus a winter Manatee tour and a kayak and horse-riding combo. Their 2 chief guides are highly experienced kayakers but most trips (2–7hrs) require no experience and are wonderfully scenic. Tours vary from $59–125 (352 589 7899, **www.kayakcentralflorida.com**).

Lake Louisa State Park: Another gem just off Highway 27 (at the west end of Highway 192), this offers beautiful countryside, with 6 lakes and rolling hills. There are over 20ml/32km of hiking trails, a picnic pavilion, swimming in Lake Louisa (with lifeguards late May–Aug), plus 20 cabins, sleeping up to 6 (8am–dusk daily, entry $5/car; 352 394 3969, **www.floridastateparks.org/lakelouisa**). Further up Highway 27 is the **Citrus Tower**, built in 1956, with panoramic views from its 22-storey glass observation deck (9am–5pm Mon–Sat, $6 adults $4 3–11s; 352 394 4061, **www.citrustower.com**); and **Lakeridge Winery**, a 127acre/51ha producing some award-winning wines with free tours and tastings (10am–5pm Mon–Sat, 11am–5pm Sun; 1800 768 9463, **www.lakeridgewinery.com**).

Revolution – The Offroad Experience: Perfect for those with kids of 16+ and keen to see the real Florida, this British-run attraction is set in 240acres/97ha of countryside with a private lake. They offer ATV (Quad-Bike), Jeep and Dune Buggy off-roading, plus the amazing JetLev adventure. The purpose-built ATV trail features 2 40min sessions of fab driving (must be 17+; 12–16 can ride with an instructor). There is a short 'test' to ensure riders are in control, then it's off over the sand-hills and grasslands on trails and dirt tracks groomed for off-road activity, but you WILL get dirty, so wear old clothes – long trousers and close-toed shoes or trainers. The **4 x 4 Experience** (in a Jeep Wrangler) can be driven by anyone with a driving licence and passengers are welcome, while the sturdy dune buggies are open to all

280lb/127kg and under 1.9m/6ft 3in. This is one of Florida's best off-road drives – novel, enjoyable and highly addictive! The **Mucky Duck** tour is self-drive in 4-passenger amphibious vehicles. The 75min experience includes training in the 6 and 8-wheel Argo UTVs and the chance to drive around and through the main lake. Drivers must be at least 18 and hold a full licence, but passengers can be as young as 4 (with safety vests and helmets provided). For real-life James Bonds, the **JetLev Blast-off Adventure** is even more novel – the chance to 'fly' a water-powered jet-pack (after full instruction) at up to 25mph/40kph and reaching 30ft/9m (bring a swimsuit as it's a water experience). It includes 30min flight time and is tricky but an absolute blast. Booking is essential on 352 400 1322 or www.revolutionoffroad. com. ATV is $75/person ($35 for ride-along); ATV & Dune Buggy or ATV & Jeep $130, or all 3 for $185. JetLev Adventure is $200. Mucky Duck tour $75/driver, $40/passenger. There are also 4–6hr **fishing adventures** for $225 and $325 (for 2) and **Target**

Archery ($45). To get there, take Highway 192 west to Highway 27; go north on 27 for 3 traffic lights; turn left on Highway 474 it hits 33, then go right for 2ml/3km and it is on the right.

◀$▶ BRITBONUS — Get $5/person off any activity at Revolution Offroad by showing your copy of the *Brit Guide* or mentioning it when booking.

OSCEOLA COUNTY

You'll find some of Florida's most scenic and nature-orientated attractions in the Kissimmee area – you just need to know where to look!

◀▶ BRITTIP — Dresses are not advisable for balloon trips and hardwearing shoes for the set-up and landing areas are essential.

Balloon trips

Florida is hugely popular for ballooning and you will often see them in Osceola County. It's a majestic experience; the utterly smooth way in which you lift off is breathtaking, but the peace and quiet, and the stunning views are awesome. It's not cheap, but it is appealing to all but young children or those with a fear of heights. It can also be a highly personal ride, with basket capacity starting at just 4 people.

Orlando Balloon Rides: The main operator in central Florida, British-run, it flies every day (weather permitting), meeting at the Convention Center at the Radisson Resort Orlando-Celebration on Highway 192 (one traffic light east of I-4) at 5.30–6.30am depending on season (the best winds are nearly always early) then transferring to the take-off site. Here you can help the friendly crew set up the new, safety-designed balloons (for 4, 8, 10, 12 or 18 passengers) one of which is also disabled-accessible. Then you fly off for 1 hour, floating serenely or sinking to skim the

treetops or one of the many lakes. After your flight enjoy a champagne landing ceremony before returning to the hotel. It lasts 3–4 hours and costs $185/adult, $95 age 4–10 (no under-4s or expectant mothers). Select hotel pick-ups is available at $10/person for the round trip, or for $25 you can be part of the chase crew and just enjoy the champagne landing. Balloonist Certificates can be downloaded from the website. Book well in advance on 407 894 5040 or **www.orlandoballoonrides.com**. Orlando Balloon Rides are also part of the Orlando Adventure Collection, a group of 7 companies with an action-themed attraction. They include Revolution – The Offroad Experience (p252), Boggy Creek Airboats (p254), Forever Florida Zipline Safari (p257), Warbird Adventures (p258), Kissimmee Helicopters and Revolution Bass Fishing. Look up **www.orlandoadventurecollection.com**.

◀$▶ BRITBONUS — Mention and show your copy of the *Brit Guide* with Orlando Balloon Rides and children (ages 4–10) fly FREE! (1 free child per paying adult). Plus, they also offer free transportation for our readers.

Thompson Aire: Top local pilot Jeff Thompson, a veteran with more than 35 years' flying, also flies every day (weather permitting), meeting at the Maingate Lakeside Resort on Highway 192, and returning there for a hearty buffet breakfast. Fares are $185 ($105 10–15s; 1 child 5–9 can fly free with a paying adult; discounts for 4 or more adults travelling together). Chase package available for non-flyers. Call 407 421 9322 or visit **www.thompsonaire.com**. Hotel pick-ups can be arranged at $15/person.

Airboat rides

The thrill of airboat rides – like flying at ground level – can be experienced on many of Florida's waterways, but especially in Osceola County. You can explore areas otherwise inaccessible to boats, skimming over the marshes to give you an alternative, close-up view. Travelling at up to 50mph/80kph means it can be loud (you will be given ear protectors) and sunglasses are also a good idea to keep stray flies out of your eyes. It is NOT the trip for you, however, if you are spooked by crickets, dragonflies and similar insects that occasionally land in the boat! In summer, a good insect repellent is essential.

BRITTIP
Look out for some great discounts and special offers on Boggy Creek's website, **www.bcairboats.com**.

Boggy Creek Airboat Rides: Take your pick from 2 contrasting sites in different parts of Kissimmee, 1 more rural while the other has more facilities. The rural site is on Lake Toho at peaceful Southport Park, all the way down Poinciana Boulevard, off Highway 192 between markers 10 and 11, and across Pleasant Hill Road into Southport Road – about a 35min drive. Boggy Creek's ½hr ride features the most modern 18-passenger airboats in Florida, skimming over the local wetlands for a close-up of the majestic cypress trees and wildlife including eagles, ospreys, snakes and turtles, as well as the ever-present gators. Southport Park feels a million miles away from the main tourist area and it is likely you'll see a variety of wildlife, especially in spring.

You don't need to book, just turn up, as boats go every ½hr (9am–5pm daily; $26.95 adults, $20.95 3–10s). Don't forget the sunscreen as you can really burn on the water. Boggy Creek

Boggy Creek Airboat Rides

also does a 1hr Night Tour ($51.95 adults, $47.95 3–10s, from 7.30pm Oct–Mar, 8.30pm Mar–Sept) for a completely different and exhilarating experience (gator eyes glow red in the dark!), but you must book in advance. Or go all out with the 45min Swamp Excursion, exploring remote areas beyond the regular tour ($56.95/person). Round-trip hotel transport is offered (call for pricing).

BRITBONUS
Brit Guide readers qualify for a free souvenir with Boggy Creek Airboats if you mention you booked after seeing them here (souvenir choice at discretion of Boggy Creek Airboats).

Boggy Creek's other (rather busier) site is at East Lake Fish Camp (reservations required), a completely different experience to Lake Toho, so it is worth trying both. East Lake also offers a 1hr Scenic Nature Tour for $43.95 adult, $38.95 3–10. Stay after your ride for a live alligator demonstration – and have the chance to hold a gator and have your picture taken! To reach East Lake Fish Camp, either take exit 17 off Central Florida Greeneway – 417 – and go 3ml/5km south on Boggy Creek Road, then right into East Lake Fish Camp, or take Osceola Parkway east until it hits Boggy Creek Road. Go left and then turn right at the Boggy Creek T-junction, then right into East Lake Fish Camp after about 2ml/3km (book on 407 344 9550 or **www.bcairboats.com**).

BRITTIP
Want an airboat ride but don't have a car? Taxis are seriously expensive but *Brit Guide* partners Florida Dolphin Tours offer a special excursion package to Boggy Creek every Mon, Wed and Sat, or Gatorland plus an airboat ride (see p000).

East Lake Fish Camp: A little gem, offering a variety of boating and fishing options (407 348 2040, **www.eastlakefishcamp.com**), a pleasant terrace and charming restaurant and gift shop (6am–8pm Mon–Thurs, until 9pm Fri–Sun). Consider arriving early for a huge all-day breakfast, or you may want to try the local delicacies – catfish, frogs' legs and gator tail. For another great slice of local eating, the Fri all-you-can-eat seafood buffet is $16.95, or try the Sun breakfast buffet for $9.95.

Wild Florida: Set on tranquil Cypress Lake, this airboat ride and wildlife reserve features ½hr, 1hr and night-time rides from their purpose-built dock (a great place for wildlife watching) with the chance to see gators, turtles, birdlife and even snakes from the safety of their 6 and 17-passenger airboats. It also features a self-contained 13-acre/5.2ha **Wildlife Park** that is home to their own collection of gators, deer, tortoises, emus, zebras, watusi cattle and water buffalo, plus an aviary and a peaceful boardwalk cypress swamp walk. You can feed some of the animals (for a small fee) and there is an excellent gift shop (remember you can't bring alligator products back to the UK) and the **Silver Platter BBQ café**, for a snack or lunch (we especially like their pulled pork!). Their alligator handling and photo opportunities (packages from $25–50; percentage of all profits goes to Florida Panther Conservation Society) are good, too, and you won't see any sign of human habitation out on the Lake. Again, you don't need to book for day tours as they go out regularly from 9am–6pm Mon–Sat (closed Sun). The ½hr tour is $25 for adults and $22 for 3–11s; 1hr is $45 and $35; 1hr private tour and night-time tour $60/person (must pre-book). All tours include Wildlife Park, or $18 and $15 on its own (407 957 3135, **http:// wildfloridairboats.com/**). To get there, take Highway 192 east to St Cloud (about 20miles/32km), turn right on Vermont Ave (12miles/19km), which becomes Canoe Creek Rd, then right on Lake Cypress Rd (a dirt road) for 2miles/3.2km. From Orlando, you can take the (toll) Florida Turnpike to 192 at Exit 244, then continue east to Vermont and follow the other directions from there.

Celebration

In 1994, the Walt Disney Company set out to build a 'new urban' neighbourhood, a model community with a friendly, welcoming spirit and strong traditional values. The result was Celebration, where picture-perfect Victorian homes mingle with smart town-houses with an array of shopping, dining and entertainment options. Today, it is a self-sufficient, bustling town with a hospital, schools, cinema and 2 hotels. On Disney's southern border off Highway 192, enter at the landmark water tower via Celebration Ave, then follow signs to the Bohemian Hotel in the town centre.

BRITTIP

For Celebration, don't stop at the first set of shops and services you come to off Highway 192. Keep going until you find Market Street and the centrepiece lake that is the proper downtown area.

Market Street shops feature delightful boutiques like **Market Street Gallery** (Disney collectables, Swarovski crystal, Lladro and gifts), **Confetti of Celebration** (speciality and customised gifts), **Sanrio Surprises** (home of Hello Kitty merchandise) and **Soft as a Grape** (casual wear for the family). Other specialists include **Enchanted Boutique** and **Woof Gang Bakery** (pet needs). There are miles of bike and walking paths, with the pretty lakefront setting, children's play area and periodic festivals. A huge event is held on American independence day 4 July, with picnics, entertainment and face-painting

Central Florida Zoo's zipline

(parking is at the town entrance, with a park-and-ride bus), while the Christmas period also sees festive events and nightly snowfall on Market Street (**http://celebrationtowncenter. com**). You can also take a ½hr carriage ride (Fri and Sat, 6–9.30pm and Sun 11am–3pm, weather permitting) at $20/person.

Segway Tours

An outstanding feature in Kissimmee/ Celebration is this super opportunity to try out the fab 2-wheeled Segway transporter and get a guided audio tour of the area as well. Ideal for young and old alike (age 14 and up), they are easy to master, fun to ride and a breeze to enjoy as you trundle along Highway 192 and around the most scenic parts of Celebration in true eco-friendly style.

ZE Tours: Choose from 3 separate tours in the company of a wonderfully personable guide (10am–4pm daily), heading out from their store in the Rock Church plaza on Highway 192 (by Marker 10; next to the Helicopter Tours) and rolling along for 70, 100 or 130mins to discover the heart of Celebration, its many lakes, paths and byways, plus lots of wildlife – from playful squirrels (which you can feed) to gators (which you can't!). There is a quick ride-around to get your 'Segway legs', then it is off in single-file, with the tranquil tour enabled by small walkie-talkies that clip on to your helmet. There are plenty of stops to ask questions and compare notes with your group, and your guide is a great source of knowledge about the town and the area (especially Disney). ZE Tours also offer bike rentals to tour Highway 192 at your leisure (and it's all completely flat). The Segway tours cost $55, $70 and $85/person (70, 100 and 130mins; 14–17-year-olds must be accompanied by a parent; minimum weight 100lb/45kg, max 250lb/113kg), or you can just try a ride-around on a Segway at $15 for 10min, $25 for 20min, and $35 for 30 min. Bike rental is from $5–25 (hourly or all day). Reservations are highly recommended for both on 863 512 0256 or online at **www.zetours.com**.

A cause for Celebration

Dining in Celebration is a real highlight. Try **Market Street Café**, a 50s-style diner serving down-home favourites such as turkey dinners or meatloaf and, or try award-winning **Café D'Antonio** for authentic Italian cuisine in a sleek, family-friendly atmosphere (407 566 2233, **www.antoniosonline.com**); Spanish-Cuban **Columbia** uses unique combinations of authentic ingredients (407 566 1505, **www. columbiarestaurant.com**); **Celebration Town Tavern**, a casual ambiance, specialising in New England seafood; **Seito Sushi**, is the place for contemporary sushi and fusion dishes; and the **Imperium Food and Wine** is an excellent option for fine wines and cocktails, plus a tempting light bite menu, including soups, sandwiches, salads and flatbreads (407 566 9054, **www.imperiumfoodandwine.com**). You should also consider the **Bohemian Bar & Grill** at the Bohemian Hotel, a contemporary American steakhouse with old-world Florida charm, while Kilwins is great for chocolate and ice-cream treats.

Forever Florida

For our money, this is one of the most outstanding non-theme-park attractions in Florida. Both a 4,700acre/1,900ha wilderness preserve and working ranch, it offers a close-up of the flora, fauna and conservation issues, plus a real taste of cracker-style life ('crackers' were 19th century Florida cowboys), as well as their own EcoPark, with 6 thrilling adventures.

Cypress Restaurant and Visitor Center: Start here with its essential 30min orientation programme into the preserve's creation. Beginning as a dream of gifted biologist and ecologist Allen Broussard, it was completed after his death (from complications of Hodgkin's disease) by his parents, Dr William and Margaret Broussard as a non-profit-making memorial to their son. The education element alone is awesome, and the 2 tours feature a strong conservation message. The 2hr **Coach Safari** is a tranquil trundle in a large-wheeled, open-sided buggy round much of the woods, swamp and prairie of the Crescent J Ranch and Conservancy. Your guide gives the lowdown on the history and environmental issues. A boardwalk along Bull Creek affords the chance to get up close with a typical cypress 'dome' and breathe the amazingly pure air. You are likely to see alligators, turtles, whitetail deer, armadillos and a host of bird life – including bald eagles and wild turkeys – as well as native cattle and horses, and you'll leave with a good understanding of the REAL Florida ($32 adults, $28, 6–12s; daily at 10am and 1pm).

Horseback Safaris: For ages 10 and over; here's the chance to enjoy Western trail rides for 90min with a native cracker guide ($65/person, book at least 24 hours in advance on 407 957 9794).

BRITTIP

Long trousers and closed-toed shoes are essential for Forever Florida's Horse Safaris. Early morning rides are especially enjoyable.

EcoPark: THE must-not-miss attraction in Central Florida for serious thrill-seekers, featuring 3 ziplines, tree-top cycling and 2 hair raising straightaway ziplines.

Zipline Safari: This 2½hr adventure starts with a short scenic hike to the launch point, which provides a breathtaking aerial view of the preserve at up to 55ft/16.8m high. The course includes 7 different ziplines, 10 observation platforms and 3 sky-bridges over 3 eco-systems. The longest run is 750ft/229m and riders reach top speeds of 25mph/40kph. The final zip brings you down to its wildlife interaction area, including a Florida panther, alligators and other animals. There are also themed 'party' events on Sat, including a Starlight Safari or Moonlight Safari on select dates, but you must book in advance ($65/person, ages 10 and up).

Cypress Canopy Cycle: This relaxing but still thrilling 45–60min pedal through the treetops takes you 25ft/7.6m up, on board a specially designed reclined bicycle suspended from an overhead steel cable. Go at your own pace, with plenty of time for photographs of the surrounding forest, wetlands and wildlife (wave at George, the 13ft/4m gator whose pond you'll ride above); $32/person, ages 10 and up.

The Thrill Pack: The Rattlesnake, Peregrine Plunge, Panther Pounce and Swooping Crane. The **Rattlesnake** is 'next generation ziplining' at its best, a 1,000ft/205m long, 20mph/32kph diving and soaring 'roller-coaster' ride from the 65ft/20m high tower. **Peregrine Plunge** launches from a 71ft/22m tower with 1,300ft/396m of line – the longest single zipline in Florida, at up to 30mph/48kph – and not for the faint of heart. But do it once and you'll want to go again. Want to get to the ground quicker? Tethered to an overhead crane and fitted into a secure harness at **Panther Pounce**, step off the 68ft/21m tower and go straight into free-fall! The effect is mindboggling, with serious bragging rights when it's over. Finally, if you thought Panther Plunge was a rush, **Swooping Crane** is a similar experience, with the added thrill factor of being hoisted 55ft/17m up, and the only way down is via the ripcord YOU have to pull. Just when you thought it was over, it's not. Spend a little time swinging back and forth while your cable – and your heart rate – settles down.

All 4 adventures are covered by the The Thrill Pack, at $65/ages 10 and up (max weight 275lb/125kg; 265lb/120kg for Panther Pounce; min weight 70lb/32kg and age 10).

BRITBONUS

$ Receive $3 off any adventure at Forever Florida when mentioning code WHOT. Reservations are required.

The Horseback Safaris can also be extended to 2 days ($199), staying in bunk-house accommodation. Forever Florida is a good 80min drive out of Orlando, 40ml/64km east on Highway 192, through St Cloud as far as Holopaw, then 7½ml/12km south on Highway 441, but is well worth the journey to experience the charm and tranquillity (407 957 9794, reservations recommended for all experiences, **www.foreverflorida.com**).

Green Meadows Petting Farm

This is guaranteed fun for kids 2–11 and their parents. It's the ultimate hands-on experience as, on the 2hr guided tour, kids get to milk a cow, pet a pig, cuddle a chick or duckling, feed goats and sheep, meet a buffalo, chickens, peacocks and donkeys and learn what makes a farm tick. There are pony rides and a play area, tractor-drawn hay rides, and the Green Meadows Express train tour. The shaded areas, free-roaming animals and peaceful aspect all contribute to another pleasant change of pace, especially as Green Meadows is barely 10mins from the hurly-burly of Highway 192. Allow 3–4hrs for your visit. Drinks, snacks and gifts are available, but it is also the ideal place to bring a picnic (on Poinciana Boulevard; 9.30am–4pm daily, last tour 4pm; $23/person, $19/ seniors, under-2s free; 407 846 0770, **www.greenmeadowsfarm.com**).

Osceola County History Center and Pioneer Village

Highway 192 (just by Marker 15) features the **Osceola County Welcome Center and History Museum**, a collaboration between the County and Historical Society, providing a small-scale but engaging look at the area's history and nature. There is a 'steamboat' entryway inside, then a tour of local history from 1867 to the present, through the 4 main 'habitats' (swamplands, pine flatwoods, oak hammocks and lakefront) with a series of tableaux and nature exhibits that depict the true rural and agricultural nature of central Florida, plus the original Indian tribes.

Outside, you can wander alongside **Shingle Creek**, the headwaters of The Everglades (free admission daily 9am–5pm; 407 396 8644, **www.osceolahistory. org**). After seeing the museum, cross over Highway 192 to Shingle Creek Regional Park for a chance to wander the hiking trails and experience Osceola nature at first hand.

Next, head for the **Pioneer Village**, just off Highway 192 on Bass Road. This delightful discovery pays real-life homage to 19th-century Florida life, with a preserved 'cracker' homestead portraying how settlers lived in the 1880s. The charming little museum traces more Osceola County history and includes a cattle camp, nature walk, school house, country store and information centre with library, plus a citrus-packing operation from nearby Narcoossee, originally started by a family from the UK! The volunteers who take you round provide a fascinating view of life here more than a century ago (on N Bass Road, just off Highway 192 by the Wal-Mart Supercenter next to Medieval Times between Markers 14 and 15. 10am–4pm Thurs–Sun; $5 adults, $2 6–12s, under-6s free).

Warbird Adventures and Kissimmee Air Museum

This is the most exhilarating ride in town, bar none – guaranteed. It's the only place we know of where, 20mins after walking in with no previous experience, you can actually be flying a 1945 T-6 Harvard fighter-trainer plane... and doing all manner of aerobatics. It's enhanced by in-flight video and wingtip camera to record every moment. Roller-coasters? They're for wimps! Mind you, this is not cheap – a 15min flight costs $250, 30mins is $430, 45mins is $590 and 1hr $740 (aerobatics on 30min flight $35 extra), while the DVD is $50 and photos $25. Nevertheless, the memory will last a lifetime and just the thought of it is thrilling. Max weight is 18st/115kg and minimum height is 4ft/122cm. Also on the same site at Kissimmee Gateway Airport is Kissimmee Air Museum, a combination warplane showcase and restoration centre where you can get up close with the exhibits, which include a Bell 47 helicopter, an open-cockpit Ryan PT-22, a Boeing Stearman biplane, its 3 T-6 Harvards and the amazing one-off Aerocar, plus small-scale offerings like a WWII rifle collection and Luftwaffe memorabilia. Other exhibits include Air Power and Pearl Harbor, with rare photos and artefacts behind the story. New aircraft include a racing P-51 Mustang, De Havilland T11 Vampire and a Ryan STA. It can all be found just off Hoagland Boulevard, ½ml/800m south of Highway 192, on the left (Air Museum open 9am–5pm Mon–Sat; $7/person, ages 6–12 $4, under-5s free; 407 870 7366, **www.warbirdadventures.com**).

POLK COUNTY

Head south from Kissimmee/Osceola County and you head into Polk territory, another of Florida's oldest-established and most authentic areas. It is home to the large-scale attractions of LEGOLAND Florida (p224) but also has its share of off-the-beaten-track experiences.

Bok Tower Gardens

For those wishing to experience the genuine peace, tranquillity and floral ambience of Florida, there is no better recommendation than this national monument and garden centre at Lake Wales, 50ml/80km to the south-west of Orlando (go west on I-4, then south on Highway 27). With one of the most unusual attractions in the state – a majestic 205ft/62.5m pink-and-grey marble **Carillon Tower:** Set in 250acres/101ha of unique parkland, this is a feast for the eyes and soul. Called the Singing Tower, the 1920s-built carillon is the centrepiece and concerts are given every day at 1 and 3pm. The Tower is wonderfully photogenic and quite stunning on a cloudless day.

Gardens: Around the Tower is a wide moat, a pond and semi-formal gardens. At one of the highest points on Florida's peninsula (all

of 298ft/90m above sea level), the view is inspiring and uncluttered, and retains an inherent peace and solitude that persuaded the founder, philanthropist Edward Bok, to grant the estate to the community in 1929. The gardens also provide a wildlife observatory, nature trails, an endangered plant exhibit, butterfly and woodland gardens and pine forests. There is a kids' play area, plus brass rubbing and art classes.

Education and Visitor Center: The award-winning centre illustrates the story of Edward Bok (don't miss the film about his impact on US society) and his vision for Bok Tower Gardens. The **Blue Palmetto Café** adds a pleasant opportunity for a light lunch and snacks, while the **Tower & Garden Gift Shop** offers souvenir items.

Pinewood Estate: For an additional fee ($6 adults, $5 5–12s, noon–4pm Mon–Sat, 1pm–4pm Sun), you can tour a fine example of Mediterranean-style architecture in this 20-room mansion, built as a winter retreat for a Pennsylvania steel tycoon in the early 1930s and lovingly maintained to show a slice of period opulence.

Getting there: Off US Highway 27 on Burns Avenue; take I-4 west to exit 55, go south on US 27 for 25ml/40km, then left on Mountain Lake Cutoff Road (2 traffic lights past Eagle Ridge Mall) and follow the signs. Admission: $12 adults, $3 5–12s (under-5s free), apart from occasional ticketed events (mainly carillon festivals and recitals). Open 8am–6pm daily (last entry 5pm; Visitor Center 9am–5pm only; 863 676 1408, **http://boktowergardens.org/**).

BRITBONUS
Receive a $3 discount off regular adult combo admission tickets at Bok Tower Gardens by producing your copy of the *Brit Guide* (includes Gardens and Pinewood Estate.)

Lake Wales

Continue on to the Lake Wales area after Bok Tower Gardens and you encounter some other local gems.

Chalet Suzanne: This eclectic yet classy family-run country inn and restaurant (a Florida original since 1931) was sadly put up for auction in August 2014 and there was no news as we went to print of any new owners or even if it would stay as an offbeat delight in this area. Look up **www.chaletsuzanne.com** for any future details..

Lake Wales: Head into the quaint 1920s town of Lake Wales and you discover **Spook Hill** (where cars mysteriously roll uphill!), **Grove House Visitor Center** (home of Florida's Natural fruit juice products – as fresh as it gets; 10am–5pm Mon–Fri; 10am–2pm Sat, seasonally. Closed Memorial Day–end of Sept) and the quaint **Museum and Cultural Center** (set in a restored 1928 Atlantic Coast Line railroad station; 9am–5pm Mon–Fri, 10am–4pm Sat).

Westgate River Ranch: out in rural Polk County is this superb dude ranch and activity centre that boasts great accommodations (including 'glamping' for those who like to camp in style) and the chance to try horse-riding, fishing, airboating, trap shooting and archery, as well as take in the exciting Saturday night Westgate Rodeo in the 1,200-seat arena. You can visit just for the day to try any of the activities or the weekly rodeo (which is followed by live music, line dancing and a family-friendly Street Party), but the accommodations are excellent and you can sample the River Ranch

Seminole County

Saloon without having to drive afterwards! It is guaranteed fun for all the family and a real taste of Florida's cowboy country. See more at **www.westgatedestinations.com** and click on River Ranch, FL..

SEMINOLE COUNTY

You may have flown into the airport at the historic town of Sanford and there are plenty of diversions to get you well off the beaten track. If you want to finish your holiday with a day or 2 in the area, there are many good hotel choices (often significantly cheaper than their big-name rivals elsewhere) and you can catch your breath after all the hectic theme-parking!

Adventures in Florida: Get into the wilds with this specialist company that features kayaking adventures along the picturesque Econlockhatchee and Wekiva rivers, with expert guides and an in-depth understanding of the flora and fauna. They offer 2–3hr trips, all-day tours and even night-time paddles, as well as expeditions and lodge-based trips further afield. Along the Wekiva River you may encounter gators, manatees, turtles and all manner of birdlife, all in total safety and with immensely personable guides. Trips must be booked in advance and cost from $40–80/person (407 924 3375; **www.adventuresinlorida.com**).

Black Hammock Fish Camp and Restaurant: One of the most fun and entertaining of the area's airboat rides is found off exit 44 of the Central Florida Greeneway (take SR 434 east, turn left on Deleon Street and left on Black Hammock Road). This quiet backwater on scenic Lake Jesup is home to Capt Joel Martin, whose ½hr tour takes you into every nook and cranny of either the east or west lake (which is crammed with some of the biggest gators in Florida). The standard rides leave every ½hr (no reservation required) and are $26.95 and $20.95 (under-11s), but there are then 1hr rides ($41.95 and $36.95), a 45min private tour ($50/person, 4 person minimum, reservations required), and a 60min night ride at $55/person (4 person minimum; reservations required; 407 365 1244, **www.theblackhammock.com**). Then grab lunch or dinner at the **Black Hammock Restaurant** (fine local delicacies, especially the catfish and gator tail, plus other dishes and a kids' menu; 11am–9pm Sun–Thurs, 11am–10pm Fri and Sat; 407 365 1244 ext 105) or visit the **Lazy Gator Bar**, with nightly drink specials 3–6.30pm.

Central Florida Zoological Park: This private, non-profit organisation puts a natural accent on the zoo theme, set in a wooded 116acres/47ha of unspoilt countryside with boardwalks and trails around all the attractions. These include more than 100 species of animal, weekend feeding demonstrations, educational programmes, a picnic area, pony rides and a butterfly garden, plus the Zoofari Outpost gift shop and, Tropical Splash Ground water play area. It's good value at $14.95 adults, $12.95 seniors (60+) and $10.95 3–12s and is open 9am–5pm daily (not Thanksgiving Day or Christmas Day). Also try **ZOOm Air Adventures**, a separate series of eco-friendly rope bridges, ziplines, guide wires and other aerial challenges through the Zoo's treetops. The 2 courses can be taken separately or combined (4ft 6in/137cm to take part), plus there are 2 children's courses (for 3–5ft/92–152cm). It costs $28.25 for the Upland course and $18.25 for the kids' versions, while the combo Upland and Rainforest costs $48.25. ZOOm opens at 9am, last adventure 4.30pm Mon–Fri, 5pm Sat and Sun (off exit 104 of I-4; 407 323 4450, **www.centralfloridazoo.org**).

BRITTIP

Visit Central Florida Zoo at the weekend and you will be offered a series of educational and enjoyable animal encounters (ranging from gators and snakes to hedgehogs).

St Johns River Cruise: At Blue Spring State Park, there's a personable 2hr nature tour of this historic waterway, with interactive narration of the flora, fauna (including manatees in winter) and history. It leaves from Orange City marina at 10am and 1pm daily, (not Thanksgiving or Christmas Day). Take Highway 17/92 north from Sanford to French Avenue and head west for 1ml/1.6km ($22 adults, $20 seniors, $16 3–12s; 407 330 1612, **www.sjrivercruises.com**).

Sanford: The heart of Seminole County, this quaint town on Lake Monroe boasts a historic centre full of brick-paved streets, antique shops and an artist colony regeneration project (Jeanine Taylor Folk Art). It is small-town America, having lost the growth battle with Orlando years ago, but it makes a peaceful diversion with the lovely Riverwalk along the lakefront. Head first for the **Historic Sanford Welcome Center** (230 East 1st Street (11am–2.30pm Mon, 11am–5pm Tue–Sat, noon–5pm Sun) and the **Sanford Museum** (520 East 1st Street) for an overview of city history, founded in 1877 by pioneering lawyer and diplomat Henry Sanford as a hub on the St John's River, the 'Nile of America.' The free museum (11am–4pm Tues–Fri, 1–4pm Sat) illustrates the life and times of the city's founder, its growth as the 'celery capital of the world' and recent life as a naval base. The historic port features the **Gator's Nest** airboat rides (from The Port Restaurant), where the 1hr tour gets up close with the river wildlife in great style ($45/adults, $35, 3–12s) at 10am and 1pm daily (book in advance, 407 892 2222, **www.thegatorsnest.com**). In the evening, the restaurant makes for memorable waterfront dining, or stop for a bite on First Street, with its many restored turn-of-the-century buildings. Try **The Corner Café** (fresh sandwiches, soups and salads) or the down home family cookin' of the **Colonial Room**. For a different dining experience, **Hollerbach's Willow Tree Café** is a genuine German diner featuring wonderful traditional food, great beers and live music Thurs–Sun evenings (11am–9pm Sun–Thurs, 10pm Fri and Sat; 407 756 4103, **www.willowtreecafe.com**). If you like the food, visit **Magnolia Square Market**, a lovely deli run by the Hollerbach family just round the corner. For a real treat, **The Imperial** at Washburn Imports (an antique store by day) is a fabulous evening bar, with delightful cocktails and craft beers.

The second Thurs in every month in Sanford features the **Alive After Five** street party 5–8pm on First Street, with music, street artists, restaurant samples and more. Tickets are $7 for food and drink. Look up details at **www.sanfordinfo.com**.

State Parks: You could, of course, just head for one of Seminole County's splendid parks and follow the well-marked trails. **Wekiva Springs State Park** offers bike rentals, hiking, canoeing, swimming, picnic areas and shelters, and **Little Big Econ** state forest has 5,048acres/2,045ha of scenic woodlands and wetlands. **Spring Hammock Preserve** offers 1,500acres/607ha of wilderness to explore and the **Lake Proctor** area has 6ml/10km of equestrian, hiking and biking adventures. There are more trails along the Econlockhatchee River at the **Econ River Wilderness Area**, while Chuluota has 625acres/253ha and the Geneva Wilderness Area 180acres/73ha, including Ed Yarborough Nature Center.

Where to stay: At Altamonte Springs, the refurbished **Hilton** is an upmarket choice without the price-tag, with large rooms, excellent amenities, a swish bar and versatile restaurant for breakfast, dinner and lunch (407 830 1985, **www.hilton.com**). At Lake Mary, the 5-year-old **Westin** still feels like new, with ultra-comfy rooms, exceptional service and the bonus of **Shula's 347 Grill**, a stylish, casual eatery featuring exceptional Black Angus steaks, signature salads, speciality dishes and a full bar (407 531 3555; **www.westinlakemary.com**). As a unique alternative, **Danville B&B** is an amazing creation in rural Seminole county. Built with a totally false front, the building opens to reveal the 'village' of Danville, which is a superbly-equipped guesthouse boasting its own pub and cinema! It is also a magnificent setting for the many weddings it hosts each year, so

advance bookings here are essential (407 349 5742, **www.danvillebnb.com**).

More info: See **www.visitseminole.com** or go to one of the Visitor Centers at Orlando Sanford International Airport (in the Welcome Center as you exit the main building) or the office at the Heathrow junction of I-4 (exit 98, go west on Lake Mary Blvd, right on International Parkway and left at AAA Drive; 407 665 2900).

CITRUS COUNTY

If you want to travel a little further, the 2 state park delights of Citrus County, on the Gulf Coast north-west of Orlando, are worth seeking out.

Crystal River Preserve State Park: Just north of Homosassa Springs, the Crystal River is home to the endangered manatee and it is possible to go swimming with these wonderful creatures, either on a self-guided or an organised tour. Winter and spring are ideal times for manatee sightings, but the park offers year-round adventure, with hiking and biking trails, kayaking, canoeing and fishing – or just pack a picnic lunch and enjoy a relaxing afternoon amid the natural beauty. You can also catch a relaxing and educational ride with Heritage Eco-Boat Tours, with a unique 1½hr look at local history (Mon, Wed, Fri, 10.30am and 1.30pm; call to confirm on 352 563 0450).

◀✚▶ BRITTIP
Never touch or disturb a wild manatee. They are protected animals and there are heavy fines, strictly enforced, for harassing them.

Getting there: Take the (toll) Florida Turnpike north to I-75, then, almost immediately, take SR44 west to Crystal River. Admission: Free (8am–dusk; 352 563 0450, **www.floridastateparks.org/crystalriverpreserve**).

Homosassa Springs Wildlife State Park: This park also showcases the manatee (via its underwater observatory), plus whooping cranes, deer, bobcats, black bear and even a hippopotamus among an active display of rehabilitating animals. There are daily programmes on its wildlife (10.30am, 11.30am, 12.30pm, 1.30pm, 2.30pm and 3.30pm), notably snakes and birds of prey, plus a hands-on children's education centre. The park's 210acres/85ha take in some of the state's loveliest landscape as well as the headwaters of the Homosassa River and this is extremely popular in the spring.

Getting there: As for Crystal River, but turn left on to CR490 just after Lecanta on SR44. Admission: $13 adults, $5 6–12s (9am–5.30pm, last entry 4pm; 352 628 5343, **www.homosassasprings.org**).

BREVARD COUNTY

Out on the Atlantic coast you'll find the beauty of Cocoa Beach's Thousand Islands. Tranquil canals wind past mangrove stands, wildlife flourishes in the still waters and the Indian River Lagoon Estuary is one of the most biodiverse eco-systems in the world.

Island Boat Lines: This family-owned enterprise offers eco-tours, fishing and the wonderful *Indian River Queen* dinner boat, recalling Mark Twain's tales of paddleboats and peaceful gentility. A relaxing 2hr 'In Search of Wildlife' eco-tour onboard Coast Guard-certified pontoon boats departs from the Sunset Waterfront Café on Highway 520 (W Cocoa Beach Causeway), passing some of the area's most impressive homes before heading into the Thousand Islands. Here you may spot bottlenose dolphins, manatees and a variety of coastal birds. Knowledgeable guides offer a wealth of info, encouraging visitors to ask questions and move about the boat for a closer look. Tours run at 10am and 2pm Mon–Sat, 2pm Sun ($28 adults, $26 seniors and military personnel, $23 2–12s; call to book on 1800 979 3370; **www.islandboatlines.com**)

Getting there: Take the Beachline Expressway (Highway 528) to Highway 1 south, then Merritt Island Causeway (Highway 520) east,

approx. 2ml/3.2km with the café on the right.

BRITBONUS

Get $8 off the regular adult price with Island Boat Lines by showing your copy of the *Brit Guide*. Book in advance, though, on 321 454 7414.

Indian River Queen: Also used for private events, this beautifully appointed triple-deck paddlewheel riverboat is open to the public at weekends, with an elegant **Date Night Dinner Cruise** for couples every Fri featuring a red carpet reception, live music, themed dinner buffet and full bar. Captain Georges and owners Penny and John provide memorable authentic Southern hospitality. Boarding begins at 6.30pm, sailing from 7–9pm ($98/couple, limit 40 couples). The **Sunday Scenic Historical Cruise:** Offers 2hr narrated tours with souvenir photo (no meal) for $35pp, select dates only (booking required on 321 454 7414 or **www.indianriverqueen.com**).

Getting there: To reach Cocoa Village Marina, take the Beachline (Highway 528) east to Highway 1, go south to Highway 520, make a slight left at Bee Line, continue to N Cocoa Blvd, turn left at King, then left at Delannoy.

Brevard Inshore and Nearshore Fishing: From Banana River Marina just off Highway 520 in Cocoa Beach, Captain Pete offers inshore fishing along the Indian River, Banana River and Sykes Creek, or Port Canaveral (summer only) for offshore fishing for snook, black drum, redfish and sea trout. The scenery is as exciting as the fishing, with rays and horseshoe crab skittering along the shallow flats through the clear water. Offshore catches include tarpon, cobia, kingfish and redfish. Florida native Captain Pete has been fishing here for 19 years and knows all the best spots. Inshore 4hr trip $200 for 1 angler, 2nd angler $75, 3rd and 4th anglers $25 each; under 10s free; offshore, 4hr trip $450 for up to 4 anglers, $550 for 6hrs, $650 for 8hrs; or night shark-fishing at $300 for 4hrs; (fishing licence, tackle, bait and bottled water, and more included; call to book on 321 302 0549, **http://orlandofishingadventures.com**).

Cocoa Beach Sportfishing: Board the fully equipped *Centerfold*, a 33ft/10m Tournament-rigged boat, and get ready for big game fishing! Troll for dolphin (the fish, not the mammal), sailfish, wahoo, kingfish, grouper and more with a crew who boast plenty of experience in finding 'the big one.' Captain Tim, along with Captains Beau and Pete, share their passion for fishing with anglers of all experience levels (novice to pro), and do it with humour and professionalism. *Centerfold* offers 9hr trips at $800, 5hr trips $600, up to 6 passengers; the 19ft custom in-shore fishing Flatsboat accommodates 1–4 passengers at $250 for 2, $300 for 3 and $400 for 4 for 4hrs, $50 per extra hour; and the new 26ft *Killer Bee* takes 1–4 anglers out for 4, 6 or 8hrs at $400, $500 or $600 (fishing licence, tackle, bait included; reservations on 321 848 2663, **www.cbsportfishing.com**). For more Cocoa Beach info, p277.

Excursion operators

For those without a car (or wanting to put their feet up for a bit), there are tours and day trips visiting as far afield as the Everglades, Miami, Florida Keys and even the Bahamas. You can see a lot if you don't mind a long day (up to 16 hours). However, if the main attraction of a trip to the Everglades is the airboat ride, you are better off going to Boggy Creek Airboats (p254).

◄■►**BRITBONUS**
$ For more info on all tours, see our special booking section online at **www.britguideorlando.net** and look up Our *Brit Guide* partners for the full range of Florida Dolphin Tours excursions – with your exclusive 12½% discount.

Florida Dolphin Tours: Make this British-owned company first on your list to check as it offers more than 15 memorable excursions, notably its swim-with-dolphins trips to the Keys and manatee swim adventure, Gatorland and Boggy Creek Airboats, plus excursions to St Augustine and an Orlando City Tour. They also feature free wi-fi on every coach and a great Christmas Dinner option. More to the point, as a *Brit Guide* partner, it offers readers a 12½% discount on all tours (see inside back cover). Choose from: **Cocoa Beach**, an excellent-value all-day trip to Cocoa beach for an afternoon of fun in the sun, an exciting airboat ride in search of gators on the St Johns River, all with a wonderful lunch ($75 adults, $59 3–9s); the **Kennedy Space Center** trip, with transportation to both Space Center and Astronaut Hall of Fame – ask about options such as including an airboat ride, Lunch with an Astronaut, or even the Ultimate Kennedy Experience (from $104 adult, $94 3–11s); **Florida Adventure Tour**, an all-day adventure (and their No.1 attraction), featuring breakfast and a 2hr boat trip on the picturesque Crystal River (with snorkel and mask to check out where the manatees swim). There are picnic lunches, airboat rides and trips to **Homosassa State Wildlife Park**, too, plus an educational briefing on manatees and a chance to see them being fed from the underwater viewing area ($119 adults, $89 3–11s); Swim with the Dolphins, its trademark tour, a holiday within a holiday: a 2-day excursion to lovely Key Largo with a 2hr dolphin programme (and the choice of an organised or informal dolphin swim), including transport, hotel on Miami Beach, dolphin swim, Everglades airboat ride, (interactive) alligator and snake-handling show, and ½-day to see Miami with shopping at Bayside or a boat tour along the inland waterway. The dolphin programme includes a full briefing and about 30mins in the water, with dolphin contact guaranteed ($209–299, $109 non-swimmers age 3–6; add Star Island boat tour for additional fee); there is also a Miami 1-Day & Everglades Tour, that packs a LOT in but the 2-day version is better value and less rushed.

BRITTIP

For something truly different and uplifting, book the Gospel Brunch at Downtown Disney's House of Blues, including round-trip transportation, admission, lunch buffet, and show. Sun, from $69.

Other tours include **limo trips** to **Chef Mickey's** character breakfast and dinner experiences, **Planet Hollywood VIP** ($79–119); **Clearwater Beach & Lunch**, a day-trip to the Gulf Coast for a beach adventure with lunch, and options to enjoy a Pirate Cruise, see the local dolphins in their own environment, go deep sea fishing AND work on your tan! ($75 and $65, plus extra fees per option); a Shopping Extravaganza, an all-day retail adventure with brunch and stops at the Orlando Premium Outlets, Super Wal-Mart and Florida Mall ($45 and $35); and **Orlando Magic** games ($89–214/person, Nov–Apr). For the latest details, be sure to check out **www.floridadolphintours**.com.

ANNIVERSARY SPOT

20 There was no Off the Beaten Track chapter in our first edition of the *Brit Guide*, but it quickly became clear repeat visitors were looking for a lot more than just the theme parks and obvious attractions. Hence, we added it as a chapter in the 1999 edition.

Further tours and day trips can be found on **www.grayline.com/Orlando/**.

Of course, you can also have a great day-trip by heading for the beaches in your hire car (see Chapter 9).

SPORT

In addition to virtually every form of entertainment known to man, central Florida is one of the world's biggest sporting playgrounds, with a huge range of opportunities to either watch or play your favourite sport.

Golf

Without doubt, the No.1 sport is golf, with almost 200 courses in central Florida. There are numerous packages for golfers of all abilities to enjoy the weather and some spectacular courses, many designed by legends like Greg Norman, Tom Watson, Arnold Palmer and Jack Nicklaus. With an 18-hole round, including cart hire and taxes, from as little as $25 (average around $75), it's an attractive proposition and quite different from British courses. If you go in for 36-hole days, it's possible to save up to $30 by replaying the same course, while it is cheaper to play Mon–Thurs than Fri–Sun, and there are often lower rates for afternoon tee-times in summer. Sculpted landscapes, manicured fairways, abundant water features and white-sand bunkers add up to memorable golf. Winter is the high season, hence more expensive, but many courses are busy year-round. Be aware some courses pair golfers with little thought for age, handicap etc., so, if 2 of you turn up, you may be paired with 2 strangers.

BRITTIP

Golf balls are inexpensive in Florida, so there's no need to bring your own. Good-quality clubs are usually available for hire, including top brands.

Virtually every course will offer a driving range to get you started, plus lockers, changing rooms and showers, while the use of golf carts is universal (including the GPS system, which gives the yardage for every shot). They feature comforts like iced-water stations and drink carts that circulate the course (don't forget to tip the trolley drivers). Some have swimming pools, and all offer a decent bar and restaurant.

Hawaiian Rumble mini-golf

Your best starting point is visiting one of the 5 Edwin Watts golf shops around Orlando for a free copy of the *Golfer's Guide* for a handy introduction to most of the courses (and perhaps some new clubs at the Watts National Clearance Center just south of Wet 'n Wild on I-Drive; 850 362 2005 **www.edwinwatts.com**). **Tee-Times USA** (1800 374 8633, **www.teetimesusa.com**) offers excellent advice and a reservation service. Visit Florida has its own golf section at **www.visitflorida.com/golf**.

Local golf pro (and *Brit Guide* friend) Chad Czarnecki recommends the website **www.golfnow.com** as a great source of tee times all over Central Florida, and usually at reduced rates. Then you can take your pick from the following representative selection:

Walt Disney World: Quick to attract the golf fanatic, Disney has 3 high-quality courses, including the 7,000yd/6,400m Palm, rated by *Golf Digest* in its top 25 (the 18th hole is reputedly one of the toughest in America), plus a 9-hole par-36 course, Oak Trail. Fees are $45–120 for Disney resort guests and $45–160 for visitors ($38 at Oak Trail) varying seasonally, with a third off Twilight Rate. Call 407 938 4653 for tee-times. Private and group lessons are available under PGA pro guidance, with video analysis and club rentals. Former Disney course Osprey Ridge is now part of the magnificent Four Seasons Resort.

BRITTIP
Some of the best tee-times at Walt Disney World golf courses are reserved for those staying at a Disney resort.

Champions Gate: Challenging and eye-catching, the 2 magnificent Greg Norman-designed courses to the south of Disney (exit 58 off I-4) are the International (a British-style links course) and the National (a more traditional style). The practice facilities, clubhouse, service and coaching (at the HQ of the renowned David Leadbetter Academy) are world class, and there are stay-and-

play packages with the superb Omni Orlando Resort; $45–142 (407 787 4653, **www.championsgategolf.com**).

Dubsdread: the oldest public course in Orlando and the only municipal one, just east of the city centre, this offers a testing 18 holes ($30–54) featuring narrow fairways and 'postage stamp' greens. It was heavily renovated in 2008 and offers a beautiful clubhouse, restaurant and pub, where the likes of Sam Snead and Ben Hogan rubbed shoulders in the past. They also have a free shuttle from some area hotels (407 246 2551, **www.historicaldubsdread.com**).

BRITTIP
Visit Dubsdread Golf Course and be sure to spend some time in The Tap Room, their speciality bar and restaurant, with a great setting for a memorable meal or just a beer and a burger.

Falcon's Fire: An outstanding course in Kissimmee, featuring the ProShot digital caddy system carts. Plenty of water around the course assures a testing 18 holes, but it is highly picturesque. $59–119 (407 239 5445, **www.falconsfire.com**).

Grande Lakes Orlando: This wonderful resort complex just off John Young Parkway is a Greg Norman masterpiece, offering 18 holes of Florida nature with a caddie-concierge service; $86–205 (407 393 4900, **www.grandelakes.com**).

Hawk's Landing: At the Orlando World Center Marriott, this beautiful course boasts extensive practice facilities, a superb shop, resort exclusivity and the world-class teaching of Bill Madonna's Golf Academy: $55–89 (407 787 3339, **www.marriottworldcenter.com**).

Hyatt Grand Cypress: A luxury experience on Winter Garden-Vineland Road ($150–175) with 3 elegant 9-hole courses and a superb 18-hole links-style offering, all designed by Jack Nicklaus; $99–195 (407 239 4700; **http://www.grandcypress. com/golf_club/**).

Kissimmee Oaks: Some majestic moss-draped oaks as well as 18 holes of memorable lakeside golf, all just 3½ml/6km south of Highway 192 in the Oaks Community off John Young Parkway $25–50 (407 933 4055, **www.kissimmeeoaksgolf.com**).

Legends Golf & Country Club: Just 25mins from Disney on Highway 27 towards Clermont, this has a pleasant layout with unusually rolling hills in a peaceful location; $37–56 (352 243 1118, **www.legendsgolforlando.com**).

Mystic Dunes: Just off Highway 192 near the Disney entrance, this course winds through native oaks and is a real test. There's a wonderful menu at the clubhouse, plus the latest equipment; $35–67 (407 787 5678; **www.mysticdunesgolf.com**).

Orange Lake Country Club: Massive vacation resort 4ml/6km from Disney offers 2 18-hole, a 9-hole and a rare par-3 floodlit 9; $30–109 (407 239 0000; **www.experienceorangelake.com/ golf**).

Shingle Creek: Arguably the cream of the crop is this world-class facility at the 5-star hotel, designed by top local architect Dave Harman and set among beautiful oaks and pines. It also boasts the superb **Brad Brewer Golf Academy**, which offers genuine state-of-the-art technology for novices and pros alike and is a real pleasure to spend time at; $49–99 (407 996 3306, **www.shinglecreekgolf. com** and **www.bradbrewer.com**). There are many others. Be sure to ask if fees are negotiable, as they can be lower at quiet times of the year. There are often reductions for seniors but check the dress code, as they can vary. Typically, you need a collared shirt, Bermuda shorts and no denim.

Fans: For those just looking to see the stars in action, Orlando has a big annual event, the **Arnold Palmer Invitational** at the Bay Hill Club off Apopka-Vineland Road in west Orlando. Held each March, it is a major tournament on the US PGA tour, with Tiger Woods, Phil Mickelson and Justin Rose all playing in recent years (407 876 2888,

www.arnoldpalmerinvitational.com). The **Players Championship** is also held at TPC Sawgrass in Ponte Vedra Beach each May, just a couple of hours from Orlando (**www.tpc.com/tpc-sawgrass**).

Mini-golf

Not exactly a sport, but Orlando's many extravagant mini-golf centres are a big hit. Several attractions and parks offer mini-golf as an extra, but for the best try the self-contained centres.

Disney's Fantasia Gardens: Next to the Swan Hotel just off Buena Vista Drive is a 2-course challenge over 36 of the most varied holes of mini-golf. The style is taken from the classic film Fantasia. Fantasia Fairways is a cunning putting course, complete with rough, water hazards and bunkers. 18 holes can take more than an hour ($14 adults, $12 children, 10am–11pm daily).

Winter-Summerland Mini-Golf: At the entrance to Blizzard Beach and divided into 2 18-hole courses, these mini works of art feature a 'summer' setting of surf and beach tests and a 'winter' variety of snow and ice-crafted holes. An adult round is $14 ($12 3–9s), a double round is half price (10am–11pm; Blizzard Beach admission not required).

Universal's Hollywood Drive-In Golf: This imaginative twin 18-hole set-up is at the entrance to Universal's CityWalk. The 2 sides are The Haunting of Ghostly Greens, a 1950s mock-horror themed selection that includes putting through a cemetery and a giant spider's lair, concluding in the basement lab of a haunted house, and Invaders From The Planet Putt, 18 holes of best sci-fi humour that feature an alien spaceship and a 30ft robot. There are also special effects, surprises (you may get a little wet!), atmospheric music and a riot of visual gags. And, while it looks good during the day it positively sparkles at night under its LED lighting system. It also stays open long after the theme parks have closed, hence is ideal for saving for late in the day. Open 9am–2am daily, it costs $15 for adults,

$13 (3–9s) for 18 holes, or $28 and $24 for both courses (9am–2am; 407 802 4818, **www.hollywooddriveingolf.com**).

International Drive: Mini-golf is a staple of the scene here, with no fewer than 6 courses in the vicinity (and be sure to see their websites for valuable discount coupons). Check out the 18-hole **Congo River** in front of the Four Points by Sheraton Orlando Studio City Hotel ($11.25 adults, $9.50 under-10; **www.congoriver.com**; 10am–11pm Sun–Thurs, 10am–midnight Fri and Sat); **Hawaiian Rumble's** 36 holes by WonderWorks on I-Drive (and in Lake Buena Vista on Apopka-Vineland Ave;) 9am–11.30pm Sun–Thurs, 9am–midnight Fri and Sat; $9.95 for 18 holes, $11.95 for 36; **www.hawaiianrumbleorlando.com**); **Pirates Cove** remains the original I-Drive set-up, with caves, waterfalls and rope bridges to test your skill over twin 18-hole courses (the Captain's Course and harder Blackbeard's Challenge; 9am–11.30pm daily; $12.50 adults, $11.50 4–12s, or $20.50 and $18.95 for all 36; **www.piratescove.net/orlando**). There is a near-identical Pirates Cove set-up at Lake Buena Vista at the back of the Crossroads shopping plaza. The unique **Putting Edge** has indoor glow-in-the-dark mini-golf at Artegon Orlando (1–9pm Mon–Thurs, noon–11pm Fri, 11am–11pm Sat, 11am–7pm Sun; $10.50 adults, $8.50 under 13s; unlimited play $2 extra) while **Volcano Island** adds 2 more 18-hole layouts, including a tricky par 45 (11am–11pm; $12.95 adults, $11.95 under 18s). Finally, the

Congo River

extensive **Gator Golf & Adventure Park** is just past Carrier Drive, next to Murphy's Arms Pub. With a variety of gator shows daily, you can sink your teeth into some challenging mini-golf (admission to park $5; golf $9.99 adults, $7.99 3–11s; gator photos, feeding and handling for additional fees; **www.idrivegatorgolf.com**).

Kissimmee: Here you'll find the scenic 36-hole **Congo River Golf & Exploration Co** set-up on Highway 192 (by Marker 12; $11.99 adults, $9.99 under-10s; 10am–11pm Sun–Thurs, 10am–midnight, Fri–Sat, **www.congoriver.com**); **Pirates Cove**, a 36-hole course next to Old Town (behind the Red Lobster, between markers 9 and 10); **Mighty Jungle Golf**, with 2 recently-renovated African-themed courses on Highway 192 by Formosa Gardens Blvd (10am–10pm Sun–Thurs, 11pm Fri & Sat; $9.95 adults, $8.95 under 12s; $2 extra for 2nd 18 holes); and **Pirates Island Adventure Golf**, off Highway 192 between marker 14 and 15 (10am–10pm).

Freshwater fishing

Freshwater fishing on central Florida's abundant rivers and lakes attracts enthusiasts worldwide. The primary draw is the chance to catch giant Florida bass – which grow to record sizes in the area's grassy waters – and view some of the wildlife in its natural environment.

To fish here you need a **Florida Freshwater Fishing License**, from the Florida Fish and Wildlife Commission (**http://myfwc.com/license/recreational/freshwater-fishing/** with a credit card). You'll be issued with a temporary licence number within minutes, enabling you to fish right away. A permanent licence will be mailed within 48 hours. A 3-day licence costs $17, 7-day $30. It's advisable to book at least 2 weeks in advance, especially at peak periods.

AJ's Freelancer Bass Guide Service: This long-running company specialises in trophy bass fishing on Lake Toho in Kissimmee. Toho is rated the best big bass lake in the USA, and AJ's holds the record for largemouth

bass – 16lb 10oz/7.5kg! Saltwater trips are also offered. All guides are experienced, full-time professionals and run trips of 4–8 hours. Rates start at $250 for a 4hr guided trip, max 3 clients per boat ($50 for 3rd person; 12 and under free). Visit the excellent website at **www.orlandobass.com** or call 407 288 9670.

Ultimate Guide Service: Another personal guide and fishing service with 36 years' experience and with trophy bass the principal aim, this is led by Captain Jim Passmore and is great for novices and even better for those seeking a real challenge. It makes for a superb day or ½ day and their attitude is notably one of low environmental impact. It costs $275 for 4hrs of fishing for 1–2 anglers, $325 for 6hrs or $375 for 8hrs (extra person $50), excluding fishing licence and lunch (407 572 5391, **www.fishcentralfla.com**).

Go bass fishing (catch-and-release) at **Walt Disney World** for $235–$270 for 2 hours for a boat with 1–5 people. It's advisable to book 24 hours in advance on 407 939 2277. For other opportunities, see **www.experiencekissimmee.com**, click Things To Do, then Nature, then Fishing & Charters.

Water sports
Florida is mad keen on water sports so, on any area of water bigger than your average pond, don't be surprised to find the locals water-skiing, jetskiing, knee-boarding, canoeing, paddling, windsurfing, boating or indulging in many other watery pursuits.

Buena Vista Watersports: This is the place for jet-skiing ($60/30 min, $105/hr; seats 2 adults and 1 child), water-skiing, wakeboard and tube rides ($55/15 min, $95/30min, $165/hr), plus rent pontoon boats, canoes, kayaks and stand-up paddle-boards ($25–125) on Little Lake Bryan by the Holiday Inn Sunspree on Highway 535 (407 239 6939, **www.bvwatersports.com**).

Orlando Watersports Complex: Just off the Beachline Expressway (528)

near Orlando International Airport, this is an elaborate facility featuring wake-boarding and water-skiing, by boat and suspended cable, for novices and experts (407 251 3100, **www.orlandowatersports.com**).

Walt Disney World: Disney offers all manner of boats (from catamarans to canoes and pedaloes) and activities (from water-skiing to parasailing) on Bay Lake, as well as the smaller Seven Seas Lagoon, Crescent Lake and Lake Buena Vista. Parasailing (from Disney's Contemporary Resort, p63) comes in 2 price categories: a Regular flight, which goes to 450ft/137m for 8–10 min, and a Premium flight to 600ft/183m for 10–12min. It costs $95–130 solo or $170–195 tandem, while boat rentals vary from $45/½ hr (21ft/6m pontoon boat) to $135/hr (personal watercraft and wave runners), and can be found at 11 Disney resorts. To book, call 407 939 0754.

Horse riding
For a more peaceful and scenic way to see some of Florida, take a tour on horseback.

Horse World Riding Stables: Out in rural Kissimmee, on Poinciana Boulevard (just 12ml/19km south of Highway 192), this gets you out into the wilds and you can spend anything from 1hr to a full day enjoying the rides and lessons. The 3 main rides through 750acres/304ha of untouched Florida countryside are the Nature Trail ($45.95 adults, $16.95 under-4s riding double with parent), a walking-only tour of 1hr for beginners aged 6 and up; the Intermediate Trail (10 and up) for 1hr ($55.95); and the Advanced Private Trail, a 1¼hr trip with a private guide for advanced riders ($79.95). There is also a picnic area with fishing pond, playing fields and farm animals to pet. Check the website for discounts (9am–5pm daily; 407 847 4343, **www.horseworldstables.com**).

Forever Florida also offers **Horseback Safaris**, an excellent way to see more of the 'real Florida' (p257).

Spectator events

When it comes to spectator events, Orlando isn't as well furnished as some cities, but there's always something for those who'd like to see a local game – and a real bonus for footy fans. There are no top-flight American football or baseball teams, but there is an indoor version of gridiron called Arena Football (the Orlando Predators at the Amway Center), plus Spring Training (pre-season) for several baseball teams (Atlanta in Disney's ESPN Wide World of Sports™ and Houston at Osceola County Stadium in Kissimmee).

Basketball: This is the main sport in town, with the Orlando Magic of the National Basketball Association (NBA). The season runs Nov–May (with exhibition games in Oct), and the only drawback is the 18,500-seat Amway Center where the team plays (on W Church Street, exit 82B off I-4) can be fully booked. Contact the Magic (407 896 2442, **www.orlandomagic.com**) to see if there are any tickets, but you'll have to call in person to buy them (from $10 in upper seats to $1,500 courtside), or try the excellent ticket resale company StubHub (**www.stubhub.com** or 1866 788 2482). *Brit Guide* partners Florida Dolphin Tours (p264) also offer Magic packages.

◀▌▶ **BRITTIP**

We rate the local sports highly if you want to experience some real Americana. You don't need to understand the game, just turn up and enjoy the excitement and fan-friendly atmosphere. Sports are a family event here.

American football: For the real thing, the nearest teams in the National Football League (NFL) are **Tampa Bay Buccaneers**, 75ml/120km to the west, **Miami Dolphins**, 3–4 hrs' drive south down the Florida Turnpike, or **Jacksonville Jaguars** up on the east coast past Daytona, a 3-hr drive on I-4 and I-95. Again, StubHub can usually give you ticket prices ($40–150) and availability (Sept–Dec). For spring training each March,

Osceola County Stadium for the Houston Astros is a real experience in local colour. Book online at **www.osceolastadium.com**, or TicketMaster (**www.ticketmaster.com**). However, the best opportunity is to head to St Petersburg on the Gulf Coast where the **Tampa Bay Rays** play at indoor Tropicana Field (Apr–Sept). Tickets are nearly always available and the indoor stadium is superb (p281).

Orlando City Soccer Club: Big news! This ambitious club will be playing in Major League Soccer (MLS), the top level of soccer in America, in 2015. They will play at the newly renovated 70,000-seat Citrus Bowl in downtown Orlando while their own stadium is built for 2016. Led by head coach Adrian Heath (ex-Everton and Stoke) and with British co-owners, they have built up a passionate and loyal following and games have become great events. Ticket prices were unknown as we went to press but the season runs from Mar–Oct, and the inaugural MLS campaign is sure to be a big event. And, if you already follow a team, you need to make 'The Lions' your No.2 club! (855 675 2489, **www.orlandocitysoccer.com**). NB: Be sure to see their website for special ticket offers once their schedule is announced in late Nov 2014.

ESPN Wide World of Sports™

Disney's big sports development is an impressive 220acre/86ha state-of-the-art complex, featuring 30 sports. It boasts a 9,500-seat baseball stadium, softball quadraplex, 10-court tennis complex, 5,000-seat indoor facility, athletics and extensive sports fields.

The Ballpark: Top of the crop for a must-see visit, this is home for spring training of baseball's **Atlanta Braves**, where the crowds flock for 16 pre-season games late Feb–late Mar (advance tickets highly recommended; individual tickets from Ticketmaster or the box office only). This is a big deal for American sports fans and games do sell out. The centre's extensive fields also cater for soccer, lacrosse, baseball and softball, and you can often see some keen sporting action just with college and school teams. **Disney's Soccer Showcase** (Sept–Jan) is a fine example of this, with some 400 skilful teams competing under the eye of various scouts. Standard admission is $16.50 adults, $11.50 3–9s, but it is also an option with Premium and Ultimate tickets (excluding special events like baseball). ESPN Wide World of Sports™ is off Osceola Parkway, on Victory Way (**www.espnwwos.com**).

Disney Soccer Academy: This series of 4-day training camps in Jun/Jul is for children 5–18, and focuses on age-appropriate coaching and technical development, small-sided games and encouragement from the stars. It costs $390/child and includes tuition by fully licensed coaches, an event T-shirt, special gift and lunch daily, plus appearances from British stars each year (1877 714 5575 or **www.midwestsoccer.net**).

Walt Disney World Marathon: A major annual event, its 17th running will be on 11 Jan 2015. Some 55,000 runners take part – including some of the world's leading athletes – drawing huge crowds and taking in all 4 Disney theme parks. Be aware the parks face some serious disruption but, as with the London Marathon, the Disney version is a great spectacle. The annual half-marathon takes place the same weekend.

Rodeo

An all-American pursuit straight out of the Old West, the **Silver Spurs Rodeo** is staged twice a year at the 8,300-seat Silver Spurs Arena. The biggest event of its kind in the south-east, it is held in Feb and early June (check website for dates). However, it sells out fast so book in advance on 321 677 6336 (**www.silverspursrodeo. com**). The event features classic bronco and bull riding and attracts competitors from as far as Canada. The arena is part of Osceola Heritage Park, which includes Osceola County Stadium (for baseball) and the Kissimmee Valley Livestock Show and Fair Pavilion. The Arena is a state-of-the-art facility and there isn't a bad seat in the house.

Motor sport

Richard Petty Driving Experience: For the ultimate in high-speed thrills, Walt Disney World has its own racetrack (next to the car park for the Magic Kingdom). Here on the 1-mile oval, you can experience one of its 650bhp stock cars as either driver or passenger at up to 145mph/233kph, with programmes devised by NASCAR legend Richard Petty. Choose from the 3-lap **Ride-Along Experience**; the 3hr **Rookie Experience** (with tuition and 8 laps of the speedway); the **Kings Experience** (tuition plus 18 laps); the **Experience of a Lifetime** (an intense 30-lap programme) and the ultimate experience of **Speedway Challenge** (50 laps, Ride-Along, shop tour with tech talk and lunch with instructor and Crew Chief). The Ride-Along will probably appeal to most (16 and over only) – 3 laps of the circuit with an experienced driver lasting just 37 seconds a lap but an unbelievable blast all the way. It's a bit like flying at ground level, is hot and noisy and you must wear sensible clothes (you climb in through the window), but it is definitely the real thing in ride terms and a huge thrill.

BRITBONUS

Show this edition of the *Brit Guide* to receive a free 2-lap upgrade when you book a full-priced Exotic Driving Experience at WDWS, and/or receive a free Ride-Along when you book a full priced Richard Petty Driving Experience at WDWS.

Preparing for the Exotic Driving Experience

You don't need to book the daily Ride-Along Experience and there is no admission fee, so you can come along just to watch (8am–1pm). The 3 driving programmes (not Tues or Thurs; Sun offers Ride-Along only) all need reservations. However, wait for the prices: $109 for Ride-Along (age 14–19 ride for $29 with paying Ride-Along adult); Junior Ride Along $69 (6–13s); $449 for Rookie; $849 for Kings; $1,299 for the Experience of a Lifetime and $2,099 for Speedway Challenge. You must be 18 or over for all but the Ride-Along (1800 237 3889, **www.drivepetty.com**).

Exotic Driving Experience: If you have ever fancied driving a super-car like a Ferrari 458, Audi R8, Porsche 997 or Lamborghini Gallardo, this Speedway offering is for you. Available either as a 2-lap **Thrill Ride** or the full 6-lap **Driving Experience**, it is a genuine taste of dream car style around a modified course, using the longest banked turn and straight of the main Oval and a hairpin turn into a street section featuring switchbacks and S-bends. The ride-along is an obvious thrill, but the driving experience is the Real Thing for car enthusiasts, with a proper driving induction followed by 6 laps with a professional instructor in the passenger seat to provide coaching and feedback. The 200mph/320kph cars will do 0–60mph/96kph in under 4secs and hit a top speed of around 120mph/192kph on the track, but it FEELS faster and the lateral G-forces and braking power are truly immense (don't do this just after a meal!). The

cars for the Thrill Ride ($105/person) are chosen at random but drivers can pick their own super-car ($199–439); over 6ft 2in/1.88m may not fit). Riders must be at least 14 (under 18s accompanied by a parent) and drivers at least 18 with full driving licence (9am–4pm, most days, but bookings advisable on 1855 822 0149; **www.exoticdriving.com**).

Daytona International Speedway: Just up the road in Daytona (take I-4 east, then I-95 and Highway 92), race fans will find more big-league thrills. The renowned Speedway hosts more than a dozen events a year, including motor-bike, stock car, sports car and go-karts. Highlights are the Rolex 24 (a 24-hr sports car event, late Jan), the famous Daytona 500 (Feb), and Coke Zero 400 (early July). The big events attract crowds of 200,000-plus and offer exhilarating sport (800 748 7467, **www.daytonainternationalspeedway.com**).

The Richard Petty Driving Experience is available here, too (16 and over only), and the $135 fee for 3 laps of the world-famous, steeply banked 2½ml/4km tri-oval includes a track tour. Or just look for the 1hr All Access Track Tour, daily on the hour from 10am–3pm ($23 adults, $17 6–12s, under-6s free) and a ½hr Speedway Tour at 11.30am, 1.30pm, 3.30pm and 4pm ($16 adults, $10 6–12s, under-6 free). There is even a special VIP Tour on specific dates (see website) at $50/person. Fascinating and fun, even for non-race fans!

OK, that's the local area sorted out; now let's take you further afield…

All ready for the Exotic Driving Experience with the Ferrari 458

9 The Twin Centre Option

While Orlando continues to get bigger and better, it is equally true there is a LOT more to see in the rest of Florida, with some magnificent twin-centre options. From St Augustine in the north-east to Key West in the extreme south (the 'Floribbean'), it's easy to find wonderful resorts, glorious beaches and more family attractions.

The beaches of the Gulf (west) coast, the Atlantic coast from Ormond Beach all the way to Miami, and the fabulous Florida Keys all feature some of the best seaside escapes in the world, while cities like West Palm Beach, Daytona, St Augustine, Fort Lauderdale, Tampa, Miami and Key West provide more Sunshine State fascination. Two-centre (or fly-drive) options are common with most tour operators, but it is also easy to arrange your own, for 1 or 2 weeks or just a night. A cruise-and-stay holiday is also a great choice, with the ports of Tampa, Port Canaveral, Fort Lauderdale and Miami within easy reach.

You can head out from Orlando in any direction in search of a great twin-centre experience. Go East to Cocoa Beach, New Smyrna Beach, Ormond Beach and Daytona Beach, all with terrific appeal and barely an hour's drive away; the sea is a degree or so cooler on the Atlantic side, and the surf and currents are more noticeable, hence this is good surfing territory, but beware possible undertows if you are travelling with children. To the north-east you have historic St Augustine about 2hrs away. To the north-west is the growing resort area of Panama City Beach. Go West for the city of Tampa and miles of pristine sands, from Clearwater Beach south to Naples and lovely Marco Island; this is better for families with younger children, while the Clearwater-St Pete Beach area is a perfect combo with Orlando (about 1½–2hrs' drive). Go South-East and you hit Vero Beach, West Palm Beach, Fort Lauderdale and Miami (about a 4hr drive). Continue South and there are the Keys, a superb 110ml/177km chain of islands linked by roads and bridges, culminating in eclectic Key West. So, heading north-east first, here's what you find.

> **BRITTIP**
> The Florida Turnpike (toll) is the main route south-east from Orlando, but it is a dull drive. If time is not a factor, take the Beachline Expressway (528) east and then I-95 or, better still, Highway 1, south for a more rewarding journey. Or go south on Highway 27 and take in the charming town of Sebring.

St Augustine

A 2hr drive up I-4 and I-95 brings you to America's oldest city. Founded by Spanish conquistadors in 1565, St Augustine is full of authentic buildings and signs of the original settlement around the imposing Castillo de San Marcos. Much of the original walled city still remains and 'old' is a much-revered term here, as 18th and 19th-century Mediterranean influences are everywhere. Walk the narrow, uneven streets of the Restoration Area to discover colonial architectural treasures, now home to gift shops, restaurants, pubs, ice-cream parlours, antique shops, quaint B&Bs and other attractions.

BRITTIP
Spanish adventurer Ponce de Leon was searching for the Fountain of Youth when he arrived at the site of St Augustine in 1513. The modern day **Archaeological Park** tells the story of his arrival and discovery of the continent of America – and offers the chance to drink the famous waters. Visit **www. fountainofyouthflorida.com**.

Tours: To see as much as possible, hop on a horse-drawn carriage, the **St Augustine Sightseeing Train** or the **Old Town Trolley Tours** for a narrated tour. For a spookier experience, walk the streets with **Ghost Tours of St Augustine**, with your guide in period costume. Other tours reveal the architectural heritage (also the product of British and colonial American rule).

Other attractions: Florida railway mogul Henry Flagler was another big influence, building some magnificent hotels for his 'passengers to paradise'. The ornate **Lightner Museum**, formerly Flagler's Hotel Alcazar, is home to his turn-of-the-century treasures, including Tiffany and other glass works of art. There's a modern theatre, art galleries, **Potter's Wax Museum**, **Ripley's Believe It Or Not Museum** and **Whetstone Chocolate Factory**. New in 2014 was the **St Augustine Distillery**, a chance to tour a working small-batch premium distillery and learn the history of the converted ice factory (free tours daily, 10am–6m Mon–Sat, 11am Sun; **http://staugustinedistillery.com/**).

Restaurants: These range from **Hot Shot Bakery** and the famous, family-owned **Columbia Restaurant**, to a modern microbrewery, **A1A Ale Works**. Golf fans should visit nearby Ponte Vedra for the World Golf Hall of Fame.

Where to stay: The premier hotel is historic **Casa Monica** (904 827 1888, **www.casamonica.com**), while the boutique **St George Inn** (904 827 5740; **www.stgeorge-inn.com**) is also a good choice, but there are numerous B&Bs, plus chain hotels like Best Western and Hampton Inn.

BRITTIP
Festivals are an integral part of St Augustine, from monthly art walk nights to annual costumed torchlight re-enactments of British occupation and the City Birthday on 8 Sept.

More info: St Augustine Visitors & Convention Bureau (1800 653 2489 or **www.floridashistoriccoast.com**).

Volusia County
Travel south from St Augustine and you arrive in this famous beach area.

BRITTIP
Look out for Speeding Through Time, a series of memorials and plaques along Daytona's Boardwalk, highlighting the world speed records set on the beaches, including those of Britons Sir Henry Segrave and Sir Malcolm Campbell.

Daytona Beach: Only 1hr from Orlando along I-4 east, this area now includes some chic hotels and restaurants, but is still family friendly. It is busiest in summer (mid-June to mid-Aug) but there is something for everyone, especially in the quieter period after Easter when there are often some good deals. The prime attraction is the good beaches (some of which you can drive on – for a $5 toll, speed limit 10mph/16kph). From these open expanses of sands, you can go boating, parasailing, biking, jet-skiing and fishing. Stay in the Oceanfront area and you are at the heart of all things beach-related, with the Pier – now including the huge Sand Blaster rollercoaster – historic Bandshell, Boardwalk and the shops and restaurants of **Ocean Walk Village**.

Here you have RC Theatres' **Ocean Walk Movies 10 Cineplex**, the fun of the **Mai Tai Bar**, **Sloppy Joe's**, **Johnny Rockets Diner**, **Cold Stone Creamery**, **Starbucks**, **Ker's Winghouse** and unique shopping at **Maui Nix Surf Shop**, **Global Candle Gallery**, **Point Break** and **Sunglass Hut**. When you're hungry, try the film-themed style of **Bubba Gump Shrimp Co** (based on the movie *Forrest Gump*). With fun decor, wonderfully casual vibe and an excellent menu, it is ideal for a quick lunch or leisurely dinner (**www.bubbagump.com** and **www.oceanwalkshoppes.com**).

◀🇬🇧▶ **BRITTIP**

Spend the day on Daytona Beach, then try some water park fun at Daytona Lagoon after 3pm, when admission is only $12.99.

Daytona Lagoon: Opposite Ocean Walk Village, this is a combination water park, go-kart track, mini-golf course, arcade and laser tag centre. The water park has a wave pool and lazy river, 7 different flumes and an area purely for toddlers (adults $27.99, children under 3ft 6in/108cm $20.99). The 18-hole mini-golf course ($7), single and double go-karts ($8–10), laser tag (must be above 3ft 6in/108cm, $7), Island Hopper kiddie ride ($3.49) and Rock Wall ($7) are all separate items. See more at **www.daytonalagoon.com**.

Historic Downtown Daytona Beach: The heart of the city is on Beach Street, with a museum of local history, restaurants, nightclubs, coffee bars and a performing arts theatre. The **Angell & Phelps Chocolate Factory** (established 1925, **www.angellandphelps.com**) is another notable curiosity. Head to the **Riverfront** in early evening when the street takes on a café society style. There are plenty of good places to eat,

but for something different try the lively **Caribbean Jack's** (right on the river at Ballough Road) or chic **Chez Paul** (on N Beach St with a view of the Halifax River). Similar upmarket choices are **Martini's Chophouse Restaurant** (on S Ridgewood Avenue) and the fine Italian dining of **The Cellar** (on Magnolia Avenue). **Vince Carter's** (on LPGA Blvd, co-owned by the basketball star) is another smart choice, with a chic Dining Room, eye-catching **Highlight Zone Sports Grill** and relaxing **Piano Lounge** (**http://vincecarters.com**).

Other highlights: Taking **The Manatee** scenic river voyage out of Ponce Inlet is a great choice. Their leisurely 2hr tours go year-round at 10am, 1 and 4pm, plus a 7pm Sunset Cruise Jun–Sept (on Inlet Harbor Rd; $25 for adults, $22 seniors, $16 children; reservations required on 386 761 2027, or **www.manateecruise. com**). Go south on Atlantic Avenue and you find even more choice of beaches and attractions, including **Sun Splash Beach**, **Frank Rendon Park** and **Lighthouse Point Park**, a 52acre/21ha stretch of nature trails, fishing, observation deck, swimming and picnicking (8am–9pm; $5/car). The tide here can retreat up to 500ft/150m and the beaches, open to the public year-round, tend to be quieter, though there can be some serious rip-tides. At the southern end of the beaches is the wonderful **Ponce de Leon Inlet Lighthouse**, with a formidable 203 spiralling steps to the top. This well-preserved monument is a magnificent re-creation of 19th-century Florida maritime life and the view from the top of America's second tallest lighthouse is superb (10am–6pm, 9pm Jun–Aug; $5 adults, $1.50 under-12s; **http://ponceinlet.org/**). It also has a lovely gift shop. Ponce Inlet has some great deep-sea fishing, too – see **www.inletharbor.com**.

◀🇬🇧▶ **BRITTIP**

Try a meal at the **Hidden Treasure Rum Bar & Grill** at Ponce Inlet for an eclectic Floridian experience.

Marine Science Center: More family-orientated fun can be found round the corner from the lighthouse, showcasing mangrove, manatee and sea turtle exhibits, a seabird sanctuary and turtle rehab facility. It has a huge artificial reef aquarium, plus static and interactive educational displays. A boardwalk and nature trail extend through the Center, which also has a gift shop (10am–4pm Tues–Sat, noon–4pm Sun, closed Mon; $5 adults, $4 seniors, $2 under-13s; http://marinesciencecenter.com/).

Daytona Speedway: Of course, this is one of the biggest draws (p272), with 2 great tours of this amazing facility that is undergoing a $400m renovation.

Three Brothers Boards: this family-run business of handcrafted stand-up paddleboards offers tours and rentals on the beautiful Halifax River, with its plentiful wildlife. Choose from the 2hr Dolphin & Manatee Adventure or the Nature Tour through mangrove trails and bird sanctuaries. You may even be inspired to try paddleboard yoga! Call 386 310 4927 or visit **www.threebrothersboards.com**.

New Smyrna Beach: Continue south on Highway 1 to this fabulous 13ml/20km stretch of pristine white sands with great surfing, shell collecting and boating at any of the many marinas. New Smyrna Beach is also a big festival destination, notably for the **Shrimp & Seafood Festival** each August and the **Jazz Festival** over a weekend in late September. Other highlights include the shopping and dining of historic and pedestrian-friendly **Canal Street**, with a farmers' market each Saturday (7am–1pm, **www.canalstreetnsb.com**), more unique shops and galleries along **Flagler Avenue** (**www.flaglerave.com**), the kid-friendly **Marine Discovery Center** and the **Atlantic Center for the Arts**. For dining, don't miss **The Garlic**, with outdoor seating under huge oaks (386 428 1600, **www.nsbfla.com**).

Where to stay: You'll find some of our favourite resorts in Daytona Beach, plus a variety of Select Small Inns (**www.daytonabeach.com/hotels/select-small-inns/**). The **Wyndham Ocean Walk Resort** is a huge ultra-modern complex right on the beach at Ocean Walk Village, with versatile 1, 2 and 3-bed condos (all with kitchens and fab views). With 3 outdoor pools, waterslide and lazy river, plus a kids' water play area, 2 indoor pools, indoor mini-golf, kids' programmes, spa and an excellent lounge and food court, it is hugely family-friendly (386 323 4800, **www.wyndhamoceanwalk.com**). The nearby **Hilton Daytona Beach Oceanfront Resort** is another large, recently renovated hotel with wonderfully spacious rooms, beachfront cabañas and suites, plus a terrific dining choice (notably Hyde Park Prime Steakhouse), 2 pools and a modern fitness centre (386 254 8200, **www.daytonahilton.com**). **Shores Resort & Spa** is a boutique choice on a quieter stretch of the beaches, (386 767 7350, **www.shoresresort.com**), while the new 10-storey oceanfront **Hyatt Place** is also a chic choice with its spacious family rooms (386 944 2010, **http://daytonabeach.place.hyatt.com**). Try **Flamingo Inn** for a great example of the Small Inns of Daytona Beach. With a tranquil oceanfront setting, heated free-form pool, tropical Key West styling and some rooms with kitchenettes (and all with fridges), it is a real boutique bargain here (386 252 7212, **www.daytonamotel.com**). More info: 01737 643 764 in the UK, 386 255 0415 in the US or visit **www.daytonabeach.com**.

BRITBONUS

For a special *Brit Guide* rate, **East Coast Paddle** offers $10 off per person on groups of 4 or more. Remember to mention the *Brit Guide* when you book.

Ormond Beach: Immediately to the north is another happening area with more smart resorts and beaches, notably at **Bicentennial Park** (with a nature walk, playground and fishing dock) and **Birthplace of Speed Park** (commemorating the first automobile race on the beach here in 1903). Don't miss **The Casements**, the

Breakfast with a difference!

Just north of DeLand in Del eon Springs State Park is the unique **Old Spanish Sugar Mill** grill and griddle house, one of Florida's little restaurant treasures. Famous for hearty cook-it-yourself breakfasts (9am–4pm; 8am at weekends), each table has an inset griddle, and you choose your ingredients and get cracking. Its speciality is pancakes (pitchers of batter provided), with all manner of fillings, but it also has bacon, eggs, ham, sausage, home-made breads, French toast, sandwiches and salads. You'll struggle to pay more than $10/person and it's great fun, as well as a local institution. However, as it is inside the State Park, there is a $6/car entry fee (386 985 5644, **www.planetdeland.com/sugarmill**). You can then try the park facilities, which include canoes, kayaks, hiking trails and boat tours (**www.floridastateparks.org**).

restored former Rockefeller House and Gardens, with free tours twice a day Mon–Sat (**www.thecasements. net**). And, for a different shopping experience, **Dunn's Attic & Auction House** takes some beating (**www. dunnsattic.com**). Stop for a meal at the fun **Lulu's Oceanside Grill** with a wonderful seafood-laden menu, great cocktails and live music on Fri and Sat evenings, **www.lulusoceansidegrill.com**). Or sample the chic **Fusion 43** (**www.fusion43.com**) or the eclectic **Grind Gastropub & Kona Tiki Bar** (**www.grindgastropub.com**).

DeLand and St Johns River Country: Just west of Daytona and home to several nature preserves (**www.visitwestvolusia.com**).

The Space Coast

Further south on the Atlantic seaboard is the 'Space Coast', home to the iconic Kennedy Space Center (p217).

BRITTIP

For good info on all Kennedy Space Center rocket launches, especially good public viewing locations, see http://spacecoastlaunches.com/.

Cocoa Beach: Closest to Orlando, barely 50mins east (on the Beachline Expressway 528, then south on Highway A1A), this area has 2 excellent public beaches plus trademark shopping at Ron Jon's Surf Shop, a massive neon emporium of all things water related. As it's the Atlantic, the sea can be chilly Nov–

Apr, but its resort style ensures good facilities (**www.cocoabeach.com**). Cocoa Beach is also home to the excellent **Planetarium & Observatory**, which holds daily shows in its large-screen cinema and world-class planetarium, plus an exhibition hall, art gallery and gift shop, all on Eastern Florida State College campus (321 433 7373, **www.easternflorida.edu/community-resources/planetarium/**). If you haven't tried an airboat ride by now, you should definitely head for **Midway Airboats** on the nearby St John River (daily from 9am; 407 568 6790, **www. airboatridesatmidway.com/**), and don't forget **Island Boat Lines** (p263).

Titusville: Head here for attractions like the **US Space Walk of Fame** (a river walk with displays of memorabilia, plaques and public art depicting America's history in space), **Merritt Island National Wildlife Refuge** (a 6ml/9km driving tour adjacent to the Kennedy Space Center) and the fascinating and rather moving **American Police Hall of Fame & Museum**, with all you ever wanted to know about the history of crime and law enforcement, and a tribute to police officers who have died in the line of duty (see **www.aphf.org** for $3 off coupon).

Aviation fans will enjoy the **Valiant Air Command Warbird Museum**, with dozens of vintage warplanes and fully guided tours through the exhibits and history of military aviation, as well as their dedicated restoration programme (**www.vacwarbirds.org**). Look out especially for the 3-day **Warbird Air Show** here in Mar.

BRITTIP
For something truly unique, **Valiant Air Command Warbird Museum** now offers regular flights on its beautifully restored vintage WWII C-47 paratroop transport plane for $175/person. Call 321 268 1941 or email vacwarbirds@bellsouth. net for full details and availability.

Melbourne: Family-friendly **Brevard Zoo** is well worth a visit here, with almost 500 animals in 5 themed areas, including the excellent Cheetah Complex in the Expedition Africa exhibit. Other highlights include Asia/ Australia, La Selva (South America), Wild Florida and Paws On Play, where children can enjoy water play, and the new Meerkat Hamlet (9.30am–5pm; $16 adults, $15 seniors, $12 2–12s; 321 254 9453, **https://brevardzoo.org/**).

BRITTIP
For top value at Brevard Zoo, consider a **Young Explorer's Package** (admission, train ride, giraffe and lorikeet feeding at $20.50, $19.50 and $16.50) or **Wild Explorer's** version (a choice of kayaking in Wild Florida or Expedition Africa, plus giraffe and lorikeet feeding at $22.75, $21.75 and $18.75).

Where to stay: Try lively, surf-themed **Four Points by Sheraton Cocoa Beach** (321 783 8717, **www.fourpointscocoabeach.com**) or **International Palms Resort** (321 783 2271, **www.internationalpalms.com**). More info: 321 433 4470 or **www.space-coast.com**.

Tampa

Going west from Orlando brings you down I-4 to the bright city of Tampa, right on a major sea bay and with some excellent attractions of its own.

Dinosaur World: Right on I-4 as you head to Tampa (and a nice stopping point by exit 17) is this family-run attraction ideal for 3–8s. With more than 200 life-sized dinosaurs in a lush, natural setting, plus walking trails, picnic area, playgrounds and gift shop, it makes a good diversion for several hours. There are no

rides, but there are various life-size animatronic set-pieces – including a triceratops and pterodactyl – along with a Prehistoric Museum featuring authentic fossils from dinosaur eggs to raptor claws and mammoth teeth. The different trails then feature more dino models with explanatory signs, plus a cave-themed video theatre, while the Skeleton Garden features 6 replica skeletons. There are also 2 play areas, for under 7s and older children, and an expanded fossil dig with fossils you can take home. The park is totally laid back and a nice change of pace from the main parks. There is no café (just drinks machines), but it does have picnic facilities and there are fast-food locations nearby, including a pizza delivery service (9am–6pm; 5pm Nov–Jan; $14.95 adult, $12.95 seniors, $11.95 3–12s, under-3 free; 813 717 9865, **http://dinosaurworld.com/ florida/**).

Florida Aquarium: In the heart of Tampa is this superb journey into Florida's waterways, coast and deep-sea elements, beautifully presented and ultra child-friendly. It starts with the Wetlands, then moves on to the new Journey to Madagascar (with lemurs and colourful chameleons), Bays & Beaches (including Sea Turtle Corner), the Touch Tank, Coral Reefs, Dragons Down Under (the amazing leafy sea-dragons from Australia), Ocean Commotion (full of interactive touch-screens, videos and podcasts) and the outdoor Explore A Shore water-play area, with squirt pools, fountains and pirate ship, plus an excellent tropical-themed Bar & Grill. Other highlights are the daily Penguin Promenade (where one of the Aquarium's penguins is brought out for a meet-and-greet), and Shark Bay, where anyone 15 and older who is scuba-certified can join the daily dive into the lagoon ($175/person, reservations required on 813 2713 4015). Other extras include a daily 20min non-scuba 'Swim with the fishes' reef swim ($75/person), a 2hr Shark Feeding programme every Sun, a daily 30min Behind The Scenes tour ($12) and a new Stingray Feeding Tour (8 and over only). There's also a daily (weather permitting) Wild Dolphin Eco-Tour on their 130-passenger catamaran, leaving from the aquarium to explore the Bay where more than 500 dolphins live, along with the occasional manatee (9.30am–5pm daily, closed Thanksgiving, Christmas Day; parking $6; $23.95 adults, $20.95 seniors, $18.95 under-12s; with Dolphin Eco-Tour, $49.90, $44.90 and $40.90; 813 273 4000, **www.flaquarium.org**; also on Tampa CityPass, p280).

◀◆▶ BRITTIP

Book tickets online for the Florida Aquarium and save several dollars on their regular prices.

Channelside Bay Plaza: Next door is a centre of shops and restaurants, which is well worth exploring for unique stores like **Lit Cigar Lounge**, **Surf Down Under**, **White House Gear**, **Del Sol** and **Quachbal Chocolatier**, plus great entertainment and dining. Choose from the fun **Fusion Flambe**, **Hooters**, **Oishi Sushi**, **Tina Tapa's**, **Splitsville** 10-pin bowling (who also own the Splitsville in Downtown Disney), lively **Wet Willie's** bar, **Thai Tani** and **Precinct Pizza**, plus **Coldstone Creamery** (great ice-cream and shakes). Like Ybor City, this is where Tampa parties – hence the restaurants and bars, many featuring live music, are hopping at weekends. There's also an **Official Tampa Bay Visitor Center** (**www. channelsidebayplaza.com**).

Lowry Park Zoo: Rated one of the top zoos in America, this lush 60-scre spread showcases manatees, koalas, elephants, tigers, penguins, giraffes and orangutans among its more than 1,000 animals. Kids will also enjoy the water-play areas, educational shows and even rides, like Gator Falls flume ride and Outback Bumper Boats. There are extensive natural animal habitats and the chance (for a few extra dollars) to interact with some of them, including giraffes and lorikeets (9.30am–5pm; $24.95 adults, $22.95 seniors, $19.95 3–11s; **www.lowryparkzoo.com**; also on Tampa

CityPass, p280). Animal lovers should also make a note of **Big Cat Rescue**, a non-profit park that sets out to rescue various lions, tigers, panthers and more that have been abandoned, ill-treated or retired from various shows. It runs 90min tours and all proceeds go into the care and rehab of the 100-plus animals. Other options include Feeder, Keeper and Private tours (3pm Mon, Tue, Wed & Fri, 10am & 1pm Sat & Sun, $36/person, over 10s only; Under-10s tour 9am Sat & Sun for $19; other tours $65–125; 1888 316 5875, **http://bigcatrescue.org**).

Museum of Science and Industry: More family fun (especially for 4–12s) can be found at this entertaining science centre, with 3 floors of educational exhibits, activities and large-screen IMAX films. Highlights include the **Kids In Charge** science play area (under-13s), **The Amazing You** (a tour of the human body), **Disasterville** (an interactive look at natural disasters) and the **High-Wire Bicycle** (ride a bike on a steel cable 30ft/9m up). Permanent exhibits include **Sky Trail Ropes Course** (with 2 ziplines) and **The Saunders Planetarium**, while the **IMAX® Dome Theatre** offers a range of films daily and there are periodic travelling exhibits. Outside is the **BioWorks Butterfly Garden** and the **Historic Tree Grove**, providing more insight into natural Florida (9am–5pm Mon–Fri, 6pm Sat and Sun; $22.95 adults, $20.95 seniors, $18.95 2–12s, includes Kids in Charge, 1 standard IMAX film and Planetarium show; additional films $8.95, $7.95 and $6.95; SkyTrail Ropes and Zipline are $20 extra with admission; 813 987 6100, **www.mosi. org**; also on Tampa CityPass, p280).

Ybor City: Tampa's other entertainment district can be found in the rejuvenated Cuban quarter of the city, where a fine mix of shops and restaurants provide a lively vibe both by day and at night. Top dining choices include **Hamburger Mary's** (tempting burgers), **Carne Chop House** (fine steaks and seafood) and **Samurai Blue** (sushi and sake) while the lively bar scene offers **Centro Cantina** and (our fave) the

Tampa Bay Brewing Co, a British-run brewpub with a varied menu, great range of beers, multiple TV screens and pool table. Find more fun at **Game Time**, an upscale arcade of games and bars and the **Improv Comedy Theatre**, busiest on Fri and Sat but bustling most nights (**www.centroybor.com**). Start at the **Visitor Center & Museum**, which shows a fascinating film on the history of the city, and the well-presented **Ybor City Museum** on East 9th Avenue (9am–5pm; $4/person, under-6s free; **www.ybormuseum.org**). You can also tour the area on the new **Electric Glide** Segway tours, a fabulous way to sight-see and have fun at the same time on these 2-wheeled machines (Mon–Wed at 10am, 1 and 3.30pm; $65/person; 1800 979 3370, **http://electricglidetours.com/**).

Much of downtown Tampa, including Ybor City and Channelside, is linked by the **TECO Line Streetcar**, replicas of authentic electric trams, with 1-way fares of $2.50 (cash only) or $5 for an all-day card. A Family All Day Ticket ($12.50, for up to 5) is available from ticket machines.

BRITTIP

Visit the Columbia Restaurant in Ybor City. Opened in 1905, it incorporates a whole city block that was gradually absorbed into this Spanish/Cuban bar-diner. Ask at the host stand if they can give you a tour, with the story of the Gonzmart family (813 248 4961, **www.columbiarestaurant.com**).

Yuengling Brewery: For a fascinating free brewery tour, try this modern facility near Busch Gardens (on 10th street, parallel to McKinley Drive, where you enter the theme park). It brews up to 9 beers (2 seasonal), including a fab lager and porter. With guided tours at 10am, 11.30am and 1pm Mon–Fri, it shows off the creative process behind the company, then offers a couple of samples! The Gift Shop is open 10am–3pm, and you are likely to see the full interior workings of the brewery, including the bottling and canning plant (813 972 8500, **www.yuengling.com**). NB:

Must wear close-toed shoes for the tour; no sandals or flip-flops; children welcome.

Where to stay: Try the boutique style of historic **Don Vicente Inn** in Ybor City, a beautiful period refurbishment of a 19th-century building with just 16 individual rooms (813 241 4545, **http://donvicenteinn.com/**). More info: Visitor Center 813 223 2752 or **www.visittampabay.com**.

BRITTIP

The new Tampa Bay **CityPass** card can provide savings on 5 main area attractions, including Busch Gardens, Clearwater Marine Aquarium, the Florida Aquarium and Lowry Park Zoo. It costs $119 adults and $99 3–9s. See more at **www.citypass.com/tampa**.

St Pete/Clearwater

Continue west and you have the gorgeous Gulf Coast, a 2hr drive down I-4 and through Tampa on I-275 south to St Pete Beach (105ml/169km) or Clearwater Beach (110ml/177km), with a string of beautiful resorts in between, all featuring white-sand beaches, water sports and far fewer crowds than you would think, plus the smart Beach Walk in Clearwater. The sea is a bit warmer and calmer on this side of Florida so is more suitable for small children. The 35ml/56km stretch from St Pete–Clearwater represents the heart of the Sunshine State beach experience and is one of the most popular 2-centre options. It has a wonderful array of attractions and averages 361 days of sun a year.

BRITTIP

Do the 'stingray shuffle' in the sea here from Apr–Oct. Whenever you are in the water, move your feet through the sand without lifting them up to ensure you alert the occasional stingray to your presence. They will then move away without bothering anyone. Neosporin is a good antiseptic if you are stung.

St Petersburg: This city, just across the Howard Frankland Bridge from Tampa, is a wonderful mix of the old and the new, with a fast-developing Art District (8 museums, dozens of galleries and counting) and a real café society feel. Take time for the world-renowned **Dali Museum** (10am–5.30pm Mon–Wed, 8pm Thurs, 5.30pm Fri and Sat, noon–5.30pm Sun; $21 adults, $19 seniors, $15 13–18s and students, $7 6–12s; **www.thedali.org**), and the **Chihuly Collection** at the Morean Arts Center, a superb showcase of the American glass artist, with guided tours on the hour every ½hr. There's also a separate glass studio and hot shop nearby (10–6pm Mon–Sat, noon–6pm Sun; $14 adults, $13 seniors, $10 students and children over 5; $5 $4, $2 for Hot Shop; combo ticket $19.95, $17.95, $12.95; 727 896 4527, **www.moreanartscenter. org**; also on Tampa CityPass, p280). Other highlights include the elegant **Museum of Fine Arts**, with its 2 interior gardens (**www.fine-arts.org**), the **St Petersburg Museum of History** (**www.spmoh.com**), and fascinating **Great Explorations Children's Museum** (**www.greatexplorations.org**). Pedestrian-friendly streets plenty of interest, while the **Bay Walk** complex adds restaurants, shops and a **Muvico** IMAX 20-screen cinema (**www.yourbaywalk.com**). Also visit the fan-friendly **Tropicana Field**, which hosts the Tampa Bay Rays baseball team (Apr–Sept) for terrific local entertainment ($10–300; **http:// tampabay.rays.mlb.com**). And try the **All About Fun Tours** from the Museum of History on 2-wheeled Segways. They are easy to master and provide a superb view of the city's miles of waterfront parks, beaches and residences with your knowledgeable guide. Ages 12 and over (max 275lb/125kg; Tues–Sat 10.30am and 2pm, Sun 12.30 and 2.30pm; 1hr tour $35, 90min $50; call for reservations on 727 896 3640, **www.gyroglides.com**).

Weedon Island Preserve: Enjoy the rich cultural history of this 3,700acre/1,500ha seaside nature park in St Petersburg. Start at the **Natural History Center** (the main entrance, confusingly, is at the back) and learn about the prehistoric and Native American settlements here (plus periodic exhibitions), then go up to the 3rd floor observation deck. There are several miles of boardwalks and trails around the tidal wetlands, which are home to a wildlife like ospreys, turtles, spoonbills, turtles, mangrove crabs, raccoons and gopher tortoises, and guided hikes on Sats at 9am (call to register; Center open 9am–4pm Thurs-Sat, free entry; Preserve open 7am–dusk; 727 453 6500, **www.weedonislandpreserve.org**). The more energetic may want to try a paddle round the shallow waters with **Sweetwater Kayaks**. This close encounter with nature (stingrays, jumping mullet and the occasional manatee) is offered on an hourly or 4hr basis (10am–4pm Mon–Fri, 9am and 1pm Sat & Sun; $40 for a 4hr single-kayak rental, $56 for double, or $17 and $25 hourly; booking advised on 727 570 4844 or **www.sweetwaterkayaks.com**).

BRITTIP

Insect repellent is essential for any visit to Weedon Island Preserve as it is not sprayed for mosquitoes, and the little pests will feed on tourists!

Beaches: You are spoiled for choice, from the 1,100acre/445ha **Fort De Soto Park** in the south to stunning **Caladesi Island State Park** in the north (regularly voted in America's Top 10). There is plenty to do, too, with the likes of **Treasure Island**, **Sand Key** and **St Pete Beach** all receiving the Blue Wave Award for cleanliness and safety. Fort De Soto Park offers free walking tours of its Spanish-American War-era fort, while John's Pass Village is an eclectic shopping district and marina full of art galleries and restaurants, plus the fun **Pirate Cruise** – a replica sailing ship offering a 2hr party cruise ($35 adults, $30 65 and over, $25 under-20s, $10 under-3s, inclusive of beer, wine and soft drinks; 11am, 2pm and sunset; call for reservations on 727 423 7824) and 90min **Dolphin Quest** boat tour at noon, 2, 4 and 6pm daily ($19.50 adults, $17.50 seniors, $15 under 20s; call for reservations on 727 392 7090). Parasailing, jet-skiing, fishing, boat rentals and tours are also popular (**www.johnspass.com**).

Dolphin Landings: A don't miss in St Pete Beach, with a pair of 51ft/15.5m yachts that sail on 2hr trips along the calm inland waterway (9.30am, noon & 2.15pm, Mon–Sat, noon & 2.15pm Sun) for close-up dolphin-watch cruises and sunset sailings, plus a Sunset Sail, 4hr trip around beautiful Egmont Key and a 3½hr trip to Shell Key, with up to 2hrs on the beach ($45 adults, $35 children; 727 367 4488, **www.charterboatescape.com**).

◀▦▶ BRITTIP

Most public beaches will have toilets, changing facilities and picnic tables, but there is usually a parking fee.

Suncoast Seabird Sanctuary: Further north at Indian Shores is America's largest wild bird hospital, caring for injured birds including birds of prey, pelicans, spoonbills and egrets. No charge but donations to visit this non-profit-making rehabilitation centre (9am–sunset, 727 391 6211, **www.seabirdsanctuary.com**).

◀▦▶ BRITTIP

Don't leave without visiting the area's top attraction, a dolphin called Winter, the star of films *Dolphin Tale* and *Dolphin Tale 2* with Morgan Freeman. Rescued from a crab trap, her tail had to be amputated and she was not expected to survive. Happily, she not only lived but has learned to swim with a prosthetic tail!

Clearwater Beach: Continue north to acres of clean, white sands and the **Clearwater Marine Aquarium**, a wonderful non-profit organisation that rescues and rehabilitates injured dolphins, turtles, river otters and more (especially good for under-12s). There are 13 main exhibits, including Turtle Cove, Otter Oasis, Shark Pass and Shipwreck Alley but much of the focus is on the area's Hollywood 'star', Winter the tail-less dolphin (see the Winter Zone.

Seminole Central

Head west out of Fort Lauderdale to Big Cypress and you find the rewarding **Ah-Tah-Thi-Ki Museum**, home to the Seminole tribe of Florida. Here you can learn about Native American culture, from its customs to the bitter 19th century Seminole Wars and its modern face as 'guardians' of the Everglades. See the Living Village and walk the 1ml/1.6km Boardwalk over the Cypress Swamp. Then try the **Billie Swamp Safari**, a 2,200-acre/1.6ha Cypress Reservation featuring close-ups of the wildlife (including snakes and gators) via its giant-wheeled buggy, airboat rides and swamp critter shows. And you can even stay overnight in its Chickee huts (1800 683 7800, **www.semtribe.com**).

There are dolphin presentations (into behaviour and care – not 'shows') 3 times a day and other interactive animal encounters, plus a **Trainer For A Day** option at $325/person. You can also do their behind-the-scenes tour, with access to all the rehab areas and a close-up of the dolphins, or 2hr **Sea Life Safari** (great for kids) that goes out on the coastal waterway. The new **Dolphin Tale Adventure** – with re-built scenes, film images, interactive kids area and mini-theater all based on the original movie – in downtown Clearwater is also included in the price if you buy tickets at the Aquarium, from where there is also a free trolley ride to the Adventure (Aquarium hours 9am–6pm daily, 10am–6pm for Dolphin Tale Adventure; $19.95 adults, $17.95 seniors, $14.95 3–12s; admission plus behind-the-scenes tour $30.90, $27.90 and $22.95; plus Sea Life Safari $38.90, $35.90, $27.90; or all 3 for $49.85, $45.85 and $35.85; 727 441 1790, **www.seewinter.com**; also on Tampa CityPass, p280).

The Beach Walk: The heart of the area is a winding beachside promenade of lush landscaping and artistic touches that links a ½-mile stretch of resorts, shops and restaurants (like the fun **Frenchy's**, **Britt's Island Grill** and **Crabby Bill's**) to Pier 60 where the daily sunset celebration (with craft

Miami nice

If you see nothing else in Miami, do spend some time in **South Beach** (or SoBe as it is known) and über-cool Ocean Drive, full of open-air cafés, art galleries and pulsating nightclubs. Tranquil during the day, non-stop at night, this is where the beautiful people hang out, or just cruise in their Ferraris and Hummers. The restored Art Deco gems twinkle at night and will use up plenty of film or a spare memory card.

stalls and music) is held. Also here is the marina where you can catch the 2hr **Captain Memo's Pirate Cruise** (10am and 2pm daily; $36 adults, $31 seniors and teens, $26 under-13s, $11 under 3s) or the **Sunset Champagne Cruise** (at 4.30, 5, 6 or 7pm, $39, $31, $26, $11; online discounts at **www.captainmemo.com**).

Caladesi Island: Further north is another of the world's most picturesque beach spots. And don't miss the annual 10-day **Pier 60 Sugar Sand Festival** each April, with even more family-friendly fun (**www.sugarsandfestival.com**).

Suncoast Beach Trolley: For those not wanting to drive, this is the perfect option (6.10am–11.25pm daily) both along the beaches and into St Petersburg for $2 a ride, $4.50 for an all-day pass and $20 for a week pass (info line 727 540 1900, **www.psta.net**).

Restaurants: The area also boasts 2,000 restaurants, of which the Key West bistro style of the 5 **Frenchy's Cafes** (Original Café, Rockaway Grill, South Beach and Salt Water Café, all in Clearwater Beach, plus Frenchy's Outpost in Dunedin), the **Daiquiri Deck/Oceanside Grill** (Madeira Beach), **Crabby Bill's Seafood** (Indian Rocks, Clearwater Beach and St Pete Beach) and the **Moon Under Water** (St Petersburg) are all worth visiting. The chic **Parkshore Grill** in downtown St Pete is ideal for a relaxing lunch or elegant dinner (727 896 3463, **www.parkshoregrill.com**), as is **400 Beach Seafood & Tap House**, which also features a fabulous

Sunday brunch (727 896 2400, **www.400beachseafood.com**).

Where to stay: A range of Superior Small Lodgings combine beachfront locations with small-scale service. Weekly rates can be from $800 for a 3-room apartment (727 367 2791, **www.floridassl.com**). Upscale hotels include family-friendly **Tradewinds Island Resorts** on St Pete Beach, a 743-room complex with great facilities and dining in a blissful location (1800 360 4016, **www.tradewindsresort.com**); the superb **Sandpearl Resort**, a 4-star choice on Clearwater Beach, with a mix of stylish standard rooms and spacious suites. The pool, bar and grill are a beachfront sanctuary, and the modern Spa has a fab array of treatments. Caretta on the Gulf offers memorable dining with an inventive fusion cuisine (727 441 2425, **www.sandpearl.com**); and the new **Hyatt Regency Clearwater Beach Resort & Spa**, an all-suite hotel at the heart of Beach Walk with fantastic pool facilities and picturesque Gulf views, plus the eco-friendly Sandova Spa, state-of-the-art gym and 2 wonderful restaurants (727 373 1234, **www.clearwaterbeach.hyatt.com**). By contrast, the **Vinoy Resort** (in St Petersburg) is the area's oldest formal hotel, a 1920s treasure that is well worth a look just for its Spanish Revival style (727 894 1000, **www.marriott.com**). Another personal favourite is the **Grand Plaza Hotel** right on St Pete Beach, where the ultra-friendly service and fresh style are ideal for a beach getaway, especially with the revolving restaurant and bar of Spinners on the 12th floor providing grandstand Gulf views (727 360 1811, **www.grand plazaflorida.com**). **Sunset**

Ah-Tah-Thi-Tiki Museum

Vistas Beachfront Suites on Treasure Island, with 1 and 2-bed suites and fully- equipped kitchens, is a top self-catering choice (727 360 1600, **www.provident resorts.com**). More info: 0208 651 4742 in the UK, 727 464 7200 in the US, or **www.visitstpeteclearwater.com**.

> **BRITTIP**
>
> Don't miss the chance to dine at the Hyatt Regency's SHOR Seafood Grill, with its dramatic show kitchen and superb local seafood dishes.

The south-west

Bradenton/Sarasota: Around 2hrs' drive from Orlando is this artsy area (take I-4 then I-75), which features the superb beachfronts of Anna Maria Island (charming and secluded beaches), Longboat Key and Venice ('the shark tooth capital of the world' and great for fossil hunters). Sarasota is year-round home to the Ringling Circus, and there are many circus-influenced offerings here, including the unmissable **Ringling Estate and Museum of Art**, which includes the unique Circus Museum and Tibbals Learning Center (the world's largest scale model of a classic circus). The **Museum of Art** features a multi-million-dollar collection of Old Masters in a palatial setting while the former family home, the dazzling **Ca d'Zan Mansion**, grounds and gardens are also part of the entry fee (daily 10am–5pm, 8pm Thurs; closed Thanksgiving, Christmas, New Year's Day; $25 adults, $20 seniors, $5 6–17s and students; **www.ringling.org**). There is superb shopping at **St Armand's Circle** in Lido Key, and the **Mote Aquarium** is also worthy of note. In Bradenton, look out for the **Village of Arts**, and the sophisticated **South Florida Museum**, which includes the Parker Manatee Aquarium and Bishop Planetarium. The Aquarium is home to Bradenton's mascot, Snooty, the world's oldest living manatee (10am–5pm Mon–Sat, 12pm–5pm Sun Jan–April and July, noon–5pm Sun; closed Mon in May, Jun and Aug–Dec; $18 adults, $16 seniors, $14 4–11s; 941 746 4131, **www.southfloridamuseum.org**). Good

food is always on the menu, and you should try another outlet of the excellent Spanish-Cuban **Columbia Restaurant** in Sarasota (941 388 3987, **www.columbiarestaurant.com**) and beachfront **Siesta Key Oyster Bar** (941 346 5443, **www.skob.com**).

Where to stay: Anna Maria Island is full of small-scale B&Bs and cute beachfront inns. The **Hyatt Regency Sarasota** is one of the top resorts in the area (941 953 1234, **www.sarasota. hyatt.com**), while the **Ritz-Carlton** is a Gulf Coast landmark (941 309 2000, **www.ritzcarlton.com**). More info: Sarasota, call 941 957 1877 or **www.visitsarasota.org**; Bradenton and Anna Maria Island, 941 729 9177 or **www.bradentongulfislands.com**.

Charlotte Harbor: Go further south (170ml/272km from Orlando) and you have the lower-key destinations of Punta Gorda, Port Charlotte, Englewood and Boca Grande. Port Charlotte is the place to be for some of the best shelling in Florida, while kayakers should try the 'tunnel of love' mangrove tunnels and other nature adventures with **Phoenix Rising Kayak Tours** (941 586 2836; **www.prkayak.com**). To immerse completely in nature, try an overnight stay on **Little Gasparilla Island**, where there are no roads, cars or shops, just miles of beaches and exceptional bird-watching and tarpon fishing. Eco-adventures can be found at **Babcock Wilderness Adventures**, with swamp buggy tours through the Telegraph Swamp (1800 500 5583; **www.babcockwilderness.com**). **Downtown Punta Gorda** has free bike rentals and a lovely walk along the Peace River where you'll feel miles off the usual tourist trail. If you are looking for 'small town America', this is it. More info: 941 743 1900 or **www.charlotteharbortravel.com**.

Fort Myers/Sanibel: It's only a short drive to the mini tropical paradise of the Lee Island Coast, featuring history and nature-rich Fort Myers and funky Pine Island. Among the many highlights are bustling family-orientated Fort Myers Beach; Sanibel Island, centred around its shell-strewn beaches; the bird-watching Mecca at the Darling National Wildlife Refuge; the jumble of shops and restaurants in Captiva Island; and Bonita Beach. Sanibel is home to the unique **Bailey-Matthews Shell Museum**, plus a quaint **Historical Village & Museum**, several wildlife attractions, canoeing, kayaking and nature tours.

Where to stay: There is a good mix of vacation homes and cottages in Fort Myers Beach and Sanibel, while the top hotels are **Lovers Key Resort** (239 765 1040, **www.loverskey.com**) and **Sanibel Harbor Marriott Resort & Spa** (239 466 4000, **www.marriott.com**). More info: 239 338 3500 or **www.fortmyers-sanibel.com**.

Paradise Coast: Continue south to the magnificent 'Paradise Coast' of Naples and Marco Island. Naples is a fresh, modern city with plenty of attractions (notably the **Museum of Art**, **Naples Nature Center** and **Corkscrew Swamp Sanctuary**, plus ultra-chic shopping) and a top beach destination. Its art-tinged ambience is well-evidenced in its 2 main areas of Fifth Avenue South, with boutique shops, sidewalk cafés and art festivals, and Third Street South, with more distinctive stores, galleries and café society atmosphere (try the **Old Naples Pub** for fine food in a relaxed ambience with an outdoor patio and live music Thurs–Sat). The beaches are mere steps away; at the municipal beach, **Naples Pier** juts into placid Gulf waters, while **Lowdermilk Beach** is fully family-friendly, with volleyball and other facilities. Marco Island is the largest of the Ten Thousand Islands, consisting of 2 main communities: Marco, known for its wide-coved beach and fine resorts, plus a multitude of fishing charters; and Goodland, with its eclectic fish house restaurants, plus fishing charters into the Everglades.

Where to stay: Pick from high-quality resorts like **Marco Island Marriott Beach Resort** (239 394 2511, **www.marcoislandmarriott.com**), Marco

Beach Ocean Resort (239 393 1400, **www.marcoresort.com**) and **Waldorf-Astoria Naples** (239 597 3232, **www.waldorfastorianaples.com**). We also like the small-scale Caribbean-tinged **Lemon Tree Inn** in Naples (239 262 1414, **www.lemontreeinn.com**). More info: 001 239 225 1013 or **www.paradisecoast.com**.

⊞ **BRITTIP**

The Naples/Marco Island area is the perfect base from which to explore the amazing Florida Everglades, though you can also reach them from Fort Lauderdale on the east coast.

Treasure Coast

Returning to the Atlantic Coast, heading south on Highway 1 brings you to an often-overlooked Florida jewel, Vero Beach. Nicknamed the Treasure Coast (for its history of shipwrecks), it boasts the intriguing **McLarty Treasure Museum** and the **Pelican Island National Wildlife Refuge**. Vero Beach itself is located on the barrier island of North Hutchinson but spreads to the mainland, with art galleries, smart shops, restaurants, small resorts and beach parks, including a boardwalk atop the dunes. Go south for another hour and you reach Palm Beach and the mainland city of West Palm Beach, foremost among Florida's chic cities. A playground of the rich and famous, Henry Flagler's **Whitehall** mansion is a highlight, while the many restaurants are places to go celebrity-watching. Also here is **Lion Country Safari**, with lions, elephants and giraffes (**www.lioncountrysafari.com**).

Where to stay: Disney's Vero Beach Resort doesn't always have availability (it is a Disney Vacation Club hotel), but is the ideal family resort on this coast (772 234 2000, **http://disneyvacationclub.disney.go.com**). In Palm Beach there is really only one place to stay (or visit) – the opulent **The Breakers**, one of America's legendary resort destinations (561 655 6611, **www.thebreakers.com**). More info: 1800 554 7256 or **www.palmbeachfl.com**.

Miami and Fort Lauderdale

From Palm Beach, you reach increasingly built-up resort territory – Delray Beach, chic Boca Raton, Deerfield Beach, Pompano Beach and Fort Lauderdale. This latter has become one of Florida's most upmarket destinations in recent years, with a great mix of resorts, shopping, attractions and beaches. It also has a canal and waterway network that makes it the 'Venice of America', with water taxis being more plentiful than the wheeled variety. Top things to see are the **Museum of Discovery & Science** (one of the state's finest), **Bonnet House Museum & Gardens**, **Old Fort Lauderdale Village & Museum** and **Las Olas Boulevard**, full of boutiques and restaurants. Shop at **Sawgrass Mills**, Florida's largest mall, which has more than 300 outlet-style stores from big-name designers. Fort Lauderdale is also a perfect stay for a few days before or after a cruise, as both Port Everglades and Miami are only a short distance away.

Where to stay: Look for their Superior Small Lodgings or the many high-class resorts now dotting the beachfront, like **Sheraton Fort Lauderdale Beach Hotel** (954 524 5551, **www.starwoodhotels.com**) and the dramatic 5-star **Ritz-Carlton** (954 465 2300, **www.ritzcarlton.com**). More info: 954 765 4466 or **www.sunny.org**.

Miami: If you have taken the 4hr drive south from Orlando, you will finally arrive in the state's biggest and most glamorous city, Miami. With superb high-rise resorts, miles of open, accessible beaches, the ultra-chic **South Beach** area (with its Art Deco District), fantastic shopping, sports, restaurants and nightlife, and an array of outstanding attractions, you could easily spend a week here. The city is actually 5ml/8km from the beach area, which runs north for almost 15ml/24km along the sprawling corridor of Collins Avenue, where you have most of the resorts and nightlife. High style is almost everywhere – **a narrated boat tour** (from the Bayside Marketplace) will show off the mansions of the rich and famous, while you should also tour Coral Gables and the older, neater Coconut Grove, with its CocoWalk shopping district and ornate Vizcaya Museum.

Other attractions include **Miami Seaquarium** on the island of Key Biscayne, the amazing **Venetian Pool** at Coral Gables and the surprising and entertaining family attraction **Jungle Island**, a combination of zoo, animal shows and gardens with great up-close encounters (**www.jungleisland.com**). You are spoiled for choice for shopping, from fashion-conscious **Bal Harbor Shops**, to the

The lovely beachfront of the Grand Plaza Hotel on St Pete Beach

massive **Aventura Mall** and funky **Lincoln Road** in South Beach. Or try the **Village of Merrick Park** in Coral Gables, a Mediterranean-style outdoor mall with more designer style, including the iconic Nordstrom department store and superb dining, notably at fab Italian restaurant **Villagio** (305 529 0200, **www.villageofmerrickpark.com**).

Miami Food Tours: When you are ready for some time away from the beach, try this fascinating insight into the Art Deco district's architecture and eclectic dining. Sample 'neighbourhood specialities' at 6 South Beach restaurants and cafés along this fun walking tour, while learning about the area's culture, history and unique building style. We give this 2 forks up! (212 209 3370; **www.miamifoodtours.com**)

Dining: This is a strong feature of Miami these days. Consider the sumptuous Latin American cuisine of **Ola Miami** (305 695 9125; **www.olamiami.com**); fresh and authentic Northern Italian trattoria offerings at **Salumeria 104** (305 424 9588; **www.salumeria104.com**); ultra-swanky **Casa Tua** (the place to see and be seen; 303 673 1010, **www.casatualifestyle.com/miami**); and the casual comforts at eclectic **Soyka**, a train station turned car collector's warehouse turned restaurant (305 759 3117; **www.soykarestaurant.com**).

Where to stay: There are boutique hotels and dazzling resorts aplenty, but there are 2 we have stayed at recently that we'd recommend every time. **The Beacon** in South Beach is the place to be when you want to immerse in the party-style buzz of Miami's Art Deco Ocean Drive and then enjoy breakfast each morning in this iconic location (877 674 8200; **www.mybeaconhotel.com**), while sumptuous **Grove Isle Hotel & Spa** gets our vote as a blissful retreat with the amenities of a luxury resort and the quiet of a secluded get-away. With its proximity to the cruise port, Grove Isle is a natural choice for a pre or post-cruise stay (305 858 8300; **www.groveisle.com**). More info: 305 539 3000 or **www.miamiandbeaches.com**.

Florida Keys

Leaving Miami behind on Highway 1 brings you to the unique realm of the Keys, a loose archipelago of 1,700 islands that arc down into the Caribbean. If you thought mainland Florida was easygoing, just try the laid-back 'Conch Republic', where shorts and flip-flops are official wear and the mix of influences merges into a 'Floribbean' culture. Scuba divers enjoy some of the world's best coral reefs, with renowned **John Pennekamp Coral Reef State Park** the highlight of miles of National Marine Sanctuary. Or try **Vandenberg Artificial Reef** off Key West, an old US Navy ship intentionally sunk in 2009 to create a man-made reef. The first city you encounter is **Key Largo**, followed by **Islamorada**, where you should stop to see **Theater To The Sea**, with its dolphin and sea-lion programmes. For fishing, some of the best charters are at Islamorada, Marathon and Big Pine Key.

Marathon is the starting point of the amazing **Seven Mile Bridge**, the unofficial 8th wonder of the world, which connects the biggest gap between the islands, while Big Pine Key is home to **Bahia Honda State Park**, one of Florida's finest beaches. Finally, the 375ml/600km drive from Orlando brings you to America's southernmost city. **Key West** is possibly the most eclectic city in the US, a mix of the laid-back and outrageous, with street performers, sidewalk artists, cafés and bars, plus the former home of Ernest Hemingway, whose residence and museum are essential viewing. You

Ola Miami

should also see **Key West Aquarium** and **Shipwreck Historeum**, and the wonderfully diverse array of shops. You must be on the harbour front, though, for the daily **Sunset Celebration**, when Key West's party spirit is in full force. The other great feature of Key West is its myriad ways to get around – you can try the Conch Tour Train, Old Town Trolley Tours, pedicabs and bicycles. Just don't expect your stay to be sedate!

Where to stay: Guest houses, inns and B&Bs are plentiful. Try **Old Customs House Inn** (305 294 8507, **www.oldcustomshouse.com**) in Key West's Old Town or charming **Banyan Resort** (305 296 7786, **www.thebanyanresort.com**). More info: 1800 352 5397 or **www.fla-keys.com**.

Cruise-and-stay

Taking a cruise is a popular pick with an Orlando stay and you'll see a lot of advertising for these well-priced 3, 4, 5 and 7-day sailings out of Port Canaveral, Tampa, Fort Lauderdale and Miami.

Disney: With its own impressive ships sailing from a dedicated Port Canaveral cruise terminal, classic design plus the usual Disney Imagineering, the vessels incorporate special features for kids, teenagers AND adults – a destination in their own right. With multiple restaurants (one for adults only), a theatre, cinema, nightclub complex, choice of bars and a gorgeous spa, plus outstanding kids' facilities, they sail to the Bahamas, Key West, Caribbean and Disney's stunning private island of **Castaway Cay**, which has an amazing array of beach amenities. It's not cheap and the short cruises can feel a bit frenzied but there is a 5-night option and winter options from Miami. They boast novel touches with their entertainment, including dazzling theatre shows and character interaction. New ships *Disney Dream* (2011) and *Fantasy* (2012) added extras like the first 'water-coaster' at sea' (a water-flume that goes OUT over the side of the ship and features a 2-deck drop); a French-themed fine-dining restaurant, Remy; Nemo's Reef splash pool for toddlers; a mini-golf course; and 5 superb kids' clubs. Book with many of the tour operators or direct with Disney on 0800 028 3179 (**http://disneycruise.disney.go.com**).

Other Port Canaveral options: (**www.portcanaveral.org**) High-energy **Carnival Cruise Lines** (all-modern hardware, party atmosphere; 1800 764 7419 in the US or 0843 374 2272 in the UK, **www.carnival.co.uk**) with 3, 4 and 5-night Bahamas voyages and 7-night cruises to the east and west Caribbean; and **Royal Caribbean** (also 2 modern, glamorous ships; 0844 493 4005, **www.royalcaribbean. co.uk**), similar 3 and 4-day trips to Nassau and its private island of Coco Cay and alternating 7-night Caribbean cruises.

Further afield: You can also catch a cruise from Tampa (**www.tampaport. com**), where you can choose from Carnival, Royal Caribbean, Norwegian Cruise Line and upmarket Holland America, with 4, 5, 7 and 14-day cruises to Mexico and the western Caribbean; busy Miami (**www. miamidade.gov/portofmiami**), with as many as 11 cruise lines in winter throughout the Bahamas and Caribbean; and Fort Lauderdale (**www.porteverglades.net/cruising**), with even more choice, including the 'world's largest ships', Royal Caribbean duo *Oasis* and *Allure of the Seas*.

Well, that represents pretty much the full range of holiday choices. Now we need to tell you about how to enjoy all the night-time entertainment…

Disney Cruise ship Fantasy

or Burning the Candle at Both Ends

If Orlando and the parks are hot during the day, they positively sizzle at night, with yet more diverse and thrilling entertainment, much of it extremely family friendly. Disney and Universal lead the way, but there is much to enjoy in the live music scene generally.

The full range runs from purpose-built entertainment complexes and an amazing range of dinner shows to a unique array of bars and nightclubs. The choice is widespread and almost always high quality. Downtown Orlando has some unique offerings, while there is more being added to International Drive all the time. Downtown Disney – which raised the bar for the big evening entertainment concept with the opening of Pleasure Island in 1987 – is experiencing a massive makeover to turn it into **Disney Springs**, which will double the current array of choice. Disney's Boardwalk Resort is also a good evening option.

BRITTIP

Photo ID is essential for most bars and clubs, even if you happen to be the 'wrong' side of 30. No ID equals no alcohol, and there are no exceptions.

DOWNTOWN DISNEY

Disney's big shopping, dining and entertainment district remains currently a 3-part adventure: the Marketplace, West Side and Pleasure Island. But, in 2013, the House of Mouse announced a new plan for a 4-part redevelopment that will keep the Marketplace and West Side (albeit with new elements and design features), turn Pleasure Island

Islands of Adventure

into The Landing, an eye-catching waterfront location of shops and dining, and add the Town Center, a big and modern 'new urban' area that will include a chic promenade. Full details are still to be announced, but completion isn't likely before 2016, which leaves the current offerings as follows (see also Shopping, p328).

Pleasure Island/ The Landing

Raglan Road: This pub features traditional live Irish music each night in its Grand Room 7.30pm–1.30am Mon–Wed, 4pm Fri, Sat, 12pm Sun, plus hourly Irish dancing. Enjoy its full bar, ample collection of genuine Irish whiskey, 9 European beers, 4 beer flights, plus local brews, great bartenders and an even better menu (p305) (407 938 0300, **www.raglanroad.com**).

Paradiso 37: This expansive, split-level bar-restaurant offers a fine array of food from the Americas (all 37 countries) plus an amazing Tequila Bar featuring 37 varieties. Live music adds to its picturesque waterfront location (p304).

More dining and live entertainment venues will be added, and The Landing should open in late 2015.

West Side

AMC® Dine-In Theaters Complex: With 24 screens and 6,000 seats plus a huge choice of snacks, drinks and even its own bar, this superb cinema multiplex shows first-run films in state-of-the-art surroundings,

Paella at Bongos Cuban Café

including the Enhanced Theatre Experience (a bigger screen, with 3D technology, 12-channel audio and digital projection) and the new feature Dine-In option, with 6 of the auditoriums converted to serve meals and drinks while you watch. The menu includes starters like wings, potato skins and onion rings, then salads, fish and chips, chicken pasta, sandwiches and burgers and yummy desserts, plus wine, beer and cocktails (tickets $8–18, prices vary by show; food and drink extra; call 1 888 262 4386 for show times; under 18s must be accompanied by an adult in Dine-In theatres; **www.amctheatres.com**). Disabled accessible; assisted listening devices available at Guest Services.

BRITTIP

Some films have added features, such as enhanced sound, larger screen, or 3-D, that will increase your ticket price. However, you can save $2 on adult tickets at the AMC® cineplex by visiting before 3.55pm.

Bongos Cuban Café: The 'big pineapple' restaurant with Latin flair has salsa music and a live band Fri and Sat nights. Sit on the outdoor balcony on a balmy evening and soak up the atmosphere (9pm–2am Fri & Sat; 407 828 0999; **www.bongoscubancafe.com**).

DisneyQuest: The most unusual element on the West Side, DisneyQuest houses 11 major adventures, such as CyberSpace Mountain (design and ride your own roller-coaster), Mighty Ducks Pinball Slam (a fun life-size pinball game), Ride the Comix! (a virtual-reality battle, this time with super-villains), Virtual Jungle Cruise (shooting the rapids, prehistoric style) and Aladdin's Magic Carpet (more virtual-reality fun in best cartoon fashion), a host of old-fashioned video games in Replay Zone, the latest sports games, a test of imagination in Animation Academy and 2 cafés – Wonderland Café, with computers and internet tables, and Food Quest, straight out of a space-age comic book.

BRITTIP

A combined annual pass for DisneyQuest and Disney's water parks at $129 adults and $99 3–9s can work out good value for multiple visits.

Two more interactive experiences are **Pirates of the Caribbean: Battle for Buccaneer Gold**, a 3-D immersion in a swashbuckling quest for pirate treasure). **Buzz Lightyear's Astro Blasters** (inter-galactic bumper cars with cannonball action! Restrictions: 4ft 3in/129cm). You enter via the Cybrolator to Ventureport and then have 4 main areas to explore: **Score Zone** (for most of the game-playing); **Explore Zone** (role-playing and virtual-reality games); **Create Zone** (hands-on activities to be your own 'Imagineer'); and **Replay Zone** (a 'moonscape' of classic games and rides). Admission: 11.30am–10pm Sun–Thurs, 11.30pm Fri and Sat. Go during the day to avoid the queues (the building admits only 1,500). A 1-day ticket costs $45 ($39 3–9s; included with all Premium and Ultimate tickets, and with the Water Parks & More option with multi-day tickets).

House of Blues: Free live music every night at the Front Porch bar, with full concerts at the separately accessed music venue next to the restaurant. The main venue offers a mix of big-name headliners (the likes of Duran Duran, My Chemical Romance, The Cult and Fall Out Boy have all appeared in recent years), up-and-coming bands and local acts. All concerts are standing room only. Tickets required, no discounts for children ($10–40 and up; 407 934 2583, **www.houseofblues.com**).

Cirque Du Soleil: The greatest show we've seen anywhere is Cirque du Soleil's La Nouba™. Twice a day, 5 times a week, the company's purpose-built, 1,671-seat theatre stages the most stupendous combination of dance, circus, acrobatics, comedy and live music in a 90min show by more than 60 performers. Unique styling, outrageous costumes and captivating sounds make this a stunning multi-dimensional assault on the senses.

The show title comes from the French *faire la nouba*, to live it up, and this it does in grand style. It features trampolines, acrobatics, trapezes, juggling and even mountain bikes, woven with comedy, innovative dance, spellbinding music and magnificent staging. Some of the stunts are jaw-dropping, notably the Chinese diabolo acrobats, BMX cycling stunts and the mind-boggling high-energy final act, Power Track/Trampoline, which features a 3D building and performers flipping and twisting in and out of the structure in quick succession. The overall effect of the constant flow of movement, sublime timing and multitude of different characters is a sheer masterpiece. A kaleidoscopic explosion of talent that never fails to amaze, it is just as exciting as when it opened in 1998. It is not cheap, but we believe it is worth every cent and a highlight of any visit to Orlando. Booking is vital and can be done up to 6 months in advance on 407 939 7600 (or **www.cirquedusoleil.com**). Shows are at 6pm and 9pm Tues–Sat, but try to be early for some excellent pre-show fun. Admission: there are 6 pricing groups, Golden Circle at $150 for adults, $125 3–9s; Front & Center, $137, $113; Cat 1, $122, $100; Cat 2, $95, $78; Cat 3, $77, $63; and Cat 4, $62, $52 (but there is hardly a bad seat in the house).

La Nouba

Splitsville: An imaginative venue in which to 'dine, dance, drink – and bowl'. Yes, it's a 10-pin bowling centre, but not like anything you've seen before. Built in best 1950s period style, this twin-level entertainment palace offers 30 lanes of bowling, multiple bars, billiard tables and a full-service restaurant, along with elegant indoor and outdoor seating, including a 1st-floor patio for a great view over Downtown Disney. The upper floor also has more a grown-up style in the evening, with DJs adding a nightclub vibe. Walk-in rates are $15/person Mon–Fri 10am–4pm and $20 after 4pm; $20/person all day Sat and Sun, but you can book a lane in advance by calling or online (10.30–1am Mon–Fri; 10–2am Sat and Sun; 407 938 7467, **www.splitsvillelanes.com**).

Other entertainment: The evening sees a variety of live music performers throughout Downtown Disney, from flamenco guitarists to classical quartets. Look for them in the West Side outside the AMC Dine In theatre, in front of Fulton's Crabhouse, and near Disney Pin Traders and T-Rex Cafe on The Marketplace side.

Disney Resorts

Disney's Boardwalk: Disney's other big evening entertainment offering is part of its impressive BoardWalk Resort, where the waterfront entertainment district contains several notable venues (not counting the excellent micro-brewery and restaurant of the Big River Grille and Brewing Works, the thrilling ESPN Club for sports fans and 5-star Flying Fish Café). **Jellyrolls** is a variation on the duelling piano bar, with the lively pianists conjuring up a humorous and often raucous evening of audience participation (7pm–2am, music from 8pm; $12 cover charge; 21 and over only). The **Atlantic Dance** club features mainly modern dance music with house and guest DJs, plus occasional live music, a huge dance floor and a great bar service and ambience. Video DJs feature on Tue, Wed and Sat, with 'duelling DJs' on Thurs and Fri, and it's especially popular on Fri and Sat nights (9pm–2am; closed Sun and Mon). It's strictly 21 and over, so bring your ID (no ID, no entry, no exceptions). The Boardwalk also features some amusing stalls and live entertainers, which add to the carnival atmosphere, while the ESPN Club features regular celebrity (American) sports guests.

Coronado Springs Resort: Inside this big Disney resort is a real hidden gem in the Rix Lounge. A bar-nightclub with a smooth ultra-lounge vibe, it features its own cocktail list, from martinis to shooters and tequila and margarita flights, plus a light-bite menu of appetisers and flatbreads. With a live DJ Thurs–Sat, it is a cool place just to go for an early-evening drink or a great full-on nightclub later on (6pm–midnight; **www.rix-lounge.com**).

ESPN Club

Electrical Water Pageant: This is another nightly (and free!) alternative, an eye-catching 'parade' that circles Bay Lake and the Seven Seas Lagoon, passing by each of the Magic Kingdom resorts in turn. It lasts just 10mins, but it's almost a waterborne version of the Main Street Electrical Parade, with thousands of twinkling lights on a cavalcade of pontoons, all set to its own music. The usual schedule is 9pm at the Polynesian Resort, 9.15 at Grand Floridian Resort & Spa (get a grandstand view in Narcoosee's restaurant), 9.35 at Wilderness Lodge, 9.45 on the shores of Fort Wilderness Resort and 10.05 at Contemporary Resort. It can also be seen outside the Magic Kingdom at 10.20pm during extended hours.

UNIVERSAL'S CITYWALK

As part of the big Universal Orlando development, this 30acre/12ha spread offers a bustling expanse of restaurants, snack bars, shops, open-air events and nightclubs. It offers a huge variety of cuisines, from fast food to fine dining, an unusual blend of speciality shops and an eclectic nightclub mix, from reggae and rock 'n' roll to salsa, jazz and high-energy disco, plus the superb Blue Man Group show and a karaoke theatre/bar. There's a $7 entry fee at the 6 clubs but you can buy a CityWalk Party Pass ($12) or Party Pass with Movie (one free film at the 20-screen Universal Cineplex; $15) for entry to all of them, while most multi-day tickets include a Party Pass. The area splits into 3, the Main Plaza (shopping and dining), Lagoon Front (dining, live music and theatre) and the Promenade (dining and nightclubs). For dining, see p307.

Blue Man Group: The most entertaining element here at the Sharp AQUOS Theatre offers a unique brand of comedy, music and multi-media theatrics, adding something completely novel to the Universal line-up. In the hands (or mouths!) of the Blue Men, mundane items like pipes, paintballs, cereal, GI-Pads, and even audience members become the instruments of wild creativity with sometimes stunning, occasionally slightly gross but always hilariously gratifying outcomes. There is a strong live music element and it can feel a bit like a rock concert. Their ability to drum up a tune on various bits and pieces is truly amazing. The wild finale, involving the whole theatre, is a real corker, and don't worry if you're seated in the 'poncho section'; the Blue Men will make sure you have adequate protection. It all adds up to an unforgettable evening of family entertainment, from $69–79 adults, $29 3–9s. Tickets are available at **www.universalorlando.com** or from the theatre box office (book online for a $10 discount).

> **BRITTIP**
> Park in Universal's multi-storey car park for all CityWalk venues – only $5 after 6pm, free after 10pm. For more info, call 407 363 8000 or visit **www.citywalkorlando.com**.

Bob Marley – A Tribute to Freedom: A clever re-creation of Marley's Jamaica home is turned into a courtyard music venue and restaurant. The bands are excellent, the atmosphere authentic and the place comes alive at night (bar open until 2am, 21 and over only after 9pm; cover charge after 9pm).

The Groove: For club-minded visitors this is a high-tech dance venue designed like a Victorian theatre but with the latest in club music, lighting and special effects (9pm–2am; 21 and over only; attire casual chic, no hats, no tank-tops).

The Groove

Hard Rock Live: Hard Rock Live is the massive mock-Coliseum styled 2,500-seat theatre with high-tech staging and sound. Big-name bands and vocal performers are on stage several times a week (Chicago, Deep Purple and the fantastic Classic Albums Live all appeared in 2014) in this slightly retro rock 'n' roll venue (407 351 5483, **www.hardrock.com**).

Jimmy Buffet's Margaritaville: Live music and 3 bars (11.30am–2am). Band (and cover charge) starts at 10pm.

Red Coconut Club: This retro dance club has a trendy, tropical vibe. With live music, signature cocktails, tapas-style menu and eclectic South Seas décor, it is a popular venue (7pm–2am Mon–Sat; 8pm–2am Sun; free admission for ladies on Thurs; 21 and over only). DJ daily, live music Thurs–Sat.

Rising Star Karaoke: It's karaoke taken to the next level, with a live band, back-up singers and a host who makes every volunteer singer feel like a star. There is a full bar with speciality cocktails, appetisers and a large selection of songs (8pm–2am nightly; 21 and over; 18 and over on Thurs only). Tues–Sat live band, back-up singers and host; back-up singers and host only on Sun and Mon.

Not breathless yet? Well, there's still the 20-screen Universal Cineplex with a capacity of 5,000 and the latest in movie comfort. There's also a Meal & Movie Deal for a film and dinner at one of the 8 restaurants for $21.95. And, of course, there's the new Hollywood Drive-In Golf (p267).

POINTE ORLANDO

This eye-catching development on I-Drive, almost opposite the Convention Center, is a mix of shops, cinema, restaurants, live entertainment and the WonderWorks fun centre (with its magic-themed dinner show). The Pointe is open all day but has notable evening appeal. Here is the full choice of night-time entertainment.

Adobe Gila's: Especially popular with locals and often packed at weekends, it stays open late and features live outdoor music and DJs several days a week. On Fri and Sat the place should be kicking from 6.30pm: on weekdays, it's likely to be 8.30pm (407 903 1477; **www.adobegilas.com**).

BB King's Blues Club: Live jazz and blues make this a fine choice for a meal or drinks and a show in this imaginative venue, featuring a main 2-storey concert hall and a variety of bars. If what you want is a real party, BB King's takes some beating, with

Jimmy Buffet's Margaritaville

live music nightly from 7pm with one of its 2 excellent house bands, plus guests (407 370 4550, **www.bbkingclubs.com**).

Cuba Libre Restaurant and Rum Bar: Offers live Latin music on Sat nights (**www.cubalibrerestaurant.com**).

Minus 5° Ice Bar: Don a Minus 5° parka or Faux Fur and a pair of gloves and party until your nose turns blue! The entire bar is made of ice—and so are the glasses—in this deep-freeze setting with LED light show, music and themed ice rooms. (**www.minus5experience.com**).

Orlando Improv Comedy Club and Fat Fish Blue: The Improv pulls in top name comedians from across the country, with shows ranging from mildly risqué to downright raucous. The theatre is intimate, making it easy for entertainers to interact with guests (often with hilarious results) and it is a terrific change of pace for a grown-up night out. Seating is first-come, first-seated, full food and drinks menu available, all shows 21 and over, with 2 performances on Fri and Sat (no shows Mon and Tue). Connected to the Improv is the bistro-style Fat Fish Blue, featuring American fare with a New Orleans accent. Full bar, a good range of speciality beers, and live music 5 nights per week. All ages welcome (407 480 5233, **www.theimprovorlando.com**).

Regal Cinema: Also here is a 21-screen movieplex (one an IMAX) that features state-of-the-art stadium seating and sound systems, where you can often see a new film before it arrives in the UK. Look for the ticket office on the ground level. For more on Pointe Orlando, 407 248 2838 or www.pointeorlando.com. For more on the restaurant choices, see p318.

Taverna Opa: A lively Greek option, with belly-dancing, other live entertainment and a great ouzo bar! 407 351 8660, **www.opaorlando.com**).

DINNER SHOWS

Another source of evening entertainment comes in the various dinner shows that are a major Orlando phenomenon. From murder mysteries to full-scale medieval battles, it's all wonderful, imaginative fun, even if the food is usually quite ordinary. It is live entertainment coupled with dinner and free soft drinks in a fantasy environment, where even the waiters and waitresses are in costume. They have strong family appeal and you are usually seated at large tables where you get to know other people, but at $40–74, they are not cheap (especially with taxes and tips). Be aware, too, of the attempts to extract more from you with photos, souvenirs and upgrades.

BRITTIP
American cinema popcorn is invariably SALTED. Sweet popcorn in the US is usually called Kettle Corn.

Disney shows

Visitors often overlook Walt Disney World's offerings unless they are staying at one of the hotel resorts, but they are certainly worth considering.

Disney's Spirit of Aloha: For an excellent night of South Seas entertainment, go to Luau Cove at Disney's Polynesian Resort. It's a bit expensive – $70–74 for adults (Category 1 main floor centre seating) and $36–40 for under-10s; or Cat 2

Rising Star Karaoke

© Universal Orlando

upper floor and sides $63–67 and $31–33; Cat 3 extreme sides or extreme upper level $59–63 and $30–32 – but good value as the 2hr show features some splendid entertainment, such as Hawaiian singers and dancers, and an amazing Samoan fire juggler, and tax and gratuity are included. The food is plentiful, with salad, BBQ ribs, roast chicken, pulled pork, vegetables, pineapple and rice, plus a pineapple bread pudding (limited kid-friendly menu). Beer, wine and soft drinks are included, and shows are at 5.15 and 8pm Tues–Sat. Make reservations up to 180 days in advance, with full payment when booking.

Hoop-Dee-Doo Musical Revue:

At Disney's Fort Wilderness Resort & Campground, this is a popular nightly dinner show that maintains the resort's Western theme, and has great food (all-you-can-eat ribs, fried chicken, seasonal vegetable, baked beans, corn bread and strawberry shortcake, plus unlimited beer, wine, sangria and soft drinks). Especially loved by children, it features the amusing song and dance of the Pioneer Hall Players in a merry American hoedown. We're slightly biased but we love this show as it's been running since 1974 and remains a Disney tradition, full of genuine wit and humour, plus a hugely energetic cast that keep things fresh every night. The Revue plays at 5, 7.15 and 9.30pm at the authentic Pioneer Hall,

Category 1 seating (main floor centre) is $66–70 for adults, $34–36 for under-10s; Cat 2 (back and balcony) $59–63 and $29–31; Cat 3 (side balconies) $55–59 and $28–30 (under-3s free; prices include tax and gratuity) and the show lasts almost 2 hours. Reservations are ALWAYS necessary and can be made up to 180 days in advance (full payment at booking).

Mickey's Backyard Barbecue:

If you can't get enough of the Disney characters, try this twice-weekly dinner show, usually Thurs and Sat, Mar–Dec at 6.30pm, at Disney's Fort Wilderness Resort. It features Mickey and the gang in a country buffet-style dinner at picnic tables under an open-air pavilion with live music, line dancing, rope tricks and other entertainment, and plenty of character interaction (great for younger children). The all-you-can-eat buffet offers barbecued pork ribs, baked chicken, hot dogs, hamburgers, macaroni and cheese, ice-cream and more. Like all Disney dining, this is a no-smoking environment. The show may be cancelled if bad weather threatens ($60 adults, $36 3–9s). To book a Disney show, call 407 939 3463.

BRITTIP
Most dinner shows can be quite chilly, especially those with animals like Medieval Times, so bring a jacket or sweater to beat the air-conditioning.

Hoop-Dee-Doo Musical Revue

Medieval Times

Spain in the 11th century is the entertaining setting for this 2hr extravaganza of medieval pageantry, falconry and robust horseback jousts that culminate in furious hand-to-hand combat between 6 knights. It's worth arriving early to appreciate the clever mock castle design and the staff's costumes as you are ushered into the pre-show hall before being taken into the arena. The show features jousting, sword-fighting and other well-scripted hand-to-hand combats, along with some superb horsemanship, with the basic idea of cheering on one of the 'Knights of the Realm' in the 6 colour-coded sections. The show also includes a dramatic musical score by award-winning film composer Daniel May, the weapons are all real and used with great skill, and there are some neat special effects. You need to be in full audience participation mode as you cheer on your knight in the traditional Good-v-Evil scenario, but kids (and many adults) get a huge kick out of it and they'll also love eating without cutlery (the soup bowls do have handles, though!). Soft drinks are included, but alcohol is Cash Bar Only. The elaborate staging is backed up by a succulent chicken, ribs and baked potato dinner and the serfs and wenches who serve you make it a fun experience. Prices, which include the Medieval Life exhibit, are $62.95 for adults and $36.95 for 3–12s. A basic Royalty Package upgrade for $10/person includes preferred seating, knight's cheering banner, souvenir cup, commemorative programme and behind-the-scenes souvenir DVD. The King's Royalty Package adds VIP first-row seating all sections or second row in the centre seating area, plus a framed group photo ($20), and the birthday Celebration Package adds a group photo per person, VIP seating, programme, banner, DVD, personalised announcement during the show and a slice of cake ($16 more). Doors open 90mins prior to show time. Times vary seasonally, so call 1866 543 9637 or visit **www.medievaltimes.com** for

reservations and details. The Castle is on Highway 192, 5ml/8km east of the junction with I-4. If you have 45mins to spare before the show, the Medieval Life exhibit is an interesting diversion. This mock village portrays the life and times of 900 years ago (with some gruesome dungeon and torture chamber scenes not for young 'uns!). Stay on after the show (the 2nd show only on busy nights) for The Knight Club, full bar service, music, dancing and the chance to meet royalty and knights for autographs and photos.

Pirates' Dinner Adventure

This show (revamped in 2013 to Rise of the Sea Dragons) features one of the most spectacular settings, with a life-size pirate ship 'anchored' in a huge indoor lagoon – and a giant animatronic dragon! It also delivers good value with its pre-show elements, plentiful food and soft drinks and after-show Pirates Bash Dream Disco. Coffee is served at the Disco and a kids' choice (chicken fingers or mac and cheese) is available if the hearty main meal of beef kebabs or chicken with rice and seasonal vegetables doesn't appeal. The story starts in period style at the Seaport Village where the Governor's Annual Gala is taking place, with entertainment provided by the magic and stories of Raddu the Gypsy King before guests are spirited off to the pirates' realm. Here, Captain Sebastian the Black is preparing to raid Treasure Bay for the booty that awaits him if he can get past the fearsome sea serpent that guards the way. The evil captain thinks he can

Medieval Times

win the day with a royal sacrifice, but the kind-hearted Benjamin Blue is ready to save the imperilled princess, even if it means fighting off the whole band of scurvy pirates. That's the cue for all manner of fights, duels, acrobatics, fights, trapeze acts and more fights, with plenty of audience participation and cheering. Highly family friendly and a big hit with kids ($65.95 adults, $39.45 3–11s, includes 1 round of beer or 2 of soft drinks during the show; see website for savings).

> **◀🇬🇧▶ BRITTIP**
> When there are 2 shows of The Pirate's Dinner Adventure in a night, opt for the later one if you want the disco bash afterwards.

There is a Governor's VIP Upgrade ($25; available in advance or at the ticket window) with an exclusive pre-show lounge, restroom and cash bar, front-row seating, guaranteed audience participation, special appetiser buffet, champagne toast, opportunity to upgrade dinner fare to Filet Mignon, Lobster Tail or Shrimp (add $14.99); or a Captain's Upgrade, with enhanced seating ($15; row 2 and 3) and discounts at the bar and gift shop. It is located on Carrier Drive between I-Drive and Universal Boulevard, and runs at 6pm, 7.30pm or 8.30pm, with appetisers served for 45mins prior to seating (407 248 0590, **www.piratesdinneradventure.com**).

Sleuth's Mystery Dinner Show

There is a $5 fee for parking but also a special Pirates Christmas Dinner Adventure show, which adds suitably festive themes.

Sleuth's Mystery Dinner Shows

This is a live version of Cluedo acted out before your eyes in hilarious fashion while you enjoy a substantial meal (with a main course choice of honey-glazed Cornish hen, lasagne with or without meatballs, or, for $6 extra, prime rib) and unlimited beer, wine and soft drinks. You can choose between 3 theatres and no fewer than 13 different plot situations (several of which have amusing British settings), including Squires Inns, Roast 'Em & Toast 'Em and Lord Mansfield's Fox Hunt Banquet (mayhem at an English banquet), that add up to some elaborate murder mysteries. The action takes place all around you and members of the audience can take some cameo roles. The quick-witted cast keep things moving and keep you guessing during the theatrical part of the 2½-hour show, then during the main part of dinner you think up questions for interrogation (but the real murderer is allowed to lie!). Solve the crime and you win a prize, but that is pretty secondary to the overall enjoyment and this is a show we enjoy a lot, plus it's a terrific choice with teens ($57.95 adults, $24.95 3–11s; times vary; 407 363 1985, **www.sleuths.com**). Also check out their periodic Stand Up Comedy Spotlight (see website for dates, times, and comedians). Sleuth's is in the plaza just past Ripley's Believe It Or Not on I-Drive, with 3 different theatres, a smart pre-dinner bar area and gift shop.

WonderWorks: Outta Control Magic Comedy

On a smaller scale but no less fun, this dinner show is at WonderWorks on I-Drive (on one corner of Pointe Orlando). A novel mixture of improvised comedy and magic, the show is accompanied by all-you-can-eat pizza, salad, popcorn and dessert, plus beer, wine and coke. Set in the intimate Shazam Theater, it features live music, special lighting effects and some slick magic tricks from illusionist (and funny guy) Tony Brent. The tricks are relatively small-scale but are served up with terrific style and plenty of audience participation. Beware of sitting too close to the stage – you WILL end up as part of the act! Twice nightly at 6pm and 8pm, it costs a good-value $24.99 for adults, $19.99 4–12s and seniors. A Magic Combo ticket for the show and access to WonderWorks (open until midnight, p235) is $43.99/$33.99 (407 351 8800, **www.wonderworksonline.com**).

Capone's Dinner & Show

This 1930s gangland version of Chicago is home to Al himself and a 'family gathering' that goes hopelessly wrong. Try to keep track of local gangster Fingers Salvatorio and his ditzy wife, Bunny-June, as they look to provide for Fingers Jnr, aka Little Pinky, and fail miserably, causing all manner of mayhem for the hapless parents, Bunny-June's sisters Babs and Bubbles, and a vengeful – if slightly dim – beat cop, ex-detective Marvel. The audience can often be at the centre of the action and there is a hilarious 'shoot-out' finale it would be wrong to reveal (but you won't mind if you are 'hit'!). A huge Italian-American buffet offers 5 types of pasta, meatballs, pizza, salad bar, a carvery and side dishes. Unlimited Bud Light, a selection of wines and cocktails, plus soft drinks, juice, Kiddie Cocktails and Mama Capone's 'dessert surprise' round out the all-you-can-eat-and-drink menu ($60 adults, $40 4–12s, 3 and under free; 407 397 2378, but see website for special deals, often at HALF price, **www.alcapones.com**).

Live music

Orlando's live music scene is lively and always changing but several venues can be relied on for quality entertainment. As already noted, the **House of Blues** and **Hard Rock Live** provide regular big-name concerts, while international acts appear at the state-of-the-art **Amway Center** in downtown (as well as the Orlando Magic, Orlando Predators and Orlando Solar Bears sports teams), including the Black Keys, Enrique Iglesias and Miley Cyrus in 2014 (**www.amwaycenter.com**). On a smaller scale but just as engaging, N Orange Avenue in downtown Orlando has 2 great venues for live music. **The Social** offers a wide range of bands and a great bar vibe (407 246 1419, **www.thesocial.com**) while **Firestone Live** – hailed as one of the freshest nightclubs in the world by *Billboard* and *Rolling Stone* magazine – is also a great choice. The latter has been a pop culture phenomenon for almost 20 years, featuring a huge range of breakthrough artists, and continues to offer a fresh, live choice (407 872 0066, **www.firestonelive.com**).

Sports bars

The Sports Bar is a particularly American invention and is well served hereabouts if you'd like to sample the way the locals follow their sport (American football is usually the biggest at weekends Sept–Jan, but basketball is also popular, along with baseball and ice-hockey).

Orlando Ale House

Orlando Ale House Group: Among the multitude of sports bars, one of our favourites has fine examples on Kirkman Road, opposite Universal Studios (407 248 0000) at Lake Buena Vista on Highway 535 near Downtown Disney (407 239 1800), on I-Drive (407 370 6688) and the newest location, Miller's Ale House in Winter Park Village (321 214 1505). The Ale Houses feature more than 30 TVs (each!), classic American bar food, including their signature spicy 'chicken zingers' and an above-average range of beers (**www.millersalehouse.com**).

Buffalo Wild Wings: Another chain worth noting has 5 Orlando locations (notably on I-Drive just south of Wet 'n Wild, 11am–2am daily, 407 351 6200; Lake Buena Vista near Downtown Disney, 11am–2am, 407 827 0444; and their newest at I-Drive 360), where masses of chicken-orientated dishes (watch out for the Blazin' sauce – it's seriously hot!) are served up in a casual, lively atmosphere, highlighted by its Buzztime Trivia System at each table and multiple big-screen TVs (**www.buffalowildwings.com**).

Other options: Also look out for the revamped **Uno Chicago** chain (**www.unos.com**) or any **TGI Fridays**, **Beef O'Brady's** or **BJ's Brewhouse** outlet. Then there is **Frank & Steins Eatery & Pub** in downtown Orlando (**www.frankandsteins.com**) and **The Pub** and **Marlow's Tavern**, both at Pointe Orlando (p319).

Disney boasts the excellent E**SPN Club** at Disney's BoardWalk Resort, a full-service restaurant with sports broadcast facilities, video games, more than 70 TV monitors, giant scoreboards and even a Little League menu for kids. Universal CityWalk boasts the **NBA City** (for basketball fans) and **NASCAR Sports Grille** (not just for motor-racing followers), with more big-screen TV style. The various British-style pubs also offer sports bar style. Try the **Orlando George & Dragon** on International Drive next to Wet 'n Wild (**www.orlandogeorgeanddragon.com**) and

Frankie Farrell's Irish Pub at Lake Buena Vista Resort & Spa (next to the Factory Stores).

Something different

Icebar: Spend 45mins surrounded by 50 tons of carved ice while sipping a chilled vodka beverage, then warm up in the Nordic-inspired Fire Lounge, at the unique venue on I-Drive just north of WonderWorks. Coats and gloves are provided or you can upgrade to a glam mock fur coat for $10, and entry fee is $19.95 (drinks not included; save $5–8 by booking online). Open 7pm–12am Sun–Wed, 7pm–1am Thurs, 7pm–2am Fri–Sat, with the first ICEBAR entry time at 7.15pm; ages 8 and up allowed 7.15pm and 8pm time slots only. No cover charge for Fire Lounge (which also features DJs), but no children. Happy Hour 7–9pm Sun–Thurs, and V 'Ice' P package at $29.95, including 1 premium drink in ICEBAR and 1 in Fire Lounge (407 426 0361 or **www.icebarorlando.com**).

◀ $ ▶ BRITBONUS
Pay for entry to the Icebar and receive a FREE pint in the Fire Lounge afterwards. Just show your copy of the *Brit Guide* for the free drink.

Howl at the Moon: If you're looking for a serious party, try Howl at the Moon on I-Drive, where the live music doesn't stop until the wee hours! An energetic piano-playing duo pound out a rockin' good time, highlighted by 'Showtime', when the whole bar joins in a choreographed dance-fest. Signature cocktails are available by the glass or the bucket(!), with drink specials nightly (21 and over only; 7pm–2am Sun–Thurs, 6pm–2am Fri–Sat; cover charge $5 Mon–Wed, $7 Thurs, $10 Fri and Sat, $7 Sun; 407 354 5999, **www.howlatthemoon.com**).

Now you'll want to know a lot more about where, when and how to tackle that other holiday dilemma – where to eat. Read on…

Dining Out

or Eat, Drink and Eat Again!

The options for dining out are omnipresent and large scale, which is excellent news as it means it's impossible to go hungry and easy to feed the family – without breaking the bank.

Variety

The variety, quantity and quality of restaurants, cafés, fast-food chains and snack bars is in keeping with the local tradition of convenience and value.

As a rule, food is plentiful, relatively cheap, available 24 hours a day, and nearly always appetising and filling. You will encounter an increasing number of fine-dining possibilities, but the basic emphasis is on value. Portions are large, service is efficient and friendly, and it's hard to come by a bad meal. The one real exception is if you dine mainly at fast food places and the likes of Dennys and Co, you won't find much fresh veg. But if you look up the vegetarian options, visit outlets like Sweet Tomatoes and ask for the vegetable option instead of fries or potatoes at other restaurants, you will find a more balanced choice. Plus, salads are almost always on the menu.

Exceptional deals

Most restaurants tend towards the informal (T-shirts and shorts are nearly always acceptable) and cater readily for families; you will always find a kids' menu, and many have activity packs. Many hotels and restaurants offer Kids-eat-free deals (from under-10 to under-14), provided parents are also dining. The age limits vary. The all-you-can-eat buffet is another common feature, where you can probably eat enough at breakfast to keep you going to dinner! Some places offer early-bird specials – a discount to dine before 6pm. Be aware that 5.30–7.30pm is peak time for many restaurants, though, and you may have to wait for a table if you arrive between 6 and 8pm.

BRITTIP
Portions are often so large, you can save money by sharing a main course. Your waiter or waitress should be happy to oblige (if you keep their tip up to the full rate).

Don't be afraid to ask for the leftovers 'to go' and don't hesitate to say if something isn't right; the locals will readily complain (politely) if they are not happy, so restaurants are keen to ensure everything is to their diners' satisfaction. And, please, don't forget to tip; the basic wage for waiters and waitresses is low, so they rely heavily on tips as part of their income and are taxed on an assumed level of tips. Unless service really is shoddy (in which case mention it), the usual tip rate is 10% of your bill at buffet-style restaurants and 15–20% at full-service restaurants. Check whether service is already added to your bill, though this is not common.

You will encounter a huge array of food types. Florida is renowned for its seafood, which comes much cheaper than in the Mediterranean: crab, lobster, shrimp (what we call king prawns), clams and oysters, as well as several dozen varieties of fish, many unusual (like mahi mahi and grouper). Latin-style cuisines, notably Cuban and Mexican, are common, and the South American influences mean the delicious citrus-marinated seafood called ceviche is often featured. There is also plenty of Asian fare, from Chinese and Indian to Japanese, Thai and Vietnamese. The big shopping malls all offer good value food courts. 'Cracker' cooking is original Floridian fare, and the speciality is alligator, either stewed, barbecued, smoked, sautéed or braised. Fried gator tail 'nuggets' are a local favourite, as are catfish and frogs' legs. And do try key lime pie!

◀🇬🇧▶ BRITTIP
An excellent section of the All Ears website run by Deb Wills lists places that cater for special diets, including veggie, at *www.allearsnet.com/din/special.htm*. Many restaurants now offer gluten-free options, too.

How to order

Ordering food can be an adventure in itself. The choice for each item is often the cue for an inquisition! You can never order just 'toast' – it has to be white, brown, whole wheat,

Café Tu Tu Tango

rye, muffin or bagel; eggs come in a baffling variety (order them 'sunny side up' for a traditional British fried egg; 'over easy' is fried both sides but still soft); an order of tea or coffee often brings the query, 'Hot, iced, lemon, green or herbal? Regular or decaf?'; and salads have more dressings than the NHS. Feel free to ask if what you fancy isn't shown on the menu.

Vegetarian options

In a country where beef is king, vegetarians often find themselves hard done by. However, there are some bright spots. Largely vegetarian restaurants include the Indian cuisine of **Woodlands** on S Orange Blossom Trail (407 854 3330, **www. woodlandsusa.com**; closed Mon), the popular Chinese of the **Garden Café** on Highway 50 close to downtown Orlando (407 999 9799), and the trendy duo of **Ethos Vegan Kitchen** on N Orange Ave, just north of downtown (407 228 3898, **www. ethosvegankitchen.com**) and **Cafe 118** in Winter Park (407 389 2233, **www. cafe118.com**) with its all-organic menu. The tapas-style **Café Tu Tu Tango** on I-Drive also serves a good variety of veggie dishes. However, most upmarket restaurants can offer a vegetarian option and will be happy for you to ask in advance. In Walt Disney World, the **California Grill** (in Disney's Contemporary Resort), **Citricos** (Grand Floridian Resort & Spa), **Le Cellier** (Canada pavilion in Epcot) and **Jiko** (Animal Kingdom Lodge) feature good vegetarian choices, while the seafood-orientated **Flying Fish** (Disney's Boardwalk) and **'Ohana** (Disney's Polynesian Resort) also serve up decent veggie fare if asked. Two good Mediterranean-style choices with vegetarians in mind are **Anatolia** (p315) and **Cedar's** (p316). Most full-service restaurants (notably **Bongos Cuban Café**™ and **Wolfgang Puck® Café** in Downtown Disney; p307) and even some counter-service outlets can cater for non-menu requests. It's always worth asking.

However, **Sweet Tomatoes** (with 5 outlets in the area, notably on I-Drive

Belly up to the bar!

If you'd like just a snack or sample of a restaurant's fare, many places offer a bar or appetiser menu, including Bar Louie, Big Fin Seafood, Bongos Cuban Café, Bravo, Bonefish Grill, Capital Grille, Carrabba's, Eddie V's, Emeril's Tchoup Chop, Fishbones, Fleming's, Fulton's Crab House, Hillstone, House of Blues, Kres Chophouse, Luma on Park, Moonfish, Morton's, The Oceanaire, Old Hickory, Portobello, Rainforest Café, Ravenous Pig, Roy's, Seasons 52, Tommy Bahama Café and T-Rex Café, plus The Crab House (for its Mon–Fri Happy Hour, 4–7pm), Brio Tuscan Grille (3–7pm Mon–Fri), Landry's Seafood House (4–6.30pm) and The Palm (5–7pm and 9pm–close).

by Kirkman Road, in the Crossroads Plaza at Lake Buena Vista and just off West Highway 192 in Kissimmee on Rolling Oaks Blvd) is a great vegetarian-friendly outlet. A buffet restaurant with some great meal deals, it has an all-you-can-eat lunch for $8.59 ($10.29 at dinner, after 4pm) that includes a vast salad counter, freshly made soups, pizza, pasta, bread and pastries, plus fruit and frozen yoghurt. The menu is healthy and the quality is consistently first class, while its website lists nutrition info. Drinks are $2.69–3.19 (refills free) and kids' meals are $3.49 3–9s and $4.99 9–12s (11am–10pm, **www.soupplantation.com**).

BRITTIP

Sweet Tomatoes is a restaurant chain we recommend highly, and you can benefit from its enhanced dinner menu by arriving a little before 4pm but still paying only the lunch buffet price.

Chamberlin's Market & Café (with 6 Orlando outlets, notably in the Dr Phillips Plaza just off Sand Lake Rd) is another choice, with home-made soups, salads, sandwiches and fruit smoothies (**www.chamberlins.com**). The **Panera Bread** chain also offers some decent veggie options (plus free wi-fi).

BRITTIP

American bacon is always streaky and crisp fried, and sausages are chipolata-like and slightly spicy. Very different from the British versions.

Eating 24/7

It's not unusual to find restaurants open around the clock (or 24/7, as they say). So here is where you can go for a snack or even a full-scale meal at 4 in the morning. **Chain restaurants:** Denny's, Waffle House, Steak & Shake, some McDonald's. **Individuals:** B-Line Diner (Peabody Hotel, I-Drive), Planet Java (Gaylord Palms Resort), Sundial 24–7 (Wyndham Lake Buena Vista) and Mainstreet Market (Hilton at Walt Disney World Resort).

Drinking

A big complaint from Brits on holiday in the US is about the beer. With the exception of a handful of English-style pubs and micro-breweries, American big-label brewery beer is generally lager, bottled or on draught (though smaller scale breweries have a more European flair). It goes down great when it's hot, but is weaker and fizzier than our own. Of course, there are exceptions (try Killian's Red, Michelob's Amber Bock, Leinenkugel's or Sam Adams beers for a fuller flavour), but don't expect a good, old-fashioned British pint. You should also look out for **The Big River Grille** at Disney's BoardWalk Resort and **Orlando Brewing** (on Atlanta Ave, just south of downtown Orlando), an organic micro-brewery with a range of distinctive brews, plus free brewery tours Mon–Sat at 6pm (407 872 1117, **www.orlandobrewing. com**). **Yuengling** – America's oldest brewery – has a plant in Tampa near Busch Gardens that also offers free tours – as well as samples! (p280). Spirits (called 'liquor') come in a large selection, but beware of ordering just 'whisky' as you'll get bourbon. Specify if you want Scotch or Irish whiskey and demand it 'straight up' if you don't want it with a mountain of ice. When you order a soft drink from a counter-service outlet, ask for 'no ice' or 'light ice' unless you want a drink with lots of ice.

There is a massive choice of cocktails and most bars and restaurants have lengthy happy hours with good prices. Good-quality Californian wines are better value than European. If you stick to soft drinks ('sodas') or coffee, most bars and restaurants give free refills. You can also run a tab in the majority of bars and pay when you leave. But be aware US licensing laws are stricter than ours and you MUST be 21 to drink alcohol in a bar or lounge. You'll often be asked for proof of age before you are served (or allowed into a club), so take your passport or photo driving licence. Don't bother to argue – no photo ID, no beer!

Magical Dining Month

Orlando has become a foodie's paradise in recent years and, to celebrate, each Sept is dedicated as Magical Dining Month, with an array of special events and a selection of top restaurants offering a 3-course prix fixe menu at $33/head, which represents a great saving on regular prices. In recent years these have included Luma on Park, La Luce (at the Hilton Bonnet Creek Resort) and Roy's on Sand Lake Rd. Check out more at **www.visitorlando.com/magicaldining**.

Where to eat

That gives you the inside track on HOW to eat and drink like the locals. Now you need to know WHERE. There are 4,000-plus restaurants in the area, so the following selection covers the main ones, grouped by style. You'll find the Fast Food and Family Favourite type in all the main areas. We also indicate a budget:

$ = most main courses under $10
$$ = most main courses $10–15
$$$ = most main courses $15–20
$$$$ = most main courses $20–$30
$$$$$ = most main course $30-plus

We also have a special section on each of the three main areas of I-Drive,

Highway 192/Kissimmee and Lake Buena Vista. But, as ever, we start with Walt Disney World.

DOWNTOWN DISNEY DINING

The heart of Disney dining can be found at Downtown Disney.

> **BRITTIP**
>
> If there are several of you drinking beer, ordering a pitcher will work out cheaper than buying it by the glass.

Pleasure Island/ The Landing

Fulton's Crab House: Good seafood is not hard to come by, but great seafood is the preserve of a handful – like Fulton's. This mock riverboat has 6 dining rooms (each with the same menu), plus the Stone Crab Lounge, which features a busy raw bar. The recently refurbished interior is filled with nautical props, photos and lithographs, giving it an eclectic atmosphere, but the real attraction is some of the freshest and most tempting fish, crab and lobster dishes in Florida, including fresh daily specials and a kid's menu. Recent additions are an excellent calamari steak and a pan-roasted mussels pasta. The Stone Crab Lounge serves lunch and dinner 11.30am–11pm, while the restaurant is open for dinner only ($$$–$$$$$; 4–11pm; 407 394 2628; **www.fultonscrabhouse.com**).

> **ANNIVERSARY SPOT**
>
> **20** Fulton's Crab House began life as the paddleboat Empress Lilly (named for Walt's wife, Lillian). In the original Pleasure Island story, it was the boat Merryweather Pleasure arrived on (hence the name Pleasure Island). It originally had a paddlewheel and funnel, which were removed after it became Fulton's.

Paradiso 37: This 'Taste of the Americas' offers a wide variety of foods, much with a Latin-tinged flavour, and live music nightly. A tempting menu includes Argentinean skirt steak, Chilean salmon, Mexican fare, plus signature cocktails and tequila. The lively style, split-level restaurant, chic bar area (inside and out) and lakeside setting mark this out for a relaxing lunch or upbeat dinner, or just somewhere to kick back with a drink or speciality coffee ($$–$$$$; 11am–11pm Sun–Thurs, 12am Fri and Sat; 407 934 3700).

Portobello: Don't overlook this Tuscan-country trattoria on the edge of the Marketplace and Pleasure Island. From the fresh bread with oven-baked garlic to the family-style menu and full wine list, there's everything from pizza to zucchini ribbons in a tomato seafood broth. We are big fans of their insistence on locally sourced fresh produce, and it really shines through in the great taste of things like the Rigatoni and Black Linguini with Florida Rock Shrimp. Old World flavours mix with New World style, while a great wine list and speciality beers complete an impressive picture, with reservations not always necessary. The addition of a fun Meatball Bar and dishes like Biramisu (Tiramisu with a local porter ale!) help to keep everything fresh and inviting, too ($$–$$$$; 11.30am–11pm; 407 934 8888; **www.portobellorestaurant.com**).

BRITTIP

For a great light lunch at Portobello, try the antipasti platter ($16), which serves 2. Their Cafe Shakerato (Italian iced coffee) is also a real treat.

Raglan Road: This Irish-themed pub, with lively music, food to match and a genuine Emerald Isle style, is where you really can enjoy the craic. Much of the restaurant's interior was shipped over from Ireland (including 4 reclaimed 130-year-old bars, plus 9 European beers on draft), establishing an authentic backdrop to an original menu created by celebrity master chef Kevin Dundon. Fresh, simple ingredients with an imaginative twist: shepherd's pie, mussels, beef stew, Irish sausages, plus excellent curries,

a range of original sandwiches at lunchtime and a Portobello mushroom vegetarian entrée. They also feature a great Sunday Brunch and special dining events (see the website). Stop in at the gift shop and check out Kevin Dundon's Full On Irish cookbook ($$–$$$; 11am–2am, 407 938 0300, **www.raglanroad.com**).

ANNIVERSARY SPOT

20 One of the biggest changes in the last 20 years has been in fine dining and the development of Restaurant Row in an area previously known for fast food and buffets. Sand Lake Road is now renowned for its 5-star restaurants and healthy options.

T-Rex Cafe: Enter the audio-animatronic world of the people who created the Rainforest Café chain: a vast series of themed areas like the Ice Cave and Jurassic Forest, which are home to all manner of roaring dinos, with meteor strikes and thunderstorms for good measure! The food is straightforward (albeit with fancy names like Woolly Mammoth Chicken and Boneyard Buffet) but portions are suitably large and it is also somewhere you can pop into just for a drink – including great cocktails – and snacks at the hugely imaginative bar area ($$–$$$; 11am–11pm, midnight Fri and Sat, 407 828 8739, **www.trexcafe.com**).

Other choices: To one side of Raglan Road is **Cookes of Dublin**, a chippie serving up real chips, beer-battered fish, gourmet battered sausages and 'Do bars' (deep-fried Snickers bars!).

BRITTIP

For reservations at any Disney restaurant, call 407 939 3463 (407 WDW DINE), or book online at **www.disneyworld.co.uk**.

The Marketplace

While The Marketplace is largely the shopping heart of Downtown Disney (p329), it also offers tempting dining.

Rainforest Café: With its safari-style

'adventures' under a spectacular volcano-topped exterior (that belches fire and smoke!), this is the place to entertain the family while they fill up on huge platefuls of chicken, pasta, steak, seafood and burgers, surrounded by audio-animatronic animals and periodic 'rainstorms', with an excellent menu for 10s and under. Stop by the Lava Lounge for a selection of small-plate appetisers from the main menu and great cocktails and other drink specials in this lakeside setting ($$–$$$; 11.30am–11pm; 407 827 8500, **www.rainforestcafe.com**).

Other choices: Ghirardelli Ice Cream & Chocolate Shop is a great option for dessert or a milkshake. **The Earl of Sandwich** serves great sandwiches and lighter meals, and **Wolfgang Puck Express** has quick-service Californian cuisine, while several **food trucks** now offer quick-bite meals, which add a fun flavour to proceedings.

BRITTIP
We think the best value at Downtown Disney is the excellent Earl of Sandwich, where one of their hot sandwiches is often enough for two.

West Side
Back in the more hip night-time district of Downtown Disney are another 5 options.

Bongos Cuban Café: Co-owned by Gloria and Emilio Estefan, the sounds and tastes of Old Havana enliven this imaginative setting, with red-hot Latin music and excellent Cuban

Portobello at Downtown Disney

fare. You'll struggle to get a tastier – or more eye-catching – platter than their speciality seafood skillet while the Skirt Steak and Roasted Chicken are equally flavour-packed ($$–$$$$, 11am–10.30pm, Sun–Thurs 11.30pm Fri and Sat; 407 828 0999, **www.bongoscubancafe.com**).

BRITTIP
The drinks menu alone at Bongos is a thing of wonder. They churn out the Cuban speciality of the Mojito by the thousand and every one is wonderfully fresh – and kicking!

House of Blues®: This cavernous combination live music venue and restaurant in backwoods Mississippi style is a must for anyone even vaguely interested in blues, rock 'n' roll, R&B, gospel and jazz – while its trademark Gospel Brunch on Sun serves up some fab food with a full gospel show (10.30am and 1pm; $40.50 adults, $20.50 3–9s). The big restaurant (11am–11pm) offers some fine fare, including seafood jambalaya, fresh fish and a host of Cajun delicacies, with live music Thur–Sat ($$–$$$$; 11.30am–11pm, 1am Thurs–Sat; 407 934 2583, **www.houseofblues.com**).

Planet Hollywood: The largest and busiest of this worldwide chain offers lashings of its film-related fun style, with a fairly standard burger-and-steak orientated menu and wonderful cocktails. Our faves – the Chicken Crunch starter and outrageously calorific LA Lasagna! ($$–$$$; 11am–12am; 407 827 7827, **www.planethollywood.com**). Planet Hollywood is also due for a major makeover in 2015 as part of the big changeover to Disney Springs.

Splitsville: OK, so it's a bowling alley, but the food and drink here are good, so you might just want to consider this as a dining option on its own. Fresh sushi is their speciality, but the menu also features gourmet burgers, sandwiches, pizza, entrée salads and main-course dishes like pulled pork, fish 'n' chips, chicken parmesan and succulent steaks. They feature signature sundaes for dessert and the cocktail menu is extremely tempting. Head upstairs of an evening and enjoy the nightclub vibe where the bowling is purely incidental and the open-air patio is a great place to chill out and watch the world go by ($$–$$$; 10.30–1am Mon–Fri, 10–2am Sat–Sun; 407 938 7467, **www.splitsvillelanes.com**).

Wolfgang Puck® Café: A rich 4-option experience from the top Californian chef: the Café, gourmet food in a casual setting; Wolfgang Puck Express, the fast-food version; the Sushi Bar for seafood and pizzas; and the Dining Room, an upscale restaurant featuring top international cuisine. It caters for just about every taste (the sushi is excellent) and is highly family friendly ($$–$$$$$; 11.30am–11pm, 6–10.30pm in Dining Room; 407 938 9653, **www.wolfgangpuck.com**).

Other choices: Grab a snack at **Wetzel's Pretzels**, with the choice of pretzels, hot dogs and lemonade; try **Haagen-Dazs** ice-cream, or coffee at the inevitable **Starbucks**; or sample more fun **food truck** offerings.

Universal CityWalk

Universal completely revamped its dining choice in CityWalk in 2014, making for even more great possibilities. There are 12 main restaurants, plus fast-food options.

Bubba Gump's Shrimp Co: This has the full Forrest Gump theme, and is heavy on seafood but also includes chicken, sandwiches, ribs, salads and more, with catchy names like Bubba's After the Storm 'Bucket of Boat Trash' (11am–midnight; 407 903 0044, **www.bubbagump.com**).

◄╬► BRITTIP
Mention you are celebrating a birthday at Bubba Gump's and you'll find you quickly become the centre of attention!

Emeril's: This is a sophisticated and vibrant 5-star journey into the cuisine of New Orleans with master chef Emeril Lagasse. Fine wines and a cigar bar enhance Emeril's Creole-based gourmet creations, and if you don't try the Louisiana oyster stew you'll have missed a real treat (lunch 11.30am–3pm; dinner 5–10pm Sun–Thurs, 5–10.30pm Fri and Sat; 407 224 2424, **www.emerils.com**).

◄╬► BRITTIP
Can't get a booking at Emeril's for dinner? Consider lunch there instead, which rarely books up. Or try its daily Happy Hour (5–8pm) with reduced prices and special small-plate dishes at the bar.

Hard Rock Café: The largest example of this worldwide chain, with its collection of rock 'n' roll memorabilia (including a pink 1959 Cadillac) and full concert venue is hugely popular, so try to get in early for lunch or dinner, with their signature burgers, steaks, fajitas, ribs and sandwiches all well worth trying. You'll also find prices in the gift shop friendlier than in the UK (11am–midnight; 407 351 7625, **www.hardrock.com/cafes/orlando/**).

◄╬► BRITTIP
After dining at the Hard Rock Café, ask for one of their Backstage Tours with a special 'rock guide'. You'll get a great insight into much of their unique memorabilia, the history of the Café (which began in London), a look inside the John Lennon-themed VIP room and a tour of the music venue's back-stage areas. An amazing – and free – treat, available 1–9pm most days.

Jimmy Buffet's Margaritaville: An island homage to Florida's laid-back musical hero, with 'Floribbean' cuisine (a mix of Key West and Caribbean), with the Volcano Bar, which 'erupts' margarita mix (!) when the blender needs filling (11am–10pm for dinner, bar and live music until midnight; 407 224 2155, **www.margaritavilleorlando.com**)

NASCAR Sports Grill: A must for motor-racing fans, with full-size stock cars and racing memorabilia, tableside plasma screens, videos and interactive games while you dine on burgers, steaks, ribs, pasta and grilled shrimp (11am–midnight; 407 224 7223, **www.nascarsportsgrille.com**),

NBA City: A huge dining experience that is sure to thrill basketball fans with its Cage dining room, interactive playground area and Club lounge where you can watch live and classic games (11am–10.30pm Sun–Thurs, 11.30pm Fri & Sat; 407 363 5919, **www.nba.com/nbacity/**).

Antojitos Authentic Mexican Food: New in 2014, Antojitos runs the culinary gambit from street food (tacos, enchiladas, fajitas) to refined twists on traditional dishes such as Paella Mexicana and Churrasco Steak, along with 203 authentic tequilas. Downstairs is the more 'street party' atmosphere while upstairs is more formal and family-style. The cocktails are superb and you can enjoy their modern Mariachi band Tue–Sat (11am–12am; 407 224 3663).

Bob Marley: Jamaican cuisine in a funky setting, featuring entrées such as curry, oxtail stew and Jamaican Jerk Chicken (4pm–10pm Sun–Thurs, 11pm Sat and Sun; 21 and up after 9pm; 407 224 3663).

Cowfish Sushi Burger Bar: Fresh and innovative, this claims to be the world's first restaurant to feature the best sushi AND the best burgers (and the trademark 'Burgushi'), with a wide variety of both in an eclectic, lively setting – including fun touchscreens at the sushi bar (4pm–midnight; 407 224 3663, **www.thecowfish.com**).

Hot Dog Hall of Fame: All manner of hot dog styles, frankfurters and stuffed dumplings from around the USA, allied to 100s of condiment variations make this a fun and unique offering (11am–2am; 407 224 3663, **www.hotdoghalloffame.com**).

Pat O'Brien's: This is a reproduction of the famous New Orleans bar and restaurant with its Flaming Fountain courtyard, main bar and duelling piano bar. Excellent Cajun food and world-famous Hurricane cocktails! (4pm–2am; 5pm–2am for the piano bar, with a $7 cover charge after 9pm; 21 and over only; 407 224 2102, **www.patobriens.com/patobriens/orlando/**).

Red Oven Pizza Bakery: Authentic artisan pizza – 5 varieties of white and red Neapolitan style – are on offer at this chic new restaurant, with some imaginative flavours all baked in their signature 900º Red Oven (11am–2am).

Vivo Italian Kitchen: Fine Tuscan dining gets a workout here, with wonderful fresh ingredients all served from an open kitchen that offers a fully customisable menu for its pasta and other featured dishes (4–11pm Mon–Thurs, midnight Fri–Sat; 407 224 3663).

Other choices: Try **Menchie's** for fab frozen yoghurt, **Breadbox** for great sandwiches, **Cinnabon** for cinnamon rolls and other pastries, **Cold Stone Creamery** for indulgent ice-cream creations and the inevitable **Starbucks** coffee house. The Top of the Walk food court also features the **Burger King Whopper Bar**, **Panda Express**, **Moe's Southwest Grill** and **Fusion Bistro Sushi & Sake Bar**. Look up more details at **www.universalorlando.com/Restaurants/CityWalk-Restaurants.aspx**.

◀▶ **BRITTIP**
Can't get in any of the CityWalk restaurants? Jump on one of the boats to the Hard Rock Hotel or Portofino Bay Hotel and you can usually dine without a wait at The Kitchen (Hard Rock), Trattoria del Porto or Mama Della's (Portofino Bay).

FAST FOOD

While it's hard to fault Disney and Universal's quality, many of their prices can be tough on the wallet. Happily, you can eat a lot cheaper in the other tourist areas and we'll now take a look at the rest of your options, starting with some familiar names. This first section is primarily fast-food outlets, all in the $ category.

The big names: You'll find plenty of **McDonalds**, plus other standards like **Burger King**, **Wendy's**, **KFC**, **Pizza Hut**, **Subway** and **Domino's**. Local variations include **Checkers** or **Hardees** for burgers, **Popeye's Famous Fried Chicken & Biscuits**, **Bojangles** or **Chick-fil-A** as a KFC

Rockin' Robin

We are delighted the **Red Robin** chain is finally in Orlando, with their first restaurant in Winter Garden Village and a big new venue at the I-Shops on International Drive. We think they feature the best burgers (and overall value) of any chain restaurant, and their variety, quality and sheer fun style is hard to beat, especially at their prices. A big menu is highlighted by almost 20 burger choices, all accompanied by endless steak fries, and they also offer fab milkshakes, sundaes and desserts, plus cocktails and drink specials. They also offer a Guinness milkshake that is truly heavenly – but not for kids! (**www.redrobin.com**).

alternative, **Taco Bell** if you'd like the cheap and cheerful Mexican option, or **Arby's** for a range of roast beef sandwiches that make a change from burgers. **Dairy Queen** offers burgers, hot dogs, pork sandwiches and ice-cream dishes, while **Little Caesar's** and **Hungry Howie's** are pizza alternatives. A more health-conscious choice is **Tijuana Flats**, with fresh Tex-Mex style in a lively atmosphere. Check out its burritos, quesadillas, enchiladas, tacos and salads – and you'll struggle to spend more than $10/person (**www.tijuanaflats.com**). Another happening local chain is **Five Guys Burgers & Fries**, who use only fresh-ground beef (never frozen), peanut oil and no trans fats. They serve up just 4 basic burgers (plus Little Burgers), hotdogs and sandwiches, and you can add your own extras from a 16-item toppings bar (**www.fiveguys.com**).

Yes, you can find proper chips in the States. They are called 'steak fries', and you will find them in most grocery stores and on some restaurant menus, (notably at Outback Steak House). Raglan Road and Red Robin serve up arguably some of the best, though.

FAMILY FAVOURITES

After all the fast food, there is a huge selection specialising in more regular fare, still with all-American style but more variety and family-friendliness. They vary from buffet

to full service, and you'll see them in many locations.

The breakfast specialists

Need to start the day by stoking up with a big breakfast? Look no further.

Bob Evans: Notable for its friendly, country-style, hearty menus (plus low-carb options) and delicious desserts, it also offers takeaway and country store choice ($; 6 or 7am–10pm; **www.bobevans.com**).

Cracker Barrel: Delightful old country store style, with mountainous breakfasts, well-balanced lunch and dinner menus, Kid's Stuff choices and an old-fashioned charm that belies the usual tourist frenzy ($; 6am–10pm Sun–Thurs, 6am–11pm Fri and Sat; **www.crackerbarrel.com**).

Denny's: A classic 24hr restaurant, its wide selection makes a traditional bacon-and-egg breakfast seem ordinary and it does an excellent range of toasted sandwiches and dinner meals, like grilled catfish, as well as a Senior Selections menu, with smaller portions for over-55s ($; **www.dennys.com**).

International House of Pancakes (or IHOP) and **Waffle House:** You will struggle to spend more than $10 on a full meal, whether on their huge breakfast platters or a sandwich with fries. Waffle Houses are open 24/7 ($; **www.wafflehouse.com**) and IHOPs 6am–midnight ($; **www.ihop.com**).

Panera Bread: As well as wonderful pastries, fresh-baked breads and sandwiches, it serves a terrific (and healthy) array of soups and salads, including vegetarian options (7am–10pm; **www.panerabread.com**).

Antojito's at CityWalk

Perkins: Also a great breakfast choice; for a hearty meal try Perkins Eggs Benedict (2 eggs and bacon on a toasted muffin with hash browns and fresh fruit), while its bread-bowl salads are equally satisfying (some branches open around the clock; **www.perkinsrestaurants.com**).

Village Inn: Massively popular with the tourist crowd is this unassuming outlet on Westwood Boulevard, just off I-Drive near SeaWorld. Unpretentious but fab value for breakfast, lunch and dinner, it serves up heaps of basic fare with friendly service, plus decadent desserts (we dare you to try their Boston Cream, French Silk or Key Lime pies!). Huge breakfast plates, all at around $7, great kids' menus and salads, sandwiches and burgers ($–$$; 6am–midnight; **www.villageinn.com**).

Buffet style

The value of the all-you-can-eat restaurants is much in evidence here.

CiCi's Pizza: With more than a dozen locations all offering a 20-item pizza spread – all made fresh every hour – plus salad and pasta options, and a couple of delicious desserts, this is an absolute bargain at $5.99 adults and $4.99 kids (11am–10pm, **www.cicispizza.com**).

BRITTIP
A buffet breakfast should keep you going until tea-time and is a good way to start a theme-park day.

Golden Corral and Shoney's: The buffet theme continues at these 2 popular choices, where the accent is again on masses of food in a pleasant setting. Golden Corral tends to be slightly newer and fresher with a Carver's Choice of roast meats, plus good vegetable selections and dessert bar (around 20 choices). There's a weekend supplement at some outlets as they add steak to the menu ($–$$; 7.30am–10.30pm; **www.goldencorral. com**). Shoney's has an à la carte menu as well as good buffets, all with a Southern accent ($; 7am–11pm; **www.shoneys.com**).

Ponderosa Steakhouse and **Sizzler:** These 2 popular, identikit, consistent but unspectacular big-chain offerings feature huge breakfast, lunch and dinner buffets. You order and pay as you enter and are then seated, before being unleashed on the help-yourself serveries. You'd be hard pushed to tell whose food was whose, but there IS a difference in price depending on location, with I-Drive tending to be a dollar or 2 dearer. Standard dinner fare includes chicken wings, meatballs, chilli, ribs, steaks (for a small supplement) and seafood, plus immense salad bars ($–$$; 7am–late evening, **www.sizzler.com** and **www.ponderosasteakhouses.com**).

The big chains

Moving up in terms of price, quality and options is this extensive array.

Applebee's: Self-styled 'neighbourhood bar and grill', this offers a rather more health-conscious menu with good salads and weight-watchers' choices as well as an array of steaks and chicken dishes, and great-value lunches ($–$$; 11am–midnight; **www.applebees.com**).

BRITTIP
Take advantage of Applebee's 2 for $20 specials, which include one starter to split, and 2 mains.

Bahama Breeze: Lively Caribbean food and surroundings, there is a pleasing individual touch and you will get good value for money here. The decor is refreshing and entertaining, and it's worth popping in just for a drink. Try the Key West Fish Tacos, calypso shrimp linguine or jerk chicken pasta ($$–$$$$; 4pm–2am Mon–Sat, 4pm–midnight Sun; **www.bahamabreeze.com**).

BRITTIP
The Bahama Breeze restaurants don't take reservations and are extremely popular in the evening. Try to arrive before 5.30pm to avoid a wait or try the Lake Buena Vista location, which can be quieter.

Pop into our 'local'

The nearest thing to a typical pub in these parts is the **Orlando/Miller Ale House** chain. Hugely popular with the locals, it features pool tables, multiple TV screens for all the sports action and a friendly, efficient style with a varied menu. It can be rowdy on weekend big-game days but is a great place to hang out with friends, bring the family or just pop in for a drink. The Ale House in Lake Buena Vista on Winter Garden-Vineland Road is also our 'local', and the new-style Miller's Ale House on I-Drive is positively vast ($–$$$; 11am–2am; **www.millersalehouse.com**).

BJ's Brewhouse: An impressive new chain to the area that features a great menu, craft beers, lively atmosphere and ultra-friendly service. The extensive menu ranges from pizza, pasta, salads and sandwiches to impressive steaks, ribs and fish dishes, hence they cater for a lot of tastes. And did we mention the great beer choice?! ($$–$$$$; 11am–midnight Sun–Thurs, 2am Fri & Sat; **www.bjsbrewhouse.com**).

Boston Market: Typical home cooking, café style, they specialise in fresh-carved meats, rotisserie chicken, decent vegetables and excellent value ($–$$; 11am–10pm; **www.bostonmarket.com**).

Buffalo Wild Wings: A huge sports bar and grill, featuring chicken wings, tenders, wraps, salads, burgers and ribs. Simple but tasty, and popular with its many large-screen TVs ($–$$; 11am–1am Mon–Fri, 2am Fri & Sat, noon–midnight Sun; **www.buffalowildwings.com**).

Café Tu Tu Tango: Another original local restaurant high on style and quality, the accent is artist-colony Spanish, with an original tapas-style menu, live music and artwork on the walls that changes daily. Vegetarians are well catered for, and you can try some succulent pizzas, seafood, salads and soups plus imaginative Mexican dishes and a well-thought-out kids' menu (11.30am–11am, Mon, Wed, Thus, Sun; midnight Tues, Fri and Sat; **www.cafetututango.com**).

Cheesecake Factory: While its prime feature is desserts (with more than 30 cheesecakes!), the rest of a substantial menu is striking in an eclectic, high-tech setting. Mexican dishes jostle with pizza, pasta, seafood, burgers, steaks and salads, plus it offers a great Sun brunch. Beware – portions are HUGE! ($$–$$$; 11am–11pm; **www.thecheesecakefactory.com**).

Chevy's: A healthy slice of Mexicana while still providing American selections, its salsa is fresh-made every hour and the tortilla chips, fajitas and tortillas are delicious ($–$$; 11am–12am Sun–Thurs, 11am–2am Fri, Sat; **www.chevys.com**).

Chili's: Also in Tex-Mex territory, it places the emphasis more on steak and ribs and less on tortillas and spices. Service is usually highly efficient ($–$$; 11am–1am Mon–Sat, 11am–11pm Sun; **www.chilis.com**).

Chuys: More Tex-Mex style, but done just that bit more authentically and fresher, with lively style and décor to back up an extensive menu that features enchiladas, tacos and fajitas as well as signature dishes like their Steak Burrito, Chuychanga and Green Chile Fried Chicken. Plus the margaritas to go with them! ($$–$$$; 11am–10pm Sun–Thurs, 11pm Fri & Sat; **www.chuys.com**).

Don Pablo's: A fairly elaborate Mexican offering with clever theming, a fun, lively atmosphere (especially round the Cantina bar) and classic, well-explained menus ($$; 11am–10pm Sun–Thurs, 11am–11pm Fri and Sat; **www.donpablos.com**).

Fuddruckers: Excellent burgers, with a huge choice (including veggie, buffalo, elk and wild boar!) and a kid-friendly style. Make your selection, find a table and wait for your burger to be cooked fresh, or choose from salad and sandwich options, plus tempting shakes, cookies and desserts ($–$$; 11am–10pm Sun–Thurs, 11pm Fri, Sat; **www.fuddruckers.com**).

Hooters: A lively place that makes no bones about its style – 'delightfully tacky yet unrefined' – this is popular with the beach-party crowd, and for the famous Hooter Girl waitresses. The entertaining menu features seafood, salads and burgers, plus Hooters Nearly World Famous Chicken Wings in 8 strengths – beware of the Samurai! ($–$$; 11am–11pm Sun–Thurs, midnight Fri and Sat, **www.hooters.com**).

Houlihan's: Classic bar-restaurant with plenty of style, cheerful service, an extensive and appetising menu (try the great entrée salads) – and huge portions (but also a mini-dessert option; $–$$; 11am–1am; **www.houlihans.com**).

Logan's Roadhouse: A fun, rustic atmosphere includes masses of peanuts in their shells (which are meant to end up all over the wooden floor!), plus a menu featuring burgers, chicken, steaks and ribs, kids' meals and express lunch selection ($$; 11am–10pm Sun–Thurs, 11pm Fri and Sat; **www.logansroadhouse.com**).

Lone Star Steakhouse: Head to Texas for its mesquite-grilled steaks, ribs, chicken and fish, with a friendly welcome and roadhouse ambience (plus more huge portions! $$–$$$; 11am–10pm Sun–Thurs, 11pm Fri and Sat; **www.lonestarsteakhouse.com**).

Longhorn Steakhouse: The newer, fancier version of the Texas steakhouse and 'Flavour of the West', this features fresh-grilled steaks, chops and ribs, plus chicken and seafood that is hard to beat at the price, with a good menu for under-10s ($$–$$$$; 11am–10pm, 11pm Fri and Sat; **www.longhornsteakhouse.com**).

Olive Garden: A rather identikit approach to Italian fare, but the light, airy dining rooms create a relaxing

Fuddrucker's

The cream of America

Orlando boasts outstanding ice-cream parlours: check out Carvel, Baskin Robbins, Dairy Queen, Marble Slab Creamery and Cold Stone Creamery, all of which make Mr Whippy seem extremely ordinary. But the perennial favourite remains **Ben & Jerry's** who have 4 shops in the main tourist areas – in Universal Studios; at Pointe Orlando; inside the food court at Orlando Premium Outlets at Vineland Ave; and at The Loop shopping centre in Kissimmee.

environment and it does a modest menu well and in generous portions. Pasta is the speciality but there is also chicken, veal, steak and seafood, plus great salads and garlic breadsticks (with unlimited refills) ($$–$$$; 11am–10pm Sun–Thurs, 11pm Fri and Sat; **www.olivegarden.com**).

Outback Steakhouse: An Australian slant on American steakhouse style, with some of the best fare – and biggest portions. Its thick, juicy, well-seasoned steaks, ribs and seafood are great, while its trademark is a large fried onion with a dipping sauce, and all at moderate prices. Good kids' menu and a real Brit visitor favourite ($$–$$$; 11am–11pm Sun–Thurs, 11am–11.30pm Fri, Sat; **www.outback.com**).

Santa Fe Cattle Co: a recent arrival in Lake Buena Vista and on Highway 27, this Western-style offering has some surprisingly neat touches in the décor and menu (and more peanuts!). Great burgers, steaks, ribs and fajitas are their stock in trade, but the chicken-fried steak, quesadillas and El Toro burrito are worth considering and the Margaritas are killer! ($$–$$$; 11am–10pm Sun–Thurs, 11pm Fri and Sat; bar to 1am; **www.santafecattleco.com**).

Smokey Bones: With a rustic, log-cabin touch and succulent, deep-smoked BBQ, it serves up fire-grilled steaks, salmon, chicken, burgers and salads. Try the BBQ platters and rib combos especially. Sports fans can also enjoy a huge array of TVs ($–$$$; 11am–11pm Sun–Thurs, midnight Fri and Sat; **www.smokeybones.com**).

A Florida steak-out

America serves great steaks and it is hard to get a BAD sirloin, T-bone or filet. For those who really want to indulge, the following (totally unofficial) ranking should help (NB: the US Dept of Agriculture grades its meat quality Standard, Select, Choice and, for the top 2%, Prime).

Standard: Beef O'Brady's, Golden Corral, Great Western, O'Charley's, Ponderosa, Sizzler, Western Sizzlin'. **Select:** Applebee's, Black Angus, Chevy's, Chili's, Copper Canyon Grill, Colorado House of Beef, Logan's Roadhouse, Lone Star, Miller's Ale House, The Pub, Rainforest Café, Red Lobster, Ruby Tuesday, Santa Fe Cattle Co, , Smoky Bones, TGI Fridays, Tony Roma's, Uno Chicago Grill. **Choice:** Amura's, BJ's Brewhouse, Brio Tuscan Grill, Cantina Laredo, Carrabba's, Jack's Place, Johnnie's Hideaway, Kobe, Le Cellier (Epcot), Longhorn Steakhouse, Marlow's Tavern, Nona Blue, Outback, Shogun, Vito's Chophouse. **Prime:** Capital Grille, Charley's, Christini's, Everglades, Fogo de Chao, A Land Remembered, Morton's, The Oceanaire, Old Hickory, Fleming's, The Palm Restaurant, Ruth's Chris, Shula's, Spencer's, Texas de Brazil, The Venetian Room, The Yachtsman (Disney's Yacht Club Resort).

Sonny's Real Pit Bar-B-Q: A national chain with no great pretensions, just masses of food of the slow-cooked barbecue persuasion served up in friendly, let's-get-messy style. The good kids' menu makes it ideal for families, and you should definitely try the ribs and coleslaw ($–$$; 11am–10pm; www.sonnysbbq.com).

TGI Fridays: Lively, eclectic style, Orlando boasts multiple offerings of this popular chain. The drinks menu is huge and the main menu is heavy on wings, ribs, burgers and steaks ($–$$; 11am–2am; www.tgifridays.com).

Tony Roma's: 'Famous for ribs', the airy decor and ambience, clever kids' menu, junior meals and melt-in-the-mouth ribs are a winning combo. You can still get chicken, burgers and steaks, but why ignore a dish that's done this well? ($$–$$$; 11am–11pm Sun–Thurs, 11am–midnight Fri and Sat; www.tonyromas.com).

Uno Chicago Grill: The place to go if you're bored with Pizza Hut, it specialises in deep-dish pizzas plus pastas, chicken dishes, steaks and salads. A recent style makeover gave Uno's a fresh, inviting new look, with extra menu choices and great lunch specials making them especially good value ($–$$; 11am–2am daily; www.unos.com).

Wildside BBQ: Another local success threatening to become a major chain, this can be found in Thornton Park and on West Highway 192 in Kissimmee, featuring delicious pulled pork, excellent ribs and their own 'secret' barbecue sauce, as well as signature salads, fresh fish and pasta. Lively bar style also offers live entertainment and sports specials ($–$$$$; 4pm–11pm Mon–Thurs, 4pm–12am Fri, 12pm–12am Sat, 12pm–11pm Sun; www.wildsidebbq.com).

INTERNATIONAL FLAVOURS

Your food choice extends beyond the obvious to an international array, featuring Chinese and Indian, but also Thai, Japanese and Italian. Some are still chains, others are one-offs.

Indian, Chinese and more

There is a wide range of Asian restaurants in Orlando, from ordinary Chinese to 5-star Japanese. Take your pick from this selection.

Aashirwad: A decent Indian choice, with an excellent lunch buffet and some seriously spicy Mughlai dishes ($–$$$; 11.30am–3pm and 5.30–10.30pm; 407 370 9830; www.aashirwadrestaurant.com).

American Gymkhana: Formerly the upmarket and stylish Raga on the upper level of the Fountains Plaza on Restaurant Row, this impressive Indian restaurant was due to get a big makeover and menu boost from Michelin-starred New York chef Vikas Khanna in late 2014, to re-emerge as a touch of Colonial India. It will feature new furnishings in period style, with a range of new-look dishes in keeping with the elegant surroundings. However, it should still feature a beautiful bar-lounge and veranda, and it is not your average Tikka Masala menu. Presentation is as imaginative as the décor but the price point is definitely higher than a typical curry-house, hence it is not a cheap night out ($$$–$$$$; 5.30–10pm Tues– Thur; 10.30pm Fri & Sat; 9.30pm Sun; Closed Mon).

Dragon Court Buffet: This locals' Chinese favourite in Lake Buena Vista serves a huge spread of fresh, appetising dishes at a terrific lunch price. With 100 items, including sushi, this is well worth trying ($$–$$$; 11am–11pm; 407 238 9996).

India Palace: An unassuming location tucked in a small shopping plaza in Lake Buena Vista, this serves good food in large amounts and with family-friendly service ($–$$$; 11.30am–11pm Tues–Sun, 5–11pm Mon; 407 238 2322).

Kobe: This brings a touch of Americana to its Japanese-themed dining, but still achieves individuality with the chef preparing the food at your table ($$$; 4pm–10pm, hours vary by location; www.kobesteakhouse.com).

◀▣▶ **ANNIVERSARY SPOT**
20 In 1995 we featured 8 Chinese restaurants in the main tourist area. Today, only Ming Court is still in business. We think that says a lot about their quality.

Ming Court: The Rolls-Royce of Chinese is this beautiful place on I-Drive, opposite Pointe Orlando, with its magnificent setting and live music most evenings. The menu is extensive and beautifully presented by friendly servers. Many dishes can be had as a side order rather than a full main course and there are extensive dim sum and even sushi and sashimi choices, plus an imaginative kids' menu. The Salt & Pepper Chicken is

Handy Manny

A perennial Brit favourite is eclectic American diner **Manny's Original Chophouse**, on Highway 27 near Haines City (8ml/13km south of the junction with I-4 and in Winter Haven). Great value and great fun, it features a steak-orientated menu with bags of local style and original décor, as well as an amazing 2-for-1 Happy Hour daily from 4–7pm. It is often packed by 6pm as locals and tourists alike flock here for the lively style and well-priced food (all steaks under $20, and many just $14–18), which also include fab burgers, ribs, fajitas, seafood and chicken, as well as their signature dishes. It may be a bit of a drive but, trust us, it's worth it. Save time with Call-Ahead seating (not a reservation). ($–$$$; 4–10pm Mon–Thurs, 10.30pm Sat, noon–9.30pm Sun; 863 422 3910, **www.mannyschophouse.com**).

one of our all-time favourites and, after 26 years in business, this is I-Drive's longest-serving restaurant ($$–$$$; 11am–3pm, 4.30pm–11pm; **www.ming-court.com**).

New Punjab: Another decent Indian on I-Drive, with fine tandoori dishes and good vegetable selection ($–$$$; 5–11pm Mon, 11.30am–11pm Tues–Sun; 407 352 7887; **www.punjabindianrestaurant.com**).

PF Chang's China Bistro: This mixes classic Chinese fare with American bistro style that makes fans of virtually all who sample it. You should try the spicy ground chicken and eggplant (aubergine), Cantonese roasted duck or Oolong marinated sea bass. There is also a good veggie selection ($$–$$$$; 11am–11pm, 10pm Sun; **www.pfchangs.com**).

Saffron: Smart and stylish Indian choice in the Plaza Venezia along Sand Lake Road, with some fab-value lunch deals and classic dinner menu that takes it into fine-dining territory. All dishes can be prepared to individual levels of spiciness and the Chicken Xacutti and Rajasthani Hara Maas are worth coming in for on their own ($–$$$; 11.30am–2.30pm, 5.30–10.30pm; **www.saffronorlando.com**).

International Drive

The majority of restaurants in this busy tourist area are of the Fast Food or Family Favourite type, but there are several individuals.

The **North** section (from Orlando Premium Outlets International Dr to Sand Lake Road) features *Fast Food:* Baskin Robbins, Burger King, Cold Stone Creamery, Dairy Queen, Dunkin' Donuts, Five Guys Burgers & Fries, KFC, McDonald's, Quiznos, Pizza Hut, Popeye's Chicken, Sonic, Starbucks, Subway and Taco Bell. *Family Favourites:* Buffalo Wild Wings, Chili's, CiCi's Pizza, Denny's, Fuddruckers, IHOP, Sizzler, Sweet Tomatoes, TGI Fridays. *International Flavours:* Aashirwad, New Punjab Indian Restaurant, Thai Silk, Shogun Steakhouse. *Home From Home:* Orlando George & Dragon. *Seafood Specials:* Red Lobster. *Deluxe Dining:* Texas de Brazil.

The **South** section (from Sand Lake Rd to Orlando Premium Outlets Vineland Ave) has *Fast Food:* McDonald's, Pizza Hut, Subway, Flippers Pizza, Taco Bell, Dunkin Donuts. *Family Favourites:* Bahama Breeze, BJ's Brewhouse, Buffalo Wild Wings, Café Tu Tu Tango, Chuy's, Cici's Pizza, Denny's, Don Pablo's, Golden Corral, Houlihan's, IHOP, Longhorn Steakhouse, Miller's Ale House, Olive Garden, Outback Steakhouse, Ponderosa, Red Robin, TGI Fridays, Tony Roma's, Uno Chicago, Village Inn. *International Flavours:* Benihana, Kobe Steakhouse, Ming Court. *Seafood Specials:* Boston Lobster Feast, Red Lobster. *Deluxe Dining:* Charley's Steakhouse, Everglades, Fogo de Chao, Vito's Chophouse and Spencer's.

Seito Sushi: Another Japanese offering from this great chain, with a formal sushi bar and a more inviting, small-scale approach ($$–$$$$; 5–10pm Sun–Thurs, 11pm Fri & Sat; 407 248 8888; **www.seitosushi.com**).

Shogun Steakhouse: This is ideal for those a little unsure of Japanese food as it is totally family-friendly with its Teppanyaki-style service, at long, bench-like tables with the chef cooking in front of you. But you can still order a no-nonsense steak or chicken ($$$–$$$$; 6–10pm Sun–Thurs, 6–10.30pm Fri and Sat; 407 352 1607, **www.shogunorlando.com**).

Tamarind: Up in Winter Park is this impressive and authentic Indian choice that features an extensive range of starters and some fabulous main courses, including excellent vegetarian dishes. Look out in particular for the imaginative Tandoori options and rice crepes or Doasa ($$$; 11.30am–3pm and 5–10pm, 10.30pm Fri & Sat (321 207 0760, **www.tamarindfl.com**).

Thai Silk: Authentic Thai flavours and contemporary décor, with soups and curries to die for. House speciality Smokey Pot is a superb stew of marinated prawns, vegetables and glass noodles in chilli ($$–$$$$; 11am–2.30pm and 5–10pm Mon–Fri,
noon–10pm Sat and Sun; 407 226 8997; **www.thaisilkorlando.com**).

Tastes of the Med

Italy, Turkey and Greece are all represented in this selection.

Anatolia: For something exotic, head for some Turkish flavours in the Dr Phillips Plaza off Sand Lake Road. With a delicious range of authentic breads, hot and cold appetisers, salads, soups, pides (Turkish pizzas), kebabs and specialities like moussaka and baklava, you can dine royally without breaking the bank. Try the babaghanoush (char-grilled aubergine with fresh herbs and spices), tabouli, kofte kebab or chicken adana ($–$$; 11am–10pm Sun–Thurs, 11pm Fri and Sat; 407 352 6766, **www.anatoliaorlando.com**).

Bravo Cucina Italiana: This fresh, inviting twist on classic Italian fare features home-made pasta, pizza, flatbreads, steaks, chops and seafood in an inviting 'Roman-ruin' decor. Casual and chic, and fun for the grown-up crowd ($$–$$$$; 11am–10pm, to 11pm Fri and Sat; 407 351 5880; **www.bravoitalian.com**).

Carrabba's: Direct from Sicily, here's casual-but-elegant dining in a festive atmosphere. House specialities include crispy calamari, chicken marsala, pasta and hand-made pizzas. The kids' menu is one of the best and the style is ultra child friendly ($$–$$$; 4–10.30pm Mon–Thurs, 4–11.30pm Fri, 11am–10.30pm Sat, 11am–10.30pm Sun; **www.carrabbas.com**).

Cedar's: Lebanese cuisine is the name of the game here, and it's some of the best chicken and lamb in town. In 'Restaurant Row' on Sand Lake Rd, this family-run Middle Eastern delight offers the full range of kebabs, falafel and hummus as well as specialities like fish tagine, grilled quail and baked kibbeh. A really different alternative and aromatic treat, with the bonus of live music and belly dancing Fri and Sat ($$–$$$$; 407 351 6000; **www.orlandocedars.com**).

Greek Flame Taverna: Another stylish offering in the Dr Phillips plaza off Sand Lake Rd, featuring Saganaki (flamed cheese), dolmades (stuffed vine leaves) and spanakopita (spinach pie), plus other classic dishes, including salads, gyros and souvlaki, ensuring a smooth taste of the Med ($$–$$$; 407 370 4627; **www.greekflametaverna.com**).

Macaroni Grill: Like Carrabba's, this chain restaurant also features a taste of Italy, with stylish, spacious dining rooms and excellent à la carte and family-style menus (serving 8–10). The pasta and wood-oven pizzas are first class and the wine list is impressive ($$–$$$$; 11am–10pm Sun–Thurs, 11am–11pm Fri and Sat; **www.macaronigrill.com**).

Pacino's: A Highway 192 feature in Kissimmee for more than 20 years, this 'taste of Sicily' features a signature open-flame oven that

Orlando George & Dragon

Landry's bonus

Regular Orlando visitors should consider joining Landry's Select Club for a great range of bonuses with 7 area restaurants, including Rainforest Café, T-Rex Café, Yak & Yeti at Disney's Animal Kingdom and upscale Morton's Steakhouse. You can sign up at any Landry's location and immediately receive $25 off a future visit while earning points towards discounts and other benefits. It costs $25 to enroll (which you earn straight back) and should pay off with 3 or more visits to any Landry's restaurant. Look up more at **www.landrysselect.com**.

delivers great pizza, seafood and steaks, as well as offering an authentic array of pasta dishes. Couples can also take advantage of their Wine Cellar setting for a romantic evening out ($$–$$$$; 4–11pm; 407 396 8022, **www.pacinos.com**).

HOME FROM HOME

Having extolled the virtues of the all-American choices, there is an array of British-style pubs that should appeal to UK visitors. All offer predictable pub grub and beers and you can happily take the kids.

Frankie Farrell's: Inside the Lake Buena Vista Resort Village & Spa is this smart pub-style restaurant and bar with an imaginative menu, excellent range of beers and live entertainment ($$–$$$; 9am–2am daily; 407 597 0214).

Hagan O'Reilley's: Rather off the beaten track in Winter Garden (about 20mins north of Disney) is this genuine Irish pub, boasting good beers, classic fare and traditional entertainment most nights. With 15 beers on tap and Happy Hour from 11am–7pm, you could easily be in the Emerald isle, although the beer garden is pure Florida! ($–$$$; 11am–11pm; 407 905 4782; **www.haganoreillys.com**).

Orlando George & Dragon: An all-British operation, this serves a hearty breakfast as well as pub fare. It stocks Guinness, Stella, Boddingtons,

Fosters, Newcastle Brown, Bass, Magners and Carlsberg, and features darts, pool, karaoke, Sky Sports and live entertainment on its outdoor patio. A good option for Christmas dinner, Sun lunch, and St George's Day, celebrated in style, plus Happy Hour daily $–$$$; 9am–2am; 407 351 3578; **www.orlandogeorgeanddragon. com**).

The Pub: This huge pub-style offering in Pointe Orlando comes from an American company with impeccable British tastes! With a magnificent bar and wide variety of cosy seating nooks, it features a fantastic mix of UK and US beers (including the fab Orlando Brewing Co), a sharp menu and multiple TV screens for all the sports action. The unique 'Pour Your Own Beer Walls' are a fun feature, as is Happy Hour Mon–Thurs 3–7pm, Wine Down Wednesdays (half-price select bottles of wine) and Jacket and Pie Night on Mon. They are also a Pub Partner of Orlando City Soccer club ($$–$$$; 11am–2am; **www.experiencethepub.com/orlando**).

Stage Door: Another friendly, family-run pub and restaurant, this has been a local fixture since 1992 and still draws a good crowd of locals and tourists, with typical fare (including a roast beef dinner on Sun after 5pm) and a good range of beers, plus live entertainment or karaoke most nights ($–$$; 11am–2am Tues–Sat, 11am–midnight Sun and Mon; 863 424 8056; **www.stagedoorpub.com**).

SEAFOOD SPECIALS

The choice of seafood eateries is equally wide and features some fun chains and excellent individuals.

Big Fin Seafood: One of Orlando's most imaginative and award-winning seafood options, in the Dellagio complex just off Sand Lake Rd. Refined but relaxed, this is a big-scale experience that offers special-occasion atmosphere, from the entrance seafood kitchen to the elegant outdoor bar (the Bar-A-Cuda – groan!). The main dining room features a grand salon style but 2 smaller rooms are more intimate,

while the Trophy Bar is ideal for a pre-dinner drink.

BRITTIP

Big Fin Seafood has possibly one of the best meal deals in town, with its Monday Dinner special, featuring a whole 1½lb Maine lobster at just $17.95.

The menu is an impressive collection of sushi, sashimi, oysters and ceviche; classic salads and chowders; meat, chops and chicken; their exclusive crab and lobster dishes; fresh fish; and tempting pastas. You can push the boat out with the $79.99 Jumbo King Crab Leg dinner or opt for their Famous Fish & Chips at $20.99. Notable are the succulent signature Swordfish Filet Mignon, lobster mac-n-cheese, crab cakes and the Shrimp or Scallop Orleans. A good kids' menu, delectable desserts (don't miss the bread pudding) and superb service all add up to a high-quality experience – but without the price tag. There is Happy Hour 5–7pm Mon–Sat, 9pm Sun, at the Bar with $6 drink selections and a reduced price Happy Hour menu ($$$–$$$$$; 5–10pm Sun–Thurs, 11pm Fri & Sat; **www.bigfinseafood.com**).

BRITBONUS

Show your copy of the *Brit Guide* at Big Fin Seafood and receive a 10% discount off your entree. Not valid with any other offers/specials.

Bonefish Grill: This chic choice can be found throughout Florida and offers both casual dining and an upmarket dinner experience, with some of the freshest fish and a terrific range of martinis and other cocktails. Non-fish fans can choose from chicken, chops, steak and main-course salads ($$–$$$$; 4–10.30pm Mon–Thurs, 11.30pm Fri and Sat, 10pm Sun; **www.bonefishgrill.com**).

Boston Lobster Feast: The place for a real blow-out on an unlimited lobster and seafood buffet. There are usually early-bird specials (4–6pm Mon–Fri, 2–4.30pm Sat and Sun), and, while it is not gourmet fare, its 40-item Lobster Feast is guaranteed to stretch the stomach ($$–$$$$; 4–10pm Mon–Fri, 2–10pm Sat and Sun; **www.bostonlobsterfeast.com**).

Eddie V's: New on Restaurant Row in 2014, this supper-club style venue features succulent seafood with live jazz-inspired music most evenings. It is a more stylish option than many counterparts but also has a more informal V Lounge that is first come, first served. The menu is a mouthwatering collection of the freshest fish and shellfish from all over the world, as well as fine steaks, backed up by a superb wine list and signature cocktails, all delivered with smooth service as befits 5-star dining (4–11pm Sun–Thurs, midnight Fri & Sat; 407 355 3011, **www.eddiev.com**).

Flying Fish: At Disney's BoardWalk Resort, the menu of this superb seafood experience is select but brilliantly presented. Its Chardonnay-steamed mussels starter is a taste sensation while the signature Potato-wrapped Red Snapper is an absolute delight, along with great scallops, steak and a vegetarian option. The Chef's Tasting Wine Dinner (Sun–Thurs, 5.30 and 8.15pm, reservations required; no under 10s) is another stand-out feature with 5 courses plus paired wines at the chef's counter in front of the show kitchen at $157/person for groups of up to 6 (4–11pm Mon–Sat, 4–10pm Sun; 407 939 3463).

Joe's Crab Shack: Another chain restaurant but with individual style, it is highly family friendly with its kids' play area and ideal if you don't want the whole shellfish thing ($–$$$; 11am–12pm; **www.joescrabshack.com**).

Landry's Seafood: This big-name company boasts a genuinely elegant touch, featuring a Fresh Fish of the Day, magnificent seafood platters and excellent salad bowl with each dish, while the service and wine list are top notch. For a special occasion, the Stuffed Flounder and Surf & Turf are ideal. Happy Hour 4pm–6.30pm with drinks specials and appetisers. Oh, and don't miss their Bananas Foster dessert and speciality Mango Mojito

cocktail! ($$$–$$$$; 4–10pm Mon–Thurs, 11pm Fri, 11.30am–11pm Sat 11.30am–10pm Sun; **www.landrysseafood.com**).

Moonfish: Another great place for seafood, you could make a feast of its appetisers alone, while its sushi, sashimi and raw bar are inspired. It's a touch avant-garde but it works well ($$–$$$$; 4.30–10.30pm, 11pm Fri and Sat; 407 363 7262; **www.talkofthetownrestaurants.com**).

BRITTIP
For something different, check out Moonfish's Sushi Chef Seasonal Creations. It also has a Happy Hour Mon–Sat (4.30–6.30pm) with bar specials and half-price sushi.

Red Lobster: Part of the Olive Garden chain and for the family market, with a varied menu, lively atmosphere and one of the best kids' menu/activity books. While lobster is the speciality, the wood-fired steaks, chicken, salads and other seafood are equally appetising, and it does a variety of combination platters ($$–$$$$; 11am–10pm Sun–Thurs, 11am–11pm Fri and Sat; **www.redlobster.com**).

BRITTIP
If the Marlow's Tavern style appeals to you, they have a 2nd location in Winter Park on S Orlando Ave, just north of Park Ave.

DELUXE DINING

This is where you can really go to town with your dining choice.

Bohème Restaurant: A magnificent menu at this tucked-away gem at the Grand Bohemian hotel in downtown Orlando. Fine seafood mixes with superb lamb, duck and seafood, with some eclectic twists and a great Sunday Brunch ($$$–$$$$; 5.30–10pm, 10.30pm Fri and Sat 407 313 9000; **www.grandbohemianhotel.com**).

Brio Tuscan Grille: With 2 Orlando locations (Mall at Millenia and Winter Park Village), this stylish

Try it all at Pointe Orlando

Dining choice doesn't come more varied than at Pointe Orlando on I-Drive. The headline restaurants are as follows:

The Capital Grille: A truly elegant dining option (also now at Mall at Millenia), with an extensive wine menu. Food includes magnificent chops, dry-aged steaks and seafood – perfect for a special night out or an upscale lunch. Complimentary valet parking (11.30am–10pm Mon–Thurs, 11pm Fri, Sat, 9pm Sun; 407 370 4392, **www.thecapitalgrille.com**).

Copper Canyon Grill: This appeals to hearty appetites with its wood-fired rotisserie chicken, hearty chicken pot pie, steaks and barbecued ribs ($$–$$$$; 11am–10.05pm Sun–Thurs, 11.05pm Fri and Sat; 407 363 3933; **www.ccgrill.com**).

Cuba Libre: This bar/restaurant adds a touch of 1940s Havana, featuring Latin-inspired cuisine with an exciting twist, from tasty tapas and ceviche to honey-mango glazed salmon – and wicked cocktails! (5pm–11pm daily, bar until 2am weekends; 407 226 1600, **www.cubalibrerestaurant.com**).

Maggiano's Little Italy: Serving exceptional family-style Italian dining with a vintage 1940s Chicago ambience – and large portions. The Flatbread appetisers are easily main-course sized, while the Family Style meals feature all-you-can-eat refills ($$–$$$$; 11am–10pm Mon–Thurs, 11pm Fri and Sat, noon–10pm Sun; 407 241 8660; **www.maggianos.com**).

Marlow's Tavern: A classic American bar-restaurant style, with (rather loud) live music. The menu is above-average (great burgers and sandwiches, but also more gourmet fare such as honey-glazed salmon, pan-seared trout and steak frites), with an imaginative cocktails and wine list ($$–$$$$; 11.30am–midnight Sun–Thurs, 1am Fri and Sat; 407 351 3627, **www.marlowstavern.com**).

The Oceanaire Seafood Room: See Top 10, p325.

The Pub: see p317.

RA Sushi Bar Restaurant: Japanese fusion cuisine and sushi bar with a varied menu, including Bento Boxes, Crispy Asian Tacos, Tempura and some creative twists on traditional favourites. Lunch and dinner, plus Happy Hour specials ($$; 11.30am–midnight Sun–Thurs, 1am Fri & Sat; 407 351 3627, **www.rasushi.com**).

Taverna Opa: Lively Greek option, with an appetising menu, from hot and cold meze to moussaka, souvlaki and signature lamb chops, but much more besides, like fine steaks, fresh seafood and a great ouzo bar. Watch for table dancing and napkin throwing! ($$–$$$$; 11am–11pm Sun–Thurs, 2am Fri & Sat; 407 351 8660, **www.opaorlando.com**).

Tommy Bahama's Tropical Café: Inspired dining in a laid-back, tropical setting. The menu is refreshing for lunch or dinner, with highlights being its coconut shrimp and tuna appetisers and seafood entrées, plus sandwiches, chicken, steaks and fab salads ($$–$$$; 11am–11pm Sun–Thurs, to midnight Fri and Sat; 321 281 5888, **www.tommybahama.com**).

Other choices: Adobe Gila's: this lively bar and Mexican cantina style features more than 50 tequilas (!), plus south-of-the-border dining delicacies like the signature Gila Wraps. ($–$$; 407 903 1477; **www.adobegilas.com**). **BB King's Blues Club:** Live jazz and blues (see p294) with a Southern comfort-food menu, such as Fried Shrimp Po Boy and Southern Fried Catfish, and a full bar ($$–$$$$; 4pm–midnight Sun–Fri, 11am–1am Sat; 407 370 4550, **www.bbkingclubs.com**). **Blue Martini:** Upmarket bar with 42 signature martinis, plus beer, wine, and cocktails. Light Fare, flatbreads and signature dishes such as Lollipop Lambchops and Main Lobster Salad (4pm–2am Mon–Fri, 1pm–2am Sat and Sun; **www.bluemartinilounge.com**). **Funky Monkey:** Eclectic restaurant/wine bar that features an imaginative Asian–American fusion menu of tapas-like appetiser plates, steaks, seafood and hand-rolled sushi ($$–$$$, 407 418 9463, noon–11pm Mon–Thurs, noon–midnight Fri and Sat, 5–11pm Sun, **www.funkymonkeywine.com**). **Hooters:** the local party place, with its famous 'Hooter Girl' waitresses and 'soon to be relatively famous' wings, burgers and seafood ($$; 11am–11pm Sun–Thurs, 12pm Fri and Sat; 407 355 3003). **Johnny Rockets:** a fun, 1950s-style diner for burgers and shakes ($; 11am–9pm Sun–Thurs, 11am–11pm Fri and Sat; 407 903 0762, **www.johnnyrockets.com**).

Italian offering makes for a superb casual lunch or romantic dinner, with delicious flatbreads, luscious salads, superb steaks and surf & turf, creative pastas and regional specialities like chicken limone and grilled pork chops, plus daily fish specials. The Tuscan country-style ambience and fresh kids' menu all add up to memorable dining. Great weekend brunch, too ($$–$$$$; 11am–10pm Mon–Thurs, 11pm Fri and Sat, 10am–10pm Sun; 407 351 8909/622 5611; **www.brioitalian.com**).

BRITTIP

At Brio Tuscan Grille, don't miss the melt-in-the-mouth beef carpaccio starter, the bistecca insalata and Shrimp Mediterranean as a fab dinner combo.

Cala Bella: At the stylish Rosen Shingle Creek Resort is this superb Italian-influenced restaurant, heavy on pasta and seafood, but with signature dishes like its sensational Cala Bella Lamb, veal piccata and Mediterranean pork. Save room for dessert – the pastry chefs are among the best in America ($$$–$$$$; 5.30–10.30pm; 407 996 3663; **www.calabellarestaurant.com**).

Cantina Laredo: A deluxe version of Mexican fare can be found in this stylish venue at The Dellagio complex on Sand Lake Road, starting with some killer margaritas and going on to delightfully fresh appetisers, superb tacos and speciality dishes like Carne Asada (grilled steak with marinated onions and chimichurri sauce) and a daily fish special. There is also a great Sunday brunch and

Taverna Opa

a good kids menu ($$–$$$$; 11am–10pm Sun–Thurs, 11pm Fri and Sat; 407 345 0186, **www.cantinalaredo.com**).

Capa: The signature 17th floor rooftop restaurant at the new Four Seasons hotel in Walt Disney World, this is superb for style, elegance – and the nightly views of the Magic Kingdom fireworks. A contemporary Spanish streakhouse, dishes range from delightful small plates, freshly shucked oysters and fine Florida seafood to succulent steaks from the wood-burning grill in the show kitchen ($$$$–$$$$$; 6–10pm; **www.fourseasons.com/orlando/dining/restaurants/capa/**).

Charley's Steak Houses: Cooking over a specially built wood-fire pit earns high marks from US meat-lovers. All the meat is specially aged, hand-cut and seasoned, making for a superb array of steaks and chops and, while it also offers fine seafood, you'd be foolish to overlook its stock-in-trade ($$$–$$$$$; 5–11pm; **www.talkofthetownrestaurants.com**).

Everglades: Tucked away inside the Rosen Centre Hotel is this beautiful Florida speciality restaurant, specialising in great steaks and fine seafood. Don't miss the Broiled Florida Grouper and melt-in-the-mouth Filet Key Largo ($$$–$$$$$; 5.30–10.30pm; 407 996 2385; **www.evergladesrestaurant.com**).

Fleming's: Check in here for finest aged prime beef and an inventive array of fresh seafood, chops, generous sides and salads, plus tempting desserts. Its award-winning wine list features 100 wines by the glass and a magnificent Reserve List for the real connoisseur ($$$–$$$$; 5–10pm Sun–Thurs, 11pm Fri and Sat; 407 352 5706; **www.flemingssteakhouse.com**).

Hillstone: A real special-occasion venue in Winter Park, the lakeside location provides a relaxed but upscale choice for a casual lunch, evening drink or full-scale dinner. Where the locals go for a 'power lunch,' it is also an evening oasis of calm and gracious service, with the

Kissimmee/Highway 192

The long stretch of this tourist corridor offers the greatest density of restaurants in Central Florida.

East section from the junction with I-4 to John Young Parkway: *Deluxe Dining:* Charley's Steakhouse. *Family Favourites:* Applebee's, Bob Evans, Chevys, Chili's, CiCi's Pizza, Cracker Barrel, Denny's, Golden Corral, IHOP, Logan's Roadhouse, Longhorn Steakhouse, Olive Garden, Perkins, Ponderosa, Ruby Tuesday, Shoney's, Smokey Bones, TGI Fridays, Uno Chicago, Waffle House. *Fast Food:* Arby's, Burger King, Chick-Fil-A, Domino's, Dunkin' Donuts, KFC, McDonald's, Pizza Hut, Quiznos, Subway, Taco Bell, Wendy's. *International Flavours:* Kobe Steakhouse, Punjab Indian Restaurant. *Seafood Specials:* Boston Lobster Feast, Joe's Crab Shack, Red Lobster. Tastes of the Med: Pacino's.

West section from I-4 all the way to Highway 27: *Family Favourites:* Applebees, Black Angus, Bob Evans, Bahama Breeze, Buffalo Wild Wings, Carrabba's, CiCi's Pizza, Colorado House of Beef, Cracker Barrel, Denny's, Golden Corral, IHOP, Longhorn Steakhouse, Miller's Ale House, Olive Garden, Outback Steakhouse, Perkins, Ponderosa, Shoney's, Sizzler, Sweet Tomatoes, TGI Fridays, Waffle House, Wildside BBQ. *Fast Food:* Burger King, Chick-Fil-A, Domino's, Dunkin' Donuts, Flippers Pizza, McDonald's, Pizza Hut, Quiznos, Subway, Taco Bell, Wendy's. *Home From Home:* Stage Door. *International Flavours:* Passage to India. *Seafood Specials:* Bonefish Grill, Joe's Crab Shack, Red Lobster.

chance to enjoy a drink on their pier or grab a window or patio table with a wonderful view of Lake Killarney. The menu varies from simple burgers and salads to epic fresh fish dishes, rotisserie chicken, succulent steaks and more. An equally good wine list, daily soup specials and signature desserts round out a superb offering, and this really is THE place to be when the sun goes down! ($$–$$$$$; 11.30am–10pm Sun–Thurs, 11pm Fri and Sat; 407 740 4005, **www.hillstone.com**)

Johnnie's Hideaway: Stylish lakefront supper club in the Crossroads plaza at Lake Buena Vista, serving a rich mix of salads, premium seafood, stone crabs, veal and succulent, dry-aged steaks. The menu is colossal, and there is also a raw bar and some of the biggest desserts we've seen, along with a charming bar area, outdoor terrace and Happy Hour 4.30–6.30pm Mon–Sat ($$$–$$$$$; 5pm–10pm, 11pm Fri and Sat; 407 827 1111; **www.talkofthetownrestaurants.com**)

Luma on Park: Head to Winter Park for this trendy 'gastropub', where the cuisine can be as simple as a well-cooked burger or pizza or a fabulous filet mignon. The mix of outdoor patio, lounge bar and restaurant makes it a chic and lively venue, with fresh contemporary cuisine. Fine

lamb, duck and fish are among the highlights, along with a great wine cellar. It also features a 3-course prix fixe menu Sun–Tue, and a special Chef's Table that should be booked in advance ($$–$$$$$; lounge bar 4–11.30pm Mon–Thurs, 11.30am Fri and Sat, dining room 5.30–10.30pm; 407 599 4111; **www.lumaonpark.com**).

Morton's of Chicago: A more upmarket style following a recent refurbishment, with a lively ambience that adds to the enjoyment of its trademark steaks, cooked on an open range. Memorable, although not cheap, especially as vegetables are extra ($$$$; 5pm–11pm Mon–Sat, 10pm Sun; **www.mortons.com**).

◀◆▶ BRITTIP
American restaurant terminology calls a starter an 'appetizer' and a main course an 'entrée'. 'Broiled' means 'grilled'.

Nona Blue: Sports fans as well as foodies will want to make a note of this wonderfully chic Lake Nona restaurant (just east of Orlando International Airport, on Narcoossee Rd), part owned by Britain's Ryder Cup golf star Graeme McDowell. Drop in for a snack at the bar or a classic burger, or go upmarket with a hand-cut steak or delicious tuna steak off their hardwood grill. They also offer fish and chips and an all-day breakfast fry-up, plus their signature G-Mac & Cheese – lobster and applewood-smoked bacon in a 3-cheese sauce over macaroni. The choice of 24 beers on tap is equally impressive and they also mix some heady cocktails, while there is both indoor and outdoor dining, with sections for sports fans to watch all the live action on multiple flatscreen TVs and quiet sections with no TVs. Golf fans can check out the McDowell memorabilia – including items from his 2010 US Open victory – and purchase Nona Blue souvenirs (priced at $18, $36 and $72, if you spot the golfing connection!), including special apparel from the G-Mac Kartel collection. ($$–$$$$; 11am–midnight Sun–Thurs, 2am Fri and Sat; 407 313 0027, **www.nonablue.com**).

◀●▶ BRITBONUS
$ Show your copy of the *Brit Guide* at **Nona Blue** and receive a special 10% discount on food, drink AND all restaurant merchandise.

Old Hickory Steakhouse: In the Gaylord Palms Resort with elaborate Everglades theming, their steak needs few gimmicks as the house speciality of certified prime-aged beef is cooked to perfection. Side dishes are extra, but the attentive service and alternatives such as oven-roasted swordfish and Maine lobster provide a memorable experience ($$$–$$$$$; 5.30–10.30; 407 586 1600).

The Palm Restaurant: Inside Universal's Hard Rock Hotel is this upmarket New York original, famous for prime-aged steaks and jumbo lobsters, served in elegant surroundings. The house speciality, jumbo Nova Scotia lobster, is spectacular. All this is reflected in the prices, and vegetables are extra, but non-hotel guests qualify for free valet parking ($$$$–$$$$$; 5–9pm Sun–Mon, 10pm Tues–Sat, 407 503 7256; **www.thepalm.com**).

Rocco's Tacos: This wildly eclectic but quality-conscious Mexican offering on Restaurant Row is great for a fun lunch or a lively evening out. Definitely start with their prepared-at-the-table guacamole and then consider one of their signature Molcajete dishes – a sizzling fajita choice served in a lava rock bowl with fresh flour tortillas. Their taco choice is equally tempting, while there is a dazzling array of margaritas and speciality drinks from their Tequila Bar, where it is party night every night! ($$–$$$; 11.30am–11pm Sun, Mon, 11.30pm Tue, Wed, midnight Thurs, Fri, 11am–midnight Sat, bar open to 2am; 407 225 0550, **www.roccostacos.com**).

Roy's: Go upmarket Hawaii style at this grand choice, where the Asia–Pacific fusion cuisine is as spectacular as the decor and service. Creator and celebrity chef Roy Yamaguchi displays his sense of style in every dish and the specialities include Macadamia-Nut Crusted Mahi-Mahi, Blackened Island Ahi and Hawaiian Braised Short Ribs as well as their own cocktails and an 'Aloha Hour' menu (5–6.30pm at the bar), with $6 appetisers, wines and cocktails. The seasonal 3-course prix fixe menu at $36.95 is a bargain, too ($$$$–$$$$$; 5.30–10pm, 10.30pm Fri and Sat; **www.roysrestaurant.com**).

Ruth's Chris Steak House: Another major chain, this also offers prime beef in a mouth-watering variety. It isn't cheap, but you'll be hard pushed to get a better steak. Simply seared, seasoned and served, they are the reason it has more than 80 locations worldwide, including in Sand Lake Rd's 'restaurant row' ($$$$–$$$$$; 5–10pm Mon–Sat, 9pm Sun; **www.ruthschris.com**).

Sanaa: This wonderfully themed dining experience is in the Kidani Village section of Disney's Animal Kingdom Lodge and features a novel take on Indian cuisine, with some imaginative variations, many served as sampler platters and, for once, not the usual huge portions. It also offers

Lake Buena Vista

The third main tourist area, this features the broadest range of choice.

East of I-4: *Family Favourites:* Bahama Breeze, BJ's Brewhouse, Carraba's, CiCi's Pizza, Golden Corral, Lone Star Steakhouse, Santa Fe Cattle Co. *Home From Home:* Frankie Farrell's. *Seafood Specials:* Landry's Seafood. *Fast Food:* Dunkin' Donuts, Subway, Wendy's.

West of I-4 (in the Crossroads area, SR 535 and Palm Parkway): *Deluxe Dining:* Johnnie's Hideaway. *Family Favourites:* Black Angus, Buffalo Wild Wings, Chevys, Chili's, CiCi's Pizza, Denny's, Fuddruckers, Hooters, IHOP, Macaroni Grill, Olive Garden, Orlando Ale House, Perkins, Shoney's, Sizzler, Sweet Tomatoes, TGI Fridays, Uno Chicago, Waffle House. *Fast Food:* Dunkin' Donuts, McDonald's, Pizza Hut, Quiznos, Steak 'n Shake, Subway, Taco Bell. *International Flavours:* Dragon Court Buffet, India Palace, Kobe Steakhouse, The Knife (South American churrascaria). *Seafood Specials:* Joe's Crab Shack, Red Lobster. *Plus:* Giordano's, a fabulous Chicago-style pizzeria serving some of the best deep-dish pizza pies, plus salads, sandwiches and pasta ($–$$$, 11am–10pm; 407 239 8900, **www.giordanos.com**).

great animal savannah views ($$$$; 11.30am–3pm, 5–9.30pm; 407 939 3463).

Shula's Steak House: Expansive and expensive, the porterhouse and prime rib steaks are outstanding, and this chain (owned by ex-American football coach Don Shula) is popular with locals at the Walt Disney World Dolphin Hotel ($$$$$; 5–11pm; 407 934 1362; **www.donshula.com**).

Spencer's: The Hilton by the Convention Center on I-Drive is home to this beautiful restaurant that features magnificent steak, chops and seafood. Side dishes (all organic, local produce) are extra, but the natural steaks are all pasture-raised without hormones or antibiotics, aged for 21 days and cooked in a custom-made grill. The prime porterhouse for 2 is outstanding, and the bittersweet chocolate soufflé is a taste sensation ($$$$–$$$$$, 5–10.30pm Tues–Sat; 407 313 8625; **www.thehiltonorlando.com**).

Texas de Brazil: A top-quality Brazilian-style churrascaria, with a wonderfully upmarket touch. Its variety of meats – each carved at the table off sword-like skewers – is superb, all beautifully cooked over its open-flame grill ($$$–$$$$$; 5–10pm Mon–Thurs, 5–10.30pm Fri, 4–10.30pm Sat, 4–9.30pm Sun, plus brunch noon–3pm Sat and Sun; 407 355 0355; **www.texasdebrazil.com**).

Zen: Asian-themed Zen at the Omni Orlando Resort at Champions Gate features a sake and sushi bar to go with its full restaurant style. An oasis of oriental charm, highlights include the Szechwan-style Beef Tenderloin and Sautéed Shrimp in Black Pepper Sauce and Spinach. Or try the superb Zen Experience – a multi-course feast ($$$–$$$$$, 6–10pm; 407 390 6664; **www.omnihotels.com**).

Our Top 10

Finally, if you fancy really splashing out, why not book in advance at one of our all-time faves for that really memorable dining experience?

A Land Remembered: This is simply the best steakhouse we've visited. Inside the golf clubhouse of the Rosen Shingle Creek Resort (but open to non-residents), it is a superbly refined

Rocco's Tacos

venue boasting exquisite service and an outstanding wine list. The menu oozes class and even features local specialities like frogs' legs, gator stew, a fresh fish selection and key lime pie. But, while the lamb, chicken and short ribs are outstanding, the steak choice is out of this world (featuring all-natural prime black Angus beef from the Harris Ranch in California). Filet mignon, New York strip, ribeye, porterhouse, prime rib, chateaubriand and a surf & turf (with lobster) are among the most succulent meat dishes you will find and, while it is pricey, we really believe it is worth every cent ($$$$–$$$$$; 5.30–10pm; 407 996 3663; **www.landrememberedrestaurant.com**).

Bice: Anyone looking for the most authentic Italian dining experience outside Italy should head to the Portofino Bay Hotel at Universal Orlando where this is as smart and smooth as they come. Genuine Tuscan style oozes out of every facet, from the formal welcome, the classic dining room, live balcony music and the authentic menu. They use only the freshest ingredients, with everything made from scratch, and it shows in dishes like the Burrata mozzarella and vine-ripened tomato starter, papardelle pasta and braised veal shank. Signature risottos are superb and roast rack of lamb a masterpiece, while the soft chocolate soufflé cake is heavenly. The wine list is impressive and Italian-orientated and the whole experience is to be savoured slowly thanks to exceptional wait staff. A 3-course meal will top $130 for 2, but it's worth it for a special occasion ($$$$–$$$$$; 5.30–10pm; 407 503 1415; **http://orlando. bicegroup.com**).

bluezoo: One of the hippest places in town (at the Walt Disney World Dolphin Hotel), bluezoo not only looks the part, but also serves some of the finest food in the Disney realm thanks to celebrity chef Todd English. With an undersea theme that benefits from superb lighting (dine later for the full effect), it has a soothing feeling, whether you are just at the bar or in one of the 3 dining rooms. Both the service and staff's knowledge are impeccable, so feel free to let them steer you around a mouth-watering menu, which includes ceviche and a raw bar. Fish is the signature dish (though chicken, beef, pork and pasta are also on offer) and seafood lovers will struggle to narrow down the choice: miso-glazed Hawaiian sea bass, swordfish, Cantonese lobster and more, or just try your choice of freshly caught fish, whole-roasted on its Teppenyaki grill with a choice of sauces ($$$$–$$$$$; 3.30–11pm; 407 934 1111; **www.thebluezoo.com**).

BRITTIP

For a great lunch or dinner alternative, visit Fogo de Chao and just sample their 30-item Salad Buffet at $24.50 per person. It is WAY more than just salad, with the likes of aged Parmesan, Italian salami and smoked salmon, and is wonderfully fresh and appetising.

Fogo De Chao: This Brazilian churrascaria is superbly authentic and flavourful, with an enchanting mix of elaborate serving style and succulent cuts of meat, all cooked on the traditional 'churrasco' skewer grill. It is a set-fee lunch or dinner, including a huge Salad Buffet (see Brit Tip), and you have a 2-sided card (red or green) to indicate to the 'gaucho' servers if you are ready for more meat. When you flip the card to green, you will be offered freshly cooked skewers of 14 different meats, from filet mignon to linguica (Brazilian sausages), along with a selection of side dishes like crispy polenta, caramelised plantains, rice, beans and heavenly garlic mashed potato. Many of the meat cuts are seasoned with garlic, sea salt, mint, Parmesan or their own special spices and they can be cooked to order, as rare or well-done as you prefer. The bacon-wrapped filet is worth coming in for on its own while the lamb chops are outrageously delicious and the marinated chicken another taste sensation. The weekday set lunch is a bargain $31.50 for the full churrascaria experience while dinner is $48.50 and Sun brunch $35.50 ($$$–$$$$$; noon–2.30 and 5–10pm Mon–Thurs, noon–3pm and 5.30–11pm Fri & Sat, noon–3pm and 5.30–9.30pm Sun; 407 370 0711, **www.fogodechao.com**).

Jiko: This favourite of ours is at Disney's Animal Kingdom Lodge and is possibly Disney's most imaginative culinary offering. Jiko ('the cooking place') features twin wood-burning ovens, a masterful menu and an exclusive selection of South African wines. The menu has Indian, Asian and African influences, with dishes like Braised Beef Short-Rib and Maize-crusted Monkfish, plus a couple of excellent vegetarian choices and a cheese plate that can be ordered as an appetiser or dessert. Its flatbreads are also a speciality and the dessert selection is totally decadent. The personal service and ethnic ambience underline the adventure of eating here, and it's the perfect venue for a romantic meal (5.30–10pm; 407 939 3463).

Monsieur Paul: Epcot's fine-dining array hits the heights with this 5-star dinner choice in the France pavilion. Under executive chef Francesco Santini and Maitre D' Phillipe Girard, this stylish but casual dining room is a true oasis of calm refinement in the theme park frenzy, with a French gourmet flair that isn't off-putting for non-foodies. Under the oversight of legendary chef Paul Bocuse, it ranges from classic dishes to innovative cuisine at the hands of Santini, with the opportunity for off-menu adventures for special occasions. Start with the Ravioli Escargot, then consider the Red Snapper in Potato Scales with braised fennel in a rosemary sauce, or the amazing Seared Scallops with Black Truffle Spaghettini in a rum cream foam. Or just opt for a simple steak, superbly presented, as the grilled Beef Tenderloin is tastebud-teasingly flavourful. But then every dish is a well-balanced taste sensation and the desserts should not be missed at any cost! There is also an excellent 4-course prix fixe menu at $89/person ($$$$$; 5.30–10pm, 407 939 3463).

The Oceanaire: Step back in time at this relaxed and stylish seafood room at Pointe Orlando. The decor, reminiscent of a classic 1930s ocean liner, and mood music lead you into a fish and shellfish wonderland, complete with a superb oyster bar. Shrimp, crab, scallops, clams, lobster and as many as 15 types of fish all jostle for attention on a sumptuous menu that also offers great salads, steaks and chicken (though you'd be crazy to ignore the seafood here). The selection varies daily according to the freshest produce available, but typical examples include 'Black & Bleu' Swordfish, Fin & Shell Fish Stew, stuffed flounder Florentine and stuffed Atlantic lobster, as well as a surf & turf option and a dozen types of oyster. Its grand shellfish platter (at $45 per person) is an extravaganza of shrimp, crab, lobster and oysters and it has an impressive wine list. Service is top-notch ($$$$–$$$$$; 5–10pm Sun–Thurs, 11pm Fri and Sat; 407 363 4801; **www.theoceanaire.com**).

Seasons 52: A trendy national chain (in the Plaza Venezia on Sand Lake Road and next to the Altamonte Mall), this offers some of the best dining in the state with the name reflecting the creative, seasonal, health-conscious menu. All appetisers, salads and soups range from 100–250 calories, the majority being either grilled or oven-roasted, and all mains are less than 475 calories. Its fish and seafood are a highlight but lamb, chicken and steaks are equally tempting and there are good vegetarian choices. The 'mini indulgence' desserts are ideal to finish a meal in style. The bar area and outdoor terrace are equally stylish, ideal for a romantic occasion ($$–$$$$; 11.30am–10pm Mon–Thurs, 11pm Fri, 11.30am–11pm Sat, 11.30am–10pm Sun; 407 354 5212; **www.seasons52.com**).

Wolfgang Puck's: At Downtown Disney, this unusual mix of styles and restaurants – 4 under 1 roof – represents some of the best family dining, with a great upmarket option in the Dining Room. The main Café is smart enough, but head upstairs and you are in seriously romantic territory, with a great view of Pleasure Island/Disney Springs and service to match. The contrast with the fun hubbub below is striking, while the menu is well thought out and varied – try the Maple Glazed Smoked Pork Chop or Seared Half Chicken, steamed seasonal fish or just opt for one of their superb steaks. There are also 2 fixed-priced menus, a 4-course for $53/head and a 3-course for $50. ($$$–$$$$ Café 11.30am–11pm; $$$$–$$$$$ Dining Room 6–10.30pm; 407 938 9653; **www.wolfgangpuck.com**).

🇬🇧 BRITTIP

Need expert local advice on dining? Check out our good friend, restaurant critic and keen foodie Scott Joseph for up-to-date news, views and insight at **www.scottjosephorlando.com**. Not only is his 'Flog' (a Food Blog) essential reading, he also offers periodic special deals for ½-price coupons at a great range of restaurants. His *Orlando Restaurant Guide* is great reading and has a free app for iPhone, iPod and iPad at the iTunes store. Just look up Scott Joseph Orlando.

And our No 1...

While it's practically impossible to single out one restaurant from this wealth of culinary delight, if pushed we'd nominate **Tchoup-Chop** (pronounced chop-chop) at Universal's Royal Pacific Resort. From the gourmet stable of New Orleans master chef Emeril Lagasse, it offers Asian-Pacific fusion cuisine in the most eye-catching setting. Service

is a team effort at each table and the superb menu is well presented and explained. Blending aromatic and flavoursome elements of Thai, Chinese, Japanese, South Seas and other Pacific Rim cuisines, Lagasse has conjured up a delectable array of dishes. Start with steamed vegetable dumplings or smoked baby-back ribs in an Asian barbecue sauce, then graduate to Sichimi Spice Ahi with crispy calamari and risotto, Szechwan Pepper Duck Confit or Hibachi Skirt Steak with purple smashed potatoes. The desserts are equally fragrant and the whole experience is a 5-star treat ($$$–$$$$$; 11.30am–2.30pm and 5pm–10pm; 407 503 2467; **www.emerils.com**).

Or... take a tip from Scott Joseph, who rates the **Ravenous Pig** in Winter Park his number 1 (and he's hard to argue with!). Taking the British gastropub idea, local restaurateurs James and Julie Petrakis have crafted a cosy hideaway that oozes charm and style, and with a menu that is superbly simple or simply superb, depending on if you just want great pub food or the full gourmet experience. Creative salads jostle with fresh pastas and a house-made charcuterie and cheese platter, as well as standards like a Pub Burger, Tacos and Steak Frites. Bookings here are highly advisable though, as its popularity is spreading ($$–$$$$; 11.30–2pm and 5.30–10pm Tues–Sat; 407 628 2333; **www.theravenouspig.com**).

But now on to another of our favourite topics – shopping...

Tchoup-Chop

12 Shopping

or How to Send Your Credit Card into Meltdown

As well as being a theme park wonderland, this vast area of Florida is a shopper's paradise, with a dazzling array of specialist outlets, malls, flea markets and discount retailers. New centres spring up all the time, from smart malls to cheap gift shops – and you can't go a few paces in the tourist areas without a shop insisting it has the 'best bargains' of one sort or another.

With so much good shopping to be had for UK visitors, there's a danger of exceeding your baggage allowance for the flight home – or your duty free allowance. American stores are genuinely fun just to browse, let alone splash out in, and you can expect to pay roughly the same in dollars as you do in pounds for items like clothes, books and jewellery, and real bargains are to be had in jeans, trainers, sports equipment and cosmetics. Almost everywhere offers free, convenient parking, while shop assistants are all polite and helpful.

Sales tax: Be aware of the hidden extra costs of shopping. Unlike our VAT, Florida sales tax is NOT part of the displayed purchase price, so you must add on 6% or 7% (it varies by county) for the final price. Also, some shops will ask for photo ID with credit card purchases, so have a photo driving licence or other ID with you.

Allowances: Your limit in the catch-all duty category of 'gifts and souvenirs' is only £390 per person. If you exceed that, you need to keep your receipts

The Emporium at Main Street USA

and go through the 'goods to declare' channel (though paying the duty and VAT can still be cheaper than buying the same items at home). Some items, such as clothing and footwear for children, do not incur a VAT rate. However, restrictions apply to all reduced-rate VAT items, so be sure to check details with HM Revenue & Customs. Your ordinary duty-free allowances from America include 200 cigarettes and 1 litre of spirits or 2 litres of fortified wine or sparkling wine and 4 litres of still wine.

> **BRITTIP**
> Don't buy electrical goods in the US – they won't work in the UK without a converter. Most games systems (notably X Box, Wii and PS3) are also NOT compatible with UK players. Hand-held games are fine.

Customs duty: You pay duty (which varies depending on the item) on the total purchase price (i.e. inclusive of Florida sales tax) once you have exceeded £390, plus VAT at 20%. You CANNOT pool your allowances to cover one item that exceeds a single allowance. Hence, if you buy a digital camera that costs £400, you have to pay the duty (at 4.9%) on the full £400, taking the total to £419.60 and then VAT on that figure. However, if you have several items that add up to £390, and then another that exceeds that, you pay the duty and VAT only on the excess item (and customs officers usually give you the benefit of the lowest rate on what you pay for). Duty rates are updated regularly and vary from 2.2% (e.g. video games)

World of Disney Store at Downtown Disney

> ## Up, up and away!
> In Downtown Disney's West Side, across the bridge from Pleasure Island, is **Characters In Flight**, a wonderful tethered balloon ride that gently soars up to 400ft/122m high carrying up to 30 at a time in a 19ft/5.7m gondola on 6min rides. It provides a fab panorama of much of the huge extent of Walt Disney World and is a great photo opportunity by day or night (8.30am–12am). It costs $18/adult and $12/3–9s. In certain weather conditions the number of passengers is limited, while it is grounded in high winds or heavy rain.

to 14% (e.g. a computer monitor) keeping in mind VAT rates change. For more info, contact the Customs and Excise National Advice Service on 0845 010 9000, **www.hmrc.gov.uk**.

> **BRITTIP**
> Pick up the *Orlando Sentinel* newspaper on Sun and you will get the full local lowdown on all the great sales for the coming week.

Alligator products constitute those of an endangered species (to UK authorities) so require an import licence. Consult the Global Wildlife Licensing and Registration Service for more info.

Downtown Disney
In many ways, the heart of Walt Disney World is its Downtown Disney district (which will become Disney Springs over the next 2 years), split into 3 linked sections: Disney Marketplace, Pleasure Island/ The Landing and West Side. This is typical Disney, a beautiful location, imaginative architecture and a host of one-off elements that make shopping a pleasure, with 48 shops and dining opportunities. A handy water-taxi links the 3 main elements of this 120acre/48.5ha plaza.

Downtown Disney can be found off exits 67 and 68 of I-4 and is well signposted (exit 68 can be congested at peak periods).

Disney Marketplace: (9.30am–11pm Sun–Thur, 11.30pm Fri and Sat; hours vary seasonally) Don't miss the **World of Disney** store, the largest of its kind, which includes **Bibbidi Bobbidi Boutique** (where young girls can have hair, make-up and nails done in true Princess style), the **LEGO Imagination Center** (an interactive playground and shop), the amazing **Art of Disney** and the new **Marketplace Co-Op** (a number of small shops under 1 roof). **Once Upon A Toy** is a gigantic toy emporium complete with a host of classic games, many with a Disney theme, for kids to try. Other worthwhile one-offs are the blissful **Basin** (for toiletries) and **Disney's Wonderful World of Memories** (for all scrapbook fans).

Young girls in the princess mood may want to take part in the daily **Princess Parade** from the World of Disney store. Held at 2pm weekdays (noon at weekends) each day, it marches in full pomp from the Princess Hollow end of the store through the Marketplace, finishing at the Carousel, where all children get a free ride. Girls can dress up (or not) as they wish, and there is NO fee to take part.

BRITTIP

Parents beware! The Bibbidi Bobbidi Boutique hair and make-up shop is hideously expensive. Packages range from $55–$245, so you may want to steer your Princess gently away!

Arribas Brothers is a big, attractive gift store. Those keen on the pin-trading hobby should check out Pin Traders. Then there's **Disney Design-A-Tee**, **Tren-D**, a cutting edge Disney fashion store for women, **Little Miss Matched** for fun and funky socks, bedding and more (popular with young girls), and **Disney's Days of Christmas**. For bargain-hunters, a section by **Goofy's Candy Company** offers **Marketplace Fun Finds** – everything at reduced prices. Dancing fountains and squirt pools (where kids tend to get seriously wet) and the lakeside setting all add to the appeal.

Pleasure Island/The Landing: This area is under complete reconstruction before it re-opens as The Landing in 2015. No shops had been confirmed as we went to press but both Raglan Road and Paradiso 37 restaurants have their own gift shops here.

West Side: Continuing into West Side (10.30am–11pm; midnight Fri and Sat) gives you the superb AMC 24 cinema complex (p290), plus another 14 retail and dining outlets. The **Hoypoloi Gallery** is one of our favourites for an eclectic range of artwork from metal to glass, while **D Street** (Vinylmation figurines and collectables) and **Pop Gallery** are also highly original. **Goofy's Candy Cauldron** is a big hit with kids, but other shops, including **Something Silver** (contemporary jewellery), **Curl by Sammy Duvall** (water sports), **Sosa Family Cigars**, **Sunglass Icon**, **Fit2Run** and the large **Harley-Davidson** store are all places you could find in the average mall and rather dull. There are gift shops for **House of Blues**, **Bongos Cuban Café**, **Cirque du Soleil**, **Splitsville** and **DisneyQuest**, though. This is also where the new **Food Truck Park** was due to open in late 2014.

International Drive

This core tourist area is awash with shopping of all kinds, from the cheapest and tackiest plazas, full of tourist gift shops, to 4 purpose-built centres. Some of the shops just north of the Sand Lake Road junction are best avoided, while the northern

The Promenade at Premium Outlets

end of I-Drive has undergone a major redevelopment. This area is also renowned for discount outlet shopping – a local speciality – offering name brands at heavily reduced prices.

Universal CityWalk: Among the most original of the 10 shops are **Quiet Flight,** for radical surf and beachwear; the retro-American decor of **Fossil** for leather goods, watches and sunglasses; **Fresh Produce** for swimwear, casual clothing and accessories; the large **Island Clothing Company for** Tommy Bahama clothing and merchandise; **Hart & Huntington Orlando Tattoo Shop** with an array of permanent tattoos, as well as clothing and accessories; and the skate-boarding chic of **Element**. Again, none of these are anything special but the huge new **Universal Studios Store** offers a wide range of park souvenirs and merchandise.

Artegon Orlando: Formerly Festival Bay, this large development at the top of International Drive is undergoing a 2-phase makeover that will change it to an artisan market, shopping, dining and entertainment complex. Anchor stores are **Bass Pro Shops**, **Ron Jon Surf Shop**, **Shepler's Western Wear** and the **Cinemark** cinema, plus **Revolutions Bowling** (an upmarket bowling centre and dining choice) and 2 eye-catching new restaurants – **Toby Keith's I Love This Bar & Grill**, with plenty of Country and Western flair, barbecue food and line dancing, and the **Berghoff Oktoberfest**, a German-style beer hall and entertainment venue. In 2015 we should see the **Oak Ridge**

Universal Studios Store

Market, farmers market stalls selling local produce, and the **Artegon Marketplace**, featuring a collection of arts and crafts stalls, including a glass-blowing studio and a unique array of gifts and collectibles (**www.paragonoutlets.com**).

Orlando Premium Outlets International Dr (formerly Prime Outlets): At the top of I-Drive, this attractive 175-shop 'lifestyle centre' has gone all out for the big, semi-open-air style that encourages people to wander the long interior promenades full of shop fronts and big-name brands. Boasting a landscaped canal running through the centre, outdoor seating, cafés, a Market Place food court, a Guest Services centre, and shuttle pick-up from 12 I-Drive/Universal area hotels (call at least 2hrs in advance on 407 858 3008) it provides a luxury touch. Major brands include the **Neiman Marcus Last Call Clearance Center**, which will attract the fashion-conscious, as will the **Hugo Boss Factory Store**, **White House/Black Market**, **Carters** and **Jones New York Outlet**. Other familiar names include **Nike Factory Store**, **Tommy Hilfiger**, **Crabtree & Evelyn**, **Banana Republic**, **Bath & Body Works**, **Ted Baker**, **Coach** and **Brooks Brothers**, plus, inevitably, a **Starbucks**. New in 2014 were **Quicksilver** clothing, **Sol** (women's fashions), **Swarovski** and **Kitchen Collection**. With its attractive food court, including the popular **Five Guys Burgers**, plus **Jack's Steakery** restaurant and the smart Italian-styled **Vinito**, you have one of the area's brightest shopping centres, that is also at the top of the I-Ride Trolley route (10am–11pm Mon–Sat, 10am–9pm Sun; **www.premiumoutlets. com/orlando**).

Pointe Orlando: Easily accessible from I-Drive, this is a good choice for an evening out with a bit of retail therapy. With 16 smart stores, you can indulge your passion for fashion at **Victoria's Secret**, **Armani Exchange**, **Chico's** and **Hollister** or stock up on gifts and souvenirs at **Bath & Body Works**, **Tommy Bahama**, SGH **Sunglass Hut**, **Charming Charlie**

A Kissimmee tradition

Old Town is home to some weekly events that appeal to locals and tourists alike and are well worth catching. The **Saturday Nite Cruise** at 8.30pm is a trademark drive-past of 300-plus vintage and collector cars (the biggest in America; viewing starts at 1pm). A **Friday Nite All American Muscle Car Cruise** features cars built between 1964 and today (viewing starts at 4pm, cruise starts at 8.30pm), while Wed night's 5pm **Little Darlin' Street Party and Cruise In** brings out the pre-1987 cars. There is live music, fairground-type stalls and prizes, and it can get fairly raucous later on, with plenty of alcoholic libations (witness the Sun on the Beach bar!).

accessories and the excellent **Tharoo & Co** jewellery.

Pointe Dining: For the full rundown on where to eat at Pointe Orlando – **Capital Grille**, **The Oceanaire**, **Johnny Rockets**, **Maggiano's**, **Cuba Libre**, **Hooters**, **Copper Canyon Grill**, **Funky Monkey**, **Fat Fish Blue**, **Tommy Bahama Café**, **Taverna Opa**, **The Pub** and **Marlow's Tavern**, plus recent additions **Blue Martini** and **RA Sushi Bar**, see p319.

Parking is at The Pointe's multi-storey car park, but several stores and restaurants will redeem your parking ticket if you shop here. It's open noon–10pm Mon–Sat, noon–8pm Sun Oct–May; noon–9pm Fri–Sat, noon–8pm Sun–Thur June–Sept; later at the bars and restaurants (407 248 2838, **www.pointeorlando.com**).

ANNIVERSARY SPOT

20 Pointe Orlando is among 4 shopping centres that have been added since we first started. When Pointe Orlando first opened in 1997, the stand-out store was FAO Schwartz. Who can forget the giant teddy bear outside?

I-Drive 360: Still under construction through 2015 is Orlando's newest entertainment and dining complex (see p237), with a selection of shops, restaurants and attractions. Next

door are the **I-Shops**, which should add even more dining and shopping opportunities, including a new **Walgreens**, the giant chemist and general store.

Kissimmee

Down along the tourist territory of Highway 192, you will again find a complete mix of outlets, with a profusion of the cheap and cheerful, but also several highly enticing possibilities.

BRITBONUS

Brit Guide readers receive FREE shopping centre coupons with the cut-out ads on the back flap of this book. Take advantage of this exclusive opportunity for added savings on your holiday shopping.

Old Town: This is Kissimmee's version of the purpose-built tourist shopping centre, an antique-style offering with an eclectic mix of shops, restaurants, bars and fairground attractions, set out along brick-lined streets. The shops range from standard souvenirs and novel T-shirt outlets to sportswear, and collectibles (check out the **Old Town General Store** for a step back in time, or the **Old Town Portrait Gallery** for period-style photos). The individual style of **Out Of This World Embroidery** offers a 'you name it, we'll stitch it' service, while **Black Market Minerals**, **Wild Billie's Gifts** and **Lucky Mouse** are all great for gift ideas. There are also 18 restaurants or snack bars. For lunch or dinner try **Tex Mex** Mexican cuisine or **Kool Katz Grill & Pub** featuring American favourites in a

Madame Tussaud's at I-Drive 360

casual atmosphere reminiscent of the Friday and Saturday Nite car cruises, while the **Blue Max Tavern** is another fun alternative. **Flippers Pizzeria** and **Bamboo Court** are also worth trying, while there are other snack outlets, with offerings from popcorn to candy and the wonderful **Sweet Dreams Ice Cream Cafe**. **Sun on the Beach** is a good nightclub in evenings (until 2am, like Blue Max). Parking is free (10am–11pm daily; ride hours vary monthly (407 396 4888; **www.old-town.com**).

Downtown Kissimmee: This offers the more local, authentic face of shopping in Florida, with the charming Main Street area featuring a range of antique shops, one-off boutiques, cafés and restaurants. Much attention has been paid to the historic district in recent years, and it is now a relaxing place for a wander and a meal. The **Welcome Station** on Main Street (formerly an old-fashioned petrol station) is a great place to start, and even has local crafts, keepsakes, and books focusing on Floridian history (9am–5pm Mon–Fri). Then look into the likes of local landmarks **Lanier's**, **Makinson Hardware** (the oldest hardware store in Florida), and **Gallery One Artists**. The authentic Mexican family style of **Azteca's** is worth trying, along with the casual sports-bar style of **Broadway Pizza**, while we fans of the smart **3 Sisters Speakeasy** wine bar and café, which has an Antique Car Show on the first Fri every month and live music Fri and Sat from 9pm–12am; 407 201 3270, **www.3sistersspeakeasy.com**). Every Tue (5pm–8pm) you can also sample Kissimmee Valley Farmers' Market in the Kissimmee Civic Center (**www.experiencekissimmee.com**).

The Kissimmee area is largely short of quality shopping otherwise, but head up to the Osceola Parkway (at the junction with John Young Parkway), which runs parallel to Highway 192, and you find the extensive developments of The Loop and Loop West, which help redress the balance. This double open-air plaza offers a unique mix of shops and restaurants, plus a 16-screen **Regal Cinema**, in a pedestrian-friendly setting, with the shops grouped around 2 large car parks. Many of the shops may not be familiar but are worth visiting. Of note at The Loop are **Ross** (a huge discount warehouse of clothes, shoes, linens, cosmetics and more), **Kohl's** (a well-priced department store), **Bed, Bath & Beyond** (household wares), **Pacific Sunwear** (beach and casual wear), **Old Navy** (clothing), **Michaels** (arts and crafts), **Sports Authority** and **Famous Footwear** (discounted shoes). There is also a hairdresser, nail salon and chemist (**CVS**). At The Loop West, look for the big department stores of **JC Penney** (clothing and housewares) and **Kirkland** (home goods), plus **Ulta** (cosmetics), **TJ Maxx** (clothing) and **DSW** (shoes), plus 16 additional shops.

In all, The Loop and Loop West boast 75 shopping and dining outlets and this has quickly become a major proposition, especially for the extensive dining choice. Take your pick from classic 1950s diner **Johnny Rockets**, **Ben & Jerry's** ice cream, the counter-service of **Pei Wei Asian Diner**, Mexican choice **Abuelo's**, **Tropical Smoothie Café** and the big-name chains of **Macaroni Grill** (p316), **Chili's** (p311), **Panera Bread** (p309), **Bonefish Grill** (p317) and the distinctive **BJ's Brewhouse** (p 311 great burgers, sandwiches, salads and steaks, plus an impressive beer choice; 407 932 5245, **www.bjsbrewhouse.com**). The shops are open 10am–9.30pm Mon–Sat, 11am–6pm Sun, later at the restaurants and cinemas (407 343 9223; **www.attheloop.com**).

BRITTIP

For something really different, don't miss **Abracadabra Ice Cream Factory**, just outside Kissimmee town centre (on North Main Street). Here, they mix fantastic creamy creations using a wonderful variety of ingredients – and flash freeze it all with liquid nitrogen for a true taste sensation! It's open 11am–10pm daily.

Disney connection

Disney collectors and lovers of theme park memorabilia will want to make note of this specialist store. **Theme Park Connection** is an amazing repository of past merchandise, collectors' items, cast-offs, old park signs, artwork, books and MUCH more. It is a touch pricey as most of its stock is rare or discontinued, and it can take *hours* to search through its warehouse-sized quarters, but you are bound to turn up a real treasure or two and revel in the astounding collection of Disney material. It is tucked away on a small industrial estate at 2160 Premier Row in Orlando, hence you should check its exact location on its website (**www.themeparkconnection.com**) or call 407 284 1934. Open 10am–5pm Mon–Fri, 10am–3pm Sat; closed Sun.

Lake Buena Vista

The Lake Buena Vista area offers 2 of the best discount outlet centres, with great range and great prices.

Orlando Premium Outlets Vineland Ave: High on your 'must visit' list, this is a huge hit with UK visitors – and it's still growing. With a fresh look and style, and a legion of big-name designers, it can be found on Vineland Avenue between I-Drive and I-4 (just south of SeaWorld; or exit 68 off I-4).

◄█▶ BRITTIP

Don't try to battle with the crowds in the main open-air car park at Orlando Premium Outlets Vineland Ave. Instead, head towards the back of the centre where you will find the 1,600-car multi-storey car park.

In all, it offers more than 170 stores of well-known brand names (like **Timberland**, **Diesel**, **Burberry**, **Giorgio Armani**, **Kenneth Cole**, **Banana Republic**, **Prada** and **Calvin Klein**) in a semi-covered pedestrian plaza, with free parking and the convenience of being at the south end of the I-Ride Trolley (main line). Other signature shops are **Samsonite Company Store**, Ecko Unltd (jeans

and sportswear), **Fendi** (stylish women's clothing and handbags), **OshKosh B'Gosh** (baby/toddler clothes), **Famous Footwear** (a mini-warehouse of footwear fashion) and **Perfumania**. Watch out also for big Disney bargains at the **Character Warehouse**. In all, there are 82 clothing and fashion stores, 35 for shoes, 25 jewellers and accessories, 12 for children's clothing and 8 for luggage. The adjoining expansion of The Promenade adds 12 additional stores, including a 2-storey **Sak's Fifth Avenue Off 5th**, **Tommy Bahama** and **Forever 21**, plus the eclectic (and distinctly lively) bar/restaurant style of **Dick's Last Resort** (**www.dickslastresort.com**).

◄█▶ BRITBONUS

Brit Guide Touring Plan clients will receive Orlando Premium Outlets' special Premier Platinum VIP Passport voucher, for significant extra savings at many shops (p41).

The food court is quite tempting, too, with 15 outlets, from **Villa Fresh Italian Kitchen** and **Maki of Japan** to **Starbucks**, **Taco Bell** and **Subway**. There is even a beer and wine café. For those without a car, there is a

Inside Sak's Fifth Avenue Off 5th

daily free shuttle service from select hotels in Lake Buena Vista. Call 407 858 3008 for reservations, which are required at least 2hrs in advance. The Lynx bus service also stops here (407 841 2279), while Star Transport has on-site taxi stands (407 857 9999). Premium Outlets is open daily 10am–11pm (9pm Sun; 407 238 7787; **www.premiumoutlets.com/orlando**).

◀▮▶ BRITTIP

Want to see a REAL shopping frenzy? Visit either Orlando Premium Outlets centre for Midnight Madness on the Fri after Thanksgiving when they open at midnight and stay open for 24 hours – and thousands pour in to shop!

Lake Buena Vista Factory Stores: Get ready for more big-name products at discount prices here, from **Fossil**, **Converse**, **Reebok**, **Jones New York** and **Van Heusen** to a budget-priced **Disney Outlet**, **OshKosh B'Gosh** superstore and (the better-priced) **Carter's For Kids**. It is another open-air plaza, with 46 stores spread over 6acres/2.5ha and with plentiful parking. It's slightly off the beaten track and therefore not quite as busy as some of the others. Recent

additions include the stylish **G by Guess**, **Lindt Chocolate Store** and **US Polo Assn**, while the **Tommy Hilfiger**, **Calvin Klein**, **Loft Outlet** and **Gap** shops have all been heavily remodelled. There is also a decent food court with a pleasant outdoor deck, and a kids' playground. Some of the stores and brand names may not be well known to us, but the likes of **Old Navy** (excellent-value casual clothing), **Perfume Smart** (discounted fragrances and cosmetics), **SAS Shoes** (think Hush Puppies, only cheaper!), **Travelpro** (luggage and travel accessories) and **Rack Room Shoes** (big names at serious savings) are worth discovering. Eclectic **World of Coffee** is both an internet café and one of the best places you could find to sip a latte and enjoy a cake or pastry, with its outdoor terrace and bird cages (plus some British snacks and chocs!). Worth noting at the neighbouring Lake Buena Vista Resort Village and Spa are the luxurious **Reflections Spa** for a bit of pampering after your day of shopping, and **Frankie Farrells Irish Pub** (p316).

The Factory Stores are on SR 535 (2ml/3km south off exit 68 on I-4) and are open daily 10am–9pm (to 7pm

Orlando Premium Outlets Vineland Ave

Our shopping tips

As we live locally, shopping is close to our hearts and we recommend the following.

Bookshop: Barnes & Noble

Chemist: Walgreens

Clothing: Marshall's and Ross stores

Disney store: Theme Park Connection

Electronics: Best Buy

Home goods: Home Goods

Mall: Mall at Millenia

Open-air centre: Winter Garden Village

Outlet shopping: Orlando Premium Outlets

Specialist store: Shepler's Western Wear

Supermarket: Whole Foods Market

Sun). Their shuttle service picks up at 60 participating hotels and condos in a 10ml/16km radius (407 238 9301, **www.lbvfs.com**).

BRITTIP
Don't miss the Lake Buena Vista Factory Stores website for an array of valuable weekly coupons and do 'friend' their Facebook page for even more special offers and discounts. Or just visit Travelpro store for a coupon booklet.

Malls

Head out slightly beyond the main tourist territory and you will discover the further choice and style of the area's many malls. They contain a huge range of shops and, if you take advantage of their periodic sales, you will be firmly back on the bargain trail. The top 2 locally are the Florida Mall and the Mall at Millenia, and both offer a contrasting experience.

BRITTIP
Need a good book? Make a beeline for Barnes & Noble, on West Sand Lake Road in the Venezia Plaza, on the South Orange Blossom Trail opposite the Florida Mall, or at the new Winter Garden Village shops. Each has a great coffee shop, too.

Florida Mall: The largest in central Florida, this features more than 260 shops, with 5 large department stores and a 16-counter food court, plus a children's play area, the lively bar-restaurant **Ruby Tuesday**, the popular fresh offerings of **Nature's Table**, **California Pizza Kitchen** and hearty **Buca di Beppo**. Located on the South Orange Blossom Trail, on the corner of Sand Lake Road, this spacious and smart mall is open 10am–10pm Mon–Sat, noon–8pm Sun. Highlights are the department stores, led by the upmarket **Macy's**, plus **JC Penney**, **Nordstrom** (with an excellent café), **Sears** and **Dillard's**. Other shops worth looking out for are **Bath & Body Works**, **Victoria's Secret**, **PacSun** (beachwear and more) and, for kids, the **Build-a-Bear Workshop**, **Game Stop** and the fun **M&M's World** store, plus trendy **Gap** and a **Zara** outlet. New in 2014 were **Call It Spring** (shoes) and **Zingara** (swimwear). Guest services offers a discount booklet with a handy international size chart to help with American sizing, while there is also

Florida Mall

The Mall at Millenia

free wi-fi throughout the mall, free wheelchair use, pushchair rental and foreign currency exchange. There are even spa and beauty treatments in the **Lancôme Institut de Beauté** in Dillard's, and the JC Penney styling salon (407 851 7234; **www.simon. com**). The Mall also benefits from the integral **Florida Hotel**, with **Cricket's Grille & Bar**.

BRITTIP

Kids – let your parents take you to the Florida Mall, then insist on visiting the huge Toys 'R Us store at the front and then M&M World inside the mall!

Mall at Millenia: If the Florida Mall is the biggest shopping venue, this is the smartest. Just off I-4 to the north of Universal Orlando (exit 78), it is the most upmarket, dramatic and technologically advanced shopping complex in Florida, with New York's most famous department stores –

The Mall at Millenia

Bloomingdale's, **Neiman Marcus** and **Macy's** – among a select number of other top-name boutiques such as **Louis Vuitton**. The entrance features a 60ft/18m glass rotunda with a flowing water garden theme and a concierge desk (valet parking is available). Then you can head in 1 of 4 directions over the marble and terrazzo floors or go upstairs to the high-quality 12-outlet food court. Try any of **Bistro Sensations** (salads, soups, wraps), **Firehouse Subs**, **Haagen-Dazs** (decadent ice cream), the authentic Mandarin-style of **Chinatown**, the fresh **Chipotle Mexican Grill** (salads, tacos and burritos) and **Southwest Grill** (succulent chicken, barbecue beef and salads), plus **Tony's & Bruno's** for Italian specialities (pasta, pizza, salads and cheesecake).

BRITBONUS

Visit The Mall at Millenia Concierge, located inside the main entrance on level 1, and show this book to receive a complimentary savings book.

The grand architecture is also focused on 5 separate courts along a flattened, serpentine S-shape, topped by an arched glass roof like a gigantic conservatory. On 2 airy levels (3 in Bloomingdale's and Macy's) and with 8 Juliet balconies connecting the 2 sides, the mall consists of a colossal amount of glass, plus a stunning

Grand Court, featuring a dozen 20ft/6m columns capped by curved plasma video screens. And, while around 20% of the 150 stores are upmarket (**Cartier**, **Chanel**, **Jimmy Choo**, **Burberry** and **Gucci**), there are many unexpected options, such as **Urban Outfitters**, **Apple**, **MAC Cosmetics** and **Anthropologie**. You will also find plenty of mainstream names like **Abercrombie & Fitch**, **Hollister**, **Gap**, **Banana Republic** and **Victoria's Secret**. The 4 main restaurants are also first class: the heavenly **Cheesecake Factory**, **PF Chang's China Bistro**, the stylish Italian of **Brio Tuscan Grille** (p320), chic **Blue Martini**, and the swanky **Capital Grille** (for that special evening out). On top of that there is the excellent fresh sandwich style of **Panera Bread**, the **California Pizza Kitchen** and a **Johnny Rockets** diner. This is also the only mall with a US post office inside (NB: Standard postcards to the UK cost $1.15). A currency exchange is available, as are international phone cards.

All in all, this takes the Florida shopping experience to a new level (10am–9pm Mon–Sat, 11am–7pm Sun; 407 363 3555; **www.mallatmillenia.com**).

Other malls: There are 3 alternatives to these popular (and busy – especially at weekends) malls. The Altamonte Mall is on Altamonte Avenue in the suburb of Altamonte Springs (take exit 92 off I-4 and head east for ½ml/800m on Route 436, then turn left); Seminole Towne Center, just off I-4 to the north of Orlando on the outskirts of Sanford (exit 101C off I-4); and Oviedo Marketplace, to the east of Orlando (right off exit 41 of Central Florida Greeneway, 417). The Altamonte Mall is the best of the bunch and well off the beaten tourist track, featuring 160 speciality shops, 4 major department stores – **Macy's**, **Dillard's**, **JC Penney** and **Sears** – and 23 eateries, including the fun **Bahama Breeze** (p310), upmarket **Seasons 52** (p325) and pub-style **Orlando Ale House** (p311). An 18-screen cinema and children's soft-play area round out the offerings.

Open 10am–9pm Mon–Sat, 12pm–6pm Sun, the Customer Service Centre offers a VIP savings book to visitors (**www.altamontemall.com**). Shop during the week and you'll feel as if you have the place to yourself!

Winter Garden Village: A final recommendation, 10ml/16km north of Walt Disney World on Highway 535 at the junction with toll road 429, which is primarily a locals' centre but still has visitor appeal. The expansive open-plan design, set around key stores like **Super Target**, **Best Buy**, **Ross**, **Marshall's**, **Home Goods** and **Beall's**, features a mix of the big names and smaller boutiques, as well as a tempting array of 21 cafes and restaurants sprinkled throughout. Look for the upmarket seafood choice of **Bonefish Grill**, the elegant **Longhorn Steakhouse**, family-style **Chili's**, **Cracker Barrel**, **UNO Chicago Grill** and **Mimi's Café**, or the counter-service options like **Five Guys Burgers**, **Panda Express**, **Coldstone Creamery** and **Chick-Fil-A**, and the first Orlando outlet of our favourite burger restaurant, **Red Robin** (**www.wintergardenvillage.com**).

Specialist shops

Wal-Mart: High on many people's lists, this warehouse-like store sells just about everything. There are 21 Wal-Marts in central Florida, 16 of which are 24hr Supercenters. The main tourist area stores are on Highway 27 (just north of 192); Highway 192 by Medieval Times (between markers 14 and 15); Osceola Parkway (at Buenaventura Lakes);

The Mall at Millenia

John Young Parkway (at Sand Lake Road); on Kirkman Road (north of Universal Boulevard); by Highway 535 and Osceola Parkway; and on Turkey Lake Road.

Other supermarkets: There are plenty of other supermarkets and you will find rather better quality at the likes of **Publix** (throughout the main tourist areas, notably on Highway 192 and 27) and **Winn-Dixie** (a major south-east US chain). But the real Rolls-Royce of food stores, **Whole Foods Market** has an Orlando branch on Turkey Lake Road, with its signature superb fresh produce emporium and plenty of chances to sample, plus a magnificent hot-food counter to grab a meal (**www.wholefoodsmarket.com**).

East End Market: For something really different head to Corrine Drive (just north of downtown Orlando) where this neighbourhood market and cultural food hub is inspired by Central Florida's farmers and food artisans. It features top local entrepreneurs, artists and chefs in a 2-storey building that also offers a demonstration kitchen, an incubator kitchen, shops and an outstanding restaurant, **Txokos Basque Kitchen**, with a small-plate seasonal menu that reflects all the local food producers (Tue–Sat 10am–7pm, Sun 11am–6pm, closed Mon; 321 236 3316, **http://eastendmkt.com/**). Don't miss **Olde Hearth Bread Co** and **La Femme du Fromage**.

Nike Factory Store on International Drive

BRITTIP

Mondays at Whole Foods Market see their superb-value Burger & Beer lunch offering for just $8, with a great range of draft beers, fab burgers and wines by the glass. In fact, it's a great bar to visit any day of the week!

For clothes, DIY, home furnishings, electrical goods, household items, gifts, toys and groceries, visit **Target** (its superstores on Highway 192 just west of Highway 535, near Mall at Millenia and Winter Garden Village are fine examples). The big chemists ('drug stores') of **Walgreens** and **CVS** also carry a surprisingly wide range of goods and almost resemble mini-supermarkets in their own right.

BRITTIP

Wal-Mart offers 1hr photo printing at great savings on UK prices, as do branches of Walgreens.

Individual outlets: Keen shoppers will want to check out other unfamiliar options. **Ross** (10 in Orlando, see **www.rossstores.com**) carries a huge range of discounted brand-name clothes, shoes, linens, towels, etc (hours vary by store, roughly 9.30am–9.30pm), while **Marshalls** (5 in Orlando, **www.marshallsonline.com**) and **TJ Maxx** (also 5, **www.tjmaxx.com**) are similar. For American sports gear visit **Sports Authority** stores (**www.sportsauthority.com**), while golfers should visit the **Edwin Watts Golf** stores (including the I-Drive clearance centre; **www.edwinwatts.com**), or any of the **Special Tee Golf & Tennis** shops. You can pick up some great deals on golf clubs in particular. By the same token, anglers can stock up on the latest gear at bargain prices at **Bass Pro Shops** (at the Artegon Orlando centre; **www.basspro.com**).

But now the shopping is done, it's time to think about the journey home…

13 Going Home

A nd so, dog-tired, lighter in the wallet but (hopefully) blissfully happy and with enough memories to last a lifetime, it's time to deal with that bane of all holidays – the journey home.

Now you have come through the last 2 weeks relatively unscathed, here's how to avoid any last-minute pitfalls.

The car

Returning the hire car can take time if you used an off-airport car depot, so allow an extra ½hr; the process is much slicker with firms that operate directly from the airports, as nearly all now do. Most airlines require you to arrive 3hrs before an international flight, so don't be tempted to leave your check-in until the last minute. The off-airport check-in facility for Virgin Holidays (at Downtown Disney by Cirque du Soleil®) is a major bonus in making this process smoother. Now you'll have time to kill, so here is a guide to the 2 main Orlando airports.

Orlando International Airport

Orlando International is 46ml/74km from Cocoa Beach and 54ml/87km from Daytona Beach on the east coast, 84ml/135km from Tampa and 110ml/177km from Clearwater and St Petersburg to the west, 25ml/40km from Walt Disney World and 10ml/16km from Universal Orlando;

so always allow plenty of time for the return journey, check-in and security procedure. The Beachline Expressway (528) can get congested in late afternoon, for example, and the Central Florida Greeneway (417) is often better.

This modern airport is one of America's biggest and rated top for passenger satisfaction. It handles more than 35 million passengers a year, busier than Gatwick and San Francisco. It can get busy at peak times, but its 1,000acre/405ha terminal complex usually handles crowds with ease, and this is one of the most comfortable airports you could find. It boasts great facilities and its wide, airy concourses make it feel more like an elegant hotel (one end is actually the airport-owned Hyatt Hotel).

New self-service immigration kiosks

Ramps, restrooms, wide lifts and large open areas ensure easy wheelchair access, and there are features like TDD and amplified telephones, wheelchair-height drinking fountains, Braille lift controls and companion-care restrooms to assist any travellers with disabilities.

The airport always aims to stay a step ahead, with environmentally friendly enhancements, smart restrooms and a wide selection of food and drink outlets. It boasts a major food court, multiple restaurant options and superb shops. A convenient 'quick turnaround' area for hire cars allows 96% of hire car companies to have onsite locations, a huge boon to visitors' ease in pick-up and drop-off.

Should you have more than 3hrs to spare, it's worth taking the 15min taxi ride to the Florida Mall.

◄▶ **BRITTIP**

You are advised to leave all luggage unlocked (no combination locks or padlocks) when you check in for your flight, as the TSA security staff open a LOT of bags during screening and have the right to access any case, locked or not. TSA-approved locks are suggested, if you prefer to lock your cases.

Landside

As with all international airports, there is a division between LANDSIDE (for visitors) and AIRSIDE (where you must have a ticket). There are 3 levels to Orlando's Landside.

- 1 is for ground transportation, tour operator desks, parking, buses and car rental agencies, plus the Virgin Atlantic baggage claim.

- 2 is for main Baggage Claim, which you negotiated on your arrival, and private vehicles meeting passengers.

- 3 is where you enter on your return journey, as it holds the check-in desks, shops and restaurants.

The main area of Level 3 is then further divided into interconnected sections:

Landside A: This houses the check-in for Gates 1–29 and 100–129. Here you'll find American Airlines, Air Canada, Southwest, JetBlue, Virgin America and Virgin Atlantic (though Virgin Atlantic departs from Gates 60–99).

Landside B: Check-in here for Gates 30–99 and Aer Lingus, BA, Delta, Lufthansa, United, Spirit, US Airways and Thomas Cook.

Once you've checked in, you can explore the East and West Halls of the Level 3 concourse. These house a good mix of shops and restaurants, plus currency exchange, information desks and ATMs, while the Hyatt Hotel is in the East Hall. The East and West Halls are linked by the restaurants, shops and services of the North and South Walks. In total, there are 91 places to shop and eat, including the food court, and it's almost like being in a smart shopping mall. Many shops feature outstanding design and even photo opportunities: see the 2 **Disney** stores, **Harley-Davidson**, **Universal**, **SeaWorld/Busch Gardens** and **Kennedy Space Center**. Other notable shops are **Lush** bath products, **Sanrio** (for all your Hello Kitty needs), **Sunglass International**, **Build-A-Bear**, **Ron Jon Surf Shop**, **Lids** (sports hats and apparel) and **Hudson Booksellers**.

Dining is another pleasure here. The 8-counter food court features **McDonalds**, **Carvel** ice-cream, **Krispy Crème** and **Nathan's Famous Hot Dogs**, as well as the slightly healthier option of **Chick-Fil-A**. **Macaroni Grill** is a tasty full-service Italian restaurant option, while **Fox Sports Sky Box** adds a multi-screen TV set-up plus counter and table service. Upstairs at the West Hall is **Chili's Too**, a cheerful, quick-service Tex-Mex bar-diner.

The East Hall is quieter and more picturesque as it is dominated by the 8-storey **Hyatt Hotel** atrium. Up the escalator is the main entrance, and, to see out your visit in style, **McCoy's Bar & Grill** (up and turn right) is a smart bar-restaurant with a superb airport view, recently refurbished and with a new menu to include a **Sushi Bar** and fabulous fresh salads, sandwiches, flatbreads and small plates ideal for sharing or lighter appetites (11am–12:30am, Sushi Bar 4–11pm; 407 825 1234, **www.orlandoairport.hyatt.com**). To go really upmarket, take the lift to the 9th-floor **Hemisphere** steakhouse (breakfast and dinner only). You'll have an even more impressive view, and its superb cuisine offers some of the best fare in the city. It's pricey, but 5-star.

◀️🇬🇧▶️ BRITTIP
If the queues at security for Gates 60–99 look long, you can use the other side, for Gates 100–129, as you end up in the same place after screening. Just remember to get the tram to Gates 60–99.

Airside

Once it's time to move to your departure gate, be aware of the 4 satellite 'arms' that make up the airport's Airside. This is where you will probably need to queue as the security screening takes time, and you should allow AT LEAST 30 minutes. The arms are divided into Gates 1–29 and 30–59 at the West end, and 60–99 (UK international departures) and 100–129 (all American domestic flights) at the East. All the departure gates are here, plus duty-free shops and more cafés.

The 4 satellites are each connected to the main building by an automated tram, so you need to be alert when it comes to finding your departure gate. There are no Tannoy announcements for flights, so you should check your departure gate and time when you check in. However, there are large monitors in the terminal with all the departure info. The usual gates are:

- 1–29: American, Aer Lingus, Air Canada and JetBlue.

- 30–59: Spirit, United and US Airways.

- 60–99: British Airways, Delta, Thomas Cook and Virgin.

- 100–129: AirTran, Southwest and Virgin America.

Although there isn't as much choice as at the main terminal, you should find the Airside areas just as clean and efficient, with the bonus of 2 duty-free shops (your purchases are delivered to the departure gate for you to collect as you board). Both stores include designer sunglasses, jewellery, handbags, fashion watches, new perfumes and a selection of travel retail exclusives.

◀️🇬🇧▶️ BRITTIP
Orlando International Airport offers free wi-fi throughout its main concourse and satellite arms.

Gates 1–29: Here you will find the first duty-free shop, a newsagents (the Keys Gift Shop), 2 **Cibo Express** gourmet markets, **Za-Za's Cuban café** and a mini food court featuring **Starbucks, Burger King, Cold Stone Creamery, Brioche Doree, On the Border Mexican Grill Cantina** and **Famous Famiglia**.

Gates 30–59: These have **Cibo Express, Pancho's Spanish Bakery and Deli, Nature's Table, Wendy's, Freshens Treats, Za-Za's Cuban Coffee,** full-service **Ruby Tuesday** and **Hudson News**.

Gates 60–99: The main satellite for UK flights offers a good **duty-free shop**, currency exchange, **Stellar News & Gifts,** the speciality **Zoom System** shop, and a mini play area.

Orlando International Airport

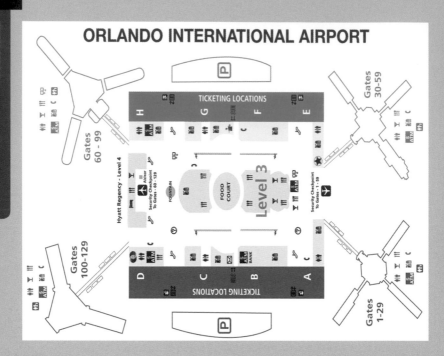

ORLANDO INTERNATIONAL AIRPORT

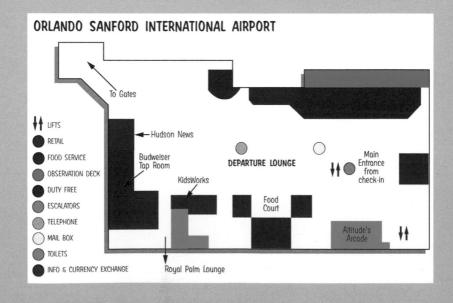

ORLANDO SANFORD INTERNATIONAL AIRPORT

To Gates

↕↑ LIFTS

● RETAIL

● FOOD SERVICE

● OBSERVATION DECK

● DUTY FREE

● ESCALATORS

● TELEPHONE

○ MAIL BOX

● TOILETS

● INFO & CURRENCY EXCHANGE

Hudson News

Budweiser
Tap Room

KidsWorks

Royal Palm Lounge

DEPARTURE LOUNGE

Food
Court

Main
Entrance
from
check-in

Altitude's
Arcade

Your chance to give something back

After having the holiday of a lifetime, all being well, you might like to know about 2 charities helping children with serious illnesses to have a memorable time here. **Give Kids the World Village** is an amazing organisation in Kissimmee, providing a week's holiday for children with life-threatening illnesses. GKTW works with wish-granting foundations worldwide to provide an unforgettable visit for children and their families. It is set up as a resort and includes meals, accommodation, transport, themed venues, donated park tickets and many other thoughtful touches in a magical setting. It's a charity we support ourselves and we hope you will, too. You can donate via its website, **www.gktw.org**.

DREAMFLIGHT takes seriously ill and disabled children from the UK on a 'Holiday of a Lifetime' to the theme parks of Orlando. They aim to bring fun and joy into the lives of children whose illnesses and treatments have brought pain, distress and disruption to their lives.

Each October Dreamflight takes 192 children in the 8–14 age group from all over the UK. For many, it will be their first time away from home and, of course, most will require medical treatment or supervision. One adult escort accompanies every two children, a high proportion from the medical professions. Helpers in Orlando accompany each child in the parks on a one-to-one basis.

Since 1987, more than 4,500 children have enjoyed what in many cases is a life-changing experience. Priority is given to children who would not otherwise be able to have such an opportunity due to their medical conditions and/or social circumstances. They meet others with similar experiences, and return with increased confidence and self-esteem. Many long-term friendships are formed between children in the groups.

For further information or to make a donation please see **www.dreamflight.org**

Thanks in advance for any contributions to these worthwhile organisations.

A food court contains **Burger King**, **Nathan's Hot Dogs**, **Carvel**, **Starbucks** and **Fresh Attractions** deli, plus the excellent table-service **Outback Steakhouse** and bar.

Gates 100–129: Offer 2 **Johnny Rivers Grill and Market** outlets, a food court with **Freshens Treats**, and **McDonald's**, plus **Starbucks** coffee shop, **Au Bon Pain** café, **Kafe Kalik** bar/lounge and 12 shops. For more details, see **www.orlandoairports.net**, which includes live flight departure and arrival info.

Orlando Sanford International Airport

Returning to the gateway for most British charter flights should be relatively simple, providing you retrace your route on the Central Florida Greeneway (following signs for Orlando Sanford Airport, NOT Orlando International) and come off at exit 49. Turn first right at the lights, then first right again on to Lake Mary Boulevard and follow it to the airport.

The efficiency of Alamo and Dollar's car return adds to the simplicity.

◀▮▶ BRITTIP
The airport turn-off sign is right after the toll plaza before exit 49 and is easy to miss; once you go through that toll plaza, take the very next turn-off.

Give Kids the World

Orlando Sanford was created as a full international airport in 1996, as an initiative between the airport authorities and several British tour operators. Thomson and Monarch plus the scheduled services of Icelandair, all use this simpler option. Of course, you are further north, so your journey time is 35min longer and you have to pay an extra $4–5 in tolls compared with the journey to and from Orlando International, but providing you follow the simple directions, you should have no problem retracing your steps here.

And, while this charter gateway is smaller than Orlando International, it boasts a spacious check-in area and works hard to make the departure as painless as the arrival, especially with its Royal Palm Lounge facility. Icelandair usually uses Terminal B for check-in; the other UK airlines check in at Terminal A. But all passengers use the same international departure lounge in Terminal A. It continues to grow, and has finished a major facility upgrade, notably in Terminal B.

There are no food or beverage outlets at the check-in level at Terminal A, but you can walk across to Terminal B where there is a **Café Ritazza** and a food court. Once checked in, you need to pass through security (allow at least 30mins) to reach the International Departure Lounge. Here you have the **Budweiser Tap Room**, which serves a good selection of international beers, and the handy food court. The 4-part outlet offers **American Grill**, **Daily Specials**, **Sweet Endings** and the aptly named **Grab-N-Go** (soft drinks, bottled water and snacks). There is then an extensive **duty-free store** (also with an increased range of merchandise), **Hudson News** for sundries, **KidWorks** for educational games, books, and toys, plus **Everything For $10**. There is also an information and currency exchange kiosk. Smoking is not permitted inside the lounge, but there is an extensive outdoor deck for smokers.

Royal Palm Lounge: The big extra here, this premium space is available to all passengers for a modest fee. It's in a separate annexe from the main lounge and is an oasis of comfort and quiet, perfect for relaxing for the last few hours of your holiday (the only things it doesn't have are beds and shower facilities!). Split into 2 distinct halves, it boasts a pleasant café bar, where you can enjoy unlimited tea, coffee, soft drinks and snacks (plus 2 glasses of beer or wine per over-21). It also provides 2 home theatre lounges, with widescreen TV and surround-sound, for recently released films; 2 quiet reading rooms; 11 computer terminals for internet access and email; a youth entertainment centre with 14 Sony PlayStation 2 consoles; a separate toddlers' playroom with soft toys and games; a smoking lounge; and a left-luggage area. The Royal Palm is billed as an airport lounge with the comforts of home and is well worth the extra cost ($30/adult, $20 4–20s, under-4s free) if you're likely to be here for 1hr or more. Most tour operators offer it in advance at a discount, or you can book on arrival or through your resort reps. With its extra capacity and facilities, this is a very satisfying way to conclude a holiday. See the Royal Palm Lounge and more about the airport at **www.orlandosanfordairport.com** or email **royal.palm@tbiusinc.aero**.

Whether you are using Orlando International or Orlando Sanford, you can also expect the return flight to be about 1hr shorter than the journey out, thanks to the Atlantic jetstreams. Nevertheless, you'll land back home rather more jetlagged than on the trip out because the time difference is more noticeable on eastward flights, and it may take a day or so to get your body clock back on local time. It is important not to indulge in alcohol on the flight if you will be driving when you land. By far the best way to beat Florida jetlag is to enjoy the memories from this trip – then start planning your next Orlando holiday!

Believe us, the lure of this theme park wonderland is hard to resist – you WILL be back!

14 Your Holiday Planner

Example: 2 weeks with Disney's 14-Day Ultimate Ticket and Orlando FlexTicket Plus

(Disney's Ultimate Tickets give 7, 14 or 21 days of unlimited admission at their 4 main theme parks, plus visits to Blizzard Beach, Typhoon Lagoon, DisneyQuest and/or Disney's ESPN World Of Sports™, valid for 7/14/21 days from first use. The Orlando FlexTicket Plus is valid for Universal Orlando's 2 parks, CityWalk and Wet 'n Wild, plus SeaWorld, Aquatica and Busch Gardens for 14 days from first use)

Day	Our Example	Your Planner
1 (Mon)	Arrive 2.40pm local time, Orlando Sanford airport; transfer to resort – check out local shops and restaurants	
2 (Tues)	Attend tour operator Welcome Meeting; rest of day at MAGIC KINGDOM	
3 (Wed)	All day at UNIVERSAL STUDIOS for the Wizarding World of Harry Potter	
4 (Thurs)	Chill out day at Disney's Blizzard Beach water park	
5 (Fri)	All day at BUSCH GARDENS	
6 (Sat)	DISNEY'S ANIMAL KINGDOM Park. Eve: Medieval Times Dinner Show (8pm)	
7 (Sun)	Have a lie-in, then go shopping at Orlando Premium Outlets and Lake Buena Vista Factory Stores	
8 (Mon)	ISLANDS OF ADVENTURE Eve: City Walk and dinner at Hard Rock	
9 (Tues)	All day at DISNEY'S HOLLYWOOD STUDIOS (Fantasmic! show at 8.30pm)	
10 (Wed)	Kennedy Space Center Eve: International Drive	
11 (Thurs)	All day at SEAWORLD (One Ocean at 3pm)	
12 (Fri)	Enjoy a UNIVERSAL ORLANDO highlights day; or chill out at Aquatica water park	
13 (Sat)	All day at EPCOT Park (IllumiNations at 9pm)	
14 (Sun)	Have a lie-in, then head for MAGIC KINGDOM Park (Wishes fireworks at 9pm)	
15 (Mon)	Gatorland/Back to airport; return flight at 5.30pm	

Busy Day Guide

NB: This is a *general* guide only as the parks do change their hours frequently and often without notice. However, this guide will still be accurate for the busiest times of the year.

Day	Busiest	Average	Lightest
Mon	Magic Kingdom, Animal Kingdom, Universal Studios	Disney's Hollywood Studios	Epcot, Islands of Adventure, SeaWorld, Busch Gardens; Kennedy Space Center, water parks
Tues	Epcot, Universal Studios	Disney's Hollywood Studios, Kennedy Space Center	Magic Kingdom, Animal Kingdom, Islands of Adventure, SeaWorld, Busch Gardens, water parks
Wed	Animal Kingdom	Magic Kingdom, Disney's Hollywood Studios, Islands of Adventure, SeaWorld	Epcot, Universal Studios, Busch Gardens, Kennedy Space Center, water parks
Thurs	Magic Kingdom	Epcot, Islands of Adventure, Kennedy Space Center, SeaWorld	Disney's Hollywood Studios, Animal Kingdom, Universal Studios, Busch Gardens, water parks
Fri	Islands of Adventure	Disney's Hollywood Studios, Animal Kingdom, Universal Studios, Kennedy Space Center, Busch Gardens, water parks	Magic Kingdom, Epcot, SeaWorld
Sat	Disney's Hollywood Studios, Universal Studios, Islands of Adventure, SeaWorld, Busch Gardens, Kennedy Space Center, water parks	Magic Kingdom, Epcot	Animal Kingdom
Sun	Epcot, Universal Studios, Islands of Adventure, SeaWorld, water parks	Magic Kingdom, Animal Kingdom, Busch Gardens	Disney's Hollywood Studios

Only here for a week? Here's our suggestion for an action-packed 7 nights in Orlando:

Day 1: Arrive; visit Epcot in evening for IllumiNations

Day 2: Up early for Magic Kingdom

Day 3: All day at Universal and Islands of Adventure

Day 4: Epcot for the day; Disney's Hollywood Studios for evening

Day 5: Disney's Animal Kingdom for the day; Magic Kingdom evening

Day 6: SeaWorld with mid-day break at Aquatica

Day 7: Hollywood Studios for the day, Epcot evening

Day 8: Shopping and return flight

Index

Acknowledgements

The authors wish to acknowledge the help of the following in the production of this book: Visit Orlando, Experience Kissimmee, Walt Disney Attractions Inc., Universal Orlando, SeaWorld Parks & Entertainment, St Petersburg/Clearwater Area Convention and Visitors Bureau, Daytona Beach Area Convention & Visitors Bureau, Seminole County Convention & Visitors Bureau, Space Coast Office of Tourism, Mount Dora Chamber of Commerce, Greater Orlando Aviation Authority, Orlando Sanford International Airport and Alamo Rent A Car.

In person: Danielle Courtenay, Amy Rodenbrock (Visit Orlando), Larry White, Sylvia Oliande, Rochelle Siegel (Experience Kissimmee), Danny Trosset, Stephanie Hunicke, Patrick Harrison, (Seminole County), Todd Heiden, Dave Coombs (Walt Disney), Tonya West (Daytona Beach CVB), Kalina Subido-Person, Damian O'Grady (Space Coast), Lindsey Towers (Alamo Rent A Car), Fiona Duncan, Kevin Gibson, Meredith Bandy, Michelle Russo (Universal), Andrea Farmer, Angelica Deluccia Morrisey (Kennedy Space Center), Chris Jones (LEGOLAND Florida), Carolyn Fennell, Larry Ell (Orlando Aviation Authority), Matt Duda (Florida Eco-Safaris), Lorraine Ellis (Get Married In Florida), Andy James, James Brown (Florida Dolphin Tours), Nick Gollattscheck, Susan Flower, Travis Claytor, Lucy Dalton, Natalie Eales (SeaWorld Parks & Entertainment), Rose Vignetti-Garlick (Downtown Orlando), Debra Ray (Church Street Business District), Sam Haught (Wild Florida), Dana Gonzalez, Matt Tuchman (Medieval Times), Dana Berry (Four Seasons Orlando), John Stine, Dipika Joshi (I-Drive 360), Laura Richeson (Richeson Communications), Scott Joseph (ScottJosephOrlando.com), Michael Caires (Orlando Sanford International Airport), Allan Oakley (Alexander Homes & Associates), Nigel Worrall (Florida Leisure), Wrenda Goodwyn (International Drive), Michelle Harris (Gatorland), Donna Ernbro (Sleuths), Gene Columbus (The Orlando Rep), Mary Deatrick (Deatrick PR for Rosen Hotels), Michelle Peters (Boggy Creek Airboats), Lorraine Gorham (Raglan Road), Lorena Garcia (Orlando Premium Outlets), Terry Lynn Morris, Jennifer Bisbee (Lake Buena Vista Factory Stores), Steve Sless (Paragon Outlets), Judy Perry (Dreamflight) and Bill Bona (Nona Blue), plus all our ATD friends!

Reader feedback via email: Evelyn Hockin, Paul Curran & Trish ffrench.

Other publications: Check out **Orlando Attractions Magazine** for information and features on this great destination – **www.attractionsmagazine.com**.

Got a red-hot Brit Tip to pass on? We want to hear from YOU to keep improving the guide each year. Drop us a line at: Brit's Guide (Orlando), W. Foulsham & Co. Ltd, The Old Barrel Store, Drayman's Lane, Marlow, Bucks SL7 2FF. Or e-mail britsguide@yahoo.com.

Photograph acknowledgements

With thanks to everyone for their help in supplying photographs for this edition.